# CLASSICS IN TRANSLATION

## Volume II: Latin Literature

# Classics in Translation

## Volume II: Latin Literature

EDITED BY **Paul MacKendrick**

AND **Herbert M. Howe**

THE UNIVERSITY OF WISCONSIN PRESS

Published 1952

The University of Wisconsin Press
114 North Murray Street
Madison, Wisconsin 53715

The University of Wisconsin Press, Ltd.
1 Gower Street
London WC1E 6HA, England

Printings 1952, 1959, 1963, 1966, 1972, 1975, 1979,
1982, 1984, 1986

Printed in the United States of America

ISBN 0-299-80896-3; LC 52-10534

# CLASSICS IN TRANSLATION

## IN TWO VOLUMES

## I: *Greek Literature*

Complete translations of Aeschylus' *Agamemnon*, Sophocles' *Antigone*, Euripides' *Medea*, Aristophanes' *Frogs*, and "The Old Oligarch"; abridged translations of Homer's *Iliad* and *Odyssey*, *The Homeric Hymn to Hermes*, and Plutarch's *Life of Tiberius Gracchus*; selections from Hesiod's *Works and ,Days*, the Lyric Poets, Pre-Socratic Philosophers, Attic Orators, Herodotus, Thucydides, the Greek Scientists, Plato, Aristotle, Epicurus, Epictetus, and Lucian; introductory essays, explanatory notes.

## II: *Latin Literature*

Complete translations of Plautus' *The Haunted House*, Terence's *Woman from Andros*, Seneca's *Medea*, and *The Deeds of the Deified Augustus*; an abridged translation of Vergil's *Aeneid*; selections from Lucretius' *On the Nature of Things*, Sallust, Cicero's speeches and philosophical works, Catullus, Vergil's *Georgics*, Horace's *Odes*, Ovid, Livy, Petronius, Quintilian, Pliny the Younger, Tacitus' *Annals* and *Germania*, Juvenal's *Sixth Satire*, and Suetonius' *The Deified Julius*; introductory essays, explanatory notes.

# CONTRIBUTORS

Smith Palmer Bovie     Alston H. Chase

Norman J. DeWitt     Charles F. Edson

Elizabeth C. Evans     Robert Fitzgerald

Eric A. Havelock     John Paul Heironimus

Rolfe Humphries     Harry J. Leon

Paul MacKendrick     Charles Pinckney

Inez Scott Ryberg     Carl Schuler

Rogers V. Scudder     Paul Shorey

Goldwin Smith     R. I. Wilfred Westgate

Dorrance S. White     Alban D. Winspear

## SARGENT PRIZE TRANSLATORS

W. S. Archibald, R. E. Bates, Marshall A. Best,
C. J. Chamberlain, Gerald F. Else, R. C. Minns,
M. M. Smith, Richard J. Walsh, and R. G. West

# TABLE OF CONTENTS

# LATIN LITERATURE

# ROMAN CULTURE: AN ESSAY

## By Paul MacKendrick

*Others, no doubt, will better mould the bronze*
*To the semblance of soft breathing, draw from marble*
*The living countenance; and others plead*
*With greater eloquence, or learn to measure,*
*Better than we, the pathways of the heaven,*
*The risings of the stars: remember, Roman,*
*To rule the people under law, to establish*
*The way of peace, to battle down the haughty,*
*To spare the meek. Our fine arts, these, forever.*
—AENEID, VI, 847–853

VERGIL's statement of Rome's mission sets up a sort of delimitation agreement: the Greeks will practise the "theoretical" arts and sciences, the Romans the "practical." If this statement of the distinction between Greek and Roman culture is sound, two conclusions follow: first, that we shall expect Roman literature—employing Horace's distinction—to be more useful than beautiful; and second, that for the understanding of Roman literature an acquaintance with its geographical, historical, economic, and intellectual background is of even greater importance than in the case of Greece. Such an analysis is in two respects of peculiar interest to us, the heirs of the democratic American tradition, because it reveals the profoundly aristocratic bias of most Roman literature, and because it suggests a number of striking analogies between the development of Rome and that of the United States.

The great boot [1] of the peninsula of Italy stretches from the Alps for seven hundred miles into the Mediterranean; in area it is somewhat larger than New England, in climate it ranges from north temperate to subtropical, with corresponding influences upon the nature of crops and people. The Alps form a mountain wall to the north; the Apennines form the great backbone of the peninsula. In the north, too, the rich bottom lands of the Po valley afford a soil richer in grain than anything in Greece; the mountain valleys are softened by grey-green olive trees, and the slopes are terraced for the growing of grapes. So the "Mediterranean triad" (grain, the vine, and the olive) grows in such abundance that importation of foodstuffs did not become necessary until, in the fourth century B.C., the large landowners began—as in sixteenth-century England—to convert productive farm land into more profitable sheep and cattle ranches. Since the harbors are better and the coastal plain wider and more fertile on the west coast than the east, Italy faces west geographically and economically: the opposite way from Greece, a fact which has its bearing upon the Romanization of the western European culture in which all Americans share.

Vergil in his *Georgics* expresses the love which Italians feel for this land of brown plain, purple mountain, blue water, and ancient hill towns perched on inaccessible crags with rivers gliding along below the ancient walls. But Italy's finest crop, he says, is *men*: the descendants of two waves of prehistoric invaders like those who over ran Greece: one of the mysterious Etruscans, who came probably from Asia Minor and made significant contributions to Roman politics, religion, arts, and the development of the Roman alphabet in which these words are written; and the other of the Greek colonists of South Italy and Sicily in the eighth and seventh centuries B.C. Like American culture, Roman culture is the product of a borrowing from all these diverse racial stocks without loss of a distinctive personality of its own. Because of this adaptability, and because of its strategic location, the city of Rome, on its seven hills, well up river from the danger of pirates on the seacoast, early became the most important market town in Italy, and began the growth we are to study, from a village of huts to a marble metropolis of a million souls, the ruler of the whole civilized world.

Roman historians divided Rome's history into three periods: the monarchy (753–509 B.C.), the Republic (509–27 B.C.), and the Empire (27 B.C. to A.D. 476).

The history of the monarchy is largely legend, manufactured by the pro-aristocratic historians and poets of later times, like Livy and Vergil, to lengthen the pedigree of their heroes. Every nation cherishes its folklore about its origins, and Romans were as fond of the tales of Romulus, Remus, and the wolf, or Horatius at the bridge as Americans are of Parson Weems' pious fictions about George Washington and the cherry tree, which are about equally well founded on fact. According to the version of the legend which prevailed in the Augustan age, Rome was founded by refugees from the Trojan War, led by Aeneas, a minor figure in the *Iliad*. But since the traditional date of the fall of Troy was 1183 B.C., while that of the founding of Rome was 753, some device had to be found to fill the gap; a series of native kings was invented, culminating in the famous twins, Romulus and Remus. Six other kings followed, until finally the aristocracy, unable to brook the harshness of the last king, Tarquin the Proud, unseated him, "liberated" Rome, and set up a republic, their ringleader being Lucius Junius Brutus, an ancestor of the "liberator," Marcus Brutus, who led the assassins of Julius Caesar.

In point of fact the republic of 509 was the product of the dissatisfaction of the Roman aristocrats—the "patricians" or "optimates"—with the monarchy, and was not in any sense a democracy such as a Greek of the age of Pericles or a modern American would recognize. It contained a majority—the "plebs"—which was without pedigree, wealth, or privilege, and the history of the Roman republic is the story of the jockeying for power of these two classes. Though it is not clear whether the patricians were the original

settlers of Rome, a group of invaders, or a king-made aristocracy, what is clear is that in historical times they had under the Roman constitution —which was actually the governing class—a monopoly of wealth and power which they did not always use to the advantage of the community as a whole.

At its outset the Roman republic gave its poorer or less well-born citizens no appeal from the decisions of the aristocratic magistrates, no opportunity to acquire property in land, no relief from debt, and no access to the highest office, the annual double magistracy called the consulship. Their sole safeguard was in the office of tribune, against which Cicero inveighs so subtly in his treatise *On the Laws*. The tribunes, plebeians by birth, and guaranteed immunity during their year of office, had the duty of protecting the plebs from unjust treatment by interposing their veto upon the act of any other magistrate.

The first stage in the gradual emancipation of the plebs was marked by the codification of the law in the famous Twelve Tables (451 B.C.). Before this date knowledge of the provisions of the law was restricted to the patrician magistrates who administered it. The new-found knowledge was bitter to the plebs, for the law was harsh and inequitable, being designed to protect the propertied class against the rest of the community, but at least they now knew the worst, and could proceed to countermeasures. Meanwhile the Tables became the basis for the massive structure of Roman law under which much of western Europe, and even our own state of Louisiana, are still governed, and to the interpretation of which many of the best minds of the next two thousand years were to be devoted.

To express their dissatisfaction with the *status quo* the plebs resorted to the device of "secession," and formal withdrawal from the political and economic life of the community, which bears a certain resemblance to the modern strike. By this means they obtained for themselves an assembly of their own, through which they were able to gain successively an increase in the number of their tribunes, the right to intermarry with patricians, access to minor offices, and finally, by 366 B.C., the privilege of standing for the consulship, ostensibly on equal terms with the aristocracy. But plebeians in power soon began to show the normal human tendency to kick away the ladder by which they had climbed, and the result of two hundred years of struggle was a combination of wealthy plebeians with patricians to reserve for themselves political, economic, and social power and prestige. Meanwhile economic progress had not accompanied political. The territorial expansion of Rome which was going on throughout this period was made possible by a plebeian army with patrician commanders, who kept the lion's share of the new land won in war. This land they farmed economically on a large scale with slave labor, driving the small farmer out of the market, forcing him to mortgage his farm, foreclosing like the flinty squire in Horatio Alger, and adding the land thus acquired to their already enormous acreage. The displaced persons thus created drifted to Rome where they formed an unemployed urban proletariat, whose votes were for sale to the highest bidder. This is the situation Sallust protests against in many of the brilliant speeches in his *Jugurtha* and *Catiline;* there was no permanent solution for it without the abolition of slavery, which no Roman seems ever to have proposed.

The parallel between the expansion of Rome and that of the United States is the more striking because it was made possible by the same virtues and resulted in the same vices: on the one hand rugged individualism, self-denial, and ability to bear up under hardship; on the other hand, irresponsibility, the cash nexus, and eventual softening of fibre. But the Romans themselves postponed the date of the decline to the time of the destruction of Carthage (146 B.C.) ; over one hundred years earlier Rome had become mistress of all Italy south of the Po, using in the process tactics not much less cruel than those involved in the winning of our own West. The territory thus won was administered in a variety of ways, ranging from full citizenship through local self-government, colonial status, and treaties of alliance. Resentment over exclusion from Roman citizenship, often refused through the shortsightedness of the landed gentry, was to be responsible for a bloody war in the last century of the republic.

The expansion of Rome had brought her into contact with Greek culture. Of Roman literature before the end of the third century B.C. we have only fragments, but they are enough to show that the Roman genius, if it had been left to develop independently, might have forged a literature worthy to stand beside any in Europe. But the Romans apparently felt a provincial sense of inferiority before the sophisticated Greeks, as Englishmen of Chaucer's time felt before the French, and Americans earlier than Whitman before the English. Further, the Greeks themselves put no premium on originality. At the time Rome came into contact with Greek culture, the Isocratean theory of imitation prevailed; the aim was not independent self-expression, but to write "what oft was said, but ne'er so well expressed." The result was, as Horace later put it, that "captive Greece led captive her fierce conqueror, and sophistication was imported into rustic Latium."

But before Roman aristocrats were to have leisure to enjoy that sophistication, which critics like Sallust said had proved Rome's ruin, nearly 150 years of struggle had yet to be faced, with the great Semitic commercial state of Carthage, in North Africa. Livy, writing under Augustus of Rome's great days, tells the story of the epic struggle between the wily Carthaginian Hannibal and the Roman aristocrat Fabius Maximus, from whose delaying tactics George Washington was to learn much which he applied to his advantage during the darkest days of the American Revolution. At the end of the struggle (146 B.C.) Carthage lay prostrate, and Rome had added to her territory Sicily, Sardinia, Corsica, Spain, and North Africa. Greece, which was declared "liberated" in 196 B.C. from Macedon, became a Roman province in the same year as the fall of Carthage; a large part of Asia Minor fell into Roman hands as a legacy from a puppet king in 133 B.C., and southern France was made a province in 120.

This enormous expansion brought, at least to the ruling class, prosperity and leisure; no longer was it true, as it had been when Carthaginian ambassadors visited Rome in the middle of the third century, that there was only one silver service in the whole city. Victorious generals brought home works of art they generally did not understand, and embassies of Greek intellectuals amazed the Romans with their versatility and erudition. Plautus, the Umbrian comic poet, is the first writer in Latin whose work survives in quantity. We have twenty plays, all from Greek originals of the so-called New Comedy, whose standard types were derived from Aristotle through the *Characters* of his pupil Theophrastus.

A generation later Roman aristocratic audiences were smiling with well-bred reserve at the comedies of Terence; the plebs preferred bearbaiting and tight-rope walkers. Terence was a member of an aristocratic literary and political coterie which centered around the person of Rome's greatest aristocratic hero, the symbol to Cicero of the Golden Age, Scipio Africanus Minor. The group also included the historian Polybius (whose analysis of the Roman constitution as a system of checks and balances impressed American Federalists); the Stoic philosopher Panaetius, from whom Cicero later borrowed heavily for his work *On Duty;* the satirist Lucilius; and the jurist Laelius, Cicero's hero in his essay *On Friendship.* It thus controlled all propaganda in the interest of the aristocratic regime, but Scipio's death in 129 B.C. under mysterious and sinister circumstances symbolized a revolt against conservative control and ushered in a bloody century which culminated in 27 B.C. with the establishment of the Augustan principate.

The points at issue between patricians and plebeians were much the same as they had been in the days of the secessions of the plebs: redistribution of public land as a solution for urban unemployment, relief for the small farmer, citizenship for the Italian allies. But the balance of power between the two classes was now held by a group of wealthy bankers, wholesale merchants, and tax farmers, called "knights," who were not eligible for membership in the Senate because their ancestors had not held high public office. To this class Cicero belonged, and he worked hard to make a coalition between it and the patrician Senate. Chief representatives of the conservative faction in this century, standing against land reform, relief, and broadening of the citizenship base, were Scipio Nasica, Sulla, Pompey, and Cicero; the great names of the opposition include the brothers Tiberius and Gaius Gracchus, Sallust's hero Marius, Julius Caesar, and Mark Antony. The defeat of the latter and Cleopatra at the battle of Actium (31 B.C.) by Julius Caesar's young nephew and heir, Octavian, later surnamed Augustus, was represented as a victory of West over East, after which Romans of all parties could join in self-congratulation. Perhaps the fact that young Cicero, the addressee of the work *On Duty,* served the year after Actium as consul under his father's enemy, may stand as a symbol of the new spirit of reconciliation.

Party strife enlisted all the resources of literature. Cicero's speeches, letters, and philosophical works provide a conservative history of Rome, to which Sallust's monographs are in part a counterweight. The dualistic philosophy of Plato and the Stoics, with its emphasis on a hierarchy of nature, a Great Chain of Being, culminating in human reason, was used to justify conservative government. While it is not clear that the philosopher poet Lucretius took part in politics, the atomic theory of the universe for which he stood did not allow for preference of one atom over another, nor for the point of view that intellectual pleasure is too precious a thing to be wasted on the lower classes; hence, in part, the diatribes against Epicureanism in Cicero's philosophical works. The lyric poet Catullus' mistress was the sister of Cicero's most implacable enemy, and Catullus himself wrote lampoons against Julius Caesar; Horace, poet and satirist, who had been a conservative at Philippi, wrote lukewarm propaganda for the Augustan regime; Vergil, out of his love for Greek literature and the Italian countryside, rose to the grandest heights of poetry of which any Roman had yet proved himself capable, as he sang in the *Aeneid* of the destiny of Rome and the pathos of human existence. Livy in a monumental work of nearly 150 volumes told Rome's story in prose, and Augustus himself—or his stepson—recorded his exploits in the monumental terseness of the inscription, in Greek and Latin, known as the *Res Gestae* or *Deeds of the Deified Augustus.*

The divinity of the ruler had long been an acceptable part of Oriental monarchy, and had come into the Greek world at the time of Alexander the Great. Augustus used it as a political device, largely in the East, specifying that no Roman citizen was to be required to worship him as a god. But Augustus and his literary circle were deeply interested in a revival of Roman religion. The natural businesslike tendency of the state cult had caused it to be so manipulated by aristocratic priests in the interests of partisan politics that Cicero had said he did not see how one priest could meet another and keep a straight face. The religion of the aristocracy in Cicero's time was one sect or another of Greek philosophy; [2] the religious sense of the common people was deeply stirred by the importation of various revivalist cults from the East, notably those of the Great Mother, Dionysus, Isis, and Mithras, which with their drama of death and rebirth prepared the way for Christianity. The Augustan revival appealed to antiquarians and lovers of the quaint rites of the Italian countryside, upon which Augustus, by means of wholesale evictions, was attempting to settle his veterans. Even the most frivolous poets of the Augustan Age are eloquent in their descriptions of rustic festival, the processions to crown the boundary stones with garlands, the simple sacrifices of milk and wine. Roman religion as a whole was even more derivative than Roman literature: the twelve major gods were identified, or "syncretized," with their Greek equivalents; the practice of observing the flights of birds, inspecting the livers of animals, and applying to human life the movements of the stars came from Babylonia and Chaldaea. The native Italic element persisted and was appealed to by the Augustan revival of animism, a belief in innumerable spirits who dwelt in the groves, fountains, and brooks, in the hearth and the larder, and who would fulfill their part of the contract with man by bringing him prosperity if he would fulfill his part by bringing them offerings, a religious attitude which by no means declined and fell with the Roman Empire.

In emperor-worship, as it finally established itself in Italy as well as in the provinces, the people of a far-flung empire found a sense of unity, of a stake in the nation, which had been lacking in the old aristocratic regime. That had been a closed corporation of aristocratic families, with a sense of extremely limited liability to promote the general welfare. In the opinion of Cicero, spokesman for the optimates, the business of the aristocrat is to govern, that of the plebeian is to know and keep his place. As in the history of our own republic, the problems were economic and social ones for which liberals, from the Gracchi to Julius Caesar, had sought a political solution. All three branches of the government, the executive, the legislative, and the judicial, were, in Cicero's consulship (63 B.C.) in the hands of the optimates, and Cicero and his

friends intended to keep them there. An electoral system which concentrated two-thirds of the votes in the hands of one-fourth of the population made bribery relatively easy, and what it cost a man to get himself elected consul he could get back by extortionate tax-collecting when he went out the following year to govern his province. Even Cicero, who was an honest man, cleared $110,000 in a single year in Cilicia, and Julius Caesar, liberal though he was, was said to have made $40,000,000 out of the conquest of Gaul. After his term as consul the aristocrat would move in the highest ranks of the Senate, which was neither an annual nor an elective body, but a self-perpetuating oligarchical cabal which for centuries preserved by dynastic intermarriages its privileged position and its vested interest in the *status quo*. The Roman constitution made no provision for a "loyal opposition"; the permanent reservoir of all political power and experience was in the ruling class, and the plebs could expect no attention to their interests save from "traitors" to that class like the Gracchi and Julius Caesar. The popular assemblies could neither initiate, discuss, nor amend proposed legislation: they could only cast ballots for magistrates whom they had not nominated, and vote yea or nay on bills proposed by the Senate. This is the government which Cicero in his *Republic* and *Laws* describes as the ideal state. In theory it represented a balance of power; in practice it was so close an oligarchy that in 115 B.C. two thousand landowners held the privilege of public office over 394,000 citizens, and thereby controlled diplomacy, commissions in the armed forces, the treasury, and the bench. They exploited conquered countries so that for well over a century the capitalist class had no capital tax to pay, and they had no interest in weakening their control by broadening the citizenship base. The system survived only because the Roman plebs were broken to discipline and were traditionally respectful of social authority. But the rise of the commercial bourgeoisie (the "knights") challenged the power of the optimates and brought about the Augustan principate.[3]

For the only choice was between voluntary social and economic reform initiated by the conservative class, or one-man rule. When Julius Caesar attempted these reforms as dictator, his assassination was represented as the "liberation" of the "republic" from a "tyranny," but it may equally well be viewed as the "murder" of a "friend of the people" by "vested interests." But Brutus and Cassius reckoned without Caesar's veterans, a citizen army which since Marius had held the whip hand, so that it was to become increasingly true that he who controlled the army controlled the state. The veterans sided with Antony and Octavian; the result was a compromise in which liberty, which had never been more than a concept to the Roman masses, was sacrificed to security, efficiency, and the Roman peace. The Senate was packed with partisans of Octavian, the key provinces were put under his control, and were supervised, budgeted, ruled by his appointees with limited power, and on the whole honestly administered. The problem of land grants and unemployment was in part met by the practice already mentioned, of settling the veterans on land confiscated from the opposition. So the ambition and feuding of the optimates destroyed a spurious republic and made forever impossible true democratic freedom for the Roman people.

Augustus boasted that he had found Rome a city of brick and left it a city of marble. Though his boast was made considerably easier to fulfill by the comparatively simple device of laying thin marble veneer over existing brick construction, it is true that Rome in his lifetime became the architectural rival of Periclean Athens. Vergil's description of the rise of Dido's Carthage, with the workmen swarming like bees, reflects the busy activity of the building program of Augustan Rome. In the plastic arts, except for the fine realistic portrait busts of the hard-headed and ruthless men of affairs of the last century of the republic, Romans had not been distinguished, for reasons of some importance for Americans: imitation sapped their creative originality, and the material expansion of the state seemed of more importance than art. But in the practical sciences of architecture and engineering the Romans had no peers. They were pioneers in the development of concrete, the arch, the vault and the dome; their military roads, stretching perfectly straight for miles across Europe, supplied the fastest and most comfortable transport Europe was to know until the nineteenth century, and indeed in some places are still in use today.

The Altar of Peace and the temple of the Palatine Apollo did not compete aesthetically with the Parthenon frieze or the Erechtheum, but they have the monumental quality which symbolizes the grandeur and the dignity of the Roman Empire. And all over the provinces, from Syria to Spain, from Britain to the edge of the Sahara, roads, temples, aqueducts, and amphitheatres testified to the unity, efficiency, and contentment, if not the liberty, of one world.

In the intellectual history of Rome, the prosperity and peace of Augustus' reign passes as the symptom of a "Golden" Age, comparable to the vitality of Periclean Athens or Elizabethan England. But the vision of greatness in Horace's "Roman Odes," Vergil's epic, Livy's history, and the *Res Gestae* is clouded in each case but the last by pessimistic reservations about the low state of public morality, the ruthlessness that is the price of Empire, and the degeneration of Romans from the high standards of virtue set by their ancestors. In short, the "Golden" Age contains within it the seeds of a "Silver" Age in the succeeding century, characterized by less sureness of touch, less supreme confidence in the future, and a general sense of failure of nerve. So in the first century A.D. in Rome, as in the fourth century B.C. in Athens, or the twentieth in the United States, there was bred in creative artists a sense of beginning decline, manifest in a spirit of nagging criticism and nostalgia for the past. There is a stage in the life of a society when criticism is healthy; that of the early Roman Empire is carping and destructive, fit prelude to a decline and fall. The pessimistic spirit was not relieved by any hopes engendered by the birth of a child in a manger in Bethlehem: Palestine was an obscure province; the earliest Christians were humble people; and the crucifixion of an alleged King of the Jews under the reign of Tiberius was a routine incident in the frontier administration of a bored Pontius Pilate. The early church forged a correspondence between the Stoic philosopher Seneca and St. Paul, but there is no evidence that they knew each other. The historian Tacitus confuses the Christians with the Jews, refers to them as "the enemies of the human race," and reports sinister allegations of mysterious atrocities in their rites; Tacitus' friend Pliny the Younger is chiefly interested in their paying lip-service to the Emperor Trajan as a god, and regards their faith as stubbornness and insanity. Meanwhile Seneca's tragedies were demonstrating the sterility of Stoicism as a rival creed; Petronius' novel, with its Babbitt for hero, was underlining the emptiness of material satisfactions; the satirist Juvenal's savage indignation was lashing at the vices of noblewomen and noblemen amid the confusion and alarms of a teeming metropolis, and Tacitus was drawing with Hogarthian strokes the picture of a conscienceless tyrant who used Christians as torches to light his garden parties. And to the north lay the threat of the German tribes, so noble, so savage, and so pure, whose descendants in 410 were to dictate terms of surrender to a humbled Rome.

The keynote of "Silver" literature is rhetorical excess, fostered by the practice of authors in reading their works for the applause of coached audiences, and by the unreality of the current educational system, which, following the Sophists of fifth century Athens, stressed the ability to make the worse appear the better reason, to embroider paradoxes, to attribute sinister motives to historical characters, and to debate impossible hypothetical cases. As in Greece, education was neither free nor public, but it was cheap, so that schoolmasters, usually Greek and often slaves, were ill paid and despised, as now. Americans will be interested to note that the earliest Roman schools were coeducational, as they never were in Greece. Education was intended to be practical, inculcating discipline, knowledge of the law, respect for authority, and propriety of conduct as well as the three R's. The Roman common people were the most literate in the world, as the wall inscriptions (graffiti) at Pompeii bear witness, but their formal education stopped at an elementary level, and higher education was class education, the sons of optimates being trained usually under the republic by being attached as law clerks to distinguished jurists. It was here they learned the importance to a future ruler of a broad general education, but its basis was still practical, its end to rule. This general education, coupled with a sense of noblesse oblige and an instinct toward sympathy, courtesy, and kindliness, was what Cicero meant by humanitas, a noble concept which runs the risk of narrowness if snobbishly applied in a democratic age. The end of Roman education in both republic and empire was to produce a polished orator, but in the empire the orator had nothing to say; hence the emphasis upon artificialities, conceits, antitheses, and quibbles which marks the literature of the "Silver" Age. In the midst of this training there was none of the Greek emphasis upon athletics for their own sake: physical education under the republic was for the sake of efficiency in war, and gymnasiums and wrestling grounds were regarded as effeminate. Tacitus is disgusted with Nero for having encouraged the spread of Greek gymnastics among Roman youth. Later emperors endowed professorial chairs, whose incumbents were not expected to criticize the regime; the educational theorist Quintilian was one of the earliest appointees. Down to the very end of the Empire Greece was the finishing school for Roman aristocratic youth, as Europe has been for Americans; Caesar and Cicero both studied there, and Athens remained important as a university town long after she became politically and economically a backwater. Oxford was not the first home of lost causes.

This education produced the administrators of the one world of the Roman Empire.[4] Their method was adaptation, "muddling through." Augustus and his successors pretended to the last that the principate was only a temporary expedient; no regular dynastic succession was ever worked out; the administrative forms of the old city-state were preserved, though sometimes to the point of absurdity (the Emperor Gaius [Caligula] is said to have made his prize racehorse consul). In the provinces, home rule was allowed to work wherever it would, and the Emperor Claudius, though vilified for it by the Bourbons of his time, with wise statesmanship broadened the base of citizenship. The breadth and complexity of the imperial administration inevitably meant the growth of a bureaucracy, the imperial civil service, which more and more placed minor powers in the hands of the bourgeoisie under the growing autocracy of the Emperor and his army. This bureaucracy carried with it all over the Empire an official culture, stereotyped and unimaginative, unable to breathe vitality into the Empire as a unit.

The relation of the emperor to his subjects came more and more to be regarded as the relation of a master to his slaves, and the slaves could be trusted not to revolt so long as the master assured them a good administration, a stable peace, bread, and circuses. Their contentment rendered quixotic the revolts of the aristocratic Stoic opposition, and illusory, as Tacitus knew, the dreams of optimates longing for the dear dead days of the republic. The Senate was the emperor's rubber stamp, the consuls were. his nominees, the law was administered by jurists whose licence depended upon his pleasure. The plebs had no political life at all, but derived what sense they had of their own importance from public and private religious associations.

The imperial army, which at its peak numbered 450,000 men, was the largest professional army the world had ever seen, but it was small in comparison to the length of frontier it had to patrol. It was a sort of Foreign Legion, largely recruited on the frontiers for service on the spot: the Roman legionary was usually of the same race as the barbarian who faced him across the wall; at the end of his twenty-year hitch he would marry a woman of his own race, but bring up his children in Roman folkways; the Roman army thus became the greatest single instrument of Romanization of western Europe. The officers were not native; they supplied the link with Rome, and they regarded military service as a career, sometimes, as in the cases of Galba, Otho, Vitellius, and Vespasian, leading to a more or less lengthy tenure of the imperial throne itself. Their enlisted men were given a lump sum or a land grant at discharge; if they chose the latter, it would be passed on to an heir if the heir would promise military service; in this device some historians see the germ of medieval serfdom.

Imperial civil administration was an improvement over that of the republic. The governor was no longer a tax collector; the emperors had enough faith in their administrators to allow the provincials to appeal, if they wished, direct to Rome; and after Claudius (41–54) numbers of provincial senators in Rome represented their province's interests there. (The provinces contributed more and more to the intellectual life of the Empire: Seneca in the first century was a Spaniard, Augustine in the fourth a North African, and there are innumerable other examples.) Local self-government handled everything but the army, appeals, and taxes; the imperial policy, like that of the British in the nineteenth century, was to achieve, with minimum violence

to local usage, a stable local system, easy to run without the need for direct intervention. With the break-up of the Empire, this system fell by default into the hands of the large landowners, and may be regarded as the basis of the medieval feudal or manorial system.

Politically the Empire was unified by the concept of Rome at its centre and the Emperor as its central personality; it was one world-wide family all akin to Rome, as symbolized in Caesar and the bureaucracy that radiated from him. The state was regarded as all-powerful and divine; there was no freedom of speech or religion; no tribunal to judge between the state and the individual; all jurisdiction was administrative action. A candidate was elected not to carry out a program but to rule. The vote of the individual citizen simply symbolized his obligation to provide a means of extracting from him his own obedience. Economically, the Empire in a typical year ran on a budget of $30,000,000. Property taxes were used to pay pensions. In return for taxes, the government provided guarantees against piracy and brigandage, and gave to commerce the advantage of a uniform language, coinage, and law, besides subsidizing aqueducts, irrigation projects, harbors, and roads. Both the subsistence level and the population rose in consequence; there were fewer foreclosures, because the government issued mortgages at low interest, the proceeds of which went to support the poor in Rome and Italy. Industry was on a workshop, not a factory basis; there was some nationalization, especially of mines. The massive public buildings in the provinces offer mute evidence that administration was too heavy for local economic life, but the Empire had never depended on a complex international exchange, so that when it broke down in the third century the debacle was not as severe as it was, say, in 1929. Slaves were few and comparatively well treated; freed slaves held high government posts, and were partners and managers in industry. The lot of the urban poor was relieved by public and private welfare funds. Fashion was still set in the cosmopolitan yet close-knit society of the capital at Rome.

The culture of imperial Rome presents a picture of unity in diversity: the government united an infinite variety of races, environments, economic interests, and social classes, which began to split up into regional cultures as soon as the central administration weakened. Greek was, for example, always a second language; Claudius and Marcus Aurelius wrote in it by preference; the Greek East was a transmission line for Oriental influences, especially Christianity. So when the Empire split, it split in two, and a part of the heritage of Plato and Pericles passed to the Byzantines of Constantinople. The West, on the other hand, had not the consciousness of kind which the Romans had had when they first conquered Greece; attempting to be less provincial, the western provinces conformed to the official culture and thereby impaired its vitality. This official culture stressed comfort, utility, and massiveness; it was flexible, reasonable, comprehensive, and consistent, but it was still a class-culture, with a penalty for subversion so harsh that it suggests, as any such harshness always does, a fundamental lack of faith in its own principles. Petronius, Tacitus, and Juvenal paint a gloomy picture of mediocre morality, with its race suicide, easy divorce, sadistic gloating over cruel spectacles, and crass materialism. There is little evidence of intellectual curiosity, or spirit of adventure and enterprise; the lugubrious succession of suicides in Tacitus bears witness to lowered vitality; the decline and fall may then be ascribed not so much to social corruption or racial degeneration as to failure of intellectual and spiritual energy: pagan philosophy was not deep-rooted in the soil, and twenty generations after Plato it was withered on the branch. Cicero's *humanitas* became a mechanism for preserving class privilege, instead of a motive force, and those who might have welcomed it if its base had been broadened turned, with the hope that springs eternal in the human breast, to what appeared to be the wider promise and warmer welcome of Christianity.

The long story of Rome has its relevance to America. American civilization is European, as Roman civilization was Greek; Americans owe to the Romans, and the Greeks, their alphabet, writing, language, basic mathematics and science, and the dominant concepts and traditions in art and music. Whatever may divide us politically, culturally America and Europe, thanks to Rome, remain one world. The American republic was founded by men steeped in the classics, in which some found an example, others a warning. But the example of the Roman republic has not sufficed to warn modern man of the dangers of imitation in literature, self-seeking in economic life, money-making as the chief end for man, or conservatism if it reckons without the rights and aspirations of the common man. Nor has the participation of the United States in world-wide empire brought with it, any more than it did to the Romans, a real desire to bridge the gap between the artist and the public, to adjust principles to changing times without compromising their essence, to be constructive rather than destructive critics, or to realize the dangers of social centralization if the individual moral fibre is not strong. The relation of the individual to society is still the central problem; it must be solved by education; the fact that here Greek and Roman education failed does not reduce the problem for modern man. George Santayana defines culture as "the diffusion and dilution of habits arising in privileged centres." It is the duty of the educated man and woman to be vigilant in the constant effort to establish at least provisionally the conditions under which the individual personality may be set free: the "open society" of which only a few Greeks and Romans, as only a few in modern times, have seen the vision.

For clearly the ideal of democracy set by Pericles has not been achieved, none of the classic heroes has saved the world, and the followers of the Christ who taught forbearance, tolerance, and bearing one another's burdens are torchlight for Nero's garden party. Successive study of succeeding ages will show that the goal has not been reached, that sorrow and sighing have not fled away, that the greatest good of the greatest number remains still only a pious aspiration. But the record has not been all failure. There have been flashes of insight and times of greatness; the Gracchi prove that democracy may still be the school of men; Scipio's dream of the rule of reason, tempered by the classical restraint of the Golden Mean and the Stoic-Christian active sympathy for the unfortunate, still gleams before us. Whether it remains a vision, or is translated into vigorous, glowing action here and now, depends on the willingness of this generation to dedicate itself unflinchingly to the unselfish service of our fellow men; in a word, to the other-regarding virtues.

# NOTES

1. The section on geography is summarized from W. C. Greene, *Achievement of Rome* (Cambridge, Mass., 1933), by permission of the publishers, the Harvard University Press.

2. In this anthology the Stoics are represented by Cicero, especially in *On the Nature of the Gods*, and by Epictetus.

3. This paragraph is summarized by permission of the publishers from R. Syme, *The Roman Revolution* (Oxford, 1939).

4. The section on the empire is summarized by permission of the publishers from S. N. Miller, "The Roman Empire in the First Three Centuries" in E. Eyre, *European Civilization* (Oxford, 1935), Vol. II.

# The Haunted House OF PLAUTUS

## Translated by Harry J. Leon

### INTRODUCTION

THE ROMANS were first introduced to drama after the Greek model in 240 B.C. by the freedman Livius Andronicus, a Greek of Tarentum. Following his example, the Roman dramatists generally based their plays, both tragedies and comedies, on Greek originals. Roman tragedy, the chief writers of which were Quintus Ennius, Marcus Pacuvius, and Lucius Accius, has perished, except for scattered quotations. The Romans, however, greatly preferred comedy, especially the type based on Greek New Comedy and known as *fabula palliata*, after the *pallium*, a name given by the Romans to the outdoor costume of Greek men, since the settings of these plays were Greek. For their models the Romans took not the older plays of Aristophanes and his contemporaries, but the so-called New Comedy of Menander, Diphilus, Philemon, and Apollodorus, who wrote in the latter part of the fourth and the first part of the third centuries B.C. and derived their themes primarily from the private life of contemporary society.

Of the large output of Roman comedy we have twenty plays by Plautus and six plays—his entire work—by Terence. The works of the other writers of comedy, the most important of whom were Gnaeus Naevius and Caecilius Statius, are lost, except for fragmentary quotations.

Of the life of Titus Maccius Plautus very little is known. Born in the Umbrian town of Sarsina (the year of his birth has been conjectured as about 254 B.C.), he knocked about with the theatrical groups in Rome and, after losing his savings in some commercial venture, was forced to do hard physical labor until success as a playwright brought him better circumstances. He died in 184 B.C.

His output of comedies was large. While many spurious plays were attributed to him in antiquity, Marcus Terentius Varro, the scholarly contemporary of Cicero, selected twenty-one plays as certainly by Plautus. It is a reasonable assumption that the twenty which have survived are those of Varro's list, especially since the oldest of our Plautine manuscripts has fragments of a twenty-first play, the *Vidularia*, which, coming at the end of the alphabetically arranged sequence, was somehow lost.

The *Mostellaria* (*The Haunted House*) is typical of many of Plautus' plays and, generally, of the author's style. The plot is loosely constructed of a series of more or less farcical episodes. The dissolute young man, the credulous old man, the clever slave, and the devoted mistress are familiar characters in Roman comedy. The language is colloquial and racy, with frequent touches of slang. Puns and wordplays (generally untranslatable) are quite common. The humor is for the most part broad and without subtleties, the only kind that could go over with a not very cultivated audience which could become unruly if its interest was not sustained. There is comparatively little character delineation. In those plays which depend on character portrayal, such as the *Aulularia* with its miser and the *Miles Gloriosus* with its swashbuckling soldier, the characterization is applied thickly.

The reader should bear in mind that the plays of Plautus were musical comedies and that verse is used throughout, even for the dialogue portions. Some parts were spoken (comparable to the blank verse in a Shakespearian play), some were delivered in a sort of recitative, and some were sung as arias or duets. The musical accompaniment was supplied by a single flute player. It may be that the singer accompanied his aria with some dancing steps, but there is no evidence either way.

The division into five acts, while it has become traditional, does not go back beyond the Renaissance. The plays may have been presented continuously, with no break, or there may have been musical interludes at certain points. On this matter we have but little information.

The normal setting of a comedy of this type was a street in a Greek city, usually Athens, with the doors of two or three houses opening on the street. By convention, the exit on the left (from the point of view of the audience) led to the harbor or to foreign parts, while that on the right led to the forum or to the country. Usually there was no change of scene throughout the play, and the whole action was supposed to occur within the two hours or so of the actual stage performance.

The costumes were standardized. Men wore the Greek *pallium*, usually a sober white in the case of older men, gaily colored in the case of young men like Philolaches and Callidamates. Women wore a *palla*, or outdoor wrap. Slaves were dressed in a tunic. Appropriate wigs were worn. It is likely that the actors wore masks after the Greek fashion. Feminine roles were played by men or boys.

In the main, the text of W. M. Lindsay in the series of Oxford Classical Texts (Oxford, 1903) has been used for the translation, although departures have been made freely from it in places where the text is corrupt or incomplete.

## The Acrostic Argument

### (Post-Plautine)

**M**anaging, while his father was away
**O**n a trip abroad, to buy and free his sweetheart,
**S**oon Philolaches squandered all, and Tranio
**T**ook charge and tricked the old man on his return,
**E**xciting him with tales that the house, being haunted,
**L**ong since had been abandoned. Then a loan shark came
**L**oudly demanding his money, for they had made
**A** loan, so Tranio said, to buy a house.
**R**equired to tell him where, he said next door.
**I**nspecting it, the father finds he's tricked.
**A**t last he is appeased by his son's best friend.

## Characters

TRANIO, city slave of THEOPROPIDES
GRUMIO, country slave of THEOPROPIDES
PHILOLACHES, a young Athenian, son of THEOPROPIDES
PHILEMATIUM, a prostitute, mistress of PHILOLACHES
SCAPHA, elderly maid of PHILEMATIUM
CALLIDAMATES, a young Athenian, friend of PHILOLACHES
DELPHIUM, a prostitute, mistress of CALLIDAMATES
THEOPROPIDES, an elderly Athenian
MISARGYRIDES (*Hate-Money*), a money lender
SIMO, an elderly Athenian
PHANISCUS, slave of CALLIDAMATES
PINACIUM, slave of CALLIDAMATES
SPHAERIO, slave of THEOPROPIDES
SUNDRY SLAVES AND ATTENDANTS

*The scene is a street in Athens, on which front the houses of* THEOPROPIDES *and* SIMO *with an alley between them. There is an altar before the house of* SIMO.

## Act I

GRUMIO (*Standing in front of* THEOPROPIDES' *house*). You'd better come out of the kitchen, you scoundrel—trying to get smart with me among the pots and pans. Get out of the house, you ruiner of our master! Wait till I get you on the farm! I'll get even with you good and plenty, if I'm alive. Get out of here, I say, you pot-sniffer. What are you hiding for?

TRANIO (*Entering from the house*). What the devil is the idea of your yelling like this right in front of the house? Do you think you're out on the farm? Get away from the house. Go back to the farm. Get out and be hanged. Get away from the door. (*Strikes him.*) How's that? Is that what you've been waiting for?

GRUMIO. Help! What are you beating me for?

TRANIO. Because you're alive.

GRUMIO. All right! You just wait till the old man gets back. Just wait till he gets back safe after you've been eating him up while he's away.

TRANIO. What you're saying doesn't make any sense and isn't true, you numbskull. How is it possible to eat a person up while he's away?

GRUMIO. You city slicker, wise guy, playboy! So you throw the farm up against me? I reckon, Tranio, it's because you know you'll be put to work at the grindmill very soon. Just a few days more, Tranio, and I'll bet you'll be increasing the population on the farm—yes, the gang that works in chains. Right now, while you feel in the mood and have got the opportunity, just drink away, squander the property, corrupt our young master—such a fine young man!—keep on drinking night and day, whoop it up, buy mistresses and set them free, feed moochers, eat in high style. Are these the instructions the old man left with you when he went away to foreign lands? Is this how he'll find his property's been taken care of? Is this your idea of the duty of a good slave, to ruin his master's property and his son? Yes, I think the lad really is ruined when he's interested in this kind of life. Before this there wasn't a young man in the whole of Attica that had the reputation of being as thrifty and as well behaved as him, but now he takes the prize for the exact opposite. This is all thanks to you and the way you're teaching him.

TRANIO. How the devil is it any business of yours to look out for me or what I'm doing? Haven't you got enough cattle on the farm to look out for, I'm asking you? We just happen to enjoy drinking and necking and bringing in dames. I'm doing it at the risk of my hide, not yours.

GRUMIO. He talks cocky, all right. Foo! (*He blows his breath.*)

TRANIO. May Jupiter and all the gods damn you! Phew! You stink of garlic! You muck-pile, rube, billy-goat, pig-sty, swill, and manure all mixed up!

GRUMIO. Well, what do you expect? We can't all smell of imported perfumes just like you do, and we can't all have the place of honor at table or eat off of such swell foods like you do. You can keep your old squabs and fish and poultry. Just let me drag out my life with my garlic salad. You're a lucky guy; I'm a poor sap. That's O.K. with me, so long as my good luck is waiting for me and your bad luck for you.

TRANIO. It looks like you're jealous of me, Grumio, because I'm having such a swell time and you're having such a lousy time. That's just the way it's supposed to be. Necking is my line, tending cattle is yours, living like a king for me, living like a tramp for you.

GRUMIO. Believe me, the hangmen will make a sieve out of you. They'll fill you full of holes; they'll drag you through the streets with your hands tied behind your back, if only the old man gets back home!

TRANIO. How do you know that this won't be happening to you ahead of me?

GRUMIO. Because I never deserved it, but you did and still do.

TRANIO. You'd better cut out the chatter unless you want to get the tar beaten out of you.

GRUMIO. Well, are you going to give me the cattle-feed to take back? Yes, give away money to disreputable characters. Go ahead and keep on like you've started. Drink away, whoop it up, eat and stuff yourselves. Use up all the victuals.

TRANIO. Aw, shut up and go back to the farm. I guess I'll go to Piraeus and buy myself some fish for supper. I'll have somebody bring the feed over to the farmhouse tomorrow. Well, what are you glaring at me for now, you jailbird?

GRUMIO. I'll bet that name will apply to you pretty soon.

TRANIO. As long as things are this way right now, I'm not worried about pretty soon.

GRUMIO. All right. But I know this much. You'll lots quicker get what you don't like than what you'd really like to get.

TRANIO. Quit pestering me now. Go off to the farm. Get a move on you. And I'm warning you that you'd better not waste any more of my time after this. (*Exit to left.*)

GRUMIO. So he's gone and doesn't care a damn for what I've said. O immortal gods! I pray for your help! Grant that our old master should get back here as soon as possible! He's been gone for three years now. Make him come back before everything's ruined, our house and our farm. If he doesn't come back, what's left will last only a few months more. I'll go back to the farm now. But there I see our master's son, all ruined now after being such a fine young man. (*Exit to right.*)

PHILOLACHES *enters from left, faces the audience, and sings.*

I've been doing lots of thinking
And I've worked my brains a lot,
   Whatever brains I've got,
To figure out what each man on this earth
Resembles most from the minute of his birth.
So I want to tell you all what I have found.
My simple parable I'll now expound.

When he's born, he's like a house,
   A brand-new house,
And I will prove it now to all of you,
So that however much you disagree,
   You presently will see
That what I say is absolutely true.
   Now if you'll lend an ear,
   I'll make the matter clear,
And all your doubts will promptly disappear.

When the house is just completed, an object to
    admire,
All men applaud the builder and they feel a
    strong desire
To use this as a model, and no matter at what
    expense
They want to build themselves a house of similar
    excellence.

Now. alas, a worthless fellow moves into this
    place.
    Lazy is he; his slaves are lazy, too,
    And to this house the harm they do
      Is simply a disgrace.
A windstorm breaks some tiles, but these he
    won't replace.
The rain comes through and soaks the walls and
    makes an awful mess;
The builder's masterpiece is wrecked, and you
    really must confess
    That the builder himself is not to blame,
    Though I really think it's a great big shame.
When repairs are slight, there are some who'll
    wait
Till the walls cave in, and it's just too late.

Well, that takes care of the house, and now I
    aim
To prove that man and house are very much the
    same.

The father is the builder of his son:
He lays the foundations with the greatest care;
To build him up no effort does he spare,
So he will be inferior to none.
    He teaches him letters
      And then ancient history
    And math and law and government
      And plane geometry,
    So that he'll be a model for
      The whole community.
When military service comes, he sends a friend
    along
To watch his boy, so he will not go wrong.
When the boy has served his time for just about
    a year,
How the building will turn out becomes quite
    crystal clear.

Now look at me: as long as I was under the
    builder's eyes,

I was a very decent lad whom none could criticize.
When I moved into my own control
And took possession of body and soul,
    I ruined—oh, so fast!—
The builder's work, which was meant to last.
First came idleness, like a wind
    Which brought the hail and rain,
And it swept away my modesty
    And left me proud and vain.
I made no repairs; then love seeped in,
    Like rain, to drench my heart.
It soaked my mind and my very soul.
    I began to fall apart.
All is ruined now: my virtue's gone,
    My name and reputation;
I am scorned by all; my head is bowed
    With grief and humiliation.
My timbers are rotted beyond repair.
To help me nobody seems to care.
It breaks my heart to think what I have been
And what I have become through vice and sin.
      Once I was best of all
      At horsemanship and ball,
      In spear and discus throw,
      With javelin and bow.
      I was so happy then,
      The happiest of men!
A model of high character for all the world I
    stood;
But now at last I realize I'm just no earthly good.

*He bows his head in shame. Enter* PHILEMA-
TIUM *and* SCAPHA *from* THEOPROPIDES' *house,
the latter carrying toilet objects.*

PHILEM. I just can't remember when I've enjoyed a cold bath more than now, Scapha, and
when I've felt so really clean.

SCAPHA. Well, everything has an outcome, just
as this year there's been a fine harvest.

PHILEM. But what has the harvest got to do
with my bath?

SCAPHA. No more than your bath has got to
do with the harvest.

PHILOL. (*Aside*). O lovely Venus! (*To the
audience*) There you see the windstorm that
swept away all my modesty, which was my roof,
so that Love and Desire rained into my heart,
and I never can repair it any more. The walls in
my heart are soaked through and this house is a
complete ruin.

PHILEM. Please look me over carefully, Scapha, and see if this dress really becomes me. I do want to please my Philolaches, my darling, my benefactor.

SCAPHA. You'll do better to dress yourself up in a charming personality, seeing that you're so charming yourself. It isn't the woman's dress that lovers love, but what's inside the dress.

PHILOL. (*Aside*). Lord love me! Scapha's a clever woman. The old hussy is smart as a whip. How cleverly she understands all the habits and feelings of lovers!

PHILEM. Come on now.

SCAPHA. What is it?

PHILEM. Why don't you inspect me and see how this looks on me?

SCAPHA. You're so beautiful that you look good in anything you wear.

PHILOL. (*Aside*). Well, for that fine compliment, Scapha, I'll make you a present today, and I won't allow you to praise my beloved for nothing.

PHILEM. Now I won't have you flattering me.

SCAPHA. You sure are a stupid woman. Say, would you rather be criticized falsely than praised truly? If you ask me, I'd lots rather be complimented, though falsely, than be blamed truly or have anyone make fun of my looks.

PHILEM. I like the truth and I want the truth to be told to me. I just hate a liar.

SCAPHA (*Admiring her*). By your love for me and by Philolaches' love for you, I swear you're gorgeous!

PHILOL. (*Aside*). What's that, you hussy? How's that you swore? By my love for her? How about her love for me? Why didn't you add that? I take back the present I was going to give you. It's too bad for you. You've lost out on what I promised to give you.

SCAPHA. You know, I really am surprised that a girl so smart as you and so clever and so carefully trained should now be acting so utterly stupid.

PHILEM. Well, just tip me off if I'm doing anything wrong.

SCAPHA. You are sure enough doing wrong in putting your hopes on him alone and being nice especially to him and turning down the others. It's O.K. for a married woman to devote herself to one lover, but not for a prostitute.

PHILOL. (*Aside*). Great Jupiter! What is this monster that is living in my house? I'll be damned if I don't kill that hag with thirst and hunger and cold!

PHILEM. I don't want you to give me any bad advice, Scapha.

SCAPHA. Anybody can see that you're a fool if you expect that he'll be your lover and benefactor for ever. I'm warning you. He'll desert you when you get older and he gets enough of you.

PHILEM. I hope not.

SCAPHA. It's what you don't hope for that happens to you lots more often than what you hope for. After all, if words won't make you believe that what I'm saying is true, learn the truth through facts. You see what I am now, but oh, what I was before! I was once loved just as much as you are now. I also was nice to just one man. But, oh dear! When my head changed its color with age, he just up and left me. That's what will happen to you, I reckon.

PHILOL. (*Aside*). I can scarcely hold myself back from flying at the eyes of that old troublemaker.

PHILEM. But he set me free exclusively for himself, and at his own expense. So I feel obligated to be at his service exclusively.

PHILOL. (*Aside*). Ye gods! What a darling creature and what a noble character! I certainly did the right thing and I'm happy to be broke on her account.

SCAPHA. You certainly are a silly creature!

PHILEM. And why?

SCAPHA. For being so concerned about his loving you.

PHILEM. But tell me, why shouldn't I be concerned?

SCAPHA. You're a free woman now. Now you've got what you wanted. If he doesn't love you on his own hook, he'll have lost all the money he paid for your freedom.

PHILOL. (*Aside*). I'll be damned if I don't beat the life out of that creature. That vicious hag is corrupting this girl with her villainous advice.

PHILEM. I can never really repay him for all that he has done for me. So, Scapha, you'd better not try to persuade me to think any less of him.

SCAPHA. Well, here's one thing you'd better think about. If you devote yourself exclusively to him now while you have your youth, you'll find yourself weeping bitterly in your old age.

PHILOL. (*Aside*). I only wish I could turn myself into an attack of asthma right now, so that I could get into that old fiend's throat and choke her to death—Oh, that vile trouble-maker!

PHILEM. I'm really under obligations to show the same grateful attitude toward him now, when I've got what I wanted, as before I got it out of him, when I was playing up to him.

PHILOL. (*Aside*). The gods can punish me all they want, if I don't set you free a second time because of what you just said, and annihilate Scapha.

SCAPHA. If you're absolutely sure that you'll always have a meal ticket and that he'll stay your lover for the rest of your life, I guess it's O.K. to give him exclusive rights and fix your hair like a married woman.

PHILEM. You know, a person's reputation is as good as money in the bank. If I only keep my good reputation, I'll be rich enough.

PHILOL. (*Aside*). By George, even if I have to sell my father as a slave, I'll much rather let him be sold, than ever let you be in want of anything or have to beg while I'm alive.

SCAPHA. What's to become of those other fellows who are in love with you?

PHILEM. They'll love me all the more when they see how I show my gratitude to one who is good to me.

PHILOL. (*Aside*). I do wish someone would bring me the news that my father is dead, so that I could disinherit myself of all my property and make her the heir.

SCAPHA. All he's got will soon be used up—the way they eat and drink day and night without anybody showing any restraint. They just plain gorge themselves.

PHILOL. (*Aside*). By heavens, I'm determined to start practising economy on you first of all. You'll get nothing to eat or drink in my house for the next ten days.

PHILEM. If you've got something nice to say about him, you may speak. But if you say anything mean about him, you'll just get a good whipping.

PHILOL. (*Aside*). By golly, if I had made a sacrifice to almighty Jupiter with the money I paid to buy her, I'd never have made so good an investment. You can see how she loves me with all her heart. What a lucky fellow I am! I've set free a lawyer to plead my case for me.

SCAPHA. Now I sée that you don't care one bit for all the other men, compared to Philolaches. So from now on, just to avoid being whipped on his account, I'll rather agree with you—that is, if you're dead sure that he'll be your lover for life.

PHILEM. Hand me my mirror and the jewel case right now, Scapha. I want to be all fixed up when my darling Philolaches arrives.

SCAPHA. It's only the woman who has no confidence in her own looks and in her youth that needs to use a mirror. What do you need a mirror for, when you yourself are the best mirror for the mirror?

PHILOL. (*Aside*). What a compliment! So you won't go unrewarded for so charming a remark, Scapha, I'll give a sum of money today as a present to you—my Philematium.

PHILEM. Is my hair all in place and arranged all right? Just look.

SCAPHA. If you're all right yourself, you can be sure your hair's all right, too.

PHILOL. (*Aside*). Oh my! Can you imagine a viler specimen than that woman? Now she's an unscrupulous yes-woman, when a minute ago she was a contradictor.

PHILEM. Hand me the face-powder.

SCAPHA. Why, what do you want face-powder for?

PHILEM. To put on my cheeks.

SCAPHA. You might as well try to bleach ivory with ink.

PHILOL. (*Aside*). Pretty clever that gag about ivory and ink! Hooray! Good work, Scapha! Good for you!

PHILEM. Well then, hand me the rouge.

SCAPHA. No, I won't. You're pretty enough as you are. Are you going to retouch a beautiful work of art with a fresh coat of paint? A young girl like you shouldn't even touch any makeup or powder or mud pack or any other kind of cosmetics.

PHILEM. Very well, take the mirror.

PHILOL. (*Aside*). Oh, damn it! She gave the mirror a kiss. How I wish I had a rock to smash that mirror's head with!

SCAPHA. Take this towel and wipe off your hands.

PHILEM. Why, what for?

SCAPHA. Didn't you just hold the mirror? I'm afraid your hands smell of silver. We don't want

Philolaches to suspect that you've received silver from anybody.

PHILOL. (*Aside*). I don't think I ever have seen a slicker wench than that one. What a smooth and clever idea that wretch thought up about the mirror!

PHILEM. What do you say to my putting on some perfume?

SCAPHA. My goodness, no!

PHILEM. And why not?

SCAPHA. Why, because a woman smells just right when she doesn't smell at all. Now take those old hags who drench themselves with perfumes and those retouched, antique, toothless creatures who try to camouflage their physical blemishes. Why, when their sweat gets mixed up with their perfumes, they start smelling right off like when a cook has mixed a lot of gravies together. You don't exactly know what they smell like, but you can tell one thing—they smell awful.

PHILOL. (*Aside*). How clever she is to understand everything! She's just the cleverest creature alive! (*He addresses the audience.*) That's true, too, as I'm sure most of you folks know, who've got old women at home for wives, that bought you with a big dowry.

PHILEM. Come and take a look at my jewelry and my dress. Does it look all right on me, Scapha?

SCAPHA. It's none of my business to worry about that.

PHILEM. But whose business is it, then?

SCAPHA. I'll tell you. It's Philolaches'. It's his lookout not to buy you anything unless he thinks it will please you. A lover buys a mistress' favors with jewelry and fine clothes. What's the use of bothering to show off before him something that he doesn't care to have? Nice clothes are all right for hiding one's age. Jewelry is O.K. for an ugly woman. A beautiful woman will be more beautiful stark naked than with fine clothes on. Besides, she just wastes her time getting dolled up if she has a bad disposition. An ugly personality messes up a beautiful outfit worse than filth. If only she's beautiful, she's more than well dressed.

PHILOL. (*Aside*). I've been holding off too long. (*He steps forward.*) What have you two been doing here all this time?

PHILEM. I'm getting dressed up in order to please you,

PHILOL. You're dressed up enough. (*To Scapha*) You go on inside and take all these trinkets away.

*Exit* SCAPHA *into the house with the paraphernalia.*

Now, my sweetheart, my Philematium, I'm just in the mood to have a little drink with you.

PHILEM. And I'm in the mood to have one with you, for whatever you like, I like too, my sweetheart.

PHILOL. Ah, those words are cheap for a thousand dollars!

PHILEM. Just give me five hundred, please. I want you to get a bargain.

PHILOL. Now that still leaves you five hundred to the good. Just figure up. I paid fifteen hundred dollars to buy you.

PHILEM. Why do you throw that up to me?

PHILOL. What, I throw it up to you, when I really feel that I'm the one to be criticized? It's a long time since I made such a good investment of my money.

PHILEM. Anyhow, seeing that I love you, I couldn't have invested my services better anywhere else.

PHILOL. Then our account of income and outgo balances perfectly. You love me, I love you, and we both think that that's the way it ought to be. If any people are happy over this, may they always be happy over their own good fortune; but if there are any who are jealous of us, may they never have any happiness at all that anyone could be jealous of.

PHILEM. (*Arranging the dining couch*). Come, take your place over here. (*She speaks to a slave.*) Boy, bring us some water for our hands. That little table there, put it right over here. See where the dice are. (*They take their places on the couch.* PHILEMATIUM *hands* PHILOLACHES *a perfume bottle.*) Will you have some perfume?

PHILOL. What do I need it for? I have essence of roses reclining right next to me.

*He sees* CALLIDAMATES *and* DELPHIUM *approaching from right.*

Why, is that my old pal on the way over here with his girl? It's he, all right. Yes, it's Callidamates coming with his girl. Hooray! Well, my darling, here are some fresh troops coming for a share in the loot.

*Enter* CALLIDAMATES, *unsteady on his feet, supported by* DELPHIUM. *A slave accompanies them.* CALLIDAMATES *sings drunkenly.*

Somebody come to Philolaches' later in the day
   To fetch me when I'm through.
Want him to come early, too.

*To a slave.*

Listen here, boy—say!
   That's the job for you.

The place where I just was—I had to run away.
Party was just dead and I got so sick,
   Had to get out quick.
Now I'm going to Philolaches' hang-out for a party,
That's a place a gent is sure of a welcome good and hearty
   With wine and food
   And a jolly mood.
Hic! Say, you don't think I'm st-st-stewed?

DEL. You always were a sot,
   Don't call this new; it's not.
CAL. How's about a kiss, what do you say?
DEL. If you insist, I guess it's O.K.
CAL. (*Kissing her*). You sure are cute! (*Staggers.*) Oops! Hold me! Wait!
DEL. Look out or you'll fall! Now stand up straight.
CAL. You are the ap-ap-apple of my eye,
   My sweetie pie,
And I'm your b-b-baby boy, my honey.
           (*He staggers.*)
DEL.    Say, this isn't funny!
You'll fall right in the street. Take care!
Let's get to our friends, who are waiting there.
CAL.    Aw, just let me fall,
   That's all.

DELPHIUM *tries to release him.*

DEL. Well, here goes.
CAL.         But I won't let go of you.

DEL. Let go, or you'll drag me down, too.
CAL. Aw, someone'll come, dear, by and by
   And pick us both up from where we lie.
DEL. He's quite pickled, I see.
CAL. P-p-pickled? You mean me?
DEL. So's you won't get hurt, just give me your arm.
CAL. Here.
DEL.    Stick by me and you'll suffer no harm.
CAL. Now, where am I heading?
DEL.         You mean you don't know?
CAL. Sure. Now I remember. I was starting to go
   Back home for a party.
DEL.         You're mixed up— and how!
   You're bound for this other place.
CAL.         Yes, I remember now.
PHILOL. (*To* PHILEMATIUM). I'd better go to meet them, dear. What do you say? He's a good friend of mine. I'll be back right away.
PHILEM. Right away is too long. So hurry, please.

PHILOLACHES *starts toward* CALLIDAMATES *and* DELPHIUM.

CAL. Hic! Anyone here?
PHILOL.         Here I am.
CAL.         Oh, Philolaches!
Best friend I've got in the world! How're you?
PHILOL. All right. God bless you! Here are places for two.
   And where do you come from?
CAL.         Well, what do you think?
From a place where they give a feller a drink.
PHILEM. Here's your place, Delphium. (*To servant*) Give him some wine.
CAL. I'm going to sleep.
DEL. (*Disgusted*).    Well, isn't that just fine!
What am I supposed to *do* with that confounded hound?
PHILOL. Just leave him and we'll start the drinks going round.

## ACT II

*Enter* TRANIO *from left, excited.*

TRANIO. Great Jupiter is trying with all his power and might to bring me and our young master Philolaches to ruin. Our hope's all shot. There is no place anywhere for confidence. Even the Goddess of Safety herself couldn't save us if she tried. I've just seen a mighty mountain of misery and misfortune over at the harbor. The master's returned from abroad and Tranio is all washed up. (*To the audience.*) Is there anyone of you guys who would like to make a little loose change? All he has to do is let himself be nailed on the cross in my place today. Where are all your tough-skinned, hard-as-nails roughnecks, or those mugs who'll go right under the enemy's siege-works to earn two bits, or those human pin-cushions who'll let their bodies be pierced by ten spears at a time? I'll give a prize of a thousand dollars to the first fellow who dashes up to the cross, but on this one condition, that his feet and hands should be nailed double. After that's been done, he can come and ask me to pay him the cash right off. But I—oh, but I'm out of luck if I don't rush straight home.

PHILOL. Hooray! Here comes the grub. There's Tranio coming back from the harbor.

TRANIO (*Panting*). Philolaches!

PHILOL. What's the matter?

TRANIO. You and me both—

PHILOL. You and me, what?

TRANIO. We're dead ducks!

PHILOL. What do you mean?

TRANIO. Your father's here!

PHILOL. What's that you've said?

TRANIO. Our goose is cooked. I say your father has come.

PHILOL. Where is he? Tell me.

TRANIO. Where is he? He's here.

PHILOL. Who says so? Who saw him?

TRANIO. I saw him myself, I'm telling you.

PHILOL. Good night! What do I do now?

TRANIO. Why the devil are you asking me what you do? You're lying on the couch.

PHILOL. Did you really see him?

TRANIO. I tell you I did.

PHILOL. You're absolutely sure?

TRANIO. Surest thing alive.

PHILOL. I'm sunk if what you say is true!

TRANIO. What good would it do me to tell a lie?

PHILOL. What am I to do now?

TRANIO. Order all this stuff to be cleared out of here. Who's that sleeping over there?

PHILOL. It's Callidamates. Wake him up, Delphium.

DEL. (*Shakes him*). Callidamates, Callidamates, wake up!

CAL. I'm awake. Gimme a drink.

DEL. Wake up! Philolaches' father is back from abroad!

CAL. (*Holding up a wine glass*). Here's to the old boy's health.

PHILOL. He's healthy, all right, but I'm more dead than alive.

CAL. Dead and alive? That's impossible.
(*Drops back to sleep.*)

PHILOL. For heaven's sake! Please get up! My father has come back!

CAL. Your father's come back? Tell him to go 'way again. What business he got coming back here? (*Drops back to sleep.*)

PHILOL. What am I to do? My father will be here in a minute to find me miserably drunk, the house full of party guests and women. It's a wretched business not to start digging a well until thirst has got you by the throat. That's the way I am, miserably trying to think up what to do, now that my father is upon me.

TRANIO. Just look at that! He's put his head down and is dead to the world. Wake him up!

PHILOL. (*Shakes him*). Won't you wake up? I'm telling you my father will be here any minute.

CAL. (*Starts up, shouting*). What's that you say? Your father? Gimme my sandals! I'll get my sword and by God, I'll kill your father!

PHILOL. Oh, you're ruining everything!

DEL. Hush up, please!

PHILOL. (*To some slaves*). Lift him up right away and drag him inside.

CAL. (*As he is carried into the house, struggling*). By God, I'll use you for a chamber pot if you don't bring me a chamber pot!

PHILOL. Good night!

TRANIO. Don't be downhearted. I'll doctor up this trouble all right.

PHILOL. I'm sunk!

TRANIO. Oh, be quiet! I'll think up some way to straighten everything out. Are you satisfied if I fix things so that when your father comes, he not only won't go inside, but will even run for dear life far away from the house? You folks just go on inside and clear all these things out of here as quick as you can.

PHILOL. Where shall I be?

TRANIO. Where you want most to be. You'll be with this girl and with that one.

DEL. Hadn't we better leave?

TRANIO. You're not going *this* far, Delphium. (*With a gesture of thumb and forefinger*) You can go on drinking inside the house, and not one drop less than you would otherwise.

PHILOL. Oh dear! I'm worried stiff about how these sweet words of yours will turn out.

TRANIO. Can't you calm down and do what I tell you?

PHILOL. I guess I can.

TRANIO. First of all, you go inside, Philematium, and you too, Delphium.

DEL. We'll both do just as you wish.

(*They go in.*)

TRANIO. May Jupiter grant that you really do so! (*To* PHILOLACHES) Now you pay careful attention to what I want done. First of all, see that the house is locked up tight right away. And don't you let anyone make a sound inside.

PHILOL. I'll see to that.

TRANIO. Just as though there isn't a soul living in the house.

PHILOL. All right.

TRANIO. And don't let anybody answer when the old man knocks at the door.

PHILOL. Is that all?

TRANIO. Have someone bring that Spartan house key out to me. I'll lock up the house from the outside.

PHILOL. I'm entrusting myself and my hopes to your protection, Tranio. (*Enters house.*)

TRANIO. It doesn't matter a darn whether it's the patron or the client that tries to help a fellow, if he has no daring in his heart. Just anybody, whether he is good or bad, finds it easy to do some wicked act on the shortest notice; but the thing to look out for, and what really takes a clever fellow, is that what he has planned and done for a wicked purpose should all turn out peacefully and without trouble, so that he won't get into some mess that will make him sorry he's alive. Now I'll fix things so that all the storm

we've raised here will turn out quietly and peacefully and not cause us any trouble at all.

SPHAERIO *comes out of the house.*

But what are you coming out for, Sphaerio?

SPHAERIO *holds out the Spartan key.*

All right, all right. You've obeyed orders perfectly.

SPHAERIO. He told me to beg you just as hard as I could to scare his father off any way at all, so that he won't come inside to him.

TRANIO. Well, you can tell him this. I'll fix it so that the old man won't even dare to look at the house, but will cover his head and run away in absolute terror. Give me the key and go back inside and lock the door. I'll lock it from the outside also.

SPHAERIO *goes in.*

Now you can tell him to come on. I'll play such games with the old man while he's still here and alive that they'll beat any funeral games which he'll get after he's dead. I'll move away from the door this way and watch from here at a distance, so that I can spring my bundle of tricks on the old boy when he comes.

*Enter* THEOPROPIDES *from left, accompanied by two slaves carrying his baggage.*

THEO. I'm surely grateful to you, Neptune, for having let me get away from you by the skin of my teeth, and just make it home. But if there ever is a time after this when you catch me placing so much as my foot upon your waters, I give you full permission to do to me then and there what you tried to do to me just now. I'm off you for good from this day on. I've already trusted you all that I was ever going to.

TRANIO (*Aside*). Well, well, Neptune, you certainly made a dreadful mistake when you missed so fine an opportunity.

THEO. After three years in Egypt I've got back home. I guess my family will be glad to see me back.

TRANIO (*Aside*). By heavens, they would be

lots gladder to see a messenger reporting that you were dead!

THEO. (*Reaches the door*). What's the meaning of this? The door is locked in the daytime. I'll knock. (*Knocks.*) Say, isn't there anyone to open the door? (*He pounds and kicks on the door.*)

TRANIO (*Approaching*). Who is this man who has come up so close to our house?

THEO. (*Aside*). Why, this is my own slave Tranio.

TRANIO. O Theopropides! How are you, master? I'm so glad to see you back safe. Have you been quite all right?

THEO. Quite all right, as you see.

TRANIO. That's just fine.

THEO. But how about you folks? Have you gone crazy?

TRANIO. What do you mean?

THEO. Why, here you are, walking in the street with not a soul keeping watch in the house and no one to unlock the door or even answer. Why, I almost broke this whole door down by banging on it.

TRANIO. Hey, did you touch this house?

THEO. Why shouldn't I touch it? I'm telling you I almost broke the door down banging on it.

TRANIO (*Horrified*). You touched it?

THEO. I did touch it, I'm telling you, and I banged on it.

TRANIO (*Groaning*). Oh!

THEO. What's wrong?

TRANIO. That's simply dreadful!

THEO. What is the matter?

TRANIO. I just can't tell you what a dreadful, what an awful thing you've done.

THEO. What do you mean?

TRANIO (*Pulling him away from the house*). Start running, for heaven's sake, and get away from the house! Run this way! Run here! In this direction, toward me!

*He starts running;* THEOPROPIDES *follows.*

Did you really touch that door?

THEO. How in the world could I bang on it without touching it?

TRANIO. Good heavens! You've absolutely ruined——

THEO. Ruined whom?

TRANIO. Your entire household!

THEO. Damn you for those ill-omened words!

TRANIO. I'm afraid you won't be able to clear yourself and your family.

THEO. What for? What is this news you're bringing me all of a sudden?

TRANIO. Say, tell those two fellows to get away from there.

THEO. (*To the slaves*). You may go.

TRANIO. And don't you fellows dare touch the house. Touch the ground the way I do.

*He bends down and presses his hands on the ground. The slaves leave.*

THEO. By heavens, won't you please tell me what all this business means?

TRANIO. For seven months now nobody has set foot inside this house, ever since we moved out.

THEO. Speak up! What did you do that for?

TRANIO. Look around you and make sure there isn't anybody listening in on what we say.

THEO. (*Looking around*). It's perfectly safe.

TRANIO. Better look around again.

THEO. There's nobody around. You can speak now.

TRANIO. A murder has been committed.

THEO. What's that? I don't understand.

TRANIO. A murder has been committed, I'm telling you—long ago, a really ancient crime.

THEO. An ancient crime?

TRANIO. Oh, we've only just lately discovered that it happened.

THEO. What is this crime you're talking about, you rascal? Who did it? Speak up!

TRANIO. A host overpowered his guest and murdered him. I guess it must have been that fellow who sold you this house.

THEO. Murdered him?

TRANIO. Then he stole this guest's gold and he buried this guest right on the spot, here in this house.

THEO. What makes you think this really happened?

TRANIO. I'll tell you. Listen. Your son had had dinner out and after he came back home from dinner, we all of us go off to bed. We fall asleep. It just happened that I had forgotten to put out the lamp. And then he screams all of a sudden, awfully loud.

THEO. Who screams? My son?

TRANIO. Sh! Shut up, listen now. He said that the dead man came to him in his sleep.

THEO. Oh, in his sleep, you say.

TRANIO. Yes. But listen now. He said that the dead man spoke to him like this.

THEO. In his sleep?

TRANIO. It would sure be a funny thing if he spoke to him while he was awake, seeing that he was killed sixty years ago. Sometimes you're just too dumb for words. Can't you keep still?

THEO. All right. I'll keep still.

TRANIO. Now listen to what that dead man said to him. "I am a stranger from across the seas, a Transmarinian. Here do I dwell. This dwelling is assigned to me, for Orcus has refused to admit me to Acheron, because I am prematurely deprived of life. Through violated faith was I ensnared. My host slew me here and buried me secretly in this house without due funeral rites— that accursed man—for the sake of my gold. Now you must get you hence. This house is damned, this dwelling is accursed!" And all the excitements, all the terrible things that have been happening here, I could hardly tell you in a year.

*A noise is heard within.*

THEO. Sh! Sh! (*Moves toward door.*)

TRANIO. Why, what in the world is the matter?

THEO. There was a noise at the door.

TRANIO (*As if talking to the ghost within*). He's the one that knocked.

THEO. (*Terrified*). I haven't a drop of blood left. The dead are summoning me to Acheron while I'm still alive!

TRANIO (*Aside*). I'm finished! Those folks in there will ruin my whole plan. I'm just dreadfully afraid that the old man will catch me at it.

THEO. What are you talking to yourself for?

TRANIO. Get away from the door! Run away, I beg you, for heaven's sake!

THEO. (*Bewildered*). Where shall I run away? Why don't you run, too?

TRANIO. I have nothing to fear. I have made my peace with the dead.

VOICE WITHIN. Hey, Tranio.

TRANIO (*Going to the door*). You'll not call me, if you're wise. I didn't do anything wrong and I didn't bang on this door.

THEO. Why are you so excited, Tranio? Whom are you talking to?

TRANIO. Oh, were you the one that called me? God help me, but I thought that dead man was complaining because you had knocked on the door. But what are you still standing here for and not doing what I'm telling you to do?

THEO. What shall I do?

TRANIO. Don't look behind you. Run away! Cover your head!

THEO. Why don't you run?

TRANIO. I have made my peace with the dead.

THEO. I know. But how about a moment ago? Why were you so scared?

TRANIO. Don't bother about me, I'm telling you. I'll take care of myself. You just keep on going and run away as hard as you can, and pray to Hercules.

THEO. (*Running off to the right*). Hercules, I pray to you!

TRANIO. And so do I pray—that he'll make you drop dead today, my old fellow. Great gods, I appeal to you! What a mess of trouble I have cooked up today!

## ACT III

MISARGYRIDES (*Entering from right*). I have never seen a sorrier year for the money-lending business than this one has turned out to be for me. I spend my whole day from morning till night in the forum, but I can't find anyone who wants to borrow a thin dime.

TRANIO. Damn it! Now I'm ruined for good! There's that money lender who loaned us the money to pay for the girl and our other expenses. The game is up unless I can think of something before the old man finds out. I'll go up to him. (*He sees* THEOPROPIDES *approaching from the right.*) But what's he coming back home so soon for? I'm afraid he's heard something about this. I'll go up and speak to him. Oh, but I'm scared stiff! There's nothing more miserable than a guilty conscience, like what's worrying me now. But anyhow, I'll just keep on mixing him up. It's the only thing to do in this situation. (*To* THEOPROPIDES.) Where are you coming from?

THEO. I've just met the man I bought this house from.

TRANIO. I don't suppose you told him about what I told you?

THEO. I certainly did tell him the whole thing.

TRANIO (*Aside*). Oh, good heavens! I'm afraid my scheme is all washed up!

THEO. What's that you're saying to yourself?

TRANIO. Oh, nothing. But tell me. You really told him about it?

THEO. I've just said that I told him the whole thing in full.

TRANIO. So he admits everything about that guest?

THEO. On the contrary, he denies it.

TRANIO. He denies it? What a scoundrel! Just imagine! Does he really deny it?

THEO. I'd tell you if he admitted it. What do you think we ought to do now?

TRANIO. What do I think, he asks? By all means, get a referee to decide between you. (*Aside*) But be sure to get one who'll believe what I say. (*Aloud*) Why, you'll win as easy as a fox gobbles up a pear.

MIS. Well, there's Tranio, Philolaches' slave— the folks who don't pay me either the interest or the principal.

TRANIO *moves to forestall* MISARGYRIDES.

THEO. Where are you heading for?

TRANIO. I'm not going anywhere. (*Aside*) I'm certainly in a fix and out of luck. I must have been born under an unlucky star. He'll be coming up to me right in front of the old fellow. I'm in a tough spot, all right. They're putting the squeeze on me from both sides at once. But I'll go up to this one first. (*He moves toward* MIS-ARGYRIDES.)

MIS. (*Aside*). He's coming toward me. It's all right. There's some hope for my money.

TRANIO (*Aside*). He looks happy, but the joke's on him. (*Aloud.*) Ah, good day, Misargyrides.

MIS. Good day to you. How about my money?

TRANIO. Aw, cut it out, you dirty dog. As soon as you come within range, you have to open fire on me.

MIS. This man is empty-handed.

TRANIO. This man sure is a prophet.

MIS. Why don't you cut out all this nonsense?

TRANIO. Why don't you tell me what you want?

MIS. Where's Philolaches?

TRANIO. You could never have met me at a better time than this.

MIS. What do you mean?

TRANIO. Come this way a minute.

MIS. (*Shouting*). Why isn't my interest paid?

TRANIO. I know you've got a strong voice. Don't yell so loud.

MIS. By heavens, I'll keep on yelling!

TRANIO. Aw, come on. Do me a favor.

MIS. What favor do you expect me to do for you?

TRANIO. Please, now, go on home. (*He shoves him toward left.*)

MIS. Go home?

TRANIO. Yes, and come back here around noon.

MIS. And will I be paid my interest then?

TRANIO. He'll pay you. Go now. (*Shoves him.*)

MIS. What's the point of my running back here or going to all that trouble and wasting my energy? Why shouldn't I wait around here till noon?

TRANIO. Oh, no! Please go on home. I'm telling you the truth. Go on, now.

MIS. But I want my interest.

TRANIO. Go on now, please.

MIS. (*Louder*). Why don't you folks pay me my interest? Why are you trifling with me?

TRANIO. By heavens, you'd better . . . (*He makes a threatening gesture, but desists.*) Oh, please go now. Listen to me.

MIS. By heavens, I'll shout his name out, too. Philolaches!

TRANIO. Go to it! Louder now! I guess you're happy now that you're yelling.

MIS. I only want what's mine. You've been stringing me along now like this day after day. If I'm a bother, just pay me my money and I'll go away. Just say "Here's your money," and you'll shut me up completely.

TRANIO. You can have the principal.

MIS. Oh no! The interest. I want that first.

TRANIO. You don't say, you filthy scoundrel! Have you come here to throw your weight around? Well, go ahead. Do anything you can. He isn't paying you anything. He doesn't owe you anything.

MIS. He doesn't owe me anything?

TRANIO. You can't collect a red cent from him. So you're afraid he'll go away and skip the country just on account of your interest, when you have your chance to get the principal back right away?

Mis. But I'm not asking for the principal. It's the interest that has to be paid me first.

Tranio. Stop being a nuisance. Nobody's paying you. Do anything you like. I suppose you're the only one around here that lends money at interest.

Mis. (*Shouting*). Give me my interest! Pay me my interest! Pay up my interest! Are you going to give me my interest right now? Do I get my interest?

Tranio. Interest here, interest there. Interest is the only word in his vocabulary. Get out of here! I don't think I've ever seen a dirtier hound than you.

Mis. You're not going to scare me now with that kind of talk.

Theo. (*Aside*). Things are getting hot over there. Although it's quite a distance, I can feel the heat from here. (*He goes up and speaks to* Tranio.) Tell me, what is that interest that this man is asking for?

Tranio (*To* Misargyrides). Now look, there's his father who returned from abroad just a little while ago. He'll pay you both the interest and the principal, so you needn't expect to bother us any more. Try and see whether he'll keep you waiting.

Mis. I'll sure enough accept anything that's given to me.

Theo. (*To* Tranio). Now look here.

Tranio. What do you want?

Theo. Who is that man? What is he asking for? Why is he calling the name of my son Philolaches and making such a fuss in your presence? What money is owed him?

Tranio. I beg of you, please have somebody throw the money in that filthy dog's face.

Theo. What? I should . . .

Tranio. Yes, order that man's face to be whacked with money.

Mis. I can quite readily stand a whacking if it's with money.

Theo. What money is that?

Tranio. It is . . . uh . . . Oh, Philolaches owes him a little sum.

Theo. How little?

Tranio. Oh, something like two thousand dollars. You don't think that's much, do you?

Theo. So that's what you call a little sum?

Tranio. Now listen. Don't you think, I'm asking you, that he's just the type for a loan shark, the most low-down class of people in the world?

Theo. I don't care who he is, what he is, or where he's from. There's just one thing I want to know and insist on knowing: What money is this? And I hear there's some interest owed in addition.

Tranio. Twenty-two hundred dollars is the amount owed him. Tell him that you'll pay it, so that he'll go away.

Theo. What? I'm to tell him I'll pay it?

Tranio. Just tell him.

Theo. I?

Tranio. Yes, you. Please go ahead and tell him. Listen to me. Promise him. Come on, now. I'm telling you to.

Theo. Now answer my question. What was done with that money?

Tranio. It's safe.

Theo. Why don't you folks pay him back then, if it's safe?

Tranio. Your son bought a house.

Theo. A house?

Tranio. A house.

Theo. Fine! Fine! Philolaches takes after his father. So the lad has already gone into business. A house, you say?

Tranio. A house, I'm telling you. But do you know what kind of a house?

Theo. How do you expect me to know?

Tranio. Gosh!

Theo. What is it?

Tranio. Don't ask me.

Theo. What do you mean?

Tranio. A perfectly swell house, out of this world.

Theo. That's certainly fine. Now, how much is he getting it for?

Tranio. For only six thousand, that's all. But he gave this two thousand as a down payment. It's from this fellow that we borrowed the money we paid the man. Do you understand? After this house was the way I told you, he right away bought himself another house.

Theo. That was certainly well done.

Mis. Say, it's getting close to noon.

Tranio. Pay him off, please, so that he won't asphyxiate us with his belching. Twenty-two hundred is coming to him, both principal and interest.

Mis. That's the amount. I ask no more.

Tranio. I'd like to see you try and ask for one nickel more.

THEO. Young man, your business is with me.

MIS. So I'll get my money from you?

THEO. You'll get it tomorrow.

MIS. I'll be going now. I'm quite satisfied if I get it tomorrow. (*Exit.*)

TRANIO (*Aside*). He can go straight to the devil! He has pretty near upset all my plans. There isn't a more repulsive class of people on earth or any with less right for existing than the loan sharks.

THEO. In what location did my son buy this house?

TRANIO (*Aside*). Oh, I'm surely stumped now!

THEO. Aren't you answering my question?

TRANIO. I'll tell you. I'm just trying to recall the name of the owner.

THEO. Come on, try to think of it.

TRANIO (*Aside*). The only thing for me to do is to pretend it's the neighbor next door. I'll say that this is the house his son bought. I have heard that a hot lie is the best kind of lie. I'm determined to say what comes to me by inspiration.

THEO. How about it? Have you thought of it already?

TRANIO (*Aside*). Damn that man—or rather, this man right here! (*Aloud*) Your son bought the house from your next-door neighbor here.

THEO. Honestly?

TRANIO. If you'll pay the money, he bought it honestly; if not, well, he didn't. Didn't he buy in a pretty good location?

THEO. Why, it's an excellent location. I really do want to take a look at the house. Go ahead and knock at the door and call someone out, Tranio.

TRANIO (*Aside*). Well, now I'm stumped again! Now I don't know what to say. The waves are driving me back a second time upon the same rock.

THEO. What's the matter now?

TRANIO (*Aside*). I simply can't think up what to do now. I'm clearly caught.

THEO. Hurry up and call somebody out. Ask him to show us around.

TRANIO. But hey! There are ladies living here. We've got to find out first if they're willing or not.

THEO. A good and reasonable suggestion. Go in and make inquiry and ask permission. Meanwhile I'll wait out here until you come out.

TRANIO (*Aside*). May all the gods and god-desses annihilate you, old man! You just insist on fighting against all my plans.

SIMO *comes stealthily out of his house.*

Why, fine! There's the owner of the house coming out just at the right time. It's Simo himself. I'll step over this way while I call a session of the Senate in my brain. I'll go over to him when I think up a plan. (*He steps into the alley between the two houses.*)

SIMO (*Singing*). What a meal! Best I've had in the longest while.
Such a feast! And my wife served it up in style.
Now she calls me to bed. No sirree! Not for me!
I got awfully suspicious
When she served me those fine dishes.
Then she said, "Come to bed,"
But after a meal I don't feel
Like going to bed. So I fled.
I sneaked quietly out the door.
I'll bet the wife is plenty sore.

TRANIO (*Aside, singing*). That old man surely is in for one most awful row.
Both at supper and in bed he'll get it from his frau.

SIMO. As I think it over, this is the hitch:
If a man gets married to a wife that's rich
And old as the hills, he'll simply dread
The hour when he has to go to bed.
In such a wife's arms
Sleep loses its charms.
So I've decided to take a walk instead.

(*To the audience*)

You folks out there, what kind of wives
You have I cannot guess;
But this I know and know right well:
I've drawn a sorry mess.
She's a pain in the neck, a plague, a curse,
And day by day she's getting worse and worse.

TRANIO (*Aside, singing*). You'll regret sneaking out, you old reprobate.
It's no use griping now or cussing at your fate.
You alone are to blame for what has occurred.
Well, I guess now's the time to approach this bird.
Now I've got him. Now my plan's all in readiness.
I can use that old goat to get out of this mess.
I'll go up. (*Aloud*) How're you, Simo? How's every little trick?

SIMO (*Shakes hands*). How's the boy, Tranio?

TRANIO. You O.K.?

SIMO. I can't kick. What're you doing?

TRANIO. I'm shaking hands with a swell gentleman.

SIMO. It's nice of you to say that about me.

TRANIO. You've got it coming to you.

SIMO. Very well. But I'm shaking hands with a good-for-nothing slave. (*Laughs.*)

THEO. Hey, you scoundrel! Get back to me.

TRANIO. I'll be right with you.

SIMO (*Hesitatingly*). How about it? How soon . . .

TRANIO. What do you mean?

SIMO. You know—uh—the things that are going on inside your place.

TRANIO. Well, what about it?

SIMO. Are you on to what I'm saying? It's perfectly O.K. Might as well have a good time. Life's so short, you know.

TRANIO. Oh! I've just come to realize that you're talking about what's going on in our place.

SIMO. You certainly are having one swell time, and it's perfectly all right. Good wine, good food, choice fish—you're sure celebrating.

TRANIO. Oh no! That's how we used to live. Now all this has become a thing of the past.

SIMO. What do you mean?

TRANIO. We're just all completely ruined, Simo.

SIMO. Now don't say that. Everything has gone smoothly for all of you up to now.

TRANIO. That's true enough, I don't deny. We have had the time of our lives. But, Simo, now the wind has deserted our ship.

SIMO. What's the trouble? In what way?

TRANIO. In the worst way.

SIMO. But hadn't the ship been safely hauled up on the shore?

TRANIO. Oh gosh!

SIMO. What's the matter?

TRANIO. I'm just completely ruined!

SIMO. How so?

TRANIO. Another ship has just come along to wreck our ship.

SIMO. I hope everything will turn out the way you want it, Tranio. But what is the trouble?

TRANIO. I'll tell you. The master has returned from abroad.

SIMO. Ah, then you're really in for it with all the trimmings: whipping, torture, chains, and on top of all, the cross.

TRANIO. I beg of you, please don't tell the master on me.

SIMO. You needn't worry. He'll learn nothing from me.

TRANIO. I'm so grateful. You'll be my patron.

SIMO. No, thank you. I don't care for your kind of clients.

TRANIO. Now to the business that my old master sent me to you about.

SIMO. First answer my question. Has the old man already found out about how you have all been carrying on?

TRANIO. Not a thing.

SIMO. So he hasn't even scolded his son?

TRANIO. No, he's just as serene as a perfectly serene sky. Now he has ordered me to ask you in all seriousness to let him look over this house of yours.

SIMO. But it isn't for sale.

TRANIO. Oh, I know that. But the old man wants to build a woman's apartment here in his own house and a bath and a promenade and a porch.

SIMO. Why, what's he been dreaming up?

TRANIO. I'll tell you. He wants to get his son married as quick as he can, and that's why he wants to build a new woman's apartment. He says that some architect praised this house of yours to him as just terribly well built. So now he wants to use your house as a model, if you don't mind. He's all the more anxious to model his place on yours because he's heard that you have very good shade here in the summer right out in the open all day long.

SIMO. But on the contrary, when it's shady every place else, the sun always sticks around here constantly from morning till evening and camps right at my doorstep like a bill collector. The only place I can find any shade at all around here is down in the well.

TRANIO. Well, if you haven't got any shade, maybe you've got a Venetian blonde.

SIMO. Now don't be so smart. Things are just the way I'm telling you.

TRANIO. Even so, he wants to inspect the house.

SIMO. He can go ahead and inspect it if he likes. If he finds anything that pleases him, he can use it as a model for his building.

TRANIO. Shall I go and call him over?

SIMO. Go ahead and call him.

TRANIO (*Aside, walking toward* THEOPROPI-

DES). They say that Alexander the Great and Agathocles were two fellows who accomplished great things, but how about me as number three? I am performing immortal deeds all by myself. This old fellow is carrying a pack and so is that other one. I've started a new racket and it's not bad. Mule drivers use mules to carry their packs, but I use people to carry mine. They can stand a heavy load. They'll carry anything you pile on them. Well, I guess I'd better speak to him. I'll go up. Say, Theopropides.

THEO. (*Startled*). Oh! Who's calling me?

TRANIO. A slave faithful to his master in every way.

THEO. Where are you coming from?

TRANIO. You know what you sent me for? Well, I've got it all fixed.

THEO. But tell me, why did you stay there so long?

TRANIO. The old man was busy, so I had to wait.

THEO. You've still got your old habits—always slow.

TRANIO. Hey, why don't you remember that old saying? You can't whistle and drink at the same time. I couldn't be both here and there all at one time.

THEO. What have you arranged?

TRANIO. You can look over the place and examine it all you like.

THEO. Then come on and take me over there.

TRANIO. I'm not delaying you, am I?

THEO. I'll be right behind you.

TRANIO. Look, there's the old gentleman himself waiting for you before the door. Just see how unhappy he is that he's sold this house.

THEO. Well, what about it?

TRANIO. He's been begging me to persuade Philolaches to let him have it back.

THEO. I should say not! Charity begins at home, you know. If we had made a bad deal, we shouldn't be allowed to back out of it. If you make a profit, you'd better take it home with you. There's no room for sentiment in business.

TRANIO. You're just holding us up by talking so much. Come right behind me.

THEO. All right. I'm at your service.

TRANIO. There's the old man. (*To* SIMO) Well, 've brought the gentleman to you.

SIMO. I'm very glad you've come back safely from your trip, Theopropides.

THEO. May the gods bless you.

SIMO. He told me you wanted to look over my house.

THEO. Yes, if it won't inconvenience you.

SIMO. Why, it's quite convenient. Go in and look around.

THEO. But how about the ladies?

SIMO. Don't you worry one bit about any ladies. You can go all about the house as you please, just as though it were your very own.

THEO. (*Aside*). Just as though it were?

TRANIO (*Aside to* THEOPROPIDES). Seeing how distressed he is, be careful not to rub it in that you've bought this house. Don't you see how sad the old fellow looks?

THEO. That's so.

TRANIO. Therefore you shouldn't give the impression of gloating over him or being too eager. Don't you even mention your having bought it.

THEO. I see your point; you've got a good idea there; it's only human decency. (*To* SIMO) Now what?

SIMO. Just go right inside and look around all you want at your leisure.

THEO. I think this is really very kind and considerate of you.

SIMO. You're entirely welcome, I'm sure.

TRANIO (*To* THEOPROPIDES). Do you see this vestibule in front of the house and the promenade? How do you like them?

THEO. Just perfectly splendid!

TRANIO (*Slyly pointing toward the two old men*). And just take a look at those posts! See what they're like. How thick they are and how dense!

THEO. I don't think I've ever seen finer posts.

SIMO. Well, I certainly had to pay plenty for them once.

TRANIO (*Aside to* THEOPROPIDES). Did you hear him say "Had to pay once?" It looks like he can hardly keep from busting out crying.

THEO. How much did you pay for them?

SIMO. One hundred fifty dollars for the two of them, not counting the shipping charges.

THEO. (*Examining them closely*). Say, they're not nearly so good as I thought at first.

TRANIO. How so?

THEO. Why, termites have eaten into both of them at the bottom.

TRANIO. It looks to me like they were cut out too early. Yes, that's the trouble with them. But even so, they'll be perfectly O.K. if you give them a coat of creosote. You know, it wasn't one of your spaghetti-eating foreigners who did this job. Look at the dovetailing in the doors.

THEO. I see.

TRANIO (*Pointing to the old men*). Just look how snugly they doze.

THEO. What do you mean by doze?

TRANIO. Oh, I meant to say how snugly they close. Are you quite satisfied?

THEO. The more I examine everything the more I am pleased.

TRANIO. Do you see that picture of a crow making fools of two old buzzards?

THEO. Why, I don't see it.

TRANIO. Well, I do. There's a crow standing between two buzzards and it's nipping away at the two of them in turn. Look here in my direction, please, so that you can see the crow. See it?

THEO. I can see absolutely no crow there.

TRANIO. Then look over there toward the two of you and since you can't see the crow, you might be able to see the buzzards.

THEO. Now to settle this once and for all, I see absolutely no picture of any bird here at all.

TRANIO. O.K. Skip it. Forget it. You're so old you can't see very well.

THEO. But this, which I can see—it all pleases me very much indeed.

SIMO. It will be worth your effort to go over it more thoroughly.

THEO. You're quite right.

SIMO (*To a slave*). Come here, boy, and show this gentleman through the house and all the rooms. I'd take you in myself, but I've got some business at the forum.

THEO. Never mind about having him take me in. I don't care to be taken. Whatever it is, I'd sooner get lost than have anybody take me in.

SIMO. I mean take you in the house.

THEO. Well, I'll go inside without anybody taking me.

SIMO. All right, go ahead.

THEO. I'll go in, then.

TRANIO. Wait a minute. I'll look if there's a dog.

THEO. Yes, please look.

TRANIO. Shoo! Go 'way, dog. Shoo! Go 'way, damn you! Go 'way to the devil! Won't you move? Shoo! Get out of here!

SIMO. There's no danger. Go right ahead. She's as quiet as a dog with pups. Go right in and don't be afraid. I'll be off to the forum.

THEO. Thank you very much. Have a nice walk.

(*Exit* SIMO *to right.*)

Tranio, see that somebody gets this dog away from the door, even if she isn't dangerous.

TRANIO. Aw, just look how peacefully she's lying there! You don't want people to think you're cranky and jittery, do you?

THEO. Oh, all right. Have it your way. Follow me this way. (*He goes into the house.*)

TRANIO. I'll sure keep close to your footsteps.
(*He goes in.*)

## ACT IV

*Enter* PHANISCUS. *He sings.*

A slave who fears trouble before doing wrong
    Is useful to his master,
But one who's a sinner and then is afraid
    Is flirting with disaster.
He may try to escape, but his chances are slim.
If he's caught, then it's just too bad for him.
Now I'm always quick to obey.
    I'm willing to swallow my pride.
The others can act as they may,
    But I'm looking out for my hide.
If a slave wants to have a good master,
    Then he'd better learn how to behave.
Bad servant, bad master, says I,
    For the master will be like the slave.
Now the slaves in our house are a sorry lot.
They disobey orders and waste all they've got.
When they're asked to go fetch the master,
    They say, "Who? Me? Oh no!"
And they sneer and they jeer
    At the one who is willing to go.
So that's how I'm here,
    Though the others declined.
I've come to fetch master,
    While the rest stayed behind.
A flogging is in store for them
    Before the day is over.
They're sure to get it in the neck,
    But I will live in clover.

*Enter* PINACIUM.

PIN. Halt and stand where you are, Phaniscus. Won't you turn around?

PHA. Don't bother me.

PIN. A conceited monkey, isn't he? Stop, you dirty moocher!

PHA. How do you mean, I'm a moocher?

PIN. I'll tell you. An offer of food will get you to do anything.

PHA. I'm looking out for myself. I like to eat. What business is it of yours?

PIN. You're stuck up because you're the master's pet.

PHA. Ouch! My eyes hurt!

PIN. Why?

PHA. They're allergic to hot air.

PIN. Aw, shut up and stop cracking such corny jokes.

PHA. You can't make me answer your abuse. The master appreciates me.

PIN. I guess he ought to appreciate his little feather bed.

PHA. If you were sober, you wouldn't say such mean things to me.

PIN. Do you expect me to listen to you, when you won't listen to me? Come along with me, you rascal, to meet the master.

PHA. All right, but please cut out this kind of talk.

PIN. O.K. I'll knock at the door. (*Knocks.*) Hey, isn't there anybody here to protect this door from great damage? (*Knocks harder.*) Isn't anybody opening up? There's absolutely nobody coming out. That's what you can expect from these dissipated characters. So I'd better be pretty careful or someone might come out and beat me up.

*Enter* THEOPROPIDES *and* TRANIO *from* SIMO'S *house.*

TRANIO. Well, what do you think of our purchase?

THEO. I'm just tickled to death.

TRANIO. You don't think we paid too much for it, do you?

THEO. I'd say that if ever a house was just given away, it's this one.

TRANIO. Well, do you like it?

THEO. Do I like it, he asks? Why, I tell you I'm just crazy about it!

TRANIO. What do you think of the woman's quarters and the porch?

THEO. Just perfectly wonderful! I don't think I've seen a larger porch even in the main square.

TRANIO. Why, Philolaches and I personally measured all the porches in the main square.

THEO. With what result?

TRANIO. This one is by far longer than any of them.

THEO. Great gods, what a splendid bargain! If he were to offer me eighteen thousand cash on the barrel head for this house, I would never accept it.

TRANIO. By heavens, if you should want to accept it, I'd never let you do it.

THEO. We have made an excellent investment of our money in this deal.

TRANIO. You can be quite sure that I was the one who advised him and urged him to do it. I'm the one who made him get the money on interest from that money-lender, and we gave it to the owner as a down payment.

THEO. You have saved the whole ship. So we still owe him four thousand dollars?

TRANIO. Not a nickel more.

THEO. He'll get it today.

TRANIO. That's a good idea, so that he'll have no excuse to back out. Just pay the money to me and I'll turn it over to him.

THEO. But I'll have to watch out so that you don't try to put anything over on me, if I give it to you.

TRANIO. Do you think I'd dare to deceive you either in word or deed even as a joke?

THEO. Do you think I'd dare not to be on my guard about trusting you with anything?

TRANIO. Is that because I've ever tried to fool you in any way ever since I've belonged to you?

THEO. Well, I've been mighty careful, thanks to the gods and to my own intelligence. I'm smart enough if I can just protect myself against you.

TRANIO (*Aside*). You said a mouthful.

THEO. Now go off to the farm and tell my son that I've come back.

TRANIO. I'll do as you say.

THEO. Tell him to come hurrying back to the city along with you.

TRANIO. O.K. (*Aside.*) Now I'll slip in this way through the back door and get to my pals. I'll tell them how quiet everything is over here and how I have got this fellow out of the way.

(*Exit into alley.*)

PHA. You know, there's no sound of any party

here like there was just before and I can't hear
the flute girl playing or anybody else.

THEO. (*Aside*). What's going on over there?
What are those fellows looking for at my house?
What do they want? Why are they looking in-
side?

PIN. I'll keep on banging at the door. (*Knocks.*)
Hey, open up! Hey, Tranio, won't you open the
door?

THEO. (*Aside*). What's all this nonsense?

PIN. Open the door! We've come to fetch our
master, Callidamates.

THEO. I say, young fellows, what are you doing
over there? Why are you breaking down that
house?

PHA. I say, old fellow, why are you asking
about something that's none of your business?

THEO. None of my business?

PIN. Unless you've just been appointed chief of
police to manage other people's affairs, to investigate and look and listen.

THEO. Say, that's my house where you're
standing.

PIN. (*To* PHANISCUS). What do you say? Has
Philolaches gone and sold the house or is this
old bird trying to put one over on us?

THEO. I'm telling you the truth. But what business do you two have here?

PHA. I'll tell you. Our master is at a drinking
party here.

THEO. Your master is at a drinking party here?

PHA. That's what I'm telling you.

THEO. Young man, you're just too fresh.

PIN. We've come to fetch him.

THEO. Fetch who?

PIN. Our master. Say, how many times have I
got to tell you?

THEO. (*To* PHANISCUS). My boy, there's nobody living in here. You know, I think you're a
decent lad.

PHA. Doesn't that young fellow Philolaches live
in this house right here?

THEO. He did live here, but he moved out of
this house quite a while ago.

PHA. This old bird is sure nuts. You're all
turned round, grandpa. If he didn't move out of
here either today or yesterday, I'm dead sure he's
living here now.

THEO. Why, nobody has been living here for
six months now.

PIN. Come out of your trance.

THEO. Who? Me?

PIN. Yes, you.

THEO. Now don't you butt in. Let me talk with
this lad here. Nobody lives here.

PHA. Yes, there does, too. Yesterday and day
before yesterday, and three days ago and four
days ago and five days ago, in fact, ever since
his father went abroad, they've never stopped
having booze parties here for any three days at a
stretch.

THEO. What's that?

PHA. They have never for three days at a
stretch stopped eating and drinking here, bringing in women, whooping it up, bringing harp
players and flute girls.

THEO. Who's been doing all this?

PHA. Philolaches.

THEO. Philolaches who?

PHA. It's the one whose father is Theopropides,
I guess.

THEO. (*Aside*). Oh! I'm ruined, if he's telling
the truth! I'll question him further. (*Aloud*) So
you say that this Philolaches, whoever he is, has
drinking parties in there with your master?

PHA. That's right, I say.

THEO. My boy, you really are dumber than
you look. Just try and think whether you didn't
stop off somewhere for lunch and drink a little
more than was good for you.

PHA. What's that?

THEO. I just want to make sure that you haven't
come by mistake to the wrong house.

PHA. I know all right where I'm supposed to
go and I recognize the place I've come to. Philolaches lives here, the one whose father is Theopropides. And after his father went away on a
business trip, he set free a flute girl.

THEO. Philolaches did?

PHA. Yeh, and the girl was Philematium.

THEO. For what price?

PHA. Fifteen.

THEO. Thousand?

PHA. Good heavens, no! Hundred.

THEO. He set her free?

PHA. He sure did set her free, for fifteen hundred.

THEO. And you say that Philolaches paid fifteen hundred dollars for a mistress?

PHA. That's so.

THEO. And he set her free?

PHA. That's so.

THEO. And ever since his father went off on a trip abroad, he's been drinking all the time together with your master?

PHA. That's so.

THEO. Well, and did he buy this house next door?

PHA. That isn't so.

THEO. And then he gave two thousand dollars to this man as a down payment?

PHA. That isn't so, either.

THEO. Oh! You've ruined me!

PHA. Why no! He's ruined his old man.

THEO. You've spoken the truth!

PHA. I sure wish it wasn't true. I guess you must be a friend of his father's.

THEO. Great heavens! His father whom you speak of is an unfortunate man!

PHA. Those fifteen hundred are just about nothing compared to all the rest he's been spending on parties.

THEO. He has ruined his father!

PHA. There's that one rascal of a slave, Tranio. Why, he could even cheat the devil out of his due. Gosh, I'm sure terribly sorry for the old man. When he finds out what's happened, it will be like a red-hot coal burning in the poor fellow's heart.

THEO. Yes indeed, if what you say is true.

PHA. What good would it do me to lie?

PIN. (*Knocking again*). Say, you in there, is anybody opening this door?

PHA. What are you banging on the door for, when there's nobody inside? I guess they've gone off to some other party. Let's go now . . .

THEO. My boy . . .

PHA. And let's continue looking for him. Follow me this way.

PIN. O.K.

THEO. My boy, don't hurry off.

PHA. Your being a free man is an overcoat for your back. But as for me, the only protection I've got for mine is to be afraid of my master and obey him. (*Exeunt* PHANISCUS *and* PINACIUM.)

THEO. I'm a ruined man! What's the use of words? From the words I hear, I haven't only just been on a trip to Egypt, but I've been carried around to solitary lands and shores at the ends of the earth, so that I simply don't know where I am now.

*Enter* SIMO *from right.*

But I'll soon find out, for there's the man from whom my son bought the house. (*To* SIMO) How are you getting on?

SIMO. I'm getting on home from the forum.

THEO. I don't suppose there was any news in the forum today?

SIMO. Yes, there was.

THEO. What was it?

SIMO. I saw a dead man being carried to the grave.

THEO. So that's news?

SIMO. Yes, I saw a dead man being carried to the grave. You know, they told me he was alive just a little while ago.

THEO. Oh, damn you!

SIMO. Why do you have so little to occupy you that you're asking about news?

THEO. You see, I've come back from abroad today.

SIMO. I'm invited out, so don't expect me to ask you to dinner.

THEO. Well, I'm not asking you to.

SIMO. But tomorrow, if somebody else doesn't invite me first—well, I'll be happy to have dinner at your house.

THEO. I'm not asking you to do that, either. But if you've got a minute, please give me your attention.

SIMO. Very well.

THEO. You have received two thousand dollars from Philolaches, according to my information.

SIMO. Never a nickel, according to my information.

THEO. Then was it from the slave Tranio?

SIMO. Much less from him.

THEO. I mean the money he gave you as a down payment.

SIMO. What are you dreaming up?

THEO. Who? I? It's you that's dreaming, if you imagine that by lying out of it like that you can cancel this transaction.

SIMO. Why, what do you mean?

THEO. The business that my son did with you here while I was away.

SIMO. You say that your son had some business with me here while you were away? Why, what business and on what date?

THEO. I owe you four thousand dollars cash.

SIMO. Good Lord, you don't owe me! But hold on, wait a minute. If you owe it to me, come across with it. You've got to pay your debts, so don't try to lie out of it.

THEO. Oh, I won't deny that I owe it to you and I'll pay it. But you be careful not to deny that you've received two thousand from us.

SIMO. Now just wait a minute. Look me straight in the face and answer me. [Tell me, what is all this about owing me money? What is the business transaction you're referring to?

THEO. I'll tell you. It's for this house that my son bought from you and gave you a down payment on.

SIMO. Oh, so he's bought this house from me? That's a new one on me.

THEO. That's why I sent Tranio to ask you to let me look at the house.] *

SIMO. But he told me that you intended to get your son married and therefore you were going to do some building at your place.

THEO. I was going to do some building?

SIMO. That's what he told me.

THEO. Oh, I'm ruined completely! I'm just speechless! Neighbor, I'm a crushed, ruined man!

SIMO. Tranio hasn't upset anything, has he?

THEO. On the contrary, he's just upset everything. He's made a fool of me today in the most outrageous manner.

SIMO. What do you mean?

THEO. It's precisely as I'm telling you. He has made a fool of me today so that I'll never get over it. Now I beg you please to give me your help and your cooperation.

SIMO. What is it you want?

THEO. Come along with me, I implore you.

SIMO. Very well.

THEO. And lend me the use of your slaves and some whips.

SIMO. You may have them.

THEO. On the way over I'll tell you all about how he made a fool of me today.

(*Exeunt into* SIMO'*s house.*)

## ACT V

### *Enter* TRANIO.

TRANIO. A guy who loses his nerve in time of trouble isn't worth a hoot. By the way, I just wonder what that word "hoot" means, anyhow? Well, after the master sent me to the farm to fetch his son, I secretly went that way through the

alley to our garden and I opened up the garden gate which is on the alley and I drew out the entire regiment, both males and females. After I evacuated all my companies from the besieged place to safety, I planned to convene the Senate of my pals. After I convened them, they actually shut me out of their session. Now that I see that I'm left holding the bag, I'm trying my best to do the same as most others do when they get into a dangerous mess. They go on messing things worse until no peace is possible. Well, I know that it's no longer possible to keep this hidden from the old man. . . .* I'll have to act fast and forestall him and arrange an armistice. I'd better hurry. But what is this noise at the door of our neighbor's house? Why, it's my master. I'd like to get a taste of what he says.

THEOPROPIDES *enters from the house of* SIMO, *accompanied by two slaves.*

THEO. You two stand right there inside the threshold, so that the minute I call, you'll jump right out. Put the handcuffs on him quickly. I'll wait in front of the house for that trickster of mine. I'll play some fine tricks on his hide today, sure as I live.

TRANIO (*Aside*). Everything's busted wide open. Now, Tranio, you'd better see what you've got to do.

THEO. I'll have to play him slyly and cagily when he comes here. I'll not show him the hook right away, but I'll let out the line gradually. I'll pretend that I don't know a thing about this.

TRANIO (*Aside*). Oh, what a mean man! There's not a smarter man than he to be found in all Athens. He's as hard a man to fool as a hunk of stone. I'll go up and speak to the fellow.

THEO. Now I'd just love to see him come here.

TRANIO. Say, if you're looking for me, well here I am right in front of you.

THEO. Well, well, Tranio, how's it going?

TRANIO. The farmers are on their way in from the farm. Philolaches will be here any minute.

THEO. You know, you've come here just at the right time. I think this neighbor of mine is a bold, bad man.

TRANIO. How's that?

THEO. Because he denies that he even knows you people.

---

* Several lines are missing at this point in the manuscripts. The dialogue in the bracketed portion is conjecturally restored from the remaining fragments.

* A few lines are lost here.

TRANIO. Oh, so he denies it?

THEO. And that you ever paid him any money at all.

TRANIO. Aw, you're kidding me. I don't see how he can deny it.

THEO. Oh, is that so?

TRANIO. I know, you're only joking now. Why, he just can't deny it.

THEO. But on the contrary, he does deny it and he claims that he never sold this house to Philolaches.

TRANIO. Well, did he deny that he received the money? Tell me that.

THEO. Why, he even offered to take an oath, if I wished, that he hasn't sold this house or received any money.

TRANIO. Why didn't you tell him you'd sue him?

THEO. I did tell him that.

TRANIO. What did he say?

THEO. He offered to let me torture the truth out of all his slaves.

TRANIO. Nonsense! He never will, I'll bet you.

THEO. But he's actually doing it.

TRANIO. No, you summon him to court right away.

THEO. Hold on! I think I'll try out his slaves first.

TRANIO. I tell you, it's a sure thing. Fetch the man here.

THEO. Don't you think I'd better call for those slaves?

TRANIO. It's about time you did. Or better still, make a formal claim to possession of the house.

THEO. No, I want to do this other thing first, cross-examine his slaves.

TRANIO. By golly, that's just what you should do. Meanwhile, I'll take over this altar. (*He goes to the altar and sits down on it.*)

THEO. What's the idea?

TRANIO. You're absolutely dumb. It's to prevent those slaves he'll offer for cross-examination from taking refuge here. I'll just sit here for you, so that the investigation won't be ruined.

THEO. Get up.

TRANIO. Not on your life.

THEO. Don't hold on to that altar, I beg of you.

TRANIO. Why?

THEO. I'll tell you. It's because I really want them to take refuge there. Let them do it. It will

be all the easier for me to win my suit before the judge.

TRANIO. You'd better keep on the way you've started. What do you want to make trouble for? Don't you know what a risky business it is to go to court?

THEO. Won't you please get up from there? There's something important I want to consult you about.

TRANIO. I'll give you my advice from here the way I am. I can think lots better sitting down. Besides, advice coming from a holy place is more reliable.

THEO. Get up. Don't trifle with me. Now look me straight in the eye.

TRANIO. I'm looking.

THEO. (*Smiling amiably*). You see?

TRANIO. I see. And if a third party should come here between us, he'd die of hunger.

THEO. What do you mean?

TRANIO. Because he could make nothing off of us. Why, we're both a pair of rascals.

THEO. I'm ruined!

TRANIO. What's the matter with you?

THEO. You have tricked me.

TRANIO. How so?

THEO. You've certainly taken me for a cleaning.

TRANIO. Well, didn't I do a good job of it? I don't see any dirt on you.

THEO. Oh, you've even cleaned all the brains out of my head! I've found out all the crimes you people have committed—yes, absolutely everything from the root up.

TRANIO. By heavens, you'll never make me get up from here if I don't want to.

THEO. Well, I'll have kindling wood stacked up around you and smoke you out, you scoundrel.

TRANIO. Please don't. I taste lots better boiled than roasted.

THEO. By heavens, I'll make an example of you!

TRANIO. So it's because you like me so much that you'll make an example of me?

THEO. Now tell me. What was my son like when I left him here on my departure?

TRANIO. He had hands, feet, fingers, ears, eyes, lips.

THEO. But that's not what I'm asking you.

TRANIO. Well, that's not what I'm answering you. But look who I see coming here; your son's friend, Callidamates. Take up the matter with me in his presence, if there's anything you want.

*Enter* CALLIDAMATES.

CAL. After I'd had a good sleep and got rid of my hangover, Philolaches told me that his father had come back from abroad and how the slave tricked him when he arrived, and he says that he is afraid to face his father. Now I alone have been chosen by the whole gang to act as their spokesman so as to make peace with the old man. And there he is, luckily. How do you do, Theopropides? I'm happy to see you back safely from your trip. Won't you have dinner at my house today? Please do.

THEO. Callidamates, heaven bless you. As for the dinner, thank you just the same.

CAL. Won't you please come?

TRANIO. Say you'll come. I'll go in your place if you don't feel like it.

THEO. You villain, are you even mocking me?

TRANIO. Just because I'm offering to go to dinner in your place?

THEO. Well, you shan't go. I'll see that you're dragged to the cross, as you deserve.

CAL. Come on, forget all that. Please have dinner with me.

TRANIO. Tell him you'll come. Why don't you say something?

CAL. Say, you, why have you taken refuge at the altar?

TRANIO. That thoughtless man came up and frightened me. (*To* THEOPROPIDES) Now go ahead and tell him what I have done. Now you have someone here to arbitrate between us. Come on, start your argument.

THEO. I say that you corrupted my son.

TRANIO. Well, just listen. I admit he did wrong, that he set free his mistress while you were gone, and that he borrowed money on interest. I acknowledge that this money has been spent. But did he act any different from the way boys of the best families act?

THEO. By heavens, I'll have to be on my guard against you! You're just too clever an orator.

CAL. Please let me decide this case. (*To* TRANIO) Get up. I'll sit down there.

THEO. Very well. You can take over this case.

TRANIO. Say, there's some trap here. Fix it so that I won't have to worry about myself and that you'll do the worrying in my place.

THEO. I don't care so much about all the rest of it as about the way he made a fool of me.

TRANIO. Well, I did right and I'm glad I did it. You ought to have more sense at your age with your white hair.

THEO. What am I supposed to do now?

TRANIO. If you're a friend of Diphilus or Philemon, tell them how your slave made a fool of you. You'll give them the most wonderful plots in all comedy.

CAL. Shut up for a minute and give me a chance to talk. Now listen.

THEO. All right.

CAL. You know that I am your son's closest friend. He came to me, for he's ashamed to face you, because he did those things that he knows you know about. Now I beg you to forgive his folly and his youth. He's your son. You know that young men of his age play around in this way. Whatever he did, he did along with the rest of us. We're the ones who are at fault. The interest, the principal, all the money spent in buying that girl, we'll pay. We'll raise the money and it will be at our expense, not yours.

THEO. There couldn't have been a more persuasive orator come to me than you. I'm not angry with him any more and I'm not mad about anything. On the contrary, even while I'm here, he can have his sweetheart, he can drink and do whatever he wants. So long as he's ashamed at having spent all this money, I'll not punish him any further.

CAL. He's really ashamed.

TRANIO. Now that you've pardoned him, what will you do about me?

THEO. You rat, you'll be strung up and horsewhipped!

TRANIO. Even though I'm ashamed, too?

THEO. By heavens, I'll exterminate you if I live!

CAL. Make a complete job of your generosity. Please let Tranio off for my sake.

THEO. I'll let you prevail on me to do anything in the world but keep from annihilating him for his rascally deeds.

CAL. Please let him off.

THEO. Just look how stubborn that ruffian is!

CAL. Tranio, be quiet if you have any sense.

THEO. Now you be quiet about asking me to do this. I'll have him horsewhipped till he's good and quiet.

THE HAUNTED HOUSE *OF PLAUTUS*

TRANIO. Oh, you don't need to do that.

CAL. Come on, now, let yourself be won over.

THEO. I don't want you to ask this of me.

CAL. Please, now.

THEO. I tell you I don't want you to ask me.

CAL. It's no use protesting. Please hold us all responsible together, for my sake.

TRANIO. What are you hesitating about? Just as if I won't get into some more mischief tomorrow! Then you can punish me good and proper for both things at the same time.

CAL. Let me prevail on you.

THEO. (*To* TRANIO). All right, you may go unpunished. You can thank him for that. Members of the audience, our play is finished. Give us your applause.

# The Woman from Andros OF TERENCE

## Translated by R. I. Wilfred Westgate and Rogers V. Scudder

### INTRODUCTION

"EVERY play has its love story," says Ovid. "That is why plays are read by all the boys and girls in Rome." The plays of Terence, written to entertain, present clever scenes and lifelike dialogues of young lovers, severe fathers, indulgent mothers, and similar persons, all as familiar today as they were in ancient Rome and Athens. All readers will have met them and can appreciate the skillful portraits which Terence draws. His clever observation of character Terence has derived in some measure from the Greek comedy-writers, Menander, Diphilus, and Philemon, who a few generations before had entertained Athens. Menander especially was admired for his accurate observation of people. "O Menander, O Life," cried the critic Aristophanes of Byzantium, "which of you copied the other?" And Quintilian declared, "From Menander's mold issued every human type."

Menander (342–291 B.C.) lived in an age which, like ours, interested itself more in personal affairs than in political principles, more in individual psychology than in patriotic exploits. Terence (185–159 B.C.) translated or paraphrased and adapted Menander's scenes for the cultivated and sophisticated society of Rome that we associate with the name of Scipio Aemilianus (185–129 B.C.). The emotions which he portrays of anxiety or hope or devotion or despair are readily appreciated by all of us today who like to watch the human scene and feel, with Terence, that "all humanity has interest for us."

On the other hand, the conventions of society have changed. It may surprise modern American readers to find a father insisting on choosing a girl for his son to marry. When the son rejects his father's choice and makes his own independently, the father takes elaborate, not to say incredible, pains to drive his son into a position of open rebellion; and the conventions of that day would then judge the boy to be guilty and would support the father's claims of paternal authority. This convention of paternal authority over young men in love seems quite alien and unconvincing to us. But except for this alien convention the modern reader will find little in the *Andria* to strain his belief and much to entertain him. "With the plays of Menander," says Wright, "love took permanent possession of the stage," and in Terence's *Andria* we see one of the earliest comedies of romantic love.

THE TEXT translated is that of Robert Kauer and W. M. Lindsay (Oxford, 1936). The translators acknowledge with gratitude some happy phrases borrowed from John Sargeaunt's Loeb translation of the *Andria*. In general they have tried to present Terence in a style to be enjoyed by American students.

---

### CHARACTERS

SIMO, a choleric and conventional old gentleman of Athens

SOSIA, SIMO's faithful freedman

DAVUS, SIMO's crafty slave, devoted to PAMPHILUS

PAMPHILUS, SIMO's son, in love with GLYCERIUM

MYSIS, GLYCERIUM's maid

CHREMES, an Athenian gentleman

CHARINUS, an Athenian youth

BYRRIA, CHARINUS' slave

LESBIA, a midwife

CRITO, an elderly traveller from Andros

DROMO, SIMO's slave and overseer

### PROLOGUE

*Spoken by one of the younger actors dressed especially for the Prologue and not representing at the moment a particular character in the play*

Your poet, when first he set his mind to writing, believed one simple task was his, that in any play he wrote he must please the audience. But he has learned otherwise. In writing his prologues he exhausts his efforts not in setting out the plot but in replying to the scurrilities of that spiteful old scribbler Lanuvinus. Now note, please, what this critic and his kind impute as a fault.

Menander wrote an *Andria* and a *Perinthia*. If you know one, you know both, for their plots are not unlike, though they are marked by different dialogue and style. What your poet found suitable in the *Perinthia* he took over and used for his own, he frankly admits, in his *Andria*. For this they reproach him and declare that it is not right thus to mingle two plays. To labor such trivial points means that they miss the whole point, for when they criticize him, they equally criticize Naevius and Plautus and Ennius. Your poet reveres these authors as his models; he much prefers their easy freedom to the pedantic accuracy of his critics. From this time forth, I warn the critics to keep silent and stop their fault-finding, lest I in turn expose their faults.

But now, friends, let us have silence and your kind attention. Try to follow the plot, then you can decide whether there's promise in your poet or not and whether future comedies from his pen deserve to be seen or to be hissed off the boards before the curtain opens.

## ACT I

*You look across a street in Athens at two city house fronts. The right one belongs to* SIMO, *the left to* GLYCERIUM. *The street would lead you, left, to the harbor and, right, to the market place downtown. Enter from the right* SIMO, *well dressed in an ankle-length white robe and a colored cloak, and carrying a long staff. Behind him comes* SOSIA *wearing a knee-length servant's tunic of grey, followed by two slaves who are dressed in coarse brown knee-length tunics; they are carrying loaves, fruit, and such-like foods.*

SIMO (*Halting near his door*). You boys take this inside.

*The two slaves enter the house.*

SIMO (*To* SOSIA). Sosia, come here a minute.

SOSIA. Right away, sir. (*Anxiously*) Is all this business going well?

SIMO. No, no. I've something quite different on my mind.

SOSIA. Is there anything more *I* could be doing to help?

SIMO. I don't need any special help from you, not in my present business, Sosia. I've always been able to count on you to keep a secret and hold your tongue.

SOSIA. I'm at your service, sir.

SIMO. From the day I bought you as a little shaver, you've always had fair and easy treatment, you know, in my house. I ended your slavery and made you free because you spent yourself freely in serving me. That was the best gift in my power, and I gave it to you.

SOSIA. I've never forgotten it, sir.

SIMO. And I've never regretted it.

SOSIA. Well, I'm very glad if I continue to give you that satisfaction, and I'm very thankful if it's given you pleasure. Only, this makes me nervous. What are you driving at, sir? When you remind me like this, do you think I've forgotten how kind you have been? Won't you tell me in a word, sir, what you want me to do?

SIMO. All right, I will. In the first place, I'll tip you off on what's happening here. This wedding, or what you think is a wedding, is not a real wedding.

SOSIA. No? Then why ever all this pretense?

SIMO. I'll give you the whole story from the beginning. This will show you my son's real character, and my own designs, and what I want you to do in this situation. You know, after he had grown up, Sosia, and was no longer a boy and was free to arrange his own life—of course, up to that time no one could tell or be sure of his real character, while as a youngster he was afraid of authority——

SOSIA. Oh yes, I know.

SIMO. ——the usual pursuits and hobbies of young men, like horses, and hunting, and some studying. He didn't go in for any one thing very heavily, just liked them all in an average way. I saw nothing to complain of there.

SOSIA. A very good principle, sir. I think that's a golden rule in life, nothing too much.

SIMO. That was his way, take people as you

find them and never worry. He gave himself up to the company he was in and joined in all their interests, never pushing his way at another's expense. That's the easiest way to win friends and be popular, and no one begrudges you.

SOSIA. A wise start in life. Nowadays friends won't take criticism, and hate it if you speak the truth.

SIMO. Now three years ago a woman moved into this neighborhood from the island of Andros, a victim of poverty, and her family never helped her. She was a fine-looking woman and still in her prime.

SOSIA. Hm. I fear trouble from that woman from Andros.

SIMO. At first she lived quietly. By thrift and hard work she made a living with spinning and weaving. But in time a lover came along with money and promises, and then another—you know how quick men are to drop their work and turn to pleasure. So she accepted the situation and set up in business. Then it happened one day that her lovers took my son along with them to keep them company. At once I said to myself, "He's caught; he's hooked." In the mornings I used to watch the servants of the lovers passing back and forth, and questioned them. "Here boy, tell me something. Who spent yesterday with Chrysis?" That was the Andrian woman's name.

SOSIA. I see.

SIMO. "Phaedrus, sir," they would say, or "Clinias" or "Niceratus"—all three were in love with her just then. "Well, what about Pamphilus?" "Pamphilus? Oh, he just paid his share for dining with them." That made me happy. I asked the same thing another day and assured myself that Pamphilus was perfectly free. In fact, I thought he had passed this test and had good self-control. When one is thrown with such people and still holds his principles unshaken, you know that he can manage his own life himself. This pleased me, and what's more, all my friends congratulated me with compliments on having such a splendid son. Not to make a long story of it, this made such an impression on Chremes that he took the step of visiting me and offering me his only daughter as a wife for my son, and a very handsome dowry with her.

SOSIA. Then what's to stop it coming off?

SIMO. I'll tell you. A few days after this visit, this woman who'd settled here, Chrysis, died.

SOSIA. That's just as well for you. Good. I felt he'd have trouble with Chrysis.

SIMO. Now in those days my son spent much of his time with the lovers of Chrysis, and he helped to arrange her funeral. All the time he seemed depressed and even broke down in tears occasionally. I took it for a good sign in those days, for I reasoned, "This boy takes to heart so the death of a woman he hasn't known long. Supposing he really loved her? And what will he do when his old dad dies?" I took all this for signs of a gentle nature and a tender heart. Well, I needn't elaborate. For the boy's sake, I went along myself to the funeral, not in the least expecting trouble.

SOSIA. Oh dear, what trouble?

SIMO. You'll hear soon. The body is carried out of the house. We join in the procession. Just then among the womenfolk present my eye fell on a girl whose face was——

SOSIA. Attractive, perhaps?

SIMO. Yes. And her expression, Sosia, so unassuming, so charming, you couldn't ask for more. She seemed to feel more distress than all the others, and her face was more attractive and finer than any other's, so I asked who she was. "The sister of Chrysis," they replied. *Then* I saw the whole thing in a flash. So *this* was his secret, and *this* explained his tears and tender sympathy.

SOSIA. I hate to think how your story will end.

SIMO. Then the funeral goes on. We follow and reach the cemetery. The body is placed on the flames. Lamentations arise. And at this point the sister I mentioned walked by mistake too close to the fire and was in some danger. Pamphilus turned deathly pale. He dropped his fine pretense of hiding his love. He ran to her and clasped her round the waist. "Darling," he cried, "Glycerium! Take care! You'll kill yourself!" She sank into his arms and wept, as if she felt at home there. Anyone could tell their love was nothing new.

SOSIA. You don't mean it!

SIMO. I came home angry and disappointed. But I still had poor grounds for scolding him. He would only have answered, "What have I done? What's wrong, Father? What's my mistake? A girl wanted to throw herself into the fire. I stopped her and saved her life." One can hardly take exception to that!

SOSIA. Quite right. If you abuse a man for saving people, what do you do when he kills them or wounds them?

SIMO. Chremes storms in the next day to see me, yelling that it was an outrage. He'd found it all out, and Pamphilus already considered this foreigner as his wife. I said flatly it wasn't so. He said it was. In the end I left him obviously not in a mood to give his consent.

SOSIA. So then you had it out with your son?

SIMO. No, because even this episode didn't quite justify any move against him.

SOSIA. Why? I don't follow you.

SIMO. "You yourself, you know, Father," he could have said, "have allowed just so much time for these affairs of mine. Pretty soon I'll be forced to fit into someone else's pattern. Till then, can't you let me lead my own life?"

SOSIA. Then what grounds are you left, sir, for ever taking any action?

SIMO. Ah! Suppose now, that he puts this girl first, above every other consideration, and refuses to get married. That will be his first false step and will give me an opening. *Now* you can see why I'm taking all this trouble, because if he does refuse, this phony marriage gives me a solid handle. And incidentally, if that rat Davus has anything up his sleeve, it will make him play his hand now when his tricks can't hurt us. That fellow will leave no stone unturned, you know, either to help my son along, or even to upset me.

SOSIA. Why ever will he?

SIMO. You want to know? He's a bad actor, through and through. If ever I catch him—— But I needn't stand talking. If things turn out as I hope, and Pamphilus falls in with my wishes, there's only Chremes left for me to manage, and I think I can get round him. Your job now is to make this wedding look convincing, scare the daylights out of Davus, and keep an eye on my son. Watch his moves and any encounters between him and Davus.

SOSIA. Very good, sir; I'll do it. Shall we go inside now?

SIMO. You go ahead. I'll come in later.

SOSIA *goes off into* SIMO'S *house.* SIMO *paces to one side and stands talking to himself uncertainly.*

I feel perfectly sure the boy won't accept this marriage. I could see Davus flinch, you know, when

he heard the wedding was on. (*The door of his house opens.*) Ah! here is Davus at my door.

*The slave* DAVUS, *in a short tunic of bright color, steps hurriedly out, looking worried and entirely lost in his own thoughts. He does not see* SIMO *and stands indecisively in the doorway. He mutters to himself.*

DAVUS. I couldn't understand at all things turning out like this. And the boss's smooth talk kept me quite nervous. What does it all mean? Even when Chremes refused his daughter, he didn't say much or get sore at us.

SIMO (*Grimly to himself*). Well, he soon will. And it's *your* hide that will feel it.

DAVUS (*Still talking to himself, busy with inward calculations*). This was his game, eh? To delude us with false success till we shut our eyes; fill us with hope and free us from worry, then jump on us like gaping fools and get us caught before we could think our way out of this wedding. (*He laughs appreciatively to himself.*) Pretty sharp, eh?

SIMO (*Aside*). What's the hang-dog saying?

DAVUS (*Still to himself*). The boss! It's the boss and I hadn't noticed him!

SIMO (*Sharply*). Davus!

DAVUS (*As if surprised*). Hello! What's up?

SIMO. Come here, at once!

DAVUS (*Aside*). What does he want with me?

SIMO. What are you saying?

DAVUS (*Surly*). What about?

SIMO (*Angrily*). You know. (*After a pause, he makes an effort to be more conciliatory, and his tone tries to be calm, even friendly.*) There's some talk that my son has fallen in love.

DAVUS. The town is all ears for news like that.

SIMO. You just listen to me.

DAVUS. Oh, I'm listening, sir.

SIMO. Now see here. It wouldn't look well if his father went spying on the boy's affairs; and of course, what he's done up till now is none of my business. While he had time to amuse himself that way, I let him follow his fancy. But that time is over, and he's got to act differently. So beginning now, I demand, and if I may put it so, I urge you, Davus, to help him back into the straight and narrow path. His circumstances are nothing unusual. All lovers feel hurt when a wife is assigned them.

DAVUS. Yes, I've heard they do.

SIMO. Well, then. Suppose in these straits a youth finds a foolish counselor, quite often his lovesick heart gets deeper and deeper in trouble.

DAVUS (*Impudently*). I don't follow, sir, at all, sir.

SIMO (*Offended*). No? You don't, eh?

DAVUS (*Goading him*). No, I don't, eh! I'm only Davus, sir, not Albert Einstein.*

SIMO (*Angrily*). Well, then, had I better be plainer in the rest of my talk?

DAVUS. Yes, you had, sir.

SIMO (*Losing his temper more and more*). If I find out today that you're up to your tricks, to spoil this wedding, or show how clever you can be, I'll slit your hide, Davus, and send you to the treadmill till they kill you there. And I'll go a step further: if ever I let you get out of there, I'll take your place myself and tread the mill instead of you. Now do you get the point? Or is this still too subtle for you?

DAVUS (*Sarcastically*). Oh no, sir. It's beautifully clear. You've made the main points very plain. No beating about the bush, sir.

SIMO. You'd be wiser to cross me in anything rather than this.

DAVUS. Don't even suggest it, sir.

SIMO. You think it's a joke. You don't fool me. Mark my words. None of your tricks now. You can't say you haven't been warned. Then watch your step!

SIMO *stalks off in ruffled dignity, going right, downtown.* DAVUS *looks after him, lost in thought, as he disappears down the street. Suddenly he pulls himself up and talks to himself rapidly.*

DAVUS. Now, Davus my boy, no time for slacking or snoozing, now that you've got the old man's views straight about this wedding. If we don't keep our wits about us, it's the end of me, or else of my young master. Which shall I do, now? That's the question. Help the boy? Or obey the old man? (*Reflects.*) Leave the boy in a jam, and he may commit suicide. Or, help him out and I face the old man with his awful temper—and he's a hard one to fool. (*He paces to and fro, then sits on the doorstep to collect his*

* The Latin here names Oedipus, who solved the celebrated riddle of the Sphinx.

*thoughts.*) The main thing is, that he's found out about his love affair and is watching me angrily for any tricks I may play against this wedding. A false step, then, means ruin. If he's out to get me, he'll find good cause to throw me into the treadmill, with his reasons and rights and wrongs. And on top of it all, there's this (*he laughs without humor*), that the woman from Andros, wife or mistress or whatever she is, is pregnant already by Pamphilus! It makes quite a story, does this little adventure, a tale of lunatics, not lovers! And whatever her child, they're going to keep it. (*He laughs scornfully.*) Just now, they're inventing some fairy tale that the girl is really a free-born Athenian. (*He adopts a mincing, sing-song tone.*) "Once upon a time there sailed from Athens an elderly trader; and he got shipwrecked on the island of Andros and was lost in the sea. But his little daughter was washed ashore alive, and was brought up by the father of Chrysis, a dear little orphan." Fiddlesticks! It sure don't sound convincing to *me*. But *they* seem to like it well enough. (*He stops as* GLYCERIUM'S *door opens, and peers towards it.*) Oh, here comes Mysis from Glycerium's house. I'll be off—to the forum to find Pamphilus, in case his father jumps on him before he knows what's happening.

*Exit* DAVUS, *right, towards town. From* GLYCERIUM'S *door appears the maid* MYSIS, *walking backwards and talking volubly with someone inside the house.* MYSIS *is elderly, fat, and flustered. She wears a long, pale green robe trailing to the ground. She calls to a servant inside.*

MYSIS. All right, all right, Archylis. I heard you the first time. You said to bring Lesbia. You know, by gum, she drinks like a fish. She's not fit to take charge when a girl's having her first baby. (*She listens for some reply.*) Do you still want me to bring her? Yes? (*She comes forward and addresses the audience.*) See how obstinate the old body is. That's because they're both old soaks, old cronies of the bottle. O dear God, give the young lady an easy time of it, please; and let the old woman make her mistakes on somebody else. (*She looks off stage, right, and sees* PAMPHILUS *coming.*) But land's sake, why is Pamphilus looking so deathly pale? I'm afraid of what's a-coming. I'll wait and see what misery this worried soul is bringing.

*She retires timid and confused to the far side of the stage so that* PAMPHILUS *does not see her for some time. Enter* PAMPHILUS *from the right. He wears an elegant, sleeved tunic and a cloak, of bright, contrasting colors. He is much excited and has evidently not met* DAVUS, *but has been taken by surprise by his father.*

PAMPH. Is this a decent way to act? Are these decent principles? Is this how fathers ought to behave?

MYSIS (*Agitated*). Whatever's up?

PAMPH. (*Talking to himself*). My God, if this isn't the limit! It was all arranged, he said, to get me married today. Wasn't I going to get any warning? Wasn't I to be consulted at all?

MYSIS (*Alarmed*). Oh my, oh my! What *is* he saying?

PAMPH. Why has Chremes changed his mind? I haven't changed *mine,* and he knows it. He said very plainly that he'd *never* consent. Is there nothing to stop him, till he's taken my girl and ruined my life? If she goes, that finishes me. Oh, I've the worst luck in the world, and nobody loves me. Oh, damn it all! Do I *have* to hook up with that Chremes girl? No one considers *my* feelings; they just ride right over me. Everything's settled *for* me, signed, sealed, and delivered. Kick me out; drag me in. What's it all for? I can only conclude that the girl's so hideous that they can't palm her off on anyone else, so they have to come to me.

MYSIS (*In consternation*). I'll never get over it! What he says is too awful!

PAMPH. And my father's part in this! To be so off-hand in a thing like this! Just came by me on the street and said, "There's a wife waiting for you. You've got to get married today. Come on; get busy; get back to the house." He might as well have said, "Come on; get busy; put a noose round your neck." It knocked me silly. Could I think of a word to say to him? Any feeble excuse? A lie? Anything? I just stood there gaping. If I'd had any warning, what could I have done? Why, I would have done something, so as not to do *this.* Well, where shall I begin? There are so many sides to the question, such a tangle of threads. I love the girl, and feel for her troubles, and the way this wedding worries her; yet I've got to consider the old man. After all, he's been very generous with me always, till now.

Have I now got to fight him? Lord! What *am* I to do?

MYSIS. Oh dear, I'm scared! If *he* don't know, where will *that* get us? It's high time he saw the young lady. No, I'll have a word with him. When a man don't know, he just needs a push, either way, to settle him.

PAMPH. (*Seeing* MYSIS *now*). Who's there? Oh, Mysis, how are you?

MYSIS. I'm O.K., Mister.

PAMPH. And how's *she?*

MYSIS. You want the truth? She's in labor. And she's terrible upset today, 'cause this was the day for your wedding. She's mighty depressed and thinks you may leave her.

PAMPH. (*Excitedly*). I couldn't even think of it! Betray her? Let her go? Break her heart? Why, she's trusted me, body and soul! I'd like to think of her as my wife, the one thing I love! A good, nice girl, and carefully brought up. And would I go and ruin her just because she's poor? Never! Not I!

MYSIS. *You* wouldn't, I know, if it was all in *your* hands; but can you face the pressure?

PAMPH. (*Aggressively*). I'm that feeble and selfish, is that what you think? I'm a crude sort of beast? No feelings or fears for a pal or sweetheart? Forget all my vows?

MYSIS (*Tearfully*). There's only one thing I know. She's too good to let go.

PAMPH. (*With great feeling*). To let go? O Mysis, her sister's last words are engraved on my heart. On her deathbed she called me; I stood close by. You were all outside; she and I were alone. "Dear Pamphilus," she began, "see how pretty she is, and how young. And you know very well," she said, "when a girl's young and pretty, it's hard to go straight and keep on your feet. Now I beg you, as you've made her promises, and are a good boy, remember your words and how lonely she is. Don't cut her adrift and leave her alone. You've been like my brother; she thinks you're wonderful and there's nobody like you; she's always tried to please you, without any reserve. I want you for her husband, to love her and guard and protect her. I'm leaving everything here to you and trust it all to your honest heart." She gave that girl to me and then she died. I've taken the girl. I've taken her, and I'll keep her.

MYSIS (*Fervently*). Oh, I hope you will!

PAMPH. Tell me, why are you on your way out?

MYSIS. I'm fetching the midwife.

PAMPH. (*More excited than ever*). Oh hurry, then, hurry! But wait! Not a word of this wedding, please. It could only make her worse.

MYSIS. All right, I see.

MYSIS *goes off left, to fetch the midwife, and* PAMPHILUS *goes into* GLYCERIUM'S *house.*

## ACT II

*A quarter of an hour has elapsed. Enter from the right* CHARINUS, *well dressed in a knee-length white tunic, and set off by a brightly colored fashionable cloak. He is followed by a slave,* BYRRIA, *dressed cheaply in a coarse brown tunic.* CHARINUS *shows every sign of despair.*

CHAR. What are you telling me, Byrria? That she *is* to be married to Pamphilus today?

BYRRIA. That's right.

CHAR. How do you know it?

BYRRIA. Downtown just now, I got the news from Davus.

CHAR. (*Distractedly*). O God! What can I do? Till now, I've had hope at least to relieve my anxiety and fear. Now hope's gone too! My nerves can't stand it, they can't, they can't. It makes me dizzy.

BYRRIA. Come, now, for goodness' sake, Charinus. You can't get what you like, so like what you get.

CHAR. There's nothing I like! Only Philumena.

BYRRIA. Oh Lord! You'd be more sensible if you'd try to get all that out of your system instead of harping on her and heaping fuel on that hopeless fire.

CHAR. It's easy enough to give advice when *you're* not in trouble, and someone else is. If you were in my place, you'd think differently.

BYRRIA. All right, all right. Have it your own way.

CHAR. (*Catching sight of* PAMPHILUS *coming from* GLYCERIUM'S *door*). Look. I see Pamphilus. I'm going to see this business through before I give up.

BYRRIA (*Aside*). What's Charinus going to do next?

CHAR. I'll appeal as man to man. I'll go on my knees to him. I'll say I'm in love. Surely *that*'ll make him put off his wedding, at least for a day or two. Meantime, something will turn up.

BYRRIA. "Something?" You mean "Nothing."

CHAR. Byrria, what's your advice? Shall I speak to him?

BYRRIA. Why not? If you gain nothing else, you'll have made him jealous—respect you as a rival who may work on his girl if he does get married.

CHAR. Damn you, you rat, with your low suspicions.

PAMPH. (*Closing* GLYCERIUM'S *door behind him*). There's Charinus. Hello there!

CHAR. Hello, Pamphilus. I'm on my way to see you. I terribly want your help and advice; you're my one hope in life.

PAMPH. I've no way of advising and no help to give. But what's your trouble?

CHAR. You're getting married today?

PAMPH. That's what I hear.

CHAR. (*Tragically*). Pamphilus, if you go through with that, you'll never see my face again.

PAMPH. What makes you say that?

CHAR. O God, I'm too nervous to speak. You tell him, please, Byrria.

BYRRIA. Who? Me?

PAMPH. What's the matter?

BYRRIA. He's in love with your fiancée, Chremes' daughter.

PAMPH. How different from me! Look, tell me something: There's been something serious between you and her, Charinus?

CHAR. Oh no, Pamphilus, nothing serious.

PAMPH. Ah! That's too bad!

CHAR. Now, as you love me, as you're my friend, please don't go and marry her!

PAMPH. I'll cooperate there! I'll do all I can.

CHAR. If that's simply impossible—if your heart's simply set——

PAMPH. My heart——? simply set——?

CHAR. Put it off, at least a few days—— so I don't have to see it—— Give me time to get away.

PAMPH. Now listen here, Charinus. I'd be mean to take credit where I didn't deserve it, you know. As for this marriage, I'm as keen to get out of it as you to get into it; keener, in fact.

CHAR. (*Gasps with relief*). You've saved my life!

PAMPH. If there's anything you can possibly

do, you or Byrria here, get busy! Rack your brains; look around; use your wits—and the girl is all yours. I'll do the same to see she's *not* mine!

CHAR. Good enough.

PAMPH. Now here comes Davus, just when I want him—always my best adviser.

CHAR. (*To* BYRRIA). Well, a fine lot of help you've given me—nothing at all that was worth having. You just get right out of it.

BYRRIA. Glad to *be* out of it.     (*Exit.*)

*Enter* DAVUS *from the right, not seeing the others. He talks to himself.*

DAVUS. What luck! What luck I'm having! Now, wherever shall I find Pamphilus, I wonder, and end his anxiety and set him up?

CHAR. (*To* PAMPHILUS). He's pleased about something, all right.

PAMPH. Nothing really; he hasn't yet heard my latest troubles.

DAVUS (*Still to himself*). I expect by now, if he's heard about the wedding, his wedding——

CHAR. Do you hear what he's saying?

DAVUS. ——he's hunting like mad for me all over town. Now, where can I find him? where run him to earth?

CHAR. Go and speak to him.

DAVUS. I know!

DAVUS *moves towards* GLYCERIUM'S *house.*

PAMPH. Stop, Davus! Wait!

DAVUS (*Stopping short*). Who ever is this that tells me to—— Oh, Pamphilus, the very one I'm after. Hello, Charinus too! Both just when I want you, right on the dot.

PAMPH. Davus, I'm ruined.

DAVUS. But just listen to this.

PAMPH. Davus, I'm finished.

DAVUS. I know what you're thinking.

PAMPH. I'm through.

CHAR. But it's *my* life, you know, that is really at stake.

DAVUS. Yes, you too; I know what's bothering *you*.

PAMPH. This wedding——

DAVUS. I tell you, I know all about it.

PAMPH. It's coming off today!

DAVUS. Don't tell me again! I know all about it. What you two are scared of is that *you'll* have

to *marry* her, and *you* (*to* CHARINUS), that you *can't.*

CHAR. Yes, that's the whole point.

PAMPH. Exactly!

DAVUS. Exactly nothing! Not a chance! I'll fix it!

PAMPH. Then be quick, for God's sake! Relieve me at once of my awful anxiety.

DAVUS. O.K., I'll relieve you. Chremes *won't* give you his daughter now.

PAMPH. How do you know?

DAVUS. I *do* know. Your father met me just now; said he was getting you married today; said a lot more that I can't tell you now—this isn't the time. So I rush off downtown to tell you the news. Then, as I can't find you, I go to my lookout. I peer in every quarter. No trace of you anywhere. Then my eye falls on Byrria, this gentleman's slave. I ask *him*. Says *he* hasn't seen you. I'm stumped. I figure, what next? Then on my way home, I put two and two together. "Look here, mighty little extra food in the house. The boss pretty glum. The wedding very sudden. It just don't make sense."

PAMPH. And where does that get you?

DAVUS (*Ignoring the interruption*). So off then at once to Chremes' place. When I get there, no crowd round his house. That makes me feel good.

CHAR. You're right.

PAMPH. Go on.

DAVUS. I hang about. All the time I'm there, I see no one go in and no one come out. No hostess in the place. No flowers. No fuss. I go up to the door, take a good look inside.

PAMPH. (*Skeptically*). Oh yeah? so that's your great proof?

DAVUS. Well, does that *look* like a wedding?

PAMPH. Well, no, I guess not.

DAVUS. Well, no, you guess not, eh? You miss the whole point! It's as plain as can be! On top of all that, on leaving the place, I met Chremes' slave. He was bringing home the old man's dinner, a dime's worth of vegetables and some sardines.

CHAR. (*Excitedly*). Oh freedom, Davus, freedom! And it's all due to you!

DAVUS. No, you can't quite say that.

CHAR. But why not? It means only one thing: Chremes won't give his daughter to Pamphilus.

DAVUS (*Coolly*). Yes, but it's silly to think that not giving to Pamphilus means giving to you!

Not unless you wake up, and see the old man's friends, and get them to help you.

CHAR. Good advice! And I'll go! though I must say I've had disappointments enough. Goodbye, then. (*Exit, left.*)

PAMPH. Well, what's my father's game now? Why all this pretense?

DAVUS. I'll tell you. Suppose he gets sore at you because of Chremes' withdrawing his consent (and Chremes still doesn't know your feelings toward the wedding), then your father, you see, puts himself in the wrong, right straight in the wrong. But if *you* go and say "No," then the blame's all on *you*. That's where the trouble will come.

PAMPH. Well, I'll go through with anything.

DAVUS. Of course, he's your father, and it won't be easy. And your girl's all alone. As soon said as done, he'll find some excuse to drive her from Athens.

PAMPH. (*Dismayed*). To drive her——? from Athens——?

DAVUS. That wouldn't take him long.

PAMPH. Then what am I to do?

DAVUS. Simply say that you'll marry Chremes' daughter.

PAMPH. (*Incredulously*). What?

DAVUS. What's the matter with that?

PAMPH. Simply say that I'll marry her?

DAVUS. And why not?

PAMPH. I'll never say that!

DAVUS. Don't say "never."

PAMPH. Don't urge me to that!

DAVUS. But just look what you'll gain.

PAMPH. Yes, I'll be shut out of *her* house, and shut up in *his* (*pointing to his father's house*).

DAVUS. That's not it at all. My view of it's this: Your father says, "Get married today, please," and you answer, "Yes, Father." What can he say to that? You'll unfix all the plans he's fixed, and you've nothing to lose by it at all. There's not the least fear of Chremes' giving his consent, so don't hesitate on the grounds that Chremes may change his mind. Say "Yes" to your father; then he can't be angry with you, he won't have the right to. As for your notion that you can easily keep her off by behaving very badly, and that no one would give his daughter to *you*, why your father would sooner find some penniless citizen willing to give you a daughter to wife than have you dragged down to Gly-

cerium's level. But if he finds you consenting, he'll be thrown off his balance. It will take him some time to find the next bride, and meantime something may turn up.

PAMPH. (*Doubtfully*). D'you think so?

DAVUS. Not a doubt of it.

PAMPH. Take care what you're getting me into.

DAVUS. You needn't say that.

PAMPH. All right, I'll say yes. Still, we've got to take care that he doesn't find out that Glycerium is having a baby by me. I've promised to keep the baby.

DAVUS (*Scornfully*). You must be crazy.

PAMPH. She begged for this promise, so she'd know that I wouldn't leave her.

DAVUS. Well, we'll see to that. But look, here's your father. Don't let him notice that you're worried.

*Enter* SIMO *from downtown, right. He does not see the others at once, and talks to himself.*

SIMO. I'm back to see what they're doing and scheming.

DAVUS (*Whispering to* PAMPHILUS). He hasn't a doubt at this minute that you will say "No." He's been rehearsing things somewhere, in a solitary spot; he thinks he's made up the perfect speech that will knock you out. But you just keep your wits about you.

PAMPH. If only I can, Davus!

DAVUS. Take it from me, Pamphilus, he won't have another word to say if you just answer, "Yes, I'll marry the girl."

*Re-enter* BYRRIA *from the left, spying on the company. He sneaks aside.*

BYRRIA. My master Charinus said to me, "Leave everything! Just keep your eyes on Pamphilus! Find out what he's doing about the wedding." That's why I'm following the old boy's trail. Ah, there *is* Pamphilus, as large as life, with Davus, too. I must get on the job, then!

SIMO (*Aside*). I see the pair of them.

DAVUS (*Whispering to* PAMPHILUS). Look out! Take care!

SIMO (*Clearing his throat*). Pamphilus!

DAVUS (*Whispering*). Act surprised when you turn and look at him!

PAMPH. Well, is that you, Father?

DAVUS (*Whispering*). That's the idea!

SIMO (*With exaggerated authority*). Today, you get married, as I said. That is my wish.

BYRRIA (*Aside*). This is the critical moment for us. Now what will he say?

PAMPH. (*Deferentially*). I've no wish but yours, Father, in this or anything.

BYRRIA (*Dismayed*). Ye Gods!

DAVUS (*Delighted*). That's knocked him right out!

BYRRIA (*Incredulous*). What's that he said?

SIMO. It does you great credit to fall in so readily with what I demand.

DAVUS (*Whispering*). What did I tell you?

BYRRIA (*Bitterly, aside*). My master, if my ears don't deceive me, has just lost a wife.

SIMO. Now, my boy, go inside. When the time comes, be prompt.

PAMPH. All right.                    (*He goes inside.*)

BYRRIA. You can't trust anybody nowadays for anything. How true it is, and you hear it everywhere, that everyone thinks about self before all! I *have* seen the girl; she was very attractive, I thought, so I don't judge Pamphilus too hardly if he wants her in *his* bed and not with Charinus. Now home with the news. I'll give them bad news and get a bad reception.
                    (*Exit, left.*)

DAVUS (*Aside*). Now Simo thinks I've got some trick up my sleeve and have stopped here for that reason.

SIMO (*Accusingly*). What's Davus got to say for himself?

DAVUS (*Impudently*). Nothing more than I had before, sir.

SIMO. Nothing, eh?

DAVUS. No, nothing, eh.

SIMO. Well, I rather thought you might.

DAVUS (*Aside*). It's taken him by surprise, all right. It's got him off his balance.

SIMO. Are you capable of telling me the truth?

DAVUS. Nothing easier, sir.

SIMO. Is this marriage against the grain for him? I mean, because of his feelings toward this foreign woman?

DAVUS. Oh no! There's nothing to that! Or if there is, it will all end in two or three days—you know how it is. After that, he'll stop worrying. He's been thinking the matter over for himself, along the right lines.

SIMO. He's done well.

DAVUS. While he was free, and youth wanted it, he enjoyed his love. It was all secret; he took good care not to let it hurt his good name, as a gentleman should. But now what he needs is a *wife;* he's set his mind on a *wife.*

SIMO. He did look to me just a shade subdued.

DAVUS. Ah yes! But it's not for that reason at all. *That* is because he feels put out with *you.*

SIMO (*Surprised*). Why with *me?*

DAVUS (*Carelessly*). It's really quite childish.

SIMO. What *is* it?

DAVUS. Oh, nothing.

SIMO. But tell me, what is it?

DAVUS. He says you certainly aren't spending much.

SIMO. Me?

DAVUS. You, sir. "There's hardly two dollars been spent on the dinner," he says. "It's not like marrying a son," he says. "And what friends can I invite to the dinner, especially at this late hour?" And I think I must say so, too, sir, that you really *are* spending very little, too little. It don't look right, sir.

SIMO (*Sharply*). That's enough from you!

DAVUS (*Aside*). I've got under his skin!

SIMO. I'll see that that's done properly. (*Aside*) Now just what does this mean? Just what *is* the game of this hardened old sinner? If ever there's trouble, he's always at the root of it.

## ACT III

*Re-enter* MYSIS *from the left, bringing with her the midwife* LESBIA, *who wears a long green dress. They do not see the men yet.*

MYSIS (*With maudlin vigor*). By Pollux, Lesbia, yes! It's just what you said: "You'll hardly find a man at all that's faithful to a woman."

SIMO (*To* DAVUS). Does this maid belong to the Andrian woman?

DAVUS (*Hedging*). What did you say, sir?

SIMO. She does!

MYSIS. But *this* man Pamphilus——

SIMO. Whatever's she saying?

MYSIS. ——has kept his word——

SIMO. My God!

DAVUS (*Aside, with suppressed indignation*). Oh, why ain't he struck deaf, or she dumb!

MYSIS. And he says that, boy or girl, the baby's to be kept.

SIMO (*In consternation*). Good God, what am I hearing? The game is up, if she's telling the truth.

LESBIA. He's a good-hearted boy, you can say that again!

MYSIS. None better. But come in behind me, and don't keep her waiting.

LESBIA. I'm a-coming.

LESBIA *and* MYSIS *enter* GLYCERIUM'S *house.*

DAVUS (*Aside*). Now *here's* a fine mess, and what's the way out?

SIMO. What does *this* mean? He can't be such a fool! A foreigner's child! (*His expression slowly clears.*) Aha! but I see it! How stupid I was not to see it at once!

DAVUS (*Mystified*). Now what *is* it he sees?

SIMO (*Aside*). So here's the first trick this fellow tries on me. They *pretend* there's a baby, as a means to scare off Chremes!

GLYCERIUM (*Inside*). Juno, Goddess of childbirth! Help me! Save me! Save me! Hear my prayer!

SIMO (*Laughing scornfully to himself*). Wow! Quick work, eh! *How* absurd! Just as soon as she hears I'm close to her door, she gets straight to work! Davus, my friend, you haven't timed your stunts too well.

DAVUS. Are you talking to me, sir?

SIMO. Or else your actors missed their cues, eh?

DAVUS. *My* actors? I don't know what you mean, sir.

SIMO (*Aside*). Suppose he had sprung this on me unawares, when the real wedding was going on. What a fool he'd have made of me! Now, *he's* stuck his neck out, and *I've* got good smooth sailing.

*The midwife reappears at the doorway, talking volubly to the maid inside.*

LESBIA. So far, Archylis, I've observed in her case all the usual symptoms of a safe delivery. First, bathe her and then give her what I told you to give, and in the right doses. I'm coming back soon. O Lord, ain't it wonderful? Pamphilus has a boy, and pray God it lives. Its father is such a good soul, not wanting to harm this dear sweet girl. (*Exit.*)

SIMO. Look, Davus, anyone would know that this was your work, if he knew you at all.

DAVUS. *My* work? What is?

SIMO. To stage things like this! Look! The midwife won't say at the bedside what to do at the birth, but comes bawling her directions from the street to the people inside. Davus, do you think I'm a fool? Do you think I am fooled by such open deceptions? You might have tried to be clever; it would show that you feared me, in case I found out.

DAVUS (*Aside*). Damned if *I'm* fooling him; he's fooling *himself*!

SIMO. I've warned you, and threatened you not to try these tricks. Did it do any good? And now I'm supposed to believe that this girl's had a child! And by Pamphilus!

DAVUS (*Aside*). Now I see his mistake! That gives me an idea.

SIMO. Well? Why don't you answer?

DAVUS. *Supposed* to believe it? You were told it would happen!

SIMO. I was told? And who by?

DAVUS. Oh, you figured it all out yourself, did you?—that was this was a frame-up?

SIMO. Don't make fun of *me*.

DAVUS. But it *was* all explained. What else would have roused your suspicions?

SIMO. Roused my suspicions? Ha! Just knowing you!

DAVUS. You don't think—— I done it?

SIMO. I certainly do!

DAVUS. Oh, you don't understand! You don't know my character!

SIMO. I don't, eh? Your character!

DAVUS. Why, if I just begin talking to you, you think that I'm lying.

SIMO. And I'm wrong, I suppose?

DAVUS. Why, now, sir, I hardly dare open my mouth!

SIMO. Well, at least I know one thing; there's *no* baby here!

DAVUS. That's right! You see through them! But nonetheless, pretty soon they're going to bring a baby out in front of this house. I'm telling *you*, Mister. And don't say afterwards it was all Davus' tricks. I don't want you to have that idea at all.

SIMO. How do you know so much?

DAVUS. I've heard things. I know. A lot of things point that way. First, the girl gave out that she was having a baby by Pamphilus; that's been proved a lie. Next, she sees a wedding under way at home and right off sends the maid for a midwife and a baby at the same time. If she don't take this step, and show you the baby, why of course the wedding goes right on!

SIMO. But tell me, when you knew they were up to this, why didn't you tell Pamphilus right away?

DAVUS. Why, who did get him away from her if it wasn't me? We all know how desperately he loved her, whereas now he's wanting a wife. No, just leave that to me; and you—well, you keep on with what you're doing about the wedding—and God help you!

SIMO. No, no. You go into the house and wait for me there, and get ready what's needed.

*Exit* DAVUS *into* SIMO's *house.* SIMO *continues doubtfully.*

He hasn't gotten me to believe all this entirely. Yet on the other hand, perhaps every word of it's true! Well, it doesn't much matter. The main thing for me is what my son promised me. So I'll go and find Chremes and ask for his daughter. If he consents, what better time than today for the wedding? He's given me his promise, so if he should get cold feet, I know that I've got every right to insist. Why, here comes Chremes, exactly when I want him.

*Enter* CHREMES *from the right. He wears a long white tunic and carries a staff.*

Chremes, I want——

CHREMES. Oh, I was just looking for you.

SIMO. I was looking for you. How fortunate!

CHREMES. Various friends have been coming to me to say that they've heard from you that my daughter and your son are getting married today. And I've come to find out whether you are crazy, or they are.

SIMO. Listen to me for a minute, and I'll tell you what I'd like from you, and that will answer your question.

CHREMES. I'm listening. Say what you want.

SIMO. I entreat you, Chremes, by all that's holy. For the sake of our friendship that began in our boyhood and has kept pace with the years, for the sake of your only daughter and my only son, whose salvation now rests in your hands, help me now and let this marriage go forward as we planned it.

CHREMES. Oh, you don't need to entreat me! As if you had to beg things before I would give them! Do you think I've changed since the day when I offered her? If it's the best thing for both of them that the marriage go on, why, give the word, and bring her here. But if it will only do more harm than good to both young people, then please look at it from both points of view, as if she were your daughter and I your boy's father.

SIMO. That's just what I want! And that's why I'm asking your consent to the wedding. I wouldn't ask you, Chremes, if the facts didn't warrant it.

CHREMES (*Sharply*). What facts?

SIMO. Glycerium and my son have quarreled.

CHREMES. What of it?

SIMO. So bitterly that I can, I hope, get him away from her.

CHREMES. Fiddlesticks!

SIMO. But it's true!

CHREMES. Yes, it's true! In the sense that "lovers thrive on lovers' quarrels."

SIMO. Well, that's the point! Let's get ahead of them while we've got time and his ardor is quenched by this quarrel! And before these women with all their schemes and crocodile tears bring back his lovesick soul to pity, let's give him a wife! I hope that, once decently married, the force of habit will save him all right from this fuss and bother.

CHREMES. That's your view of it! But I don't think he's capable of being faithful to my daughter—and he's got to, if he marries her.

SIMO. How shall we ever know if we don't take a chance?

CHREMES. But it's a serious matter to take that chance with one's own daughter.

SIMO. Really, doesn't the difficulty all come down to this? On one hand, there might have to be a separation, which heaven forbid! On the other hand, if the boy is put straight, look at all the advantages: first, you'll have restored a son to your old friend; then you'll get yourself a faithful son-in-law, and your daughter a faithful husband.

CHREMES (*Yielding*). Very well. If you feel it's right, if you're sure of your ground, I hate to put any obstacle in your way.

SIMO. Chremes, I've always thought the world of you, and with good reason.

CHREMES. But tell me——

SIMO. What?

CHREMES. ——how do you know they're quarreling?

SIMO. Davus told me himself, and he knows all their plans. He's urging me to hurry up this wedding as fast as I can. You don't think he'd do that unless he knew my son wished it, do you? You shall hear for yourself. Hey there, call Davus. Oh, there he is, coming out of the house.

*Enter* DAVUS *from* SIMO'S *house.*

DAVUS. I was just coming to see you, sir.

SIMO. What is it now?

DAVUS (*With innocent curiosity*). Why aren't they bringing the bride? It's getting towards evening.

SIMO (*To* CHREMES). You hear that? Up till now Davus, I've rather feared that like the common run of slaves you might try and cheat me, especially as my son is in love.

DAVUS. Me, sir? You thought that *I'd* do that?

SIMO. I thought so, and I've been so distrustful that I've been keeping from you what I'm going to tell you now.

DAVUS. And what is that?

SIMO. You'll hear in a minute, for I'm beginning to have a little confidence in you.

DAVUS (*Gratified*). At last you appreciate my real nature, sir.

SIMO. That wedding *was* not going to take place.

DAVUS. What? It wasn't?

SIMO. I pretended it was, just to test you and my son.

DAVUS. You don't say, sir!

SIMO. It's a fact.

DAVUS (*Admiringly*). Well, well. I never could have figured that out. Lord, what a clever arrangement!

SIMO. And listen to this. After I sent you inside, I met Chremes here, by a stroke of good luck.

DAVUS (*Aside*). My God, are we ruined after all?

SIMO. I'm telling him what you told me just now.

DAVUS (*Aside*). What next?

SIMO. I've asked him for his daughter's hand and have managed to get his consent.

DAVUS (*Aside*). That's the end of it!

SIMO. What did you say?

DAVUS. I just said, "How splendid!"

SIMO. Now, Chremes has no further objections.

CHREMES. I'm going straight home to have her get ready, and then I'll be back to tell you the news.                    (*Exit.*)

SIMO. Now, Davus, I must ask you, since you alone have brought about his marriage——

DAVUS (*Aside*). Oh, yes, *I've* done it all!

SIMO. ——try to straighten out my son.

DAVUS. Oh, I'll try, so help me!

SIMO (*Eagerly*). Now's the time you can do it, while he's exasperated with her.

DAVUS. You needn't worry.

SIMO. Well then, where is he now?

DAVUS. No doubt he's at home.

SIMO. I'll go and tell him just what I've told you.                    (*Exit into his house.*)

DAVUS (*Alone on stage*). For what can save me from that awful mill? There's no chance of my getting out of it. I've mixed up everything. I've cheated the master and landed the boy in this marriage. I've done just what Simo didn't expect and Pamphilus doesn't want. Curse my cleverness! If I'd left things alone, they'd have come out all right. (*He catches sight of* PAMPHILUS *entering from* SIMO'S *house.*) But there is Pamphilus. If I only had a tall cliff to jump off!

*Enter* PAMPHILUS. *He does not see* DAVUS *at first.*

PAMPH. Where's the scoundrel that's ruined me?

DAVUS (*Aside*). Ah, this is the end of me.

PAMPH. But I must say I've brought this on myself, being so helpless and no-account, to have put my fate into the hands of that worthless slave! It serves me right for being a fool. But he won't get away with it, not altogether.

DAVUS (*Aside*). I'll play safe ever after, I know that, if I get out of this!

PAMPH. Whatever can I say to my father now? Shall I say I *won't* marry her when I've just said I will? I haven't the face! I simply don't know what to do with myself!

DAVUS (*Aside*). Well neither do I, though I'm thinking my hardest. I'll say I'll find something. I must just play for time.

PAMPH. (*Catching sight of* DAVUS). Aha!

DAVUS (*Aside*). He's seen me.

PAMPH. (*To* DAVUS). Look here, my good fellow, what have you got to say? You've got me in a hell of a fix. (*Ironically*) Your advice!

DAVUS. I'll get you out!

PAMPH. Get me out?

DAVUS. Why yes, Pamphilus.

PAMPH. No doubt, just as before.

DAVUS. Better, I hope.

PAMPH. Oh, I'm to trust you again, scoundrel! *You'll* straighten out this whole hopeless business? See whom I've relied on! You've gotten me out of a very peaceful state only to throw me into what? A wedding! Didn't I say this would happen?

DAVUS. Yes, sir.

PAMPH. Then what do you deserve?

DAVUS. The gallows. But give me a minute to recover my wits; I'll find a way out.

PAMPH. Oh, damn it, I haven't got time now to thrash you as I'd like! I've got to look out for myself at once. I can't take it out of your hide now.

## ACT IV

*Enter* CHARINUS *from the left, talking excitedly to himself.*

CHAR. Would you believe it? Can you conceive it? That anyone could be so heartless as to gloat over others, and pile up his pleasures from another man's troubles? Is it fair? The very worst people are those who can't bring themselves to say "No" when they should; but when the time comes to make good their promises they're forced to show their true colors. They're afraid to say "No" and yet have to say it. So then they throw all shame away, crying, "Who are you, anyway? You're nothing to me! Give up *my* girl to you? Look here, I've got to think of myself first." And if you then say, "But you promised," they're not bashful then, when they should be. When there's no need to be bashful, that's when they are. Well, what's my next move? Go up and protest against all he has done? Heap reproaches on him? You may say it will do me no good. It will, though, a lot! I'll make him good and sore and relieve my own feelings.

PAMPH. Charinus, my folly has ruined us, you and me, unless the gods help us.

CHAR. You call it folly, eh? In the end, that's your only excuse! You have broken your word!

PAMPH. What d'you mean, in the end? And my only excuse?

CHAR. Do you still think I'll pay any heed to your words?

PAMPH. What *do* you mean?

CHAR. You never fell for her till I said I loved her. I judged your disposition, like a sap, from my own.

PAMPH. You've got it all wrong!

CHAR. You weren't happy enough, I suppose, with your girl till you'd robbed me of my love and cheated my hopes. Well, then, take the girl.

PAMPH. Take the girl? O Lord, you don't know what deep waters I'm in, damn it all; or what worries this precious jail-bird of mine has heaped on my head.

CHAR. Nothing strange about that, if he takes after you.

PAMPH. You'd never say that if you knew my true feelings.

CHAR. I know, I know. You've quarreled with your father, and now he's in a rage and hasn't been able to get you to go through with the wedding today.

PAMPH. That's not it at all! Just to show you how little you know of my troubles, there wasn't any wedding being arranged for me today! There *wasn't* anyone giving me a wife today!

CHAR. Very likely indeed! And then you were forced into it—by your own free will!

PAMPH. Wait! wait! You still haven't got it!

CHAR. I've got it enough to know that you're going to marry her.

PAMPH. Why *do* you keep plaguing me? Listen to this: he never stopped goading me to say "Yes" to my father, begging and pleading till at last I gave in.

CHAR. And who might "he" be?

PAMPH. Davus.

CHAR. Davus? Why?

PAMPH. I don't know, except that it was a bad day for me when I ever listened to him.

CHAR. Is this the truth, Davus?

DAVUS. It is, sir.

CHAR. It is, eh? You scoundrel! I hope you are damned with the fate you deserve. Why, if all his enemies had wanted to pitch him into this wedding, that's exactly the advice they all would have given.

DAVUS. I've missed a trick, sir, but I'm still in the game.

CHAR. You are, eh?

DAVUS. We've failed one way, sir, so now we'll try another. You surely don't think that to fail once or twice means we'll fail all the time!

PAMPH. Oh no, of course not! Just put your mind to it, and I'm sure you'll arrange me not one but two weddings.

DAVUS. Pamphilus, as your slave I owe this to you, to try night and day with all my might to help you, and even risk my life. It's your part to pardon me if things don't turn out as we hoped. I've failed so far with what I've done, but I'm still working hard. If you can find a better way out, dismiss me.

PAMPH. I'd like to! Get me back where I was when we started.

DAVUS. Yes, I will.

PAMPH. Well, do it at once!

DAVUS. Just wait, now. I hear Glycerium's door opening.

PAMPH. That's none of your business.

DAVUS. I'm figuring things out.

PAMPH. You are, eh, at last?

DAVUS. When it's ready you shall have it; it won't take me long.

*Enter* MYSIS *from* GLYCERIUM's *house. She is talking to* GLYCERIUM *within as she appears.*

MYSIS. Now wherever your Pamphilus is, I'll take care to find him and bring him back with me. Just don't you fret, precious.

PAMPH. Mysis!

MYSIS. Who is it? (*She turns and sees* PAMPHILUS.) Oh Pamphilus, I'm that glad to see you.

PAMPH. What's the matter?

MYSIS. She told me to beg you, if you love her—my mistress, I mean—to come right away. She's dying to see you.

PAMPH. Oh damn it all! My troubles are beginning all over again! (*To* DAVUS) Look how completely you upset both Glycerium and me with all your fussing! She's calling for me because she must have heard that the wedding's going on.

CHAR. How simple to have had it all quiet if this fellow had only kept quiet!

DAVUS (*Defiantly*). Go on! Stir him up! As if he weren't crazy enough by himself!

MYSIS. Yes, sir, that's just it, and that's why she's feeling so low now, poor thing.

PAMPH. Mysis, I swear by all that's holy, I will never leave her! No, not if the whole world turn against me. I wooed her; she's mine; we suit each other. I've had enough of those who want to separate us. Only death can take her from me.

MYSIS. I'm so relieved!

PAMPH. Apollo couldn't speak any truer than that. If we can make my father believe that I'm not responsible for stopping the wedding, well and good. If we can't, then I'll make him believe—it's easy enough—that I *am* responsible. Now, how does that strike you?

CHAR. (*Dryly*). It strikes me that you've ruined us both.

DAVUS. I'm getting an idea.

PAMPH. Oh grand! I know what you'll try——

DAVUS. I promise I'll fix this for you.

PAMPH. You need to, right now.

DAVUS. I have it, right now.

CHAR. What is it?

DAVUS. It's for *him*, you know—not you. Don't get me wrong.

CHAR. All right, then.

PAMPH. Your plan, now. Let's have it.

DAVUS (*Decisively*). Time's short enough for action, let alone talking. Don't think I can spend time giving all the details. Both of you, move along. You'll only be in my way.

PAMPH. I'll go and see Glycerium.

(*Exit into* GLYCERIUM's *house.*)

DAVUS (*To* CHARINUS). And you, where will you go?

CHAR. Shall I tell you the truth?

DAVUS (*Ironically*). Oh of course! Here we go—a long speech.

CHAR. What can you do for *me?*

DAVUS. What more do you want? I've given you time, getting the wedding put off for a day! Isn't that enough?

CHAR. But Davus——

DAVUS. But what?

CHAR. (*Pleading*). Arrange for *my* wedding!

DAVUS. Absurd!

CHAR. Do come to me, if you can think of anything.

DAVUS. No use coming. I'm not thinking of your troubles.

CHAR. But still, if you do——
DAVUS. Oh, I'll come if I do.
CHAR. I'll be at home.            (*Exit, right.*)
DAVUS. Now, Mysis, wait here a little, till I come out.
MYSIS. Why?
DAVUS. You must.
MYSIS. Well, hurry up.
DAVUS. I'll be back soon, I tell you.

*Exit* DAVUS *into* GLYCERIUM'S *house.*

MYSIS. There's nothing you can count on! God help us, I thought this Pamphilus would be the greatest blessing in the world to my mistress— a friend, a lover, a husband who'd face anything. But now see what grief he's caused her! She's paying quite a price now for the pleasure she's had. Here comes Davus. Man alive! What on earth are you doing?

DAVUS *reappears from* GLYCERIUM'S *house, carrying the baby in his arms.*

DAVUS (*Urgently*). Mysis, you're a smart girl. Right now I need all your brain-power to help my schemes.
MYSIS. Whatever's the idea?
DAVUS. Quick, take the baby; put it on the doorstep.
MYSIS. You mean, on the ground?
DAVUS. Here, take some of these branches from the altar; put them under him.
MYSIS. Why don't *you* do it?
DAVUS. Because, if by any chance I have to swear to my master that I didn't put him there, I can do it with a clear conscience.
MYSIS. Oh, are you beginning to get a conscience? Give him to me.
DAVUS. Hurry up, and I'll tell you what next. Oh my God!
MYSIS. What is it?
DAVUS. The bride's father is coming—in the middle of everything. I can't follow my first plan.
MYSIS. I don't know what you're talking about.
DAVUS (*To himself*). I'll pretend I've been coming along too, from this way, from the right. (*Whispers urgently to* MYSIS.) Now, Mysis, back up my story if you have to say anything. Don't fail.
MYSIS. I've no idea what you mean! But I'll

stay if you need me. You're cleverer than me, and I don't want to spoil your plan.

*Enter* CHREMES *from the right. He does not at first see* MYSIS *or the baby.*

CHREMES. I'm back again, now that I've got things all ready for my daughter's wedding, and am going to have her fetched. (*He sees the baby on the doorstep and gives a violent start.*) Bless my soul, now! What's this? A baby! Good heavens! Woman, did you put it here?
MYSIS (*Perplexed and helpless*). Oh dear! Where's he gone to?
CHREMES. Can't you answer me?
MYSIS. He's nowhere about! Oh Lord! Oh dear! Oh dear! He's gone off and left me!
DAVUS (*Talking busily to himself to suggest preoccupation*). Oh my! Oh my! Oh my! What confusion downtown! So many men there squabbling at law! And the price of grain's gone up! (*Aside to audience*) I dunno what else to say!
MYSIS (*Indignantly*). You just tell me, will you, why you left me alone?
DAVUS (*Affecting surprise*). Eh? What's this nonsense you're talking? (*He discovers the baby.*) Ho! Mysis! Where did this baby come from? Who put him there?
MYSIS (*Astonished*). Are you out of your mind? You ask me such a question!
DAVUS. Why, who else should I ask? I don't see anyone else.
CHREMES (*Mystified*). I wonder where it did come from.
DAVUS (*In a menacing tone*). Will you answer my question? (*He follows his question with a blow.*)
MYSIS. Ouch!
DAVUS (*Whispers*). Come over here to my right.
MYSIS (*Follows to left of stage*). Are you crazy? Didn't you yourself——
DAVUS (*Whispers*). If you speak one word except what I ask you, look out! (*Aloud*) Abusing me, eh? Now: where did he come from? Answer directly!
MYSIS. Why, from our house!
DAVUS (*Scornfully*). Aha! Not surprising at all that her mistress should play a trick like that! No better than she should be!

CHREMES (*With dawning suspicions*). Surely this maid belongs to the woman from Andros?

DAVUS (*Pretending righteous anger*). D'you think we're the people to stand for your nonsense?

CHREMES (*Decisively*). I came just in time!

DAVUS. Hurry up, now! Take that child off the doorstep. (*Then whispering to* MYSIS) Wait! Don't stir a foot from this place!

MYSIS. Now God's curse light on you! You frighten me to death!

DAVUS. Do you hear me? Or don't you?

MYSIS (*Miserably*). What do you want?

DAVUS. Lord! Still asking questions! Come, now. Whose baby is it you've put here? Speak up!

MYSIS. Don't you know?

DAVUS. Don't you worry about what I know. Just tell me what I want to know!

MYSIS. Your master's.

DAVUS. Which of my masters?

MYSIS. Pamphilus.

CHREMES. Ah!

DAVUS (*Incredulously*). What? Pamphilus?

MYSIS. Well, isn't it?

CHREMES. How right I was in always steering clear of this marriage!

DAVUS. What a villainous thing to do!

MYSIS. What are you shouting about?

DAVUS. Is this the baby I saw being brought to your house last evening?

MYSIS. What a thing to say!

DAVUS. It's true. I saw Canthara coming in, bulging with something that she was hiding.

MYSIS (*Outraged*). Thank God there were some respectable women present when the child was born.

DAVUS (*Pompously to himself*). Certainly she's very much mistaken in the man for whom she's concocted this scheme. I can just hear her saying, "If Chremes sees the baby lying on the doorstep, it will stop the wedding!" It won't! It will only make him keener!

CHREMES. Good Heavens! It will *not*.

DAVUS (*Indignantly to* MYSIS). Now look here. I give you fair warning. Take that baby away, or I'll trundle him into the middle of the street, and bundle you after him, into the mud.

MYSIS. Lord, man, you must be tight!

DAVUS. One lie after another! Already I've heard that you go whispering around the town

that the woman is a free Athenian citizen——

CHREMES (*Pricking up his ears*). How's that?

DAVUS. ——just so they can say that the law will *make* him marry her.

MYSIS. Well, and isn't she an Athenian citizen?

CHREMES (*To himself*). What a ludicrous muddle! And what a narrow escape I've had!

DAVUS (*Pretending to see* CHREMES *for the first time*). Why, who's here? Oh, Chremes, sir, you're just in time. Listen to this.

CHREMES (*Stiffly*). Yes, I've heard every word.

DAVUS. You've heard every word?

CHREMES. Yes, from beginning to end.

DAVUS (*To* MYSIS). D'you hear that, you? Such wickedness! They should take out this woman and crucify her. This is the gentleman I was talking about. Don't think you're just fooling with Davus!

MYSIS (*Begins to weep*). Oh dear, poor me! Dear, good old gentleman, I swear I've told no lies!

CHREMES. I know the whole story. (*To* DAVUS) Is Simo at home?

DAVUS. Yes, sir.

*Exit* CHREMES *into* SIMO'S *house.*

MYSIS. Here, keep your hands off me, you brute. If I don't tell Glycerium everything you've done——

DAVUS. You simpleton! Can't you see what we've managed?

MYSIS. How could I?

DAVUS. Why, he's the bride's father! There was no other way to get him to know what we want him to know!

MYSIS (*Crossly*). Well, you might have warned me.

DAVUS. But don't you see it's much more effective if you act natural than if you've been coached!

## ACT V

*There now enters from left,* CRITO, *in traveling dress—long white tunic, broad hat, long staff. He looks about him and talks to himself.*

CRITO. This is the street, they say, where poor Chrysis lived, preferring to get rich here in questionable ways to being poor and virtuous at home. At her death all her property reverted to me by law. Ah, here are some people that I can ask. Good evening!

MYSIS (*After carefully looking at the stranger*). For pity's sake! Who's this I see? Ain't it Crito, the cousin of Chrysis?

CRITO (*Looks carefully at* MYSIS). Why, Mysis! How are you?

MYSIS. And you, Crito?

CRITO. And Chrysis? She is really—— ah——

MYSIS. Ah, yes, we've lost her, alas! And we're all in sore trouble.

CRITO. Why, what's happened to you? How are things here? You're all right, I trust?

MYSIS. We? Oh, so-so. We do what we can, as the saying goes, since we can't do as we choose.

CRITO. Tell me about Glycerium. She's in touch with her family?

MYSIS. If only she were!

CRITO. Not in touch with them yet? Then it's a great mistake for me to be here at all! Dear, dear, if I'd known, I'd never have sailed. She's always been considered the sister of Chrysis, so of course she gets all the property of Chrysis. Indeed it would be very hard for me, a foreigner here, to take the matter to court—quite useless, in fact, as the failures of others show very plainly. And she probably has now some friend and protector, being quite grown up when she left home. With regard to me, people would only call me a cheat and a beggar, a legacy-hunter; and what's more, I *don't* want to take the property from the poor girl.

MYSIS. Oh you dear, good man! You keep to the good old ways, sir!

CRITO. Bring me to her, please. I can at least see her, now that I've come this far.

MYSIS. Yes, of course, sir.

CRITO *and* MYSIS *enter* GLYCERIUM's *house.*

DAVUS. I'll follow this couple. I wouldn't want old Simo to see me just now.

(*He follows them into* GLYCERIUM's *house.*)

CHREMES *and* SIMO *appear from* SIMO's *house. They are in vigorous dispute.*

CHREMES. Enough! enough! My friendship towards you has gone far enough, and I've run risks enough. Now stop your pleading! In trying to accommodate you, I've nearly spoilt my daughter's life.

SIMO. No! no! This is the very moment I must beg, or rather, demand, that you keep your promise and carry it through.

CHREMES. How unfair you are when your feelings run away with you! Just to have your own way, you don't care what you ask. If you did, you wouldn't keep heaping such unfair demands upon me.

SIMO. What unfair demands?

CHREMES. What a question! Here was a young man already engaged in another love affair and quite shuddering at the idea of matrimony when you pushed me into giving my daughter to him— to a life of domestic discord and a most precarious marriage. You expect me to cure your lovesick son no matter what it may cost my daughter. Well, you had your way and I agreed when it seemed reasonable. Now it's unreasonable. You'll just have to face things. People say that that girl is a citizen. And she's had a baby. Just leave us, please, out of the whole affair.

SIMO. I solemnly implore you in the name of heaven not to listen to such people. It means everything to them if they can discredit him. That's their purpose in everything they've said and done. Remove their motive, and they'll soon stop.

CHREMES. You're quite wrong. I saw Davus with my own eyes, arguing with her servant.

SIMO. Well, what of it?

CHREMES. They were having an argument, all right. Neither of them knew I was there.

SIMO. No doubt you are right. In fact, Davus told me a while ago that's what they would do. I forgot to tell you, but I meant to.

DAVUS (*To* GLYCERIUM *within, as he comes from her house*). Now, don't worry, I tell you.

CHREMES. There's Davus! Look at that!

SIMO. Which house did he come from?

DAVUS (*Still to* GLYCERIUM). The stranger and I will fix it.

SIMO (*Exasperated*). *Now* what mischief is he up to?

DAVUS (*To himself*). Neatest thing I ever saw. Right man, right place, right time!

SIMO. Oh the villain! Who's he so pleased with now, I wonder.

DAVUS (*Still to himself*). It's all clear sailing now.

SIMO. I'll speak to him at once.

DAVUS (*Notices* SIMO *and gives a start.*) It's the boss. What am I to do?

SIMO (*With mounting rage*). See here, my fine fellow!

DAVUS. Oh Simo, sir, and Chremes, sir. Everything's ready in the house now.

SIMO. You've taken good care of it all, eh?

DAVUS. You can send for the young lady whenever you wish, sir.

SIMO. Very fine indeed! That's all we were waiting for! You just tell me this: What are you doing in that house?

DAVUS. Me, sir?

SIMO. Yes.

DAVUS. Me, sir?

SIMO. Yes, you!

DAVUS. Why I went in there, sir, just a minute ago.

SIMO. I said "what," not "when"!

DAVUS. Along with your son, sir.

SIMO (*Dismayed*). What? Is Pamphilus in there? That cuts me to the quick. Didn't you say they'd had a quarrel, you dog?

DAVUS. They have.

SIMO. Then why is he in there?

CHREMES (*Laughing*). What do you think the boy's doing? Why, enjoying his scrap!

DAVUS. Not that at all, Chremes. Just let me tell you of their terrible plot. Some old man has come along, and he's in there right now. Such gall! But he's a smart one! To look at him you'd think he was somebody, with his serious face and honest way of speaking.

SIMO. And what's *he* got to do with it?

DAVUS. Nothing, except what I heard him say.

SIMO. And what *did* he say?

DAVUS. That he knew Glycerium was a freeborn Athenian.

SIMO (*Turns towards his house and summons his slave-driver furiously.*) Hey, Dromo, Dromo!

DAVUS. Why, what's the matter?

SIMO. Dromo!

DAVUS (*Pleading*). Listen to me!

SIMO. If you say one word more—— Dromo!

DAVUS. Listen to me, *please!*

*Enter* DROMO *from* SIMO'S *house with a rope, accompanied by other slaves.*

DROMO. What do you want, sir?

SIMO. Pick him up and take him indoors as quick as you can.

DROMO. Who?

SIMO. Davus.

DAVUS. But why?

SIMO. Because I say so. Take him away!

DAVUS. What have I done?

SIMO. Take him away!

DAVUS. If you find that I've lied, you can kill me!

SIMO. I'm not listening.

DROMO. I'll shake you up a bit.

DAVUS. Even if it's all true?

SIMO. Yes, even if it's all true! Tie him and keep him tied! Here, tie his hands to his feet. Come now, to it! God, if I'm spared I'll teach you today to cheat your master, and I'll teach that boy to cheat his father! (DAVUS *carried off.*)

CHREMES. Come, don't lose your temper.

SIMO. There's a grateful son for you! Chremes, can't you feel for me? What I have to suffer because of that boy! (*He calls in at the door of* GLYCERIUM'S *house.*) Hello, Pamphilus! Come out of there, Pamphilus! Have you no sense of decency?

PAMPH. Who's calling me? (*He appears at the door.*) It's my father! Oh heavens!

SIMO. What have you to say for yourself, you absolute, you utter——

CHREMES. Come, now. Stick to the point and don't call him names.

SIMO. As if there were any names that he didn't deserve! Is this *your* story too, that Glycerium's a freeborn citizen?

PAMPH. They say that she is.

SIMO. "They say!" Oh what gall! Does he know what he's saying? Not a bit sorry for what he's done? Look! Is there a blush to show signs of a conscience? No backbone! No principle! No regard for convention, or law, or his old father's wishes! Just wants his girl, even if it means ruin and shame!

PAMPH. How unhappy you make me!

SIMO. Bah! Is it only now, eh, that you feel unhappy, Pamphilus? Long, long ago, you should have used that word "unhappy"—yes, on the day you first resolved that, come what might, you must have your own way. But what's that to *me?* and why should *I* worry? Why should *I* rend my heart, and distress my grey hairs for this fellow's folly? Am *I* to be punished for this boy's sins? Not I! No, let him take her! Away with him, and let him live with her!

PAMPH. O father!

SIMO. What d'you mean, "O father"? You don't want *me* for a father! You've found yourself a home, a wife, a family, regardless of your father's wishes. You've made them declare that the girl's a free citizen. All right, have your way!

PAMPH. But father, listen a minute.

SIMO. What is there to say?

CHREMES. Still, let him speak.

SIMO. All right, let him speak.

PAMPH. I confess that I love her; and if I've done wrong, I confess that too. I put myself in your hands, father. Punish me as you choose. Give what orders you like. Shall I take a wife? Shall I give up my love? I'll face it as best I can. But this only I ask of you, that you don't think I bribed this old gentleman. Let me clear myself by bringing him to you.

SIMO. Bring him to me?

PAMPH. Please, father.

CHREMES. That's reasonable.

PAMPH. Please let me do this.

SIMO. All right.

*Exit* PAMPHILUS *into* GLYCERIUM'S *house to fetch* CRITO.

Anything, Chremes, that will show that the boy's not lying.

CHREMES. Even a great fault needs no great punishment, between father and son.

PAMPHILUS *re-enters accompanied by* CRITO.

CRITO (*Cheerfully*). No need to urge me! Any one of these reasons would make me comply— the fact that you ask me, or the fact that it's true, or my wish to help Glycerium.

CHREMES (*After gazing intently at the newcomer*). Do I see an old friend from Andros? Is it Crito? It is!

CRITO. And how are you, Chremes?

CHREMES. What brings you to Athens so unexpectedly?

CRITO. Well, I am here! But can this be Simo?

CHREMES. It is, indeed.

CRITO. You are looking for me?

SIMO. Ha! You! Do *you* say that Glycerium's a freeborn Athenian?

CRITO. Do you, sir, deny it?

SIMO. You've come primed here to say this!

CRITO. Now what do you mean?

SIMO. You needn't ask! Do you think you can get away with that sort of thing? enticing young gentlemen into mischief—well-brought-up and innocent of the world—and deluding them with your temptations and promises——

CRITO. Are you mad?

SIMO. ——and then patching up their unsavory affairs into marriages?

PAMPH. Oh dear! I'm afraid the stranger can't stand all this!

CHREMES. Simo, if you knew him, you wouldn't think that of him. He's a fine, reliable man.

SIMO. He, fine? He, reliable? It's all much too smooth. Here he arrives on the very day of the wedding, though he's never been here before. Just the man to invite one's belief, eh, Chremes?

PAMPH. (*Aside*). If I weren't afraid of my father, I could give him some good advice now, in return for all his.

SIMO (*Furiously to* CRITO). You crook!

CRITO. What's that again?

CHREMES (*Soothingly*). It's his way, Crito; please overlook it.

CRITO (*Angrily*). Just let him mind his manners, then. If he persists in speaking so, he'll get an earful in return. Do I bother you or care about you? This is your own affair, and you've got to deal with it. As for my story, we can soon tell whether it's true or not. (*He speaks more quickly.*) Some time ago an Athenian citizen was shipwrecked on Andros and this girl with him, a small child. Being destitute, he turned first to Chrysis' father.

SIMO. He's warming to his story!

CHREMES. Come, let him speak!

CRITO. Must he keep interrupting like this?

CHREMES. Continue.

CRITO. It was a kinsman of mine that took him in. In that house I heard from the man's own lips that he was an Athenian. In that same house he died.

CHREMES (*Eagerly*). What was his name?

CRITO. His name? Wait a moment.

PAMPH. Phania.

CHREMES. Oh heavens!

CRITO. Now, by God, I think his name *was* Phania. In fact, I know it was. He said he came from Rhamnus.

CHREMES. Oh Jupiter!

CRITO. Many other people in Andros heard these same facts, Chremes.

CHREMES (*With mounting excitement*). May it be as I hoped! And now, tell me, what of the girl? Did he say she was his daughter?

CRITO. No.

CHREMES. Whose was she?

CRITO. His brother's.

CHREMES. She is certainly mine!

CRITO. What's that?

SIMO. What's that you're saying?

PAMPH. Don't miss this, Pamphilus!

SIMO. What makes you think that?

CHREMES. This Phania was my brother!

SIMO. I knew him. I know he was.

CHREMES. He left Athens to avoid the war and follow me to Asia Minor. At that time he was afraid to leave the girl in Athens. This is the first time I've heard what became of him.

PAMPH. (*Exultingly*). Now I can hardly contain myself, I'm so excited by fears and hopes and joy at this sudden, this wonderful news.

SIMO. Indeed, I'm delighted, perfectly delighted that you've found your daughter.

PAMPH. I'm sure you are, father.

CHREMES. Yet there still is one doubt that troubles me.

PAMPH. Damnation! You deserve to be troubled, with all your scruples. You'd try to find knots in a bulrush.

CRITO. Well, what is it?

CHREMES. The girl's name is wrong.

CRITO. Why, bless me, she did have a different name when she was little.

CHREMES. What was it, Crito? Can't you remember it?

CRITO. I'm trying to think.

PAMPH. (*Aside*). Shall I let his forgetfulness spoil all my happiness when I can remedy things myself? I'll tell you, Chremes. The name you're hunting for is Pasibula.

CHREMES. Pasibula! That's it!

CRITO. Yes, that's it!

PAMPH. I've heard it from her a thousand times.

SIMO. I know, Chremes, that you know that we are all perfectly delighted over this.

CHREMES. Lord help me, I do, indeed.

PAMPH. As for the rest, father——

SIMO. I'm quite reconciled to the situation now.

PAMPH. O my dear, good father! And Chremes isn't changing his mind about my wife, now that I have her?

CHREMES. All is well—unless your father has something else to add?

PAMPH (*Worried*). Do you?

SIMO. Of course not! I agree.

CHREMES. Her dowry, Pamphilus, is twelve thousand dollars.

PAMPH. I'll accept that, too.

CHREMES. I want to see my daughter at once. Do come with me, Crito, for I don't believe she'd recognize me.

SIMO. Why not have her brought over to our house? (CHREMES *and* CRITO *go into* GLYCERIUM'S *house.*)

PAMPH. A good idea. I'll entrust that to Davus.

SIMO. *He* can't do it!

PAMPH. Why not?

SIMO. He's engaged in something more important, more pressing.

PAMPH. Oh? What is it?

SIMO. He's been chained up.

PAMPH. (*Reprovingly*). Father! It's not fair to chain him up.

SIMO. Ha! ha! But I had him chained down!

PAMPH. Do have him let loose, please.

SIMO. All right, I will.

PAMPH. But at once!

SIMO. I'm going inside now.

(*Exit into his own house.*)

PAMPH. Oh happy, lucky day!

*Enter* CHARINUS *from the right, unnoticed.*

CHAR. I want to see what Pamphilus is doing. Ah! there he is!

PAMPH. (*To himself, not noticing* CHARINUS). You'd hardly believe that I believe this is true! But it is! Yes, thank God, it is! You know, what makes the gods live on forever is that their pleasures go on forever. Well, I'll go on forever if nothing spoils my present joy. Now, whom do I *specially* want to hear my whole story?

CHAR. (*Aside*). What makes him so happy?

*Enter* DAVUS, *limping and stiff.*

PAMPH. Here's Davus! He's the very first one I'd choose! He'll be really glad, gladder than anyone, to hear of my pleasure.

DAVUS (*With signs of pain*). Where's Pamphilus?

PAMPH. Davus!

DAVUS. Oh, Pamphilus.

PAMPH. (*Enthusiastically*). You don't know what luck I've had!

DAVUS. No. But I know what luck I've had!

PAMPH. Yes, so do I.

DAVUS. That's how it always happens; my bad news reaches you before your good news reaches me.

PAMPH. Dear Glycerium has found her parents.

DAVUS. That's good.

CHAR. Ha!

PAMPH. Her father's a great friend of ours.

DAVUS. Who *is* he?

PAMPH. Chremes!

DAVUS. It makes a good story!

PAMPH. All that remains is for me now to marry her!

CHAR. (*Aside*). He's dreaming! His obsessions are all coming out in his dreams!

PAMPH. And as for the baby, Davus——

DAVUS. Oh stop! Stop! I've never heard of such luck in my life.

CHAR. (*Struck with the happy thought*). Why then I'm saved too! —if their story is true. I'll speak to them.

PAMPH. (*Seeing* CHARINUS *advance*). Who's that? Oh Charinus, you've just come at the right moment.

CHAR. It's wonderful!

PAMPH. Have you heard?

CHAR. Yes, heard it all. (*Earnestly*) But don't forget me in your prosperity. Chremes is entirely in your hands now. I know he'll do anything you wish.

PAMPH. I won't forget you. But I can't bear to wait till he comes out. Come inside with me. He's in there now, with Glycerium. Davus, you hurry home and bring servants to carry her over to our house. Don't waste time! Don't hang around!

DAVUS. Yes, sir.

*Exit* PAMPHILUS *with* CHARINUS *into* GLY-CERIUM'S *house.* DAVUS *watches the door close, then addresses the audience.*

Now don't wait for them to come out again. The ceremony will take place inside. Whatever else there is that needs to be done will take place inside.

*Exit* DAVUS *into* SIMO'S *house. The* MUSICIAN *steps forward before the curtain and speaks to the audience.*

MUSICIAN. Now give them a hand!

# TITUS LUCRETIUS CARUS *On the* Nature of Things

## Translated by Alban D. Winspear

## INTRODUCTION

IN MOST departments of creative activity and artistic achievement, the Romans regarded themselves as inferior to the Greeks. In the field which Lucretius made his own—the poetical exposition of philosophical doctrine—they have no need to hang their heads in shame. For majesty of theme and subject matter, for sustained eloquence of exposition, for acuteness of philosophical insight and argumentation, for poetical imagery and musical cadence, and for the sheer enthusiasm of scientific passion, the Greeks—despite the philosophical contributions of Leucippus, Democritus, and Epicurus—produced nothing to rival Lucretius. Indeed I am not sure that, as regards all these qualities, Lucretius is not the greatest poet that ever lived.

Of Lucretius the man, apart from what we can infer from his great poem, we know singularly little. There is a legend of dubious validity and perhaps scandalous intent, that he was driven mad by a love philtre administered by a jealous woman, composed his poems in the lucid intervals of insanity, and died at the zenith of his ripened powers by his own hand. There is a debatable connection with Cicero (the renowned Marcus or his less famous brother) who may or may not have revised or edited the manuscript. At all events Marcus shows a proper appreciation, commendable in a philosophical opponent, of Lucretius' poem—"many flashes of genius and yet much art." The poem itself gives us a picture of an educated and aristocratic Roman familiar with the life of the *haut monde,* its luxurious palaces and country houses, its ostentation and vulgarity, its boredom with the banquet of externals. Yet Lucretius does not show much awareness of the exciting world around him—the crucial days of Rome's greatest civil wars. At one point he appeals to his goddess patron for peace,

I cannot carry out this task of mine with mind at peace
At such a crisis of my country's fate.

Negatively, the troubled times sent him to a creed of escape, a passionate opposition to the desire for wealth and power, a residence in what, following Lucretius, we have come to call the ivory tower.

Lucretius was before all things the poet of the scientific outlook, of philosophical materialism, of opposition to religion in creed and rite and myth. This opposition was his deepest passion; it gave rise to some of his most moving poetry, two passages of which are reproduced below. In his consideration of human evolution in general, this opposition leads him to some of his most majestic speculations—they are of the kind which we should now call anthropological—as to how this belief in the gods originated. It leads him to his most profound philosophical speculations. Against religion and a belief in the supernatural, which so many put forward to explain the origins of the universe and its government, he puts forward his atomic philosophy. And this opposition to religion, finally, accounts for his central ethical philosophy, his teaching about how man ought to live.

"There are two moments in Lucretius' zoology" writes Leonard, "that are notably Darwinian: the effect of organic adaptation and of domestication upon the preservation of the species; the survival value of swift legs, for instance, and of man's cooperation, both of which kept the earth stocked with animal life . . . [and] the Lucretian reiteration against teleology, that is, design in Nature, a favorite idea of Aristotle and of Lucretius' own much-scorned Stoics. Not only are there no Gods planning ahead from without; but Nature herself, he says, from within herself is not planning ahead: she merely grows, and things happen and particular functions develop out of what happens." *

The theory of special creation Lucretius sharply attacked, as well as any notion of design in nature. The earth is mortal, made without divine intervention and

---

* W. E. Leonard and S. B. Smith, *T. Lucreti Cari de Rerum Natura* (Madison, 1942), p. 60.

destined in its time to perish. In good naturalistic terms he explains what force and what cause started the various courses of the sun, the journeys of the moon, the position of the earth in the center of the universe, the cause for day and night, the reasons for eclipses. Then he discusses the origins of animal and vegetable life. His exposition deals with the origin of man, the ways of life of primitive folk, without fire or tillage or the arts of Lucretius' own relatively advanced civilization. Mankind, he thought, began to modify its savage ways as a result of family life and the mutual care of children. Nature taught men language. Out of gesture and speechlessness man evolved the habit of speech. Men learned to control fire out of the original gift of the lightning. Fire was not, as in the old Greek myth, the supernatural gift of a semidivine, though rebellious, Prometheus.

Lucretius' account of the rise of civilization is interesting. Kings founded cities and citadels as a refuge and stronghold for themselves. Gold was discovered and this destroyed honor; men will always follow the party of the rich. Then there came the rebellion of the poor and revolutions. And so magistrates were devised to temper the stubborn clash of rich and poor. Just as he denied that fire had been given to any semidivine Prometheus, so he believed it was not a goddess Athena who gave to men control of the various arts—of metal-working, of warfare and all its various techniques, weaving, agriculture with its various skills, music and the knowledge of the stars. It was the race of men, toiling endlessly, that created these advances in technique and civilization. And this, little by little, has advanced life to its high level and has stirred up from its depths the great tides of war. In his account of evolution, Lucretius ponders deeply the origin of religion and belief in the gods. His conclusions are reproduced in the passages selected for translation below.

Lucretius and his school, the Epicureans, were pioneers in the development of the atomic theory. His position was quite simple. The whole universe could be explained in terms of atoms and space without postulating the intervention of the gods. Atoms, he thought, were falling endlessly in space, infinite space, combining, clinging together, forming infinitely rich and infinitely various combinations of things, to explain all the rich complexity and variety of the world as we know it. The whole material universe, the world of life and human activity, too, is in constant flux and change—some things coming into being and some passing away. But the sum of all things remains the same. The only reality is the changing world of matter. Even man's institutions and his thoughts are reflections of the changing material scene. The only changeless is the material substratum— the stuff from which the world and all that is in it is made. There is no ideal unity beyond the many. The universality of the world lies precisely in its materiality. Change is uniform and predictable and can, therefore, be

reduced to law. There is no room in the world of Lucretius for surprising or supernatural occurrences, for miracle or divine caprice. "Nothing can come to be from nothing by divine decree." All change is slow change, everything proceeded by slow and imperceptible degrees; *nihil per saltum facit natura*, nature does nothing by leaps (though the poet, as opposed to the philosopher, does ample justice to the explosive moments in nature and history when, of a sudden, in the twinkling of an eye, the old is swept away, the new is born).

Two postulates were necessary for this school of thinkers in explaining the physical and social universe— atoms and space. Granted these two principles, they felt that everything in the world could be explained without bringing in the gods at all. The atoms (which he calls by many names) were solid, indestructible, and invisible. They are constantly in motion, begetting and destroying worlds and all that in them is. They are of many sizes and shapes; this accounts for differences of quality, texture, and shape in the world of things. Lightning will penetrate where fire will not, because it is composed of finer atoms. Light will pass through horn (the ancient equivalent of glass) on the side of a lantern when water will not; wine through a strainer when oil will not, for the same reason. Condiments and pickles tickle rather than wound our sense because their atoms are not smooth nor altogether hooked with jagged barbs, but slightly angled out. Hard substances are composed of hooked atoms; fluids of round smooth atoms which will not easily cohere (he uses a heap of poppy seed as an example). The sea is at once fluid and bitter. Its atoms must, therefore, be mixed—some smooth and round, but with painful rough ones mixed therein. This explains why it is possible to separate the salt from the water; why salt water can be purified and freshened if it filters through the ground.

The number of atomic shapes was, he held, limited; the number of each shape, infinite. Although the texture, hardness, softness, etc., of things are dictated by atomic shapes, their color, odor, taste, and temperature are not. Worlds are infinite in number but finite in time. Our world is already in old age, has passed its creative prime.

In all this the reader may detect many crudities, many signs of inadequate theory or control of fact. He may be tempted to compare modern atomic theories to Lucretius' disadvantage. It would be more just, I think, to reflect how extraordinary is the insight; how exciting these analytical anticipations of the modern scientific world outlook, in spite of the inadequate scientific apparatus with which these men worked, in spite of their relatively primitive concepts of scientific method.

Lucretius was at one with the materialists of all ages in his concept of scientific method. He wanted his thinking to be understandable to the common man. He was careful to use simple, strong, plain, direct words and to use them in their natural meaning. He apologizes to his reader when he is forced to use a technical term from Greek philosophy for which there was no natural Latin equivalent. Logic chopping and the—to him—niggling arguments of his idealistic opponents he most heartily despised. When he contemplated the power of the senses to give knowledge to men he experienced a tremendous emotional uplift. All knowledge comes ultimately from sense experience. Reason cannot test or judge the senses because it owes its existence to them. And yet his atomic theory, involving unobservable entities, is sheer poetry unless reasoning connects it with sense experience. This is one of the many contradictions inherent in Lucretius' strange personality. One sense cannot correct another, sight, hearing, and so on. Nor can one sensation correct another, for they are all equally true.

Lucretius' opposition to religion is the key to his views on ethics, on the question how is it best for man to live. His answer to this question is twofold—positive and negative. On the negative side, Lucretius' answer is clear, articulate, resolute. Men must not live as most men now do, in a constant struggle for power and wealth. Avarice, ambition, lust, he thought, brought men no lasting happiness. No man has ever been more sensitively aware of the haunting dissatisfactions that dog mankind even in the midst of wealth and plenty and success. Most men do not know what they want for themselves. Man's greatness, well-being and happiness cannot be found in a multitude of possessions. He cannot find happiness or a well-nourished ego in wealth or success or pride of birth. Man's yearning for all these things is an expression of fear, of insecurity and consequent inner dissatisfaction. If only mankind could banish fear of insecurity! And here Lucretius makes a remarkable assumption. All these fears and agonies and strivings can be reduced to one fear—the fear of death. And the fear of death is poignant because men fear eternal torments after death. If then, Lucretius argues, we can banish once for all the fear of unending torments which men think await them when they die, then all fears will be done away and man can live in perfect peace, happiness, tranquillity. Here then is the reason, deep, urgent, compelling, for the study of philosophy. All human life is in question, not what one is to do in the next hour. To put his point of view briefly, bluntly, Lucretius believed that for the attainment of tranquillity of mind the most important single thing was the study of physics, a knowledge of the atomic philosophy. Out of this study would proceed the full emotional and intellectual realization of universal law, cause and effect, operative everywhere in the universe. Man would come to realize that nothing ever comes from nothing by divine decree but that all things are governed by order, regularity, consistency—in a word, by law. And so, he thought, fear would be banished, fear of the gods, of death, and of the torments after death. Thus mankind, embracing the "passionless

bride, divine tranquillity," would come to lead a life that was altogether godlike. Was not that how the blessed gods themselves lived in the spaces between the stars? Not in a multitude of possessions, not in wealth, fame, eminence, or power could man find his inner satisfaction. Rather by renouncing all these things he might find peace. In passage after fervent passage our poet sings the praises of the simple life.

As an ethical thinker (at this particular stage of social and intellectual development) Lucretius was conscious of a paradox between his ethical teaching, which demanded freedom of the will for its realization, and his physics, which postulated the universal rule of law. This paradox he tried to solve, not too satisfactorily, by the doctrine of the swerve of the atoms. The atom swerve serves a twofold purpose in his system—it accounts for creation, for the passage from the homogeneous world of atoms to the heterogeneous world of things, and it accounts for freedom of the will by introducing an element of caprice into the very heart of things. In so brief an introduction to Lucretius' great poem there is no space for a discussion of this paradox. To many it has seemed a blemish on his system—notably to Cicero, who dismissed it as a puerile fiction. But whatever one's conclusion on this particular matter, there can be no doubt of Lucretius' general position in the history of thought. He has given us the most mature expression of philosophical materialism to come down to us from classical antiquity, and the most eloquent and poetical exposition of that creed of all time.

In this rendering of select passages from *De Rerum Natura*, mindful of Plato's admonition that the musical man in tuning a lyre does not try to outdo the musical man who has achieved perfection of pitch, I have not hesitated to borrow occasional phrases and even lines from Keats, Shelley, Gray, Tennyson, Cyril Bailey, and William Ellery Leonard where these seem to me to have attained perfection of rendering. No regular verse form can hope to reproduce the cadence of the Lucretian hexameter, and the attempt to use one can only result in distorting the thought by fitting it to the English meter. Prose, on the other hand, abandons any suggestion of the original poetic form without making possible the emphasis of verse. The translation of the *De Rerum Natura* has therefore been rendered in rhythmical lines of irregular length in order to adapt the verse to the ideas of the original rather than to expand or contract the thought of the poet to fit the verse scheme.

I am aware that to some it may seem impertinent to challenge comparison with Leonard's masterly verse rendering of the poem. I can only plead that if Leonard were here, he would be the first to applaud and encourage the attempt.

THE TEXT translated is that of W. E. Leonard and S. B. Smith (Madison, 1942).

## *From* Book I

*Invocation to Venus*

In this magnificent exordium or introduction to the poem as a whole the poet addresses the goddess Venus, as founder and patron of the Roman race, as the traditional goddess of love, as the symbol of fertility in nature, and as a deity who has power to give peace, because she had influence with her lover, Mars, the god of war.

Mother of Aeneas' clan, of men and gods delight,
Venus, all-fostering, who under gliding stars in sky,
Dost make to teem ship-bearing sea, fruit-bearing earth;
Since every race of living things, through thee
Conceived, is born and sees the light of sun;
Thee, goddess, thee the winds do flee, and heaven's clouds,
Thee and thine advent;
For thee the checkered earth pours forth its lovely flowers,
For thee expanses of the sea do smile,
And tranquil sky does gleam when bathed in light.
When first the vernal face of day is seen,
The living breath of Zephyr is unlocked and strongly blows.
Then first the birds in sky give word of thee,
Thee and thy coming,
Touched as they are in heart with power divine.
And then the beasts of field are driven wild,
To leap gay meadows and to swim swift streams.
And so, a captive of thy charm, each thing in hot desire,
Will follow thee wherever thou dost go to lead them on.
Yes, and through seas and hills and headlong streams,
The leafy homes of birds and grassy fields,
Thou dost put sweet love in the hearts of all,
And make them reproduce their race,
Kind after kind.

Since thou alone art Nature's queen,
Without thy help can nothing come to shining shores of light.
Nothing is gay without thee, nothing beautiful.
I want thy help in writing verse,

The verse I try to write for Memmius, my friend.
(Hast thou not willed that he excel at every time, in every thing?)
So, goddess, give eternal beauty to my words;
Grant me that while I write
Fierce war on land and sea may sleep and rest.
For thou alone canst grant to mortal man
Peace and its blessings,
Since Mars, in arms all-powerful, rules the fierce works of war,
Thy lover, Mars, who often sinks upon thy breast,
Completely overcome by love's eternal wound,
And so, in thine embrace,
His shapely head pillowed upon thy breast,
He gazes on thee, feeds his eager eyes with love,
His whole soul hangs upon thy lips.
Do thou, Divine, embracing him reclined, with holy frame,
Pour out sweet whispered words, O Goddess famed,
And beg the quiet of peace for Roman folk.
I cannot carry out my task with mind at peace
At such a crisis of my country's fate,
Nor could my Memmius betray his stock,
Or heedless be, and fail the country's safety.
[1–42]

*Lucretius gives reasons for his opposition to Roman institutional religion.*

When human life lay foully prone upon the ground
Conspicuous to see,
Crushed by creed and myth, like ponderous weights,
Which like incarnate horror from the skies looked down
And lowered over men with visage grim,
A man of Greece first dared to raise his mortal eyes against,
And even stand against and fight.
And him no fables told of gods could daunt,
Nor heaven with lightning flash or thunderbolt dismay;
But only stirred the more the valorous splendor of his mind.
He longed to be the first to crack the cramping bonds of nature.
And so his splendid strength of soul prevailed.
Outside he went, beyond the flaming ramparts of the world,

And ranged the infinite whole in mind and
thought's imagining.
And from his mental voyages to us brought back,
Like conqueror crowned in victory, the news of
nature's laws,
Of what could come to be and what could not,
The code that binds each thing, its deep-set
boundary stone.
And so religion in its turn
Is trampled under foot and trodden down
And man is made like god by one man's victory.

One fear I have in this long argument,
That even Memmius might think
We're impiously dabbling in profane philosophy
And setting wanton foot on sin's broad way.
Rather religion has itself begot
Impious and bloody deeds.
Think how at Aulis Grecian chiefs, picked lead-
ers of mankind,
Stained altars of the chaste and huntress queen
With maiden's blood in obscene rite and wanton
sacrifice.*
And she, poor girl, the fillets on her maiden locks,
Adorning either cheek,
Saw father stand by sacral stone, steadfast but
somber;
The slaves of sacrifice with swords concealed
To spare a father's natural sympathy; †
The clansfolk weeping at the doleful spectacle;
In tongueless terror down she fell and swooned.
Poor girl, it could not help at all at such a time
That she had long ere this been first to call him
father.
For borne aloft in rough men's hands,
Not tenderly, like bride in husband's grasp
(To altar led the escort, not to wedlock's home),
No wedding hymn but funeral chant accompanied
her
Who chastely died by wanton act,
Just when love's consummation should be hers.
And so she died,

* This is Lucretius' account of a well known episode,
the sacrifice of Iphigenia by her father, Agamemnon.
When the Greek fleet was delayed by contrary winds at
Aulis, the soothsayer Calchas announced that the goddess
Artemis had been offended, and could only be propitiated
by the sacrifice of the child of one of the leaders. Agamemnon summoned his daughter Iphigenia, under pretence of marrying her to Achilles, and offered her up.
† Scholars usually regard this as having only local
force, "beside him." I think they miss a characteristic
piece of savage Lucretian irony "on account of him," i.e.
"out of deference to his feelings."

A sad and sacrificial victim at a father's blow,
That jealous god, by butchery propitiate,
Might grant auspicious voyage to the fleet.
That is religion, these its monstrous acts.

Memmius, you too will want to fall away,
Even you,
Quite vanquished by the fear-provoking words of
priests.
How many things can priests invent,
Vain myths to sap a lifetime's reasoning
And muddy fortune's goods with fear!
No wonder; for if men could see
There is to misery a fixed, ordained end,
In some way they'd find strength
To stand against religion and the threats of
priests.
But as it is; no principle is there,
No chance to rally and stand fast,
Since fear of endless torments makes us shrink
from death.          [80–110]

*The creed of religion vs. the creed of science*

And so this darkened terror of the mind must
be dispelled,
Not by the rays of sun or gleaming shafts of day,
But Nature's laws, by looking in her face.
Our first beginning must set out from this:
No thing can come from nothing by divine de-
cree.
For, you see,
Fear so possesses every mortal heart
Because so many things are seen to happen
On earth and in the sky for which men find no
cause.
They think these happen by divine decree.
Wherefore when we have seen
That nothing comes to be from nothing
Then more clearly we shall see
The object of our search,
And when each thing can be created
And how can come to be
Without the help of gods.

For if everything came to be from nothing
Every species could be random born.
There'd be no need of seeds.
Man could arise from sea,
The scaly race of fish from earth,
Birds could explode from sky.

And beasts both wild and tame, by random birth
Could roam ploughland and wilderness alike.
And fruits on trees would never stay the same,
But change.
All creatures could produce all offspring.
If all things did not have their procreant seeds,
How could they have a fixed and changeless
mother?
But as it is,
Because each thing is made from certain seeds,
From these the thing is born and comes to shores
of light,
When stuff appropriate to each
And proper elements are there;
All things cannot come from everything,
Because in everything there is a separate hidden
power.

Again, in spring we see the rose,
In summer, corn; the grapes at autumn's prompt-
ing.
Why? But that seeds of things together come;
When time is ripe the fashioned thing appears,
When season's right and teeming earth brings
forth
The tiny fragile things in safety to the shores of
light?
But if they came to be from nothing,
They would suddenly explode to birth
At random times and inappropriate seasons of the
year,
Because, you see, there'd be no elements
To keep them from cohering and from birth,
Till time is ripe.
Nor need there'd be of space for things to grow
If they could grow from nothing.
Babies would suddenly be men,
And shrubs would swift and sudden leap from
earth.
But nothing now like this occurs
Since all things slowly grow from proper matter,
As is right,
And as they grow retain their natural kind.
So you may know that all things wax
From atom stuff appropriate. This, too, is true:
Without the showers at proper seasons of the year,
Earth could not produce her gay and teeming
brood.
Nor without food
Could nature nurture living things in kind,
Nor save their life.

So you must rather think
That in the multiplicity of living things
Are common elements, like alphabet in words,
Than that a thing can come to be without its
atom stuff.

Then, why could not nature fashion men so
huge
That they could pass on foot through ocean's
depths
And with their strength of arm tear hills apart?
Or men whose length of life could far surpass
A man's allotted span?
Surely because there is atomic stuff assigned to
each,
Determining what can come to be.
And so confess we must
That nothing ever comes to be from nothing,
Since things need "seeds,"
That each created thing can be produced
And brought to air's soft breezes.

Last argument:
We see that well-worked fields surpass a wilder-
ness,
That man by toil of hands can bring forth better
crops.
Therefore, atomic particles must lurk in earth,
Which we, by turning fertile glebe, subduing sod,
Can bring to birth.
If there were not, we'd see all things improve,
Without the agency of human toil, spontaneously.
[146–214]
[The omitted portion describes the properties
of atoms, maintains the existence of void, or
empty space, and asserts that everything else is
either property or accident of these two. Rival
theories—of Heraclitus, Empedocles, and Anaxagoras—are refuted, and the book ends, after the
eloquent passage on the poet's theme, with a
proof that the universe is infinite.]

*The poet's theme*

Come hear the rest, come lend your ears
To more prophetic strain.
I know how difficult my topic is.
Fame is the spur that touched my heart with
hope
And branded breast with burning love of Muses.
Touched with Fame's spur, I feel my spirit glow;

I tread the trackless heights,
Not trodden earlier by foot of man.
I love to press towards unsullied rills and drink.
I love to pluck fresh flowers and weave
A splendid garland for my head,
In those rare heights whence ne'er before
The Muse has plucked a flower for any man.

My fame is this: I touch a mighty theme
And burst religion's bonds from human minds.
Then too, I write on murky theme translucent
    verse
And coat on everything the Muse's charm.
In this, I think, I'm not unreasonable.
As doctors do when they give horrid drugs to
    boys,
First smear the glass around with honey's golden
    sweet.
The child's young age, detecting no deceit,
Drinks goodness down in bitter guise.
He's cheated, not betrayed.
He's rather turned to health again.
Just this do I.
To some who have not tasted it,
This creed of mine may seem too grim.
Too many shrink away from it.
And so I wanted to expound for you
Deep wisdom in Pierian song
And coat the bitter drug of reason with the Muse's
    charm.
In this way I might hope to hold your mind
To theme both high and hard,
Until you'd mastered nature's shape and form.
                                          [920–950]

## *From* Book II

### *The Tranquil Life*

O sweet it is, when, on the mighty sea,
The wind stirs up great billows,
One's own foot firm on steady earth,
To watch another's troubles.
Not that we find delight in other's strugglings,
But that it's sweet to look on troubles
From which oneself escapes.
Sweet, too, to look
When cavalcades of war contend upon the plain,
And one is safe.
But far surpassing everything in bliss it is
To occupy the high, serene, embattled eminence,
The ivory tower,

Whose battlements are thought and high phi-
    losophy,
The wisdom of the wise.
Here you look down and see, like tiny ants,
Men scurry to and fro, wandering here and there,
Seeking to find the hidden path of life,
Well spent and ordered.
You see them battle with their wits,
Pit lineage 'gainst lineage,
Working night and day with sinews and with wits,
To gain the crown of wealth, the pride of power.
Men's wretched minds, men's blinded hearts!
In darkness deep, in peril sore,
This little life of ours is passed,
Not to see that nature asks for nothing
But that, body free from pain and mind from
    care,
We can enjoy sweet peace of mind and spirit.

Few things we see our body really needs;
Enough to keep us free from pain.
Though these few things can serve up many
    luxuries—
Pleasant enough at times.
Nature herself feels not the loss
If gilded effigies in sumptuous halls
With flaming torches in their raised right hands
Do not bring light to midnight feasts;
If gold and silver shimmer not and glint;
If music echo not from lacquered and from gilded
    beam.
Without all these, in grassy nook reclined,
A stream, a shady tree instead of luxury,
Needing no wealth, men tend their bodies' needs
And find sufficient bliss,
Spring on the mountains, flowers in every mead.

Tortured by sickness and by fever racked,
Does woven tapestry or deep rich purple glow
Bring healing quicker, as a bed, than peasant's
    cloak?
And so, since neither fame nor family nor wealth,
Can heal your body, can they help your mind,
Unless perhaps, when your own legions strengthen
    self-esteem
(You see them marching swift on open plain in
    mimic war,
You judge them both alike in arms, in spirit like,
Strengthened with great reserves and power of
    cavalry),
In face of all their strength do superstitious fears

Flee headlong from the mind?
Does martial strength banish the fear of death,
Leave mind relaxed, or spirit free from tension?
But if we see that martial strength is only trivial
    mockery,
That really human fears and carking cares,
Dread not the clash of arms, the javelin flight,
And boldly move 'mid kings and high estate,
Bend not the knee before the sheen of gold,
Not reverence rich tailoring of sumptuous cloth,
How can you doubt that freedom from external
    things
Is sovereign gift of reason?

Is not all life in darkness spent?
Like tiny boys who tremble in the dark
And think that anything may come,
We, also, tremble in the light,
And shrink from things that in themselves, are
    no more terrible,
Than what boys fear in dreams and fancy sure to
    be.

*The movement of the atoms*

Come now, I will unfold and tell
What movement of the atom stuff made things
And broke them down again when made,
And what compulsion's brought to bear on them,
And what velocity's assigned to them,
To fall through mighty void.
You lend attentive ears.
Matter assuredly is not close packed;
We know, because we see that things grow small,
And all things, like a river, flow away in time's
    long lapse;
And yet the sum of things remains the same.
The reason is that bodies moving from a thing
Diminish what they left, augment the thing to
    which they come.
The one grows old, the other waxes strong.
Yet even with the new they don't remain.
And so the sum of things is ever new
And all things mortal live by give and take.
The generations wax, the generations wane;
In time's brief span all living things are changed,
Like runners in a race they pass life's torch.
                                [1–79]
[The omitted lines deal with the kinetics of the
atomic theory: the incessant movement of the
atoms, their velocity, and their universal down-
ward motion due to weight.]

*The swerve of the atoms*

In the system of Lucretius, the swerve of the atoms
plays a twofold role. It accounts for the making of the
universe of things out of the homogeneous atom stuff;
and it accounts for freedom, free will in human beings.

I long that you should grasp this point, too, in
    our search.
When atoms fall straight downwards through the
    void,
Impelled by their own weight,
At some chance time and some chance intervals
    in space,
They swerve a bit,
So slightly that you scarce can call it swerve.
Unless they did, eternally straight down they'd fall
Like raindrops in a storm. Unless they did,
There'd be no clash nor clinging in the atom
    stream.
Nothing could nature e'er create.

If any think
That weightier atoms swifter through the void
    are borne,
And hence come movements which give shape to
    things,
In this he's clearly wrong.
When objects fall straight down through water or
    thin air,
The heavier faster falls, just because the medium
Checks not all things in equal measure equally,
But rather faster yields to heavier things.
And empty space can never, anywhere, check
    things in flight.
Its nature makes it yield.
And so both heavy things and light
Are borne at equal pace through silent void.
The heavy cannot strike the light by swifter
    flight,
Nor cause the clashes nor the variant motion—
Nature's way of making things.
And so once more, once more, I'm moved to say,
Atoms must swerve the tiniest bit.
If not, we're forced to think
That bodies sideways fall—
They clearly don't.
This is apparent, this is manifest.

That bodies of themselves can never sideways
  move;
But fall straight down, as you yourself can see.
But who is there who sees that *nothing* ever
  swerves
From straight-down movement of its perpendicu-
  lar path?

Once more, if movement always is to other
  movement linked,
And if the new comes ever from the old,
As in determinist argument;
If atoms in their swerve do not fresh start
To break the bonds of Fate;
If cause may follow cause in infinite time,
Whence comes free will for living things on
  earth?
Whence comes this power, I say, snatched from
  the grasp of Fate,
This Will whereby we move wherever fancy
  prompts?
For move we do
At no fixed times, and no fixed intervals of space,
Wherever fancy prompts.
Assuredly at times like these
Man's purpose is the starting point;
His purpose stirs the motion in his limbs.

You've seen on race tracks, when the barrier's
  down,
The eager strength of racing horse
Cannot set limbs in motion half so fast
As eager mind conceives.
The total sum of matter through the frame
Must be aroused, and so stirred up
That every limb may follow mind's swift prompt-
  ing.
So you may see
The start of motion comes from out the heart;
The mind's firm will gives it the starting point.
And thence it spreads through all the frame and
  limbs.                                [216–271]

[The omitted lines discuss the permanence of
matter and motion.]

*Atoms vary in shape.*

Come now, in order learn of atoms, how diverse
  they are,
How differently they're formed with differing
  shapes.

Not in the sense that few are like in form,
But generally they're everywhere not all alike.
Nor should we wonder: atoms so many, atoms
  limitless,
Need not always, everywhere, be similar in size
  and shape.

Then, too, the race of men,
The voiceless, scaly fish that swim the seas,
Glad herds, wild beasts, the various birds
Which haunt the joyful banks, the springs, the
  pools,
That flit through distant glades,
Take any one you want as specimen:
You'll find it differs slightly from its kind.
This, too, is how a child can know its mother;
  mother, child.
We know they can, and beasts no less than men.

Often outside the lovely shrines of gods
On incense-breathing stone of altar
A calf is slain.
Its breast pours out a hot and reeking stream of
  blood.
Its mother in her loss wanders the grassy glades
And seeks the footprints in the ground of tiny
  cloven hoof.
And everywhere she turns her longing eyes
For sight of loved one lost.
Again she stands and fills the leafy glades with
  loud lament;
Often comes back to old familiar stall,
In hopes to find him.
Her heart is pierced with yearning for her loved
  one lost.
Nor can green willows or the dew-fresh grass,
Nor old familiar streams, up level with their
  banks,
Bring joy to heart or heal the pang of loss.
The sight of other calves in meadows lush helps
  not.

Thus every creature loves and needs its own;
Horned goats are recognized by tiny kids with
  tremulous bleating.
Butting lambs in pasture know their mother's call.
Nature demands that each return for milk to
  mother's udder.
Grains, too, kind by kind are never quite alike.
Take any one you want as specimen,
You'll find it differs slightly from its kind.
The same in shells that paint the lap of earth,

Where sea with gentle waves
Beats on the thirsty sand of winding shore.
And so I must insist these things must be:
The atoms are by nature made, not all alike,
Not turned out by factory's mass production.
Differ then they must.                    [333–380]

[But though this variety is not infinite, atoms
of any given form are infinite, and combine
variously. Atoms are without color, heat, sound,
taste, smell, or sensation; they make up infinite
worlds which come into being and pass away by
Nature's decree.]

### *From* Book III

*In praise of his teacher Epicurus: the moral
value of his philosophy*

Into thick darkness came of old bright light.
You do I follow, you, who brought the light
To show us what is good and bad in life,
You do I follow, glory of the Grecian race,
And in your footsteps firmly plant my own.
Not that I want to rival you; affection makes me
          want to imitate.
How can a swallow vie with swans
Or kid with little tottering limbs
On race track vie with mighty practised horse?
You are the father of my mind, discoverer of
          nature.
From your books, O seer renowned,
You give a father's precepts in philosophy.
As bees in flowery meadow suck each flower,
So we your golden words repeatedly;
We feed on them and find them golden,
Worthy of eternal life.
Soon as your thought, born of a godlike mind,
Begins to thunder forth on Nature's laws,
Then all terrors from our spirits flee;
The ramparts of the world are torn apart.
I see the atoms' pageant streaming through the
          void.
The power of godhead is revealed,
The quiet untroubled haunts of deity,
Which are not shaken by the wanton winds,
Nor lashed from cloud with rain.
No snow falls white nor frost assails;
Cloudless the air that covers them, and heaven
          bounteously smiles,
And sky is bathed in light.

Nature supplies them all they need for tranquil
          life
And nothing ever mars "their sacred everlasting
          calm."
Guided by you, we never catch a glimpse of Hell's
          recess.
Earth cannot block our vision. We can see
Whate'er goes on in space beneath our feet.
And so, thinking your thoughts
And with your guidance mastering science
A kind of godlike pleasure comes on me,
Pleasure and horror mixed,
Because your power of mind has left the works
          of nature naked to my view.

Now since I have discoursed on atoms and have
          shown
What kind they are, how different in shape,
And how, self-moved, they ever fly,
In motion everlasting e'er impelled,
And how from atoms every object can be made,
Now I must tear up by the roots and cast away
That fear of death,
That fear that sullies mortal life from end to
          end
And pours the murk of death on everything,
Leaves no man's pleasure pure and unalloyed.

For though men often say disease and infamy
More dreadful are than deepest depths of Hell
And though they hold that soul is blood or wind
(Whichever theory they are clinging to),
And so they claim they need not our philosophy
Yourself can judge that this is done for pomp and
          arrogance
Rather than deep belief. For these same men,
Exiled from country, banished from human sight
Black with the blackest crimes, gnawed by a hun-
          dred cares,
Live all the same.
Wherever wretchedness and anguish place them,
They worship all the same,
Butcher their sleek black bulls and give their
          offerings
To guardian spirits of the dead.
Their troubles turn their mind to creed and cult.
And so it's good to watch men in adversities,
By mounting dangers pressed.
At times like these men pour their deepest
          thoughts from depth of breast.
The mask is torn away, the face remains.

Then too, the lust for power and place and
    wealth,
Motives which make men pass the bounds of law,
And join in crime and struggle night and day
With all their might to scale the heights of wealth,
These wounds of life are too much nurtured by
    the fear of death.
Men see that infamy and biting poverty
Are far removed from pleasant tranquil life,
A kind of lurking at the gate of death.
These things they want to flee, spurred by false
    fear.

    And so in time of civil war they build their
        wealth.
Their lust for gold outruns all bounds.
In piling wealth they slaughter heap on slaughter.
With hardened heart they gloat when brother dies.
A kinsman's banquet they both hate and fear.
Likewise from this same fear envy can wear
    them down.
This man, they see, has power,
While that one wins respect and walks in fair
    renown.
And I, they'll say, am doused in murk and mire.
Some die to win their statues and their fame.

    And sometimes, even through their fear of
        death,
Hatred of light and life takes hold of men.
With heavy hearts they kill themselves,
Forgetting that the fear of death caused all their
    woes.
The fear of death makes one man sully honor,
Another crash through friendship's bonds,
Wanton, in short, with every human tie.
Often have men, seeking to skirt the shoals of
    death
Played false to fatherland and parents, too.
Like tiny boys who tremble in the dark
And think that anything may come,
We also tremble in the light and shrink from
    things
That in themselves are no more terrible
Than what boys fear in dreams and fancy sure to
    be.                                    [1–93]

[The omitted lines discuss the nature and formation of the soul, and give proofs of its mor-
tality.]

*Lucretius with his arguments tries to banish
the fear of death.*

Death then is nothing, affects us not at all,
Since soul is held to be of mortal stuff.
And just as in the past we knew no ill
When Punic hosts from all sides rushed to war,
When all the earth beneath the lofty shores of
    sky,
Trembled in dreadful battle,
And men could doubt which side was doomed for
    fall
And loss of empiry on land and sea alike;
So, when we're dead,
When soul and body out of which we're formed,
    one entity,
Are torn apart in death,
Nothing can touch our sense at all or move our
    consciousness,
(For we shall not be alive to know)
Even if ocean were with land confused and sea
    with sky.

    Even if mind's structure and the power of soul
        have consciousness,
Still that can nothing mean to us, we who're
    created what we are,
One creature by the wedlock and the mating of
    our body to our soul.
Even if time could collect again our particles of
    matter after death,
Arrange them once again as once they were;
If it were given us to live once more,
That fact could nothing mean to us at all,
When once is burst the self-succession of our
    consciousness.
Even now, we care not for the "self" that once we
    were,
No torment for that "self" e'er touches us.
If one gives thought to time's immensity,
And atom's motions in their infinite variety,
This you could easily conceive,
That this atomic structure out of which we're
    made
Might once have found before exactly same ar-
    rangement.
But this we cannot grasp at all with grip of
    memory.
The pause of life has intervened;
The movements of our consciousness

Have wandered far and wide.
If pain and grief are due to touch a man
That man must live and be to feel these things.
Since death has taken this away,
Forbids the man to be whom pain might strike,
From this we learn there's naught to fear in
    death;
That once a man is dead he cannot be in misery,
That there's no difference if he never had been
    born,
When death immortal once has snatched our mor-
    tal life.

So when you see a man lament
That after death his body rots away,
Is licked by flames or torn by teeth of beasts,
This you must know;
His words do not ring true,
Some hidden goad is lurking in his heart,
Even while his verbal creed
Denies the fact of consciousness in death.
He does not (here's my view)
Follow his verbal creed nor grounds thereof.
He does not fully tear his roots from life and
    throw himself away.
He unconsciously assumes a part of him remains.
For when a man, while still alive,
Pictures his body after death,
Imagines birds and beasts are gnawing at the
    corpse,
Indulges in self-pity,
His thought has failed to free his sense from that
    poor corpse,
Confounds it with himself and thinks the body
    "he."
And so he groans that he was born a mortal man,
And does not see that in real death there'll be no
    second self,
To live and mourn the dead and stand in lamen-
    tations,
While the self outstretched is torn or burned.
For if, when dead, it's evil to be torn by teeth of
    beasts,
Why is it not as bad to lie on scorching flames and
    shrivel up?
Or suffocate in honey when embalmed?
Grow stiff with cold when sleeping under weight
    of ponderous slab?
Or feel oppressed and ground by weight of earth
    above?

No more, they say, no more, can joyful home
    fires welcome you,
Nor loyal comely wife,
Nor children be the first to share a father's kiss
And touch the heart in joyful wellsprings of con-
    tent.
No more, they say, can you be prosperous and
    guard your own.
Poor wretch, they say, how wretchedly
Has death's accursed single day snatched life's
    best gifts.
But this they do not say: "You'll want these
    things no more."
For were their vision clear, did words conform to
    it,
They'd free themselves from every pang of fear.
Just as you are when lulled in sleep,
So will you be through all unending time,
Completely free from every care and grief.
But we are inconsolable in tears
While body shrivels on the awful pyre.
And time can ne'er assuage the eternal pang of
    grief.
*This* is the question we must put to him.
"What is so bad in this?
If mortal creature turns to rest and peace,
Why should you waste away in torments of un-
    ending grief?"

Often do men do this when banqueting
(Wine cup in hand, their brows with garlands
    crowned):
Propose a toast and say,
"Brief is the span of bliss for little men,
Soon it is past and never can you call it back
    again."
As though in death this were the worst of tor-
    ments,
That thirst should parch our throat and scorch
    our palate.
As though desire for any *thing* could lurk within.
No mortal man can long for self and life
When flesh alike and mind are deep in sleep.
And sleep, for all we care, can endless be;
No longing for ourselves can linger on.

And yet in sleep atomic movements wander
    through our flesh
Not far at all from those that bring us conscious-
    ness,

When man springs up from sleep and gathers wits
  again.
Much less, I say, can death affect us, if there can
  be a "less"
Than what we know is nothing.
In death the particles, more widely spread,
Let no man wake and stand again,
When once the cold release from life has hold of
  him.

Another argument;
Let Nature, like a judge, find sudden utterance,
Upbraiding one of us in words like these:
"Is death so great a thing then, mortal man,
That you abandon self to sickening grief?
Why do you weep and groan at death?
If life was good for you and all its joys
Have not drained off, like water poured in cracked
  receptacle,
And left untasted,
Why do you not, like guest at feast of life,
Slip peacefully away, with mind serene, poor
  fool,
Grasp quiet and nothingness?
But if your pleasures all have slipped away and
  life is burdensome,
Why add some more which in its turn will slip
  away
And never give you zest?
Should you not rather make an end to life and
  toil?
For insofar as I devise and calculate
Nothing is left of pleasure, not a thing.
The same monotonous sameness always, every-
  where.
But if you're not by years weighed down,
Nor limbs worn and decayed,
Still all this yet will come to you,
Even if span of life should many generations over-
  pass,
Even if death should never come."

What answer can we make?
Admit we must that Nature's plea is just,
Her brief well grounded and well argued.
But if some older man, advanced in years, com-
  plain
And mourn his death, poor wretch, more than
  he should,
Were it not right that Nature grow more shrill:
"Enough of tears, you oaf, check your complaints.

You've tasted every joy of life
And now you waste away.
But you looked before and after
And sighed for what was not.
So life has slipped away from you, hated and
  spoiled,
And now before you know, Death stands at your
  head,
Before you can depart,
Sated and filled with feast of things.
So now, forget possessions, be your age;
Serenely yield them to your sons, as yield you
  must."

Rightly, I think, would Nature plead,
And rightly would she shriek and scold.
The old order changes, yielding place to new.
No man goes down to Hell, or loathsome Tartarus.
There must be matter that new things may grow.
These, too, will follow you when they have lived
  their life,
Just as the things before you died, so die will
  they.
Life's law still holds, that thing must grow from
  thing,
And life is something we can rent, not own.

Consider, too how nothing means the endless
  past to us,
Before our birth.
This mirror of the future nature now holds up,
After our death.
Does that seem sad, does that seem grim?
It seems to me more tranquil far
Than any kind of sleep.              [830–977]

*The argument against the fear of death, con-
tinued*

This, too, please tell yourself from time to time;
Ancus the good is dead,
A better man than you a thousand times, you
  greedy fool.
And many other kings and potentates are dead,
Who once were great in power, ruled mighty
  folk.
And that great king who bridged the Hellespont,
And led his troops by land from side to side,
On foot, on horse, crossed salty deep, insulting
  ocean's waves,
Yet he is dead. He's left the light of day

And poured his soul abroad from dying frame.
And Scipio is dead, war's thunderbolt, the
  scourge of Carthage.
He gave his bones to earth like any unknown
  tramp.
And too, the finest brains in science or art,
Boon comrades of the Muses:
Homer himself, the peerless, sceptred, crowned,
Is laid to sleep like others.
Even Democritus, when creeping age
Warned him that mind and memory were grow-
  ing dim,
Of his own will met death, gave up his life.
And Epicurus, too, is dead,
Teacher and prophet, for his life is spent.
(He topped the human race in genius,
Blotting out rivals as the rising sun dims stars.)

Do you then hesitate to die, think it unjust?
You who in life are already partly dead,
Who pass the greater part of life in sleep,
Snore on your feet and never cease to dream,
And drag around a mind drugged with dull
  fear,
And never know what ails you,
Oppressed on every side with many a care,
And staggering like a drunk in mind's blind
  blundering.
If men,
When once they feel a massive burden in their
  heart,
Oppressing, weighing down,
Could also know the source, the cause,
They would not live their life as now we often
  see men do;
Not knowing what he wants, one runs from
  place to place
As though that way he'd lay his burden down.
He often leaves his spacious home and goes out-
  doors,
Because he's bored at home.
And then goes back again as suddenly, finding
  outdoors no good.
And then he drives his nags in headlong haste
To country home as if to fight a fire,
Or else devotes himself to sleep and seeks ob-
  livion,
Or sometimes rushes back to city home to visit
  that again.
In this way every man is striving to avoid him-
  self.

But no man as we know can lose himself.
This self will cling to him against his will.
Because he's sick and never grasps the cause of
  his disease.
But were perception clear,
Then man would soon abandon everything,
Devote themselves to physics and philosophy.
What is in question, after all,
Is not one hour but all eternity,
What fate awaits man after death.
                              [1023–1075]

*From* Book IV

[The omitted lines are on vision, sensation,
and thought, and on bodily functions, leading to
a passionate denunciation of the passion of
love.]

*Lucretius discourses on sex and love.*

This pleasure, then, is love for us, thence comes
  the name.
Hence, first of all,
The drops of love's sweet passion into heart dis-
  tilled
Are followed by cold care.
Though she, beloved object, is afar,
Yet pictures of her haunt the eyes;
Her lovely name, the ears.
And yet it's best to banish love's imaginings
And fast from food of love; turn the mind else-
  where,
Indulge your lust with any one at hand,
Not focus it on one and so pile up
Mountains of grief assured.
The sore will grow and fester if you feed it.
Day by day the madness grows, the pang more
  piercing,
Unless love's wounds you scramble with fresh
  strokes,
And loiter after lady of the streets,
Before you're chained to one
(Unless in studies new you can absorb the mind).
He who shuns love does not lose love's reward.
He picks a pleasure less alloyed with pain.
For surely pleasure's purer when you're fancy
  free.
And lover's passion, even at possession's hour,
Tosses about in dark, blind blundering.
He hesitates what first he should enjoy with hand
  or eye.

What they have pursued they tightly squeeze,
And cause the body pain,
And often fasten teeth in lips, smite mouth with
    kisses—
The pleasure is not pure, and secret goads lurk
    there,
Bidding them hurt whate'er it be that has induced
    their madness.
But Venus gently mitigates these pains in love;
Sweet pleasure mingled checks the bites.
Here is his hope that passion can be quenched,
Even by the body that induced the flame.

But nature objects and makes it happen just
    the other way.
Alone of human appetites love is like this:
The more it feeds, the fiercer flames desire.
For food and drink are taken in the limbs,
Possessing their allotted parts of human frame;
Desire for them is easily assuaged.
But from the lovely face, complexion fair, of
    loved one
Nothing lover gleans for pleasure save some pic-
    tured images,
At which fond hope doth grasp like straws in
    wind.
Just as in dreams a thirsty man may long to
    drink,
But water is not there to quench his thirst,
He strives in vain to grasp at water's images,
And still feels pangs of thirst,
The while he thinks he drinks from torrent
    stream,
Just so in love, Venus mocks lover with these
    images;
He cannot sate his lust through gazing on love's
    frame.
And though his hands move aimless over all,
He cannot wring a piece from lovely limbs.

Even when at the last,
Lovers embrace and taste the flower of youth,
Sweet augury of coming bliss
When Venus plants her seed in female form,
With eagerness, they press, body to body, lip to
    lip,
And intermingle moisture from their mouths,
'Tis all in vain.
He cannot shave away a fragment from beloved
    flesh
Or bury life in passion of a mutual ecstasy.

Just this at times they seem to wish to do,
So gladly are they held in Venus' bonds,
While limbs grow loose and liquid in love's
    ecstasy.

And when accumulated lust has left their limbs,
A little while they feel a respite from desire.
And then the rage returns, passion revisits them;
They long to grasp again the object of desire.
They cannot find device to conquer their disease;
In doubt they waste away from secret wound.

Think too,
They dissipate their strength and spend their
    energy.
They pass their life under another's sway.
Work is neglected, name and fame grow sick and
    faint.
Fortune meanwhile is spent, lavished on eastern
    scents,
Corinthian shoes, dainty and sweet, to grace a
    lady's feet.
Yes, and great emeralds flashing green are set in
    gold.
The lover's ardor constantly wears out
The sheer and purple gown.
It's used too hard, and drinks up Venus' sweat.
Their wealth is spent in bands and ribbons for
    their hair.
Islands and mainlands send their gorgeous stuffs.
Wealth is poured out on linens, dainties for the
    feast,
Games, frequent toasts, perfumes, garlands and
    wreaths.

But all in vain, for from the fount of charms
There ever flows a bitter drop even 'mid the
    flowers,
Some pang of conscience, surging of remorse,
That life should pass in idling and wantonness.
The lady, perhaps, has dropped a heedless word
To torture him and left its sense in doubt—
A word that lodged in lover's consciousness
And burned to flame.
Or else he finds her eyes too restless, fears another
    man;
Or finds a gleam of malice in her smile.
Even when love goes well these problems rise.
But when love's crossed or hopeless, torments
    countless throng,
Which you could see in darkness with shut eyes.

So it is better far, exactly as I've cautioned you,
To be on guard beforehand, be on guard, be not
    enticed.
To shun entanglement in snares of love,
That's not so difficult.
But once entangled in its mesh, to break away
    again,
And burst the bonds of love's entanglement—
    that's hard.                    [1058–1148]

It's not divine decree or supernatural ordering,
That helps an ugly woman win man's love.
A girl can often win her prize herself
By modest bearing and by neat array.
Easy you'll come to think you'd find
A life with girl like this.
Is not a stern resolve by frequent little blows worn
    down?
The hardest rock in time's long span will crack,
If frequent blows of water keep on pounding it.
                                    [1277–1287]

## *From* Book V

*In praise of Epicurus and his achievements in
moral enlightenment*

What talent's adequate to write a poem
To match the insight of this seer's philosophy?
Or whose command of words is great enough to
    match his merits,
Deserve the gifts he's given from heart and brain?
No mortal, as I think.
If I can speak as demonstrated majesty of theme
    demands,
He was a god, a god, I say, O Memmius renowned.
He first brought reason's gifts to man's life's
    ordering,
That which we've come to call philosophy.
His thought has brought the barque of human
    life
Out of the billows, lodged it safe in port;
Out of the inky black and stress of midnight
    storm
Placed it in clear and calm and dazzling light.
Could any god accomplish more than this?

Think of the other gifts we call divine.
Ceres, the legend states, brought grain to men,
    and Bacchus, wine.

Without these gifts man's life can still go on.
Distant tribes, they say, have never needed them.
Without a mind at peace no man lives well.
And so 'tis right that we should think him god,
Whose consolations, known afar, bring peace of
    mind.
If you think Hercules a greater benefactor of
    mankind,
You're clearly wrong.
What damage could Nemaean lion with yawning
    jaws
Or bristling boar of Arcady do to mankind?
Or Cretan bull, or hydra with its palisade of
    poisonous snakes,
Or threefold might of triple-bodied Geryon . . . ? *
And all the other monsters of this kind which
    were destroyed.
But even were they not,
What harm, I say, could they have done alive?
No harm, at all, I say.
Even today earth teems with terror and with
    savage beasts,
In glades and mighty mountains and deep woods.
Their haunts we can avoid, if that's our wish.
But if the heart's not pure, what perils and what
    wars
We have to enter, if we wish or not!
What pangs of care can rive an anxious heart!
What terrors, too!
And what of pride and lust and wantonness!
And what of luxury and sloth!
And so the seer who banished all these sins
By words, not arms,
Should we not number him among th' immortal
    gods?
And this the more because he used to speak in
    good and godlike words
About the gods themselves,
And by his reasoning reveal the stuff of things.
I follow in his footsteps, think his thoughts,
And teach by what stern law all things are made,
And how they must abide in it,
Nor break the strong decrees of time.
First of all the mind, we've learned, consists of
    mortal stuff,
Unable to endure through endless time,
Though visions do in sleep perplex and cheat the
    mind;
(We seem to see the dead who've lived their life).

---

* Lucretius has here detailed other fabled monsters of
legend.

*The argument of the Fifth Book*

Now the unfolding of my thought brings this
    point next:
I must show the cosmos likewise made of mortal
    stuff,
And how the meeting of material particles
Created earth and sky and sea and stars and moon
    and sun.
And then what living creatures came to be on
    earth,
And what could never be.
And how men learned to speak,
Communicating thought in various tongues
By naming things.
How fear of gods has entered human hearts,
A fear which round the world keeps holy places,
Fanes and lakes and groves, altars and images of
    gods.
And then I will expound
The wanderings of the sun, the paths of moon,
How steersman Nature governs them.
So we'll not think spontaneously or free of will
They move on yearly courses, well disposed to
    man,
Producing crops and creatures for his need.
And most of all not think that blessed Providence
Could move the years and seasons.
For even men who've fully learned that gods lead
    carefree lives
If ignorant of laws by which things move,
Those things in chief which happen overhead,
    up in the sky,
They're drawn to ancient creed and cult again;
Imagine savage tyrants overhead,
Strong to accomplish anything
Because, poor fools,
They know not what can be and what cannot,
The law that binds each thing, its deep-set bound-
    ary stone.

*The world is not eternal or divine.*

Now for the rest, no longer dallying with prom-
    ises,
Consider first: the seas, the land, the sky.
Three natures, triple body, triple form so much
    alike,
One day, my friend, in just one day will hurtle
    down to ruin.
The massive structure of the universe
That lasted many years will fall apart.
I know full well how strange a thing,
Stupendous to the mind, is this my doctrine,
That earth and sky will one day fall in ruin,

How hard it is for words like these of mine
To win belief!
It's always so when novel thought assails the
    mind;
Ideas beyond the reach of sight and touch
Which always give the easiest access to the heart
And temples of the mind. But speak I will.
Maybe the very fact will bring belief—
Perhaps you'll feel an earthquake, see the earth,
The whole earth shaken in a moment's time.
May pilot Fortune steer us from this fate;
May thought, not horror, make us realize
The whole might fall one day in rending, sound-
    ing crash.

Before I approach this point, tell destiny, more
    certainly,
More sacredly, than Pythian priestess
Speaking from the laurelled shrine
And tripod of the Delphic god,
I've many consolations to unfold in verse.
So will you not,
Checked by the bridle bit of ancient creed,
Think earth and sky and sun, and sea and stars
    and moon,
Because divine in structure, must endure
Through endless time.

So you'll not think it right
That man, like giants rebellious, should torments
    face,
For crime of shaking with his thought the walls
    of universe,
Wanting to quench the glorious sun in heaven,
Branding immortal fact with mortal speech.
These things are not divine,
Not worthy to be numbered with the gods;
Rather they give us hint of what is far removed
From living motion and from consciousness.
We surely cannot think that mind and conscious-
    ness
Are linked with every object bodily;
Trees cannot live in air, nor clouds in salty sea,
Nor fish in fields, nor blood in logs, nor sap in
    stones.
Fixed law ordains where each thing lives and
    grows.

So mind can never be without the brain,
No consciousness apart from blood and cells.
For, if it could, it's far more plausible
That mind should lurk in head or shoulders,
Even in the heels or any other part of man;
At least the human vase remains the same.
But since, even within our human frame
There is a law, a fixed determination
Where mind and soul can live apart and grow,
We must the more deny that outside mortal frame
And human form the soul could live
In crumbling sods of earth or in the fire of sun,
In moisture or the lofty shores of sky.
For these are not endowed with consciousness
    divine,
Since they're not even quickened with the breath
    of life.                                    [1–145]

[Lucretius in the omitted lines attacks theology
and teleology: the world had a beginning and is
mortal; the movements of the heavenly bodies
can be explained by physics. The youth of the
world can be explained without supposing the
existence of gods; this includes an explanation of
the origin of vegetable and animal, as well as of
human life.]

*The life of primitive man*

The human race was harder far in early days
    than now,
As you'd expect, since hard earth brought it forth.
Its bones within were harder, solider;
Its sinews binding flesh were tougher far.
Its hardy strength could hardly be assailed by
    heat or cold
Or novel food or any flaw in human frame.
Age after age while sun sped through the sky
They lived their life like wandering beasts.
No sturdy ploughman held his curving plough;
No skill was theirs to till the field with iron share,
Or plant young shoots in earth,
Or prune high trees with knives.
The gift of sun and showers, spontaneous bounty
    of the earth,
Was boon enough to please their hearts.
Under the acorn-laden oaks they gained their sus-
    tenance;
Or dined on berried arbute
(These you've seen, in winter red;
Much larger were they in the days of old).

Besides all this, the flowering youth of earth
Bore other fare as rough, plenty for wretched
    men.
To quench their thirst the rills and rivers called,
As now from mighty hills the water's fall
In loud and solemn tones calls thirsty roving
    beasts.
Or in their wanderings they came to know
The woodland church of Nymphs and lingered
    there.
For they knew
That water gliding there in bounteous flood
Washed the wet rocks and trickled over mosses
    green,
And sometimes welled and burst its banks
And rushed o'er level plain.

Not yet did man know how to serve himself with
    fire.
He had not thought to clothe himself with skins,
Use spoils of chase for body's covering.
Men dwelt in woods and glades and hollow moun-
    tain caves;
And hid their shaggy limbs in brushwood piles
When blows of wind or rain forced them to hide.

They could not think of social good
Or know the fine restraint of common codes or
    laws.
Whatever booty fortune gave, the individual
    seized;
His only learning was to live and thrive himself.
Venus herself joined lovers in the woods in
    primal ecstasy;
Sometimes a mutual love joined man and girl,
Or else the violent strength of male, unbridled
    lust.
Or else she was by little gifts seduced—
Acorn or arbute or the choicest pear.
Relying on their wondrous strength of hand and
    foot
They followed hard on track of woodland beast
With mighty clubs or stones to hurl.
Most they subdued; a few they'd dodge and hide.
When night came on they laid their naked limbs
    on earth
Like bristling boars,
And wrapped themselves around with leaves and
    foliage.
Nor did they look for daylight and the sun
With wailing loud,

Or wander panicked through the fields in black
of night;
But deep in silent sleep they waited patiently
Till sun with rosy torch brought light to sky.
For since from babyhood they'd learned to know
Light following darkness, turn by turn, and dark-
ness light,
They had no sense of wonder or of fear,
No sense of apprehension lest the sun should
ne'er return,
And earth be buried always in unending night.
Their fear was rather this, that savage beasts
Might make night restless for a wretched folk.
They left their home, abandoned rocky roof
If foaming boar or mighty lion approached.
At midnight oft they'd leave their leaf-spread
couch
To savage and unwelcome guest.    [925–987]

*The evolution of man and human institutions*

And when, as time went on, they'd mastered
fire,
Gained themselves huts and skins to cover them,
One man, one woman in a single hut together
lived,
And tiny ones around them growing up they
saw,
Then first the human race learned gentler ways.
Now used to fire,
Their freezing limbs would shrink from cold
Beneath the vault of sky.
Excessive sex wore down their savage strength,
And children with their blandishments
Subdued their elder's haughty will.

Then neighbor oft to neighbor pledged his
word
Eager to form a friendship and refrain from
mutual harm.
And pity they'd evoke for girls and children, too.
When these with piteous cries,
Pathetic gestures, and the broken word
Would teach the primal law of moral life,
That all should spare the weak.
Yet concord was a lesson hard to learn.
Most of mankind was loyal to its pledge.
Else would the human race in earliest times have
failed
Nor wealth of progeny sufficed, destruction to
avert.    [1011–1027]

Here I'll anticipate your silent questionings.
'Twas lightning's flash that first brought fire to
man,
And from that source all heat of flame is spread
abroad.
Even to this day we see that many things burst
into flame,
Sparked by the fire from heaven,
When heaven's blow has brought the gift of heat.
Again, when branching tree is lashed by winds,
Sways to and fro and surges with its boughs
Against another tree,
Fire often flashes forth,
Induced by friction of a bough on bough.
In either way fire may have come to man.

Now kings began to lay out cities and to choose
Sites for their citadels, to give protection
To their persons, and a place of refuge.
And flocks and herds and fields were parcelled
out
As individual holdings,
Given to men pre-eminent in bearing, talent,
strength
(For comeliness was vital then, strength of
physique prevailed).

Then came a fell invention—property—the
power of gold.
This undermined the power of strong and noble
men.
The faction of the rich quite generally,
Sucks in a man though strong and nobly born.
So if a man would guide his life aright
By reason's principles,
Plain living with a mind at peace is wealth in-
deed.
The little that he needs man never lacks.
But men have longed for wealth and power pre-
eminent,
To build a strong foundation under life,
That wealth enable them to lead a life of quiet
tranquillity,
But all in vain.
While mad to scale the dizzy peaks of honor and
of fame,
They've made the path of life with dangers teem.
Often they think their striving's reached the peak.
But envy, like a thunderbolt,
Has hurled them down to noisome depths.
Since envy like a lightning flash

Sets topmost heights ablaze,
Whatever is pre-eminent most generally.
Better to be a subject with a mind at peace
Than hold the kingly power and kingdom's sway.
Permit men, then, to sweat away the blood of life
Worn out in vain;
Fight their way forward on ambition's narrow
    way.
Vain is the wisdom gleaned from lips of other
    men,
Vain fantasy by hearsay, not experience, won.
Such spurious insight cannot help mankind.
It never has, it never will.

And so the kings were killed,
The ancient prideful majesty
Of thrones and scepters trampled down.
The glorious majesty that hedged a king was
    stained with blood,
Crushed 'neath the people's feet,
And mourned its ancient high estate, now lost.
The object once of fear, it now in squalor lies.
The ancient polity, I say, is trampled down.
Each single man, self-centred now,
Plays his own hand, seeks gain for self alone.

To check all this,
The cleverer men established magistrates
And founded laws that subject folk might will-
    ingly obey.
The human race, wearied of passing life in mu-
    tual violence,
Lay faint from feuding.
And so spontaneously it would submit to statutes
And the woven web of laws.
Because each single man sought vengeance for
    himself
More savage than allowed by equal laws,
On this account they tired of private retribution.

And so it comes about that fear of punishment
Has come to spoil and spatter every joy of life.
His individual deeds of violence hem a man in,
Returning like a boomerang on him from whom
    they sprang.
Nor can he pass his life in peace and quietness,
If once his deeds of violence
Break through the accepted common pacts of
    peace.
And even if he hides his sins from all mankind,
    all gods,

Still lurks the fear that some day they'll be
    known.
Often a man by talking in his sleep or raving in
    delirium
Has bared an ancient crime which he'd kept
    hidden long.    [1091–1160]

*Origin of belief in the gods*

And now the cause
That spread belief in deity through mighty folk,
And filled our towns with shrines,
And prompted men to institute the rites of solemn
    sacrifice,
Which linger even to this day on festal days and
    in great places
(Whence, even now, horror is branded in our
    human hearts,
Compelling men to found new shrines of gods and
    celebrate
On festal days),
All this it's not so hard to tell in words.
Even in ancient times the human race
Perceived with waking eyes the glorious shape of
    gods;
Much more in sleep, they thought they saw
Bodies of supernatural size and form.
To forms like these was consciousness assigned,
Because men saw them move their limbs,
Utter proud words proportionate to their size and
    mighty strength.
Immortal life men gave to them,
Because their face appeared from time to time,
Their form remained.
But most of all because they thought
That creatures blest with strength like this
Could not be overcome by any force.
They thought their lot must better be than ours
Because no fear of death could harass them.
And, too, because in dreams they could perform
Many miraculous deeds in manner effortless.
And then men marked in due array the ordered
    laws of sky,
The splendid pageant of the seasons of the year,
But did not know the cause.

And so they sought escape,
By handing all things over to divine control,
By thinking all things ruled by gods' decree.
They placed the temples and abodes of gods above
    the sky,

Because the sun and moon revolved through sky,
The moon and day and night,
The splendid stars of night,
Night-wandering torches and the flitting flames,
And clouds and sun and showers and snow and
winds,
Lightnings and hail and rapid thunder claps,
Those turbulent, tremendous threats.
O hapless race of men,
When deeds like this to gods assigned
Were joined to petty vengefulness.
What groans for you, what wounds for us,
What tears for later ages!

This is not holiness, before the sight of men,
Day after day to crawl up to a stone
(The ritual veil on head)
And never miss an altar;
Nor prostrate lie before the shrines of gods, with
outstretched palms,
Nor slaughter hecatomb on hecatomb,
Nor weave a litany of vow on vow.
No! Holiness is this—
To contemplate with mind serene the whole.
When we lift eyes to great celestial temples of the
world,
Aether above, studded with twinkling stars,
And let thoughts roam on heaven's immensity,
The ordered course of sun and moon and stars.
Then this reflection starts to stir and wake and
raise its head,
That this tremendous power of god might turn on
us,
This power that moves the constellations
In their endless, restless way.
The lack of scientific thought assails the doubt-
ing heart—
No knowledge how the cosmos came to be and
how 'twill end,
How long the ramparts of the universe
Can bear the task of endless, restless journey-
ing,
Or whether, gifted by divine decree with endless
life,
And gliding endless down the grooves of time,
They can defy the strength of time's eternity.

And, after all,
What mind escapes the sudden flash of fear, fear
of the gods,
When lightning's dreadful stroke

Makes parched earth tremble and the great sky
crash?
Nations and peoples tremble,
Shrink and huddle limbs together out of fear,
terror of gods,
The thought that now's the time
For some foul deed, for some proud word,
To suffer retribution's torment.
Or when the force of furious wind at sea
Sweeps fleet and admiral and horse and foot in
headlong rout,
Does he not beg in prayer the peace of god,
That heaven will bless with calmer seas and favor-
ing winds?
But all in vain, for nonetheless,
He's caught in whirling hurricane and helpless
borne
To shallow waters and to Death.
A mighty hidden force so tramples down
All human strength,
Holds under foot and seems to make mock of
The pomp of power and power's relentless instru-
ments.
Again, when all of earth trembles beneath our
feet,
Cities are shaken to their fall,
Or threatening rock and quake,
What wonder that mankind contemns itself
And leaves place in its thought
For mighty power and marvellous strength of
gods
To govern all things?                [1161–1240]

*Lucretius continues his account of the evolu-
tion of human institutions.*

Nature herself, creative Queen of everything,
Gave men a pattern how to sow and graft.
Berries and nuts would fall from trees,
And then, when time was ripe, put out their shoots
in swarms.
From Nature, too, men learned to graft a wand to
parent stem,
Plant shrubs in soil.
And various ways they learned to till their smiling
fields,
Domesticate both fruits and beasts
By care and constant tending.
And day by day they beat the woodland back,
Back up the mountain slopes, and made the val-
leys yield a place for crops.

That so they might on hill and plain
Have meadows, pools, and streams,
Corn land and vineyards that bring joy to men,
And grey-green belts of olive trees
Checkering the landscape over hill and vale and
    plain.
As even now you see the countryside
Made beautiful with various charms,
Where men have made it gay by planting trees,
And fenced it in around with fruitful shrubs.

    To imitate the liquid notes of birds,
Man learned long, long ago,
And much before he'd learned to sing in com-
    pany sweet songs,
To entrance the ear.
The west wind whistling through the hollow reeds
First taught the country folk to breathe through
    scrannel pipes.
Then bit by bit they learned the sweet lament—
The elegies that flutes poured forth,
Their holes by fingers stopped.
Through pathless glades the sweet sound made
    its way
And forest deeps, through fields by shepherds
    left,
Through lovely resting place.
So bit by bit time brings each thing to view,
And reason raises it to shores of light.
These tunes would soothe their minds, delight
    their ears,
When they lay stuffed with food.
(That's when all pleasure brings delight.)
For often, as we've said, in grassy nook reclined
A stream, a shady tree instead of luxury,
With no great wealth they tend the bodies' needs,
And find sufficient bliss,
Spring on the mountains, flowers in every mead.
Then you'd hear jokes and talk and pleasant
    laughs
(The rustic muse was strong),
And life was gay and mirth made garlands for
    their heads
Of flowers and leaves.
And round they'd dance
With random step and clumsy limbs.
With heavy foot their rhythmic tread would beat
    on mother earth.
This made them laugh in merry mood.
All things, like children, in the childhood of the
    race,

They found both strange and new.
So to the wakeful came the solace of sweet sounds,
To guide the erring voice through many a tune,
Follow the endless windings of a song,
To pipe on reeds with curling lip.
Even to-day,
Policemen and sentries hold this old tradition
    fast,
Have learned to keep the rhythm of a song,
But find therein no greater bliss
Than woodland folk of earthborn men
Found long ago.
For what is here and now pleases men most,
    seems best,
Unless there's something sweeter that we've
    learned of old.
But generally the better thing found later on
    destroys the old,
And makes us like it less.

    And so it is
That man has come to like his fare of acorns
    less,
Abhor his reed-strewn couch.
Garments of skins, no longer fashion's peak,
Were envied long ago.
The first to sport such luxury, I think,
Was ambushed, slugged and put to death.
And yet in killing him
They tore the coat apart, stained it with blood,
And could not sell for gain.
Of old 'twas skins;
Now gold and purple vex men's lives with care,
And weary them with constant, endless wars.
We are to blame, I think.
Cold used to torture earthborn men
As they lay naked on the earth without the
    warmth of pelts.
But we're not harmed without our purple cloth,
With massive golden ornament.
We only need a poor man's cloak to keep out
    cold.

    And so the race of men toils endlessly, in vain.
It wastes its time in fruitless cares
Because it's never learned the end of gain
And how far pleasure true can go.
And this has drawn life's ship to stormy seas,
Stirred up great tides of war.
The watchful wardens of the firmament, the moon
    and sun,

Traversing with their light the whirling vault of
    sky,
Taught men that seasons of the year revolve,
That all things move by some fixed plan,
In fixed and due array.

And now, fenced in with mighty wallèd towers,
Man lived his life.
The land was parceled out in plots and fenced
    and tilled.
Then ocean's level wastes bloomed with the sails
    of ships.
Men learned to make a compact,
Seal a bond between allies for mutual aid;
Then poets first began to sing immortal deeds
    in glorious verse.
(The alphabet was new when first the poets sang.)
Therefore, our age knows nothing of the past,
Except where science points out the bits of evi-
    dence.

And so man made his way.
Experience, the tireless search of eager mind,
Has taught him many things—
Of ships and walls and laws, weapons and roads,
Of how to till the soil and how to dress;
And all life's prizes, life's delights,
Pictures and songs and statues finely wrought.
He's learned them stage by stage and bit by bit.
So step by step time brings each thing to view
And reason raises it to shores of light.
Thing after thing grew clear in human hearts
Until man's art assailed perfection's peak.
                [1361–1457]

### From Book VI

[Book VI gives an atomic explanation of
meteorological phenomena and terrestrial curi-
osities, on the one hand thunder, lightning, and
thunderbolts, waterspouts, clouds, and rain; on
the other, earthquakes, the sea, volcanoes, the
Nile, pestilential lakes, curious fountains, and
the magnet. The climax comes in the description
of pestilences, especially the plague at Athens,
where the poet follows Thucydides, but adds to
his source a curious note of fascination with the
gory details of horror that is peculiarly his
own.]

### The great plague at Athens

A plague like this and gusty waves of death,
In Athens long ago filled fields with dead
And left its roadways desolate.
Born deep in Egypt,
Over swimming fields and wide extent of sky
It made its way and brooded at the last o'er all
    the folk
Of Cecrops' famous town.
In serried ranks they felt the sting of fell disease
    and death.

And first they felt the head with fever burn
And both eyes flare with inflammation red.
The blackened throat within was choked with
    blood,
While ulcers blocked the path of voice and ut-
    terance.
The tongue, the vocal spokesman of the brain
Would ooze with blood,
Weakened with evils, slow in movement, rough
    to touch.
When through the throat the onset of disease
Had filled the breast and touched the very heart,
Then all the warden fortress of their life was
    broken down.
The breath poured noisome odors from their
    mouth,
Smells like the stench of rotting flesh, when
    thrown outdoors.
And straightway all the strength of mind and all
    the body's energy
Grew faint and dim,
As if the victim, even now, were at the gate of
    death.
And with their aching torments ever came
Anguish unutterable, mingled sobs and groans.
Continuous vomiting by night and day doubled
    them up,
Caused spasms in their weary limbs,
And broke their weary bodies down and wore
    them out.
In no case could you feel the surface and the
    topmost skin
Burn with excessive heat.
Rather the skin felt lukewarm to the touch.
And yet the whole was red with ulcer's flame,
As is the case when sacred fire burns through the
    limbs.

Within, meantime, the man was burning up
    right to the marrow bones.
A fiery furnace blazed beneath his ribs.
No coverlet, though light and thin, would help at
    all,
Only a cooling breeze.
And some would hurl their sick and burning limbs
In waters cold, immerse their bodies bare in cool-
    ing waves.
Many leaped headlong into cold, deep wells,
Striving with open mouths to quaff a cooling
    draught.
A thirst unquenchable, parching their scorching
    frames,
Made endless water seem like tiny drops.
Respite was none for evil; there they lay, done up.

In silent panic Medicine muttered low,
When sufferers rolled their weary fevered eyes—
Heralds of death.
And many other signs of death were there to
    note—
The troubled mind, in anguish plunged and fear,
The furrowed brow, the fierce and frenzied face,
The ringing ears, plagued and possessed with
    noise,
The quick tense breathing or great sudden pants,
The shining sweat that gleamed on neck and
    throat,
The thin rare phlegm, with yellow flecked and
    salt,
That coughing scarce could bring up through
    the throat.
Then in the hands the sinews would contract.
All limbs would tremble, and the cold
Inched slowly up the body from the feet.
To the last moment nostrils were compressed,
The tip of nose was sharpened like a quill.
Then eyes were hollowed, temples, too,
Skin hard and cold, a drooping grin on mouth,
Brow drawn and swollen.
A little later and the limbs were stiff in death.
And on the eighth bright day of shining sun,
Perhaps the ninth, they yielded up their life.

And if a man escaped the doom of death,
Yet afterwards a slow decay awaited him,
Noisome with ulcers and the bowels' black flux.
In many a case, while head would ache,
Foul blood flowed from his nose.

In this way ebbed away his whole reserve of
    body's strength.
If he survived this horrid flow of tainted blood,
Still the disease invaded nerves and limbs and
    even genitals.
In many a case, fearing the gates of death,
They suffered self-castration with a knife.
Some lingered on, deprived of hands and feet,
And some of eyes,
So firmly had a morbid fear of death seized hold
    of them.
For some all memory of things slipped right
    away—
They knew not who they were, or where.

And though the corpses lay in serried ranks
    piled up,
The dogs and birds avoided them,
So strong the stench they made.
Or, if they tasted, straightway drooped,
Struck by swift death.
In those days hardly any bird appeared at all,
No gloomy creatures issued from the woods.
They mostly fell, and drooped and died.
The loyal strength of dogs, though fighting hard,
Laid down its life, their corpses strewn through
    every street.
The dire power of plague would wrest
All power from all their limbs.

Meanwhile the sad untended funerals
Were rushed in rivalry, like contests at the games.
Nor could a single cure suggest itself,
To heal all men alike.
What aided one and gave him strength
To draw life-giving air and gaze upon the temples
    of the sky,
To others brought destruction, death.
In all the havoc, this was most pitiable:
When a man saw himself entangled in disease,
As though condemned straightway to death,
His courage fled. He'd lie with grieving heart
And look for death and pour his spirit out.
The dire contagion of the greedy plague
Passed on from man to man,
Like havoc through a flock of woolly sheep or
    horned kine
And so the plague heaped pyre on funeral pyre.
Too covetous of life and dreading death
Some paid for cowardice by coming to an end

Hard and disgraceful,
Deserted, shameful, and bereft of help.

[1137–1242]

Again had death filled temples of the gods
    with lifeless folk,
Every sacred shrine
Was cumbered and befouled with lifeless clay,
Where vergers made a place for suppliants.
By now the worship of the gods, the awful power,
Counted for naught.
The press of present grief quite vanquished it.
The ancient rites of sepulchre were out of use.
The whole of normal life was broken up,
So every man in grief laid out his own.
The sudden horror, squalor, poverty
Brought men to venture deeds unknown, un-
    heard.

Often they'd place their own beloved dead on
    stranger's pyre
And brawl and battle, even shed some blood,
To leave them there and then touch off the pile.*

[1272–1286]

--------

\* The notes in the Leonard-Smith edition of the poem on these final lines are worth quoting:

"The whole ending of the poem presents a terrifying picture of the vanity of religion, of the belief in divine providence, and of the due performance of ritual. . . .

"There is something utterly horrible about this final scene, the folk desperately scurrying about and fighting for the burial of their beloved—as if Death really did concern them!—and preserving to the very end this one supreme and unrewarded *pietas*, the concern for their own dead, which opens the poem, has yielded in the end to the awful will of Death. Such a conclusion would probably have appealed with especial force to a poet whose temperament is marked by a profound and brooding melancholy."

# SELECTIONS FROM SALLUST

## *Translated by Paul MacKendrick*

## INTRODUCTION

C. SALLUSTIUS CRISPUS (86–*ca.* 34 B.C.), is one of the few ancient authors to show any sympathy for the common man; opponent of Cicero, partisan of Caesar, tribune of the people, quaestor, praetor, and proconsul of Numidia, he has not gained in reputation by having the courage to oppose the senatorial class. According to the aristocratic tradition, he was once horsewhipped for an intrigue with another man's wife, was expelled from the Senate on a morals charge, and enjoyed his magnificent gardens on the Pincian Hill at the expense of the provincials he had robbed as governor. However real these sins may be—and they can be matched from the life story of many an optimate—the allegation of them was sufficient to drive Sallust from public life; he devoted the years of acute civil war to writing about party strife instead of participating actively in it.

Sallust invented the historical monograph: he selected episodes in Roman history to illustrate the successive stages in the struggle of democratic power against the insolence of the nobles. His one work of connected history, an account of the years 78–67 B.C., is not preserved, having perhaps fallen victim to opposition censorship, though for this theory there is no positive evidence. The episodes Sallust chose to treat were the war against the Numidian prince Jugurtha and the conspiracy of Catiline, both as examples of aristocratic mismanagement. The selections here printed from the *Jugurtha* present two speeches on the bad record of the aristocracy, an analysis of party strife in Rome, an account of the election of the "new man" Marius as consul, and a character sketch of the aristocratic dictator Sulla. The selections from the *Catiline* include Sallust's account of his motives for writing history, a grim picture of the decline and fall of the Roman Republic, a fine chiaroscuro of the gloom in Rome during the conspiracy, lightened by the revulsion of the plebs when they discovered Catiline's true character, a critical comparison of the rival leaders Cato and Caesar, and the story of the final battle, where among the corpses of friends and loved ones, men were occasionally able to recognize even an enemy.

Sallust is the first of the triumvirate of Roman historians which includes Livy and Tacitus. He shares with Livy a nostalgia for the earliest days of Rome, when

men were so noble and so poor. He rivals Tacitus in his cynicism and in his ability to evoke the atmosphere of crack-up, the mood of an age of anxiety. But the historian to whom Sallust would most like us to compare him is Thucydides. Literary critics of the Roman Empire compared the speeches in the two historians and did not find Sallust wanting. The style of both is difficult and full of abstractions almost too heavy for language to bear, and both possess to a high degree the talent of grasping what is generic in a situation without falsifying what is unique. Both had seen the ideal vision of a great movement for liberation fade into a mere struggle for power, and both write therefore with a high pessimism. For Sallust should not be romanticized into a Shelley, with a view of "man, equal, unclassed, tribeless, and nationless"; if he sympathized with the common man, it was with a view to enlisting his vote for Caesar; Sallust shares with Carlyle a "great man" theory of history; the struggle, for him, is not one between the classes and masses but between rival dynasts struggling for the soul of the ordinary man. In this insistence upon the corruptive force of money, he anticipates Toynbee: faced with the challenge of Empire, Rome had failed to respond. But of all historians ancient or modern to whom Sallust may be compared, he probably has the closest affinity to the Florentine Niccolo Machiavelli. Both wrote in retirement with a political ideal in mind; each has an undeserved bad name; both study men, unearth natural causes, are champions—from whatever motive—of the forgotten man; and it would have been better for both if Nature had endowed them with a less powerful intellect or a more genial temper.

FOR THE *Jugurthine War* and the *Conspiracy of Catiline*, the text used is that of A. W. Ahlberg (Leipzig: Teubner, 1938); for the letter *To Caesar on the Commonwealth*, that of A. Kurfess (Leipzig: Teubner, 1930). Occasional turns of phrase have crept in from J. C. Rolfe's admirable translation (reprint of the second edition, Cambridge, Mass., and London, Loeb Classical Library, 1947). For the *Catiline*, notes in the school edition of Professor H. E. Butler (Oxford, 1921) have been found especially useful.

## THE JUGURTHINE WAR

This tale (published about 41 B.C.) of battle, siege, and intrigue in North Africa (118–105 B.C.) attracted the historian because "in this war for the first time measures were taken against the insolence of the Roman nobility." The man who took the measures was the plebeian Gaius Marius, fellow-townsman of Cicero, seven times consul, reorganizer of the Roman army, chief representative of the popular party in Rome between the fall of Gaius Gracchus and the rise of Julius Caesar. Marius, simple, brave, uncorruptible, is the hero of this work; the composite villain is the corrupt Roman nobility who put Rome up for sale "doomed soon to perish, if she finds a buyer." Jugurtha, the Numidian prince over whose territory the Roman nobles haggle as they mismanage the war, is presented as a noble savage corrupted by Roman aristocrats into believing that bribery can accomplish miracles. He bribes the Roman Senate into giving him the choicest half of Numidia, then besieges the other heir, captures him, and tortures him to death. This is an insult to the prestige of the Roman Senate as arbitrator, and an army is therefore sent into North Africa. It dallies while Jugurtha makes money talk to the consul in command. In the first passage below, Memmius, tribune of the people, is stirring the Roman populace to rage at the bungling in Africa by recounting the previous bad record of the nobility.

*Memmius on the bad record of the Roman nobility*

31 . . . "If the public interest did not outweigh all other considerations, fellow citizens, there is much that would keep me from making you this speech: the strength of the party in power, your mood of resignation, the general lawlessness, and most of all the thought that nowadays to be an honest man is more of a risk than a distinction. I am actually ashamed to remind you how for the past fifteen years you have been the plaything of a minority's insolence, how disgracefully your partisans have been murdered without your lifting a finger, how laziness and slovenliness have so corrupted your spirit that you do not even now rise up against your enemies where they are most vulnerable, but persist in being afraid of those who ought properly to be afraid of you. Nevertheless my spirit moves me to face the strength of the opposition. At least I will make trial of the freedom of speech my father left me as my inheritance. Whether I do so in vain or to some purpose rests in your hands, citizens.

"I do not urge you to follow your ancestors' example and take up arms against injustice. There is no need to resort to violence, nor secession; let each of your enemies go to Hell in his own way. After the murder of Tiberius Gracchus (*they* said he was plotting to make himself king) the loyalty of the Roman people was investigated; after the slaughter of Gaius Gracchus and Gaius Fulvius also many a mother's son of your class was murdered in prison; in both cases it was not the law but the whim of the opposition that put an end to the carnage.

"But suppose that restoring its right to the people is the same as trying to make oneself king; suppose they had a right to exact whatever vengeance cannot be exacted without shedding citizen blood. In the old days you took it hard, but you took it in silence, while the treasury was plundered, while kings and free peoples paid taxes to a few nobles, who kept for themselves the lion's share of both the credit and the profit. Then *they* thought nothing of having gotten away with crimes of this magnitude, and so in the long run the laws, your rights, and everything human and divine have all been handed over to the enemy. And the doers of these deeds feel neither shame nor regret, but stalk about in their self-conceit under your noses, showing off their priesthoods and their consulships, and some of them their triumphs, just as if they had earned them instead of stealing them.

"Even slaves that are bought for gold do not stand for unjust orders from their masters; are you, citizens, who were born to rule, going to tolerate servitude meekly? But who are these men who treat our commonwealth like an occupied country? They are arch-criminals, whose hands are bloodstained, whose avarice is monstrous. They are guilty as sin and proud of it, men to whom loyalty, decency, duty, honor, and dishonor are all merely matters of profit and loss. Some of them rest secure in the murder of tribunes of the people, others in crooked trials, many in the shedding of plebeian blood; in short, the blacker the crime, the safer the criminal. Their crimes should trouble their conscience; instead, your cowardice troubles yours, while they are unified by a common desire, a common hatred, a common fear. That unity among the 'good' is called friendship; among the 'wicked,' partisan spirit. But if you were as vigilant about liberty as they are enthusiastic about tyranny, you may be sure the commonwealth would not be in its present ruinous state, and the privileges it is yours to bestow would be in the hands of the best candidates, not the most shameless. Your forebears, to get their due and establish their rights, twice took arms, seceded, and occupied the Aventine Hill [494 and 449 B.C.]; will you not strive with all your might for that liberty, which is your heritage from them? And you should strive the harder, because it is a greater disgrace to lose what has been gained than never to have won it in the first place.

"If you ask, 'What then is your proposal?' I reply that it is to take vengeance on the traitors, not by force of arms, which is more their due than it is your duty, but by legal procedure and Jugurtha's own evidence. If he is submissive, he will of course obey your orders, but if he ignores them, you will have firm grounds for judging the nature of that peace or surrender which assures impunity to Jugurtha, a fortune to a few key men, and losses and disgrace to the commonwealth. But perhaps you have not yet had your fill of their tyranny; perhaps the present occasion suits you less well than the days when kingdoms, provinces, law, equity, trials, war and peace, in short everything in heaven and on earth were in the hands of a minority, while you, the Roman people, triumphant over your foes, rulers of all nations, considered yourselves lucky to keep the right to draw your breath. For which of you, at any rate, dared refuse your chains?

"For my part, though I think it the depth of disgrace for a man worth his salt to take an insult lying down, I could stand your forgiving arch-criminals—who after all are citizens—if your forgiveness would not inevitably result in your ruin. For they are so lacking in decency that it means nothing to them to have gotten away with their crimes, unless they snatch from you the right to further misdeeds, while all you will have is the perpetual worry of knowing that you must either be slaves or fight for your freedom. For what possible confidence can you have in their good faith or singleness of purpose? They want to be tyrants, you to be free; they want to commit crimes, you to prevent them; finally, they are treating our allies like enemies, and our

enemies like allies. Can there be peace and friendship between men whose intentions are so different?

"Therefore I warn you, I urge you, not to let so great a crime go unpunished. It is not a mere question of cheating the treasury or extorting money from the allies; these are serious matters, but we are so used to them that we think nothing of them. This is a case of betraying the senate's authority and your sovereignty to a mortal enemy; at home and abroad your country has been put up for sale. Unless there is an investigation, unless the guilty are punished, what choice will we have, except to knuckle under for life to those responsible? For to do what you please with impunity is to be a king. What I urge upon you, citizens, is not that you should take more satisfaction in the wrongdoing than in the uprightness of your fellow-citizens, but that you should avoid ruining the innocent by pardoning the guilty. Besides, in public life it is far better to forget a good turn than a bad one: a good man simply grows more reluctant to do good if you neglect him, but a bad one grows more vicious. Moreover, if there were less lawlessness, you would not be in such constant need to barter liberty for security."

[Memmius' speech results in Jugurtha's being brought to Rome under escort, but the only consequence is further delay. Meanwhile, bribery works its will in the Roman army in Africa, which is defeated and made to pass under the yoke in token of submission. Panic ensues in Rome, and legal action is finally proposed against the traitors, as Memmius had advocated, but one of the chief recipients of Jugurtha's bribes is appointed a chief investigator. This circumstance gives Sallust opportunity to make the following comment on the course of party strife in Rome since the destruction of Carthage (146 B.C.).]

*Party strife in Rome*

41 The system of parties and factions, and, in short, every evil practice, began in Rome a few years before [1] as a result of inactivity and a plentiful supply of what mankind most highly prizes. For before the sack of Carthage the people and the Senate of Rome ran the state between them smoothly and moderately, and there was no competition between the citizens for prestige and power: fear of the enemy kept the state on the

straight and narrow path. When that fear disappeared from their minds, its place was of course taken by the love of luxury and the insolence which always accompany prosperity. So the ease they had dreamed of when times were bad proved, after they had got it, to be more harsh and bitter than the bad times themselves. For the nobility began to make a mockery of their privilege, and the people to do the same with their liberty, and they grabbed and squandered and wasted, every man for himself. So everything was torn in two, and the commonwealth, which was in the middle, was ripped to pieces.

But the nobility, thanks to its cliques, was more powerful, while the strength of the people, dissipated and divided among so many, was of less avail. Military and domestic administration was in the hands of a minority; the treasury, the provinces, public office, military decorations,[2] and triumphs were in the hands of the same men; the people bore the burden of military duty and poverty; the generals divided up the spoils of war among the few: meanwhile the parents or little children of the soldiers, if they had one of the nabobs for a neighbor, were evicted from their homes. So, along with power, selfishness without limit or discretion invaded, desecrated, and laid waste everything, holding nothing important or sacred, until it wrought its own destruction. For as soon as men from the noble class were found who preferred true glory to unjust power, there began to be movements in the state, and strife between citizens began to arise like an earthquake.

42 For after Tiberius and Gaius Gracchus, whose ancestors in the Punic War and in others had added much territory to the commonwealth, set about liberating the people and exposing the minority's crimes, the nobility, guilty and therefore apprehensive, took counteraction against the Gracchi, acting sometimes through the allies in Italy and in Latium, sometimes through the Roman knights, who had withdrawn from the popular party in the hope of association with the aristocracy; and first they murdered Tiberius, and then a few years later Gaius (who was following the same policy) though one was tribune of the people, and the other a Commissioner for Colonies; M. Fulvius Flaccus [3] was a fellow victim. Admittedly the Gracchi were so eager for victory that their mood was hardly moderate

enough. But if the nobility had been honest men, they would rather have lost the fight than avenge their injuries as they did by malpractice.

So the nobility, taking advantage of this victory to satisfy their whims, dealt the death blow to many, some with the sword, some by exile, and earned for themselves thereafter from the people rather terror than obedience. This situation has often ruined great states, when one party wants to beat the other by fair means or foul, and to wreak more than usually savage vengeance upon the conquered. But if I were to treat of party strife or of the general nature of political society either point by point or in keeping with the importance of the subject, time would fail me sooner than my material.

[A new general, Metellus, noble but honest, outmaneuvers Jugurtha both in war and in diplomacy, aided by his able lieutenant, the commoner Marius, whose ambitions he discourages. The following chapter tells how Marius, at long last given leave from the African army to go to Rome, is elected consul and placed in command against Jugurtha, relieving Metellus—a strong expression of popular disapproval of the aristocratic regime in general.]

*Marius, elected consul, takes command against Jugurtha*

73 Metellus . . . sent Marius home, since he had repeatedly asked for leave, and Metellus thought that a lieutenant who was serving against his will and disliked his commanding officer was of little use to him. And at Rome, when the contents of the despatches on Metellus and Marius became known, the common people were glad to believe what was said about both. The general's noble rank, which had formerly earned him credit, now counted against him, while Marius' humble origin made him still more of a favorite. But in both cases party prejudice carried more weight than the men's actual merits or defects. Besides, radicals in office egged on the mob, in every assembly accusing Metellus of capital crimes, but praising Marius to the skies. Finally the common people were so worked up that all the craftsmen and farmers, whose livelihood and financial credit depended on the labor of their hands, left their work and followed after Marius, since they considered honoring him of more importance than earning their living. The upshot

was that the nobility was defeated at the polls and for the first time in many years the consulship went to a "new man." And afterward when the people were asked by the tribune of the people, T. Manlius Mancinus, whom they wanted to run the war with Jugurtha, they all in a body said, "Marius."

[Meanwhile in Africa Metellus, who has gained several successes over Jugurtha, hears the bad news that his second in command is to relieve him. Marius, in Rome, recruits a new army and in the following bitter speech attacks the aristocracy.]

*Marius against the aristocracy*

85 "I know, citizens, that there are many who have not used the power they have gained in the same humble spirit with which they asked you for it: at first they are hard-working, obsequious, and moderate; later they carry on shiftlessly and insolently. But mine is the opposite view: for since the commonwealth as a whole is more important than the consulship or the praetorship, administering the state ought to require more responsibility than merely running for office. I know perfectly well how big a job, with your invaluable help, I am taking on. It's a more thankless business, citizens, than you think, at the same time to run a war and not dip too deep into the treasury, to draft men into military service without making them angry, to take the responsibility for everything at home and abroad, and to do so in the face of criticism, opposition, and party politics. Besides, if others fail in their duty, their long pedigree, the heroism of their ancestors, the family money and the money they married, and their many hangers-on are all an excellent defense; in my case, my hopes are centered in myself alone, and valor and honesty must be my safeguard, for other resources are undependable.

"This too I know, citizens, that everyone's eyes are focused on me, that fair-minded and honest men are on my side—since my good deeds benefit the state—but that the nobility is looking for a point of attack, which is all the more incentive for me to work hard, so that you will not be tricked and so that their efforts will go for nothing. From childhood until now I have been used to hard work and danger. I have no intention, citizens, of abandoning, now that I have won your approval, the way of life I used to fol-

low for its own sake before you gave me your support. Those whom ambition has prompted to pretend they are honest find it hard to be moderate when they attain power; for me, who have set myself a high standard of conduct all my life, honesty has already turned from habit into second nature.

"You have commissioned me to fight the war against Jugurtha, and the nobility has taken it very hard. I beg you, consider in your hearts whether it would not be better to change your minds, whether you should not send on this or any other like errand one of that clique of nobles, a man of long pedigree and a gallery of family portraits, and no military experience. The result, of course, will be that in his sublime ignorance of such matters he will fuss, be confused, and choose some man of the people to remind him of his duty. For it often happens that the man you commission general looks for someone to be general over him. And I know people, citizens, who never began to read history and Greek tactical handbooks until after they were elected consuls: these fellows have got the cart before the horse, for doing the job comes after election in point of time, but in actual practice demonstration of competence comes first.

"Now, citizens, compare me, a 'new man,' with them in their arrogance. What they know generally at second hand and by burning the midnight oil, I know in part from observation, in part from my own personal experience; what they learned from books, I learned from active duty. Now is the time to judge for yourselves which is worth more, words or deeds. They look down on my lack of background, I look down on their laziness; what I have against me is low birth; what they have against them is bad reputation. I believe that human nature is the same for everyone, but that the noblest man is the bravest one. And if it were now possible to ask the fathers of Albinus and Bestia [4] whom they would prefer as sons, me or them, what other answer do you suppose they would give than that they wanted as fine children as possible?

"But if they are right to look down on me, they are doing the same to their own ancestors, whose nobility, like mine, began in honorable action. They envy me the honor I have won; then let them envy my hard work, my integrity, the risks I have run, since it was through these that I earned the honor. But these men, spoiled and arrogant, lead their lives as though they scorn the honors you have to offer; then they campaign for them, as though their conduct had been honorable. They are simply fooling themselves if they expect to enjoy simultaneously two complete opposites, the pleasure of laziness and the rewards of virtue. And when they make speeches before your assemblies or in the Senate, they even devote the bulk of their oration to the praise of their ancestors: they think that by the mention of *their* bravery they themselves become more distinguished. Quite the contrary. For the more distinguished the life of their ancestors, the more shameful becomes their own indolence. This is exactly the way the matter stands: ancestral fame focuses as it were a beam of light upon posterity, which does not allow either the virtues or the vices of this generation to lie in the shade. I confess my inadequacy, citizens, in the matter of ancestors, but there is something that is far more distinguished—my own deeds, and they give me the right to speak. Just see how unfair the opposition is. The virtue they lay claim to by inheritance they will not let me claim as my own, on the pretext that I have no family portraits and that my nobility is brand new; and yet nobility is certainly something which it is better to have earned than to have inherited and then defiled.

"Of course I know perfectly well that if they wanted to speak in rebuttal, their speech would be florid, eloquent, and well organized. But since after your lavish kindness to me they have seized every opportunity to rend us both limb from limb with slander, I did not think it right to hold my tongue, for fear someone would interpret my retiring nature as a guilty conscience. For, at least in my own opinion, no speech can injure me; actually, if they speak the truth, they must speak well of me, and if they tell lies, my life and character will refute them. But since they are casting reflections on *your* judgment, because you have placed on my shoulders the honor of your highest office and the responsibility of a critical campaign, look at it from every possible angle and see whether you ought to regret it. I cannot, to win your confidence, make a great show of family portraits, triumphs and consulships in my family tree, but if the situation demands, I *can* show you my awards for valor, my banner, my medals and other military prizes, and my scars

besides; they are all in front. Those are my family portraits, those are my patent of nobility, not a heritage left to me, as my opponents' has been to them, but the product of my own hard work and risk of life and limb.

"My speeches are not carefully planned; I don't think that is important. True courage can stand on its own feet; *they* need artifice, to cover up their dirty deeds with pretty words. I have never learned Greek literature, either; I had little stomach for the subject, especially since it has not made its professors any more honest. But these subjects I have studied, and they are far more useful to the state: to strike at the enemy, to stand constant watch, to fear nothing but disgrace, to endure heat and cold with equal indifference, to sleep on the ground, to bear up under the double burden of poverty and hard work. These are the lessons with which I shall urge on my troops; I shall not be stingy with them and lavish with myself; I shall not make my reputation at the expense of their sweat. This is what is truly useful, this is the kind of command that befits free citizens. For to be a harsh disciplinarian with an army while you yourself live a life of ease is to act like a plantation owner, not a general. It is by actions like mine and others like them that your ancestors made themselves and the republic famous. And this is what the present nobles rely on, though they are themselves of very different character, and yet they look down their noses at us who pattern ourselves upon the men of old, and claim all the offices in the state, not on grounds of merit but as though they were their due.

"But these men in their overweening pride are very far wrong. Their ancestors left them every proper inheritance: wealth, pedigree, the glorious memory of their deeds; courage they did not leave them; they could not: it is the only thing which can neither be given or received as a gift. They say I am uncouth and boorish in my manners, because my dinner parties are not very stylish and because I do not put a higher value on some play-actor or chef than I do upon my estate-steward. It is a pleasure to admit it, citizens. For I learned from my father and other venerable men that luxury suits women, but hard work suits men, that the reputation of all good men ought to be higher than their bank accounts, and that a man can be prouder of armor than of fine furniture or interior decoration.

"Well, then, let them indulge their pleasure and their own standard of values: let them make love and drink; let them pass their old age as they have spent their youth, in banquets, in a state of unconditional surrender to their bellies and the most unseemly part of their bodies; let them leave dust and sweat and other things of that sort to us, who find them more agreeable than dinner-parties. But that is not the way it is. For when these shameless fellows have disgraced themselves with their carryings-on, they are off in hot pursuit of the rewards that belong to the virtuous. And so—the rank injustice of it!— easy living and laziness, the worst of vices, do not stand in the way of their votaries, but are the ruination of the undeserving commonwealth.

"Now that I have made them a rejoinder in keeping with my character, if not with their vices, I shall speak briefly about the state of the nation. First of all, don't worry about Numidia, citizens. For everything which up to now has been Jugurtha's safeguard, you have stripped away: greed, amateurishness, and a swelled head; then, too, the army there knows the country, but, so help me, it has had more hard duty than good luck, for the greater part of it has wasted away through the greed or the rashness of its leaders. You, then, who are of age for service, put your shoulder to the wheel along with me and do your patriotic duty, and don't worry about past disasters to other men or about domineering generals. I personally will be with you as adviser and comrade in time of danger, on the march or in battle, and our interests shall be the same in everything. And assuredly with the gods' help everything is waiting for us: victory, prize money, citations. But even if these rewards were in doubt or far in the future, yet every good citizen should come to the republic's rescue all the more because no one ever achieved immortality by shirking, and no parent has ever hoped for his children that they should live forever, but rather that they should live good and honorable lives. I should make a longer speech, citizens, if mere words would make the timid more courageous; but as it is, for those who are ready I think I have said more than enough."

[Marius' speech fires the populace to action, and he is able to reorganize the Roman army on a volunteer basis, and with it to win battles but not the war. As his prestige in Africa is increas-ing, Sulla, the aristocrat who was destined to be his deadliest rival, arrives; in the following chapters Sallust describes his character.]

*The character of Sulla*

95 While this campaign was going on, the quaestor L. Sulla arrived in camp with a large cavalry force which he had been left behind in Rome to recruit from Latium and the allies.

But since the course of events has brought this great man to our notice, it seems appropriate to say a few words about his life and habits. . . . Sulla was a noble of a patrician clan, of a family then almost extinct because of the slackness of his ancestors, equally well educated in Greek and in Latin, of remarkable intelligence, a pleasure-seeker, but even more a seeker after glory; he liked soft living when he was not on duty; but pleasure never interfered with his work, except that he might have been better ad-vised in the matter of his wives; [5] he was elo-quent, able, and made friends easily. His talent for concealing his true purpose was incredibly subtle, and he was lavish with many things and especially with money. No man was luckier than he before his victory in the Civil War, but his luck was never greater than his merit, and many have hesitated to say whether his luck or his courage was the greater. For as to what he did afterward, shame would vie with repugnance were I to discuss it.

96 After Sulla, then, arrived in Africa, as I have already said, and proceeded to Marius' camp with the cavalry, he may have been inex-perienced and untrained in war before, but in no time at all he became the cleverest officer in the army. Besides, he was polite to the soldiers and called them by name; he did favors for many when they asked him, and for others of his own accord. He was reluctant to take favors, but he paid them back sooner than borrowed money, at the same time dunning nobody, but rather striv-ing to have as many as possible in his debt. He was ready for a joke or a serious talk with the lowest ranks. On a detail, on the march, or on watch he was everywhere at once, but he did not meanwhile ape those perverted by ambition and damage the consul or any good man by malicious gossip. But he would never, in councils of war or in action, allow anyone to get ahead of him, and

indeed he got ahead of most of the others. So his conduct and his personality rapidly made him a favorite with Marius and the men.

[Sulla finally ends the war by persuading a rival chief to betray Jugurtha to Marius, and Sallust ends his story with Marius' re-election to the consulship and his triumph (January 1, 105 B.C.).]

## THE CONSPIRACY OF CATILINE

The struggle between nobility and commons which Marius had apparently won for the *plebs* was renewed and won for the nobility by Sulla, whose excesses in turn gave rise to the discontent which culminated in the conspiracy of Catiline, supported more or less openly by the millionaire Crassus and the liberal Julius Caesar. Catiline, feeling that he had been defrauded of the consulship to which Cicero was elected (63 B.C.) put himself at the head of an armed band, which was defeated and its ringleaders executed, Catiline himself having died in battle. For his part in these executions Cicero himself was later exiled by the popular party, while Caesar, whatever his part in the conspiracy—and Sallust does all he can to exonerate him—was ever afterward in the ascendant, until he too was brought low by the conservative assassins' daggers on the fateful Ides of March, 44 B.C. Sallust's monograph, which probably appeared about a year later, opens with the following preface on his reasons for writing history.

*Introduction: Sallust's reasons for writing history*

*1* All men with ambition to be something more than the other animals ought to strive with might and main not to pass their lives unsung, like the beasts whom nature has made to creep upon the earth and indulge their appetites. But our strength is centered in the mind and the body taken as a whole: the mind gives commands, the body obeys them; the one we share with the gods, the other with brute beasts. This seems to me to be an additional motive for seeking our reputation with the resources of brain rather than brawn and, since the life we have to enjoy is short, for making our memory last as long as possible. For the reputation won through wealth and beauty is fickle and fleeting, but virtue keeps its fame for eternity.

But there has long been a controversy among men as to whether bodily strength or mental efficiency brings wars to a more successful end. For before you begin you must act deliberately, and after you have deliberated you must act swiftly. So each element, incomplete in itself, needs the help of the other.

*2* Therefore in the beginning kings—for that was the first name given to governing power on earth—disciplined themselves in different ways, some their minds and others their bodies: for mankind in those days still practised unselfishness; each man was content with his own. But after Cyrus in Asia, and the Spartans and Athenians in Greece, had begun to subjugate cities and nations, to treat lust for power as a motive for war, and to think "the greater the Empire, the greater the glory," then at last hazard and experience taught mankind that cunning in war is worth more than brawn. But if the mental efficiency of kings and generals were as strong in peace as is it in war, man's life would be steadier and have fewer ups and downs, and we should not see transition, change, and confusion everywhere. For control is easily kept by the same devices by which it was won in the first place. But when laziness replaces hard work, and lust and arrogance replace self-control and fair dealing, man's fate changes with his character. So power passes always to the best from the less good.

Ploughing, seafaring, building—all depend on mental efficiency. But many, enslaved to their bellies and their beds, pass their lives without education or culture, like strangers in a strange land, and to them, quite contrary to nature, their bodies are a pleasure, their souls a bore. I do not think it matters much whether they live or die; they leave no record either way. On the other hand there is one sort of man, and one only, who seems to me to be really living and having profit of his soul: the man who, with a job to do, is in quest of reputation for a deed well done or a profession honorably followed.

But life is so full of a number of things that nature gives us our choice of paths to follow. *3* It is a fine thing to exalt our country in action, it is no mean thing to exalt her with words; fame can be won in peace or in war; and many, both men of action and men who recount their deeds, have won renown. But in my opinion, though equal prestige does not attach to the writer and the doer of the deed, yet writing history seems especially difficult: first because his words must match the deeds; second because the majority of readers attribute criticism to malice and jealousy, whereas when an author records the high courage and fame of good men, each reader calmly accepts what he himself thinks easy, but treats anything beyond that as fiction.

When I was young and ambitious I was attracted, like many others, to a political career, where I found many barriers to advancement, for if a man was unassuming, frugal, and honest, he made no headway against a rival who was forward, lavish with bribes, and greedy. Though my mind was unused to evil ways and viewed this state of affairs with scorn, yet I was young and inexperienced, and there was so much dishonesty around me that it won me over, too, and held me fast, and, though I differed in character from the wickedness of the rest, yet honest ambition made me a victim to the same jealous gossip as the others.

4 Therefore, when once after many worries and dangers I found peace of mind and decided I must pass the rest of my life far removed from politics, I had no intention of wasting valuable leisure in idleness and laziness, nor of making the slavish employments of farming or hunting my goal in life. Rather I decided to go back to a plan I had started but had been kept from by the vice of ambition: to write a history of the Roman people in episodes, selecting what seemed worth remembering, a decision confirmed by the freedom of my mind from any ambition, fear, or party prejudice.

Therefore I shall give as honest and brief an account as I can of the conspiracy of Catiline; for I think the unusual nature of his crime and the resultant danger to the state makes this a particularly memorable chapter in Roman history.

[Sallust then describes briefly the character of Catiline, whose worst side, he says, was brought out by the decline in Roman morals at the time.]

*Decline of Roman morals*

5 . . . Since the period of which I am writing brings up the subject of civic morality, my subject seems to encourage me to review past history and discuss briefly our ancestors' domestic and foreign policy, so as to show their concept of government, the greatness of the heritage they left us, and the way in which the state, changing little by little from the finest and the best, turned into the worst and the most depraved.

6 My authorities say the city of Rome was founded and first inhabited by Trojans, refugees led by Aeneas, vagrants and wanderers. They were joined by the Aborigines, an uncivilized race, lawless, rulerless, free and uncoerced. After these two groups had met within the same walls, the story of how easily they were made one, despite differences in race, language, and customs, is a remarkable one: so quickly was a scattered and wandering mob turned into a harmonious state. But after their state, more populous, civilized, and extensive, was apparently flourishing and strong, then, as often happens, they began to be envied on account of their wealth. Neighboring kings and peoples therefore made war on them, and they had few friends to help them: for the rest were frightened and steered clear of danger. But the Romans screwed up their courage at home and in the field; got busy, made ready, encouraged one another, went to meet the enemy, and by armed force protected their liberty, their country, and their parents. Afterwards, when their valor had warded off the danger, they came to the rescue of their allies and friends, and established diplomatic relations more by doing favors than by receiving them. Their government was based on law, and it bore the name of monarchy. Picked men, whose bodies were enfeebled by age, but whose minds were mighty in wisdom, formed a Council of State: either because of their age, or because their responsibilities were paternal, they were called "Fathers." Later on, when the monarchy, which had stood at first for the preservation of liberty and the public welfare, had degenerated into arrogance and tyranny, they changed their constitution and created a pair of rulers with an annual term: thus they thought men's minds would be least able to grow arrogant through unlimited opportunity.

7 But this was the time when everyone began to lift his head higher and to show his versatility. For kings trust the good less than the wicked, and they are always a little afraid of

other men's merits. But the republic's record of growth in a short time is extraordinary, once independence had been won: such was the ambition that possessed the people. First of all the young men, as soon as they were old enough for war, went into camp and learned military science by experience, and preferred fine armor and war horses to wine and women. So to men like these there was no labor that seemed abnormal, no stronghold too rugged or too high, no enemy under arms too formidable: valor everywhere held sway. But their hardest fight for glory was with one another: they vied with one another to strike down the enemy, scale the wall, and be seen doing it. This to them was riches, prestige, and high nobility. They were greedy for praise and generous with money: they wanted their glory to be great and their wealth honorable. I could mention places where the Roman people with a handful of men routed huge armies of the enemy, or what naturally fortified cities they took by siege, but such matters would take us too far from our subject.

*8* But surely Fortune is all-powerful; she brings fame or obscurity according to caprice rather than merit. The history of Athens, in my opinion, was famous and noble enough, but somewhat less important than her reputation indicates. But because she had a crop of very talented writers, Athenian exploits pass everywhere for the most famous in the world. So the bravery of men of action is famous in proportion as the talents of men who could praise it are extraordinary. But the Roman people never had such a stock of talent, because the wiser they were the more they had to do with practical matters. No one exercised his mind apart from his body, and all the best men preferred deeds to words, and praise of themselves by others rather than tales of others' prowess by themselves.

*9* Therefore high character was cultivated at home and abroad; harmony was at its height; selfishness was at a minimum; what was just and good prevailed among them not by convention but by nature. They worked quarrels, disagreements, and strife out of their system against the enemy; the only competition between citizen and citizen was for the prize of courage. Their religious ceremonies were magnificent, their households simple, their friendships devoted. They took care of themselves and their country in two

ways: by daring in war and fair-dealing when peace came. I consider the best proof of this to be that they more often court-martialed men who had joined battle against orders and who withdrew too slowly when retreat was sounded, than those who ventured to abandon the battle flag or leave their post when defeated; while in peacetime they ruled by kindness rather than by fear and would rather forgive an injustice than avenge it.

*10* But when hard work and just dealing had built the republic, when mighty kings had been vanquished in war, and fierce tribes and great nations forced to surrender, when Carthage, the rival of Roman rule, had been completely wiped out, and every land and sea lay open, Fortune began to go berserk and throw everything into confusion. Those who had found hard work, risks, and the harsh fortunes of war easy to bear found peace and riches, apparently so desirable, to be actually a burden and an agony. So first the lust for money grew, and then the lust for power; these were the timber, as it were, of which all their woes were built. The proof is that greed perverted integrity, dependability, and every other good quality, and replaced them with arrogance, cruelty, atheism, and the doctrine that everything has its price. Ambition prompted many a man to double-dealing, to thinking one thing and saying another, to judging friendships and enmities not by merit but by profit, and to value a good appearance above a good heart. These vices were at first of gradual growth, and were sometimes even punished; but afterward the pollution moved in like an epidemic; the city was changed, and her government that had been the fairest and best in the world became cruel and unendurable.

*11* But at first it was more ambition than avarice that fired men's minds, ambition being the closest of the vices to virtue. The desire for prestige, office, and power is the same in good men and bad, but the former strive for them by an honest course, while the latter, because of defects of character, try to gain their ends by trickery and cheating. Avarice includes the love of money, which no wise man has ever wanted: as though it were steeped in deadly poison it makes a man's body and soul effeminate, is always boundless and insatiable, and can be neither sated by feast nor cured by famine. But after

L. Sulla, having taken over the state by force of arms, came to a bad end from a good beginning, everyone fell to plundering and thievery, one man coveting a house, another lands; the winning side showed neither self-control nor forbearance, but committed foul and cruel crimes against their fellow citizens. Besides, Sulla, to assure the loyalty of his Asian Expeditionary Force, had flown in the face of tradition and had relaxed discipline and been too democratic. The pleasure resorts had had no trouble in corrupting the once fierce spirit of soldiers on leave; it was there that the army of the Roman people first learned the pleasures of women and wine, and became connoisseurs of statues, paintings, and silverware, and robbers of them, too, whether they were public property or privately owned; here they first learned to sack temples and to defile everything human or divine. Therefore, after these soldiers had won the victory, they left nothing to the vanquished. Good fortune puts even wise men's principles to the test, to say nothing of the effect of victory upon the ruined characters of men like these.

*12* As soon as men began to worship money, with fame, privilege, and power as the result, honesty began to fall into a decline, poverty to be considered disgraceful, and refusal to cheat as ill will. So, as a result of prosperity, high living and selfishness along with arrogance began to infect the young: they stole, they squandered; cared little for their own property, coveted that of others; paid no heed to purity of mind or body, or indeed to anything in heaven or earth, had no standard of value or sense of proportion. It is worth while to compare the town houses and estates, built up of late till they are as big as whole cities, with the temples of the gods built by our forefathers, deeply religious men. The temples were adorned with their piety, their houses with their good name, and they took nothing from the vanquished but the right to do wrong. But the men of our time, on the contrary, cowards that they are, have committed grand larceny; everything that those heroes of old, in spite of their victory, had let our allies keep, the men of our time have stolen, just as though the proper use of sovereignty were to commit injustice.

*13* What is the use of mentioning things which are unbelievable except to eye-witnesses: that private citizens, in no small numbers, have turned mountains upside down and decked over the sea? Such people seem to me to have made a mockery of their wealth: for they have been in hot haste to misuse shamefully what they might have possessed with honor. But lust, vice, gluttony, and the rest of the evidences of sophistication had moved in on them just as greed had: men turned effeminate, women offered their virginity for sale in the public square; they ransacked the ends of the earth and the seven seas for delicacies; they took siestas they did not need; they did not wait for hunger or thirst, cold or fatigue, but anticipated them all in their decadent living. All this egged on the young men to crime, when their family wealth gave out: a mind used to evil ways could not easily do without its satisfactions, and so abandoned itself all the more wastefully to all kinds of profiteering and extravagance.

[Such, according to Sallust, was the economic, social, and political climate which made Catiline what he was. The historian recounts Catiline's past, his marriage, his early revolutionary designs, and the names and motives of his accomplices. In the following passage, Sallust gives the gist of a speech of Catiline to some of these earlier conspirators.]

### Speech of Catiline to the conspirators

*20* "If your courage and trustworthiness had not been in my judgment tried and true, opportunity would have knocked in vain; great prospects, even the power within our grasp, would have meant nothing, and if I thought you cowards or waverers I should not swap security for this risky business. But because on many great occasions I have found you brave and loyal, I have dared to embark upon a great and glorious plan. A further motive has been my recognition that your idea of good and bad is the same as mine; for to have the same likes and dislikes is the one solid basis of friendship.

"You have all individually before now heard what my plan is. All the same, I grow more and more angry every day, when I consider how we shall have to live, unless with our own hands we set ourselves free. For ever since the government fell under the sway of a few nabobs, they have invariably been the ones to whom the kings of the East have paid their tithes, and whole peoples and tribes their taxes; all the rest of us, however industrious or honorable, and irrespective of pedigree, have been an unrequited and impotent mob, knuckling under to men who would be afraid of us if the term 'government' had any meaning. And so all the thanks, the sovereignty, the honor, the wealth is either in their hands or where they want it; *we* get the left-overs: risk in war, defeat at the polls, cases in court decided against us, and destitution. Tell me, how long are you going to stand it, my band of heroes? Is it not better to die like men, and have done with it, than to lose like cravens a cursed and dishonorable life, in which you are the plaything of other men's arrogance? I have all the more reason for asking the question because, as gods and men are my witness, victory is in our hands; we are in the prime of life, and we have brains, while time and affluence have put *them* in their dotage. We have only to get started, and the course of events will make the rest easy. For who on earth who is a man at heart can stand their having surplus wealth to squander in building on the sea and levelling hills, while our income is not enough even for the necessities of life? Who can stand their building two or more houses in a row, while we have not even a hearth that we can call our own? Though they buy paintings, statues, and *objets d'art*, tear down brand-new buildings, and build others in their place; in short, though in every way they torment and harry their money like an enemy, yet their greed is so insatiable that they cannot spend it all. We on the other hand face want at home, debt in business; our situation is bad, our prospects still worse: to sum up, what choice have we but to possess our souls in misery?

"But what if you should rise up? Look! Liberty, that liberty of which you have often dreamed, is before your eyes, and wealth, honor, and fame besides: all these are the prizes Fortune offers to those who win. The facts, the times, your poverty, the splendid spoils of war are more eloquent advocates than any speech of mine. Put me at your head, or as a soldier in the ranks: neither my wits nor my strength will ever desert you. My hope is to carry our program as consul, with your help, unless perhaps my mind deceives me and you are readier to be slaves than masters."

[Catiline binds the conspirators with a solemn oath, but the plot is betrayed, and Cicero is elected consul. Catiline nevertheless continues his plans but fails in a scheme to murder Cicero. The con-spirators raise an army of paupers and thieves in Etruria, and the Senate declares a state of emergency. In the following passage Sallust describes the resultant gloom in Rome.]

### Gloom in Rome

31 The situation stirred the city to its foundations, and its whole appearance was changed. Instead of the carefree frivolity which years of peace had produced, suddenly there was gloom on every face: men fussed and fidgeted, put no trust in any place of refuge, nor in any person, were in a state that was neither war nor peace, and assessed the danger each by his own fear. Besides, the women, struck by fear of war such as Rome's greatness had prevented their feeling before, began to fret and to pray, to ask what was to happen to their poor little children, to pester their husbands, get into a state of nerves, and forget their arrogance and their life of luxury in their despair over their own and their country's fate.

[Cicero denounces Catiline, who leaves Rome, but appeals by letter to influential men there. The conspirators' Etrurian army asks terms of the opposing general, who advises them to throw themselves on the mercy of the Senate. The Senate prepares for war. At this point Sallust again surveys the sorry state of things in Rome, and in the following passage compares it with her past greatness.]

### Rome's present sorry state

36 . . . This was the time when, in my opinion, the sovereignty of the Roman people was in the deepest depths of misfortune. For though from the rising to the setting of the sun the whole earth groveled before its armed might, and though at home there was in abundance that peace and prosperity to which mankind attaches highest value, yet there were Romans who persisted obstinately in working their own and their country's ruin. For in spite of rewards offered by senatorial decrees, out of so large a population the reward induced not one to betray the conspiracy, and not one of Catiline's accomplices deserted his camp: such was the violence of the disease which like a plague had affected the minds of a majority of the citizens.

37 It was not only the ringleaders whom this

madness deranged; the common people as a whole, in their eagerness for revolution, were on the side of Catiline's scheme, as one would expect from their character. For invariably in politics those who are without means are jealous of good men and give preferment to the wicked; they hate the old order and long for the new, and because they hate their own lot are eager to change everybody else's. In the midst of riot and treason they do not have to worry about supporting themselves, since poverty is a position it is not hard to keep up without a deficit. But the common people of the city were hotheaded for a number of reasons. Rome was like a sewer into which had flowed first of all men with the greatest reputation for slanderous and impudent tongues, next, those who had wasted their substance in riotous living, and finally, all those whose morals or criminal records made home too hot for them. Besides, many remembered Sulla's victory, and because they had then seen some common soldiers made senators, others so rich that they lived in banqueting and luxury like kings, each man now hoped for a similar reward of victory if he took up arms. Furthermore, the young men, who had formerly eked out a miserable living by the sweat of their brow on the farms, were now attracted by private and public doles, and preferred idleness in town to hard labor in the country. These and all the others waxed fat on their country's ills. Therefore there is the less cause for wonder that paupers of bad character but great expectations paid as little attention to their country's interests as they did to their own. Besides, those who after Sulla's victory had seen their parents proscribed, their property confiscated, and their freedom limited, viewed the coming of war almost as calmly as the others. Again, anyone who belonged to any other party but the senatorial would rather see his country in revolution than himself less important. This then was the menace which after many years had recoiled upon the state.

*38* For after the tribunician power was restored in the consulship of Pompey and Crassus [70 B.C.], hot-blooded young men, monopolizing this key position, began their rabble-rousing by denouncing the Senate, and added fuel to the flame by bribery and promises, thereby making themselves powerful public figures. Against them the majority of the nobles put up a terrific struggle under the pretext of defending the Senate, but really out of pure self-interest. For, from that time on, to put the truth bluntly, though all the politicians alleged honorable motives, some "the defense of the people's rights," others "the increase of the Senate's authority," all were really using the general welfare as an excuse to compete for personal power. Their competition was neither temperate nor restrained; both sides were merciless in victory.

[In recent years the common people had been more and more ground down, but even if Catiline had won, it would not have solved the problem. Nevertheless, some of his partisans tried to persuade certain Gallic allies of Rome to join the revolt, others fomented riots in the provinces and in Italy itself, while the conspirators in Rome, it was alleged, planned to set fire to the city and murder their parents and the consul Cicero. The latter, however, forestalled them by arresting the chief conspirators and their dupes. The result was a revulsion of feeling among the common people.]

*Revulsion of feeling among the common people*

*48* Meanwhile the common people, once the plot was disclosed, though at first in their desire for revolution they were only too eager for war, now changed their minds and cursed Catiline's proposals, while they praised Cicero to the skies, showing as much joy and happiness as if they had been rescued from slavery. For they thought that while other acts of civil war would bring them more profit than loss, the proposed burning of the city, would be cruel, would go too far, and would spell their utter ruin, since they all lived from hand to mouth and owned nothing but the clothes they stood up in.

[Attempts having been made to implicate Caesar and Crassus, as well as to set some of the arrested conspirators free, Cicero called a meeting of the Senate to ask advice. Sallust reports the speeches of Caesar, who counsels moderation (i.e., not execution, but confiscation, disfranchisement, and life imprisonment), and of Cato the Younger, who moved the death penalty and carried the day. The two men's speeches give Sallust an opportunity for the following reflections on the cause of Rome's greatness, and upon the characters of the two speakers.]

## Cato and Caesar

53 . . . In the course of much reading and conversation about the heroic deeds of the Roman people at home and abroad, on land and sea, I have grown fond of speculating as to what special quality has sustained them in these exploits. I knew that time and again they had with a mere handful of men fought against whole divisions of the enemy; I learned that with a small treasury they had waged war with millionaire kings, that in addition they had often endured the bludgeonings of chance, that the Greeks had ranked ahead of the Romans in eloquence, the Gauls in military prestige. And as I turned it all over in my mind I concluded that it was the distinguished excellence of a minority of citizens that had brought it all about, and that they were responsible for the triumph of poverty over riches, of few over many. But after the state began to decline because of soft living and laziness, our country was still great enough to absorb the vices of its civil and military leaders, and yet survive; yet she was like a mother past the age of childbirth, and so for many years Rome produced practically no one of real excellence. But within my memory there have been two men of infinite excellence, but very different personality, Marcus Cato and Gaius Caesar. And since the course of events has brought them up, I have no intention of silently passing by the opportunity to reveal with all the skill at my command the nature and character of both of them.

54 They were, then, about evenly matched in pedigree, years, and eloquence. They were alike in loftiness of mind, and also in reputation, but their reputations were different. Caesar's claim to greatness was his good works and his openhandedness; Cato's the consistency of his conduct. The former grew famous for gentleness and sympathy, the latter's reserve enhanced his prestige. Caesar won his fame by gifts, relief, and pardons, Cato by never wasting his money. The one was a refuge for the down-and-out, the other the terror of the wicked. Men praised the affability of the one, the steadiness of the other. Finally, Caesar had from the first made up his mind to hard work and long hours; in his concentration on his friends' interests he neglected his own; he never refused any gift worth giving; what he wanted most was a high command, an army,

a new war, where his talents might shine. Cato, on the other hand, aimed at moderation and decorum, but above all at aloofness. He did not compete in riches with the rich nor in party politics with the politician, but with the industrious in excellence, with the temperate in morality, with the guiltless in unselfishness; he preferred to *be* good rather than to seem so: and so the less he courted reputation, the more it followed in his train.

[In accordance with Cato's motion, the arrested conspirators are executed. Catiline himself, with his army, is forced into battle, addresses his men for the last time, is defeated and dies fighting.]

## Catiline's end

60 . . . When Catiline saw that his troops had been routed and that he was left alone with a handful of men, he remembered his ancestry and his former prestige, rushed in to the thickest of the fray, and there fell sword in hand, his body pierced through and through.

61 But when the battle was over it became clear how boldly and courageously Catiline's army had fought. For almost every man covered with his body when he died the position he had won in the fighting while there was still breath in his body. A few in the center of the line who had been routed by the general's bodyguard lay a little apart, yet even these had fallen with all their wounds in front. But Catiline was found far from his men, among the bodies of the enemy, still breathing a little, and still showing in his face the fierceness of spirit that had been his when he was alive. Finally, from the whole army not one free citizen was taken alive either in the battle or in flight: proving that they had been no more sparing of their own lives than of those of the enemy. For their part, the army of the Roman people had won no happy or bloodless victory. For the best fighters had either died in battle or been carried from the field critically wounded. Besides, many who had come out of the camp to see the sights or to rob the corpses, when they turned over the bodies of the enemy found in some cases a friend, in others an acquaintance or a relative; there were some also who found enemies they recognized. And so throughout the army there was a surge of mingled joy and tears, mourning and exultation.

## TO CAESAR ON THE COMMONWEALTH, II

A separate manuscript in Rome contains the text of two documents, ascribed to Sallust, purporting to give advice to Julius Caesar about constitutional reform, including the passing of laws against extravagance, relief of unemployment, equalizing of military service, a dole of grain to veterans, a fairer method of voting in the centuriate assembly and the Senate, and increase in the size of the latter. Though the fact that Caesar put most of these suggestions into practice may be used to prove either that the documents are genuine or that they were written after the fact, the weight of respectable scholarly opinion now inclines in favor of their genuineness. The following extract from the second of these can be dated 51–49 B.C.; it contains an account of the class struggle in Rome, with an explanation of the degeneracy of the plebs, and concludes with a recommendation of the course which Caesar actually adopted: the enlargement of the citizen body and the settling of the new citizens in new colonies.

*Reforms needed to abate the class struggle*

5 I believe in the tradition of our forefathers, that the state has been divided into two factions, the patricians and the plebeians. In the old days the highest authority was in the hands of the patricians, but the plebeians had by far the greater strength of numbers. And so the state suffered frequent secessions, which constantly reduced the nobles' power and increased the people's rights. But the source of the people's freedom of action was the fact that no one's power was above the law, and if a noble took precedence over a common man, it was through good repute and heroic deeds rather than wealth or arrogance: no matter how humble a man's station, either in farming or in military service he had enough for himself and his country, and lacked nothing that any honest man might want.

But when unemployment and poverty began to drive them one by one from their farms and forced them to become vagrants, not knowing where they might lay their heads, they began to cock an eye at other people's property, and to put their liberty and their country up for sale. So little by little the common people, formerly in the saddle, with whole nations at its beck and call, began to go to pieces, and exchanged slavery as individuals for the supreme power which once all had shared. Our proletariat, therefore, primarily because of its ingrained bad habits, and secondly because it has straggled into every possible trade and walk of life, with no cohesive principle whatever, seems to me at least to be quite incompetent to control the government. But with an injection of new citizens I have high hopes that they will all rise up and strike a blow for liberty, since surely the new citizens will want to keep the freedom they have, while the old will want to throw off their shackles. I advise you to mingle the new with the old and set them up in colonies: the result will be a richer military establishment and a lower class kept by prosperity and honest employment from conspiring against the state.

6 Of course I am not so blind as not to foresee how the nobles will rant and rage when this project is proposed. How they will bluster, crying out that the whole state is turned upside down, that this amounts to the enslavement of those who have been citizens all along, and finally that this will become a monarchy instead of a free republic, when one man's misplaced generosity grants citizenship to enormous numbers of people! But for my part I have made up my mind to this: it is criminal to curry favor for oneself at the expense of the general welfare, but it is ridiculous and cowardly to fail to promote the general welfare simply because it happens to be also to an individual's advantage.

## NOTES TO *THE JUGURTHINE WAR*

1. I.e., before the events which Sallust is describing (before 115 B.C.).

2. Reading *loriae* "laurel crowns" with Bernays.

3. M. Fulvius Flaccus was consul 125 B.C., a member of the Gracchan Land Commission, the first to propose citizenship for Rome's Italian allies, a colleague of C. Gracchus in colonizing of Carthage (122 B.C.); he was murdered in the rioting of 121 B.C.

4. Sp. Postumius Albinus, aristocrat, consul 110 B.C., shared the disgrace of his brother Aulus, who surrendered to Jugurtha and permitted a Roman army to "pass under the yoke" in token of abject submission. L. Calpurnius Bestia, also an optimate, consul 111 B.C., was condemned by a "popular" investigating committee along with Albinus, for having come to terms with Jugurtha.

5. He had four.

# SELECTIONS FROM THE SPEECHES OF CICERO

*Translated by Norman J. DeWitt*

## INTRODUCTION

MOST OF US know, in a general way, that Marcus Tullius Cicero was one of the most distinguished characters of classical antiquity—a "great" man in his way; and if we have studied the history of European culture extensively, we know too that few have influenced man's words and ideas so deeply as Cicero—in education, philosophy, political theory, public speaking, and the arts of literary composition.

To supplement this general concept of Cicero's importance, suppose we look at him now in his own day and age. He lived, of course, in the period when the old Roman republic was in process of disintegration, when time-honored attitudes and traditions were being shown to be incapable of adjustment to new political, social, and economic problems. We think of Cicero along with Julius Caesar, Pompey the Great, Brutus, Cassius, Mark Antony, and others of whom almost everyone has heard in one way or another. Cicero's political career began in earnest when, at the age of forty-two, after he had achieved an amazing record as a trial lawyer, he was recognized by conservative landowners and capitalists as the best man available to do, as some of them are reported to have said, a dirty piece of work: to stop what they regarded as a dangerous revolutionary movement led by Lucius Sergius Catilina. Catiline was in fact organizing an armed uprising. Cicero was elected one of the two consuls for the year 63 B.C. The other consul was an unimportant character. Soon many of the leading conspirators were in jail, where they were later executed, and Catiline left town in a hurry, later losing his life fighting bravely with his army in the country to the north of Rome. This was Cicero's "finest hour." As he remarked rather frequently (*too* frequently, some thought) in later years, he had saved his native land. Through the complex and tortuous political maneuvering that marked the dying republic, to the time of his own death at the hands of Mark Antony's agents in 43 B.C., Cicero remained a respected but helpless bystander. For a short time only, in the period following

Caesar's assassination in March, 44 B.C., did he again figure prominently in politics. The reasons for his failure are not hard to understand. In practical politics, money talks. In Rome, the army also talked; the politician who had legions back of him could be very persuasive. Cicero had neither money nor legions; he had to do his own talking.

But in spite of his lack of political power, Cicero still looms large in the records of his period, mainly because he provides most of the records himself. His amazing fluency brought him a victory of sorts, and one that he desired: to be remembered by posterity. The lives of few great historical figures are so well documented; none perhaps so well documented by their own writings. Hundreds of Cicero's own private letters have been preserved; they give us uninhibited insights into the man's character such as students of history rarely have available.

When we realize that Cicero was a great man, in a certain way, and worth knowing about, we naturally ask, "What kind of a man was he? What was he like?" If we were to read widely in the modern studies of Cicero, we would find that he was a champion of freedom and an advocate of economic royalism; a great liberal and a die-hard conservative; a great philosopher, a mere journalist and popularizer; a great moralist and an unscrupulous special pleader. He has been called a weakling, vacillating, a typical intellectual liberal (as opposed to the man of action), shallow, vain, superficial, unoriginal, hypocritical, stuffy, pompous. He has also been called one of the master minds of western civilization. In a way, Cicero was all of these things—he was, after all, a human being, and he has told us too much about himself for us to make a hero of him.

There are two things about Cicero that we really need to keep in mind. First, we should recall that he was what the Romans called a *novus homo*, a "new man": that is, he was the first member in the history of his family to be elected consul. And second, we should remember that he was one of the ablest barristers or courtroom lawyers in the history of legal process.

Cicero came from a small town about sixty miles southeast of Rome, Arpinum; his family was very respectable, and well connected in Rome itself. But in the smart set at Rome, among the "four hundred," Cicero was still a "new man," from the "wrong side of the tracks." He did not rate socially, compared, for example, to members of the Claudian family, whose ancestors had held the consulate generation after generation and had left the family name on the Appian Way (the full name was Appius Claudius) and on one of the great aqueducts which supplied Rome with pure water. So it seems to us today, at any rate, that much of Cicero's vanity, his lack of sureness, and many other disabilities, stemmed from what we call an inferiority complex, a feeling of insecurity. He was always anxious to be what he knew he was not, and to be classed with the "best" people.

It was a good thing and a bad thing to be a "new man" in old Rome. Throughout the long history of the republic, high office and public responsibilities were handed around among members of the traditional ruling families—something like the sixty families which have been said to control American finance through interlocking directorates. Both good and bad things may be said of these Roman families: their good qualities helped ensure that the republic lasted as long as it did, a long time in the history of governments; their inability to adapt themselves to new conditions helped to destroy them and their Republic. It is to their credit that from time to time they did admit to office exceptionally capable "new men" like Cicero; they should have done it oftener. But soon these new men and their families became as exclusive as the rest of the group; and the system perpetuated itself.

Next, we need to understand that Cicero was not a lawyer in the modern sense; in old Rome there were no professional lawyers depending for their living upon the practice of law. As we shall see, fees were not charged for legal services. All young men of independent means who belonged to the traditional ruling families could look forward to the law as a career; and the law courts in those days were much more closely related to politics than they are with us (although a high proportion of our congressmen, senators, and cabinet members have been trained as lawyers). The main emphasis in Rome, so far as members of the "best families" were concerned, was on public speaking, both in the courts themselves and in general politics. Court was held in the open air in the Forum, and the *corona*—the audience—was sometimes as important as the court itself, as spectators indicated their feelings by applause or ominous silence. Any man who had need to go to court could represent himself and do his own talking. But it was much better to get one of the well-known leaders, specially gifted in work of this sort, to act as a mouthpiece and do the talking before the jury. These distinguished trial "lawyers" were not hired, and

they received no fees—to take money for services rendered would have been considered highly improper.

Whether a man got a good lawyer or not depended a great deal upon what we call "pull" or "drag." Suppose Pansa, who lived in a small Latin town, were involved in an important suit coming up in court in Rome. He would not go directly to one of the great *oratores*; the procedure was much more complicated than that. Pansa would probably go and see his neighbor Calvus, whom he knew to have important friends in Rome. One of these important friends might be Pollio, who knew Cicero (or some other important *orator*) very well. The upshot would be that Pansa, Calvus, and Pollio would all go and call upon Cicero—and a handful of other leading citizens of Pansa's home town would probably go along, too, just for the effect. Cicero liked to stand in well with the small towns, so very probably he would have agreed to take Pansa's case. In so doing, he acquired what the Romans called *gratia*. A number of important people in one of the small towns were placed under obligation to him; he became their "patron," and they became his "clients." When the next election came around, they might swing a large number of votes his way. Or, if Cicero were not a candidate himself, he could perhaps swing these same votes to some favored candidate. And apart from this, the social and political importance of a Roman gentleman was measured by the number of clients he had, especially when, as custom was, the clients dropped around to the house early in the morning to pay their respects and to walk downtown in a procession with him to the Forum where everyone could be properly impressed.

It is in this context, then, that we are to think of Cicero as a "trial lawyer." He had, of course, remarkable gifts for this sort of work; and his entire education, beginning at a very early age, was directed toward the development of these gifts. Curiously enough, the long process of education as Cicero himself described it, ending in the fully trained courtroom lawyer, was simply general or liberal education as we know it today in theory. In fact, this kind of education originally had a very practical purpose that is often overlooked.[1] The legal process, the court of law, is the place where all human activity is ultimately reviewed; and the trial lawyer therefore needs to be acquainted with the general principles, the basic objectives and ideas, of all that men do. He needs to understand human behavior ("psychology," we call it), philosophy,[2] natural science, medicine, art, music, political science, economics, history, and so forth. He need not be a specialist in any field—not even in legal science itself, because he can always get the expert in jurisprudence to "brief" him on that—but he must understand always the general principles and objectives and procedures in any given branch of human activity. And he needs, along with this knowledge, the fullest possible mastery of language, so that he can talk intelligently, pleasingly, convincingly, and persuasively about everything that men do and think privately and in public. So, in effect, the all-round liberal education that Cicero described was his own education, the practical training of a Roman trial lawyer.

Cicero himself, the product of training combined with natural genius, possessed amazing verbal facility. He had a sharp and ready wit, as a courtroom lawyer must have. His witticisms were famous in Rome and were in constant circulation. Julius Caesar prided himself on his ability to tell the difference between a genuine Ciceronian remark and one that was merely foisted on him. Roman wit was inclined to be rough; and much of Cicero's humor consisted of what we would call the "dirty crack." He was a master of the sharp retort and his tongue gained him more than one enemy.

But his mental ability went far beyond skill in repartee. He had what the trial lawyer needs: the knack of absorbing a great deal of information in a short time—like a good student—sorting out the unessentials, stressing the key points and general principles, then re-expressing them for the uninformed listener or reader more clearly and more understandably than the specialist in any particular field. This is, of course, simply what any well-educated person should be able to do; it is also what a lawyer needs to do in presenting the essential facts of a case, the basic issues. Even in his essay-dialogues, Cicero was still the courtroom lawyer, still presenting a case, and—we should always remember—never able to shake off the habit of slanting the evidence or distorting the facts with consummate skill, for the sake of the case at hand. And in all his cases, whether in dialogue-essays or actual court addresses, he had complete command of his own language, the same smooth competence that we detect when we hear a first-class symphony orchestra led by a skilled conductor. Of course, public taste in Cicero's time (and the lack of radios and public address systems) favored a style of writing and speaking that we consider too "rhetorical" today, but Cicero could do whatever he wished as the occasion required: simplicity, grandeur, hard-hitting brevity, pathos, humor—the old trial lawyer could provide them all.

One other aspect of Cicero's forensic skill helps us to understand what sort of man he was. In his own writings on public speaking, he points out that a successful orator must be a certain kind of actor, with as much skill and training as any stage actor. And the orator must be sensitive to the emotions of his listeners so that he can play upon them—just like an actor. It follows, of course, that Cicero was an actor himself; he had a tendency to play to the gallery, to be very sensitive to the opinions of others. And since Cicero *was* an actor, a very gifted one, we should not read his speeches as though we were reading written prose, like a magazine article. They need to be read with imagination, like the lines of a play, because they were written by and for an actor.

And thus we see something of the man Marcus Tullius Cicero. He had very grave faults. Attached as he was to the cause of the "best people," he was sorely lacking in social vision. His writing often reveals a strong reactionary slant. He had no solution for current problems; indeed, he did not really know what the problems were. He thought in terms of the Forum and a narrow political clique when it was time to weigh the future of a system stretching from the English Channel to the Near East, embracing many different peoples and many different cultures. His natural talents, which made him a great barrister and a great writer, kept him, like Isocrates, from being either a successful politician or a great leader. Trained in analysis, too often he saw both sides of a question and was afraid to commit himself to either. Invariably he was pleading a special case, watching the reactions of the jurors. Winning a verdict was more important, often, than telling the truth.

But in his later years, resentful, forced out of public life, he took up his greatest case. Hating dictatorship and absolute government for what it had done to him, he turned his gifts as a pleader, his genius at clarification and simplification, toward writing dialogue-essays [3] in which he stated the brief for the moral and political ideals of European civilization. In so doing, he became counsel for that attitude of civilization which we sometimes call the West.

TEXTS TRANSLATED are the Oxford Classical Texts, edited by A. C. Clark and W. Peterson: *On the Agrarian Law* (Clark, 1909); *For Cluentius, For Murena, For Caelius* (Clark, 1905); *For Sestius* (Peterson, 1910); *For Milo* and *Philippics* (Clark, 2nd ed., 1910).

# AGAINST RULLUS

## (On the Agrarian Law II)

One of the oldest political issues in Rome was that of the *ager publicus* ("public land"). In the course of its conquests, beginning in the early years of the Republic, the Roman state itself took over a great deal of land, some of it very good for farming. Sometimes this land was sold at auction, the proceeds accruing to the state. Sometimes a colony of Roman citizens was settled on it, a tract being allocated to each individual. Often the land was rented, with leases extending over very long periods. Land so leased was frequently used for large-scale farming by wealthy proprietors. The tenants could not be dispossessed unless the state required the land for some other purpose than agriculture. Now the most powerful vested interests in Rome were those related to real estate; and any radical movement of have-nots was therefore likely to involve questions of land and property-ownership. Frequently wealthy landowners had leased public lands for so long a time that they regarded their "use" as amounting to actual ownership. Hence they resisted vigorously any attempt to terminate their leases by formal state action and to distribute the land among propertyless citizens.

Illegal holdings of public land by "vested interests" had been one of the main issues during the turbulent careers of the Gracchi two generations before Cicero's day; and the issue was still a lively one when Cicero became consul for the year 63 B.C. One of the new tribunes for the year, Publius Servilius Rullus, when he took office on December 10, 64 B.C., proposed a land law which gave unprecedented authority to a Commission of Ten. The terms of the law were very cleverly—too cleverly, as it turned out—drawn up to give tremendous advantages to the popular party. Cicero spoke against the law on the occasion of his first appearance as consul, on January 1, 63 B.C. in the Senate. Later he delivered a speech against Rullus' new law before the popular assembly, the first part of which speech we read here in translation. Note how carefully Cicero leads up to his attack on the law itself—a law which was, and was designed to be, a rallying point for discontented elements in Roman society. The real author of the law is generally supposed to have been Julius Caesar, who was fishing in troubled waters. If Caesar *was* the author, the bill may have been a very shrewd move to force Cicero to take up a definite stand on the side of vested interests, and at the same time a move to foster antagonism between the *nobiles* and *populares*.

*Introduction: Cicero the "new man"*

*1* Fellow Romans: this is a procedure grounded in custom, established by our forefathers, that men who have won the honor of portrait busts of themselves for their families through your kindness should hold their first assembly by combining complimentary remarks about earlier members of their own families with grateful references to your kindness. In this inaugural address a certain number show that they deserve the high rank attained by their elders; most of them, however, create this impression— they make it look as if the public had owed such a great debt to their ancestors that there is still a balance due to the descendants.

As for myself, fellow Romans, in front of you I am not in a position to talk about my ancestors—not that they weren't men such as you see my brother and myself to be, sprung as we are from their blood and brought up in their teachings, but because they never achieved public distinction and the glamor of high office conferred by you.

*2* Now I am afraid that for me to talk about myself here before you would seem conceited; to say nothing, ungrateful. You understand that it is very difficult for me personally to mention in detail the activities by which I have reached this high office; and I cannot possibly overlook your very great kindness. For this reason, I am going to speak with calculated restraint, so that when I refer to what I have received at your hands— this unique evaluation, and why I have been thought worthy of the highest honor you can grant—I may express myself, if the occasion arises, in reasonable terms, in the belief that you, the very persons who are responsible for this evaluation, will still hold the same opinion of me.

*3* I am the first new man after a very long interval, almost longer than our day can remember, whom you have made consul. That position, which the nobility was holding, hedged in and guarded in every possible way by distinction of birth and family, you have broken open; and as I lead the way, you have indicated your desire that in the future it should remain open to merit. And not only did you elect me consul, which is in itself a very high honor, but you did so in a way in which few members of the great families have been elected in this state, and not one new man before me.

For assuredly, if you will be good enough to look at the record in connection with new men, you will find that those who won the election for consul without any previous defeat were elected only after hard work,[4] day in and day out, and at a definitely opportune time: they ran for consul many years after they had been praetors, and considerably later than they might have under the laws setting the minimum legal age.[5] What is more, those who became candidates as soon as legally eligible were not elected without first suffering defeat. You will find that I am the only one of all the new men we can remember who ran for consul as soon as it was legal and was elected as soon as he ran, so that this high office bestowed by you and sought at the exact moment of my eligibility was obviously won, not at a time when a second-rate opponent gave a good opportunity, nor dunned out of you by protracted supplications, but by sheer merit.

4 Yes, fellow Romans, it is a very great distinction which I have just mentioned—that I was the first new man after so many years upon whom you bestowed this honor, that it happened the first time I ran, that it came in the first year in which I was legally eligible, but for all of that, nothing can be finer and bring greater distinction than this: at the electoral meeting at which I was chosen, you did not hand in your ballots in secret as a guarantee of your liberties, but you openly avowed by unanimous acclamation your good will and enthusiasm for me. And so it was not the final sorting of the ballots but your rallying to the voting places at the outset, not the successive reports of the announcers but the unanimous voice of the whole Roman people that declared me consul-elect.

5 This remarkable, this extraordinary favor on your part, fellow Romans, in my own mind I consider a reason for very great satisfaction and pleasure, yet it brings me proportionately greater responsibility and worry. That is to say, fellow Romans, there are coursing through my own mind many thoughts, serious thoughts, that allow me no portion of peace either by night or by day: first, for safe-guarding the consulship, which, while a difficult and serious problem for anyone, is especially so for me, since there is no prospect of indulgence for my mistakes, and scant prospect of praise, grudgingly expressed at that, if I succeed; if I am in doubt, there will be no advisors I can trust; and I see no likelihood of dependable support from the nobility if I get into trouble.

6 But if I were being drawn into any sort of crisis by myself, fellow Romans, I could face the future with less anxiety; but I suspect that there are certain men who, if they think that I have made a slip in any matter accidentally, to say nothing of intentionally, are going to abuse all of you thoroughly for having preferred me to all my old-guard competitors. However, so far as I am concerned, fellow Romans, I think it is better to endure any kind of treatment than to fail to carry on my consulship in such a way that in all my acts and in all my decisions you will be praised for my election and for the mandate you

have given me. Add to this the fact that in my case there is this very laborious task, this very difficult procedure in carrying on as consul, in that I have made up my mind not to recognize the same terms and understandings as my predecessors in this office, some of whom have been at considerable pains to avoid coming here where you could see them, while others have not been very energetic at putting in an appearance. On the contrary, I am not only going to state here on the rostra,[6] where it is very easy to do so, but I have already stated in the Senate itself, (which does not seem to be quite the place for such remarks) in that first speech of mine on January 1, that I am going to be a consul of the people. 7 Actually, since I realize that I have been elected consul, not by the support of all-powerful individuals, not through the preponderant influence of a few, but by such a unanimous decision of the Roman people that I was ranked far ahead of men of high social standing, I cannot possibly help being a man of the people in this office and in all my life.

*What is it, in troubled times like these, to be a people's consul?*

But I badly need your wisdom in helping me to interpret the force of this word "people." A very serious misconception, you know, is flourishing as a result of the double-dealing of persons who do not mean what they say; actually they are attacking and undermining the interests, to say nothing of the welfare, of the people, while they are doing their best in their speeches to gain a reputation as friends of the people. 8 I am well aware, fellow Romans, what the condition of the republic was when it was given into my charge on January 1—full of worry, full of apprehension, a condition in which there was no disaster, no misfortune, which right-minded citizens were not apprehending and ill-intentioned citizens were not hopefully awaiting. All sorts of violent plots were being reported against this present form of government and against the state of law and order to which you have a right, some to be in preparation, some to have been set in motion the moment I became consul-elect. All feeling of security was taken from the business world, not by the impact of some unprecedented disaster, but as a result of suspicions and general uneasiness concerning the law courts, by the prospect of the nullification of verdicts already delivered. People thought that new dictatorships, new powers—not just extraordinary military powers, but royalistic—were being sought.

*9* Since I not only suspected all this but saw it very clearly—after all, it was not going on in the dark—I stated in the Senate that I was going to be a people's consul in the administration of this office. By that I meant, what is so much in the people's interest as peace abroad? You can see that not only living creatures which nature has endowed with feelings, but even the houses and fields seem to enjoy it. What is so much the people's as liberty? You can see that it is longed for, not only by human beings, but even by dumb animals, and put ahead of everything else. What is so much in the people's interests as law and order, peace at home? It is such a gratifying thing that you and your forefathers and all stout-hearted men believe the most irksome tasks to be worth undertaking in order that the people at long last may enjoy law and order, especially when accompanied by dominion and general respect abroad. What is more, here is another reason why we owe our forefathers special praise and gratitude: as a result of their efforts it was made possible for us to enjoy peace at home, law and order, without paying a penalty. In view of these facts, how could I not be a consul of the people, fellow Romans, when I see all these things, peace abroad, liberty in keeping with your name and race, law and order at home—in short, everything that is dear to you, everything that is worthwhile, all entrusted to me and, in a certain way, handed over collectively for legal guardianship to me as consul?

*10* And I may say, fellow Romans, that you should not think it welcome and to the interests of the people when some generous measure is proposed which in words may make a brave show but cannot in practice by any means whatever be put into effect without draining the public treasury. And these disturbances of the legal processes are not to be rated in the interest of the people, either—the invalidation of verdicts already delivered, the restitution of civil rights to men already condemned, things which are usually the final stages in the collapse of broken-down states already in hopeless condition. And if certain persons promise land to the Roman people, if they are working up one thing under cover and holding out something else, playing on your hopes and resorting to plausible pretences—these persons are not to be rated as friends of the people, either.

*Cicero does not oppose land laws as such; but every new bill has to be examined on its own merits.*

To be perfectly honest, fellow Romans, I certainly cannot denounce land laws themselves as a class. That is, I recall that two very famous, very able men, very great friends of the Roman people, Tiberius and Gaius Gracchus, settled the people on public lands—lands previously occupied by private individuals. And I am not the kind of a consul who, like most consuls, thinks it a crime to speak well of the Gracchi, men by whose good policies, good sense, and good laws I am aware that many departments of the administration were reorganized. *11* And so, when it was reported to me, immediately after my election as consul, that the tribunes-elect of the people were writing up a land law, I was very anxious to learn what they had in mind; the reason being that since we were both going to exercise official responsibilities in the same year, there ought to be some understanding between us in the interests of good government. *12* When, in a friendly way, I made advances and endeavored to participate in their discussions, I was kept in the dark, I was shut out; and when I made it clear that if the law seemed to the advantage of the Roman people, I would support it and help to get it passed, in spite of this they turned down my generous offer—they said I could never be brought around to approving any form of generosity to the people. I put an end to further offers to be of service; I was afraid that persistence might be thought to be either designing or interfering. In the meantime they did not leave off holding secret meetings, bringing in certain private citizens, combining the darkness of night and mystery with the secrecy of their meetings. You will easily guess at the seriousness of my fears, as a result of these developments, from your own worries during this time. *13* At length the tribunes took office. Publius Rullus' opening speech aroused great anticipations because he was the chief promoter of the land law and acted tougher than any of the others. The instant he was elected he practised putting on a new look, using a different tone of voice, and walking with a different gait. He went around with his clothes shabbier, his person unkempt and shaggy, his hair longer, with more whiskers, so that he seemed to be giving everyone notice, by his expression and general appearance, of violent action to come from the tribunate and of a threat to the constitution. I was awaiting the man's law and his first speech. At first no law is proposed. He orders a meeting called for December 12. People come running to the meeting, all expectation. He unwinds a pretty long speech; it sounds terrific. There was just one thing about it that seemed wrong to me: in all that crowd nobody could be found who could understand what he meant. Whether he did this for the sake of covering something up, or whether he likes this kind of speaking, I have no idea. Even so, some of the brighter people standing in the assembly had a suspicion that he wanted to say something or other about a land law. Finally, when I become consul-elect, in due time the law is released to the public. At my instructions a number of copyists get busy at the same time and bring me an exact copy of the law.

*To Cicero, the merits of Rullus' land law are dubious.*

14 I want to assure you, fellow Romans, I want to assure you in every possible way that I approached the reading and the study of this law with this thought in mind: that I would back it and promote it if I found it to be suitable and useful to your purposes. Now it is not because of any instinctive dislike or open disagreement or deep-seated hatred that the consulate has taken up sort of a war against the tribunate, although subversive and irresponsible tribunes of the people have many a time been opposed by loyal and fearless consuls and many a time the vicious ambitions of the consul have been checked by the power of the tribunate. It is no conflict of powers but an incompatibility of individual character

that causes the disagreement. 15 And so in this spirit I took this law in my hands; I desired very much to find it framed to your advantage, the kind of a law that a consul who was a friend of the common people in fact, and not just in his speeches, could honorably and gladly support. And from the first section of this law to the last, I tell you that I find, fellow Romans, no thought, no undertaking, no enactment, other than this: that ten kings shall be set up to control the treasury, the collection of revenues, all the provinces, the entire state, the allied kingdoms, the free peoples—in short, under the name and pretense of a land law, ten lords of the entire earth are being created.

And so I maintain, fellow Romans, that this lovely people's land law gives you nothing, makes a present of everything to certain men, holds out land to the Roman people with one hand and takes away even their liberty with the other, increases the wealth of individuals, drains off the wealth of the people, and finally—this is absolutely outrageous—through the agency of the tribune of the people, whom our forefathers meant to act as a guard and a watchman of our liberty, absolute tyrants are set up over the citizen body. 16 After I have put all these facts before you, fellow Romans, if you think they are not true, I shall bow to your authority and change my attitude toward this law; but if you recognize that a plot is under way against your freedom under the name of government generosity, do not hesitate, with your consul standing back of you, to defend this freedom which was won for you with much blood and sweat by your forefathers and inherited without any effort on your part. [In the rest of the speech, Cicero analyzes the provisions of the bill, hammering home the point that the true intent was not the welfare of the people but the establishment of a dictatorship. The bill, even if we allow for Cicero's partisan bias, does seem to have over-reached itself; and the people voted it down.]

## IN DEFENSE OF CLUENTIUS

The speech which we are going to read here in part provides a good example of Cicero's skill as a trial lawyer. Cicero's main purpose was to get his client, Aulus Cluentius Habitus, acquitted of a charge of trying to poison

one Oppianicus. Many critics think that this address to the jury fairly represents Cicero at his best. Cicero was forty when the trial took place (in 66 B.C.); he had not yet become deeply involved in politics. The introduction very carefully sets the stage for the damaging evidence against his client's enemies which forms the main part of the address; and while we are very likely to conclude that Cluentius was as pure as the driven snow and could never have thought of poisoning anyone, it is worth remembering that Cicero himself afterwards remarked, not without pride, that he had "thrown dust in the jury's eyes."

The background of the trial itself was extraordinarily complicated. It is at least necessary to remember that eight years previously Cluentius (the present defendant) had prosecuted Statius Albius Oppianicus, father of the Oppianicus who brings the present charge. (Note that in the Roman legal process there was no public prosecutor, like a District Attorney; each individual who had been wronged or put in jeopardy himself laid the charge and was responsible for the prosecution. The state merely provided the machinery by which this might be done.) In the earlier trial, Cluentius had charged that Oppianicus Senior had attempted to poison *him*; and the jury voted for the conviction of Oppianicus. But the circumstances under which the verdict was reached led to suspicions that someone had bribed the jury. Cicero in his review of the earlier case informs us that while public opinion was convinced that Cluentius had bribed the jury to gain the conviction of an innocent man, in fact it was Oppianicus who had *tried* to bribe the jury to render a verdict of "Not Guilty." The case then became a public scandal, since members of the Senate at that time made up the juries; and one of the tribunes of the people made political capital at the time out of the alleged corruption of a senatorial jury.

In the second trial with which we are immediately concerned here, it was necessary, in effect, for Cicero to retry the first case, and to prove that Cluentius had been innocent of bribery and that Oppianicus Senior was a thoroughly bad character. Cicero no doubt believed that the best defense was attack. It was also necessary to combat the general atmosphere of scandal. In so doing, Cicero introduces us to Sassia, Cluentius' mother, as disagreeable a female as can be found in the annals of crime, and Oppianicus, who makes all other murderers, in history or in fiction, look like amateurs. We wonder, too, if we are given here a view of private life and morals in a decadent society. Some critics have seen in the careers of Sassia and Oppianicus an explanation of what was wrong with Rome. But while we are scarcely given a portrayal of the old Roman virtues here, we should remember that the legal process deals with the abnormal, and that murder trials and divorce proceedings give a somewhat one-sided sociological view. It might be added that the favorite murder weapon among the Romans was poison. Proof of use was difficult; there were no scientific methods available that might prove, in the event of an autopsy, that some person or persons unknown had slipped a little toadstool juice in Uncle Cornelius' after-dinner wine.

*Introduction: Cicero will follow the prosecution in dividing his speech into two parts.*

1 Gentlemen of the jury: I noticed that the prosecutor's remarks were divided roughly into two parts, in one of which I thought that he was relying with considerable confidence on the long-standing prejudice against the earlier trial held with Junius as judge, while in the other part he seemed to touch, merely as a matter of form, rather nervously and half-heartedly, on the business of poisoning, the charge which this court has been set up by law to investigate. Therefore, I have definitely decided to observe this same division between the prejudice and the charge of poisoning in my remarks for the defense, so that everyone can understand that it is not my intention to avoid the issue by saying too little or to obscure it by saying too much. 2 But when I think over the problem of how to develop either line of argument, one of them—the one which is appropriate to your court and to a legally constituted investigation of a case of poisoning—seems to require of me little time and no great effort in refutation, whereas the other, which is somewhat remote from a legal process and is more suited to mass meetings stirred up in defiance of law and order than to the quiet moderation of the court—I can see how much trouble and how much work there is going to be in its treatment.

*Cicero expresses the hope for an unprejudiced hearing*

3 But in the face of this difficulty, gentlemen, I find consolation in the well-known fact that it is your practice, when you hold a hearing on criminal charges, to look to the attorney for their complete refutation and not to think that you are under obligation to contribute anything to the defendant's acquittal beyond what his counsel can gain by way of clearing his client of the charges, or can establish by proof. On the other hand, in dealing with prejudice, you are under obligation, as you go over the case among yourselves, to take into consideration the arguments which we should make and not those which we do make. Now, in this case, so far as the actual charges are concerned, only Aulus Cluentius is on trial; in the matter of prejudice we are all on trial. For this reason, I am going to conduct one half of my case in the form of a classroom lec-

ture, and the other half in the form of a plea. In the first half, I shall have to ask for your careful attention; in the other half, I must earnestly beg for your good will. No counsel, you know, can hope to combat prejudice without your support and the support of men like you.

4 As a matter of fact, so far as my part in the case is concerned, gentlemen of the jury, I don't know which direction to take. Am I in a position to say that the well-known scandal over the bribery of the bench in that other trial never existed? Can I say that it was never ventilated in public meetings, pulled to pieces in the courts, made the subject of remarks in the Senate? Can I wipe from men's minds such strong impressions, so deeply fixed, formed so long ago? That is beyond my talents. It is for you, gentlemen of the jury—it is for you to help my innocent client, to save him, trapped in this disastrous scandal, which is like some destroying flame, a house on fire, involving us all.

5 Yes, even though in other places truth has little room in which to stand secure, little strength, here in this place it is ungrounded prejudice that should be weak and feeble; prejudice may lord it over a mass meeting, but in a court of law, prejudice should lie low; prejudice may have force in public opinion and in the gossip of the uninformed, but it should be cast out by the minds of men who know the law and hold fast to reason; it may make sudden and powerful attacks, but as time goes by and the case is judicially reviewed, prejudice should age and fade away. And, in brief, let us hold fast to that definition of fair trials which has been handed down to us by our fathers of old, that in courts of law guilt is punished without prejudice, and if there be no guilt, prejudice is put aside.

6 For this reason, gentlemen of the jury, I have these requests to make of you before I begin to speak of the case itself. First of all, I ask what is only fair: please do not bring into this court any preconceived opinions—you know, we will lose our influence as judges and our reputations, too, unless we review cases here according to the facts alone and do not apply to cases judgments we have brought with us from home. The second request is this: assuming that you have already formed any opinion, if it is dislodged by logic or weakened by my pleas, or, in short, by truth itself uprooted, don't fight back, let your preconceived opinions go, either gladly or from a sense of jus-

tice. And finally now, as I go on to discuss each point in the charge and refute it, do not make any mental reservations as to points on either side, but wait to the end and let me work out my argument in my own way; when I have come to the summing up, then you may review in your own minds anything that I may have left out.

*This long-standing prejudice will end here, if you will deal with it impartially.*

7 Gentlemen of the jury, I, for one, have no trouble in realizing that the other side of the case I am undertaking has been heard for these eight long years, that it is a case in which irresponsible public opinion itself has all but found my client guilty and silently passed sentence on him. But if any kindly god will let me have your good will long enough to hear me, I shall certainly guarantee to convince you that a man has nothing to fear so much as prejudice; that an innocent man, when prejudice has been aroused, has nothing to hope for so much as a fair trial, which is the only place where at long last any true end and destruction of slander may be found. And so I have high hopes that if I am able to do what I propose, to bring out in detail and clear up the various points of my case, this place and the jury on which you sit, which *they* thought would be a thing of dread and terror to my client, Cluentius, will at last be a haven of refuge to his unhappy storm-tossed fortunes.

8 Although there is a multitude of things I might say before I come to the case itself, about the prejudice which is dangerous to all of us, still I prefer not to keep you too long in suspense by holding off the main part of my argument; and so I shall come to the actual charge—with this appeal, gentlemen, which I know I may have to use rather often, to listen to me as if this case were now being pleaded for the first time, as in fact it is, and not as if it had often been argued already, but never with the facts properly established. I mean that this is the first day on which there has been any opportunity to dispel the actual charges against Cluentius; before today the whole case has been involved in errors of fact and prejudice. And so, while I reply clearly and in a few words to an accusation of many years' standing, I am asking this favor of you, gentlemen of the jury— listen to me carefully, please, as you have already begun to do.

*The charge*

**9** The charge is that Aulus Cluentius bribed the court to secure the conviction of a personal enemy, an innocent man, Statius Albius Oppianicus.

*Oppianicus' crimes*

I shall prove first, gentlemen—since the core of all this frightful prejudice was the charge that an innocent man was done in by bribery—I shall prove that no one was ever brought before the bar of justice on more serious charges or on weightier evidence than Oppianicus. I shall prove in the second place that previous judgments had been passed on Oppianicus by the judges who subsequently condemned him, judgments of such a nature that he could not possibly have been acquitted by them, or by any other judges, for that matter. After I have established this, I shall then prove something I perceive is very much needed, that bribery in that [earlier] trial was not attempted by Cluentius, but against Cluentius. And I shall see to it that you understand that [earlier] case from beginning to end—what the facts themselves warranted, what rumor added to it, to what extent prejudice has fanned the flames. . . .

*Cluentius was driven to prosecute Oppianicus because Oppianicus had wronged him.*

**11** Aulus Cluentius Habitus, gentlemen, father of this man, my client here, in character, reputation, and family background, was not only the most outstanding man in the town of Larinum to which he belonged, but in that whole neighborhood and district. He died when Sulla and Pompeius were consuls [88 B.C.], leaving a son of fifteen, my client here, and a grown-up and marriageable daughter. The girl, shortly after her father's death, married Aulus Aurius Melinus, her cousin on her mother's side, a young man who was considered at the time to be of unusually fine character and good repute among those of his own age. **12** This marriage, highly exemplary as it was, accompanied by all domestic concord, suddenly aroused the unspeakable passions of a wicked woman—a shameless person, leagued, too, with crime. You see, Sassia, mother of this Cluentius Habitus—yes, his mother shall be named all through this case, his mother, I repeat, although she treats her son with all the hate and cruelty due a public enemy—and she shall at no time hear of the criminal outrages she has committed in such a way that she shall lose the name of mother that nature has given her—I mean the more tender and the more loving the very name of mother is, the more you will consider deserving of detestation the unexampled crime of this mother who for many years, and now more than ever, yearns for the death of her son.

*Cluentius' mother fell in love with her own son-in-law.*

Well, then, she, Cluentius' mother, fell head over heels in love with this young Melinus, her son-in-law, in defiance of all decency. At first, but not for very long, at that, she exercised self-restraint in that lust as well as she was able. Then she began to burn so madly, to be so carried away by the flames of passion, that nothing could restrain her desire: not her sense of shame, not her chastity, not her maternal instincts, not the family disgrace or the public scandal, not her son's grief or her daughter's broken heart. **13** The young husband's fancy, not yet strengthened by wisdom and understanding, she enticed with all those arts by which the young can be snared and captured. The daughter was not only tortured by the anguish natural to all women so wronged by a husband, she was unable also to bear the terrible thought that her mother was her husband's mistress—a thing she felt she could not even complain of without doing something very wicked—she wanted no one else to know of her terrible trouble; she began to pine away with grief and tears, held close in the arms of my client here, her very loving brother.

**14** But look! There's a sudden divorce, which seemed likely to cure all her woes. The girl Cluentia separates from Melinus; not sorry, considering how she had been wronged; not glad, considering that she was leaving her husband. Yes, and then it was that this extraordinary mother, this woman of distinction, started celebrating right out in the open, triumphant with joy, having won the battle with her daughter but not with her lust—she didn't want her reputation damaged overlong by dark suspicions—she has the marriage bed made up and decked out, the very marriage bed which had been made up two years before for her daughter's wedding in the very same house—after her daughter has been bundled out. Mother-in-law marries son-in-law without ceremonies, without any wedding guests, everything foreboding a black future.

*15* Oh! To think of this woman's wickedness— unbelievable it is, and not heard of in a lifetime, except in connection with this one woman! What unbroken, untamed passion! What unique and brazen effrontery! Wasn't she afraid at all, if not of the vengeance of Heaven and the scandal among men, at least of that wedding night itself and those marriage torches? Wasn't she afraid at the door of the bedroom? Her own daughter's bridal couch? Or even the walls themselves which had witnessed that other union? No, she broke through and trampled down every scruple in her mad passion; lust overcame shame, audacity overcame fear, madness overcame reason. *16* Her son found this disgrace hard to take, affecting as it did his family, his relations, his good name; and to his troubles were added also the daily complaints of his sister and tears without end. However, he came to the conclusion that he should do nothing more positive, in spite of his mother's outrageous conduct, than to put an end to all associations with her, being afraid people might think that he was not only aware of, but actually approved of, the conduct that he could not look upon without the keenest anguish if he kept on seeing her.

*Cluentius disowned his mother, and a feud sprang up between them which has been the cause of all his troubles since.*

*17* You have now heard how the clash between my client and his mother began. You will realize how it affects the case when you hear what comes next. Now I am well aware that no matter how bad a mother is, it is still not exactly proper to mention a parent's depravity at the trial of a son. I would not be a fit man to take on any case, gentlemen, if I did not acknowledge this principle shared by all human beings and deeply fixed and planted in human nature—I who am retained for the defense of men in peril. I fully realize that men should not only keep quiet about their parents' misdemeanors, but should also endure them with resignation. Still, I hold that only those things should be endured which can be endured, and that silence should be maintained only when it can be maintained.

*18* In all his life my client Cluentius has seen no disaster, faced no peril of death, feared no

evil, that was not worked up and furthered by his mother. He would now be reticent about all his troubles—yes, he would allow them to be veiled by silence if not by oblivion—but naturally, the way things are going now, silence is absolutely out of the question. I mean to say that this trial here, my client's present jeopardy, that indictment, the whole crowd of witnesses ready to testify, were originally tricked out by his mother, and at this moment are being lined up and made ready for action with all the wealth and resources his mother has. To top it all, she has just swooped down on Rome from Larinum in person, to lay her son low for good. Here she is—a brazen woman, wealthy, cruel. She is lining up the prosecution, she is lining up the witnesses, she loves to see my client's unshaven face and untrimmed hair, his garb of mourning [as the customary appearance of the accused in a Roman trial]; she longs for his destruction, she is eager to shed the last drop of her blood if only she may see his poured out first. If you do not perceive that all these statements represent the facts in this case, you are at liberty to conclude that I am merely irresponsible in naming her as the guilty one; but if they are revealed clearly in all their wickedness, you will be bound to pardon Cluentius for allowing me to say these things; you would be bound *not* to pardon me if I failed to say them.

*An attempt to poison him drove Cluentius to prosecute.*

*19* At this point I shall summarize the charges on which Oppianicus was found guilty in the earlier trial, so that you can understand the resolute attitude of Aulus Cluentius and the idea that lies back of the prosecution. And first I will explain the reason for the prosecution, so that you may see that Aulus Cluentius was forced to act by sheer necessity. *20* When he had actually detected the poison which his stepfather Oppianicus had fixed for him, and it was not a matter of guess-work, but a matter of tangible and visible proof, he laid a charge against Oppianicus. How resolutely and painstakingly he conducted the prosecution, I shall tell later; at the moment I wanted you to know that there was no other reason for laying a charge, that the one reason was to escape the threat to his life, the daily plots against his person. And so you

understand that the charges laid against Oppianicus in the earlier trial were of such a nature that
the prosecution had nothing to fear and the defense nothing to hope for, I shall outline a few
items of the charge brought at that trial. When
you know what they are, none of you will be
surprised that the defendant's lack of confidence
in his case found a way out in Staienus and
bribery. . . .

[Here Cicero tells of an unsavory incident in
which Oppianicus had been involved, but with no
direct bearing on Cluentius' family troubles.]

*Oppianicus commits multiple murders; he falls
in love with Cluentius' wicked mother.*

25 And this is small stuff: hear the rest, and
you will be surprised not that Oppianicus was
finally convicted but that he should have enjoyed
his freedom for a considerable length of time.
26 First, take a look at the nerve of the scoundrel. He conceived a passionate desire to marry
Sassia, Cluentius' mother, the woman whose husband, Aulus Aurius, he had murdered. Whether
his lack of shame in proposing to her was greater
than his lack of feeling, if she accepted him, it is
hard to say; but anyhow, note the humane feelings and consistency of both of them. 27 Oppianicus asks Sassia to marry him, and he keeps after
her. She on her part was not taken aback at his
effrontery, she did not scorn his shamelessness,
and least of all did she shrink in horror from the
house of a man spattered with the blood of her
husband, but because he had three sons—that is
why she declined the marriage with distaste. Oppianicus, who had lusted to get his hands on
Sassia's money, decided he should find in his
own house a way of removing the obstacle to the
marriage. He had with him his infant son by
Navia [a divorced wife]; but a second son by
Papia [another divorced wife] was being brought
up at his mother's, at Teanum in Apulia, about
18 miles from Larinum. Suddenly, without giving any reason, he sent for this boy from Teanum.
This was an unusual thing for him to do, unless
on the occasion of games or on holidays. The
poor mother sent the boy along, not suspecting
anything wrong. Oppianicus had pretended that
he was setting out for Tarentum—on that same
day the boy, who had been seen in public in
perfect health about five o'clock in the after-

noon, was dead before dark and cremated before
dawn. 28 And news of this terrible bereavement
reached the mother by common gossip before any
member of Oppianicus' household reported it.
She—when she heard that she had lost her only
son, as well as the privilege of burying him—at
once, half out of her mind, went to Larinum and
held services again, even though the child was already in his grave. Not ten days had passed before the other son, the baby, was murdered. And
so, Sassia goes right ahead and marries Oppianicus, lightheartedly, with all her hopes
realized. No wonder; she found herself being
courted, not by presents from her fiancé but by
the funerals of his sons. And Oppianicus, in contrast to other men who are inclined to be anxious
to make money for the sake of their children,
reckoned it a pleasure to sacrifice his children for
the sake of money.

29 I know, gentlemen, I know how profoundly,
in keeping with your human sympathies, you
have been shocked during this brief review of
Oppianicus' foul deeds. I ask you, then: what
were the feelings of those who had not only to
listen to such a review, but to pass judgment on
it? . . .

[Cicero re-emphasizes the guilt of Oppianicus
as brought out in the earlier trial; and insists
that in spite of the intervening death of Oppianicus, his record is still pertinent to the present
trial.]

30 Is there anyone who can even suspect, when
he has heard all these facts, that Oppianicus was
an innocent man framed and overwhelmed at
that [earlier] trial?

In a lump sum, then, gentlemen, I shall give
you the rest of the story, so that I can get to
events that are more relevant and more closely
attached to my client's case. Bear in mind, please,
that it is not my task to accuse the late Oppianicus; yet, since I should like to convince you
that the court was not bribed by my client, I am
using this as the primary basis of my defense,
that Oppianicus, as found guilty, *was* thoroughly
guilty and an out-and-out scoundrel. He gave a
glass of wine to Cluentia, my client Cluentius'
aunt, and she, with her glass half-finished,
screamed that she was dying in terrible pain. She
lived no longer than she spoke—yes, with these
very words, as she screamed, she died. And in
addition to the sudden death and the statement

of the dying woman, all the usual traces and signs of poison were found on her body. And with the same kind of poison he did away with his brother Gaius Oppianicus.

*31* And this isn't all. Even though the murder of a brother seems to climax every other form of crime, still, in order to lead up to this act of horror, he paved the way in advance by other crimes. That is, his brother's wife Auria was pregnant and was thought to be coming close to the time when the baby was to be born. He then poisoned the woman so that his brother's progeny might perish along with her. Then he turned to his brother, who, too late—since he had already drained the deadly glass of wine and was crying out about his wife's death and his own—wanted to change his will, but died in the very act of declaring his intentions. Thus Oppianicus murdered the wife so that he would not be barred by her issue from inheriting his brother's property; and he robbed his brother's children of life before nature could grant them the light of day; and by this token he made it known to all that no way was barred, that nothing could be sacred, to a man from whose criminal daring not even the protection of a mother's body could save his brother's children. *32* I recall that when I was in Asia Minor a woman in Miletus had taken a bribe from heirs next in line and had caused a miscarriage by the use of drugs. She was sentenced to death; and rightly so, because she had taken away from the father his hopes, the prospects of continuing the family name, the perpetua-

tion of the clan, the heir of the household, and from the community, a prospective citizen. How much more severely does the same violation of the law deserve to be punished in the case of Oppianicus! For the reason that the woman simply inflicted torture upon herself by doing violence to her own body; Oppianicus, on the contrary, effected the same result through the torture and death of another person's body. Other men, it seems, cannot undertake the murder of a number of relatives in one individual; here we have come upon Oppianicus, who was able to kill more than one in one body. . . .

[Cicero thus far has reported only a few of Oppianicus' murders; before the report is finished, very little is left of Oppianicus' character. Cicero then reviews the matter of bribery alleged in the trial that had taken place eight years before, and shows that in fact it was Oppianicus who, through a disreputable character named Staienus, had tried to bribe the jury. As for the charge in the present trial, that Cluentius had tried to poison Oppianicus Junior, Cicero made light of it. The main charge was that at a dinner party given by Oppianicus, a young man named Balbutius picked up a drink intended for Oppianicus, drank it, and promptly dropped dead. Cicero asked how the poison, if there was any, got in the drink; and suggests that the innocent victim merely had indigestion. The monster Sassia is at the bottom of it all, and Cicero in his peroration begs the jury to save his client from such a mother.]

## IN DEFENSE OF SESTIUS

Sestius, a devoted friend and supporter of Cicero, was one of those who had been most active in bringing about his recall from exile in 57 B.C. Together with Milo (about whom we shall read later) Sestius took an active part in the gang warfare which characterized this period. Early in 56, Clodius (Cicero's old enemy, whom we shall meet in the *Address in Defense of Milo*) brought an indictment against Sestius, charging the use of force and bribery in electioneering. Since the prosecution was obviously an attempt to hit at Cicero through his friend, Cicero quite naturally acted for the defense, using this attack upon a member of the conservative party as an excuse for a definition and defense of the whole party's platform and principles.

We have in the following pages a brief excerpt from the end of the defense of Sestius in which Cicero sets forth

his views on the "best people" [7] in Roman politics. To many readers today Cicero's remarks seem to have a curiously contemporary significance. What that significance may be is perhaps best left for the reader to decide. In addition, however, to what it tells us about Cicero, the speech reveals one aspect of Greek and Roman political life that was more important than one might think: the extreme sensitivity of men in public life to the winning of honors and titles for their own sake, somewhat akin to the sensitivity of Orientals to "face."

*Who are the best people?*

*96* In this community, men who are anxious to take part in politics and to distinguish themselves have always been of two kinds: some have desired to be regarded as, and to be, representatives of the common people; others have desired to be regarded as, and to be, representatives of the best people. Those who desired what they did and what they said to be agreeable to the rank and file were regarded as representatives of the common people, while those who behaved in such a way as to win the approval of every good citizen were considered representatives of the best people.

97 Well, who are these "best people?" There are more of them than you can count—if you ask me [addressing his opponents]—and we could not carry on without them: they are the originators of public policy, they are the men who belong to the same party as these leaders, they are the members of the upper classes who are eligible for the Senate; they are the Roman citizens of the small towns and the country districts; they are business men; there are also descendants of freedmen [former slaves] among the best people.

As I say, the members of this class are widely scattered and on various levels of society, but the class as a whole, make no mistake, can be described and defined very briefly. All men belong to the best people who are law-abiding, are not naturally unscrupulous, not fanatics, not up to their ears in debt. And so, Vatinius, let us take it as an established fact that those whom you named a "family compact" are men beyond reproach, levelheaded and financially secure. Men who have due regard for the wishes, the best interests, and the opinions of these people in governing the state are to be considered as the most solid and the most distinguished citizens, as leaders in the community—as defenders of the best people and as included among the best people themselves.

*How to judge the best people*

98 These pilots of the ship of state—what is the goal, then, upon which they are to keep their eyes and by which they are in duty bound to plot their course? Something that is of priceless value, the one thing to be desired by all right-thinking, loyal, well-to-do citizens: the preservation of law and order and the respectful treatment of all citizens who deserve well of the community. Men who are in favor of this are all judged to belong to the best people; those who put it into effect are

considered great men and preservers of the state. In other words, it is not right for men to be so carried away by the glamor of a political career that they do not look out for law and order; and they should not willingly accept any form of law and order that is inconsistent with the proper treatment of citizens who deserve well of the community.

*Foundations of law and order*

Now here are the foundations of this law and order with due honor given those who deserve it; here are the basic elements which must be protected by our leaders and defended even at the risk of life itself: our respect for our religion, our system of omens, the power of the officers of the state, the authority of the Senate, our laws, our traditions, our courts, our judicial process, our financial standing, our provinces, our allies, the glory of empire, our armed forces, our public treasury. 99 To be the defender and protector of these things, so many and so important are they, is a task calling for a high order of courage, a high order of skill, and a high order of steadfastness. All these qualities are required because, among so large a number of citizens, there are a great many who—fearing the law and being well aware of their own misdemeanors—are on the lookout for radical movements and political upheavals, or else, because they are born fanatics, thrive on civic dissension and agitation, or, because of the money they owe, would rather go up in flames with everyone else than to have their own little fire. When people like these find backers and leaders for their own fool ideas and vicious enterprises, political hurricanes are stirred up; and those who have demanded for themselves the helm of state must be on the alert and strive with all knowledge and all concentration to preserve those things which I declared a moment ago to be fundamental and basic, and to stay firmly on their course and reach that harbor of law and order where proper respect is paid to those who deserve it. 100 Gentlemen of the jury: if I were to tell you that this course of action is not rough and steep going and beset with dangers and treachery, I would not be telling you the truth—all the more so because I have been aware of it all my life, and what is more, beyond the lot of other men, I have learned it by my own personal experience.

*Good citizens are slow to act.*

The constitution of our republic is attacked in greater strength and by greater numbers than it is defended, for this reason: irresponsible characters who have nothing to lose not only get excited when anyone gives them the nod, but also rise up against the government of their own accord, whereas good citizens somehow tend to be rather slow—they ignore trouble in its early stages, but in the end, of sheer necessity, they are finally forced to do something, so that it happens not infrequently that they put things off too long and take action too late, and while they are willing to maintain a state of good order even without the proper treatment of deserving citizens, they lose both good order and that kind of treatment themselves. *101* Moreover, would-be defenders of our constitution, if they are inclined to be unstable characters, have a habit of going over to the other side; if they are a little timid, they give up completely; only such men as your own father was, Marcus Scaurus [addressing directly one of those present in court], stand firm and endure to the end for the sake of the constitution. He resisted all trouble-makers from the time of Gaius Gracchus to the time of Quintus Varius; *there* was a man whom no show of force, no pressure, no fear of making enemies ever caused to waver; or, for example, Quintus Metellus, your great-uncle on your mother's side, who, when he was censor, black-listed Lucius Saturninus, a man who was riding high in the favor of the popular faction; and when he had used his power as censor to bar the would-be Gracchus from the Senate in the face of rioting by the populace, who were infuriated by this denial of eligibility, and when he had been the only one to refuse to take the oath to abide by that law which he considered unconstitutional, he preferred to give up his right to live in Rome rather than to budge from his convictions. Or, to pass over examples from earlier history—of which there is an abundant supply, in keeping with the high repute of this government, and not to mention the name of some one of those who are now living—such a man was the late Quintus Lutatius Catulus: neither storms of personal peril nor the glamour of high office ever could, by fear or by hope, move *him* from his determined course of action.

*Precedents from the past*

*102* In the name of the immortal gods! You who seek true distinction, praise, and undying fame—I implore you to imitate these examples! These are magnificent examples, these are divine, these are deathless; their report goes far and wide, they are given over to the record of the ages, they are handed on to generations yet to be. To imitate them is no easy thing—I do not deny it; the risks are great—I admit it;

> many are the pitfalls for
> good citizens . . .

has been truly said; but

> what so many envy and so
> many desire, is folly . . .

for you, says the poet,

> to seek, unless you carry
> through to the end with the
> greatest pains.

I should prefer that the same poet [8] had not said in another passage for our ill-intentioned fellow citizens to seize upon,

> let them hate, so long as
> they fear.

As you know, it was to young men that he had given the former excellent advice.

*Things are better now.*

*103* However, this course of political action, this general attitude, was once more to be feared when, at many points, the enthusiasms of the masses or the advantage of the common people clashed with the best interests of the state as a whole. A law to regulate voting was being brought in by Lucius Cassius; the common people thought that their freedom was the issue at stake; the leading citizens were unable to agree among themselves, and when it was a question of the security of the best people, they were afraid of the irresponsibility of the masses and the reckless use of the ballot. Tiberius Gracchus was for passing a land law; the common people liked it; it seemed that the fortunes of the poorer classes were about to be established; the best people fought against the measure because they saw that it set class against class, and because—since men of means were being dispossessed of property they had held for a long time—they thought that the constitution was being stripped of its best defenders. Gaius Gracchus was for bringing in a relief law; the proposal was welcomed by the common people, since rations were to be supplied on a lavish scale without their having to work for them; right-minded citizens resisted the bill because they thought that the common people were being enticed away from thrift to idleness; and they also foresaw the exhaustion of the public treasury.

*Law and order prevail.*

*104* Even within our own memories many incidents have arisen—which I pass over advisedly—in this struggle which involves the conflict between the greed of the common people and the wisdom of our leading citizens. At this time, however, there is no longer any issue over which the common people disagree with our duly elected officials and leading citizens; they are not asking for a thing; they are not anxious for a radical change of government, and they are happy in their own peaceful condition and the respect paid to all good citizens and the good name of the state as a whole. And so, since the common people of Rome cannot be stirred up with the promise of lavish government handouts, since the lower classes, being fed up with such violent disorders and class wars, are welcoming law and order, agitators and trouble-makers now have public meetings on hire. In their proceedings they do not make it their aim to say or propose what the people in attendance will like to hear, but by purchase and hire they see to it that no matter what they say, the meeting will seem to like to hear it.

*105* Now can you gentlemen possibly imagine that the Gracchi or Saturninus or any one of those men in the good old days who were regarded as champions of the popular party ever had anyone in a public meeting on his payroll? Not one ever had, because the lavishness of their

proposals and the prospects of the advantages they set forth used to excite the mass of the people without any actual bribery. Accordingly, although in those days leaders who belonged to the popular party were naturally offensive to men of conservative views and public experience, yet their standing was high because of the favorable verdicts of the common people, and by every form of recognition. There used to be applause for them in the theater; they used to carry by the ballot the measures for which they had fought; people loved their names, the way they spoke, the way they looked, the way they carried themselves. Moreover, those who were opposed to this class of popular leaders were considered persons of importance and high standing; they had much influence in the Senate, very much influence among good citizens, but the mass of the people did not like them; their proposals were often voted down; as a matter of fact, if one of them had on some occasion received a round of applause in public, he used to be very much afraid that he had done something wrong. And in spite of all this, if there was any crisis of major importance, the same common people used to be heavily influenced by their prestige.

[The remaining forty-one paragraphs of the speech continue the emphasis begun above upon the fact that no one wants revolution. The charge of rioting against Sestius is denied and is used as an excuse for an invective against a partisan of Caesar, Vatinius, "the best-hated man of his time," who was ambitious for the consulship and of course a good hater of the party of the "best men." After a digression to encourage the young conservatives to imitate their ancestors who made Rome great, Cicero in his peroration urges the acquittal of his client on the ground that Sestius contributed to the orator's return from exile, and that acquittal will make for law and order and keep the discontented under control. Sestius was acquitted, and showed his gratitude, and his conviction of the truth of Cicero's words in this speech, by passing over to Caesar's party after the battle of Pharsalus (48 B.C.)]

# IN DEFENSE OF MURENA

As we have seen, 63 B.C. was Cicero's great year, during which he served as consul and "saved the Republic" by

revealing and putting an end to Catiline's conspiracy against the "best people." As consul it was his duty—and he was keenly aware of it—to ensure that the elections for the following year's consuls were properly held, so that there might be no interruption in the administration of public affairs. One of the unsuccessful consular candidates for the year 62 B.C. was Servius Sulpicius Rufus, an old friend of Cicero and one of the most distinguished figures in the history of Roman law.

While Sulpicius had political ambitions, he was better known as a *juris consultus*, a gentleman "learned in the law." In this connection we need to remind ourselves again that there was no legal profession in Rome as there is with us. Theoretically any member of the Roman office-holding class could act as a *patronus* or pleader (*orator*) and speak on behalf of his clients in court. Some, like Cicero, with special aptitude or training, were better known as *patroni*, and their services were more often solicited by those who were unable, or felt unable, to do their own speaking. Or again, a member of the office-holding class might be elected to the position of *praetor*, which meant that in his capacity as presiding judge in court, he might have to define the issues in a suit, analyze a problem of law, try to determine the applicable principles, and establish a *formula* according to which the decision in a case would have to be made. While the ordinary member of the office-holding class naturally knew a good deal of law—a great deal more than the average American—he was still an amateur, with the law merely one of the aspects of his political career.

Consequently, to fill the need for specialists in the law, a class of experts gradually arose during the history of the Republic who devoted their lives to the study of legal principles. They were, like the *patroni* or *oratores*, still not professionals in the modern sense: they did not take fees for their services, since they were men of independent means. (Their remuneration came, of course, in the ordinary way of Roman society and political life: I do you a favor and then you do me a favor.) But if any point of law came up that was beyond the knowledge or competence of the ordinary judge or *praetor*, *orator*, or litigant, it was customary to consult one of the *juris consulti*. While the interpretations and opinions of these men had no standing in the official court system under the Republic, still, since they were regularly consulted by judges and litigants, their expert advice was gradually fed into the stream of Roman law as it developed and adjusted itself over the course of generations to new problems and new conditions. Under the Empire, the emperor regularly chose a group of *juris consulti* to act as a sort of cabinet of legal advisers; and while decisions in cases where there had been an "appeal to Caesar" were issued as coming from the emperor himself, they were in fact the judgments of men who had devoted their lives to the study of law and its basic principle of *aequum et bonum* (equity and right).

Servius Sulpicius was the most distinguished authority on law in Cicero's time. (Compare what Cicero says about him in the last of our selections, *Philippic* IX.) When Sulpicius was defeated in the elections held late in 63 B.C. for public offices in 62, he brought suit, charging that his opponent Murena had won by illegal means. Sulpicius was seconded, in his prosecution, by Marcus Porcius Cato "the Younger," a man famous, as Sallust tells us, for his rigid ethical principles, one who was felt to personify in his habits of life the incorruptible rectitude of the Stoic philosophy—an admirable gentleman, perhaps, but scarcely a lovable character. It may be recalled that Cato was given the cognomen "Uticensis" because he committed suicide at Utica in North Africa in 46 B.C. rather than give up his allegiance to the old Republic and give in to Caesar.

In defending Murena, Cicero undertook a task of some personal delicacy, for he naturally did not wish to offend either Sulpicius or Cato; and the speech as a whole is a masterly job of tactful verbal maneuvering and evasion of the actual issue, whether Murena was really guilty of bribery or not. (He was acquitted.) One of the best parts of the speech is the one we read here, where Cicero, in order to show that Murena, though not a lawyer, was worthy of the consulship, makes fun of lawyers in such a way as to make it impossible for Sulpicius to show any resentment, no matter how annoyed he may have been. And at the same time Cicero manages to make the gentleman learned in the law seem completely inferior to the warrior skilled at arms. But after reading this speech, we should turn to our final selection from Cicero's addresses to read his last words on his old friend Sulpicius.

NOTE: In addition to the difficulty of following any legal procedure, the layman will have added difficulty in following Roman procedure because of the visual ritualism involved. Since Roman law had reached an advanced stage of development before literacy and the keeping of records became general, it was felt necessary to resort to many devices which would enable witnesses to see and remember what was being done. For example, if you had seen a Roman being attacked in the street by someone and he wished to call you as a witness in a suit for assault and battery, he would reach out and give your ear a gentle tug. This would mean that he was laying claim to what you had heard (and by inference, seen), and by tugging your ear, he makes the whole procedure vivid and memorable. Likewise, today when the groom, in the marriage ceremony, slips the ring over the bride's finger and says "With this ring I thee wed," he is performing a vivid and memorable act in the presence of witnesses who will remember the ceremony independent of any written documents. In the procedure ridiculed by Cicero in the selection here, a piece of sod from the farm in question has actually been brought into court, and the hearing involves the pretense of leaving the court and going out to the farm where the action fictitiously takes place. What makes the whole thing so silly, Cicero suggests, is that the sod—representing the farm—is in court all the time, and nobody really goes anywhere. We might add that the court is not a hall or a building, but, according to the Roman saying, wherever the *praetor* is, there is the court.

### The Law vs. the Army as a profession

*19* The discussion now involves the remaining period of time up to the present; it was employed by the two of them in entirely different ways. Our Servius went in for civilian duty here in the city along with me, giving expert legal opinions, drawing up legal instruments, looking out for clients' interests—work full of worry and irritation; he has learned the civil law, he has worked long hours at night, he has assisted in many suits, he has put up with the stupidity of many, he has suffered from their highhandedness, he has swallowed their stubbornness, he has lived to suit the convenience of others, not his own. It is a very praiseworthy thing, and appreciated by everyone, that one man should work so hard at such a science as is helpful to so many.

*20* In the meantime, what was Murena doing? He was a staff officer with the gallant and brilliant Lucius Lucullus, a commander of consummate ability; and as a staff officer, he had charge of an army, gave combat orders, took part in hand-to-hand fighting, defeating substantial elements of the enemy forces, took cities—some by frontal attack, some by siege; he passed through Asia Minor, that wealthy and likewise luxurious country, without leaving a trace of graft or high living; and his experiences in a very bitterly fought war were such that he directed many momentous actions without his commander-in-chief, and his commander-in-chief none without him. And what is more, even though I am speaking in the presence of Lucius Lucullus himself, at the same time, to avoid seeming with his permission to make free with the facts, I may say that everything I have mentioned is supported by official communiqués in which Lucius Lucullus gives all the credit that a commander who is neither self-seeking nor jealous was bound to accord to another in sharing the glory.

*21* Murena and Servius are both men of the highest standing, both very important persons, to whom I, with Servius' permission, should like to grant the same and equal honor. But I do not have Servius' permission; he scoffs at military

life, he attacks the entire staff officers' system, he thinks that the consulship is the prerogative of this routine work and these everyday jobs. "So you were in the army, were you?" he says. "So you never came near the Forum all these years? So you were out of town all this time, and when you do turn up after a long absence like that, you think, do you, that you can run for the consulship against men who have practically lived in the Forum?"

First of all, about that routine work of ours, Servius: you have no idea how tired of us men can become, how fed up they can get. In my own case, I may say that always being on exhibition has greatly increased my personal popularity, but at the same time, when people were fed up with me, it took great personal efforts on my part to overcome their feelings. And perhaps this applies to you, too. It might have done neither of us any harm to have been missed, at that.

*22* But let that pass. Let us get back to our comparison between pursuits and professions. How can you doubt that in reaching the consulate, military distinction brings much more honor than that of the legal profession? You stay up late at night so that you can give an opinion to those who consult you; he does it so that he can arrive at a military objective with his army at the strategic moment; the crow of the cock gets you up in the morning, the blare of the bugle gets him up; you draw up a legal line, he draws up a battle line; you see that your clients are not taken in, he sees that towns and camps are not taken; he knows and understands how the enemies' forces may be kept out, you do the same with rain water from your neighbor's drains and spouts. He is experienced in extending boundary lines, you in locating them. And—why argue about it? I must say what I think—the excellence of military achievement outweighs all others. This is what established the name of the Roman people, this is what brought everlasting fame to this city, this is what has forced the entire world to acknowledge our dominion. All our affairs at home, all these fine pursuits of ours, the applause and hard work here in the Forum, are watched and guarded by the military virtues. As soon as there is a whispered suspicion of trouble, our peaceful arts at once are stilled.

*23* But since you seem to me to be fondling that legal science of yours like a darling daughter,

I am not going to let you labor any longer under a delusion like that—the feeling that what you have come to love so ardently is something important and distinguished. I have always considered you worthy of the consulship and every other office because of your other qualities, self-restraint, solidity of character, sense of justice, sense of honor, and all that; but I shall say this—there is no superhighway to the consulship in that profession of yours. That is, all the pursuits which endear us to the Roman people necessarily possess some praiseworthy claims to merit and popular utility.

24 The greatest public honors go to those who are noted for their military achievements; everything, as you know, relating to our government and the permanence of the state is believed to be strengthened and defended by these men. Again, it is of the greatest service for us to be able to reap the fruits of their good counsel or the risks they take, in our private lives as well as in public affairs.

Again, it carries great weight and is laden with honor, that ability to speak well, and it has often turned the scales in the election of a consul—to be able, with word and thought, to sway the minds of the Senate and the people, and those who sit on the judgment bench. It is a question of finding a consul who may, on occasion, by the sheer power of words, put a radical tribune in his place, who may divert an excited mob from its course, who may stand up against a proposed handout to the people. This is not surprising when you consider that because of this power men who were not of noble birth have often risen to the consulate, especially when this same gift brings with it many feelings of gratitude, lifelong friendships, great enthusiasms. Of all of these, there is nothing in that skilled trade of yours, Sulpicius.

*The pettiness of the legal profession*

25 In the first place, there can be no distinction in such a petty profession: its basic material is small-scale, preoccupied as it is almost with individual letters of the alphabet and punctuation marks. And then, even if there used to be a certain amount of respect for your pursuit among our forefathers, since your mysterious professional secrets were published, it lost its lofty position and is now looked down on. Whether

an action at law could begin or not, at one time few men knew; the public did not have a list of the days on which the courts could sit; a great deal of power lay in the hands of those who were consulted for legal opinions on points of procedure; people asked them to name good days, just as if they were astrologers. A certain Gnaeus Flavius turned up [304 B.C.], a secretary, who got busier than a bee, so that people could learn the business days and the holy days by heart, and swiped the wisdom of the jurisconsults from these very cagey fellows themselves. And so the lawyers, who were furious, and were afraid that when the schedule of business days and holy days was published and mastered, people could go to law without their help, made up certain rigmaroles so that they would have a finger in every pie, too.

26 Of course a suit could have been handled very nicely like this: A man says, "The farm in the Sabine country is mine." "No, it's mine," says the other man. Then comes the decision of the court. The legal experts would have none of it. "The aforesaid farm," says the legal expert, "which is in the territory called Sabine . . ." Wordy enough; but look here. What comes next? "I hereby affirm and declare on the basis of the common law of Roman citizens that it is mine." And then what? "From that place there [gesture indicating where the other litigant stands] I summon you out of this court to engage in an action-at-law for possession." The man who was being sued for the property had nothing to say himself in answer to such a wordy and contentious opponent. Then the same professor of law switches over from one actor to another in the manner of a Latin flute-player on the stage. "From that place there where you stand [gesture] from which you summoned me for an action-at-law for possession, I in turn summon you out of this court to the aforesaid farm."

In the meantime, just so the judge won't think he's a fine lucky fellow himself and able to say something *he* thought up, a song and dance has been made up for him, too. And while it is silly all the way through, it is at its worst in this phrase: "To them and to the witnesses on both sides being here present and alive, I hereby declare and point out that way there [gesture]: go your way to the farm." That legal genius of ours was right there to show them which way to go. "Come your way back from the farm." They came back with the same guide. This used to sound foolish, I imagine, even back in the days of our bearded ancestors—that human beings, when they had duly taken their stand in the proper place, should be told to go away and then immediately be told to come back to the very same place from which they had started. Everything that follows is shot through with the same kind of foolishness. "Whereas I spy you in court," and this one: "Do you, the plaintiff, hereby declare due cause for your claiming title to this property?"

As long as this nonsense was a professional secret, people used to look up to those who had it in their keeping; however, once the secrets were made public and passed around from hand to hand and looked into carefully, people found that there was absolutely no sense to them, that actually they were full of foolishness and double-talk. *27* That is, while a great many splendid principles have been laid down by the laws,[9] they have been largely distorted and perverted by the misplaced ingenuity of the lawyers.

Our forefathers decided that all women, because of the infirmity of their judgment, should be subject to the power of a guardian. These lawyers invented classes of guardians who would be subject to women. Our forefathers did not wish forms of family worship to disappear; by the genius of these lawyers, old men were forced to go through fictitious marriages to get rid of these rites.[10] In a word, they kept to the letter but left out the spirit of justice from the entire common law, so that simply because in somebody's law book they had found this name "Gaia" [equivalent to "Jane Doe"] used as a specimen, they thought that all women who go through a fictitious marriage are called "Gaia." Moreover, the following has always seemed remarkable to me: that so many human beings, such clever fellows, have never been able to decide, after so many years, whether the right phrase is "the day after tomorrow," or "the third day," whether "judge" or "arbitrator," "case" or "suit." *28* And so, as I said, there never has been any distinction, much less popularity, worthy of the office of consul in that profession which is made up entirely out of imagination and fictions. I mean that this business that is available to all and equally at the disposal of myself and my opponent Sulpicius—it cannot have popular appeal under any condition. And so you have now

lost not only the prospect of passing out favors as a political investment, but even that privilege which you enjoyed at one time—"May I call upon you as a consultant?"

No one can be considered wise in that form of wisdom that has no standing at all anywhere outside of Rome, and none in Rome when the courts are not in session. For the same reason, no lawyer can be considered an expert, because they all disagree with one another about something they all know. What is more, the law can't be considered difficult, for the reason that it is embodied in a few not very obscure writings. And so, if you make me get mad—I'm *such* a busy man—the day after tomorrow I'll hang out my shingle as a lawyer. I mean by that: in the case of actions at law which are instituted on the basis of written formulas, all the formulas have been put in writing; and yet there is nothing so strictly worded that I couldn't add, "As to the case in question . . ." [thus making the formula applicable to the case in hand]. Moreover, the questions about which advice is sought may be answered at very little risk. If a man gives the right answer, he will appear to have given the same advice as Servius Sulpicius; but if he gives a different answer, people will think that he is an authority on disputed points of law and that he makes a specialty of them.

### The trial lawyer vs. the "paper-work" lawyer

*29* For these reasons, not only is the military glory I have mentioned far ahead of your legal formulas and actions-at-law, but the practice of pleading is far superior to that occupation of yours when it is a matter of winning public office. And so I think a great many men at first much preferred pleading, but when they could not make a success of it, they fell back upon that pursuit of yours in particular. Just as among Greek musicians, so they say, those who can't succeed as harpists become flute-players, so we see here in Rome that those who can't graduate as pleaders take refuge in the study of law. Public speaking involves immense work, immense profit, immense distinction, and immense popularity too. That is, people come to you, so to speak, for the preservation of their health, while from pleaders they seek the salvation of their very lives. What is more, your considered opinions and decisions are often upset by a good speech, and without the defense of a speaker they cannot be made to stand. If I had attained any reasonable degree of proficiency in the field of public pleading myself, I should speak about its merits more sparingly; I am not referring to myself at all now, but to those who have been or are now distinguished speakers.

*But for political life the army is the best preparation.*

30 There are just two professions that can put men in the highest grades of public esteem: one is the general's, the other is the pleader's, because by one the blessings of peace are preserved, by the other, the perils of war are repelled. At that, other qualities count for a good deal in themselves, justice, integrity, a sense of right and wrong, a sense of restraint and moderation—and in those qualities, Servius, everyone knows that you stand very high. But right now I am talking about pursuits that have to do with public office, not about this or that man's good personal qualities. All those pursuits are dropped the instant some new disturbance sounds the call to arms. In other words, as a gifted poet [Ennius] and a very good authority says, "Once wars are declared, there is driven from our midst" not only that wordy imitation of wisdom of you lawyers, but even the mistress of civil life, "philosophy; action is ruled by force, the pleader is pushed aside"—not only the pleader who is a tedious speaker, and long-winded, but even "the good ones; the unshaven soldier is loved"—but, as for your profession, it is kept out in the cold. "Not out of the court to engage in an action at law," says the poet, "no, they seek redress by cold steel."

If this is so, Sulpicius, I think the courts should give way to the barracks, the peace and quiet of civil life to military service, the pen to the sword, the shady places where we chat to the hot sun; in a word, let that pursuit be foremost for which our city is foremost in the world.

[The passage translated above represents about one seventh of the entire speech. In the remainder, Cicero gives an independent account of his proceedings in the conspiracy of Catiline (secs. 50–52); chaffs Cato for his Stoicism (60–62); touches upon the actual charge of bribery on which the whole case turns (54–83); and in his peroration (83–90) exhorts the jury to consider the good of the state, and be merciful.]

## IN DEFENSE OF CAELIUS

Marcus Caelius Rufus, friend of Cicero, was one of the many able and sometimes brilliant young men-about-Rome whose careers, in the dying years of the Republic, were symptomatic of the unhealthy state of society and politics. Careers in the service of the state, which had promised active and useful lives to young men of the office-holding families in the good old days, were no longer open to those who were unwilling to act merely as agents of the "Big Three"—Pompey, Crassus, and Caesar. There were too many young men with wealth, talent, and nothing important to do. Consequently they tended to devote their energies and talents to a great many things that were supremely unimportant, judged by the standards of a healthier society.

This background of restlessness and frustration is reflected, in many of its aspects, in the poems of Catullus. In his famous first address to Lesbia, he turns, in a revulsion of feeling, from the praises of his beloved, to a final stanza which elaborates the theme of *Otium, Catulle, tibi molestum est*—"to live in idleness, Catullus, is a bad thing for you. . . ." Curiously enough, if, as we generally believe today, Lesbia was actually Clodia, sister of Publius Clodius Pulcher, then it is equally possible that the man who displaced Catullus in Clodia's affections was Caelius Rufus, in whose defense Cicero is acting in the address we read here. Clodius and Clodia were both bitter personal enemies of Cicero; and Cicero on more than one occasion paid his respects to Clodia in terms that were sharp, witty, and sometimes unprintable.

Caelius, in his turn, came to a parting of the ways with Lesbia, with results that are the occasion of Cicero's address here. In April, 56 B.C., Clodia, through her representatives, accused Caelius of having tried to poison her and of having failed to return a considerable sum of money that she had given him (in order, as it turned out, to contrive the assassination of an Egyptian ambassador named Dio). The scene of the alleged crimes was Baiae, a favorite pleasure-resort of the Romans by the sea not far from Naples. How the Roman upper set conducted itself there may be inferred from Cicero's speech. The prosecution was formally initiated by an otherwise unimportant and gullible young man, Sempronius Atratinus, supported by other prominent Roman *oratores*. In prosecuting Caelius, however, Clodia made a bad mistake, since she gave

Caelius, and Cicero who acted for him, an opportunity to deal with her as few women have been dealt with in a court of law. (We should remember that the rules of procedure were very loose in comparison with Anglo-American courts where, under a careful judge, Cicero would have been required to confine himself to the question of whether Caelius did or did not try to poison Clodia and did or did not embezzle money from her.)

In the prosecution, much was made of Caelius' character and morals; and in this connection Cicero was at somewhat of a disadvantage, for Caelius was far from being a lily-white character. Notice in the translation how Cicero deals with this aspect of the prosecution. His skill had the usual result; his client was acquitted, and like Sestius, later went over to Caesar, but not for long; he soon joined Milo against him, and died in 48 B.C., in battle against Caesar's army.

*Introduction: there is something fishy about this case.*

*1* Gentlemen of the jury: if there should happen to be any person now present who is unfamiliar with our laws, our courts and our procedures, he would certainly wonder what is so frightfully important about this present case, because at a time of holidays and free shows, when all public business is suspended, this trial is the only one going on; and he would have no doubt that the defendant is accused of such a horrible crime that the state will collapse if it goes unpunished.

In the same way, when he heard that there is a law requiring an official court investigation, on any day at all, into the cases of radicals who belong to subversive organizations, who picket the Senate under arms, assault the magistrates, and attack the Constitution, he would not disapprove of the law; he would ask what the charge was before the court. When he heard that no overt act, no deliberate provocation, no breach of the peace, was up before the court, but that a young man of brilliant mind, hard-working, popular, was being prosecuted by the son of a man whom he is summoning and has summoned into court himself—and what is worse, that the attack on the young man was being backed by the wealth of a woman of decidedly loose morals—our surprised friend would not criticize the loyalty of Atratinus himself to his father; he *would* conclude that the woman's passions ought to be cooled off, he *would* consider, gentlemen of the jury, that you are overworked if you cannot take time off even when everyone else is having a vacation.

*2* Well then, if you are willing to listen carefully and form a true conclusion about this case as a whole, you will come to this decision, gentlemen: no one would have been likely to come downtown to prosecute this case if he had any choice in the matter, and when he had come downtown, he would not have entertained any hope of success unless he were backed by somebody's unendurable passion and overbitter hatred. But personally I do not blame Atratinus, a fine young man of broad interests, a close associate of mine, who can be excused on the grounds of loyalty to his father, or, if you like, necessity or mere youthfulness. If it was his own wish to prosecute, I attribute it to loyalty; if he was told to prosecute, I attribute it to necessity; if he had any hopes of succeeding, I attribute it to his adolescence. As for the others who are involved, they have no excuse whatsoever; in fact, they deserve the most vigorous kind of opposition.

*Cicero answers misrepresentations of his client's character.*

*3* And so far as I am concerned, gentlemen of the jury, this seems to be the best way of introducing the defense of young Marcus Caelius here: for me to reply first to the statements made by the prosecution with a view to misrepresenting my client's character and for the sake of undermining or wrecking his reputation. His father has been used against him in various ways; they say that either he was not a very glamorous figure himself or that he has not been treated very becomingly by his son. So far as Marcus Caelius' standing is concerned among his acquaintances and elders, he can easily answer all charges against it without saying a word—even without a speech from me. Next, as for those older men who, on account of their advanced age, do not know him so well, because for some time they have been taking less part with the rest of us in the activities of the Forum, let them be assured of this: whatever distinction may be attached to a member of the business and financial class in Rome, which surely can be very great, Marcus Caelius has always enjoyed and today enjoys it in the highest degree, not only on the part of his own associates, but also with everyone who may have had some real reason for being acquainted with him. *4* Moreover, being the son of a member of the financial order [the "knights"] should not be entered on the books as a charge against him by the prosecution—not when these gentlemen are jurors and not when I am acting for the defense.

Next, as for what you said about his loyalty to his father: there is, naturally, my personal opinion, but there is assuredly the judgment of his parent. What my opinions are, you will hear from the witnesses; what his parents feel about him, the tears of his mother make plain—and her unbelievable dejection, the garb of mourning worn by his father and this ever-present air of grief of which you are aware, and the atmosphere of mourning.

*5* Next, as for the point that the young man is not esteemed by his fellow-townsmen: no higher honors were ever conferred upon anyone, gentlemen, than upon Marcus Caelius in his absence: they made him a member of their municipal senate when he was out of town, and although he was not a candidate in person, they bestowed upon him rank that they had refused to many who *were* candidates. And to match this, they have now sent carefully selected representatives both of senatorial rank and members of the Roman business class to accompany a delegation to this court with complimentary remarks about Caelius, impressive and gracious.

I think I have laid down the basis upon which I shall conduct the defense; it is absolutely unshakable if founded upon the deliberate judgment of his own people. That is, the character of my youthful client could not possibly be established firmly enough to satisfy you members of the jury if he did not find favor with his father, such a fine gentleman, to say nothing of his home town, so well known and so respected. *6* As a matter of fact, to return to myself, from a small town like this I also started out and gained fame among men; and the story of my hard work here in the Forum and my plan of life has worked its way into the esteem of men somewhat more widely than the good wishes and approval of my fellow townsmen could secure. . . .

[Here Cicero reviews one by one the specific charges made against Caelius' character, including his close relationship with Catiline in the period immediately preceding the conspiracy of 63 B.C. Cicero deals with this in the same way as

he is forced to deal with most of the charges against Caelius: a great many young men did the same things or behaved in the same way, he says, and condemnations of Caelius in these respects are simply condemnations of the follies of youth in general and not of one man. We return to the translation at the point where he turns to another of the prosecutors, Herennius, and dismisses him largely through the use of ridicule. Turning next to another prosecutor, Balbus, Cicero reverts to the general misconduct of young men through which he leads naturally to a personal attack of his own on Clodia. Throughout, and especially when he deals with Clodia, one has the impression that Cicero is thoroughly enjoying himself.]

*The prosecution takes an overpuritanical view of my client.*

*25* Now I noticed, gentlemen of the jury, that you listened very attentively to my good friend, Lucius Herennius. While you were held in large part by his display of brains and by his particular style of speaking, there were still times when I was afraid that his address, so subtly developed in the direction of incriminating my client, might gradually and step by step make an impression upon your minds. You recall that he said a great deal about high living, about the sexual conduct, a lot about the frailties of youth, a lot about habits and morals; and although he is the kind of a man who is gentle in his way of life as a whole, and accustomed to engaging very pleasantly in that kind of sweet humanitarianism which almost everyone by this time enjoys, in this trial he wore a very long face, he acted like a kind of paternal uncle, a guardian of morals, a schoolmaster; he scolded Marcus Caelius as no parent ever scolded a son; he delivered a long lecture on incontinence and intemperance.

Need I say any more, gentlemen? I felt forgiving toward you for listening so attentively especially because I personally was in a shiver over that cold and frozen oratory of his. *26* And first was the part that moved me least, where he said that Caelius was a close friend of my client Bestia, that he had dined at Bestia's house, paid regular visits to his house, was supporting his candidacy for the praetorship. I am not disturbed by things that are obviously not true; that is, he said that certain persons had dinner together who either are not in court or are forced to tell the same story. No, and I'm not shocked, either, by his charge that Caelius was a fraternity brother of his in the Lupercalia, a primitive fraternity, quite obviously of pastoral and rustic origin, of the brothers of the Luperci, whose well-known woodland rendezvous was instituted before laws and civilization, inasmuch as they not only, as fraternity brothers, lodge indictments against one another but even make references to the fraternity in speeches for the prosecution, so that people will think that they are afraid that anybody may not know all this!

27 But let it go; I am answering the charges that have alarmed me more.

There was a long-winded lecture on the subject of fancy living, milder than ever, with more argument than roughage in it—and consequently listened to more attentively. This reminds me of Publius Clodius—my *friend!*—when he orated in such a vigorous and forceful manner at the top of his voice, full of fire, viewing every subject with alarm. Even though I used to think highly of his flow of words, still I was never afraid of him. You see, I had seen him lose out when he tried to sue in a good many cases.

*Sowing of wild oats does not last forever.*

Now, Balbus, I am answering you first—with your kind permission—if I may, if it is proper for me to defend a man who never said "no" to an invitation to dinner, who has sported in the gardens, who has helped himself to the perfume, who has seen Baiae. 28 Well, to be truthful, I have seen and I have heard of a good many persons in Rome who not only took a sip of this kind of life and touched it, so to speak, with their finger-tips, but even gave their youthful years completely over to gay living, but sooner or later they came out of it and became "solid citizens," and were serious and well-known men. In other words, everyone concedes a certain amount of fun to this period in life, and nature herself is generous with the desires of youth. If only these desires break out in such a way that they do not ruin anyone's life, do not break up anyone's home, they are usually viewed good-naturedly and tolerantly. 29 But you seemed to me to want to fan up a certain amount of prejudice against Caelius by exploiting the bad name that is attached to young men in general. And so all that silence with which

your remarks were greeted was due to this: we were thinking of the weaknesses of many when only one defendant was under discussion. It is easy to make a charge of extravagant living. The day would soon fail me if I were to try to bring out all that I could say on that point: a speech on seduction, adultery, the insolence of youth, prodigality, has boundless possibilities. Allowing that you place before us no particular defendant, but simply faults of that kind in general, the charge can be made with considerable weight and at considerable length.

But it is up to you and your good sense, gentlemen, not to be sidetracked from the defendant, and not to apply to Caelius as a man and as the defendant those stings with which your sense of responsibility and your sternness are armed—since it is against a fact of life, the faults, the morals of the times that the prosecutor has whetted them, since Caelius is unfairly being made the victim of a certain amount of prejudice based not upon the specific charge against him but upon the faults of many. 30 And so I do not venture personally to reply to your strait-laced remarks as I should. That is, it would be my privilege to make excuses for the lapses of youth and to ask that they be pardoned. No, I say, I do not venture to do that; I am not falling back on the excuses owed to youth; I put aside all the rights granted to young men. I ask only for this: if there is any general prejudice at this time of life attached to huge debts, to rebellious attitudes, to the passions of youth—and I see that this prejudice is very considerable—still I beg that the offenses of others, the faults of youth and these times, may not be allowed to harm my client. And at the same time I, who make this request—I do not refuse to make the most careful reply to the charges which are assembled exclusively against my client here.

*The charges against Caelius: embezzlement and poisoning*

Now there are two charges: one relates to money, the other to poison. In both charges the one and the same person is involved. The money was procured from Clodia, the poison was procured to give to Clodia, as is said. All the other matters are libels, not charges—more fit for a mud-slinging match than for a public enquiry. "Adulterer, rotter, embezzler" is name-calling, not prosecuting at law. That is, there is no basis for these charges, no foundation; these are empty words uttered by an angry and irresponsible prosecutor. *31* Of these two other charges I see the author, I see the source, I see a very definite name and person. Money was needed; he got it from Clodia, he got it without a witness, he had it as long as he wanted. I see the characteristic mark of a certain notorious friendship. He also wished to murder her; he hunted up poison, he tampered with her slaves, he got the dose ready, he named the place, he bought the poison on the quiet. Again, I see violent hate arisen, with a very bitter breaking-up of friendship. In this case, gentlemen, we have to deal exclusively with Clodia, a woman who is not only notable but notorious—a woman about whom I would say nothing if it were not a matter of defense against a criminal charge. *32* But you are aware, Gnaeus Domitius [11]—you are a man of exceptional good sense—that our business is with this woman only. If she did not say that she had lent Caelius money, if she did not claim that he had prepared to poison her, we are simply bad-mannered if we introduce into this case the mistress of a household in any way other than that which the sanctity of married women requires. But if we leave that female out of the picture and have left no charge, no resources left to the prosecutors of Marcus Caelius, what is our duty as counsel for the defense other than to fight back at those who are hounding him? And of course, I would do this with plenty of vigor, if I were not hampered by my feud with that female's boy-friend— her brother, I had an impulse to say; I always make a mistake here. Now I am going to proceed with considerable restraint, and I will not go any farther than my regard for truth and the case itself compel me to. And, naturally, I have never felt that I should engage in hostilities with women, certainly not with the woman all the men have regarded as every man's woman rather than any man's enemy.

*Cicero addresses Clodia in a parody of the old-fashioned manner.*

*33* But first, I would still like to ask her whether she would like me to deal with her sternly and severely in the good old-fashioned way, or whether she would like me to be easy-going and

gentle and polite. If she likes that old-fashioned austerity in the good old-fashioned way, I shall have to rouse up from the shades one of those characters with real whiskers—not with one of these cute little goatees that she is so crazy about, but the shaggy type that we see on old statues and portrait busts—to give the woman a good talking-to and do my talking for me so she won't, by any chance, get angry with me. Well, suppose some member of her own family rises from the dead—preferably the famous Appius Claudius Caecus ["the Blind"]; naturally, he's the one who'll feel least pain—he won't be able to see her. If he does rise from the dead, he'll certainly deal with her and speak to her along this line:

"Woman, what business have you with Caelius? What business have you with a mere youngster? With one not a kinsman? Why were you so friendly with him that you lent him money? Why so unfriendly that you were afraid he would poison you? Hadn't you seen your father a consul? Hadn't you heard that your father's brother, your grandfather, your great-grandfather, your great-great-grandfather, [your forefathers], were consuls?

*34* "And lastly, didn't you know that you were, until recently, the wife of Quintus Metellus, a highly distinguished citizen, a fine soldier, a great patriot, who, the moment he set foot outside his doorway, outranked almost every other citizen in character, reputation, and distinction? When you came from such fine old stock and had married into such a distinguished family, why this affair with Caelius? Was he a relative of your husband's by blood or by marriage, a close friend of your husband? No, none of these. Then what was this, unless it was irresponsible passion?

"If the portraits of your male ancestors had no influence on you, did not even my daughter, the illustrious Quinta Claudia, remind you to be her rival for domestic honors in the glory of womanhood? Did not the famous Vestal Virgin, Claudia, remind you, who would not allow herself to be dragged from the chariot by a hostile tribune of the people, as she embraced her father riding in his triumph?

"Why did your brother's vices influence you, instead of your father's and your grandfather's virtues, traced as far back as my time—not only on the men's side but also on the women's side of the family? Did I myself squeeze a treaty of peace out of Pyrrhus so that you could day by day make pacts for your shameful affairs, did I build an aqueduct so you could enjoy it in unchastity, did I pave a highway [the Appian Way] so that you could revel along it in the company of other women's husbands?"

*Cicero pierces Clodia with the shafts of his own wit.*

35 But, gentlemen, why have I brought in a person of such authority that he makes me afraid that he, Appius, may suddenly turn the tables on me and begin to accuse Caelius with that well-known censorial dignity of his? But I shall take care of that a little later, and in such a way, gentlemen, that I am sure that I can give Marcus Caelius' private life a clean bill of health in the face of the most strait-laced critics. But as for you, madame—you see, I am now speaking to you myself with no third person brought in—if you think to make good what you do, what you say, what you insinuate, what you plot, what you contend, you have to render an accounting of, and explain the why and wherefore of, such close associations, such constant companionship, such intimate relationships. The speakers for the prosecution, needless to say, toss around references to sexual abnormalities, infatuations, adulteries, night clubs, beach resorts, dinner parties, cocktail parties, song fests, chamber music, boating parties; and at the same time they indicate that they have no objection to your making these references. Since you chose to bring these matters down into the Forum and place them before the court—in what thoughtless and impetuous frame of mind, I have no idea—you should either explain them away and show them to be falsified, or admit that neither your charges nor your evidence is worth believing. 36 If, on the other hand you wish me to treat you a little more politely, this is what I'll do. I'll get rid of that old man who is almost a village character in his harshness. I'll take someone from the group right here—preferably your little brother [Clodius], who is the most citified member of the family. He loves you very much. Because of some phobia or other, I imagine, and certain groundless fears of the dark, he always used to go to bed with you, like a little shaver with his big sister. Imagine what he says to you:

"Why are you so upset, sister? Why are you so beside yourself?
Why do you raise an outcry and make a mountain out of a molehill?" [12]

You glimpsed a nice young fellow next door; he had *such* a nice complexion and was *so* tall, and his face and his eyes intrigued you; you wanted to see him oftener; you were at the same garden parties with him quite often; you are a woman of noble birth and you want to ensnare with your powers that son of a family with a frugal and economical father. You can't do it. He kicks, scorns, repels you; he doesn't think your gifts are worth *that* much. On your way to someone else! You have a garden by the Tiber, equipped with every convenience, at the spot where all the boys come for a swim; here you are at liberty to make dates every day. Why do you keep bothering this chap who turns you down flat?

[After further attempts to minimize the charges against Caelius' morals, Cicero sums up the argument.]

*Clodia is so immoral that it is hard for a man in her company to be considered the guilty one.*

48 But if there is anyone who thinks that young men ought to be forbidden to have relations even with women of easy virtue, he is certainly strait-laced—I cannot deny it; but such thinking is out of step not only with the freedom of this generation but also with the traditions of our forefathers and what they allowed. That is, when has this not been a regular thing, when has it been reprimanded, when has it not been allowed—in short, when was it that the unpermissible has not been permitted?

At this point I shall state the case clearly, naming no woman, simply leaving the thing open. 49 If some unmarried woman opens her home for the passion of all who may present themselves, and if she openly sets herself up in that kind of business, makes arrangements for parties with men who are no relation to her at all, if she does this in Rome, in the gardens, in Baiae, with large crowds in attendance, if, in general, she plays that kind of a role not only in the way she carries herself, but in her dress and those who walk with her, not only in the glances she throws and her loose talk, but also in hugging, kissing, beach parties, boat parties, dinners, so that she appears not only to be a hussy, but a bold and brazen hussy at that . . . If some young fellow happened to be in this woman's company, which do you think he would be, Lucius Herennius—an adulterer or a customer? Would it be his desire to take her chastity by storm or to satisfy his passion? *50* Now I am ignoring the wrongs you have done, Clodia; I am putting aside my own painful recollections: I am passing over the cruel things you have done to my friends when I was not there to protect them; let not what I have said be said about you. But I am putting this question directly to you, since the speakers for the prosecution say they received the charge from you and have you as a witness to the charge: if there were a woman of the kind that I have just described, entirely unlike you, in her way of life and by her principles a woman who sold her favors, do you not think that it would be very disgraceful and very shocking for a young man to have done a bit of business with her? If you are not that kind of a woman, and I should prefer that you were not, what is there for the prosecutors to bring up against Caelius? And if, on the contrary, the prosecutors would have you be that kind of woman, why should we for the defense have any fears of this charge—if you despise her? On this basis, give us a means of approach and a basis for the defense. That is, either your sense of decency will allow us the defense that nothing with intent to injure was done by Marcus Caelius, or else your lack of decency will give both Caelius and the rest a very ample opportunity to defend themselves.

[Sections 51–55 of the speech dismiss the charge of embezzling; secs. 56–69, the charge of poisoning. Then, in a long peroration (70–80), Cicero reviews his client's career, stating that he has been the victim of a good law perverted by a bad woman; that he will soon come to the end of sowing his wild oats and settle down as a respectable member of the party of "good" men. Finally, the orator points, in the most hoary of rhetorical clichés, to the pathetic figure of his client's aged father, and asks that Caelius be acquitted for his sake. The jury swallowed the bait, and the wily Cicero, by again evading the issues and playing upon prejudice, racked up another victory.]

# IN DEFENSE OF MILO

Publius Clodius (or Claudius) Pulcher, a Roman politician both prominent and notorious, was killed in a fight on the Appian Way not far south of Rome in January, 52 B.C. So far as we can determine from the accounts which have survived, Clodius, with his personal bodyguard of about thirty slaves, was attacked by a much larger gang led by his rival Titus Annius Milo. The death of Clodius caused a political uproar. Pompey [the Great] proposed and carried a law through the Senate providing that Milo should be tried by a special court with a "blue-ribbon" jury hand-picked by Pompey. This was, of course, a deviation from time-honored procedures regularly established for trying cases of conspiracy and homicide, and Cicero, as we shall see, took exception to it in his address to the jury. But the irregularity was indicative of the high state of tension in Roman politics at the time; and Pompey was probably right in his decision that the normal processes of law could not in this instance be operated in an orderly fashion.

So great was the tension, in fact, that when it came to his turn to address the court, Cicero was unable to speak with his usual composure. What we read here is unquestionably a version of the address written after the event as an example of what Cicero wished he *had* said. The opening sentences, from this point of view, seem to be an apology, or at least an explanation, of why, on the actual occasion, he had done rather badly. This was one case that Cicero lost. His client Milo was condemned; and as a result Milo was forced to leave Roman territory. He took up his residence at Massilia (now Marseilles), then a pleasant Greek city. There he is said to have remarked dryly that it was a good thing that Cicero had not delivered the speech in the revised and published form; otherwise he (Milo) would never have been able to enjoy the excellent Massilian sea food.

The murder of Clodius was the climax of a story going back a good many years—a story involving Cicero in curious ways, as well as involving the whole tangled web of personalities in Roman politics at this time. Clodius from his earliest years had shown a marked aptitude for rascality in a period when private and public rascality tended to reach the level of an art. But late in the year 62 B.C. Clodius achieved a degree of virtuosity that was unique even in Roman society.

One of the oldest and most solemn religious observances among Roman ladies of high station was that of

Fauna, the Bona Dea—the Good Goddess—a divinity entirely feminine, associated with purity and chastity. The rites were held once a year, for Ladies Only. All men were barred from the house, and even pictures of men were modestly curtained over, presumably to keep them from peeking. The ceremony for 62 B.C. was to be held at the home of Julius Caesar, with his wife, of course, acting as hostess. In a prankish and perhaps curious mood, Clodius dressed up as a woman and with the connivance of a maidservant managed to make his way into the house. His voice, however, gave him away; and in the confusion attendant upon discovery, Clodius was able to get out of the house at—one infers—a high rate of speed. The sequel, naturally, was as fascinating a scandal as Rome had enjoyed for a long time. It led, incidentally, to Caesar's divorcing his wife with the oft-quoted remark that "Caesar's wife must be above suspicion."

Clodius was elected one of the quaestors for 61 B.C., and presently his enemies, eager for an opportunity to make political capital, managed to impeach him for an act of impiety. When the case came to trial, Clodius' defense rested on the point that he couldn't possibly have been recognized at the festival of the Bona Dea because he was out of town at the time—at Interamna, in fact, about 50 miles away. Unfortunately for his future peace of mind, Cicero punctured the alibi by testifying that he had seen Clodius in Rome about three hours before the time when he claimed to have been in Interamna—conclusive proof, in view of the speed of travel in those days. Although his alibi had been destroyed by unimpeachable testimony, Clodius managed to gain an acquittal by bribing and intimidating the jury. From this time forward, Clodius' passionate desire to "get" Cicero was checked only by Caesar's control of Clodius and his use of Clodius to threaten Cicero into a cooperative mood. When Cicero refused to work with Caesar, Crassus, and Pompey in the political deal that was made between the three in 59 B.C., Caesar gave Clodius his way, with the result that in 58 B.C. Cicero was forced to go into exile. Clodius secured the enactment of laws confirming Cicero's banishment (for having executed Roman citizens without due process of law in mopping up the Catilinarian conspiracy in 63), burned his home on the Palatine, Rome's most select neighborhood, and destroyed his two country houses (at Tusculum and Formiae).

Gradually, however, public opinion organized in favor of Cicero's recall. When Clodius' one-year term of office was ended, he was no longer able to do anything as a public official to prevent Cicero's return. Therefore at this point Clodius introduced a new element into Roman politics: gangs of roughnecks maintained purely for the purpose of making trouble and creating calculated public disorders. Clodius used his gangs to try to break up public meetings held in favor of Cicero's recall. Later he made the mistake of trying strong-arm methods on Pompey himself, who then encouraged his henchman Milo to

form gangs of his own. Thenceforth gangster violence was a commonplace of Roman politics and political meetings and elections until the fracas on the Appian Way in which Clodius lost his life.

*Introduction: Let the jury do its duty fearlessly, even in the face of threats of force.*

*1* Gentlemen of the jury: I am afraid that it is a shame for me to be nervous as I begin the defense of a very brave man—especially so because Titus Annius Milo is more disturbed for the welfare of the government than for his own welfare—and that it is most unbecoming for me not to bring the case a greatness of spirit equal to his . . . yet the unusual setting of this unusual court brings dismay to my eyes; wherever they turn they fail to find the familiar appearance of the Forum and the time-honored procedures of the law. I see that the place where you [the jury] are now seated is not surrounded by a ring of spectators, as once it was; we are not enclosed by the customary crowd; (2) and those squads of soldiers whom you observe on guard duty in front of all the temples, even if they are posted there to prevent disorder, do something to a speaker . . . so that, though in the Forum and in front of a jury, though surrounded by troops for our own security, we cannot even be freed from fear without a certain fear.

If I thought that these precautions were aimed against Milo, I should yield to the occasion, gentlemen; I should consider that in the midst of such display of military force, the pleader had no place. But the good judgment of a wise and just man, Gnaeus Pompeius [Pompey the Great], renews my strength and reassures me; and I am sure that he would not consider it in keeping with his own sense of justice to surrender to the weapons of the military a man whom he had entrusted to the verdict of a jury; and I am sure he would not consider it in keeping with his great intelligence to arm the undisciplined and excited mob with public authority. *3* And so those swords and spears there, those officers and their squads, speak of protection, not of threats; they tell me to be not only calm but bold; and they promise to my defense of Milo not only their support but at the same time a silent hearing.

The rest of this great throng—which of course consists of my fellow-citizens—is with me to the last man; and of all of those you see watching from every point of vantage where any part of the Forum can be seen, waiting for the verdict in this trial here, there is not one, apart from his support of Milo's merits, who does not think that this day's issue concerns himself, his children dear, his country, and his future.

A single class will include our opponents and our personal enemies: those who have been fattened by the insane conduct of Publius Clodius, with all its looting and burning and general destruction in the community—men who were urged only yesterday at a mass meeting to dictate the verdict you should give; and if any uproar from them should happen to arise among you, it should warn you to keep on the roll of citizens [not to exile] a man who has always disregarded this class of men and their loudest shoutings when your well-being was at stake.

4 With this in view, be with me in your minds, gentlemen of the jury; and if you have any fears, put them to one side. For if ever the power was yours to sit in judgment on brave and loyal men, if ever yours to judge your fellow-citizens who have served their country well, if, in a word, an occasion was ever given to chosen men of the most honorable rank, by their conduct and their votes to make known their support of a good citizen and brave—as they often have by the expressions on their faces and their words—assuredly at this time that power is completely yours to settle whether we, who have always been devoted to your service, shall be in unending misery and mourning or, long abused by our most worthless fellow citizens, shall at long last be refreshed and cheered by you and by your protection, by your high character and wisdom. 5 I mean this, gentlemen: could anything be contrived or said with greater toil, with greater thought, with greater pains on behalf of us two than such a decision, we who have been led to public life by the prospect of rewards of high distinction and cannot go without the fear of fearful punishments? For my part, I have always thought that those other storms and tempests, at least in mass meetings, were Milo's to endure, because he always thought his feelings were always with loyal citizens as opposed to malcontents; but in a trial, and in this court in which men of the highest standing from all classes of citizens sit in judgment, I never thought that with such men as agents Milo's enemies would ever

have any hope of blotting out his future, to say nothing of his renown in days to come.

6 However, in this case, gentlemen, I shall not take unfair advantage of Milo's career as tribune and all the good things he has done for the welfare of the community. Unless you can see with your own eyes that a conspiracy against Milo was formed by Clodius, I am not going to plead with you to waive the present charge in consideration of my client's many distinguished services to the state; and I am not going to ask that if the death of Publius Clodius has meant your survival, you should on that account write it up to the credit of Milo's merits rather than to the good fortune of the Roman people; but if Clodius' plot becomes clearer than this sunshine, then and not until then shall I beg you and implore you, gentlemen, that if we have lost all else, this right may yet be left to us: that we be free to defend our lives without fear of penalty from the reckless weapons of our foes.

*Ignore appeals to prejudice: there is such a thing as justifiable homicide.*

7 But before I come to the part of my argument which is relevant to the case before you, I think I should refer to the charges which have been bandied about repeatedly in the Senate by our enemies, and at mass meetings by agitators, and a little while ago by the prosecution. I want you to be able to see the matter before the court plainly and with all possibility of error removed. They say that it is a sin that the man who has slain by his own admission one of his fellow human beings should gaze upon the light of day. In what city, let me ask, do these silly fools think they are arguing the point? Don't they know that they are arguing it in the same city which has witnessed as its first capital case the trial of the courageous Marcus Horatius who, even before the city had gained its freedom [from the kings, in 509 B.C.], was still acquitted by the assembly of the Roman people, although he confessed that he had slain his own sister by his own hand? 8 Or is there anyone who does not know this: that when an inquest is held over a case of homicide, the commission of the act is either denied categorically or it is claimed that the act could be justified in right and law on legal grounds? Unless, I suppose, you think that Publius Africanus was of unsound mind when he

was questioned by Gaius Carbo, a tribune of the people, who was trying to start trouble in a public meeting by enquiring what Africanus thought about the death of Tiberius Gracchus—and Africanus answered that he thought Gracchus had been rightfully killed. And by the same token, the great Servilius Ahala [tyrant-slayer of 439 B.C.] and Publius Nasica and Lucius Opimius [arch-enemy of Gaius Gracchus] and Gaius Marius, and the Senate when I was consul, could not escape being considered wicked, if it is wicked for citizens who break the law to be killed. Similarly, gentlemen, it is not without good reason that gifted poets, too, have recorded in their dramas how a man had slain his mother to avenge his father's death and was acquitted by a sentence that was not only divine in origin but also came from the wisest of all goddesses [Athene-Minerva], at a time when the opinions of men were divided [Orestes in the *Eumenides* of Aeschylus]. *9* In view of the fact that the Twelve Tables state that a burglar by night may be killed by any means whatever without fear of the law, and a burglar in the daytime if he defends himself with a lethal weapon, who is there to think that there should be a penalty no matter how a man is killed, when he sees that on certain occasions a sword is put in our hands by the laws in order that we may kill a man?

*Milo was using force only to repel force.*

All right, then; but if there is any occasion when homicide is justifiable, and there are many such occasions, certainly it is not only justifiable but even imperative when violence is repelled by violence. When a military tribune, a relative of the commander, in the army of Gaius Marius tried to commit an indecent assault on a soldier, he was killed by his intended victim; you see, that fine young man preferred to place himself in jeopardy of the law rather than to submit to dishonor. And that great general absolved the young man of any offense and freed him from peril of the law. *10* In fact, what unjustifiable death can be inflicted on a bandit or a gangster? What is the idea of our personal bodyguards, our own swords? We should certainly not be permitted to wear them if it were not permissible to use them in any way. And so, there does exist a law, gentlemen, not a written law, but a law of nature, which we have not learned, inherited, or read in

a book; from nature herself we have picked it up, absorbed it, copied it; we come to it because we are made that way, not by learning; because we have assimilated it, and not as the result of training. Consequently, if our lives come into any unexpected peril, where we face the attack of hold-up men and their deadly weapons, every means of preserving one's life is legitimate. *11* That is to say, the laws are silent in the face of deadly weapons, and they do not ask us to wait for their judgment, because the man who decides to wait will have to pay a penalty that he does not deserve before he can exact one that is deserved. And yet in its very wise way, and more or less by implication, the law itself offers the right of self-defense; it does not forbid killing a man, but it does forbid carrying a deadly weapon with homicidal intent, so that when all the facts of a case and not the carrying of a weapon are being reviewed, the man who has used the weapon for the purposes of self-defense is not judged to have carried the weapon with intent to kill someone. Therefore, let this principle remain as the background of the case, gentlemen; for I have no doubt that I shall make good in your judgment my case for the defense if you will remember this—and you cannot forget it—that it is lawful to kill a gangster.

*It is alleged that the Senate has already declared Milo's act against the public interest.*

*12* Now comes the point that is often put forward by Milo's enemies, namely that the Senate has formally passed judgment that the fight in which Publius Clodius lost his life was contrary to the public interest. The fact is that the Senate has approved that act by formal vote, to say nothing of its expressions of sympathy. How many times have we dealt with this matter in the Senate! What expressions of agreement from the entire body—how outspoken, how unmistakable they were! That is to say, when, at the Senate's most crowded meetings, have there been found four or at the most five who did not express their support of Milo's case? That is what those half-dead mass meetings held by that half-baked tribune [quite literally—the tribune Munatius Plancus had been burned in the fires set by hoodlums] make clear. Every day he used to denounce my dominating influence in envious terms, charging that what the Senate passed represented my wishes, not its own feelings. Incidentally, about that dominating influence—if that is what it is to be called, rather than a moderate amount of authority in good causes resulting from my great public services, or a certain degree of popularity among good citizens because of that hard work of mine in the line of public duties—call it dominating influence by all means, just so long as I use it for the preservation of loyal citizens and against the insanity of traitors.

*13* But as for this court of inquiry here, although it is not unjust, still the Senate has never held that its establishment was necessary. That is, there are laws, there are legal procedures dealing with both homicide and armed assault already in existence; and the death of Publius Clodius did not cause the Senate to grieve and mourn to such a degree that a new kind of inquiry had to be set up. As you know, the Senate was deprived of the power to determine by what kind of court he was to be tried on charges of moral degeneracy.[13] Is it believable that the Senate considered it necessary to set up a special court to investigate his death? If that is so, why did the Senate vote to the effect that the burning of the Senate House, the attack on the house of Marcus Lepidus, and the slaying in question here were against the public interest? Because no violence is ever resorted to among citizens of a free republic that is not contrary to the public interest. *14* The reason for this is that self-defense of that sort against violence is never desirable, but there are times when it is necessary. Unless, of course, that day on which Tiberius Gracchus was killed, or the day on which Gaius [Gracchus] was killed, or the day on which the weapons of Saturninus were crushed to earth, even though it was in the interest of the state that they should be crushed, still did not inflict a wound upon the state. And it was in accordance with this principle that I personally gave as my formal opinion, when it was established that there had been a homicide on the Appian Way, that no one who had defended himself had acted contrary to the interests of the state; but since the case contained elements of violence and treachery, I left the question of criminal charges to a jury but expressed my disapproval of the thing in general. Consequently, if that crazy tribune there had permitted the Senate to carry out its intentions, we would not now be having a special inquiry. That is,

the Senate was for voting that the inquiry should be held under existing laws, merely out of turn on the calendar of scheduled cases. The motion was voted on clause by clause at the demand of someone or other—I don't have to publicize everybody's misdemeanors. In this way the rest of the Senate's resolution was invalidated by a hired veto.[14]

*It is alleged that Pompey has condemned Milo already.*

*15* "But," it may be objected, "Gnaeus Pompeius expressed his judgment on the fact and on its legal aspects by his motion; that is, he introduced a measure dealing with the homicide which had occurred on the Appian Way in which Publius Clodius was killed." What, then, *did* he move? Why, that an inquiry should be held, of course. The next question is, what is to be inquired into? Whether the homicide took place? But the fact is established. By whom committed? But that is well known. Accordingly Pompeius saw that even where the fact is admitted, a plea of self-defense can still be admitted. If he had not seen this, that the individual who confesses the fact has a chance of acquittal, just as he sees my client and me admitting it, he would never have ordered an inquiry and he would never have given you *this* letter which in judgment spells preservation rather than *that* letter which spells disaster.[15] As for myself, I really think that Gnaeus Pompeius has not expressed a serious judgment against Milo; on the contrary, he has definitely laid down the principle you ought to keep before you in arriving at a verdict. That is, he who does not impose a penalty upon confession, but gives an opportunity to make a defense, has concluded that it is the circumstance of death, not the fact of death, that needs to be looked into. *16* No doubt he will soon tell us about this step that he took on his own initiative, whether he thought of it as something due to Publius Clodius or necessary to meet the political emergency.

*Historical precedents: previous murders have gone unpunished.*

A most distinguished man, a champion of the Senate, and, incidentally, in view of those troubled times, almost a patron and protector of the Senate, was killed in his own home—Marcus

Drusus, tribune of the people, an uncle of our juryman here, this very brave gentleman, Marcus Cato. There were no bills brought before the people on the subject of his death; no inquiry was voted by the Senate. How great was the grief in this city, as our fathers have told us, when that attack was made at night on Publius Africanus [16] when he was asleep at home! Who did not then give way to groans? Who did not burn with indignation that the man for whom everyone desired immortality was not even permitted to await his natural death in the course of time? There wasn't any special enquiry voted into the death of Africanus, was there? Of course not.

*17* Why so? The fact of murder is the same whether the victim is a public figure or someone unknown. Granted, that is, that there is in life a distinction between the honors paid to the great and those paid to the lowly; let death, at any rate, when it is the result of crime, be governed by the same penalty for all, and by the same laws—unless it happens that a man is more of a murderer when he has murdered his father, and when his father is an ex-consul, than if he were a nobody; or if the murder of Publius Clodius is more shocking because he was killed among the monuments of his ancestors—as you know, our opponents keep repeating this, as much as to say that the great Appius Claudius the Blind paved that highway [the Appian Way], not for the use of the public, but to provide a spot where his descendants might hold people up and get away with it. *18* And so, I suppose when Publius Clodius killed a distinguished Roman financier, Marcus Papirius, on that same Appian Way, that act was not subject to punishment! That is to say, it was a member of one of the first families of Rome who had murdered a mere businessman among the monuments of his ancestors—today, how dignified and heroic the name of the *Appian* Way makes everything sound! Earlier, when it was smeared with the blood of a respectable and harmless man, nobody ever mentioned it; now it is dragged in over and over again after it has run with the blood of a hoodlum who had murdered his own father. But what's the use of mentioning all these incidents? They arrested a slave of Publius Clodius in the temple of Castor; Clodius had put him there to murder Pompey; when the dagger was wrenched from his hand, he began to confess; after that, the Forum had

to get along without Pompey, so did the Senate, so did the public in general; he took shelter behind the doors and walls of his home, not behind the rights that the laws and the legal process gave him. *19* No special legislation was proposed, was it? No special kind of court was decided on, was it? Yet if the facts, the man, the occasion, called for such action, certainly in this case they were all most demanding; the assassin had been planted in the Forum, right in the lobby of the Senate; moreover, he was planning death for the one man upon whom the future of the state depended—at a time in the history of our government when if this one man had gone down not only the state but entire peoples would have crashed to ruin. Unless, of course, the attempted assassination of Pompey should not be punished because it failed to come off, just as if it were the outcome of actions of which the laws take cognizance and not the intent—the failure of the plot gave us less cause for grief, but it was certainly no less punishable.

*Pompey is not prejudiced, simply just.*

*20* How many times I have escaped myself from Publius Clodius' deadly weapons, gentlemen, and his bloodstained hands! And if sheer good fortune, perhaps my own, perhaps that of the state, had not preserved me—now tell me: who would have passed a law to have my death investigated?

But I am just being stupid when I go so far as to compare Drusus, Africanus, Pompey, and myself, to Publius Clodius. Those acts could be put up with; no one can accept the death of Publius Clodius calmly; the Senate is in mourning, the businessmen and financiers are heartbroken, the whole community is spent with grief, the small towns are wearing sackcloth and ashes, the colonies are overcome, and last but not least, the very fields are mourning for a citizen so kindly, so helpful, so gentle. *21* No, gentlemen, no, this was certainly not the reason why Pompey thought a court should be set up by law; but wise as he is, and endowed with almost prophetic vision, he saw many implications: Clodius was his enemy, Milo is his close friend; if he took part in the universal rejoicing, he was afraid that the sincerity of the reconciliation which had taken place might be questioned; he also saw many other implications, but this one in particular: no matter how harsh the terms of his legislation, you jurors would still have no qualms in arriving at a verdict. And so he selected none but the leading lights from our distinguished political groups [senators and financiers]; and he definitely did not—as quite a few people keep saying—he definitely did not shut out my friends in the selection of the jurors. You *know* this just man never thought of *that*; and even if he had desired to, he never could have managed it in choosing good men and true. For the political support I enjoy is not confined to those personal intimacies which cannot extend very widely, because one's personal associations can be shared only with a few; but if I do have any influence, this influence is based on the fact that public life has brought me in contact with the good [17] and loyal citizens. When Pompey chose his jurors from the best of these, and believed at the same time that his personal integrity was most deeply involved, he could not possibly have chosen men who were not my supporters. *22* Yes, and as for you, Lucius Domitius—the fact that he wished you to preside in this investigation—he was looking only for a sense of justice, dignity, tolerance, and integrity. His enactment was that the presiding judge should be an ex-consul—I imagine because it was the function of the leading citizens to resist the irresponsible attitude of the masses and the recklessness of men who have no principles. He appointed you by preference from the men of consular rank; he knew that from boyhood you had given convincing proof of your scorn for the insanities of the people's party.

*Statement of the case: Clodius' projects and character*

*23* Well then, gentlemen, to get on finally with the case and the indictment: if a full confession of the fact is not unprecedented; if no judgment other than what we wish has been passed by the Senate; if the sponsor of the law still wished the matter of justice to be discussed, even if there was no exception taken to the facts of the case as stated; if the jurors who were selected and the judge who was appointed are the kind of men who can investigate the case justly and wisely, then just one thing is left, gentlemen: your duty is to consider only this point—which of the two [Milo or Clodius] was guilty of conspiracy against the other. And in order that you

may get a clearer view of this in the light of actual proofs, please give me your attention while I outline briefly what happened.

*24* Publius Clodius decided to throw the government into disorder with all sorts of crooked deals during his term of office as praetor. He saw that the elections had been dragged out so long in the preceding year that he would be able to hold his praetorship for a few months only. He had no respect for that high office, as other men have; all he wanted was to avoid having Lucius Paulus as praetor along with himself—a man of exceptional character—and he was looking for a solid year in office in which to get his claws into the government. So he suddenly gave up his proper year [the first in which he was old enough to be eligible] and put his name down for the next year, not because, as is usually the case, of some religious scruple but so that he could have, in his own words, a full unbroken year for the praetorship—that is, to overthrow the constitution.

*25* The thought kept coming to his mind that his praetorship would be crippled and powerless if Milo were consul. Added to this was his realization that Milo was going to be elected consul by the unanimous choice of the Roman people. So he made a deal with Milo's opponents, but on this condition: that he should have the complete direction of their campaign, even if they didn't like what he was doing—that he should carry the entire campaign on his own shoulders, as he said more than once. He was all for calling the electoral divisions together, for acting as go-between, for putting a new Colline district on the books which would be made up of the lowest type of citizen. The more he tried to create confusion, the stronger Milo became every day. When Clodius, ready as he was for any kind of crime, saw that Milo—a man of courage, his worst enemy—was sure to be elected consul, as he learned from the unequivocal talk, to say nothing of the votes, of the Roman people, he began to work out in the open and say in so many words that Milo would have to be put out of the way. *26* He brought down out of the Apennines [mountains] a crowd of roughneck foreign slaves with whom he had looted public forests and raided Etruria—you have seen them. He made no bones about the thing; I mean that he said over and over again quite openly, that if Milo's consulship could not be taken from him, at least his life could. He often hinted at this possibility in the Senate, said it openly at mass meetings. What's more, when that gallant gentleman, Marcus Favonius, asked him what he expected to get out of all this raging around while Milo lived, he said that in three days, or four at the most, Milo would be dead—a remark that Favonius at once passed on to Marcus Cato here.

*Time, place, and opportunity were all favorable to Clodius' murdering Milo, not the other way round.*

27 In the meantime, Clodius learned—and it was not hard to find out—that Milo, who was dictator of Lanuvium by title, was under formal religious and legal obligations to take a trip to that town on January 18 to declare the election of one of the municipal priests. Accordingly, Clodius himself suddenly left Rome the day before; the idea was—as was later found to be a fact—to ambush Milo in front of Clodius' country place. Moreover, his departure was such that he made a sacrifice of his personal attendance at a noisy public meeting which was being held that same day; his furious inspiration was there sadly missed; and he would never have sacrificed his attendance at the meeting if he had not wished to keep an appointment at the scene of the crime.

28 Now Milo had been in the Senate that day up to the time of adjournment; he went home, changed his clothes and his shoes, waited a while for his wife to get ready—as we all do—then started so late that Clodius could have been on his way back to Rome that same day, if it had been his plan to do so. Milo was met by Clodius on horseback, ready for action, no coach, baggage, none of his usual Greek pals, no wife—which practically never happened; while our alleged conspirator here, who had planned this trip with murder on his mind—as *they* say—was riding with his wife in a carriage, wrapped up in his overcoat, accompanied by a large, awkward, dainty, effeminate retinue of maids and house-boys. 29 Milo meets Clodius in front of the latter's country place at about five o'clock, or close to it. At once an attack is made on my client by a number of armed men stationed on higher ground; they block the road and kill the driver; but when Milo threw off his overcoat, jumped out of the carriage, and began to defend himself energetically, then those who were with Clodius, swords in hand, separated into two parties—some ran to the back of the carriage to get at Milo from the rear; others, apparently under the impression that he was already dead, began to cut down the slaves who were following. These slaves, who were loyal to their master and had presence of mind, were cut down—some of them, that is; others, seeing that a fight was going on around the carriage, and being kept from going to their master's rescue, when they heard—and that, too, from Clodius himself and believed him—that Milo had been killed, these slaves of Milo—as I say, openly, and with no idea of shifting the blame from my client, but to state the facts—without the orders and without the presence of their master, did what every master would wish his slaves to do in such circumstances . . . [i.e., killed their master's enemy].

[The remainder of Cicero's speech consists of an attempt to prove that Milo was the object of a deliberate conspiracy—the intended victim of premeditated murder—and that therefore in bringing about the death of Clodius he had acted merely in self-defense. Hence the review of the law of self-defense in the part of the speech we have read here.]

NOTE: We have an independent account of the fight given by Asconius, a scholar of the first century A.D. We are told that the meeting took place quite by accident, that Milo's gang started the fight, and that Milo's bodyguard, which was much the larger, included two gladiators—the equivalent of professional "trigger-men." Clodius was wounded and carried into a tavern. When Milo heard of this, realizing that here was a fine opportunity, he ordered his slaves to drag Clodius out into the road and finish the job. The corpse was left lying on the Appian Way. In other words, according to this account, Milo was guilty of a deliberate act of homicide.

# AGAINST ANTONY

## (Philippic II)

The assassination of Julius Caesar in the lounge of the theater built for Rome under the direction of Pompey the Great was one of the most dramatic events in European history, but it was badly planned. Those who took part in the murder, most notably Brutus and Cassius, apparently believed that once Caesar was put out of the way, the Republic would be automatically "restored." Instead, the history of political events in Rome following the Ides of March, 44 B.C., is simply a record of confusion until again the scene was dominated by powerful personalities. One of these was Marcus Antonius (Mark Antony).

For a while, after Caesar's death, there was an uneasy restoration of senatorial administration in which Cicero took his part. During the summer of 44, his outlook became pessimistic; and he retired from active participation in politics. Meanwhile Antony had shown himself extraordinarily difficult to get along with in the Senate. For no good reason, Antony took offence at Cicero's absence from a meeting of the Senate on September 1. The next day Cicero attended and delivered what is now called the "First Philippic." The speech was conciliatory, in the main, but Cicero was unable to keep out of it a certain undertone of criticism. The sole effect was to irritate Antony into making a violent reply. Cicero made no answer at the time, but he retired to one of his country places and at leisure composed a speech in which he turned all his distinguished powers of abuse against Antony. This was the famous "Second Philippic," parts of which we read here in translation. As he wrote it, Cicero developed the feeling that he was playing the part of a new Demosthenes, fighting for liberty against military power and aggression, just as the great Athenian orator had done in his time. The "Second Philippic" was circulated as a pamphlet late in November; it was never delivered as a speech in the Senate, although one would infer from reading it that it had been.

Then, in December 44, Cicero returned to the city and opened a powerful speaking campaign against Antony, who had meanwhile retired to northern Italy. But the following summer came the decisive event. A new figure had entered upon the political scene in the person of Julius Caesar's grandnephew, Octavian, later known—and better—as Augustus. A lad of eighteen when Caesar died, but incredibly shrewd, he had won the support of Caesar's legionary veterans and began gradually to speak with more and more authority. Suddenly Antony and Octavian joined forces; with overwhelming military power against them, Cicero and the senators were doomed. The net effect of Cicero's "Second Philippic," as it turned out, was merely to make Antony his irreconcilable enemy. When the power lay with Antony, his men hunted Cicero down and killed him.

*Introduction: Antony's attack upon Cicero is a proof of treason.*

*1* Through what destiny of mine, gentlemen of the Senate, am I to say that this has come about: in these twenty years no one has been a public enemy without at the same time declaring war on me, too? No—and there is no need, either, for me to mention the name of any man; without being reminded, you are calling names to mind. Those men whose names you know paid me greater penalties than I had wished; I am surprised, Antonius, that you are not shuddering at the ends to which they came, those men whose actions you are taking as a pattern now. And this that I shall mention caused me less surprise where those others were concerned—as you know, not one of them was my enemy of my own free will, all were attacked by me for the republic's sake—you, unharmed even by so much as a word of mine, attacked me unprovoked with abusive language so that you might be thought more venturesome than Catiline, madder than Clodius; and you thought your break with me would win you favor with disloyal citizens.

*2* What am I to think? That I am held in contempt? I am not aware of anything in my way of life, in my standing in the community, in my record of achievements, or in these moderate abilities of mine, that Antonius can scorn. Did he think that in the Senate he could most easily undermine my reputation? This body that has borne witness to the good administration of the state by many famous citizens—to me alone for having saved it? Is it possible that he wished to enter a public-speaking contest against me? Well, that *is* a generous gesture! I mean, what fuller, richer subject is there than for me to speak on my own behalf and against Antonius, too? This is, of course, the answer he did not think he could justify himself before men of his own kind as an enemy of his country unless he were an enemy to me. *3* But before reply to him in connection with the other matters, I shall say a few words about the friendship which he charges me with having violated, because in my judgment that is the most serious charge of all. . . .[18]

*Antony accuses Cicero of breach of friendship, adducing a personal letter as evidence.*

7 But he even read aloud a letter which he said I had sent him—this uneducated low-brow who has no idea of how things are done. I mean to say, what person who had even the slightest acquaintance with the way gentlemen do things, ever brought out and read in public a letter that had been written to him by a friend—because of some offense that had occurred in the meantime? Doesn't this simply mean that you take away from life life's good fellowship, that you take away the private conversations of friends who are parted from one another? What a lot of jokes one so often finds in letters which fall flat when they are read in public! How many serious thoughts there are which still should not be made known under any circumstances! 8 Let this do for his bad manners; now take a look at his incredible stupidity.

What have you to say in answer to me now, my fluent friend—fluent, as you seem to be to Mustela [Weasel] and Tiro [two of Antony's roughneck stooges]? Since they are standing right now in sight of the Senate with drawn swords, I shall rate you as a splendid speaker, too, if you show me how you propose to defend them on a murder charge. But tell me now, what would be your answer if I were to say that I never wrote you that letter? By what evidence would you prove me the writer? Possibly by the handwriting? That's a field in which you have a very profitable knowledge.[19] How could you prove it? It was written in the hand of a secretary.

I am beginning to envy you your teacher who taught you how to be a blockhead for so large a tuition fee—how large a fee I shall reveal presently. 9 That is, what could be less the mark—I do not say of a lawyer, but of a man—than to make an allegation of such a nature against an opponent that when the opponent has denied it in a word, the one who raised the allegation cannot proceed any farther? But I do *not* deny it; and in this connection I convict *you* not only of lack of breeding but also of lack of good

sense. Now what word is there in that letter that is not full of civility, desire to be helpful, kindly intentions? And that is what your charge amounts to: that in this letter I express a high opinion of you, that I write as if I were writing to a fellow citizen, to a good man, not to a gangster and a criminal. But I am still not producing your letter, even though I could rightfully do so, since I was attacked first by you—the letter in which you ask that with my approval you might recall someone from exile; and you give me your word that you will not do this unless it is agreeable to me. And you got what you wanted from me. Naturally; why should I stand in the way of your unlimited gall, which the authority of this body could not hold in check, nor public opinion in Rome, nor any laws at all? 10 But after all, why should you have been asking me, if the man you were asking for had already been brought back home by a law of Caesar's! But obviously he wanted me to have the credit in a matter where not even he himself could gain any, what with the law already having been passed.

[Cicero now deals with Antony's attacks upon his consulship and with the charge that he had refused to surrender the body of Antony's stepfather for burial. At the same time Cicero works in some interesting remarks on the subject of Antony's private life, and characterizes Antony's earlier speech against him as inconsistent and clumsy.]

*Antony charges that Cicero was behind Clodius' murder.*

21 You said that the murder of Publius Clodius was my idea. Well, what would people have thought if he had been killed in the Forum, while the Roman people were looking on, at the time when you went after him with a sword and would have dispatched the business right there if he had not thrown himself into a stairway of a bookstore and held off your attack with a barricade? As a matter of fact, I admit that you had my good will in this proceeding, but not even you say that it was my idea in the first place. Now as for Milo, I couldn't even have given him my good will; I mean that it was all over before anyone could suspect that he was going to do it. But, you say, it *was* my idea. I suppose Milo was the kind of a man who could not do a public service on his own. But, you say, I was happy

about the whole thing. So what? When the entire community was so happy, was it my duty to look sad? 22 However, there was an official inquiry set up into the death of Clodius—not set up, I must say, with much wisdom; I mean, what was the point of a new law ordering an inquiry into homicide when there was already a regular process of inquiry set up by existing laws?—but still, an inquiry there was. And so, whereas no one said a word against me when the issue was alive, here we find you saying it after so many years.

*Antony charges that Cicero caused the civil war.*

23 As for your bold statement—a long one, too—that the friendship between Pompey and Caesar was broken up by my doing, and for that reason it was my fault that the Civil War started, you were wrong more or less about the whole thing; but what is most important, you were wrong about the dates.

Personally, I did everything I could, when Marcus Bibulus, a prominent citizen, was consul, to the full extent of my efforts and abilities, to win Pompey from his partnership with Caesar. Here Caesar had better luck than I; that is, he broke up the close associations between Pompey and myself. But after Pompey had surrendered himself completely to Caesar, why should I have tried to draw him away from Caesar again? To hope for success in that would have been foolish, to urge it, impertinent. 24 However, two occasions did arise when I tried to give Pompey some advice against Caesar; I wish you would criticize them adversely if you can. One item was that he should not extend Caesar's command in Gaul for five years; the other was that he should not permit a proposal to be carried that Caesar be allowed to file his candidacy for the consulship without being present in person. If I had succeeded in persuading him on either one of these two points, we should never have fallen into this pitiful condition.

Yes, and what is more, I personally—when Pompey had already transferred to Caesar all resources, all his own and all those of the Roman people, and too late had begun to recognize the evils that I had foreseen long before, and when I saw that a cursed war was being inflicted upon our country—I personally never relented in my role as the prime mover in urging peace, co-operation and reconciliation; and that comment of mine at the time is well known to many: "Pompey, how I wish that you had refrained from going into a partnership with Caesar in the first place, or from breaking off that alliance later on! The one would have been a mark of your stability; the other, of your foresight." These, Marcus Antonius, were always my policies in relation to Pompeius and the republic; if they had prevailed, the republic would now be standing; it would be you, with your outrageous actions, your bankruptcy, and your infamy, that would have collapsed.

*Antony charges that Cicero planned Caesar's murder.*

25 But that is ancient, this is current history—that Caesar was killed according to my plan. And now, I am afraid, gentlemen of the Senate, that you may think that I have done something terribly unethical—that I have planted a ringer in the ranks of the prosecution who will deck me out with my own distinctions and with those of others, too. I mean, who ever heard of my name among the partners in that magnificent enterprise? Whose name, I may add, among their number was ever kept dark? Kept dark, did I say? Whose name was not made public at once? I would be more inclined to say outsiders had boasted of their association with the act, when they were not on the inside at all, than that anyone who was on the inside would have wished his name to be concealed. 26 What is more, how likely is it that among so many men, some not very well known, some quite young, who were not keeping any name dark, my name could have stayed under cover?

Why, if instigators had been wanted by those who played a leading role in freeing the republic, should I have egged on the Bruti, one of whom saw the bust of Lucius Brutus [20] every day, the other, the bust of Ahala? [21] Well, then, were men with ancestors like these to ask advice from strangers rather than from their own circle, and somewhere outside rather than in their own homes? Well, what about this? Gaius Cassius, born in a family that could not stand any man's domination, not even superior authority—I suppose he wanted my backing? A man who would have dispatched this business, even without the help of these distinguished men, in ·Cilicia at the mouth of the Cydnus river, if Caesar had moored his ship, as he had previously decided, on the one bank instead of the opposite.²² *27* Gnaeus Domitius—the death of his distinguished father, the death of his uncle on his mother's side, the removal of his prospects of high office, did not arouse him to recover his liberty, but my influence *did?* Did I talk Gaius Trebonius into it? Why, I would not have ventured even to suggest it. To him the republic owes an even greater debt of gratitude because he placed the liberty of the Roman people ahead of one man's friendship and preferred to avert dictatorship rather than to be a partner in it. I suppose Lucius Tillius Cimber took my lead as his adviser? My admiration for his participation in that incident was stronger than my belief that he would do so—that is, admiration for the reason that he was unmindful of favors rendered, but mindful of his country. Well, what about the two Servilii—shall I call them Cascas or Ahalas? And it is your considered opinion that these men were motivated by my influence rather than by their affection for the republic? To go through the rest of the names would take too long; and this fact in itself is to the state a fine tribute that their number was so many, and to themselves, a glory.

*28* But bear in mind how far this sharper has proved my guilt. "When Caesar had been killed," he says, "at once lifting high his bloody dagger, Brutus called out Cicero's name and congratulated him on the recovery of liberty." Why me, of all people? Because I knew about the plot? See if this wasn't the reason for calling me by name: because Brutus had accomplished something almost identical with my own accomplishments, he called me in particular to witness that he had come forward to emulate my glorious deeds.

*29* Now, you prize blockhead, don't you understand that if what you assert against me, to have wished for Caesar's death, is a crime, then to have been glad when Caesar died is also a crime? In other words, what is the difference between a man who advises an action and one who approves of it? Or what does it matter whether I wished it done or was glad that it was done? Is there any man, then, with the exception of those who enjoyed Caesar's monarchy,

who did not want that incident to take place or failed to approve of it when it did?

Everyone, therefore, is to blame; that is, all respectable citizens, so far as was in their power, killed Caesar; some lacked a plan, others the courage, some the opportunity, but none the desire. *30* But see how dumb the man is—or I should say, that jackass. That is, he said, "Brutus, whose name I mention with all honor, held up his bloody dagger and called out 'Cicero!' We must understand from this that he was in on the plot." So I am being called a criminal—I, whom you suspect of having suspected something; Brutus, who held his dripping dagger up before him, is given honorable mention by you? All right; be as dumb as I said you were in your statements; what you do and what you express as your opinions are much worse. Make up your mind, Mr. Consul, make up your mind about this sometime, what you choose to be the status of the Bruti, Gaius Cassius, Gnaeus Domitius, Gaius Trebonius and the rest in this deed; sleep it off, I say, and breathe out the fumes of your hangover. Do we have to bring torches to wake you up when you go to sleep over momentous issues like these? Are you never going to understand that you have to make up your mind whether the men who took part in that deed are guilty of homicide or are vindicators of our liberty?

[Cicero deals in some detail with Antony's inconsistent behavior in the period following Caesar's assassination. He then defends his own course of action in 49 B.C. during the Civil War, takes up Antony's charge that no one had thought well enough of him to leave him any inheritances; and finally goes over from defense to the attack in the latter half of his speech.]

*Antony offered Caesar a kingly crown upon the Lupercal.*

*84* But I do not want my speech by any chance to skip the very prettiest example of all the many performances of Marcus Antonius; so let us get to the Lupercalia.

He makes no bones about it, gentlemen of the Senate; you can see that he is upset; he is perspiring; he is turning pale. Let him do anything he likes, so long as he doesn't vomit the way he did in the Portico of Minucius. What defense can there be for such disgraceful conduct? I am *so* anxious to hear where the fat fee paid to his professor of public speaking comes in—that is, where the Leontine land will pay off.[23]

85 Your colleague [in the consulate—Caesar] was sitting on the rostra, on a gilded chair, wearing a wreath and a purple toga. You go up the steps, you go up to his chair—even if you were Lupercus, you should have remembered that you were a consul, too—you hold out a crown. All over the Forum there were groans.

Where did that crown come from? I mean, you didn't pick up something that somebody had thrown away: you were bringing something that you had carefully thought out and rehearsed at home. You scoundrel, you tried to put it on his head; the crowd groaned. He kept pushing it away; they cheered. We have found you, then— you traitor—to be the one and only man who was willing to propose an autocracy and to have your own colleague in the consulship as autocrat, and at the same time to feel out how much the Roman people would bear and endure. 86 Why, you even tried to play for pity; you tried to throw yourself at Caesar's feet as a suppliant. Begging for what? To be a slave? You should have asked it only for yourself; your life from boyhood shows that you would submit to anything, that you very easily provided your services.[24] You certainly didn't have that as a mandate from us in the Senate and from the Roman people!

What wonderful eloquence that was when you sounded off in a public meeting without a stitch of clothing on![25] What could be lower than this, what could be more disgusting, what could be more deserving of all the punishments in the book? You aren't waiting, are you, for us to stick you in the rear with a pitchfork?[26] What I am saying now, if you have the slightest particle of feeling, is cutting you—this speech is drawing blood.

I am afraid I may be impairing the glory of heroic men, but I am moved by resentment and I shall speak out: what is more essentially wrong than that the man who pushed the crown away is dead—everyone admits he was rightfully killed —while the man who tried to put it on his head is living?

87 But he even ordered this entry in the public records under the heading "Lupercalia": "To Gaius Caesar, dictator with unlimited tenure, Marcus Antonius, consul, offered the kingship by order of the people; Caesar refused to exercise it."

Now I begin to be less and less surprised that law and order worry you, that you not only hate Rome but the light of day, too, that you associate with the lowest kind of thugs not only at parties but day in and day out. That is, where in a state of peace will you find firm footing? What place can there be for you under the laws, and in the courts of law which you tried to the best of your ability to abolish and hand over to the autocracy of a king? Is this why Lucius Tarquinius was driven out, why Spurius Maelius [by the omnipresent Ahala] and Marcus Manlius were put to death—so that many centuries later a king might be set up at Rome—an unholy thing—by Marcus Antonius?

*Antony's illegal and two-faced conduct in Rome on and after the Ides of March*

88 But let's get back to the auspices, on the subject of which Caesar intended to take formal action in the Senate on March 15.[27] I ask you: what would you have done then? As a matter of fact, I kept hearing reports that you had come primed because you thought that I was going to say something about the faked auspices—which we still had to observe. The fortune of the republic cancelled action for that glorious day; the death of Caesar didn't cancel your decision relating to the auspices, did it? But I have incidentally mentioned an occasion which I must digress to mention before I deal with those matters which my speech had begun to discuss.

How you ran! How scared you were that glorious day! How you despaired of life, what with your guilty conscience, when you got safely home unobserved—thanks to the mercy of those who wished you to be spared, if only you would be sensible, after your rapid exit. 89 Oh, my predictions of things to come—how true they have always been—how useless! I kept telling those liberators of ours on the Capitol Hill, when they wanted me to approach you and urge you to defend the constitution, that you would promise anything so long as you were afraid; but that the instant you stopped being nervous, you would be your old self again. So, when the other [exconsuls] were going back and forth to your house, I stuck to my original opinion; and I didn't see you that day or the next day, and I did not believe that any co-operative arrangement could be set up by any deal between the best citizens and the most bitter enemy of their country. Two days later I came into the Temple of the Earth—unwillingly, I may say, since armed guards were posted at all the entrances. *90* What an opportunity was that day for you, Antonius! Even though you have suddenly come forward as my enemy, still, I am sorry for you, because you stand in the way of your own glory.

Heaven be my witness! What a hero, and how great you would have been, if you could have maintained the frame of mind you had on that day! We should be enjoying the peace which had been secured by a hostage in the person of a lad of noble birth, the grandson of Marcus Bambalio.[28] However, it was fear—no full-time teacher of duty—that made you behave; what made you misbehave was something that never leaves you when fear is gone—your unbounded effrontery. And even at the time when people thought you to be a true supporter of the constitution—with me dissenting, of course—you presided at the funeral services for the tyrant—if you can call that a funeral service—in a way that was crime at its worst.

*91* That was *your* lovely memorial address, that was *your* moving appeal for pity—that was *your* rousing call to action. You—you, I say, put a light to those torches by which Caesar was only half cremated and by which the house of Lucius Bellienus was set on fire and burned down. It was you who directed those attacks against our homes which we fought off by sheer hand-to-hand fighting—attacks made by destitute characters, slaves for the most part. Again, for all of that, it was you who, on the following days in the Capitol—after you had wiped from your face the soot of those fires, as it were—proposed and carried truly splendid decrees of the Senate to the effect that after March 15 no official listings of exemption from taxation or any other special privilege should be posted. You yourself remember what you said about restoring exiles, what you said about exemption from taxation. Yes, and best of all, you abolished forever from the republic the title of dictator; by this move, incidentally, you did seem to have developed such a hatred of royal power that you were for abolishing the evil omen of that name because of the recent fear of the dictator. *92* The constitution did seem to others to be established, but no, not to me—

I was apprehensive of all sorts of shipwreck with you at the helm. Did he fool *me*, then?

In other words, he couldn't be unlike himself very long, could he? While you senators looked on, notices were being put up all over the Capitol, and exemptions from taxes were being sold not only to individuals singly but to entire states; citizenship was no longer being given out to one at a time, but to whole provinces. Consequently, if these measures stand, and they cannot if the republic is to stand, not only, gentlemen of the Senate, have you lost your tax revenues, but even the domain of the Roman people has been lessened by this man's private market. . . .

[Sections 93–114, omitted here, deal with Antony's alleged ill-gotten private wealth, his confused domestic affairs, his drunkenness while engaged in public business, and his illegal imposition of martial law upon Rome. But at least he did declare the dictatorship abolished.]

*Peroration: Let Antony repent and mend his ways.*

*115* Therefore, call before your mind, Marcus Antonius, that glorious day on which you abolished the dictatorship; keep before your eyes the joy of the Senate and the Roman people, compare it with this monstrous marketing which you and your friends have conducted; then you will understand how great is the gulf between gain and glory. But truly, just as certain people, under the effects of some illness and because of some numbness of the senses, do not appreciate the pleasant flavors of their food, so lustful men, greedy, criminally inclined, do not have the capacity to enjoy the taste of true fame. But if the prospect of true fame cannot lure you to right action, cannot fear, either, distract you from conduct of the foulest sort? You do not fear the courts of law. If this is because of your innocence, I compliment you; but if it is because your position rests on force, don't you understand what a man really ought to fear when his lack of fear of the courts is on that basis? *116* But if you are not afraid of brave men and fine citizens because they are kept from your person by an armed bodyguard, your own partisans, believe me, will not put up with you very long. Moreover, what kind of a life is it to be afraid of something from your own followers day and night? Unless, of course, you have men bound to you by stronger obligations than Caesar had in the case of some of these by whom he was killed, or unless you are to be compared to him in any respect. In him there was a great mind, a powerful brain, logical ability, a tenacious memory, literary talent, capacity for taking pains, power of reflection, application; he had accomplished feats in war, however disastrous to the constitution, that were still great; having planned for many years for absolute rule, he accomplished what he had in mind through great exertion and at great hazards; by public shows, by public works, by bonuses to veterans, by public feasts, he used to woo popularity with the unlettered populace; he had bound his own followers to his side by gifts, his opponents by a show of forgiveness—in short, he had already brought to a free community the habits of slavery, partly out of fear, partly out of passivity.

*117* I can compare you with him on the basis of your passion for power, but in other respects you are not in any way comparable. But out of the many evils which he has branded upon the republic, there has arisen this much good: he has taught the people of Rome how far to trust each man, to whom they may entrust themselves, and against whom they should be on guard. Don't you reflect upon these troubles and don't you perceive that it is enough for resolute men to have learned how fair an enterprise it is, how welcome an achievement, how glorious in name, it is to strike down a tyrant? Or do you suppose that when men would not put up with Caesar, they will put up with you? *118* Believe me, they will compete with one another hereafter as they run to do this work, and no opportunity that is slow to come will be waited for.

Come back to your senses sometime, I beg of you; think of those from whom you have sprung, not those with whom you live. Deal with me as you will, but come back into the good graces of the republic. But take thought for your own future; I will publish my own manifesto. In my youth I defended the republic; I shall not desert it in my age; I scorned the swords of Catiline; I shall not be in dread of yours. What is more, I would cheerfully offer my body if by my death the state can recover its liberty, so that at long last the pangs of the Roman people may bring to birth that with which it has so long been in labor. *119* Indeed, if in this very temple some twenty years ago I said that death could not come out of due season to a man who had been consul, how much more truly do I say that it cannot come out of season to an old man! Yes, to me, gentlemen of the Senate, today death is even something to be wished for, now that the honors I have won and the services I have performed are things of the past. Two things only do I pray for: one, that at my death I may leave the Roman people free—no greater boon than this could be given me by the immortal gods; second, that the outcome of life may be for each man as each man deserves of the republic.


## SERVIUS SULPICIUS RUFUS: IN MEMORIAM
### (Philippic IX)

In the selections we read from Cicero's address in defense of Murena we saw that Servius Sulpicius Rufus was an old friend of Cicero's who, presumably, could take a joke; again in a letter written by Sulpicius on the occasion of Tullia's death, the depth of feeling between Cicero and his old friend was evident. Here, in this address to the Senate early in 43 B.C., Cicero pays his last respects to Sulpicius. It is unfortunate that the occasion was what it was, for in view of the cause of Sulpicius' death—his mission to Antony to demand that he raise the siege of Mutina—any honors paid to him would at the same time focus attention on Antony's misdeeds. In fact, it is difficult to avoid the conclusion that the main purpose of the address was political. But politics being what they are, Cicero need not be blamed overmuch for turning Sulpicius' death into propaganda against Antony; and we may allow ourselves to see at the same time occasional evidences of sincere feeling.

### Cicero's introduction

*1* Gentlemen of the Senate: I should prefer that the immortal gods had made it possible for us to be moving a vote of thanks to Servius Sulpicius here alive instead of trying to find some way of paying tribute to him now that he is dead. No,

I have no doubt that if our distinguished fellow citizen could have presented a report to you on his appointed task, his return would have been gratifying to you and of advantage to the state—not that Lucius Philippus and Lucius Piso were lacking in either determination or attention to business in such a critical assignment; but since Servius Sulpicius was more advanced than they in age, and more advanced than anyone in good judgment, he left the entire personnel bereaved and weakened when he was suddenly taken away from the mission.

2 Yet, if honor ever has been deservedly paid to an envoy in death, we shall find that never was it more deserved than in the case of Servius Sulpicius. Other men who have been overtaken by death while on diplomatic duty left home to face the unknown hazards of life without any fear of death; even though Servius Sulpicius went on his way with some prospect of reaching Marcus Antonius [Mark Antony], he had none of returning home. Although he was so afflicted that he had little confidence in his powers of resistance if hard work was going to be added to his ill health, he did not refuse to try to be of some service to the state if he could, so to speak, with his last breath. And so the rigors of winter, the snow, the length of his journey, the roughness of the road, his failing health did not hold him back; and when he had come to the point of seeing and conferring with the man whom he had been sent to meet, he passed away in the very act of discharging his duty conscientiously and thoughtfully.

3 Therefore, as on other occasions, so here too. Gaius Pansa, you have done a fine thing in urging us to honor Servius Sulpicius and in having said so much in full measure of praise for him. I would not add anything to your remarks except my vote if I did not feel that I should say something in reply to my distinguished friend Publius Servilius, who has expressed the opinion that the honor of a statue should be conferred on no one unless he met his death as a result of an actual physical attack while on diplomatic duty. However, gentlemen of the Senate, it is my interpretation of the feeling of our forefathers that they thought it was a question, not of the manner of death, but of the actual cause. That is to say, when the mission itself was the cause of death, they wished to create a visible memorial, so that men might face the

responsibility of diplomatic duty in dangerous wars with greater confidence. Therefore we should not try to find precedents among the enactments of our forefathers; we should try to interpret the general policy which created the precedents themselves.

*Cicero cites precedents.*

4 Lars Tolumnius, King of Veii, put four representatives of the Roman people to death at Fidenae; their statues stood on the rostra down to a time I can myself remember. They deserved the honor. To compensate for their brief span of life, our forefathers gave to those who had died for their country a memorial that would last forever.

On the rostra we see the statue of a man who was renowned and great, who was the first to attain the consulship in that family which was afterwards so rich in stout-hearted men—Gnaeus Octavius. In those days, no one begrudged the tribute paid to a newcomer to political life, no man failed to pay honor to his character. But Octavius' mission was one in which there was no suspicion of danger. That is, he had been sent by the Senate to investigate the attitude of the kings and free peoples [in Asia Minor], and in particular to see the grandson of King Antiochus, the king who had given our forefathers a battle, and to tell him that he could not maintain a fleet and keep elephants—Octavius was assassinated in the municipal gymnasium at Laodicea by a man named Leptines. 5 In recognition of his loss of life, a statue was given to him by our forefathers, which was destined to be an honor to his descendants for many years. It now remains as the sole memorial of so distinguished a family. That is to say, in his case and in the case of Tullus Cluvius, Lucius Roscius, Spurius Antius, and Gaius Fulcinius, who were murdered by the king of Veii, it was not the blood shed in their dying that brought the honor, but the fact itself of death met in the service of their country.

*Sulpicius died while on duty.*

Therefore, gentlemen of the Senate, if some accident had brought the death of Servius Sulpicius, I should of course be distressed that our country had suffered so severe a blow, but it would be my feeling that his death should be marked by general grief rather than by a monument. But now who doubts that it was the mission itself that deprived him of life? As you know, death was in his company when he left home—the death which he might have escaped by his own attentions and the constant care of his fine son and his devoted wife. *6* But, since he saw that if he did not acknowledge your authority, he would not be like himself, and that if he did acknowledge your authority, the responsibility he had assumed would involve the end of his own life, he chose at a time when his country was facing a grave crisis to die rather than to seem to be of less assistance than his utmost to his own country.

In many towns along the route he followed he had the opportunity to rest and look after himself. There were also the generous invitations of his friends—consistent with the standing of so distinguished a man—and the urgings of his colleagues on the mission to relax and think of his own life. Yet, hurrying, hastening, anxious to carry out your instructions, he persisted to the end in his steadfast purpose, in spite of his illness. *7* When Sulpicius arrived, Antonius was much disturbed because the conditions reported to him in your instructions had been drawn up at the instance and the advice of Sulpicius; and he made it plain how much he hated the Senate when he received the death of the Senate's adviser with such insolent delight.

*Antony was the murderer.*

Antonius therefore killed Servius Sulpicius just as much as Leptines killed Octavius and the King of Veii killed the men I mentioned a moment ago. The man who was the cause of death surely inflicted it also. For this reason I think that it is pertinent for the record of future generations as well that it should be plain to see what the judgment of the Senate was concerning this war. The statue itself will bear testimony that the war was so important that the death of an envoy won a memorial of honor.

*8* But if you are willing to recall, gentlemen of the Senate, the excuse Servius Sulpicius made for declining the mission, no doubt will remain but that we are repairing by honor to the dead the injury we did to the living. You, gentlemen of the Senate—this is a serious charge to make, yet I must make it—you, I say, you took the life of Servius Sulpicius. When you saw him excusing himself as a sick man, more by the fact than by the words, you were of course not cruel—what could be less appropriate to this body?—but when you so confidently expected that there was nothing that his influence and wisdom could not bring about, you withstood all his excuses and forced the man who had always considered your unanimous decision as having great weight to forego his objections.

*9* Yes, and when the urging of the consul Pansa was added, more moving than the ears of Servius Sulpicius had known how to resist, then at the last he took me and his son to one side and spoke in such a way as to imply that he placed your authority ahead of his own life. Astounded at his resolute spirit, his son and I did not venture to oppose his wishes. His son, a man of unique devotion to his father, was deeply moved; my own grief did not fall far short of the son's emotion; but each of us was forced to give way to Sulpicius' greatness of character and the weight of his words when—accompanied, I may say, by the hearty compliments and congratulations of all of you— he promised to do what you wished and not to dodge the risks of the policy in which he himself had been the prime mover. We saw him to the city limits the next morning as he hurried to carry out your instructions. I may add that as he left he spoke to me in such a way that what he said seemed to anticipate what was to come.

*The character of Sulpicius*

*10* Give him back, then, gentlemen of the Senate, give him back the life which you took away: the life of the dead, as you know, lies in the memory of the living. Ensure that the man whom you, all unknowing, sent to his death may gain life everlasting at your hands. If, by your vote, you erect a statue on the rostra,[29] the forgetfulness of time to come will never obscure the remembrance of his mission.

His other achievements, I do not need to tell you, will have been entrusted to the memory of all men by many splendid memorials. Always will his reputation on the lips of all the living pay homage to his character, steadfastness, and sense of honor, and his exceptionally conscientious foresight in guarding the interests of the state. Yes, and his amazing, unbelievable, so to speak, and almost superhuman knowledge in the realm of legal interpretation, in the exposition of the principles of equity—that will not be silenced, either. All men of all time in this community who have had any competence in the science of law, if they were brought together in one place, would not be a match for Servius Sulpicius. For he was a master of justice no less than of jurisprudence; (*11*) he always referred specific propositions originating in statutory and common law to a flexible standard of equity, and he did not like to take cases to court when he could settle them out of court. He does not, therefore, need a statue as a memorial to these accomplishments; he has other memorials, and greater ones. This statue will bear witness to his honorable death, those other things will be a memorial to a life of enduring renown, so that the monument now in question will vouch rather for the Senate's gratitude than for a hero's fame.

*Sulpicius' son*

*12* The devotion of the son will also appear to have had considerable influence upon the honor we pay to the father. Although he is not with us today, overcome as he is by his grief, your attitude ought to be precisely the same as if he were present. I may say, by the way, that he is so overwhelmed that no man has ever grieved for an only son as he grieves for his father. And of course it also involves the good name of the son of Servius Sulpicius, as I see it, that he should seem to have secured due honor for his father. Even so, no finer memorial could Sulpicius have left than the likeness of his own character, his manliness, his steadfastness, his sense of duty, his great intellect—his son, whose sorrow can be lightened by this honor as by no other form of consolation.

*The specific proposal*

*13* And now as I call to mind the many conversations I have had with Servius Sulpicius in the course of our friendship, it seems to me that a bronze likeness, one showing him on foot, will please him more—if there is any awareness in death—than a gilded one showing him on horseback, the kind that was first erected for Lucius Sulla. Servius Sulpicius, you know, had a remarkable attachment for the conservative customs of our forefathers, and he strongly criticized the extravagances of our own day. Accordingly, just as if I were going to ask him about his own preferences, I move—just as if I were doing it with his authorization and consent—I move that we erect a bronze statue showing him on foot. And this, of course, as a memorial of honor, will lessen and soften the deep-felt grief and sense of loss that affects all citizens.

*14* And this motion of mine, gentlemen of the Senate, is necessarily endorsed by the motion of Publius Servilius, who has expressed the opinion that a tomb should be erected at public expense for Servius Sulpicius, but not a statue. I mean to say that if the death of an envoy without bloodshed and without any attack involving a weapon does not call for honor, why does he propose the honor of a state burial, which is considered to be the greatest honor that can be paid to the dead? Again, if he extends to Servius Sulpicius what was not extended to Gnaeus Octavius, why does he think that what was voted for Octavius should not be voted to Sulpicius? As a matter of fact, our forefathers voted statues for many, tombs at public expense for few. But statues are worn away by the weather, the malice of man, and the passage of time; the sanctity of the grave is in the earth itself, which cannot be molested or obliterated by any physical means; and so, while other honors fade away, the grave becomes more sacred with the ages

*15* Therefore, let this great man's statue be added to by the honor to which I refer—a man to whom no honor can be paid undeserved. Let us now show our appreciation in honoring the death of a man to whom our gratefulness cannot be shown in any other way. Let there be also marked with infamy the irresponsible effrontery of Marcus Antonius waging an unholy war; that is to say, once these honors have been conferred on Servius Sulpicius, the testimony as the repudiation and rejection of the mission by Antonius will last for all time.

*The formal motion*

On the basis of these considerations, I now move: *Whereas* Servius Sulpicius Rufus, son of Quintus, a member of the Lemonian electoral division, at a time of grave national crisis, suffering as he was from a serious and critical illness, placed the authority of the Senate and the welfare of his country ahead of his own life, and fought against the violent and overwhelming nature of his illness in making his way to the place where the Senate had sent him, to the camp of Marcus Antonius; and when he had all but reached Antonius' headquarters, overcome by his illness, he lost his life at a time of national crisis; and his death has been in keeping with a life lived in complete integrity and honor, a life in which Servius Sulpicius was often of great service to the state, both as a private citizen and in public office; and

*16 Whereas* a man of this distinction has met his death while in service of the state, it is the will of the Senate that, by vote of this body, a bronze statue showing him on foot should be set up on the rostra, and that around this statue a place five feet square shall be reserved for his children and their descendants for viewing the games and gladiatorial shows, inasmuch as he died for his country, and that the reason therefor shall be inscribed on the base of the statue; and that Gaius Pansa and/or Aulus Hirtius the consuls, if it shall seem good to them, shall instruct the City Quaestors to let a contract for the construction of the base and the statue and for their erection on the rostra, and shall see to it that the

contract monies be appropriated and paid to the contractor; and

*Whereas* the Senate has heretofore shown its authority in the funerals of, and in the distinctions conferred upon, brave men, it is the will of the Senate that Sulpicius' funeral shall be conducted with all ceremony; and

*17 Whereas* Servius Sulpicius Rufus, son of Quintus, of the Lemonian electoral division, has deserved so well of the republic that he ought to be honored with these marks of distinction, the Senate votes, and considers it in the public welfare, that the Curule Aediles suspend their rulings concerning funerals in the case of the funeral of Servius Sulpicius Rufus, the son of Quintus, of the Lemonian electoral division; and that Gaius Pansa, the consul, designate for the burial a space of thirty feet square in the Campus Esquilinus, or in such place as may seem good to him, where Servius Sulpicius may be buried; which plot shall also belong to his children and their descendants, and shall be furnished at public expense with clear title for such place of burial.

[The motion was carried.]

# NOTES TO SELECTIONS FROM CICERO'S SPEECHES

1. See selections from Quintilian, below.

2. See selections from Cicero's philosophical works.

3. See translations of his philosophical works.

4. E.g., Marius. See the selections from Sallust.

5. The consuls had to be forty-three years old.

6. See note on Philippic IX, 10.

7. Cf. the "Old Oligarch's" remarks on "decent" people in his *Constitution of Athens* (Vol. I).

8. Accius (170–*c.* 85 B.C.), Roman tragic poet, of whose work only fragments now remain. The passage quoted is from his *Atreus.*

9. Cicero is to enlarge on this theme later, in his treatise *On the Laws,* translated in part below.

10. If a woman with expensive family worship to keep up married a childless old man, the responsibility for the rites was transferred to him, but ceased forever at his death.

11. The praetor, or judge, before whom the case was tried.

12. Author unknown.

13. In connection with the Bona Dea, see the introductory note to this selection.

14. The motion was in two parts: (a) that the riot in

which Milo was involved was not in the public interest; (b) that an extraordinary hearing be held. Part (a) was carried; the tribune Plancus then vetoed part (b), and Pompey then appointed his blue-ribbon jury.

15. Jurors were given two tablets, one with A—"*absolvo,* I acquit," and another with C—"*condemno,* I condemn." The juror discarded one; the other, which he turned in, was his vote.

16. The Scipio of the *Dream.*

17. In the sense in which Cicero uses the term in *For Sestius.*

18. Antony had complained in this connection that Cicero, in spite of his presumed friendship, had appeared in court against him, and that Cicero had made a poor return for favors that Antony had done him. Cicero's retort was that a man of Antony's low character was not in a position to do anyone favors.

19. Referring to Antony's supposed forgery of documents after Caesar's death. Antony had taken over Caesar's secretarial staff and all his files.

20. One of the traditional founders of the Roman republic in 509 B.C.

21. The mother of Marcus Brutus was Servilia, whose

ancestor Gaius Servilius Ahala supposedly killed an aspirant to kingly power in 439 B.C. On Ahala, cf. *For Milo*, sec. 8.

22. During the Civil War.

23. Cicero had earlier twitted Antony for giving two thousand acres of tax-free public land to one Sextus Clodius, an alleged expert in rhetoric.

24. An allusion to certain scandalous allegations that Cicero had made earlier.

25. Another reference to Antony's elocution, at a wild party with some of his friends.

26. The police in ancient times used an instrument somewhat like a pitchfork to make prisoners step lively.

27. As a member of the college of augurs, Antony had reported the auspices unfavorable when Dolabella was elected consul. As presiding consul, Antony declared Dolabella's election illegal. The question was, had Dolabella been elected or hadn't he?

28. Sarcasm: Bambalio was Antony's father-in-law, elsewhere described by Cicero as "no account."

29. Speakers' platform in the Forum, so called, in the plural, because it was decorated with the bronze beaks (*rostra*) of ships captured in war. Modern practice uses the singular, rostrum.

# SELECTIONS FROM CICERO'S PHILOSOPHICAL WORKS

*Translated by Paul MacKendrick*

## INTRODUCTION

IF A MAN who has been an eloquent and successful trial lawyer and eminent in public life, a man, for example, like William Jennings Bryan, suddenly in his sixties turns to the writing of philosophy, it is interesting to speculate about his motive. To be sure, all thinking men are interested in the history of thought. It is equally certain that philosophy offers certain consolations to those who, like Cicero, grieve for the death of a beloved daughter. Again, a statesman whose party is out of power suffers from enforced leisure which philosophizing may occupy. There is some merit, too, in popular treatment of abstruse subjects, in the compilation of an encyclopedia of the best thoughts of the Greeks on the theory of knowledge, rhetoric, politics (*On the Republic, On the Laws*), religion (*On the Nature of the Gods, On Divination*), and ethics (*On the Chief End of Man, Tusculan Disputations, On Duty*). But the most interesting, and perhaps even the most important motive may be propagandistic. It is possible to argue that there is a certain unity in all of Cicero's thought, that his orations, letters, rhetorical and philosophical works all tend toward the same end: the justification of the role of the conservative party in Roman politics. The central core of his argument, borrowed from Plato, Aristotle, and the Stoics, is: "The rule of reason is the law of the universe; reason in Rome is found chiefly in the *optimates*' party; therefore the *optimates*' party should rule the universe." Many of the selections here presented illustrate this thesis, though an effort has been made to show also what objective justification there is for Cicero's influence upon western thought in the Middle Ages and the eighteenth century.

Of course Cicero did not suddenly begin to philosophize on the day his daughter died. He tells us himself (*On the Nature of the Gods*, I, 6) that he was philosophizing most when he looked least like it, and it is true that his earliest education, chosen for him by an ambitious father with an eye on a public career for his son, included phil-osophical study as a part of his training in public speaking. Before he was twenty he had met the most distinguished philosophers of his day, and the controversies of the Stoics, the Epicureans, and the Academics became very real to him as he heard them argued by experts in his own house. In fact, the impact of Greek philosophy might be said to have hit him, at an impressionable age, as a new religious sect may hit a particularly devout community. His earliest published work was a translation of Plato; during his travels abroad (79–77 B.C.) he listened to lectures in philosophy in Athens and in Rhodes. Even in his poetry, of which in charity to his memory the less said the better, he mentions his philosophical studies. Down to the time of his consulship he was doing more reading than writing in philosophy, to which he turned by instinct in times of personal danger or depression. But he still hoped, even in exile, for glory as a statesman rather than as a philosopher. Yet as the influence of Julius Caesar and his party increased, Cicero was pushed more and more into the political background and into an attempt to justify in theory the regime of the optimates which had failed in practice. The dictatorship of Caesar gave him the leisure he least wanted, and in less than two years he turned out the enormous bulk of his philosophical works. One last political battle, that against Mark Antony, proved fatal; Cicero paid with his life for being unable to practise the philosophic calm which he preached so often to his readers.

Of the works themselves Cicero professed no high opinion; he says of them (*Letters to Atticus*, XII, 52, 3) : "They are mere copies; they cost me no trouble. I simply supply the words, of which I have plenty." The deprecatory remarks of Cicero, like those of Brahms about his symphonies, are not intended to be taken seriously. But originality is one thing and influence is another; Cicero's philosophical works have impressed the mind of western man far beyond their intrinsic merit, and that is the justification, if any is required, for the space they occupy in this anthology. Furthermore, since the Greek Stoics are fragmentary, sententious, or late, the selections from Cicero, especially from *On the Nature of the Gods*, represent here the Stoic philosophy of the Roman republic. St. Augustine's conversion was influenced by Cicero's philosophy; St. Ambrose adapted Cicero's work *On Duty* to the duty of a Christian priest; St. Thomas Aquinas' chapters in the *Summa* on Natural Law go back to Cicero's treatise *On the Laws*; Hugo Grotius' work in international law is indebted to the Stoics as interpreted by Cicero; and the American Federalists, though not Jefferson, turned the ideas of Cicero's *On the Republic* to use in framing the American Constitution. The works excerpted here, then, form the cornerstone of the conservative tradition. The question how durable that cornerstone is forms one of the burning problems of our troubled time.

This introduction is not intended to suggest that it is not worth while to try to follow the course of Cicero's arguments, since he is simply writing political propaganda. Whether that was his intention or not, and whether he was unconsciously influenced by that or not, he does in many places offer us arguments, clearly stated, popular without being vulgar, which were for many centuries all that most western Europeans knew of the important

idealist tradition. Cicero's own view about philosophizing appears below (*On the Nature of the Gods*, I, 10) · ". . . in philosophical discussion the proper object . . . is feeling the weight of reason." It would be uncandid in the translator to conceal his own conviction that this weight has too often been thrown upon the side of privilege, but the selections have been chosen to allow the reader to make up his own mind, and there is no intent to belittle the importance of the idealist tradition, either historically or as a mental exercise.

THE TEXTS on which translations of these selections are based are the following: *Scipio's Dream*, F. E. Rockwood (Boston, 1903), with Arabic numbers referring to the smaller paragraphs of the Teubner text; *On the Laws*, Du Mesnil (Leipzig: Teubner, 1879); *On the Chief End of Man*, Miss W. M. L. Hutchinson (London, 1907), to whose notes the translator is indebted; *Tusculan Disputations*, J. E. King, Loeb Classical Library (Cambridge, Mass., and London, 1945), in the use of which every effort has been made to avoid the influence of King's translation; *On the Nature of the Gods*, O. Plasberg, revised by W. Ax (Leipzig: Teubner, 1933); *On Divination*, C. F. W. Muller (Leipzig: Teubner, 1889); *On Old Age* and *On Friendship*, R. Klotz (Leipzig: Teubner, 1855); *On Duty*, C. Atzert (Leipzig: Teubner, 1932).

## SCIPIO'S DREAM, *FROM* ON THE REPUBLIC

*Scipio's Dream* is a part of the sixth book of the fragmentary work, *On the Republic*, which Cicero wrote between 54 and 52 B.C., during the active years between his exile (58–57 B.C.) and his provincial governorship (51–50). This was a period of increasing liberal influence in the Roman republic, centering in the rivalry between the conservative Cato and the liberal Julius Caesar, who was increasing his prestige and his income by his successes in Gaul and Britain. Cicero, as spokesman for Roman conservatives, apparently felt, as he was to feel in his later philosophical works also, that the time was more than ripe for rallying the upper class round a political and philosophical ideal. He found the basis for it in the *Republic* of Plato and the *Politics* of Aristotle, applying their theories to the practical problems of the Roman state as he saw them. Essentially, his position was that "the leisure, independence, and self-interest, which the ownership of property entailed, and the intelligence which a superior education promoted, gave to the upper class a right both to determine the general policy and to attend to the administration of a state." [1]

The essay *On the Republic*, consequently, is less a systematic work of political theory than the lively small

talk of a group of cultivated men influenced by party and class prejudice, about the need for "good and honest" men ("decent citizens," the Old Oligarch would call them) to participate actively in public life. Following the Platonic tradition, Cicero casts the work in the form of a dialogue held by a group of aristocrats at leisure in the golden age before the beginning of apparent success for the liberal reforms of the Gracchi (129 B.C.). The group were typical of aristocrats of the time in that they had mostly held the consulship, were interrelated by marriage, had studied philosophy, and were experts in the law. They represent, in short, a later phase of the famous Scipionic circle, which had supported and perhaps collaborated in the writing of Terence's comedies.

The first book of the treatise defends the life of a statesman, defines the commonwealth, describes its degeneration, and takes the actual Roman aristocratic republic of 129 B.C., with its system of checks and balances, as the type of the ideal state. It is interesting for Americans to note that this balanced constitution, as described by the Greek historian Polybius (also a member of the Scipionic circle), profoundly influenced the writing of the American Constitution. In the second and third books,

Cicero gives a brief resumé of Roman history as he sees it, and, like Plato, mentions the ideal statesman and the necessity for justice in the state. In the fragmentary fourth book, social classes, moral standards, the influence of the drama, and especially education were probably among the subjects discussed. In Book V, old fashioned aristocratic virtue is praised in the person of the ideal statesman. In Book VI, with which we are primarily concerned, Cicero is apparently following the model set by Plato when he ended his *Republic* with a vision of judgment, the Myth of Er (Vol. I, p. 346), wherein he aims to show the reward of the good man in the after life. One of the interlocutors wants a statue raised to the aristocrat who murdered the liberal Tiberius Gracchus. To this the younger Scipio replies that the aristocrats have a more durable reward than mere statuary, and then proceeds to describe the bird's-eye view of the universe and the conservative's reward in it, given him in a dream by his grandfather. This famous Roman, the elder Scipio, was the hero of the Second Punic War, in which his victories gave Rome the rich province of Spain and the position of the greatest Mediterranean political, military, and commercial power.

*Scipio's Dream* should be read in comparison and contrast with Plato's Myth of Er, and the reader should bear in mind that however much Plato may have been above the actual political battle of his time (and this is an open question), Cicero was definitely in the midst of it and wrote his *Republic* as a part of the propaganda battle between Roman conservatives and Roman liberals. Eternal life, thus considered, is not for everyone, but for those who have given security, support, and increase to the fatherland: in short, the Roman aristocracy. It is their devotion to the conservative cause which will lead to their life of eternal blessedness among the wonders of the universe and the music of the spheres. By comparison with this happiness, mere earthly reputation and memorials are of little worth, for entrance to heaven is based not upon these but upon aristocratic virtues and a sense of *noblesse oblige*. It is the activity of the conservative mind, which is the microcosm of the mind of God, that gives men like Scipio (or Cicero) their best hope of heaven; members of rival philosophical schools, and, by implication, rival political parties must be purged of much dross before they can be admitted. Ironically enough, it is possible that the ideal of the *princeps*, or philosophical director of the state, which Cicero works out here, was used by Caesar's great-nephew and heir Octavian (later the emperor Augustus) to give an aura of respectability to his bourgeois one-man rule, which Cicero, if he had lived, would have abominated.

To say that *Scipio's Dream* is a work of propaganda is not to deny its literary merit. It is written in Cicero's most polished periodic style, and its descriptions, strongly influenced by Stoic physics, of heaven, earth, and the music of the spheres have exerted a profound literary influence

in the Middle Ages and modern times. With the Myth of Er, it forms a part of the dream literature of western Europe, as represented by the story of Jacob's ladder in Genesis, the Revelation of St. John the Divine, Dante's *Divine Comedy,* and *Pilgrim's Progress.* It is perhaps indicative of the central importance of politics in Greek and Roman life ("Man is by nature a *political* animal") that in none of these visions is the life to come so squarely based on political activity in this world as in the dreams described by Plato and Cicero. Symbolic of the change from the classical to the Christian point of view is the fact that our sole manuscript of *On the Republic* was erased in the Middle Ages—which knew *Scipio's Dream* from another source—to make room for a commentary on the Psalms by St. Augustine, and not rediscovered and deciphered until 1820.

*The younger Scipio, on duty in Africa, dreams of his grandfather.*

VI, 9 "After I had reported in Africa to the consul, Manius Manilius, as military tribune (you recall) of the Fourth Legion, what I wanted most was to meet King Masinissa, who was for good reasons a very close family friend. When I paid him a visit, the old man embraced me, the tears streaming down his face, then looked up to heaven and said: 'Thanks to the sun in the highest, and to the moon and stars, that before I die I see in my kingdom and under my roof a Publius Cornelius Scipio, the very mention of whose name refreshes me, so clearly stamped on my mind is the memory of that splendid and invincible man, his grandfather.' Then I asked him questions about his kingdom, he asked me about our republic, and that day passed for both of us in a long conversation.

10 "After a regal banquet, we prolonged our talk far into the night. My grandfather was the sole subject of the old king's conversation; he remembered the things he had said as well as the things he had done. Then, when we parted for the night, I fell into a deeper sleep than usual, because I was tired from my journey and had stayed up late. (I believe the subject of our conversation was responsible for what followed; for it quite often happens that what we think and talk about has an effect on our sleep, as in Ennius' account of his vision of Homer, whom of course he used often to think and talk about during his waking hours.) At any rate my grandfather appeared to me, in a likeness which I recognized more from his portrait bust than from personal

recollection. To tell the truth, I shuddered when I saw who it was, but he said, 'Be brave; fear not, Scipio, and hand on my words to posterity.'

*Scipio's grandfather foretells the young man's future honors and possible murder.*

*11* "From a high place brightly illuminated by full starlight he pointed down toward Carthage, and said, 'Do you see that city, which once I humbled before the Roman people, now taking up again the old war, and incapable of keeping the peace? Now you have come, a mere private, to besiege it. Within these three years you will become consul and overturn it, and thereby earn in your own right the nickname "Africanus," which up to now you have worn as a mere inheritance. When you have destroyed Carthage, you will hold a triumph, you will become censor, you will go on missions to Egypt, Syria, Asia Minor and Greece; in your absence from Rome you will again be elected consul; you will win a major war, you will level Numantia to the ground. But when you ride again in your triumphal chariot onto the Capitoline Hill, you will find the republic in turmoil over the policies of my grandson Tiberius Gracchus.

*12* " 'This is the time, Africanus, when you must reveal to your fatherland the keenness of your mind, your talents, and your judgment. But at this time too I see destiny opening before you a parting of the ways. For when the years of your life have completed seven times eight solstices, and when these two numbers, each of which is considered perfect for a different reason, in nature's round have reached the sum that is foreordained for you, the whole state will turn to you alone and to your proud name; it is to you that the Senate, all the aristocrats, the allies, Latin and Italian, will look for guidance; on you alone the state will depend for security; in short, you will be needed as dictator to restore public order, if only you escape the treacherous hands of your own kin.' At this point Laelius broke out into an exclamation, and the rest uttered heavy groans, but Scipio smiled gently and said, 'Sh! You'll wake me from my dream! Hear the rest of my story; it will take only a little while.'

*Incentives to patriotism: eternal life for good conservatives*

*13* " 'But to spur you on to greater eagerness to preserve the republic, Africanus, be assured of this: for all who have given security, support, and increase to the fatherland, there has been ordained in heaven a special place where they may enjoy in blessedness eternal life; for to that director god who rules the universe there is nothing, at least on earth, closer to his heart than that united assembly of mankind, joined together under law, which we call the State, whose rulers and preservers, sent from heaven, to heaven return.'

*Incentives to conservatives: the true life is the life after death.*

*14* "At this point, stricken as I was by fear not so much of death as of plots within my own family, I plucked up courage to ask him, 'Are you, and my father Paulus, and the others whom we think of as dead, really still alive?' 'The truth is,' he replied, 'that it is those who have escaped from the bonds of the body as from a prison who are really living; your so-called life is the real death. Look! Your father Paulus approaches.' As I caught sight of him, I dissolved in tears, but with an embrace and a kiss he bade me stop my weeping.

*This blessedness may not be attained by suicide*

*15* "As soon as I could check the flood of tears and speak, I said, 'Most reverend and best of fathers, since this life of yours is really life, as I have just heard my grandfather say, why do I stay on earth instead of hurrying to come to you?' 'That is not the solution,' he replied. 'For unless that God, whose temple is all that your eye can see, releases you from this galling prison house of the body, you cannot gain entrance here. For man was given life on condition that he would inhabit that globe, the earth, which you see in the midst of this firmament, and the source of man's soul is those eternal fires which you mortals call planets and stars, which, as spheres each endowed with the living breath of divine minds, complete the circuit of their orbits with a speed that wakes our wonder. Therefore both you, my son, and all loyal Romans must keep your souls in the custody of your bodies, and not leave mortal life unbidden by him by whom your souls were given you. Otherwise you will appear to have deserted the post among men assigned you by God.

*But by a life of devotion to the conservative cause*

" 'But, like your grandfather here, like me who begot you, Scipio, practise justice and loyalty, virtues which, important as they are in the case of parents and kinsfolk, are most important of all as they affect the fatherland. Such a life is the road to heaven and to this assemblage of those who have finished with mortal life, and, released from the body, dwell in that place which you see.'

*Which will lead to an eternity among the wonders of the universe.*

16 "Pointing to a ring of light blazing with uncommon splendor among the other flames, he continued, 'And this, as the Greeks have taught you, you call the Galaxy or Milky Way.' As I looked at it, it seemed to make the rest of the heavens wondrous bright. Moreover there were stars there such as we never see from this earth, and all of a size beyond our wildest conjecture; the smallest of these was the moon, farthest from the sphere of heaven, closest to the earth, shining with a borrowed light. Furthermore, the stellar spheres were far larger than the earth. The result was that the earth itself seemed to me so small that I was vexed at the small size of our empire, which gives us access to the merest pinpoint, as it were, of earth.

*The nine spheres, the planets, and the stars*

17 "As I kept looking down, my grandfather said, 'How long, pray, will your mind remain earth-bound? Do you not see that you have come into the temple of the sky? The universe, you must know, is built of nine circles or rather hollow spheres, one within the other, of which one is the sphere of heaven, the outermost, embracing all the rest, identical with God himself, the all-highest, limiting and containing the others; studded in this heavenly sphere are the eternal rolling orbits of the fixed stars; and beneath it are the seven spheres which revolve the opposite way from the heavenly sphere; one of these spheres is occupied by that planet which on earth men call Saturn. Next comes the glow of that good-omened and health-bringing planet called Jupiter; next below is Mars, red and hateful to the earth; next, about half-way between

heaven and earth, comes the sun, the leader, chief, and regulator of all other sources of light, the mind and guiding principle of the universe, so large that it surveys and fills all things with its light. One of the two orbits that follows close upon the sun is Venus, the other Mercury, and in the inmost sphere the moon turns, lit by the sun's rays. Beneath the sphere of the moon there is nothing that is not mortal and frail, except the souls granted as a gift of the gods to the race of men, but above the moon all things are eternal. For the core of all the hollow spheres, the ninth, the earth, does not move, but is the lowest, so that all heavy objects gravitate toward it of their own weight.'

*The music of the spheres*

18 "After I had collected myself following the amazement with which I viewed the spheres, I asked, 'What is this music, so mighty and so sweet, that fills my ears?' 'It is the driving motion of the spheres themselves that produces it,' he replied; 'though the intervals that separate them are unequal, yet the spheres are arranged in an exact proportion; the harmony of bass and treble makes a series of matched chords. For so mighty a motion cannot proceed in silence, and naturally at one extreme of the universe the sound is high, at the other low. That is, that outermost orbit, the heavenly one that carries the stars, because it moves the fastest, moves with a high-pitched, lively sound, while this lowest, or lunar, sphere moves with a deep bass note. I leave the ninth, the earth, out of account, for it remains forever fixed, and motionless in one place, occupying the midpoint of the universe. But the other eight orbits, two of which (Mercury and Venus) move at the same speed, strike seven notes with fixed intervals. This number is the key of almost everything; imitating this music with stringed instruments and the voice, expert musicians have opened for themselves a pathway back to heaven, just as others have whose massive intellects have followed divine pursuits in the midst of this human life.

19 " 'When the ears of mere mortals are filled with this music, they grow deaf; indeed, hearing is the dullest of your senses. Just as the people who dwell in the high mountains at the cataracts of the Nile have lost their sense of hearing entirely, because the roar is so deafening, even so

this music, resulting from the turning of the whole universe at high velocity, is so great a thing that men's ears cannot hear it, just as you cannot look straight at the sun without its rays blinding your eyes.'

*By comparison with this eternal life, the reputation of the conservative on earth is unimportant, because limited in space and time.*

"Marvel as I did at this, I could not keep my eyes from perpetually looking at the earth.

20 "Just then my grandfather said, 'I perceive that you still cannot take your mind off the habitat and abode of men; but if it seems to you to be as small as it really is, keep this heavenly sphere ever in view, and despise that mortal one. For what reputation can you gain from the converse of mere men, or what glory that is worth the striving? You see from here that the earth is inhabited only here and there in confined spaces, and that desert wastes lie between these inhabited blots or patches. You see too that dwellers on earth are not only so cut off from one another that there can be no intercommunication; but that some live in the same longitude as you but in the opposite latitude, others in the same latitude but in the opposite longitude, while still others live at the antipodes. Surely you cannot expect your reputation to spread among any of these.

21 " 'From here also you can see that this same earth is girdled round, as it were, by several zones, two of which, as far apart as possible, and supported by the opposite poles of the heavens, you see to be frozen solid, while the middle and widest zone is parched by the heat of the sun. Only the remaining two are habitable. The South Temperate Zone, where, from your point of view, men walk upside down, has nothing to do with Romans; this other, buffeted by the north wind, where you live—see how small a part of it belongs to you. For the whole territory you inhabit, narrowly limited from north to south, wider from east to west, is nothing but a sort of tiny island, surrounded by that sea which though on earth you call it the Atlantic, the Great Sea, the Ocean, or some grandiose name, is really, as you see, quite infinitesimal.

22 " 'Out of the area of this known and inhabited world, small as it is, how likely is it that your name, or that of any one of us, can climb

the Caucasus which you see here, or swim the Ganges there? Who at the other ends of the earth, east or west, north or south, will hear your name? When you have lopped off these areas, surely you see what narrow limits your fame would have to spread itself in. As for those who actually do talk about us, how long will they do so?

*In the passage of the millennia of the Great Year, temporal reputation will be forgotten.*

23 " 'And this is not all. Even if *our* posterity should want to hand on to theirs the eulogy of any one of us which they received as a heritage from their fathers, the floods and conflagrations which must occur at fixed intervals would make it impossible for us to achieve a temporal, much less an eternal glory. In any case what does it matter that posterity will talk about you, when you consider that your ancestors never did? And yet those same ancestors are at least as numerous as posterity, and they were certainly better men.

24 " 'These considerations become especially striking when you reflect that not one of those who can hear our name mentioned have memories a year long. For men unscientifically calculate a year on the basis of the revolution of the sun alone, a single star; but when all the stars return to their starting point, and after eons the whole heaven again looks the same as it did at the beginning, then that can really be called the revolving cycle of a true year, and in it I scarcely dare to mention how many generations of men are included. Perhaps I can express it this way. When the sun suffers eclipse in the same quarter of heaven and on the same day of the year as once it seemed to men to do, at the time the soul of Romulus made its way hither, and when all the constellations have been called back to the positions they held then, you may consider the year to have come full circle; but you must know that of that year scarce a twentieth part has so far passed.

*Entrance to heaven is based not on vulgar reputation but on virtue and nobility.*

25 " 'If then you have no hope of return hither to heaven, where great and eminent men find their just reward, consider on the other hand how little that petty human reputation is worth, which can scarcely last the smallest fraction of a single year. If therefore it is your wish to look

on high and contemplate this dwelling, this eternal home, you will not debase yourself to seek the good will of vulgar men, nor centre your hopes upon any rewards that mere men can give. Let virtue, shining by her own light, attract you to the true reward. As for what others may say about you, leave that to them, in the assurance that there will be gossip in any case. Remember that all such gossip is confined to these zones which you see; no man's reputation, for good or ill, ever lasted forever. Men die, and their fame is buried; posterity forgets, and reputation is snuffed out.'

26 "When he had finished, I said, 'Grandfather, if it is really true that for those who have deserved well of the fatherland a straight path, as it were, leads to the gate of heaven, in that case, even though from boyhood I have followed in your footsteps and my father's, and have given you nothing to be ashamed of, now that you have revealed to me so great a reward I shall strive all the more vigilantly.'

*It is the mind and not the body that attains eternal life.*

" 'Strive you must,' he answered, 'and keep in mind that it is not you that is mortal, but this outward body; for what your mere outline reveals is not the real you; essentially it is each person's mind that *is* that person, and not the bodily shape which the finger can point to. Know then that you are a god, if indeed energy, thought, memory, and foresight are godlike. For the mind is ruler, director, and mover of the body, which it commands exactly as the great director God rules this universe; and as the eternal God himself moves the universe which is in part mortal, so the eternal mind moves the body which is subject to decay.

*It is the godlike motion of mind or soul that makes the world go round.*

27 " 'For what is always in motion is eternal; but whatever is the source of motion to another object and itself derives its motion from some source must find the limit of its existence in the limit of its motion. Only the self-mover, since it never deprives itself of motion, never stops, but is rather the source and origin of motion for other moving objects. But such a first principle

has no starting point; for all things originate from a first principle, while the first principle itself can originate from no other thing; for what came into being from some other source would not be a first principle; but if it never begins, it never ceases either. For once a first principle has ceased to exist, it will not come into being again from some other source, nor create another first principle out of itself; at least it will not, if it is true that all things must start from a first principle. That is why the first principle of motion rises out of what is self-moved; but this self-mover cannot be born or die, or else the whole heavens would fall of necessity and all nature come to a stop and find no other source of motion which would impel it to start its motion again from the beginning.

28 " 'Since then it is obvious that whatever is self-moved is eternal, who can deny that self-motion is the natural attribute of souls? For whatever is moved by an external force is without soul or inanimate; but what has a soul or is animate has within itself the source of its own motion; for this self-motion is the unique quality and force of the soul; and if it is the only thing in the universe which is self-moved it is clearly not subject to birth and is therefore eternal.

*The conservative's use of his divine mind in politics is his best hope of heaven; Epicureans cannot be admitted without a long term in purgatory.*

29 " 'Use it therefore to the best ends. For example, it is the best man's sense of responsibility for the security of the fatherland which rouses the soul and uses it so as to make it wing its way more swiftly to this its proper dwelling-place. This it will do the more rapidly, if, while it is still enclosed in the body, it will look abroad, and, in the contemplation of the things beyond the body, will withdraw itself as far as possible from it. For when men surrender themselves and, as it were, cater to the bodily pleasures, which desire impels them to minister to, they violate the laws of gods and men, and their souls, when they escape the body, flit about the earth itself and return not to heaven until after many centuries of torture.'

"My grandfather's image faded away: I was loosed from the bondage of my dream."

# ON THE LAWS

The theory of Plato's *Republic* was followed in his old age by the grim practicality of his *Laws*, based at least in part on actual Athenian legal procedure. Cicero, immediately after writing his *Republic*, set to work on a treatise *On the Laws* (ca. 52–46 B.C., never finished) in which actual Roman law is idealized as the Roman constitution is idealized in his earlier work. Ostensibly in dialogue form, the book consists largely of long monologues by the author. The central core is the administrative code laid down in Book III, 6–11, which, with all its imperfections from the point of view of the modern liberal, gives evidence of the genius for administration which held the Roman Empire together, and to which all modern government is indebted. The other speakers are Cicero's brother Quintus and his publisher, the millionaire Epicurean Titus Pomponius Atticus. The scene is Cicero's ancestral villa on the River Liris near Arpinum; the dramatic date, 52 B.C.

In his *Laws*, as in his *Republic*, Cicero reveals himself both as the defender of the *status quo* and as the popularizer for all succeeding ages of some of the fundamental ideas of western legal and political theory: e.g., the Stoic concept of Natural Law which underlies the American Declaration of Independence, and the Stoic concept of the Law of Nations which underlies man's aspirations toward One World. Both these concepts Cicero borrows from the Stoic view of man as a rational animal, deriving his reason from God and sharing it with all other men, who are therefore his brothers and to be treated with equity. But closely connected with this reasoning is the idea of the hierarchy in nature, the Great Chain of Being, which Cicero uses to justify the control of the state by his—the conservative or *"optimates"*—party. The selections which follow have been chosen to bring out both sides of Cicero's thought: balancing the high ideal of the law in I, 15–23, and the fine passage on *noblesse oblige* (III, 30–32), we have the deeply prejudiced remarks on the impiety of Cicero's enemies (II, 42–43), the subtle condemnation of Rome's most democratic office, the tribunate (III, 19–26), and the highly undemocratic condemnation of the secret ballot in elections (III, 34, 37–39).

In the first fourteen paragraphs of Book I, omitted here, Atticus urges Cicero to write a history of Rome. Cicero rejoins that he would be eager to do so if leisure permitted, but that first there is required an analysis and interpretation of the laws about which Roman history is largely built. From this beginning arises the discussion which follows.

## From Book I

### Introduction: Importance of Law, philosophically considered

*15* ATTICUS. If you ask what I, at least, expect of you, it is this. Now that you have written a *Republic*, or ideal state, you should, it seems, next write a *Laws*. For that is, I see, what your master, your favorite, your beloved Plato has done.

MARCUS. As he describes it, he, Clinias, and Megillus the Spartan, on a summer day in Crete, among the cypress glades of Cnossus, with many pauses for rest, talked about public administration and the best laws. Is that what you want me to do, as we walk or rest among these tall, slim poplars on this shady green river bank? Do you want us to investigate these same matters, a little more fully than lawyers usually do?

*16* ATTICUS. Those are exactly the things I want to hear.

MARCUS. How about Quintus?

QUINTUS. There is nothing I would rather listen to.

MARCUS. And quite right, too. For this is the way to look at it: there is no kind of discussion that makes clearer nature's gifts to human kind, or the number of superb thoughts in the mind of man, (indeed, it was to cultivate these gifts and make something of them that we were born and entered into the light of day), or the nature of human association in society. For only when these subjects have been expounded can the origin of law and justice be found.

*17* ATTICUS. Then, differing both from most of our contemporaries, who emphasize the praetor's edict, and from the elder generation of legal experts, who set great store by the Twelve Tables, you would derive law as a subject for study from the inmost depths of philosophy?

MARCUS. Yes, for in this conversation, Atticus, we are not investigating proper legal procedure or considering what our opinion would be in a given case. These things are important, to be sure, and many famous jurists have treated them in the past, while in our own day Sulpicius is an expert of the highest authority; but in this discussion we ought to embrace the whole subject of law and justice in such a way as to reduce our so-called "civil law" to a position of minor and restricted importance. For this is what we must do: expound the nature of law, derive it from the nature of man, consider the laws under which states ought to be ruled, and finally, treat of the collected and published laws and decrees of peoples, among which our own so-called "civil law" will not be least conspicuous.

*18* QUINTUS. You are taking up the investigation as you should, Marcus, at the very source. Any other interpretation of civil law opens the way to mere litigation, not justice.

MARCUS. That is where you are wrong, Quintus. It is not knowledge of the law, but ignorance of it, that leads to litigation. But that is a subject I will come back to. At the moment, let us consider the origins of justice.

*Definition of law: the universality of Natural Law*

The experts, then, usually begin with law, on the whole rightly, as long as they define it (as they do) as the highest reason, innate in nature, commanding right action and forbidding the contrary.[2] When this same reason has been firmly fixed in the mind of man, the result is law.

*19* And so, the experts think that law is practical wisdom, whose function it is to order right action and forbid transgression, and they think it derives its Greek name (*nomos*) from a word (*nemein*) implying giving each one his own, while I think our word (*lex*) is derived from the verb "to choose" (*legere*). For they emphasize equal distribution when they talk about law, and we emphasize choice, but actually both ideas belong in the definition. If this definition is correct, as I at least always think of it as being, it is right that we should derive the origin of justice from law, for law is a natural force, it is the thinking mind of the man of practical wisdom, it is the standard of judgment for justice and injustice. But since our whole discussion is concerned with the people's thinking on the subject, we shall have to use ordinary speech from time to time and say that law is what the mob calls it,

that which decrees its meaning in writing either by commanding or by forbidding. But let *us* derive the beginning of established justice from that highest law which was born centuries before any law was written down or any state founded.

*20* QUINTUS. Yes, that will be more convenient, and wiser, in keeping with the nature of our discussion as we have begun it.

*The origin of justice in Natural Law*

MARCUS. What is your pleasure, then? Shall we investigate the origins of justice itself? When they have been found, we can put the results of our investigations unhesitatingly under the right headings.

QUINTUS. Yes, that is the way I think it ought to be done.

ATTICUS. Record my vote along with your brother's.

MARCUS. Then we must retain and preserve the constitution of that *Republic* which Scipio took six books to prove ideal. All our laws have to be adapted to that type of state, but, more important, we must sow the seed of good moral character and not prescribe everything in writing. So I shall look for the root of justice in nature. It is under her guidance that our whole discussion should evolve.

ATTICUS. Precisely. With a guide like that, at any rate, we can hardly go wrong.

*21* MARCUS. Then do you grant us this, Atticus—for I know Quintus' opinion—that all nature is ruled by the immortal gods' power, nature, reason, force, mind, divinity, or whatever attribute I can use to make my meaning clearer? For if you don't grant that point, we shall have to arrange our argument with that particularly in mind.

ATTICUS. I grant it, if you insist. I am the readier to do so because the warbling of the birds and the purling of the streams keeps me from worrying about any of my fellow Epicureans' overhearing.

MARCUS. That, we must certainly not let happen. For, as good men should, they usually get quite angry at any such admission, and they won't stand for it at all if they hear that you have betrayed the very first principle of that excellent man Epicurus: "God does not worry in the slightest about himself or others."

ATTICUS. Please go on, for now that I have

granted your point, I want to see where it leads me.

*Law links man and God in one great community.*

MARCUS. I won't be too long about it. This is where it leads. That provident, sagacious, complex, sharp-witted animal, with so long a memory, so full of reason and judgment, which we call man, has been brought to birth by God the all-highest in very exalted circumstances. For he is the only one of all the numerous natural types of living creatures who shares in the power of reason and thought, which the others are entirely without. Moreover, what is more divine than reason, not merely in man, but in all heaven and earth? And when reason has reached the finish of maturity, it is properly called wisdom. *23* Therefore, since nothing is better than reason, and since it exists both in man and in God, the prime link between man and God is the bond of reason. Moreover, those who share reason, share right reason also. And since law is right reason, we ought to think that law also links man with the gods. Furthermore, those who share law, share justice also. Moreover, those who share law and justice ought to be considered to belong to the same state, all the more so if they obey the commands of the same authorities. Moreover, they obey this heavenly hierarchy, this divine mind, this omnipotent God, so that this whole universe ought to be considered a single state shared by gods and men. And as in states, by a system which I will discuss in its proper place, one's status is determined by one's family relationships, so in nature, but much more magnificently and pre-eminently, men are bound together by their family relationship to the gods. [The rest of Book I embroiders this theme of the Great Community, emphasizing man's duty to live in friendship with his neighbor. Friendship is the subject of a separate essay by Cicero; personal friendship was the basis of the *optimates'* political influence. If justice is a natural thing, it does not depend on the flux of opinion, or upon mere utility, as the Epicureans hold. The question of the origin of law leads to the question what is the highest good (treated in Cicero's essay *On the Chief End of Man*). Philosophy is to be praised for leading us to the recognition of the true law and, more important, of our true self,

with accompanying awareness of our duty. Book II is concerned with divine or canon law, which is discussed here on the ground that God has a priority over man. The discussion is based on the definition of Natural Law in Book I.]

*From* Book II

*Civil law must correspond to the unwritten law of God's reason: what does not, aims at corruption and is no law.*

*11* QUINTUS. I agree, brother, that law is identical with what is right and true, and that it does not stand or fall with the alphabet in which it is written.

MARCUS. Then just as the divine mind we were discussing is the highest law, so law is reason when it is perfected in man; and it is perfected in the wise man's mind. But the pieces of changeable and temporary legislation which are laid down for peoples are called laws more by courtesy than because they deserve the name. For the Stoics use some such arguments as these to show the praiseworthiness of any law properly so called: it is certainly evident that laws were invented for the security and preservation of citizens and states, and to assure a quiet and happy life for man; that the inventors and ordainers of such statutes proved to their fellow-citizens that they would write and pass laws under which, once they were approved and accepted, the people might live honorably and happily; and what they called "laws," of course, were pieces of legislation put together and passed with this ideal in mind. Consequently one might properly interpret those who lay down pernicious and unjust decrees for the populace as going back on their promises and professions, and their legislation as anything but "law." Thus it may be crystal clear that in the very interpretation of the word "law" there is the force and meaning "the act of *choosing* what is just and true." *12* Therefore I ask you, Quintus, as the Stoics do: if, because it lacks something, a state ought to be considered as nothing, is the thing which it lacks to be considered among good things?

QUINTUS. Yes; among the greatest.

MARCUS. Now when a state lacks law is it therefore to be considered of no account?

QUINTUS. Undeniably.

MARCUS. Then law must be included in the category of good things.

*13* QUINTUS. I quite agree.

MARCUS. But among the peoples of the world much legislation is passed which is pernicious and unhealthy. What are we to say about that? Do these deserve to be called laws any more than if a set of brigands had held a meeting and passed them? For doctors' prescriptions cannot be said to be sound if ignorant, unskilled practitioners prescribe poisons instead of proper medicines; similarly in a nation, any chance piece of legislation cannot be called a law, even though the populace has accepted it, ruinous as it is. Law then is the distinction between what is just and what is unjust, expressed in accordance with Nature, the oldest and chiefest of all things. And in accordance with Nature human laws are set up, punishing the wicked, preserving and protecting the good.

[Having set up an absolute standard for law, according to which conservatism is good, innovation bad, Cicero sets up his ideal code of religious law, emphasizing the importance of the aristocratic clan-cults, and of religion as useful to the state; he would forbid any religious ceremony not approved by the state, especially nocturnal rites or "mystery" religions; and he would have the priests supervise all public games. This brings him to the subject of music.]

*The influence of music on morals*

*38* Since public spectacles are divided into those in the circus and those in the theater, the circus shall be used for competition between man and man, in running, boxing, and wrestling, and for horse-racing, to last until it is determined who has won. In the theater there shall be music, vocal, on stringed instruments, and on woodwinds, but it must be moderate, as prescribed by law. For I agree with Plato that there is nothing that influences immature, malleable minds so easily as musical chords; it is impossible to overemphasize their power whether for good or for evil. For music excites men who are relaxed and relaxes men who are excited. Sometimes it keys men up; sometimes it unnerves them. Many Greek states attached importance to preserving their traditional music, but when their national character degenerated and became effeminate, they changed their music, too, and (according to some authori-

ties) were depraved by this sweet corruption. It is also possible that when their high moral standards lapsed on account of other vices, there was room in their ears and their souls, changed as they now were, also for innovations in music. *39* This is why Plato, at least, the wisest and by far the most learned man in Greece, especially feared relapse in music. For he said it was impossible to change musical modes without changing the public laws. Now I do not think such innovation is especially to be feared, but I do not think we should ignore it, either. But this I do view with alarm, that audiences that used to derive a high moral pleasure from the melodies of old poets like Livius and Naevius now leap up and twist their necks and roll their eyes to the rhythm of the new music.

[Continuing his commentary on religious law, Cicero insists on the preservation of traditional usages, and lays down punishments for religious violations, especially violation of oaths. God always punishes the wicked, he says, and he cites as evidence his enemy Clodius.]

*All Cicero's enemies are impious and have received their just reward.*

*42* The crimes of wicked citizens sullied religious justice when I was sent into exile; my household gods were driven from their shrine and in its place was built a temple not to Liberty but to Licence; I was driven from the very shrines I had saved. Run over the sequel quickly in your mind (for there is no point in naming names). I had a statue of Minerva, protectress of our city. Though all my property was confiscated and I was ruined, I would not allow unholy men to violate her; I took her from my house to her father Jupiter's. The verdict of the Senate, of Italy, of all nations has named me Preserver of the Fatherland. What greater distinction could come to a man? But of those whose crimes have weakened religion and laid her low, some lie prostrate in their turn, their gangs broken up and scattered, while the criminal ringleaders, more completely irreligious than the rest, have not only suffered disgrace and remorse of conscience, and lost their lives, but have even been denied funeral rites and burial.

*43* QUINTUS. Yes, I know their fate, brother, and I give the gods due thanks for it, but too often we see sacrilege turn out quite differently.

MARCUS. If we think the wicked go unpunished,

Quintus, that is because we do not properly understand what divine punishment is, but are carried away by mob opinion and fail to discern the truth. We judge human suffering in terms of death or bodily pain or mental anguish or judicial condemnation. I admit that these are the ills that flesh is heir to and that they have happened to many good men. But the punishment of crime is a sad business, and quite apart from the inevitable consequences is in itself a heavy burden to bear. Men who would never have been my enemies unless they had hated their fatherland, we have watched as they became the victims of the fires of their lust, their fear, or their conscience, their every act prompted in turn by fear and by scorn of religion; but the verdicts that we have seen them force through by bribery were the verdicts of men. The gods remain uncorrupted.

[Book II concludes with a detailed commentary on funeral customs, including a provision that patricians be buried separately from plebeians.]

### From Book III

[Book III, on administrative law, opens with a preface justifying the existence of superior and inferior in the state as a part of the law of Nature.]

### Ruling and being ruled

*2* MARCUS. You see then that the function of the magistrate is to preside, and to lay down what is right, useful, and conformable to law. For magistrates preside over the people as the law presides over magistrates, and it can truly be said that a magistrate is a speaking law, the law a silent magistrate. *3* Furthermore, it is a magistrate's official power that is best adapted to natural justice and to the terms of our compact with Nature, which is my definition of Law. Without this power nothing can endure; neither a household, a state, a noble family, the whole human race, the whole nature of things, nor the universe itself. For the universe obeys God; land and sea obey him; and the life of man bows to the decrees of the supreme law. *4* But let us come to matters closer to us and better known: once upon a time all ancient peoples were ruled by kings. This type of official power was offered at the beginning to the justest and wisest men, and that was the practice in our Roman commonwealth, as long as it was ruled

by kings; next the royal power was handed down to the next generation, as it still is in nations which now have kings. Objectors to royal power wanted to be free not from all obedience, but from obedience always to the same person. For my part, since I am legislating for free peoples and have already stated in six books *On the Republic* what my views are on the best sort of commonwealth, I shall on this occasion adapt my laws to the type of state I approve of. *5* We must, then, have administrative officials, whose foresight and hard work are indispensable to the state and whose organization embraces the entire state government. But it is not enough to prescribe to them the limits of their authority; the citizens, too, must know the extent of their obligation to obey. For the good governor has had in the past to obey, and the reasonable subject appears worthy some day to be a governor. So the subject must have grounds for hoping that he will some day be a governor, and the governor must keep in mind that he will soon have to be a subject. And I add to my preamble, following Charondas in his *Laws*, that the citizens shall love and cherish their magistrates, as well as be obedient and submissive to them; indeed my favorite Plato calls those who revolt against their magistrates "Titans," after those who revolted against the gods. So much for preamble; now for the laws themselves, if you please.

ATTICUS. For my part I am pleased both with the preamble and with your whole arrangement of topics.

### Cicero's ideal administrative code, based upon actual Roman practice

*6* MARCUS. Commands shall be in accordance with law, and citizens shall duly and unprotestingly obey them: the forms of coercion open to the magistrate against the disobedient or dangerous citizen shall be fines, imprisonment, or flogging, subject to the veto of equal or higher authority, or of the people, to whom there shall be the right of appeal. After the magistrate has given his opinion or proposed a fine, there shall be a trial before the people to determine the amount of the fine or the nature of the penalty. On military service there shall be no appeal from the commanding officer; the orders of a commanding general shall be unalterable law.

There shall be a number of minor magistrates

with limited authority and various functions: in the army they shall command the troops to whom they are assigned, and be their *military tribunes:* on home duty they shall be the treasurers of public money, and have charge of prisons and executions; they shall mint bronze, silver, and gold money; they shall be judges in lawsuits; they shall carry out the decrees of the Senate.

7 There shall be *aediles,* or superintendents of police, the dole, and the annual festivals, and this office shall be their first step in rising to higher rank.

The *censors* shall make a census of the population by age, number of children, number of slaves, and income. They shall have charge of the city's temples, streets, water supply, treasury, and taxes. They shall divide the citizens into tribes, and then into divisions by wealth, age, and rank. They shall enroll the young men in the cavalry and infantry. They shall discourage bachelorhood. They shall regulate public morals. They shall permit no dishonor in the senate. There shall be two of them, and they shall hold office for five years; the other offices shall be annual. The office of censor shall never be allowed to lapse.

8 The arbitrator of justice, who shall try to assign for trial private lawsuits, shall be the *praetor:* he shall be the administrator of the civil law: sharing his authority shall be as many praetors as the Senate shall decree or the people order.

There shall be two magistrates with the authority of kings: from their functions as leaders, arbitrators, and givers of counsel they shall be called praetors, judges, and *consuls.* In the army they shall have the supreme command, subject to no one. The safety of the people shall be their highest law.

9 No one shall hold the same office twice without an interval of ten years; the appropriate age for holding a given office shall be fixed by law.

But when there is a major war or revolution, one man shall hold consular power for not longer than six months, if the Senate so decrees, and if he is named under favorable auspices, he shall be *dictator;* his *master of the horse* shall have the same powers as a praetor.

But when there are neither consuls nor dictator, there shall be no other magistrates; the patricians shall take the auspices, and produce one of their number with power duly to conduct the election of consuls.

Major and minor officials and ambassadors, with permission of the Senate or people, may leave the city; they shall wage just wars justly; they shall spare our allies; they shall restrain themselves and their staffs; they shall extend Roman glory; they shall return home with honor.

No man shall serve as ambassador for personal profit.

The ten men whom the people shall elect to assist them in case of violence shall be their tribunes, and their veto and recommendations shall be valid. Their persons shall be sacrosanct. They shall not allow the office of *tribune of the people* to fall vacant.

10 All officials shall have the right to take auspices and to preside as judges. The *Senate* shall consist of ex-magistrates; its decrees shall be binding; even if an equal or higher power vetoes them, they shall be preserved in writing. The senatorial order shall be free from vice, and they shall set an example to the rest of the citizens.

When elections, verdicts, bills, and protests are ratified by vote, the vote shall be known to the aristocracy, and open to the plebeians.

But if a situation arises which is beyond the jurisdiction of the existing magistrates, the people shall elect a responsible official, and give him power to act.

The right to call and to preside over meetings of the people and of the Senate shall be in the hands of the consul, the praetor, the dictator, his master of the horse, and the officials chosen by the patricians to conduct consular elections; the elected tribunes of the people shall have the right to preside over the Senate, and shall lay necessary legislation before the people.

Meetings of the people and Senate shall be orderly.

11 If a senator is absent without cause, he shall be fined; senators shall speak in order of rank, and briefly; they shall be experts on the political situation.

There shall be no violence in the *popular assembly.* An equal or greater power shall have the right of veto. But if there is any disturbance in a meeting, the responsibility shall rest with the instigator. Whoever vetoes bad legislation shall be considered a useful citizen.

Presiding officers shall take the auspices, abide by the findings of the public *augur,* and file published notices of proposed legislation in the public archives after they have been read. They shall not consider more than one bill at a time; they shall inform the people of the facts and permit them to receive information from officials and private citizens.

Bills against individuals shall not be proposed. Trials on capital charges shall be held only before the largest[3] assembly and before those placed by the censors on the citizen-rolls.

Neither candidates, officeholders, or ex-officeholders shall give or receive presents.

Violation of these statutes shall be subject to appropriate penalty.

The censors shall faithfully preserve the text of these laws. On going out of office, the magistrates shall render an account to the censors, but shall not thereby be exempt from the provisions of the law.

[Cicero appends to the text of his ideal statutes—which closely resemble the actual administrative law of the Roman Republic in his time—a commentary on its various provisions. The following passage is taken from the commentary on the office of tribune of the people.]

### The tribune of the people

19 MARCUS. The next law authorizes the power of the tribunes of the people in our republic. On this subject there is no need for discussion.

QUINTUS. But in God's name, brother, I want to know what you think of the tribunate, for I personally think it is a nuisance, born in revolution for the fomenting of revolution. If we care to recall its origins, we find that it came into being in the midst of civil war, after the occupation and siege of parts of the city. Then, after it had been quickly killed, as the Twelve Tables bid us do with extraordinarily deformed infants, it was very soon brought into being again somehow, and reborn, more foul and disgusting than ever. For is there any crime for which it has not been responsible? At the very beginning, true to its treacherous origins, it wrenched all privilege from the patrician class, gave the whole lower class equality with the highest, upset and confounded all class distinctions, and even after it had destroyed the prestige of the governing class, it still never was wholly inactive. 20 For, not to

mention Gaius Flaminius,[4] and incidents of so long ago that they already seem like ancient history, let me ask you what rights the conservatives had left when Tiberius Gracchus' term as tribune was over? Yet even five years before that the lowest and meanest man alive, the tribune Gaius Curiatus, threw into prison the consuls Decimus Brutus and Scipio Nasica—and what distinguished men they were! *That* had never happened before.[5] Didn't Gaius Gracchus change completely the *status quo* in the commonwealth by his ruinous legislation and by those daggers which he said himself he had thrown into the forum so that the citizenry could slit each other's throats with them? Then there are Saturninus, Sulpicius, and the rest, whom the commonwealth couldn't even get rid of without the use of cold steel. 21 Yet why should I cite examples from ancient history and from other men's lives when I could be quoting our own recent experience? Who would ever have dared, who would ever have hated us enough to think of undermining our position if he had not been able to sharpen a tribune's dagger against us? And when these desperate criminals could find no tool in any household or in any clan, they decided, in a dark hour for the commonwealth, that they must upset the whole clan-organization. It is our glorious and everlasting distinction that no tribune could be found to act against us at any price except a man who could not even legally *be* a tribune.[6] 22 But when he was found, what a carnage he created! It was prompted by the irrational, desperate, sinister raging of a foul monster, set aflame by the fury of the mob. And so in this business I strongly approve of Sulla's legislation, which deprived the tribunes of the people of the opportunity for injustice, while leaving to them the right of giving relief. As for our colleague Pompey, in every other respect I praise him to the skies, but about his attitude to the tribunician power I have nothing to say; it is one which I do not want to censure and which I cannot praise.

23 MARCUS. You see the faults of the tribunate very clearly, Quintus. But in any prosecution it is unfair to list the bad points, highlight the defects, and omit the good points entirely. Why, with such a procedure one could criticize the consulship itself, by a mere catalogue of the errors of consuls whom I do not care to mention. Now I admit

that the tribunician power has some inherent bad features, but they are the price we pay for the good which the office was set up to do.

You say that the power of the tribune of the people is too great. Who denies it? But the power of the people themselves is much more savage and much more violent, yet because it has guidance, it is sometimes gentler than if it had none. For a leader takes into account that he proceeds at his own risk, a thought that never enters the head of the impulsive mob.

24 You say the tribunes sometimes inflame the people. But they often appease them, too. Is a board of tribunes ever so hopeless that not one of the ten is in his right mind? Why, it was a colleague, ignored and even removed from the board of Tiberius Gracchus, who finally overthrew him. What struck him down was his denial to a colleague of the right of veto. Note here how wise our forefathers were. The mere concession of this power by the patricians to the plebeians caused an armistice, snuffed out a revolution, found a compromise whereby men of trifling importance thought they were on equal terms with the chiefs of state, which was the only way to preserve the government. You cite the Gracchi, and you could have mentioned many others besides; in a board of ten, you will always throughout history find some who are dangerous; perhaps even the majority have been irresponsible radicals. But meanwhile no one looks askance at the highest class, and the people put up no risky fights for their rights.

25 It follows then that either our kings should never have been driven out or that liberty should have been granted to the people in fact and not merely in theory. As it is, liberty has been granted on such terms that the people have been induced by a number of admirable practices to yield to the authority of the governing class. As for my own case, model brother that you are, it came up while the tribunician power was at its height, but I have no quarrel with that power as such. For it is not true that the plebeians were roused to hold a grudge against me; the prisons were emptied, the slaves were incited to revolt, and there was besides even fear of armed force. My quarrel was not with that nuisance Clodius, but with a political crisis, and if I had not yielded to it, the fatherland would not have reaped any

lasting profit from my services, as the event proved. For as it turned out, there was not a man, I will not say merely among free men, but even among slaves worthy of freedom, who did not hold the security of my person close to his heart.

26 But even if what I had done to preserve the state had not pleased everyone, and even if the flaming resentment of a howling mob had driven me into exile, and even if the power of the tribunes had roused the people against me, as Gracchus roused them against Popilius or Saturninus against Metellus,[7] I should have endured it, brother Quintus, and I should have found my consolation not so much in the Athenian philosophers whose job it is to comfort us, as in the heroes who, driven out of Athens, preferred exile from an ungrateful city to residence in a wicked one.[8] As for your failure to approve Pompey's policy toward the tribunate, there is one thing I think you do not quite allow for: what he had to follow was not the best procedure, but the inevitable one. He knew that the state ought not to include the office of tribune, but since the people had fought so hard for it when they did not know its advantages, how could they do without it when these advantages were known? It was the act of a statesman not to abandon criminally to a member of the popular party an office which on the one hand was not dangerous, and on the other was so popular that it could not be abolished.

[Cicero proceeds with his commentary on the detailed provisions of his administrative law. In connection with the clause stating that the Senate shall set an example to the rest of the citizens, he makes a classic statement of the position that privilege brings responsibility, that *noblesse oblige*.]

### The aristocrat's duty

30 MARCUS. "The Senate shall set an example to the rest of the citizens." If we attain this end, we shall have attained our final goal. For the state is improved and set right by the restraint of its governing class just as much as it is infected by their selfishness and vice. The great Lucullus, whom we all know, is alleged to have made a very neat reply, when he was criticized for the splendor of his villa at Tusculum. He said he had two neighbors; the one higher up the

hill was a knight, the one lower down an ex-slave. "They have splendid villas," he said; "I ought to be allowed to have one, since the lower classes are permitted to own them." Don't you see, Lucullus, that you are yourself responsible for their wanting one? If you didn't build one, they wouldn't be permitted to. *31* For otherwise who would endure such fellows, with their villas crammed with statues and paintings, some of them stolen from the state, others from the very shrines and temples? There is not a man who would not root out such greediness, if the very men who ought to be rooting it out were not in the grip of the selfsame greed.

Bad as the sins of the governing class are, that is not so great an evil as the fact that the governing class has numberless imitators. For it is plain to see in history that the character of the state has always reflected the character of the men in authority; upon a change in the morals of the governing class ensues a similar change among the populace. *32* This is scarcely less sound an axiom than Plato's dictum that political revolutions follow upon changes in musical styles. My opinion at any rate is that when the life and livelihood of the nobility changes, the *mores* of states change also. Immoral aristocrats, then, are the more dangerous to the state, because they are responsible not only for their own vices, but for injecting them into the body politic. They bar progress not only because they are corrupt, but because they corrupt others, and they do less harm by their sin than by their bad example. This axiom, extended to the whole patrician class, can be applied even more specifically; for a few men—very few—in positions of trust and honor have it in their power to corrupt or set to rights the morals of the whole state.

[Cicero next justifies his provision that the vote should be free but not secret; he advocates empowering the patricians to inspect each ballot before it is cast.]

### The secret ballot

*34* QUINTUS. Everyone knows that the secret ballot has stripped the patricians of all their power. A people who while they were free never felt the lack of it, under the pressure of a powerful and domineering governing class actually demanded it. Actually history records severer condemnation of political bosses in the days when there was a voice vote than since there has been a secret ballot. The men in power have given the people places to hide, where the secret ballot may conceal a harmful vote while the aristocracy is unaware of individual popular opinion; whereas the proper solution is to cure the populace of its perverse fondness for legislation which is not in the aristocratic interest. Therefore no patrician has ever proposed or sponsored a measure like yours. . . .

*37* ATTICUS. I have never yet approved of a popular party measure; what I always say is, that the ideal commonwealth is the kind Marcus here set up when he was consul, where the power rests with the aristocracy.

*38* MARCUS. Well, I see you have killed my legislation without a ballot. But for my part, though Scipio has spoken eloquently enough on his own behalf in my six books *On the Republic*, I am granting freedom to vote to the people in such a way that the possession and use of political power shall be in the hands of the patricians. My law on voting ran as follows: "The vote shall be known to the aristocracy, and open to the plebeians." Its intention is to cancel all subsequent legislation which may in any way protect the secrecy of the ballot by forbidding the inspection, questioning, or challenging thereof. Marius' law even made the approaches to the polling-place narrow. *39* If these laws are made, as is usually the case, to prevent dishonest elections, I have no fault to find, but if it is true that they are not strong enough to stop electoral corruption, then by all means let the people have their ballot as a guarantee of their liberty, as long as it is offered voluntarily for inspection to any really substantial aristocratic citizen, so that liberty may consist in the very fact that the people are given an opportunity of honorably doing a favor for the aristocracy. This same sense of liberty is responsible for the situation you mentioned, Quintus, that fewer are condemned by the secret ballot than by the old voice vote, because it is enough for the people to feel they have the authority. As long as they keep the ballot, their whole remaining inclination is to submit to authority and to show a sense of obligation. And so, except for votes that are influenced by wholesale donations, do you not see that if bribery can be got rid of, the people in voting are bound to ask the opinion of the aristocracy? Therefore our legislation preserves the semblance of liberty, preserves intact the authority of the aristocrats, and removes a bone of contention.

[In the remaining nine paragraphs of the work as we have it, Cicero concludes his commentary on the administrative law, and permits himself to be persuaded to discuss legal procedure and the legal basis of the Roman magistrates' authority in the following books, now lost.]

## ON THE CHIEF END OF MAN

The five books De Finibus Bonorum et Malorum, the longest and one of the most ambitious of Cicero's philosophical works, were published in August, 45 B.C., shortly after the death in childbirth of his beloved daughter Tullia. It is dedicated to M. Junius Brutus, the murderer of Julius Caesar. In plan it consists of three dialogues, in which the ethical philosophy of the Epicureans (Books I and II), the Stoics (Books III and IV), and the "Old Academy" (Book V) are successively expounded and criticized. Cicero aimed to show that neither pleasure, the life in accordance with nature, nor self-sufficient virtue are adequate ends for man, but only upon the first of these —the Epicurean view—is his attack really savage, and even here he admits that individual Epicureans' lives are better than their precepts. The attacks upon Epicureanism are to be compared with Lucretius' propounding of the doctrine, which Cicero is said to have edited. The motive for Cicero's attacks upon Epicureanism is at least in part his feeling that an ethical theory in which each man is invited to consult his own interest, and an atomic physics in which one atom is much like another, cut at the root of the collectivist, hierarchical philosophy upon which rested the domination of the Roman state by Cicero's party of *optimates*. But Cicero's critique also involves much close reasoning, as study of Book I, 18–26, will prove. The selections translated from Books I and II epitomize Cicero's attitude toward Epicureanism. The selection from Book III puts into the mouth of the *optimates*' leader, Cato the Younger, the enemy of Catiline (See Sallust, *Catiline*, 54), the Stoic view of the brotherhood of man in One World, the world of the Roman Empire. The selections from Book V reveal the reverence with which Cicero, despite his patriotism, views the historical associations of Athens; present him as a sympathetic observer of child development; involve an allegorical interpretation of Homer; and conclude with a definition of justice as a world-wide linking of the "best" men.

As Book I opens, Cicero is discussing Epicureanism with his friends the Epicurean L. Manlius Torquatus (praetor 49 B.C.; he fought against Caesar in the Civil War, and died during it) and C. Valerius Triarius the Stoic. The scene is Cicero's villa at Cumae; the dramatic date is 50 B.C.

*From* Book I

[Cicero defends Latin against the scorn of Greek-lovers. He feels he can still serve his countrymen by contributing to their higher education, and he cannot find a worthier theme than that supreme problem of philosophy, "What is the chief end of man?"]

*The importance of philosophizing in Latin about the chief end of man*

10 I never stop wondering where the present scorn of things Roman came from. This is certainly not the place for lecturing, but this is the way I feel, and I have often argued that the Latin language is not only not poor in vocabulary, as is commonly thought, but is actually richer than Greek. For, at least since there have been any models to follow, when has the language of our good orators or poets fallen short of the Greeks either in richness or in taste?

For my part, as far as court cases, hard work, and running risks are concerned, I don't think I have deserted the position of trust in which the Roman people have placed me. And so I certainly ought, so far as in me lies, to work hard also so that my efforts, my study, and my burning the midnight oil may make my fellow citizens wiser men. My quarrel is not so much with those who prefer to read Greek, provided they really read it, and not merely pretend to. My interest is in being of service to those who wish to use both languages, or to those who, provided they have works of philosophy in Latin, do not particularly feel the lack of Greek. 11 As for those who want me to write on other subjects, I ask them to be reasonable. On the one hand I have written a great deal, more than any other Latin author, and will perhaps write more, if I live long enough; and on the other hand any man who has got used to careful reading of my philosophical works will give as his opinion that there is no reading that is more important. For what is there in life that is so well worth inquiring into as the whole field of philosophy? And within that field, the subject of this book is most important: what the end of life is, what its ultimate goal, what the standard is to which all conclusions about right living and proper conduct ought to be referred, what Nature pursues as the highest good among desirable objects, and what she avoids as the ultimate evil. I admit that on this subject there is the most extreme disagreement among the philosophers, but who will think that my investigation into what is best and truest of all that life has to offer is not in keeping with the position of importance which everyone attributes to me?

[Cicero proposes first to discuss the clearest and simplest theory of man's aims, that of Epicurus. First, by request, he lists his objections to the Epicurean science, logic, and ethics.]

*Epicurean physics*

18 Though there is much in the physics both of Democritus and of Epicurus that I do not approve of, my chief objection is that of the two objects of physical investigation—(a) the material out of which each object is made, and (b) the force that makes each object—they talk about the material but leave out of account the efficient cause. But this is a flaw in the structure of both their theories: Epicurus' own particular set of ruins is this: he thinks Democritus' separate and impermeable atoms fall downward by gravity in straight lines, and that this is the natural motion of all bodies.

19 Then it occurs to this brilliant theorist that if every atom falls downward in a perfectly straight line, no atom can ever touch another, so almost in the same breath he smuggles in a fiction: he says the atom "swerves" just the least possible amount, which brings about those embraces, couplings, and cleavings of the atoms to one another, out of which the world and every one of its parts are made. Not only is the whole theory a childish fiction, but it does not even do the job he wants it to. For in the first place he invents this swerve as a random thing (for he says that the atom swerves without a cause, which is the worst crime a physicist can commit), and

in the second place he thereby deprives his atoms, without reason, of that very motion that he assigned to them in the first place; i.e., the natural downward motion in a straight line of all bodies having weight; but he has not attained the end, for the sake of which he made up his theory. 20 For if all the atoms swerve, none will ever meet; or if some swerve and some fall straight downward by gravity, my first objection is that this is tantamount to assigning areas to the atoms, in one of which they will fall straight down, and in the other swerve; my second objection is (and this is a bog in which Democritus too is stuck) that this unruly rush-hour crowd of atoms could never create the splendor of the universe which we see about us. Furthermore, no good physicist believes that matter is anything but infinitely divisible, and Epicurus would not have thought it was, either, if he had been willing to learn geometry from his friend Polyaenus instead of actually teaching him that there was no truth in it. Democritus thinks the sun is large, as he should, being a scholar and a master geometrician; Epicurus thinks it is perhaps a foot wide; for he thinks the sun is about as big as it seems to us to be, with a little leeway more or less. 21 And so the views he borrows he makes a mess of; the views he follows all belong to Democritus: atoms, void, the images they call "films," whose impingement upon us are the cause not only of vision, but of thought; his theory of infinity itself, which they call the "boundless," is all derived from Democritus, and so are the innumerable worlds, which come into being and pass away as a daily performance. And though I in no sense approve of any of these theories, still I don't want Democritus, whom others praise, to be traduced by the man who did all his plagiarizing from him.

*Epicurean logic*

22 Not content with these errors, in that other part of philosophy, having to do with investigation and discourse, which is called logic, this wretched philosopher of yours seems to me at least to be utterly stripped and weaponless. He does away with definitions; he teaches nothing about division into genus and species; he does not follow tradition in the construction and conclusion of syllogisms; he does not demonstrate the solution of dilemmas or make distinctions

between types of ambiguity; he makes sensation the criterion of truth; once sensation has mistaken falsehood for truth, his view makes any distinction between the two impossible.

*Epicurean ethics*

23 In ethics, he attaches the greatest importance to pleasure and pain, which Nature herself, according to him, ordains and stamps with her approval. He makes the seeking of pleasure and the avoidance of pain the sole basis of conduct. Though it is possible to argue for pleasure better, i.e., less slavishly, than he, as Aristippus and the Cyrenaics have done, yet in my opinion there is no ethical system less worthy of human kind. For to me at least Nature has brought us into being and shaped us for higher ends than pleasure. I may be wrong, but this at any rate I do think: that the mere sensation of physical pleasure was not enough to have made the first Torquatus earn his nickname by wrenching that famous neck-chain from his enemy; nor was it for pleasure that he fought with the Latins in his third consulship in the Battle of the Veseris. On the contrary, by beheading his son for disobedience he apparently deprived himself of many pleasures, since he placed the claims of official authority ahead of natural paternal love. 24 What about that later Torquatus, the one who was consul with Gnaeus Octavius? You don't think he was considering his personal pleasure, do you, when he was so severe with Decimus Silanus' son, whom he had adopted? Ambassadors from the province of Macedonia accused the son of accepting bribes during his term as governor. The senior Torquatus put the case on the calendar of his own court, and after hearing both sides, gave it as his judgment that his son had not shown the same sense of responsibility in office that his ancestors had, and banished his son forever from his sight. I shall say no more of the risks, the hard work, the pain that many an aristocrat has endured for the sake of the fatherland and his own kind. It is not merely a question of deriving no pleasure; it amounts to an actual renunciation of pleasure; and there was no pain they were not willing to undergo, rather than shirk any part of their duty. I pass rather to cases which prove my point equally well but may appear more trivial. 25 Is it just for pleasure's sake, Torquatus, that you and Triarius

here devote so much energy to literature, history, research, reading the poets, and committing so many lines to memory? Don't tell me, "That is my idea of pleasure, just as doing their duty was that of my ancestors." That is not the kind of pleasure that Epicurus defends, or his pupil Metrodorus, or any other Epicurean who knows or teaches the philosophy of pleasure.

The question is often asked, why there are so many Epicureans. There are other reasons, but what most attracts the majority is their notion that Epicurus says that right and honorable conduct of itself brings happiness or pleasure. These worthies do not realize that if this is true, reason is completely overthrown. For if it conceded, leaving the body out of account as the standard of pleasure and pain, that such conduct is pleasant in and for itself, then virtue and scholarship ought to be pursued for their own sake, which is the very last thing Epicurus wants to maintain.

26 This, then, is why I disapprove of Epicurus' ethics. For the rest, I could wish either that he himself had been better educated (for, as you must agree, he does not exactly have the cultivated man's knowledge of scholarly subjects), or that he had not discouraged other men's studies.

[The remainder of Book I is devoted to Torquatus' defense of Epicurus against the charges mentioned in the first twenty-six paragraphs, chiefly on the ground that Epicurean pleasure is not merely sensuous, but is of the highest kind that the wise man can conceive. In Book II Cicero returns to the attack with a reply to Torquatus, in which he emphasizes that only reason can decide what the chief end of man is, and that reason rejects every theory of the chief end which either includes pleasure or rejects virtue. In this connection he gives an unforgettably vivid picture of the profligate's life (sec. 23). We may then choose between theories of the chief end which involve virtue and those which involve pleasure. If Cicero can show that there is something moral which is an end itself (i.e., desirable for its own sake) he will have refuted the Epicurean theory that pleasure is desirable for its own sake. This refutation will involve definitions and examples of what is meant by the term "moral" which are set forth in sec. 45.]

## From Book II

### The profligate's life

**23** What is the point of saying, "I have no fault to find, provided men put some limit to their desires"? This is the same as saying, "I have no fault to find with profligates, provided they are not profligate." Or likewise, "I have no fault to find with the wicked, provided they are good men." Epicurus, Puritan that he is, does not think that luxurious living as such ought to be criticized. And to speak God's truth, Torquatus, if the highest good is really pleasure, he is perfectly right in not thinking so. For I should hate to imagine prodigals, as you usually do, as people who vomit onto the table and have to be carried away from banquets and next day in spite of their hangover fall to guzzling again; men who boast that they have never seen a sunset or a sunrise, and who squander their patrimony and then live in want. None of us thinks that profligates of that sort live a pleasant life. But let us take the sophisticated ones, men of taste, who have the best chefs and pastry cooks, and fish-ponds, fowl and game preserves, all stocked with the rarest species; men who avoid drunkenness, whose wine is drawn, as Lucilius says, from a full jar, and has lost its tang by straining. Suppose they have their private theatricals and the supper parties afterwards, the pleasures without which Epicurus cries that he knows not what is good in the world; let there be even good-looking boys as cupbearers, and everything that goes with luxurious living: clothes, plate, statuary, landscaping, a palace; never shall I admit that even prodigals like these really live good and happy lives. . . .

### The quarrel between virtue and pleasure

**44** Epicurus' theory puts us to more trouble to refute, (a) because he uses the term "pleasure" in a double sense (the usual meaning, and "privation from pain"), and (b) because he and his friends and many successors have defended this usage, and somehow the people always make common cause with those who have the least authority but the most energy. If we do not succeed in refuting them, we might as well desert the whole cause of virtue, honor, and good repute. And so, when the other theories are set aside, the quarrel that remains is not between me and Torquatus, but between virtue and pleasure. This quarrel Chrysippus,[9] at any rate, that brilliant and hard-working philosopher, does not consider beneath his dignity; he considers that the entire decision as to which is the highest good depends upon a comparison between the claims of pleasure and of virtue. For my part I think that if I can show that there is something called morality which is worth seeking for its own sake as a motive force, your whole theory falls to the ground. And so when I have defined "morality" with appropriate brevity, Torquatus, I shall proceed to attack as much of your position as my memory permits.

### What is morality?

**45** By morality, then, I mean that which is in itself praiseworthy, without any consideration of reward or profit, when no motive of expediency whatever is involved. Its nature can be understood not so much by this definition (although the definition does contribute something) as by the universal judgment of mankind and by the pursuits and conduct of the aristocracy, who perform many an action from one motive only, because it is the proper thing to do, because it is right, because it is honorable, even though they see that they will gain nothing by it. For though men differ from the beasts in many other ways, the chief difference is that they have reason, which Nature has given them: a quick and vigorous mind, capable of carrying on many activities simultaneously; keen-scented, so to speak, seeing the causes and connections of things, making analogies, connecting discrete impressions, linking the future with the present, and controlling all the circumstances of coherent life. Reason makes man desirous of association with mankind and of adapting himself by his nature, his language, and his habits, to life in society, so that, beginning with holding his household and family dear, he insinuates and involves himself further and further with the society first of his fellow citizens and then of all mankind, and, as Plato wrote to Archytas, remembers that he has been born not for himself alone but for his fatherland, for his own kind, so that a very small part of him is left for his own use. **46** Reason brings to birth in man the desire of seeing the truth. The most obvious example of this is our eagerness, in leisure moments, to know even what the motions of the heavens are. Starting from these beginnings, we come to love all truth; that is, loyalty, candor, dependability; and to hate everything that is empty, false, and deceptive, as for example fraud, perjury, malice, and injustice. Reason has about it something spacious and magnificent, adapted for giving orders rather than obeying them, treating all human vicissitudes not merely as bearable, but as trivial; it has a certain loftiness and exaltation, fearing nothing, yielding to no one, always invincible.

[Cicero goes on to accuse Epicurus of advocating morality merely because it pays. This is counterfeit virtue, which no public man could profess without ruining his reputation.]

*Pleasure not a proper motive for political action*

74 What does it look like, Torquatus, that you as an Epicurean, in spite of the name you bear, your talents, and your high reputation, do not dare to speak out publicly and say what you are doing, what you are thinking, what you are aiming at, what your standard of value is, your motive for wanting to carry out your aims, and finally, what it is in life that you hold most valuable? Now that you are about to enter into office and mount the rostrum to address the assembly (at which point you ought to tell what your principles are going to be in your judicial decisions, and perhaps also, if you choose, say a few words about your ancestors and yourself in accordance with tradition), what would I have to pay you to get you to say that in your praetorship you intend to make pleasure the motive for your every action, and that you have never in your life done anything with any other motive? "Do you think me crazy enough," you say, "to talk like that before the uninitiate?" Say it all the same; say it in court, or, if you are afraid of the spectators, say it in the Senate. You will never do it. Why not, unless because such talk is disgraceful? Then aren't you ashamed to talk like that in front of Triarius and me? . . .

*Cicero admits that Epicureans are often better than their creed.*

81 In every art, pursuit, or science, even in virtue itself, the very best is rarely found. Epicurus himself was a good man, and many Epicureans

have been in the past and are now constant in their friendships, serious and consistent in their whole way of life, making their decisions on a basis not of pleasure but of sense of duty. These facts simply increase the prestige of an honorable life and decrease that of the life of pleasure. For some of them live in such a way that their lives refute their professions. And as in other cases what men say is thought to be better than what they do, so what the Epicureans do seems to me to be better than what they say.

[So there is no room for virtue in the Epicurean system. Furthermore, if pleasure is the supreme good, pain is the chief evil, and you Epicureans are ill-equipped by your life of pleasure to endure pain with patience. Finally, if pleasure is the supreme good, the supreme good is the same for man and beast, so what is the use of pursuing liberal studies? In short, man is a paragon, and born for a higher end than pleasure.]

*Man is born for a higher end than pleasure.*

111 But if it is true that pleasure is the chief end, we are far and away surpassed in our capacity for it by the beasts, for whom without the need for toiling the earth herself pours forth from her rich store all sorts of food in abundance, whereas we support ourselves with difficulty or not at all, though we seek sustenance by the sweat of our brows. But all the same I cannot bring myself to think that the highest good for man is the same as a beast's. For in that case what is the use of reason, that great instrument for acquiring proficiency in the highest arts, what is the use of so many highly advanced liberal studies, so brave an array of virtues, if they are all acquired for no better reason than for pleasure? 112 Xerxes massed an immense force, navy, cavalry, and infantry; he bridged the Hellespont, dug a canal past Mt. Athos, so that he marched on the sea, and sailed on the land. Suppose that after he had spent so much energy to attack Greece, someone asked him the reason for so huge a preparation and so great a war, and suppose he said, "I wanted to bring back some honey from Mt. Hymettus." Would not so great an effort then seem entirely unmotivated? Consider in the same way the wise man, equipped and embellished with so great and impressive a store of arts and virtues. Unlike Xerxes, he does not walk on the

sea, or sail on the mountains; but his mind embraces the whole heaven and the whole earth, with the sea besides. If we say that what he is seeking is pleasure, we shall be saying that he has made all these mighty preparations for the sake of a bit of honey. *113* Believe me, Torquatus, we have been born for something higher and more magnificent, as the soul and the body both testify: the soul with its unlimited capacity for memory (like your own, Torquatus), with its ability, almost as uncanny as second sight, to foresee consequences, with its innate sense of propriety serving as a restraint upon selfishness, with its staunch watch over justice for the protection of human society, with its solid, steady contempt for pain and death in the midst of hardships that must be undergone and perils that must be faced; the body too proves my point; when you consider your limbs and your senses, they will seem to you, like the other parts of your body, not merely to accompany the virtues, but to minister to them. *114* But if in the body, the seat of pleasure, many qualities must rank ahead of pleasure, qualities like strength, health, speed, beauty, what do you think will be true of the soul? In it the most learned men of old thought there was something celestial and divine. But if pleasure were the highest good, as you Epicureans say, the most desirable thing would be to pass days and nights at the height of uninterrupted pleasure, with all the senses steeped in and reacting to all possible sweetness. But what man worthy of the name of man wants to pass even an entire day in this unworthy sort of pleasure? It is true that the Cyrenaics are not reluctant to embrace the life of pleasure; you Epicureans are more restrained about it, but they, perhaps, are more consistent. *115* But let us extend our mental survey beyond those skills leading to virtue, so important to our forebears that they dubbed those who lacked them "unskilled." I now ask whether you can possibly suppose that artists like Phidias, Polyclitus, or Zeuxis,—not to speak of poets like Homer, Archilochus, or Pindar—kept their eye solely on pleasure as they practised their art. Shall the craftsman attach more importance to beauty of form than the distinguished citizen to beauty of conduct? The reason why so many of you have missed the mark so widely for so long is surely that the man who fixes on pleasure as the highest good is making his decisions

not with that part of his soul where deliberative reason dwells but with the appetitive element, the most unreliable part of all. I ask you this question: if the gods exist, as even you believe, how can they be happy, seeing that they are incapable of sensual pleasure? Or if they are happy without this sort of pleasure, why are you so reluctant to let the wise man possess his soul in the same way?

[Cicero reminds Torquatus that no hero, Greek or Roman, of fact or fiction, ever gained his reputation by being an efficient pleasure-seeker, nor do we assess the promise of young men on the basis of selfish hedonism. The pursuit of pleasure, in fact, is subversive of political morality, since it destroys that desire to give and receive benefits which builds the *concordia ordinum*—the working compromise among senators, knights, and plebs which was Cicero's political ideal. Torquatus himself, Cicero says in conclusion, would prefer the labors of Hercules to a life of ease, provided he could be of service to those in need. Torquatus refers the argument for rebuttal to Epicureans more expert than he, and the book ends.]

### From Book III

[In Book III (dramatic date 52 B.C.; scene Cicero's villa at Tusculum), Cicero turns to the Stoic view of the chief end of man, presenting as spokesman the most distinguished Stoic of his day, Cato the Younger. For the Stoics, virtue is the chief end, and it consists in the exercise of choice between good and evil. As a result of his choice, the wise man lives in conformity with his experience of the laws of Nature, and is always happy, whatever his external circumstances. In his relation to externals, the sage is guided by his sense of duty, which sometimes counsels suicide, even though he may be completely happy. He sees the universe as One World, the city state of the gods and of the whole human race; as citizens of this One World, it behooves us to set the common good before our own.]

### The Stoic world commonwealth

*64* The Stoics hold that the universe is ruled by the divinity of the gods, and that it is as it were the common city-state of men and gods. Each of us is a part of this universe, from which it naturally follows that we should put the common advantage before our own. For just as the laws put the common security before the security of individuals, so the man who is good, wise, law-abiding, and aware of his duty as a citizen gives greater consideration to the common good than to that of any individual or to his own. Not even the man who betrays his fatherland is more to be condemned than the man who deserts the common good for the sake of his personal good or security. Therefore it follows that the man who courts death for the commonwealth's sake is worthy of all praise, because it is fitting that the fatherland should be dearer to us than our very selves. A notorious and heartless quotation circulates to the effect that when we are dead, we care not whether the whole earth goes up in flames (it is usually quoted in a commonplace Greek verse). In opposition to it, let me cite the certain truth that we ought for their own sakes to consider also the welfare of those who come after us.

### The Stoic universal law of common citizenship

65 This same sense of the intimate association of souls has brought about the practice of making last wills and testaments. The fact that no one wants to live in complete solitude, not even if pleasures are his in infinite abundance, makes it easy for us to understand that we have been born for close human association, a sort of natural community. Moreover we have a natural impulse to be as useful as possible to the maximum number of people, especially in the teaching of philosophy and in handing on to posterity the precepts of practical wisdom. 66 And so our propensity for teaching as well as learning is so strong that it is hard to find any one who does not pass on to others what he knows himself. And just as Nature has given bulls the instinct to fight for their calves with all their might and main against lions, even so those who have the resources and the ability (like Hercules and Bacchus) are naturally spurred on to the preservation of the human race. And even when we give Jupiter the title of Best and Greatest, or when we worship him as Savior, as God of Hospitality, as Supporter of Armies, what we mean is that the security of mankind is in his keeping. It would be terribly inappropriate to demand that the immortal gods cherish us and care for us while we ourselves are negligent and mean in our treatment of one another. Therefore just as we use our limbs [by instinct] before we learn why we have them, so we are linked by a natural instinct in the bonds of a civil community; if it were not so, there would be no room for justice or benevolence. 67 But though the Stoics believe that bonds of justice exist between man and man, they do not think that there is any such link between man and the beasts. So Chrysippus well says that all other animals are born for the use of men and gods, but that men exist to live together in society, so that men may without injustice use beasts to their own advantage. And since man's nature is such that a sort of universal law of common citizenship links him to the human race, the man who abides by this law will be just, the man who departs from it unjust. But just as, though the theatre is public property, each spectator may be said to have a right to the seat he occupies, even so in our one world there is no objection to the law which grants to each man the ownership of private property.

[His sense of the community of mankind, Cato continues, will lead the Stoic sage to want to take part in the administration of government. As he does so, he will make friendships and administer justice for their own sakes, and not for the sake of expediency. The sage will also study dialectics and physics for their own sakes, and not for the sake of their applications. The book ends with Cato's sketch of the perfectly balanced and adjusted Stoic sage, whose mind is his kingdom and his riches.

In Book IV, Cicero attacks the Stoic view of the chief end of man as unoriginal, artificial, overintellectual, illogical, and ostentatious.]

### From Book V

[At the opening of Book V, the dramatic date shifts back to 79 B.C. and the scene changes to Athens, where Cicero, Quintus, Atticus, and others are introduced as they stroll to Plato's famous Grove of Academe, discussing the influence upon the imagination of places associated with famous men.]

### The historical associations of Athens

1 We decided to take an afternoon stroll to the Academy, which at that hour is not at all

crowded. And so at the appointed hour we all met at Piso's [10] house. Then, as we talked on a variety of subjects, we covered the three-quarters of a mile between the Dipylon Gate and the Academy, and when we got to its justly famous promenades, it was as deserted as we had hoped. 2 Then Piso said: "I don't know whether it is a natural instinct or a mistaken notion, but when we see places which we know that famous men have much frequented, we are more excited—as I am now—than when we hear their deeds or read their works. For I am thinking of Plato, who, they tell us, began here the practice of philosophizing in dialogues; his little gardens over there do not merely remind me of him; they seem to conjure up his very figure before my eyes. Speusippus taught here, and Xenocrates, and his pupil Polemo; that very garden seat there that we have seen was his. Of course when I look at our Senate House in Rome (the old one, I mean, not the new, which seems all the smaller to me since it has been enlarged), I always think of Scipio, old Cato, Laelius, and first of all my grandfather Piso; for that is the sort of power that places have to stir reminiscences; so that there is good reason to recognize the aid that places can give in developing the faculty of memory." [11] 3 Quintus rejoined: "You are absolutely right, Piso. For as I was on my way here the deme of Colonus caught my eye, and Sophocles, who lived there, flashed before my eyes; you know how fond I am of reading his works. Though it was only a shadowy vision, his spirit moved me all the same to a more profound recollection of Oedipus coming here and asking in that tenderest of odes the names of these very places we see before us." [12] And Atticus added, "As for me, butt that I am of your jokes for my devotion to Epicurus, I spend most of my time, as you know, with my favorite Phaedrus [13] in the Gardens of Epicurus, which we have just passed, but I follow the old proverb, and am mindful of those who are still living; yet I couldn't forget Epicurus even if I wanted to; we followers of his school have his portrait not only on our walls but even on our drinking-cups and our rings."

4 At this point I joined in and said: "Our friend Atticus, it seems, will have his joke, and perhaps he has a right to it, for he has settled himself so firmly in Athens that he is practically a citizen of Attica and is likely to derive his nick-name from that fact; but I agree with you, Piso, that it does happen that we think harder and better about famous men when their favorite haunts remind us of them. For you remember the time in our travels together when we reached Metapontum and had to see the place where Pythagoras used to sit, and the place where he died, before I even looked up our host. Today, too, when we are in a place which contains even more traces of famous men than the rest of Athens, this garden seat here excites me most; it once belonged to Carneades; his well known face appears before my eyes, and I imagine that the very seat itself, bereft of his mighty talent, misses the sound of that famous voice." 5 Piso said: "Everyone has commented now; what about your cousin Lucius? Does he enjoy feasting his eyes on the place where Demosthenes and Aeschines used to fight it out? For every man is attracted most by his own specialty." "There's no need for you to ask," said Lucius, blushing. "Why, I actually went down to Phalerum, to the spot where they say Demosthenes used to practise speaking, so as to get used to dominating crowd noises with his voice. Afterward I turned a little to the right off the highway to visit the tomb of Pericles. But such spots are without number in this city; wherever we tread, we set foot upon a bit of history."

[After this introduction, Piso proceeds to expound the doctrines of the successors of Plato and Aristotle (the "Academics" and "Peripatetics") on the chief end of man, which they held to consist in virtue plus natural goods, which will enable a man to live in harmony with his own nature at its highest stage of evolution. If man were born fully self-conscious, his chief good would be evident to him from infancy; as it is, he only gradually advances from the first blind impulses of Nature to an understanding of his own special powers and their goal. Even children, however, show as it were germs of those virtues which reason develops.]

*The development of children shows the germ of reason.*

41 . . . At first the desires of our soul aim only at self-preservation, but when we begin to make distinctions and understand what we are and how we differ from the rest of living creatures, we then embark upon the course we were

born to follow. *42* We see an analogy in the beasts, who at first do not move from the place where they were born, but then each is moved by his own appetite, and we see baby snakes crawling, ducklings swimming, blackbirds flying, young bulls using their horns, little scorpions using their stings; in short, each one's nature is his guide to life. It is the same way with the human race. For new-born babies lie there at first as though they were entirely lifeless, but when they gain a little strength, they use both their minds and their senses, to sit up, use their hands, and recognize their nurses; next they begin to enjoy the company of children of their own age; they like to be with them; they love to play, and they begin to listen to little stories. If they have anything left over, they like to give it to others. They begin to be more inquisitive about what goes on at home, and to be capable of study and learning, and they want to know the names of people they see. In their games with their playmates, if they win, they are beside themselves with joy; if they lose, they are downcast and depressed; all of which is far from accidental. *43* For Nature apparently has created human faculties for the perception of every virtue, and therefore children are moved instinctively by the images of virtues whose seeds they have within them; for these seeds are the prime elements of nature, and when they grow, virtue begins, as it were, to germinate. For we have been born and made to contain in us the first principles of action: love of our fellow man, liberality, and gratitude. Our souls are adapted for containing wisdom, commonsense, and courage, and rejecting their opposites, so that those sparks, as it were, of the virtues which I have said we see in children are not accidental; from them philosophical reason ought to be kindled, so that we can follow reason as leader as though it were a god, and so come to the goal that Nature has set before us. For at the risk of repetition let me say again that in tender years and in the undeveloped mind can be detected the natural faculty as though through a mist; as the soul progresses and grows stronger, it does indeed recognize that natural faculty, but in such a way that it can progress still further, though it is in itself still incomplete.

[Not only the instinct of self-preservation proves that virtue is the Chief End of Man; another proof is that each part of us has its own tendency to perfection. This accounts, both in children and in adults, for the irrepressible desire for knowledge, which operates within us like a Siren's song; it is the cognitive faculty striving to realize its own end.]

### The Siren song of knowledge

*48* . . . The innate love of learning and knowledge is so strong in us that beyond doubt the nature of man is irresistibly attracted to study without any ulterior motive. Do we not see how not even a whipping can discourage boys from contemplation and investigation of the nature of things? Why, even when they are driven away, they come running back to it. See how proud they are of a piece of information, how eager to impart it to others! How fascinated they are by parades, fairs, and similar spectacles, so that for the sake of them they will endure even hunger and thirst! What is the conclusion then? Do we not see that those who are fascinated by liberal studies and arts take no account of their health or their income, but, captivated by love of learning and science itself, will endure anything, and compensate by immense effort and trouble for the pleasure they get from learning? *49* I think Homer saw a little of the truth of this in the lines he wrote about the Sirens' song. For it was not the sweetness of their voices or the novelty and variety of their songs that used to entice passing sailors; they came because they professed to want wide knowledge, so that it was love of learning that made men cleave to the Sirens' rock. . . .

*But we are born, not only for contemplation, but for action as well, and the noblest action is justice, as manifest by men in society.*

*65* In every moral act . . . the most illustrious thing, and the one that has the widest range, is the tie that binds man to man, a sort of alliance for the distribution of advantages. This natural human affection has its origin at our very birth, because our parents love us, and our whole family is linked by marriage and blood relationship. Gradually it creeps beyond the walls of the individual house, first to blood relations, then to relations by marriage, then to friends, neighbors, fellow citizens, and allied states, and finally to the whole compass of the human race. This affection of the soul, which gives to each his own and handsomely and equitably protects this close-linked alliance of man with man that I have been talking about, is called justice, and linked to it are piety, benevolence, liberality, kindness, courtesy, and the like.

[The conclusion is that all systems of philosophy place the chief end of man in the pursuit of happiness; they differ only in their definition of terms. Atticus congratulates Cicero on having outdone the Greeks on their own ground, and the whole party adjourns to Atticus' town house.]

# TUSCULAN DISPUTATIONS

The five books of the *Tusculan Disputations*, so called from Cicero's villa at Tusculum where the discussions are supposed to have taken place in 46 B.C. between Cicero and several unidentified young men, were published in 44 B.C., before the murder of Julius Caesar. Like the work *On the Chief End of Man*, the volume is dedicated to Brutus. The subject is ethical: the minimum essentials of a happy life, treated under five heads (cf. Cicero's own outline of the work: *On Divination* I, 1). The first essential (Book I) is not to fear death; Cicero, in contrast to Lucretius, believes the means to this end is belief in the immortality of the soul (cf. Plato, *Phaedo*). Second (Book II), to be truly happy a man must be able to endure pain. Third (Book III), he must learn not to be a prey to anxiety. Men of Cicero's troubled generation felt their anxiety neuroses as keenly as Kierkegaard, Sartre, and the Existentialists; the selection here printed prescribes philosophy as the medicine of the soul in terms which would not appear strange to modern psychoanalysts. Fourth (Book IV), true happiness depends upon the control of the sensations of excessive joy, fear, and desire. The passage translated on the passion of love is almost as savage as Lucretius' (*On the Nature of Things*, IV, 1037–1287), and reminds us that Cicero made a marriage for money which ended in divorce. Book V asserts the final Stoic point, against Aristotle and Piso's position at the end of *De Finibus*, that virtue alone is sufficient to a happy life. The point is illustrated by examples of vice (Dionysius of Syracuse) and of virtue (Archimedes of "Eureka" fame), and by an eloquent picture of the happiness of the Stoic sage who has contracted his desires to fit his means. The final passage in the book harks back to *Scipio's Dream*, as Cicero insists that honors from the mob are not necessary to happiness, and reflects bitterly upon democracy's alleged hatred for the superiority of virtue.

## From Book III

### Philosophy, the medicine of the soul

5 . . . Leaving other ills aside, what bodily ailments can be worse than these two, anxiety and selfish desire? But how can we believe that the soul cannot minister to its own diseases, when as a matter of fact it is the soul that has discovered medicines for the body? Now the body, with nature's help, is often strong enough to cure itself, but not all who have undergone cures get well immediately, whereas souls with a will to be cured, and in obedience to the precepts of the wise, will without question be cured. 6 A medicine for the soul actually exists: philosophy, whose help we do not have to seek outside ourselves, as we do when the body is ill; rather we must struggle with all our might and main to be to ourselves our own doctors.

[For philosophy removes the weakness in our natures, and shows that anxiety is not natural but mere indulgence of the will; men simply think they suffer anxiety; philosophy can persuade otherwise. Book IV discusses the other disorders of the soul: delight, lust, distress, and fear. Under the head of lust Cicero discusses love and how to control it.]

## From Book IV

### The passion of love

68 All one has to do is to concentrate hard in order to see how disgraceful the lover's happiness is. Those who are beside themselves with happiness when they enjoy the delights of love are disgraceful, and those who lust after such delights with their souls on fire are scandalous. Indeed that thing vulgarly called love—and I swear I can find no other word to use—is so trivial that I can see nothing which in my opinion can be compared to it. . . . 74 The proper prescription for the man in love is to show him how trivial, how contemptible, how absolutely worthless the object of his love is, how easily his passion can be satisfied elsewhere or in another way, or even ignored entirely. In some cases the victim should

be made to concentrate on other interests, problems, and concerns—business, for example; often, as in the case of sick people who are not getting well, he must be cured by a change of scene. Some even think an old love should be driven out by a new one, like one nail by another. *75* Moreover it is most important and necessary to warn him of the power of the passion of love; for of all the disturbances of the soul there is surely none more impetuous, so that, even if you are reluctant to charge the lover with actual excesses like debauchery, seduction, adultery, or, to cap the climax, incest, all of which are reprehensible vices, the upsetting of the mind in love is in itself disgusting, quite apart from perversions. *76* For entirely aside from love's excesses, how essentially trivial ordinary love is!

> Wrongs, suspicions, quarrels, making up,
> War, then peace again; if you should try
> To use *your* mind to make her make up hers,
> 'Twould be the same as going sanely mad.[14]

This wobbly fickle-mindedness is enough to scare anyone off by its very perversity. One must also use the same proof that is used in the case of other disturbances of the soul, that it is all a matter of opinion, judgment, and the will. For if love were natural, everyone would be in love, and forever, and with the same object; it would not be the case that one man is put off by shyness, another by taking thought, a third by surfeit.

[In Book V, Cicero's thesis is that virtue is itself sufficient for a happy life, a thesis which he denied in the last book of his *On the Chief End of Man*. Philosophy deserves all praise for making this clear. Consider Pythagoras' reply to the man who asked him how philosophers differ from other men.]

### From Book V

#### The contemplative life

*9* Pythagoras said that the life of man seemed to him to be like that Olympic festival which used to be held with all sorts of splendid competitions before an audience drawn from the whole of Greece. At the Olympics, some men, at the peak of training, competed for the glory and prestige of a crown; others came to make money by buying and selling; but one group, far the noblest, were after neither applause nor gain, but came to see the sights, and to observe carefully the participants and their methods. In the same way, he said, we, as though we were visiting a crowded festival on a trip from another city, are visitors in this life, on a journey from a life of quite another kind. Some of us slavishly seek prestige, and others money; but there are some rare beings who decide that everything else is worthless, and contemplate with loving care the nature of things; these men call themselves students of wisdom, or philosophers, and, as at the festival the noblest thing to do is to look on, acquiring nothing for oneself, so in life the contemplation and comprehension of nature far outranks all other interests.

#### Socrates and the New Academy

*10* Pythagoras did not simply invent the name; he extended the field of philosophy as well; when . . . he arrived in Italy, he made that part of it known as Magna Graecia famous for the excellence of its institutions and laws, both public and private; perhaps another time we might discuss his teaching. But in the early days of philosophy, down to the time of Socrates, who was the pupil of Archelaus [15] the pupil of Anaxagoras, the subject-matter of philosophy was mathematics and physics, the coming-into-being of things and their passing away, and these early philosophers did careful research into astronomy in all its branches: the size of the stars, their distances apart, their orbits. Socrates was the first to call philosophy down from heaven and settle her in cities; he even brought her into the homes of men and forced her to inquire into their lives and conduct, and into the nature of good and evil. His complex dialectic, his varied interests, his massive intellect, all piously recorded in writing by Plato, produced several dissenting schools of philosophy, of which I follow by preference the one closest to Socratic usage, which involves concealing my own opinion, relieving others of the burden of error, and striving for probability in all discussions. This was the method followed by Carneades in his brilliant and voluminous works, and it is the method I have followed both in other discussions and recently at my Tusculan villa.

[Our subject is the sufficiency of virtue for living happily, which is not the same as living well.

In our previous discussions, we saw that we cannot enjoy a happy life if our soul is disturbed; i.e., a prey to vice instead of the seat of virtue.]

### The peace of mind of the Stoic sage

15 . . . The turbulent tossing of souls whipped up to heights of passion by unconsidered impulses to repel all reason leaves no room for the happy life. For who can help being miserable when he lives in fear of omnipresent death and ever-threatening pain? Furthermore, the same man often lives also in fear of poverty, a bad name, dishonor, ill health, blindness, or, worst of all, enslavement, which often falls to the lot, not of individuals only, but of mighty nations; how can a man be happy in the face of fears like these? 16 What about the man who does not merely fear that these evils *will* happen, but actually endures their onslaught here and now? Heap upon the same man exile, bereavement, childlessness; how can a man crushed under the weight of such an avalanche be anything else but the most miserable man alive? When you see a man on fire with mad lust, indulging his ravenous appetites with insatiate greed, and, the deeper he drinks of the most exquisite pleasures, the more parched with unquenchable thirst, would you not call him the most unhappy of mortals? When you see a man beside himself with empty and trivial frivolity, swollen with promiscuous desire, does he not seem as unhappy to you as he seems happy to himself? These are the unhappy men; happy men on the other hand feel no fear, the gnawing of no anxiety, the impulse of no lust; no empty frivolity drives them out of their minds and dissolves them into enervating ecstasies. Just as, when we say the sea is calm, we mean that not even the slightest breath of air ruffles the waves, so we perceive that the mind is in a state of quiet satisfaction when there is no disturbance to move it. But if there exists a man who can endure the buffets of fortune and every human ill, whatever may befall him, so that fear and anxiety cannot get at him, and if this same man is not covetous, is not carried away by an empty pleasure of the soul, is there any reason why he should not be happy? And if this happiness is brought about by virtue, is there any reason why virtue of itself should not suffice to make men happy?

[It might be argued that there are other goods besides virtue which may produce the happy life, but virtue is the only good, and moral goodness is best. The example of Dionysius the Elder, tyrant of Syracuse 405–367 B.C., shows that vice brings misery.]

### The tyrant's happiness is illusory.

57 From the time when he came to the throne at the age of twenty-five, Dionysius was tyrant of Syracuse for thirty-eight years. How beautiful and prosperous this city-state was, which he kept under the heel of bondage! We have it on good authority that his manner of life was temperate, that he was a keen and hard-working man of affairs, but that injustice and wrong-doing were innate in his nature, and therefore from the philosophic point of view he must seem the most unhappy man in the world. For he could not attain the objects of his desire even at a time when he thought he was all-powerful. 58 He was born of aristocratic stock in an honorable station in life (though the authorities differ on this point), and he had plenty of friends and relations of his own age to associate with; he even had about him, in the Greek fashion, a number of young men who were in love with him, but he trusted none of them. Instead, he drew his bodyguard from the slaves he had selected from wealthy families and set free, and from a group of foreigners and savages. Such was the nature of the prison into which he had locked himself because of his criminal lust for power. Why, he would not even trust his neck to a barber, but taught his daughters to shave him; and so, like the meanest serving-maids or employees of a beauty shop, a king's daughters cut their father's hair and beard. And when they grew up, he would not trust even them with the razor, but bade them singe his hair and beard with red-hot walnut shells. 59 He had two wives, Aristomache of Syracuse and Doris of Locris, but he would never visit them at night without first having a careful search made. He had a wide moat dug round the bed, crossed by a wooden draw-bridge which he would personally raise after he had locked the bedroom door. He did not dare stand on an ordinary platform, but used to make his speeches from a high tower. 60 Once when he wanted to play tennis, of which he was very fond, he took off his shirt, so the story goes, and gave his sword to one of his boy-loves.

At this point one of his friends said jokingly, "You've put your life in his hands," and the boy smiled. Dionysius ordered them both put to death: the friend, for suggesting a way to murder him, the boy, for having laughed his approval, and he was sorrier for this act than for anything else he had done in all his life, for he had executed one whom he dearly loved. This is the way that headstrong men are split in two by their passions: to satisfy one, you must reject another.

*The sword of Damocles*

61 But this very tyrant passed his own judgment on the extent of his own happiness. Once one of his parasites, a man named Damocles, was talking about Dionysius' army, his power, the grandeur of his reign, his overflowing wealth, the majesty of his palaces, and said that no one had ever been happier than he. The tyrant said, "Well then, Damocles, since you like my sort of life so well, should you like a taste of it, to see what I live like?" Damocles said he would. So Dionysius had him perched on a golden couch covered with a handsome tapestry magnificently embroidered; he had several sideboards set with vessels of silver and embossed gold; then he ordered boys hand-picked for their beauty to stand by the table and wait upon Damocles at his slightest nod. 62 There was perfume, and garlands; incense was burning; tables were set with the rarest of delicacies: Damocles thought he was a lucky fellow. In the midst of all this splendor Dionysius ordered a gleaming sword to be let down by a horsehair from the ceiling, to hang over the neck of this happy man. The result was that Damocles did not even look at those handsome waiters or the finely-wrought silver, nor touch a morsel of food; finally, the garlands slipped off his head, and he said to the tyrant beseechingly, "Let me go away; I don't want to be happy any more." Does that seem enough of an admission on Dionysius' part that a man can find no happiness in anything, when some terror is always hanging over his head?· . . .

*Dionysius is the type of vice; his fellow townsman, the scientist Archimedes, is the type of virtue.*

64 I can imagine nothing more foul, unhappy, and hateful than the life of Dionysius. I shall not contrast it with the life of scholarly philosophers like Plato and Archytas; rather I shall raise up from his dusty diagrams a humble little man of the same city who lived many years later, Archimedes. When I was quaestor in Sicily I found his grave, though the Syracusans did not know where it was, and even said there was no such thing. It was entirely surrounded and covered with briers and brambles, but I found it by recalling some doggerel said to be inscribed on his tomb, which said that on top of it there was carved a sphere and a cylinder. Well, after I had surveyed the situation carefully (the tombs being very numerous round the Agrigento Gate) I noticed a small column sticking up just a little out of the brambles, with a sphere and a cylinder on top. I at once told the Syracusans, whose men of distinction were with me, "I think that is what I was looking for." A number of men were sent in with sickles to clear away and open up the site. As soon as a path had been made, we approached the base of the column; about half the epitaph could be read, though the last half of the lines was worn away. And so a famous Greek city, once a learned one as well, would not have known the whereabouts of the tomb of its most brilliant citizen if a man from Arpinum had not shown them where it was.

But I digress. Of all the people, who have even the most casual contact with the Muses, that is, with the teaching of liberal studies, who would not rather be the mathematician than the tyrant? If we compare their way of life, we find that the mind of the one was nourished on the intellectual pleasure of scientific research and method, which is the sweetest thing that souls can feed on, while the mind of the other was fed on murder and wrongdoing, with fear as its companion day and night.

[From Archimedes and other philosophers, Cicero, to prove that virtue suffices for a happy life, constructs a composite picture of the Stoic sage, somewhat like Cato's at the end of the *De Finibus*. The description of the heavens is a close parallel to that in *Scipio's Dream*.]

*The Stoic sage*

68 Let us assume a man of talent in the liberal arts, and let us spend a little while constructing him in our imagination. In the first place he must have genius, for virtue is not an easy companion

to slow wits. Then he must have an eager impulse to track down the truth, which is what produces those triplets of the soul: first, knowledge of the physical universe and explanation of the workings of Nature; second, a code prescribing a way of life, what to choose and what to avoid; third, an ability to draw conclusions and detect fallacies, upon which exact argument and sound judgment depend. *69* How happy must the soul of the wise man be, since it spends its days and its nights in such preoccupations! He sees the movement and the revolutions of the whole universe, and he sees the stars, studded in heaven at fixed intervals, adapting their motion to its own, he sees seven others following their own widely separated orbits, some high, some low, whose planetary motion follows a fixed, proportionate, and definite orbit; this constant astronomical observation excited the philosophers of old and spurred them on to further investigation. Thus began the investigation into the origin of species; the seeds, as it were, from which all things were conceived, came into being, and grew to maturity, the beginnings of each species, animate or inanimate, endowed with speech or mute; the nature of life and death, and how man passes by turns from one to the other; where the earth comes from and how the force of gravity holds it in balance; how the hollows of the earth contain the sea, and how all things of their own weight seek always the center of the universe, which is the lowest of the spheres.

*70* When the soul spends its days and nights in such speculations, it hits upon the knowledge of the precept of the God of Delphi, that the mind itself should know itself and feel its connection with the divine mind, which fills it with joy that cannot be satisfied. For reflection upon the nature and the power of the gods kindles a zeal for imitating their eternity, when the soul refuses to think of itself as rooted in the short span of human life and sees the causes of things linked together in the bonds of necessity; yet, as they flow from eternity to eternity, guided by the intelligence of the divine mind. *71* When the wise man concentrates on, looks up at, or rather surveys all the divisions and boundaries of the universe, how calmly his soul turns to the contemplation of this terrestrial, human sphere! Hence arises the science of Ethics, the branches of virtue burst into their various blooms; he

discovers what the ultimate good is, at which Nature aims and what the ultimate evil, the standard by which we should regulate doing our duty, the pattern we should choose to govern our life. At the end of such investigations as these, the conclusion is reached with which we are concerned in the present discussion, that virtue is self-sufficient for the happy life.

*72* There follows in the third place the method and science of logic, which permeates every branch of philosophy, defining objects, distinguishing figures of the syllogism, linking major and minor premises, drawing universal conclusions, judging truth and falsehood; a science at once very useful in analysis, pleasurable to the liberally-educated, and worthy of the philosopher.

But this is what our wise man does with his leisure time; now let him pass to the conservation of the commonwealth. What could he do that would bring him more distinction, since he has wisdom to discern his fellow citizens' advantage, justice to keep him from turning his office into private gain, and all the other virtues in their infinite number and variety? Add the fruit of friendship, which for the philosopher means a turn of mind and a way of life in tune, note for note, with his own, together with the deep pleasure of daily and intimate association. What, then, does such a life lack to make it happier? It is so filled with infinite and varied joy that the goddess of Fortune herself must yield precedence to it. But if to rejoice in such goods of the soul, that is, in virtues, is to be happy, and if all wise men enjoy these pleasures, it must be admitted that they are all happy.

[The wise man can be happy even on the rack. And his happiness does not depend upon conventional views of the value of external goods, as several examples prove.]

*Contract your desires to fit your means.*

*90* Could a Scythian like Anacharsis succeed where Roman philosophers have failed, in counting money worthless? A letter of his is quoted as follows: "Anacharsis to Hanno, greeting: My garment is a Scythian blanket, my shoes the calluses on my feet, my bed the earth, my sauce is hunger; I live on milk, cheese, and meat. You may come to me, then, as to one at peace, but as for those gifts you delight in, give them to your fellow citizens or to the deathless gods." Nearly every philosopher, of every school, except those whose natural viciousness made them lose the straight and narrow path of reason, has been capable of this same attitude. *91* When a mountain of gold and silver was carried past in a parade, Socrates said, "How much there is that I don't want!" When Alexander's ambassadors brought Xenocrates fifty talents, a large sum for those days, especially in Athens, he invited them to dinner at the Academy and set before them a meal that was adequate enough, but without display. Next day they asked him whom they should pay the money over to. "What!" he replied, "Didn't yesterday's picnic show you that I have no need of money?" But when he saw how downcast they were, he took thirty minae, to avoid the appearance of turning up his nose at the king's generosity. *92* But Diogenes, certainly, was freer with his tongue, as befits a Cynic. The story goes that when Alexander asked him if there was anything he needed, he said, "For the moment, just don't stand in my light!" For apparently Alexander had interfered with his sun-bathing.

[The wise man holds in check all desires, whether of pleasure, food, wealth, or honor. He is particularly scornful of honors from a democracy, for he knows how the mob hates the superiority of virtue.]

*Democracy the leveller*

*104* We must understand therefore that popularity with the mob is not to be courted, nor lack of notoriety to be feared. "I came to Athens," Democritus says, "and no one there recognized me." How steadfast the dignity of the man, who counts it glory that glory is not his! Are flautists and lute-players to use their own judgment, rather than that of the mob, about pitch and tempo, while the philosopher, though he belongs to a more distinguished profession, must investigate, not the truth, but the mob's caprice? What is stupider than to scorn them as individuals as though they were day-laborers and savages, but to think that they amount to something when taken as a group? *16* The wise man will scorn our petty ambitions and reject honors from the mob even when they are offered to him voluntarily; but we do not learn to scorn them until it is time to repent their acceptance. Heraclitus has a remark about Hermodorus, the most distinguished man in Ephesus; he says that every man in Ephesus should be put to death because, when they exiled Hermodorus, they decreed: "Let no man stand out among us, but if one appears, let him live in another place and among another people." Is not that what happens in every democracy? Do they not hate the superiority of virtue? Was not Aristides exiled (for modesty compels me to use Greek examples rather than Roman) because he was too just? How many inconveniences men avoid who have no contact whatever with the mob! For what is pleasanter than retirement among one's books—those books in which we read of the infinity of natural objects, and, in our own world, of heaven, earth, and sea?

[Philosophers scorn exile and ill health, too, and they all, even Epicurus, agree that virtue suffices for a happy life. Cicero decides to write down for Brutus a summary of these conversations, both for their practical value and because it will help him pass the time which hangs heavy on his hands without political activity.]

# ON THE NATURE OF THE GODS

Cicero published his three books of theology in 44 B.C., possibly in the very midst of the rioting following Caesar's murder. The work is again dedicated to Brutus; the scene is the town house of the statesman and Academic philosopher C. Aurelius Cotta, the dramatic date 77–75 B.C. The aim is to show the attitudes of the various philosophical schools toward the questions of the existence and nature of the gods and their government of the universe. The Epicurean position, that gods exist but are unconcerned with the world, is stated in four pages and refuted in twenty-six (Book I). Book II states the Stoic position, that the gods exist at the apex of a hierarchy of the universe, that the heavens declare the glory of God, and the firmament showeth his handiwork, that animal adaptation to environment, and human reason, are evidence that the gods exist. Book III contains an Academic refutation of the Stoic position, including a remarkable passage, for which unfortunately there is no space here, suggesting that in the present parlous state of the world it might be a better thing if human reason did not exist, and that in any case it has made such a mess of things that it is sorry evidence for the existence of a benevolent god.

Cicero's critique of Epicureanism here is particularly savage; he uses every trick of the prosecuting attorney, including appeals to emotion instead of logical argument. A possible reason is that the Epicureans attacked not religion in the sense of the individual's attempt to get into a right relation with the power manifesting itself in the universe, but religion as manipulated by Cicero's *optimates* party as a device to control the "lawless desires, unreasoning anger, and violent spirit" (Polybius, 6, 56) of the mob. Any attempt to abolish a belief in the political function of the gods was dangerous, from the point of view of the ruling class in Rome; to stem the Epicurean tide may then have been one important motive for the perfect spate of philosophical essays which Cicero produced in the years 45–44 B.C. It is possible to argue that the reforms of Caesar were undermining the divine right of the *optimates*, and that the people were beginning to realize, as the Stoic poet Manilius put it fifty years later, that if they had strength in proportion to their numbers, the universe would go up in flames.

### From Book I

[Cicero in his introduction stresses the importance and difficulty of the subject, and the variety of opinions on the existence of the gods. Some doubt, some deny; those who believe there are gods differ about their nature; the Epicureans deny that they have any regard for human affairs; the Stoics say that they arrange the universe for the good of man; the Academics refuse to dogmatize, and confine themselves to criticism of other views. As for Cicero himself, though he has been always interested in philosophy, he is now more absorbed by it than ever, as an occupation for enforced leisure, as a patriotic duty, and as a consolation for the loss of his beloved daughter Tullia. He sympathizes with the Academic point of view; it provokes independent thought.]

### Variety of opinions about the nature of the gods

*1* Generally speaking, Brutus, philosophy contains many a subject which so far has never been satisfactorily explained, but, as you well know, research into the nature of the gods is particularly difficult and particularly obscure. And yet it is the fairest subject the soul can know, and the

most important for the guidance of religion. The opinions of the experts on it are so varied and so conflicting that it ought to go a long way to prove that the beginning of philosophy is lack of knowledge,[17] and that the Academics show common sense in refusing to commit themselves where the facts are uncertain. For what is more disgraceful than forming opinions rashly, and what is so rash and so unworthy of the reputation for consistency of a philosopher as either to hold a false opinion or to defend unquestioningly a point of view which one has not explored enough to grasp and understand?

*2* For example, on this subject the majority (in accordance with the greatest probability and with the position nearly all of us are naturally led to) have said that the gods exist, but Protagoras said he could not make up his mind, and Diagoras of Melos and Theodorus the Cyrenaic [18] thought there were no gods at all. And even those who have said the gods exist have so many and such conflicting opinions that it would take forever to list them. For many statements are made about what the gods look like, where they live, and how they pass their time, and philosophers argue about these matters with the maximum difference of opinion; but the greatest argument of all rages about the crux of the matter: whether they are entirely inactive, never exert themselves, and are entirely free from responsibility for governing the universe, or whether on the other hand by them all things were made and set up from the beginning to be directed and set in motion for ever and ever. Unless this dispute is resolved, men must wallow in the depths of error and ignorance about subjects of the greatest importance. *3* For there have been and are now philosophers who think that the gods are entirely careless of human affairs. If their opinion is sound, what meaning can piety, holiness, or religion have? For all this worship ought in purity and chastity to be paid to divinity, if the immortal gods notice it and grant any favors in return to the human race; but if the gods are unable or unwilling to help us, if they do not care about us at all or notice what we do, if there is nothing that can flow from them into the life of man, why should we worship the immortal gods, or honor them or pray to them? Moreover, as in the case of the other virtues, so also with piety; it cannot consist in a mere empty profession. When piety goes, holiness and religious observance go with it, and when these go, the result is an upset and muddled life; (4) and I am not at all sure that with religious piety gone, public confidence, human society, and justice, the one most distinctive virtue, do not go with it.

But there are other philosophers, great and famous ones, too, who think that the whole universe is controlled and directed by the divine mind and reason. And they think further that the gods are considerate and provident about human life; for their view is that fruits, vegetables, the weather, the seasons, and the phases of the moon, whereby all the fruits of the earth come to maturity and ripen, are gifts of the immortal gods to the human race. It is these philosophers who have assembled much of this book's contents, which is of such quality that it almost seems to have been manufactured by the immortal gods for human use. But against them Carneades has argued so fully that he rouses in every man who is not lazy a desire to track down the truth. 5 For there is no subject on which there is such wide disagreement, not only among laymen, but among experts as well; in view of the variety and conflict of these opinions, one thing is certainly possible, that none of them is true; but the other is certainly impossible, that more than one of them is.

*Cicero's motives for philosophizing*

As I argue my case, I can appease kindly critics and refute jealous fault-finders, so that the one group may regret their censure and the other rejoice in their new-found knowledge; for those who give friendly advice deserve to be instructed; those who make hostile attacks deserve to be disdained. 6 Moreover, I see that a great deal of talk has been current about my books, several of which I have published within a short time, and that comment has been divided between those who wonder where I got my sudden zest for philosophizing, and those who want to know what certain knowledge we have on each subject; I have even felt that many of my readers are surprised at my special approval of that philosophy which is alleged to take away the light and to shed as it were a shadow of darkness on nature, and at my unexpected sponsorship of a school long since deserted and abandoned. But my taking up philosophy is no sudden thing; from my

earliest youth I have devoted no ordinary pains and effort to it, and I was philosophizing most when I looked least like it; witness my orations, crammed with the opinions of the philosophers, and my friendship with scholars, who have always lent distinction to my house, chief among them Diodotus, Philo,[19] Antiochus, and Posidonius, who were my teachers. 7 And if all philosophical precepts are to be judged by their effect on a man's life, I think that both in my public and in my private life I have done what reason and philosophical authority dictated. But if anyone asks what impelled me to put this down on paper so late in life, there is nothing easier to explain. For retirement bored me, and the state of the nation was such that it had to be guided by the responsible judgment of one man. So in the first place I thought that for the nation's sake philosophy ought to be explained to Romans,[20] because I thought that it made a great deal of difference to the prestige of our state that such weighty and distinguished subjects should come within the scope of Latin literature. 8 And I am the less apologetic for my plan because I note in how many men I have obviously inspired an impulse to write about philosophy as well as to learn about it. For many who were educated in Greece used to be unable to tell their fellow-citizens what they had learned, because they distrusted the competence of Latin to express what they had learned from the Greeks; but I seem to have made such progress in this quarter that now even in vocabulary we Romans are not outdone by the Greeks. 9 Another inducement to concentrate on philosophy was sickness of soul, the result of a stroke of undeserved bad luck; if I could have found any greater relief for this ailment, I should not have taken particular refuge in philosophy. I could find no better way to enjoy this relief than to devote myself not to reading books merely, but to surveying philosophy as a whole. Now one becomes best acquainted with all its parts and branches, when whole investigations are set forth in writing; for there is a remarkable cohesion and interlocking of subjects in philosophy, so that one is linked to another, and they all seem to be fitted and bound together. 10 But those who want to know what my own opinion is on each subject are more inquisitive than they need be; for in philosophical discussion the proper object is not yielding to authority but feeling the weight of reason. I will even go so far as to say that the authority of professors often stands in the way of those who want to learn; for the student tends to leave off using his own judgment, and to treat as settled what he sees to be the conclusion of the teacher he approves of. And so it is my practice to reject the alleged practice of the Pythagoreans, who, so the story goes, when anyone asked them what the proof was of some philosophical proposition, would reply, "He said it himself," "himself" being Pythagoras: a mind made up beforehand carried so much weight that authority would prevail even when it had no reason behind it.

[The undogmatic approach is especially important for a subject like theology. The reader may make up his own mind from Cicero's account of a meeting in Cotta's house, where the views of the Epicureans, Stoics, and Academics were expounded respectively by Velleius, Balbus, and Cotta, with Cicero as audience. Velleius begins, by ridiculing Stoic theology and cosmology; next he surveys the history of philosophy, from Thales to Diogenes of Babylon,[21] and shows that their views, like those of poets and Eastern sages, are steeped in error. Epicurus, on the other hand, while convinced that the gods exist, believes that they are free from passion, and therefore not to be disturbed by creating and directing worlds, which move by atomic motion, not by fate. There is no such thing as fate, and therefore inquiry into it by such devices as augury is nonsense.]

*Epicureans and their gods are free from care.*

51 VELLEIUS. You Stoics, Balbus, are always asking us Epicureans what the life of the gods is like and how they pass their time. To be sure it is in a way more blessed and more overflowing with every good thing than anything else that can be imagined. For our god does nothing, is involved in no occupations, expends effort on no work, rejoices in his own wisdom and virtue, and knows for certain that he will always have maximum pleasure for eternity. This god, let us say, is truly blessed, whereas yours is completely overworked. 52 For suppose God himself *is* the universe; what could be less leisurely than to turn about heaven's axis at a stupendous speed without a single moment off, unless you argue that there is nothing blessed about leisure? Or suppose that there is a god *in* the universe itself, directing

it, guiding it, keeping steady the orbits of the planets, the changes of season, the orderly succession of nature, keeping a constant eye on land and sea, watching over the life and convenience of mankind. What a troublesome and laborious business that god is involved in! 53 But we Epicureans define the blessed life as one in which the soul is carefree and exempt from every chore. For the same man who taught us the rest of our philosophy taught us that the universe was made by Nature, that she had no need of a workshop, that the job which you Stoics claim cannot be done without divine ingenuity is so easy that Nature has made, is making, and will make universes without number. But because you do not see how Nature can operate without the agency of some mind, you act like the tragic poets: since you cannot work out the solution to the plot, you take refuge in God. 54 But you would certainly not feel any need of him if you had eyes to see the immensity, the boundless size of the zones stretching in every direction, into which the mind, though it cast itself and extend itself ever so far and ever so wide in its pilgrimage, yet never sees the farthest coast upon which it may rest. Now in this unmeasured expanse of length and breadth and height there flies about an infinite number of countless atoms, which in spite of the intervening void, nevertheless cling together, and, hooking on to one another, form a continuity; and out of this are formed the contours and outlines of natural objects, which you think cannot be shaped without bellows and anvils. And so you have placed upon our necks an eternal master, for us to fear day and night. For who would not be afraid of a god who foresees everything, plans everything, notices everything, and thinks everything is his business—an inquisitive and busybody god? 55 This is the origin of your predestined Necessity, which you call Fate, so that you say that whatever happens results from eternal truth and a chain of causes. How highly should we value this philosophy, whose supporters, like so many old crones, and ignorant ones at that, think that everything happens by fate? The result is your "mantic art," which is called divination in Latin, which would steep us, if we were willing to listen to you, so deeply in superstition that we would have to kowtow to inspectors of entrails, observers of the flights of birds, soothsayers, warlocks, and interpreters of dreams. *56* Released from these terrors by Epicurus, and set free, we have felt no fear of the gods, who, we know, are neither making trouble for themselves nor looking for any for anyone else, and in piety and holiness we worship Nature, who stands above and before all things.

[Cotta replies with an Academic criticism of Velleius' Epicurean theology, especially its reliance on the common consent of mankind, and its making of gods in man's image. Why have the Epicurean gods limbs if they are inactive? Epicureans scoff at the argument from design, but, as long as their gods are inactive, they have no valid substitute to offer. The gods of popular religion have at least the virtue of being of some use.]

*Academic critique of Epicurean theology*

*99* COTTA. But perhaps you do not heed even this argument, that not only in man but even in a tree whatever is extra or useless gets in the way. What a nuisance it is to have one finger too many! Why? Because the five you have do not want another, either for show or for use. But your Epicurean god has not merely one finger extra, but one head, one neck, shoulders, sides, belly, back, knees, hands, feet, thighs, and shins. On the other hand, for the purpose of your god's kind of immortality, of what use are these parts of the body or his face itself? (The argument applies even more to the brain, heart, lungs, and liver, for they are life's dwelling-place; facial expression has nothing to do with life's durability.) *100* And yet you find fault with those, who from the evidence of Nature's splendid and mighty works; from the sight of the universe itself and its parts, heaven and earth and sea, and its badges of rank, the sun, moon, and stars; from their knowledge of the ripeness, the changes, the succession of the seasons, have suspected that some natural force above and beyond us exists which has created all this, and moves, directs, and guides it. Even if such men reach false conclusions, they enable me to see what they are getting at: but what great and extraordinary work can *you* point to which seems to have been created by the divine mind, and which may be lead you to an inkling that the gods exist? "I have in my soul," you say, "an ingrained concept of God." Of Jupiter with a beard, and Minerva with a hel-

met; you don't think god is really like that, do you? *101* How much better is the procedure of the uninformed mob, who assign not only man's limbs, but even the use of them, to their god; for they issue him a bow, arrows, a spear, a shield, a trident, a thunderbolt; and even if they do not see acts which may be acts of God, they still cannot imagine a do-nothing deity. The very Egyptians, objects of ridicule as they are, hold no beast sacred unless they derive some benefit from it; the ibis, a long-legged bird with stiff legs and a long, horny beak, for instance, kills an immense number of snakes. The ibises saved Egypt from a plague by killing and eating the winged snakes which were carried in on the African wind from the Libyan desert, so that the snakes did no harm by their fangs when they were alive, nor by their odor when they were dead. I could talk about the usefulness of the mongoose, the crocodile, and the cat, but I don't want to be long-winded. So I shall wind up by saying that at any rate it was the usefulness of beasts that prompted the barbarians to worship them, whereas in the case of your gods not only is there no evidence of usefulness, but there is no evidence of any activity whatever. *102* Epicurus says, "God has nothing to interfere with his leisure." Such a god, like a spoiled child, thinks there is nothing better than a vacation. But even children, in spite of being on holiday, amuse themselves with play of some kind: do we want our vacationing god to be so sluggish from inactivity that if he should so much as move, we should be afraid he could not be happy? The Epicurean argument not only robs the gods of motion and divine activity, but it makes men lazy, too, if it is true that so long as God is *doing* anything, not even he can be happy.

[Cotta devotes the rest of Book I to showing that Epicurean principles are fatal to true religion, and ends with the suggestion that Epicurus only pretended to believe in the gods, in order to avoid the people's hatred. In Book II, Balbus undertakes to expound the Stoic theology under four heads: divine existence, the divine nature, divine governance of the universe, divine benevolence. As we take up the text, Balbus is arguing that the gods exist because there exists a hierarchy (the "Great Chain of Being") in the universe, beginning with vegetables, proceeding through animals and man, with his potentialities for virtue and wisdom, and needing God to crown all and to give all other things a mark to strive toward. If the universe contains all things, it must contain that which is supremely good; what is supremely good is wisdom; what is supremely wise is God; therefore God exists. *Q.E.D.*]

*From* Book II

*Stoic theology: the hierarchy of Nature*

*33* BALBUS. And even if we want to proceed from primitive and incomplete natures to the ultimate and perfect ones, we arrive of necessity at the nature of the gods. For we notice, first, that nature supports the fruits of the earth, to which she grants simply protection while they take root and grow. *34* Next, she has given animals sense-perception and motion, and appetite, which attracts them to healthful food and repels them from what is poisonous. She has given more than this to man, for she has added reason, whereby the soul's appetites are regulated, being sometimes allowed to run free, and sometimes reined in. The fourth and highest level includes those who are born naturally good and wise, in whom there is innate from the beginning a self-consistent right reason, which must be considered higher than man, attributable to God, and therefore to the universe, in which that perfect and absolute reason must inhere. *35* For it cannot be said that in any ordered arrangement something in the nature of an end and finishing touch does not exist. For just as in the vine or in cattle, unless some force interferes, we see nature take its own course to an end; just as a picture or an artifact or any other product of human skill has an effect as of a finished piece of work, so also in nature as a whole, and to a much greater degree, some end is necessarily accomplished and brought to perfection. This is all the more certain because, while many external forces can prevent particular natural objects from reaching perfection, nothing can stand in the way of universal Nature, because it contains and controls all natural objects. Therefore that fourth and highest level must exist, since no force can attack it. This is the level at which we suppose the Nature of all things to exist; since it naturally excels all things, and since nothing can stand in its way, it follows necessarily that a universe endowed with mind and with practical wisdom exists.

[After proving that the stars, too, are divine, Balbus passes to his second subdivision, the divine nature. God is not made in man's image; He is spherical, and revolves. Nature operates creatively, artistically, and providentially because God is in it. The gods the people worship are personified abstractions, or heroes, or natural forces. Pure religion and undefiled is this: to worship one divine being in holiness and purity, and without superstition.]

*Stoic theology: true religion*

*71* The best, purest, holiest, and most pious worship of the gods is this, that we should revere them always with mind and voice pure, single, and undefiled. For it did not need philosophers to tell our ancestors that there is a distinction between religion and superstition. Those who used to pray and make sacrifices all day long that their children might have superabundant length of days were called "superstitious," a term which later was more widely applied; those on the other hand who industriously study and reread all that is legible pertaining to divine worship have been called "religious" from "re-legible," just as elegant people derive their name from the verb "to elect," diligent people from the verb "to be diligent," intelligent people from the verb "to be intelligent"; in all these words the same idea of "legibility" inheres as in the word "religion." This is how it happens that when we call one man "superstitious" and another "religious" the one is a term of opprobrium, the other a term of praise.

[After this etymological nightmare, Balbus proceeds to his third point, the divine governance of the universe, of which the chief proof is the famous "argument from Design," which deduces the existence of the watchmaker from the existence of the watch. The world's order is too marvelous to be the result of a fortuitous concourse of atoms. Only familiarity, as Aristotle tells us, blinds us to the divine marvels of the universe.]

*The Stoic argument from design*

*95* Suppose that beings existed who lived underground in fine, well-lighted houses, adorned with statues and pictures, and equipped with every convenience which ostensibly happy people enjoy in abundance. Suppose further that they had never gone above ground, but had it on hearsay that a divine force existed. Then suppose that one day the jaws of the earth yawned open and they were able to make their way out from their hidden dwellings to the regions which we inhabit. Suppose there suddenly burst upon them the sight of the earth, the sea, and the sky, that they saw for the first time mighty clouds and blustering winds, and the size, the beauty, and the efficiency of the sun, making daylight with its rays spread all over heaven. Imagine next that night cast its shadows over the earth, and they saw the whole of heaven studded and adorned with stars, and the varied light of the waxing and the waning moon, the risings and the settings of the heavenly bodies, and their orbits, fixed and unchangeable through all eternity. At the sight of these, surely their first thought would be that the gods exist and that all these wonderful works are the works of God. . . .

98 Let us look first at the whole earth, set in the midpoint of the universe, solid, spherical, and made into a ball by the gravitation of all its parts, clothed in a garment of flowers and plants and trees and fruits, in number beyond belief, in diversity that cannot cloy. Think too of springs flowing cool in all seasons, of rivers with their pellucid waters, of river banks clothed in grass-green, of high vaulted caves, rough rocks, tall mountains looming up, fields stretching away to the horizon; and think of the hidden veins of silver and gold, and the limitless supply of marble. 99 How many different kinds of animals there are, both tame and wild! Think of the birds, flying and singing, the flocks feeding, and the life of the beasts of the forest! And what shall I say of the race of men, who, appointed as it were as custodians of the earth, suffer it not to breed too many wild beasts nor to turn into an uncultivated wilderness of weeds; men, by whose labors the countryside, the islands, and the seashore gleam with the bright pattern of houses and cities? If we could see all this with our souls as we see it with our eyes, no one could look at the whole earth and still be of two minds about divine reason.

[Balbus describes the sea and the sky in the same ecstatic vein, quoting at length from Cicero's translation of the astronomical poet Aratus. The whole of these wonders is held together, he says, by a sort of cosmic sympathy.]

*Divine governance of the universe according to the Stoics: cosmic sympathy*

119 I don't want you to think me tedious on the subject of the movement of the stars, and especially of those called "planets" or "wanderers." The harmony resulting from their different rates of speed is such that while the most distant one, Saturn, is ice-cold, the middle one, Mars, is red-hot, and the one between, Jupiter, glows with a moderate heat. Two stars below the level of Mars are under the sun's influence, while the sun itself fills the whole universe with its light, and lights up the moon, which in turn controls pregnancy, childbirth, and the ripening of growing things. Anyone who is not moved by this dovetailing of the universe, this dress parade of nature, sympathetically, as it were, keeping safe the cosmos, has, I am convinced, never given astronomy a second thought. . . .

*Divine governance is further proved by the adaptation of animal life to preserve the individual.*

121 Consider the number of species of animals, and how much energy is expended to the end that each may survive according to its kind. Some have hides to protect them, others are clad in fleece, still others bristle with quills. We see them covered with feathers or with scales, armed with horns, or equipped for flight with wings. Nature, too, has provided for each animal, in lavish abundance, its appropriate fodder. I can list point by point what there is in the shapes of the animals, what cunning and subtlety in the arrangement of their parts, what remarkable construction in their limbs so that they can hold and devour their food. For every inner part has come into being and been placed in such a way that not a one is superfluous, not a one unnecessary to survival. 122 Nature, too, has given to beasts both sense perception and appetite, so that the latter gives them their impulse to take their proper food, the former the ability to distinguish things harmful from things wholesome. For animals approach their food by walking, gliding, flying, or swimming; some of them eat by opening their mouths and using their teeth, others tear at food held in their claws, others use their curved beaks; they suck their food, they graze on it, they swallow it whole, or they chew it. Some of them are so close

to the ground that they can easily reach food there with their beaks; the taller ones, (*123*) like geese, swans, cranes, and camels, have the length of their necks to help them. The elephant even has a handlike trunk, because the size of his body makes it difficult for him to get at his food. To the animals that feed on others Nature has given either strength or speed.[22] Some are given cunning devices, like the spiders, one species of which weaves a web, and devours whatever gets stuck in it, while another species keeps a watchful eye out, as it were, unobserved, and seizes on and consumes whatever falls into its clutches. The mussel ("pina" in Greek), has two big shells that open wide; it enters into a sort of partnership for food-getting with the tiny shrimp: when little minnows swim between the open shells, the shrimp notifies the mussel, which thereupon clamps its shells shut with a snap. So animals of very dissimilar species go food-hunting jointly, (*124*) and the question is whether they make some arrangement between them, or whether they are associated by natural instinct from the moment of their birth. There is no less cause for wonder in the case of aquatic animals who are born on land; crocodiles, for example, and mud turtles, and some kinds of snake, born out of water, make for it as soon as they can. Another example: we often put hens to sit on ducks' eggs; when the ducklings hatch, the hens care for them like mothers, since they have hatched and reared them, but then the ducklings leave the hens and run away, with the hens in hot pursuit, the very first time they see water, which is as it were their natural home: so deep an instinct of self-preservation has nature implanted in living things. I have even seen in writing that there exists a bird called the spoonbill, which gets its food by flying up to diving sea birds; when they come up out of the water, having caught their fish, he holds their heads under with his beak until they give up their catch, which he then makes off with. There are also written accounts of this same bird's practice of filling its crop with shellfish. When the stomach's heat has digested them, the spoonbill vomits them up again, and then sorts out the edible parts from the shells. *125* Then there are the sea frogs, whose practice is said to be to cover themselves with sand and move along near the water's edge; when fish come up to them, looking for food, the frogs pounce on

them and eat them. There is a sort of instinctive war between the kite and the crow, so that they break each other's eggs wherever they find them. Who can fail to marvel at this one of Aristotle's many observations: when cranes cross the sea, migrating to a warmer climate, they form a triangle, whose apex forms an airfoil; then, as the triangle broadens out on either side, the birds use their wings as oars to make flying easier; the base of the cranes' triangle, too, is helped along like a ship by winds from dead astern; and the bird behind rests its head and neck on the back of the bird flying in front; the leading bird cannot do this, because he has no place to rest, so he flies to the rear to rest, and one of the birds that has been resting takes his place, and they keep up this shifting for the whole flight. *126* I could multiply examples of this sort, but you see the kind of thing I mean. . . . *132* It is impossible to enumerate the conveniences afforded by rivers, the ebb and flow of tides, the forest-clad mountains, the salt-beds at a great distance from the sea, the earth full to bursting with wholesome remedies, and finally, the countless necessary arts that minister to life and sustenance. Even the alternation of day and night contributes to the survival of living things by assigning one period to activity and another to rest.

So from every source and every argument the conclusion is that everything in the universe is marvelously managed by the plan of the divine mind for the security and preservation of all things. . . .

*But the hand of providence is best seen in the structure and nature of man.*

*147* Now the man who does not see that the human soul and mind, with its capacity for reason, judgment, and common sense, has been perfected by divine solicitude, seems to me to be himself lacking in these very faculties. I wish you would let me borrow your eloquence to talk about them, Cotta; if it were done in your manner, how intelligent we mortals would appear, what a capacity we should be shown to have for logical grasp of the connection of conclusion with premises! This logical faculty, of course, enables us to judge what follows from what, to draw our conclusions rationally, to define particulars and comprehend them in a syllogism; and from this arises scientific knowledge of natural forces and categories, a knowledge as distinctive as any possessed by God himself. How important those faculties are which you Academics undermine and abolish! For it is with the senses and the mind that we perceive and grasp things outside ourselves, *(148)* and when these externals are brought together and compared, we derive from them the skills which are necessary partly to support life and partly to make it pleasant. How distinctive and divine is that force of eloquence which you always call the queen of the arts! In the first place, it enables us to learn things of which we are ignorant, and to teach what we know to others; next, we use it to exhort and to persuade, to console the afflicted and to guide the timid out of the way of fear; to restrain the overeager and to quench the fires of lust and anger; it links us in the bonds of laws and of statutes, and of dwelling together in cities; it distinguishes our lives from those of brute beasts. *149* You cannot believe, unless you pay close attention, how many devices nature has wrought for us to use in speech. For in the first place an artery stretches from the lungs to the inner part of the mouth, whereby the voice, starting from the mind, is caught up and uttered. Then the tongue is situated in the mouth and fenced about with teeth; it shapes and limits unduly loud sounds, and when it strikes the teeth and other parts of the mouth makes the sound of the voice distinct and clipped; and so we Stoics usually compare the tongue to the pick, the teeth to the strings, the nostrils to the sounding board which echoes to the string in music.

*150* What convenient servants to innumerable skills are the hands that Nature has given to man! The contraction and extension of the fingers is easy because the ligaments and joints are flexible, and they make any motion without difficulty. And so, by the motion of the fingers, the hand can be made to paint, mould, carve, or produce sounds on stringed or wind instruments. This ministers to our pleasure, but the hands serve our needs too, in agriculture, building, weaving or sewing of garments, and in the working of bronze or iron; and as a result we have made all our progress toward the things that the mind has discovered and the senses perceived, by the application of craftsmen's hands, so that we can be housed, clothed, and protected, and possess cities, walls, houses, and temples. *151* It was by the

works of man's hands that the variety and abundance of our food was discovered. For much of our farm produce is procured by the labor of hands, and either eaten at once or stored away for future use, and besides we eat land and water animals, and birds, some of which we hunt, and others we raise domestically. We even break in four-footed beasts as draft animals, whose strength and speed adds to our own. We put loads on some animals and yokes on others; we turn the razor-sharp senses of elephants and the keen scent of dogs from their natural uses to our own; we extract from the depths of the earth the iron that is so necessary for agriculture; we discover the deep-hid veins of copper, silver, and gold, so useful, and so decorative. We cut down trees and use the lumber both from those that we raise in nurseries and from those that grow wild, partly to burn for warming our bodies and for cooking food, and partly for building, so that we can use the protection of houses to ward off heat and cold. *152* Timber has important uses in shipbuilding; sea voyages supply all sorts of products from all over the world; and we mortals alone have control over the two most violent things in nature: the winds and the sea; because we have skill in seafaring, we use and enjoy many maritime products. Men have dominion over all the earth's conveniences also: we enjoy meadow and mountain; ours are the rivers, ours the lakes; it is we that plant grain and trees; by irrigation we make the earth fertile; we dam rivers, dig channels for them, change their courses; in short, with our hands we try to make as it were another nature in the nature of things.

*153* Has not human reason made its way even into the heavens? For we are the only living creatures who understand the rising, setting, and orbits of the stars; the human race has defined the length of the day, the month, and the year; it has investigated the eclipses of the sun and moon and has predicted them for all subsequent time, however far in the future. As the mind contemplates these phenomena, it comes close to an understanding of the gods; out of that understanding rises piety; with piety is connected justice and the other virtues, out of which there comes into being a blessed life equal and similar to that of the gods, since it yields to the life of the heavenly beings only in respect of immortality, which has nothing to do with the good life.

By setting forth these facts, I think I have shown adequately how far human nature ranks ahead of all other animate things. As a consequence, it should be understood that neither the shape and position of our limbs nor the remarkable vigor and ingenuity of our minds can have been brought to pass by mere chance.

[Balbus concludes Book II with examples of divine solicitude for man. In Book III, Cotta subjects the Stoic theology to an Academic criticism, taking up each of Balbus' four points in turn, after which Cicero announces his personal preference for the Stoic position, and the dialogue ends.]

# ON DIVINATION

This work, a sort of appendix to *On the Nature of the Gods,* published early in 44 B.C., advances in the first book a series of arguments in favor of attempting to discover the unknown by supernatural means. The argument based on political usefulness of divination in controlling and blocking new legislation is not the least important. The second book presents the arguments against divination, at the same time insisting that while superstition should be rooted out, true religion, as an ancestral institution, should be encouraged. The Emperor Augustus in his religious revival followed Cicero's advice. The book opens with a survey of Cicero's encyclopedic philosophical works and studies and a statement of his motives for writing.

## From Book II

*Cicero summarizes his philosophical works.*

*1* As I have devoted long thought and research to the question how I might be useful to as many people as possible, and not deprive the state of the benefit of my judgment, I have found no better way than by handing on to my fellow citizens a guide to the liberal arts, a goal which I think I have now reached in several volumes. For I wrote as eloquent an invitation as I could to the study of philosophy in my *Hortensius;* and I illustrated the branch of philosophy which I consider least arrogant and most logical and elegant, in the four books of my *Academics. 2* And since the basis of philosophy is the choice of the chief end for man, I cleared this up in five books dedicated to clarifying the position of each philosopher on the subject, and stating what might be said in opposition to him. Soon after, five more books of *Tusculan Disputations* revealed the minimum essentials of a happy life. Book I is on despising death, Book II on bearing pain, Book III on relieving anxiety, Book IV on other disturbances of the soul, and Book V embraces the subject

which best illustrates philosophy as a whole; for it demonstrates that virtue alone is sufficient for a happy life. *3* After these works were published, I finished three books *On the Nature of the Gods,* which includes the results of all investigation of this subject. To finish it off in full or even overflowing measure, I began to write the present books *On Divination;* if I add to them, as I intend, a book *On Fate,* I shall have done full justice to the whole subject. With these books should be grouped the six *On the Republic,* which I wrote when I was at the helm of the ship of state. It is an important subject, closely related to philosophy, and treated at great length by Plato, Aristotle, Theophrastus, and the whole tribe of the Peripatetics. What comment shall I make on my *Consolation?* It was certainly good medicine for me, and I think it will be a real help to others also. In the midst of my other labors I recently tossed off the book I dedicated to Atticus *On Old Age;* and since it is primarily philosophy which makes a man good and brave, my *Cato* ought to be included in this catalogue. *4* And since both Aristotle and Theophrastus, men distinguished both for their keenness of mind and for the extent of their works, have linked the rules of rhetoric with philosophy, I think my oratorical works ought to be included in the philosophical list. There will then be the three *On the Orator,*[23] a fourth called *Brutus,* and a fifth, *The Orator.*

## Philosophy as political action

This is the list to date; I was eager to treat the rest, with my mind so well prepared for the task that if a more important matter [24] had not stood in the way, I should have left no branch of philosophy unexposed to the light of Latin literature. For what better or more important contribution can I make to the state than to educate and instruct the young, especially considering the present low state of public morals, which has caused such a degeneration of our young people that everyone's help is needed to rein them in and curb them? 5 I do not expect, I do not even ask, that all our young folk should turn to the study of philosophy. All I ask is just a few; few though they be, their hard work can be a widespread influence in the state. In fact, I am reaping the reward of my labors even from men already well along in life, who find my books a comfort; their eagerness to read makes my desire to write grow stronger day by day; and I find that I have more readers than I had thought. It would be a splendid thing, and a legitimate source of pride to Romans, if they felt no inferiority before Greek philosophical literature; 6 and I shall fill that gap if I carry out my plans. For my part, it was a serious national crisis that gave me my motive for expounding philosophy. In the midst of civil war I could neither come to the rescue of the state, as had been my wont, nor stand idly by, and I found nothing better to do; nothing, at least, that was worthy of me. My fellow citizens will forgive me, then, or rather thank me, for not having gone into hiding while the state was under monarchical rule, nor having deserted, nor worried, nor acted like a man angry with an individual or with the times, nor having been so lost in praise and admiration of another man's fortune as to regret my own. For this is the very thing I learned from Plato and from philosophy, that constitutional changes are perfectly natural, and that states are ruled sometimes by an aristocracy, sometimes by a democracy, and occasionally by a tyrant. 7 When our state suffered this latter change, I was deprived of my former duties and began to renew my philosophical studies, so that my mind could have this special relief from its troubles, and that I might be of whatever use I could to my fellow citizens. For I have used my books as my political action, and as my arguments in support of the policy I advocate; 25 and I had thought of philosophy as my substitute for statesmanship. But now, since I have begun again to be a counselor of state, I have to devote my time to that, or rather I have to devote to it my every thought and care, and all the time I ought to spend on philosophy is what I can spare from public duties and responsibilities.

[Cicero argues, against the Stoics, that we have no evidence from any source that divination is a science; it is either fortuitous or fated; if the former, the future cannot be predicted; if the latter, what is the use? He surveys the various forms of divination, and quotes Cato's famous remark, that it was a wonder soothsayers did not laugh in each other's faces when they met. In connection with his treatment of astrology, he argues that heredity and environment influence us far more than the stars.]

*Heredity and environment*

94 Is it only a minor mistake on the part of the astrologers not to realize that they have left entirely out of account the power of the parental seed, which is of fundamental importance in birth and procreation? For no one can fail to see that in appearance, in character, in many of their habits and impulses children take after their parents. This would not be the case, if the responsible agency were the phase of the moon and the arrangement of the constellations rather than the natural force of heredity. 95 Does not the fact that persons born at the very same instant have different characters, different lives, different experiences go at least some way to prove that the time of birth has nothing to do with one's life history? Unless perhaps we think that no one was conceived and born at the same instant as Scipio. For who was ever born that could match him?

96 Furthermore, does anyone doubt that many who were born with some unnatural defect were made whole and set right either by natural means, when nature had reinstated herself, or by the surgeon's art? For example, those whose tongues clove to the roof of their mouths, so that they could not speak, had them slit with a scalpel and set free. Many have even removed a natural defect by concentration and exercise; for example, Demetrius of Phalerum writes that Demosthenes could not pronounce his "r's," but practised until he could say them very plainly. But if these defects had been implanted by or inherited from a star, no power on earth could change them. Again, do not different environments breed different sorts of men? It is easy, in speech at least, to cover the ground, and show what an incredibly vast variation and difference there is, physically and mentally, between Indians and Persians,

Ethiopians and Syrians. *97* And that proves that environment has more effect than the moon on human birth.

[Predictions of "inspired" prophets, and interpretations of dreams, are equally fallacious. We must distinguish between religion and superstition, and preserve the one while we confound the other.]

*Religion versus superstition*

*148* To be perfectly frank, superstition has pervaded all nations, borne down heavily upon everyone's mind, and taken advantage of human weakness. I have already made this statement in my books *On the Nature of the Gods;* my chief point in this argument has been the same. Apparently we should do ourselves and our countrymen a great deal of good, if we were to root superstition out entirely. But I want it clearly understood that I do not want religion destroyed along with superstition. For it is the wise man's business to protect ancestral institutions by retaining the old rites and ceremonies. That there is some eternal Being who stands out above the rest, and that the human race ought to revere and admire Him, is an admission that the beauty of the universe and the orderliness of the celestial bodies compels us to make. *149* Therefore, just as religion, being associated with natural science, ought actually to be propagated, so every root of superstition ought to be weeded out. For it looms over you, presses hard upon you, and pursues you wherever you turn, whether you listen to a hedge-priest or to the interpretation

of an omen, whether you make a sacrifice or watch the flight of a bird, or visit an astrologer or a soothsayer, or if there is lightning or thunder, or a bolt from the blue, or some monstrous birth or prodigious occurrence. And since something like this is nearly always happening, you can never, if you are superstitious, gain a moment's peace. *150* Sleep looks like the refuge from every care and worry. But it too is the source of many fears and vexations. In themselves dreams would be rather scorned than heeded, if philosophers had not stood sponsors for the interpretation of them, and not the most contemptible philosophers, either, but some of the keenest, who can tell a logical argument from a fallacy, and who are considered just about the last word. If Carneades had not made a stand against their excesses, for all I know they might now be considered the only philosophers that counted. It is against these that practically my whole argument and discussion is directed, not because I hold them in special scorn, but because they seem to defend their point of view with great keenness and common sense. But since it is characteristic of the Academy never to insert its own opinion, to give its approval to what seems probable, to compare the opposing briefs, and express whatever can be said against any given point of view, and, never using the force of its own authority, to leave the listener's mind open and unprejudiced, we shall hold to this practice handed down from Socrates, and use it among ourselves, with your permission, brother Quintus, as often as we can.

# ON OLD AGE

In this dialogue, dedicated to Cicero's friend and publisher Atticus and published in 44 B.C., Cato the Elder, the type of old-fashioned Roman virtue, is imagined to be denying, in a discussion with Laelius and Scipio the Younger (dramatic date 150 B.C.) the alleged disadvantages of old age; that it deprives us of the active life of the man of affairs; that it involves physical weakness; that it denies us nearly all pleasures; and that it is the threshold of death. We may suppose that Cicero, broken at sixty-two by a life of personal and political tragedy, wrote the essay as a piece of self-consolation. In the first passage below Cato is discussing pleasures, with special

emphasis on the pleasures of love. (Cf. *Tusc.* IV, 68, 74–76.)

*The pleasures of old age*

*46* CATO. For my part, because I love to talk, I enjoy also those banquets that begin in the afternoon, with young fellows like yourselves as well as with men of my own age, and I am grateful to old age, because it has increased my fondness for conversation, but taken away my greed for food and drink. But I don't want to appear to declare war to the death on pleasure, which is perhaps after all a natural instinct up to a point. To those who enjoy the pleasures of the table, I say that I have not noticed that old age lacks good appetite, either. I for one like our tradition of appointing a toastmaster, and I enjoy the conversation that begins by ancestral custom at the head of the table when the drinks are served, in tiny, chilled glasses, as Xenophon describes them in his *Symposium*, iced in summer, warmed in the sun or by the fire in winter. I regularly keep up this practice even on my Sabine estate, and every day I join my neighbors at a dinner party which we spin out until late at night with conversation on as many subjects as we can think of.

47 It will be argued that old men do not enjoy so much of what I may call the titillation of the senses. True, but we don't feel a sense of longing, either, and one is not bothered by what one does not miss. Sophocles made a good answer, when in his old age someone asked him whether he still enjoyed the pleasures of love. "God forbid," he replied; "I have been as glad to escape from them as from a harsh and crazy master."

[Old men have still the pleasures of study, and of farming, like Cincinnatus called from the plough to the dictatorship. (Cato had written a treatise on agriculture, a sort of *Old Farmers' Almanac*, full of hard-headed practical advice.)]

*The satisfactions of farming*

56 In the old days those who enjoyed farming did not have a pitiable old age, did they? For my part, I don't see how any life can be happier, both because of the satisfaction of doing one's duty, inasmuch as agriculture keeps the whole human race alive, and because of the pleasure of it which I have already mentioned, and from the overflowing bounty of all provisions which feed man and provide sacrifices for the gods; since some people would miss these creature comforts, by mentioning them I am renewing diplomatic relations with pleasure. For if a landowner is a good farmer and keeps at his job, his wine cellar, oil vats, and larder are always chockfull; his whole farm is well stocked, with enough and to spare of ham, goat meat, lamb, chicken, milk, cheese, and honey. And then there is the vegetable garden, which the farmers themselves call their spare side of meat. Even spare-time pursuits like fowling and hunting add to the

larder. 57 Do I need to say any more about the green meadows, the orderly rows of trees in the orchard, or the beauty of the vineyards and olive yards? I shall cut it off short. Nothing can match a well-cultivated field for rich return on investment or beauty of appearance, and old age, far from slowing down our enjoyment of farming, actually invites and attracts us to it. For where can an old man find a better place to toast himself in the sunshine or by the fire, or enjoy a more wholesome coolness of shade trees and running streams? 58 Let others, then, enjoy feats of arms, riding, throwing the javelin, fencing, tennis, swimming, and running, so long as out of their many recreations they leave to us old men our dice and our knuckle-bones, these to be used only when we feel like it, for old age can be happy without them.

[The greatest advantage of old age is the political influence it brings. As for bad temper and miserliness, these are vices not of old age but of individual character. Not all wine sours as it ages. Finally, men fear old age because it brings them close to death. This is a one-sided view.]

*Death is no hardship to wise old age.*

66 There remains the fourth consideration, which especially seems to bring anxiety and worry to men of my age: the approach of death, which certainly cannot be far distant from old age. How much to be pitied any old man is, who in all his long life has never seen that death is to be scorned! As a matter of fact, if it completely snuffs out the soul, death ought to be ignored, and, if it leads us to a place where we may have eternal life, it ought actually to be wished for. Certainly there is no third alternative. 67 What then have I to be afraid of, if after death I am going to be either not unhappy or positively happy? For that matter, no one is stupid enough, however young he is, as to be positive he will live till evening. Why, youth runs more fatal risks by far than I do. Young people fall ill more easily, they are harder to cure, and the course of the illness is more serious. And so few ever reach old age; otherwise life would be better and more sensible. For it is the old that have intelligence, reason, and judgment: if there had never been any old men, there never would have been any governments at all. . . .

*70* An actor, to please his audience, need not appear all the way through the play, as long as he gives satisfaction in the scenes he does appear in. In the same way the wise man need not continue to appear until the final curtain. A short life is long enough for good and honorable living, but if you should live longer, you need regret it no more than a farmer, when the sweetness of springtime is past, regrets the coming of summer and autumn. For youth is like spring, giving promise of the harvest to come, while the other two seasons are planned for reaping the harvest and gathering it in. *71* For the harvest of old age, as I have often said, is the rich memory of benefits received. Besides, everything that happens in accordance with Nature ought to be numbered among the good things. Now what is more in accordance with Nature than for old men to die? When death comes to the young, it is against Nature's will, and she fights against it. And so the death of a young man seems to me like the quenching of a flame by a torrent of water; but when an old man dies, it is as though the flame of its own accord, without the application of external force, is used up and goes out. Just as green apples are hard to pick from the tree, while those which are ripened to maturity fall of their own accord, so it requires force to take life away from young people, but only ripeness to take it from the old. And that ripeness is so pleasant to me at least, that the closer I come to death, the more I seem to come within sight of land and to be coming at long last into harbor after a far voyage.

[Cato cites historical and literary examples of men who have met death bravely; to every thing there is a season, and a time to every purpose under the sun.]

*76* All in all, at least in my opinion, when one is tired of everything one is tired of life. Boyhood has certain interests, but adolescents do not miss them, do they? Nor does a man in steady middle age long for the renewal of the pleasures of early youth. Middle life has its pleasures, too, but they are not sought for in old age. Old age has certain interests of its own, but they fail, just as those of earlier ages do, and when that happens, being tired of life makes the time ripe for death.

[After citing various views on the after life, Cato gives his own; he looks forward to the survival of his fame, and to happy meeting with his friends in the hereafter.]

## The joys of Heaven

*82* No one will ever persuade me, Scipio, that your father Paulus, or your two grandfathers Paulus and Africanus, or his father and his uncle or many other distinguished men who do not need listing, would have put so much effort into being remembered by posterity unless they knew in their hearts that posterity would remember them. Or, if you will pardon an old man's bragging, do you think that I would have undertaken so many offices both civil and military, working day and night, if my fame was to be bounded by the same limits as my life? Would it not have been far better to pass a leisurely, quiet life without any effort or struggle? But somehow my soul rose up and always looked forward to posterity as though it would begin to live only when it had departed this life. But if it were not true that souls are immortal, an aristocrat's soul would not make a special effort to achieve immortal fame. *83* It is a fact that the wiser a man is, the more calmly he dies; only fools make hard work of dying. Does not the farsighted soul, with wider vision, seem to you to see that death is embarking upon a better life, a point of view not granted to those of duller vision? In fact I am beside myself with eagerness to see the fathers of both of you, whom I loved and saw much of, and it is not only they, my personal acquaintances, whom I am anxious to meet, but also those famous men whom I have heard of, and read about, and even written about myself. You may be sure there is no one who will find it easy to hold me back once I have started on that journey, or to boil me into youth again as though I were Pelias.[26] And if any god should grant me, at my age, to become a boy again and squall in my cradle, I should refuse point-blank; I should not want to be called back from the finish-line to the starting block when my race was all but run. *84* For what advantage does life hold, or rather, what trouble does it not hold? But suppose it does have advantages; certainly it has also either satiety or a limit. I do not want to whimper over life, as many have done, and wise men, too, nor am I sorry I have lived, since my way of life has not led me to think I was born in vain, and I depart from life not as from a house, but as from an inn. For Nature has given us a hostelry to stay at, not to dwell in forever. O day bright beyond the others, when I shall set out for that divine assembly and meeting-place of souls, and leave this vile medley of confusion! For I shall go to meet not only the heroes I have mentioned, but my son Cato, too, than whom no finer man or better son was ever born. I cremated his body; it would have been more fitting if he had cremated mine. His soul, not deserting me, but looking back at me, went off to the very place whither it knew that I, too, would have to come. I have the reputation for having borne my loss bravely; not that I bore it with equanimity, but I consoled myself with the thought that the parting and the separation between us would not be long.

*Conclusion: old age is to be borne lightly, whatever its sequel.*

85 Well, Scipio, you and Laelius have said

that you often marvel at how lightly I bear my old age. These are the reasons why, far from finding it troublesome, I find it positively pleasant. But if I am wrong in believing that the human soul is immortal, I am glad to be wrong, and I do not want my error wrenched from me while I live: but if when I am dead I shall feel nothing, as certain trifling philosophers hold, I shall in that case have no fear that dead philosophers will laugh at my error. But if we are not to be immortal, yet for a man to be snuffed out when his time comes is something to be wished for. For Nature sets a limit to life as she does to other things. Moreover, old age is the last act of life, and, as at a play, if we find it boring, we ought to make our exit, especially if we have already had our fill.

This is what I had to say about old age; I hope you both come to it, so that you can prove by your own experience the truth of what you have heard from me.

## ON FRIENDSHIP

The dialogue *On Friendship* (44 B.C.), put by Cicero into the mouth of Laelius, the friend of Scipio the Younger, begins with an expression of sorrow at the latter's recent death (dramatic date, 129 B.C.), which broke up one of the most famous friendships in history. The subject of friendship having been mentioned, Laelius is easily prevailed on to discuss its theory and practice with his son-in-law, C. Fannius (consul 122 B.C., soldier and historian), and Q. Mucius Scaevola (consul 117 B.C., and one of Cicero's teachers in the law). Starting with the premise that it is possible only between "good" men, he then defines the term "good" and "friendship." Apart from its ethical value, the subject is important for the light it throws upon the importance of personal relations between the "good" men of the *optimates* party in assuring to themselves majority votes at elections and in the passage of legislation favorable to themselves. The emphasis upon friendship in Plato (*Lysis*), and Aristotle (*Ethics* VIII and IX) may in part be due to similar considerations.

*Friendship impossible save between good men*

18 My first instinct is to say that friendship is impossible except between good men. Now I am not going to cut to the bone in my analysis of

"good," like the hair-splitters, who may be right, but contribute little to any generally useful purpose, when they deny that anyone is a good man unless he is a "sage." So be it; but the sagacity they are talking about is something no human being ever achieved, whereas we ought to consider the quality as it is in the usage of daily life, not as we may imagine it or wish it to be. I shall never admit that Gaius Fabricius, Manius Curius, or Tiberius Coruncanius,[27] whom our ancestors called wise men, were "sages" according to the criteria of these logic-choppers. Let them keep their vague but arrogant term, as long as they admit that the men I have named were good men. But they will not even consent to that compromise; they insist that the term cannot be used except of a "sage." 19 Let us then proceed with the brains God gave us, as they say. Those whose life and conduct is such that they can be counted on to be trustworthy, impartial, courteous, and generous, who are not greedy, lustful, or overbold, but rather steadfast, like the men I just named, are the men whom we ought, in keeping with their reputation, to call good, because they follow, to the limit of human ability, Nature, the best guide to living well. For, as far as I can see, we were born into a mutual association, which grows closer with contact, so that fellow-citizens have a higher claim on us than foreigners, and relatives than strangers; for though in the latter cases nature herself has produced the friendship, it still has not a firm base. Now friendship has this advantage over blood-relationship: you can have the latter without good will, but not the former. *20* To understand best how potent friendship is, look at it this way: out of the limitless association of mankind, which Nature herself links together, this is a thing so concentrated and focused that the whole of natural affection links together two people, or not many more.

### Friendship defined

For friendship is nothing more or less than the harmony of all things human and divine, plus good will and affection, and save for wisdom, I find it difficult to conceive of a better gift of the immortal gods to man. Some give first place to riches; others mention good health, political power, public office; many even argue for pleasure. But this last is an end for beasts, while the others are fleeting and undependable, resting, as they do, not upon our own judgment but upon the fickleness of fortune. Now those who say that virtue is the chief end, say very well, but virtue itself is what produces friendship and holds it together, and without virtue friendship cannot exist in any way.

[Friendship has more ends in view than any other object of desire; a friend is another self (Aristotle, *Ethics*, 1166A32). In politics, for example, friendship has great cohesive force.]

### The many advantages of friendship

*23* Of all the many great advantages of friendship, none is more conspicuous than that it projects the spotlight of good hope into the future and does not permit the soul to grow weak or to fail. For he who looks upon a true friend looks upon another image of himself. Therefore though friends are away, they are at hand, though they are needy, they overflow with riches, though they are weak, yet they are strong, and—a hard saying,—though they are dead, yet do they live, be-

cause the honor, the remembrance, the longing of their friends follows so eagerly after them; so their death seems happy, and the life of their friends full of praise. But if you were to abstract from the nature of things the link of good will, no household, no city could stand, and not even country life would continue. If this is hard to understand, dissension and discord can give us an insight into the power of friendship and harmony. For what household is so steadfast, what state so firmly based, that it cannot be completely overturned by hatreds and discords? This will give us a basis for judgment about how much good there is in friendship.

[Laelius next discusses the origin of friendship, which he finds in Nature, rather than, like the Epicureans, in the relative strength of one friend and weakness of the other.]

### The origin of friendship

*32* Those who, like beasts, make pleasure their sole standard disagree [with those who seek friendship for its own sake], and no wonder. For those who abase all their thoughts to so earthy and contemptible a level are incapable of looking up and seeing anything lofty, magnificent, and divine. Therefore let us banish them from our conversation, while we ourselves come to the understanding that feeling fond of someone, or kindly-intentioned affection, arises by nature, when once the object of friendship has been proved to be of moral worth. Seekers after moral worth move closer to it and cleave to it, so that they may profit from their association with the man they have begun to be fond of, and from his way of life: their love is in a state of parity and balance, and they are readier to earn favors than to demand them; and this becomes an honorable competition between them. This is the way in which the greatest profit will be derived from friendship, and thus it will be sounder and truer to derive its origin from nature than from weakness. For if it were profit that cemented friendships, loss would dissolve them, but since Nature is immutable, it follows that true friendships are eternal.

[The question how to make friendships endure leads to the discussion of how far a friend should go in doing what a friend asks; honor must come first, lest evil associations corrupt the state into revolution, as C. Gracchus appeared to the *optimates* to be doing at the dramatic date of this dialogue.]

### The limits of friendship

*40* Let this law of friendship then be ordained, that we neither ask our friends to act dishonorably, nor act so ourselves if we are asked. For both in the case of sins in general, and specifically in the case of crimes against the state, it is a low and quite unacceptable excuse to confess that the deed was done for the sake of a friend. This remark is now especially apt, Fannius and Scaevola, because we are now placed in a position where we must take a long view of what may happen to the commonwealth. We have already swerved considerably from the path and course marked out by our ancestors. Tiberius Gracchus attempted to set up a monarchy, or rather actually was a king for a few months. *41* Need I ask whether the Roman people had ever heard or seen such a thing before? I cannot speak without tears of what Tiberius' relatives and friends, who followed him even after his death, did in the case of Publius Scipio. Because of the recent punishment of Tiberius Gracchus we have endured Carbo as best we could. What we should expect from Gaius Gracchus' tribunate I should not like to guess: we are gliding imperceptibly along a path which, once it starts, slips headlong to destruction. You see in the matter of the ballot what a deterioration has already set in, first because of the Gabinian law, and then two years later because of the Cassian.[28] I think I see the people divorced from the Senate, and major affairs of state being settled at the whim of the mob. For more people will learn how to bring about such a revolution than how to resist it. *42* What is the point of all this? That without associates no one makes any such attempt. Good men must be taught that if they happen unawares to have fallen into this sort of friendship, they should not think themselves inseparably bound to friends who are doing some great wrong: for the disloyal,[29] a punishment ought to be put on the statute books, with a punishment no less for those who have followed than for those who have led in treachery.

[Expediency is not the end of friendship, and between like-minded men it should have no limits, regardless of rank or duration or maturity. But we should not make friends too hastily; once we have made them, we should not flatter them. Finally, what creates and preserves the bond of friendship is virtue, such as was pre-eminent in Scipio.]

### Friendship based on virtue: Scipio as example

*102* But since human affairs are frail and fleeting, we have always to keep on the lookout for people whom we may love and by whom we may be loved in return: for if love and good will are taken out of life, enjoyment goes with them. For me, at any rate, though Scipio has been snatched suddenly from us, he still lives and will always live: for what I loved in that great man was his virtue, and the breath of life has not gone out of *that*. It is not I alone who have the vision of it, I who have always known it well; it will be brilliant and splendid to men of after time as well. No one will ever undertake a major task with courage and hope without thinking that he ought to take Scipio's memory and image as his model. *103* As a matter of fact, of all the gifts which nature or good luck has granted me, I have nothing to compare with Scipio's friendship. In it I found agreement on public questions, advice on private ones, and a delightful relaxation. So far as I know, I never offended him in the slightest, and I never heard from him an unwelcome word; our households were as one, we ate together at the same table; we were constant companions not only on military service, but in our travels and our country vacations.

*104* Do I need to speak of our constant study and research, in which, far from the public eye, we spent all our leisure time? If the fond recollection of this shared life had died with him, I should not be able to bear, no matter how hard I tried, my sense of the loss of this most intimate and loving friend. But my memories are not dead; on the contrary they are nourished and strengthened by thought and reflection. Besides, even if I were completely deprived of them, my very advanced years would still bring me great solace; for I shall not have to miss him much longer. Then, too, all brief sorrow, however deep, should be endurable.

This is the end of my speech. As for you, I urge you to rank friendship a close second in your esteem to that virtue without which it cannot exist.

# ON DUTY

The treatise *On Duty*, published in the second half of 44 B.C., is Cicero's last and is by many considered his finest philosophical work. It is cast in the form of a letter to his son, a student in Athens, who at the time, as undergraduates will occasionally, was himself giving some evidence of neglect of duty. Octavian made him consul in 30 B.C. to lend color to the pretext that he was reviving the Republic. The theme is the duty of the Roman gentleman to live his life with a sense that his position of privilege brings with it a responsibility to society. (Cf. *On the Laws* III, 30–32.) In Book I, the whole duty of man is linked to the four cardinal virtues, Wisdom, Justice, Courage, and Temperance; in Books II and III, Cicero shows that there is no real conflict between a wise man's sense of his moral responsibility and his own self-interest. The argument, though derived from Stoic sources, is copiously illustrated from Roman history, interpreted with a strong bias against popular leaders like the Gracchi, Marius, and especially Julius Caesar. The work has had a strong influence upon the ethical teaching of the Christian church, as well as upon the eighteenth century concept of the gentleman.

## From Book I

### *Importance of combining Greek and Latin studies*

*1* Son Marcus, you have now spent a year, and that year in Athens, listening to Cratippus,[30] so that you ought already to have more than enough instruction in philosophy because of the high standing in the field both of your teacher and of the city of Athens itself, the former being able to broaden your knowledge, the latter to set you an example. Nevertheless, since I have always found it to my advantage to combine Latin with Greek, not in philosophy only, but in my practical work as an orator, I think that you ought to do the same, so that you may acquire equal fluency in either tongue. Apparently I have been of great assistance to my countrymen in this field, so that even scholars, to say nothing of those who have no Greek, feel that they have acquired from me some information and some basis for judgment. *2* Because I feel Greek is important, you will hear lectures from the chief philosopher of our time, and your education may take as long as you like; you ought to want to study as long as you have no regrets about your

progress. But if you read my philosophical works, which do not differ much from the Peripatetics, since we both aim at being followers of Socrates and Plato, you may still use your own judgment about philosophical doctrine—I will not stand in your way—but you will certainly enrich your Latin style. I should not want it thought that I say this out of vanity. For while I yield to many in my knowledge of philosophy, on the other hand if I take as my own specialty the field I have spent my life in, that is, oratory, the art of speaking clearly, elegantly, and to the point, I think I have some right to claim it as my own. Therefore I strongly urge you, my son, to read closely not my speeches only, but also my philosophical works, which have already virtually reached the same level of excellence. The speeches have a more forceful style, but you ought also to cultivate the even and moderate philosophical tone. *3* As a matter of fact, I do not note that any of the Greeks has yet succeeded in working in both fields and acquiring both the style appropriate to the courtroom and the quieter tone of philosophic discussion.

[The subject of moral duty is both useful and important, though Epicureans cannot be trusted to treat of it. It has its theoretical and its practical side, and may be discussed under the heads of conflict between honorable actions, conflict between expedient actions, and conflict between what is honorable and what is expedient. The question whether an act is morally right or wrong depends on whether the act is in accord with one or more of the four cardinal virtues, Wisdom, Justice, Courage, and Temperance.]

### *Instinct and reason*

*11* To begin with, self-preservation; that is, preservation of corporeal life, is a natural attribute of every living creature, as is also the avoidance of everything that seems harmful, and the seeking out and acquisition of the necessities of life, food, shelter, etc.[31]

Another common trait of all living things is the desire for procreative union and the love of offspring. But the greatest distinction between man and beast is that the beast is moved only by his senses, and adapts himself only to the present, with little awareness of past and future, while man, because he shares in reason (whereby he distinguishes sequences of cause and effect, sees the causes of things and is not unaware of their consequences and what we may call their antecedents, compares like events, and joins and links the present with the future), easily foresees the whole course of his life and prepares in advance what is necessary for its progress. *12* Nature also, by the force of reason, links man with man [32] in common language and common life, implants in him from the beginning a special love for his offspring, gives him an impulse to desire the existence and increase of the population and, to that end, to be eager to acquire whatever contributes to a comfortable livelihood, not for himself only, but for his wife, his children, and the others whom he holds dear and has the responsibility for. This responsibility challenges the mind and makes it more efficient.

*13* The unique characteristic of man is the tracking down, the search for truth. And so whenever we are free from essential business and responsibilities, we have a strong desire to see, hear, or learn something new, and we consider necessary to the good life the knowledge either of things that were unknown before or of things worthy of admiration. Thence we deduce that whatever is true, uncompounded, unadulterated, is particularly adapted to the nature of man.

To this desire for seeing the truth there is linked a seeking for pre-eminence, so that no mind well formed by nature wants to obey anyone who does not teach it precepts or give it just and legitimate orders which are of some use; this independence gives rise to magnificence of mind and scorn of human vicissitudes.

*14* The power of nature and reason is conspicuous also in the fact that man is the only animal who senses what order is, and decorum, and moderation in word and deed. And so no other animal has man's feeling for the beauty, charm, and dovetailing of parts in visible objects. Now nature and reason transfer this sense of fitness by analogy from the eyes to the mind, so that a man thinks that self-consistency and order ought to be preserved far more in exercise of judgment and in his own action than in the works of external nature. Further, the result is that man in general is careful not to do anything unseemly or effeminate, and in particular not to let sensual pleasure control his thoughts or actions. From all these natural tendencies combined arises that moral goodness we are looking for, which exists as such even though it is not recognized, and moral goodness rightly so called is praiseworthy by nature, even though no one praise it.

### Duty and the four cardinal virtues

*15* So, son Marcus, you see the very outline and expression, as it were, of moral goodness, which, as Plato says, if our eyes beheld it, would rouse a wondrous love of wisdom. But every moral act rises from one of four categories: it is involved either in the perception of truth, i.e., mental ingenuity; or in the preservation of human social relationships, the giving to each man his due, and the keeping of one's word in contracts; or in the breadth and strength of a lofty and invincible soul; or in the order and restraint of all speech and action which is the essence of moderation and temperance. Now though these four virtues are mutually linked and interlocked, yet specific kinds of duties arise from each; e.g., the pursuit and discovery of truth inheres in the category I first described, under which we place theoretical and practical wisdom, and this is the virtue to which the business of pursuing truth is appropriate. *16* For in measure as a man's perception of the highest truth in a given situation is most acute, and in proportion to his speed and keenness in seeing and working out causation, we customarily and rightly consider him especially wise in theory and in practice. So truth is his province; it is as it were the material he handles and works with.

*17* Moreover, the other three virtues are faced with the necessity of providing and protecting the prerequisites to the carrying on of human life, so that the union of mankind in society may be preserved and the excellence and magnificence of the human mind may shine forth in increasing man's resources, in providing conveniences for man and his family, and particularly in being able to despise these very external goods that man has provided for himself. Finally, order, consistency, moderation, and the like are involved in that category which is concerned with action of some kind, and not merely with contemplation.

[Cicero proceeds to discuss in order the relation of the virtues to duty; first Wisdom, then

Justice and Liberality, then Courage, with which he associates that magnificence of soul which leads the truly good man to have the moral courage to do his duty unselfishly as a public servant despite the obvious attractiveness of the contemplative life. On this point Cicero is closer to Aristotle than to Plato.]

*Moral courage: the retired life*

69 Now there are many at present, and there have been many in the past, who in pursuit of this peace of mind that I have been talking about have withdrawn from affairs of state and fled to the refuge of retirement, among them the best-known and by far the most distinguished philosophers and numbers of men of high seriousness who have not been able to stand the conduct either of the people or of princes, and have lived in the country enjoying their estates. 70 Their aim was like that of kings: to lack nothing, to obey no one, to live independently, the essence of independence being to live as you please.

Therefore, though men eager for power have this desire for independence in common with these men of leisure whom I have mentioned, the former think they can acquire independence by having great wealth, the latter by being satisfied with the little they have. On this subject we ought not to scorn completely the opinion of either side, but the life of the men of leisure is easier, safer, and less annoying or overbearing toward others, while the life of those who adapt themselves to public affairs and the carrying on of important business is more profitable to the human race and better calculated to attain fame and distinction. 71 Therefore we ought perhaps to yield a point to those who do not take part in affairs of state, provided they devote their extraordinary talent to philosophy, and to those who have withdrawn from public affairs because of the impediment of poor health or some other quite serious reason, since such men hand over to others both their right to office and their credit for holding it. But if those who have no such motive allege that they despise the power and titles that the majority admire, in my opinion their attitude deserves not only no credit, but even positive condemnation. Insofar as they despise fame and think it nothing worth, it is hard not to approve of them, but the ground of my criticism is that they seem to regard the trouble and inconvenience of political

life in general, and defeat and failure at the polls in particular, as a disgrace of some kind, and beneath their dignity. For some people, when things go wrong, are not consistent: they condemn pleasure with the utmost strictures, but are too weak in the face of pain; quite inconsistently, they are careless of fame but crushed by gossip.

*The duty of public service*

72 But those to whom nature has granted what it takes for a public career ought to cast aside all hesitation, run for office, and administer the government, for there is no other way for the city to be ruled or a man's magnanimity to be made manifest. Men embarking on public careers no less than philosophers, and perhaps even more, must cultivate magnificence [33] and that scorn of human vicissitudes which I talk about so often, as well as peace of mind and freedom from worry, at least if they are going to live without anxiety and in a dignified and consistent way. 73 This is easier for the philosophers, since there are fewer things in their lives open to the blows of fortune, since their needs are less, and since if any misfortune befalls them, their fall cannot be so heavy. Therefore not without reason greater emotions of the soul are aroused in public men than in those who lead lives of retirement, which is all the more reason why the former must practise magnanimity and free themselves from anxiety. Moreover, a man who embarks upon a public career should be careful not to consider merely how honorable an action is, but also whether he has an opportunity of carrying it out; and in this connection he must take care not to let laziness lead him to premature despair, nor eagerness to overconfidence. Finally, before you tackle a job of any kind, you must prepare yourself for it diligently.[34]

[But peace has her courage, no less renowned than bravery on the battlefield, as Cicero's own career bears witness. As for physical courage, discretion is the better part of it, but self-sacrificing patriotism deserves the highest praise. Courage must also be shown in public administration, which must be nonpartisan, thorough, unselfish, and nonvindictive.]

*Public administration must be nonpartisan.*

85 In general future heads of state should cleave to two Platonic precepts [*Rep.* 342E,

420B]: first, they should so safeguard their fellow-citizens' advantage that they should forget their own and make the general welfare the standard of all they do; and second, they should attend to the whole body politic, and not concentrate on one part at the expense of the rest. The administration of the state is like a guardianship: it must be carried on to the advantage of the wards, not the trustees. Moreover, whoever favors one part of the citizen body and neglects another introduces something completely destructive into the state; i.e., sedition and discord. The result is that some seem to favor the people, others the aristocracy, while few act in the interests of the citizenry as a whole. *86* This partisan policy caused great discords among the Athenians, and in our state not only sedition but even pestilential civil war, which any responsible, courageous citizen, worthy to be chief of state, will shun and despise, devoting rather his whole attention to the common weal, and not pursuing wealth or power, but administering the state as a whole so as to serve everyone's interests. He will not trump up false charges to invoke hatred or jealousy of anyone, and in general will so cleave to justice and honor that he will run any risk of offence, however heavy, to preserve them, and risk death rather than desert them. *87* In general, canvassing for votes and competition for office is a particularly wretched practice, about which the same authority, Plato, well says [*Rep.* 488B], "Those who compete to see who shall run the government are no better than sailors arguing about which of them shall steer the ship." He also advises us [*Rep.* 467C] to consider those men our enemies who bear arms against us, not those who want the government run in accordance with their judgment. An example of the latter case is the difference of opinion between Scipio the Younger and Q. Metellus,[35] which was without rancor.

*88* Indeed, we ought not to listen to those who think that we ought to get into a towering rage with our enemies, and say that this is a characteristic of the great-souled and courageous man; for nothing is more praiseworthy, nothing worthier of a great and famous man than a placid and forgiving disposition. Indeed, among free people and impartial laws one ought even to practise affability and what is called serenity of mind, for fear our anger at those who interrupt us at inconvenient times or make impudent requests

may drive us into an unprofitable and offensive surliness. Nevertheless mildness and clemency ought to be approved in such a way that provision is made for applying in the public interest that severity without which the administration of the government is impossible. But all punishment and correction ought to be free from insult; the standard aimed at should be the advantage of the state, not of the man who administers the punishment or verbal reproof.

*89* We must be careful, too, that the punishment is not greater than the crime, so that for the same offense some are flogged while others do not even get a tongue-lashing. Furthermore, in administering punishment anger must be strictly forbidden; for a man who punishes in anger will never hold to that famous mean between too much and too little, which appeals to the Peripatetics, and rightly so, provided they do not approve of wrath and call it a profitable gift of nature. Indeed, anger ought in all circumstances to be rejected, and it is to be hoped that chiefs of state will be like the laws, whose motive for punishment is not anger, but the desire to see justice done.

[It takes courage, too, to face prosperity. To be humble, also, sometimes requires courage, as does magnanimity in public and private life. Cicero next passes to the fourth of the virtues, temperance, and under this head first discusses propriety, which he defines as conformity of action to the dignity of human nature, whether in literature or in life.]

### *Temperance: propriety and the moral virtues*

*95* This propriety I speak of applies, therefore, to every moral action, and in such a way as to be obvious, no far-fetched reasoning being required to perceive it. For there is a certain appropriateness perceptible in all virtue, which can be separated from it more in theory than in practice. Just as physical charm and beauty cannot be separated from good health, so this propriety we are talking about is all bound up with virtue but is distinguished from it when we consider it. *96* Its definition, moreover, is twofold; for we distinguish a universal propriety involved in all honorable action, and another subordinate kind, applicable to the separate categories of individual honorable acts. The former is usually defined about as follows: Propriety is that which conforms to the dignity of man precisely in the area where man's nature differs from that of the other animals. The philosophers define the subordinate part thus: Particular propriety means conformity to nature in such a way that moderation and temperance are made manifest together with the outward appearance appropriate to a free man. *97* That this is what propriety means, we can judge from that kind of propriety which the poets observe, which is usually more fully treated under another heading.[36] We say the poets preserve the proprieties when the action and words are worthy of each character; for example, if Aeacus or Minos should say, "Let the people hate us, so long as they fear us," or "The father himself serves as his sons' tomb," it would seem inappropriate, because we follow the tradition that they were just men; but if these same speeches are assigned to Atreus, they evoke applause, for the speech is worthy of the character. But the poets will decide from the character what is appropriate to each person; upon us, on the other hand, nature imposes the character, one of great superiority, far excelling the other animals.

*98* Therefore the poets, in the midst of a great variety of characters, will decide what suits and is appropriate to even the vicious ones, but since Nature has assigned us our parts in life's drama— the roles of self-consistency, moderation, temperance, and modesty—and since she trains us not to disregard them in our conduct towards our fellow man, we see clearly the wide range both of that universal propriety which applies to all honorable acts, and of that specific kind observable in each individual virtue. For just as physical beauty, on account of the neat dovetailing of the parts, attracts the eye and is a source of delight precisely because all the parts are charmingly harmonious one with another, so this propriety, life's jewel, inspires the approval of those who associate with it, because of the orderliness, the consistency, and the moderation of every word and deed.

[The main duty prescribed by propriety is the subjecting of the appetites to reason. Propriety is manifest in outward appearance and inward self-control, in conversation (conduct in the home), and even in the observance of the minor fine points of etiquette.]

### Propriety in outward appearance

*130* Now since there are two kinds of beauty, one involving charm, the other dignity, we ought to consider charm a feminine attribute, dignity a masculine one. Therefore let every unmanly frill be removed from our outward appearance, and let us beware of any similar fault in our gait or our gestures. For the gait appropriate to the frequenters of a wrestling school is often rather offensive, and actors' gestures are by no means always free from absurdities, while in both categories correctness and simplicity win approval. Good color should add to dignity of outward appearance, and physical exercise to good color. One should strive also for neatness, not excessive nor to a fault, but just enough to avoid the charge of boorish and unpolished slovenliness. The same principle should be applied in dress, where, as in most other cases, the mean is best. *131* We ought also to avoid effeminate slowness in our walk, so as not to look like litter-carriers in a procession, and we should not hurry too fast, a practice which brings about shortness of breath, a change of expression, and distortion of the features, and thereby shows clearly a lack of self-possession.

### Propriety in inward self-control

But we must work far harder even at keeping our inner emotions in accordance with Nature. We shall succeed, if we carefully avoid worry and hysteria and hold our mental attention fixed upon the preservation of propriety. *132* The inner emotions are of two kinds: thought and appetite. Thought is mainly concerned with discovering the truth, while appetite impels us to actions. We must therefore see to it that we employ thought to the best possible ends, and that we make appetite obedient to reason. . . .

### Propriety in conversation

*134* Conversation, in which the Socratics excel, should be gentle and not in the least long-winded, and there should be charm in it. It should not be treated as private property, on which others are forbidden to trespass; rather, in general conversation as in everything else one should not take variety amiss. The prime consideration should be the subject matter: if it is serious, we should talk seriously; if it is frivolous, with charm. We should attach importance to not letting conversation betray any moral fault, which is bound to happen especially if we make a practice of talking about people behind their backs, belittling them either in jest or in earnest, with gossip or invective. . . .

*The little things that count*

145 Serious breaches of etiquette, like singing in the Forum or other major eccentricities, are readily apparent and need no special advice or warning; but we must studiously avoid what appear to be slight slips which most people would not even notice. However little a flute or lyre may be out of tune, the expert always notices, and in the same way we should be careful in life to avoid any chance disharmony, and all the more because harmony of action is a higher and a more important thing than harmony of sound. [We may correct our lapses from propriety by observing others and by heeding the criticisms of the wise; as for the laws of the state, they are the fixed code of duty, not to be violated save in exceptional cases.]

*The laws of the state are rules of duty.*

148 There is no need for axioms about action in accordance with tradition or with civil institutions, which are themselves axioms, and no one ought to be deceived into thinking that because some action or words of Socrates or Aristippus were contrary to the tradition or practice of states, anyone is free to do the same. For these men acquired this freedom by conferring special and superhuman benefits upon mankind. . . .

*There is a distinction between vulgar and liberal occupations.*

150 Now about which trades and pursuits are liberal and which vulgar, the standard doctrine is this. Occupations like tax-collecting or money-lending, which incur the hatred of mankind, are especially disapproved of. Vulgar and unbecoming a free man are the occupations of all hired laborers whose labor rather than their skill is being paid for; for in these cases the very wages carry with them the obligation of servitude. We must also think of those persons as vulgar who buy from wholesalers for immediate sale; for they can make no profit without a certain amount of lying; but nothing is baser than empty pretensions. All craftsmen are involved in vulgar skills, for there is nothing that can be considered liberal about a workshop. Skills that minister to pleasure, "fishmongers, butchers, chefs, sausage-stuffers, fishermen," as Terence says,[37] ought to be definitely disapproved. Add to the list, if you like, *parfumeurs*, dancers, and gamblers.

151 But those skills which involve greater practical wisdom or more than average utility, like medicine, architecture, or teaching honorable subjects, are honorable for those to whose social class they are appropriate. Commerce on a small scale ought to be considered vulgar; but if it is heavily capitalized, operates over a wide area, and benefits a large number of people without false pretensions, it is not much subject to criticism; and if the merchant, glutted or rather contented with his profit, makes a practice of coming often, as it were, from the high seas into harbor, and from there to his country estate, it may even seem possible to justify praising him. But of all profitable occupations, there is none better than agriculture, none richer, none pleasanter, none worthier of man in general or the free man in particular. But since I have treated this subject adequately in my work *On Old Age*, [56–57], you may refer to the relevant passages there.

[Book I ends with an estimate of the relative importance of duties: those which issue in social action come first; among these religious duties take precedence. Duties to the state come next, then duty to the family. These three combine into what the Romans meant by *pietas*.]

*From* Book II

[After defending his own interest in philosophy, Cicero shows that if we try to separate what is expedient from what is morally right, wisdom degenerates into mere cunning.]

*Expediency and morality not to be separated*

9 Now we have a choice of five ways of doing our duty: two pertain to propriety and honor; two to the conveniences of life—wealth, resources, property; and the fifth to the exercise of judgment in choosing among the other four. If ever a conflict should seem to arise among these, the division of duty which I want you to be best acquainted with, the one involving honor, goes by the board. But my present subject is "ex-

pediency." Our habit in the use of this word has been careless, has got out of line, and has gradually reached the point where we distinguish the honorable from the expedient and suppose that there is such a thing as an honorable act that is not expedient, or an expedient one that is not honorable. This point of view is a deathblow to the whole life of man. Philosophers of the highest authority therefore have devoted much honest labor to a strict theoretical distinction among three confused categories: for they hold whatever is just to be also useful; likewise, whatever is honorable is also just, from which the conclusion is that whatever is honorable is also useful. Those who fail to see this waste their admiration on men who are merely cunning and clever and who turn wisdom into a vice. Their error must be rooted out and their opinion changed to the point where they hope and realize that it is by honorable purposes and just acts, not by fraud and evil-doing, that they can attain their ends.

[It is expedient that there should be association and intercourse between man and man. Personal affection gives power its best security; this is the essential difference between the old republic and the new despotism.]

*Personal affection once bound together the Roman empire; it does so no longer.*

26 As long as the empire of the Roman people was held together by the good that it did rather than by the harm, wars were fought either on behalf of our allies or of the empire, and ended either mercifully or with minimum severity; our senate was the port of refuge for kings, tribes, peoples, and the highest aim of our civil and military officers was to win praise for fair dealing and good faith in the defense of our provinces and allies. 27 And so what we had then might better have been called a world trusteeship than an empire. For some time now this practice and this discipline have been gradually breaking down, but after Sulla's victory we abandoned it altogether; for no action against the allies any longer seems unjust, when citizens themselves have been treated so cruelly. So in Sulla's person an honorable cause won a dishonorable victory. For he had the effrontery to say, when he had set up his auction block and was selling in the forum the goods of aristocrats, of rich men, and, worst of all, of his fellow-citizens, that he was selling his own booty. His example was followed by one [Julius Caesar] who in an impious cause, and after an even more disgraceful victory, did not merely confiscate the goods of individual citizens, but included whole provinces, whole territories in a single category of destruction.

[After discussing how to win friends and influence people, by money, or by personal service, Cicero turns to the rules of expediency as they apply to public service, and discusses the duties of the governor: to provide for the security of property, keep down taxes, provide the necessities of life, be free from avarice, and especially to avoid radical measures for the redistribution of wealth; Cicero's example is to be followed here, not Caesar's.]

*Historical examples of self-denial: Scipio and others*

76 Panaetius praises Scipio—and why should he not?—because he was free from avarice. Yet Scipio had other even higher qualities. Credit for freedom from avarice belongs not to one individual, but to the whole era. Aemilius Paulus made a prize of the whole Macedonian treasury, which was enormous; he contributed so much money to our treasury that one general's prize money cancelled everybody's taxes. But he brought nothing into his own household but the eternal memory of his name. Scipio followed his father's example and was made no richer by the sack of Carthage. What about Scipio's colleague as censor, L. Mummius? He grew no richer, did he, from the sack of Corinth, one of the richest cities in the world? He preferred to enrich Italy rather than his own household; though the enrichment of Italy seems to me to have contributed to the spiritual enrichment of his household as well. 77 To return to the point, then, no vice is lower than avarice, especially in chiefs of state and governors of commonwealths. For to turn the state into a source of personal profit is not only morally reprehensible; it is contrary to all the laws of god and man. And so the oracle of the Pythian Apollo, that it would be avarice and nothing else that would ruin Sparta, seems to have been a prophecy not only for the Spartans, but for all wealthy peoples. But there is no easier way for heads of states to enlist the good will of the common people than by freedom from avarice and by the practice of self-restraint.

*The ruinousness of the welfare state*

78 Those on the other hand who call themselves members of the popular party, and therefore embark on programs for the redistribution of public lands to drive owners from their property, or think that debts should be cancelled, are undermining the foundations of the state. In the first place they are undermining cordial class relations, which cannot exist when money is taken away from one class and given to another. In the second place, they are undermining justice, which entirely disappears if a man is not to have the enjoyment of his own property. For the essential of a city or a state, as I have said above, is that every man should have the free and unfettered control of his own property. 79 But in the process of ruining the state they have not even gained the favor they suppose. For the man from whom property has been taken is an enemy, while the man to whom it has been given even pretends he did not want to take it, and especially where debts are involved conceals his satisfaction, for fear of seeming to have been insolvent. But the victim of the injustice remembers his grievance and flaunts it, and even if the wrongful recipients outnumber the wronged and unwilling donors, the former cause does not on that account prevail, because the basis for judgment in these matters is influence, not majority. For where is the justice, when a man who has owned no property for many years or even centuries before gets the property, while the man who has been a property owner loses it?

80 It was for this kind of unjust program that the Lacedaemonians exiled the ephor Lysander, executed King Agis [the Fourth, 241 B.C.]—an unprecedented act—and from that time on, in consequence, suffered so much discord that tyrants sprang up, the aristocrats were banished, and the world's most famous constitution fell into ruins. And it was not the only one to fall, but it overturned the rest of Greece by contagion, which started with the Lacedaemonians and then spread. Furthermore, was it not quarrels over land grants that proved the ruin of our own Gracchi, the sons of that distinguished gentleman Tiberius Gracchus, and the grandsons of Scipio?

*A better system: Aratus of Sicyon*

81 The man who deserves his high reputation for dealing with this problem is Aratus of Sicyon. After his city had been held for fifty years by tyrants, he set out from Argos, entered Sicyon secretly, and got possession of the city, surprised and assassinated the tyrant Nicocles, and restored six hundred exiles, who had been the richest men in town, thereby at his arrival setting the state free. But he observed that goods and possessions presented a serious problem, because on the one hand he thought it most unfair that his restored exiles should be in want, other owners now enjoying their property; and on the other hand he felt it was no great piece of justice to oust from their property those who had held it for the past fifty years, seeing that in so long a period much of it was held by bequest, much by purchase, and much by dowry, all with clear title. His conclusion was that he ought neither to take the property away from its present owners nor fail to satisfy the former ones. 82 Therefore, once he had decided that what was needed to settle the claims was money, he said he wanted to go to Alexandria, and told his people to let the matter rest until his return. He went to visit Ptolemy [II Philadelphus], with whom he had diplomatic relations. Once he had told the king that he wanted to set his fatherland free and had explained the reasons, this man of distinction had no difficulty in obtaining from the rich monarch a sizeable loan. He brought the money back to Sicyon and called into council with him fifteen of the chief men of the city, who formed with him a joint panel for hearing the cases both of those who held other people's property and of those who had lost their own; and by assessing the value of the property, he managed to persuade some to take money in lieu of property they now held, and others that it was more convenient to accept a certain sum in cash than to recover their land. The upshot of it was that harmony between classes was established and everyone went away happy. 83 A great and worthy man, who should have been born a Roman! That is the fair way, direct dealing with the citizens, not as I have seen twice in my lifetime, setting up an auction block in the forum and putting Romans' property at the mercy of the bark of an auctioneer. But that Greek, like the wise and excellent man he was, thought it best to ask everyone's advice, which is the wisest and most intelligent thing a good citizen can do: not to divide his fellow citizens' sense of their own interests, and to include everyone under the same code of justice.

*Good government will prevent debts being contracted.*

But the opposition says, "Let the landless live rent-free on other men's property." What? So that, after I have bought the property, built my house, kept it up, and spent my good money, you should have the enjoyment of it against my will? How does that differ from stealing their own property from one group, and giving property they don't own to another? *84* What is the aim of cancellation of debts, if not that you buy a farm with my money, and then you own the farm while I whistle for my money? Therefore provision ought to be made, by one of a number of feasible methods, to prevent the incurring of debts, on the ground that they make the state suffer. Certainly the proper method is not for the rich to lose what they have, while debtors make a profit with other people's money. For there is no stronger bond for the commonwealth than credit, which cannot exist, unless debts are paid when due. No more positive action was ever taken toward this end than in my consulship. All sorts and conditions of men resorted to armed force on the issue, but my strenuous resistance relieved the state of the whole problem. Never had there been more people in debt, never had there been a better or an easier method of payment; for once the hope of cheating the creditors was dashed, the paying of the debts was a necessary consequence. But now the present winner [Julius Caesar], who was the loser then, has worked out at last, now that he is no longer in debt, the plan he devised when he owed everyone money. His love of wrong-doing is so ingrained that he takes delight in it even when he has no motive.

*85* From the kind of largesse, then, which takes away from some and gives to others, the guardians of the state will abstain, and will devote special effort to guaranteeing property rights on a basis of fair legal procedure, and to removing the obstacle of jealousy that stands between the rich and the holding or recovering of their property. In addition, they should use every available means of civil and military policy to increase the public holdings through expanding the empire, enlarging the public lands, and tapping more sources of revenue. This is the business of great men, this is what our ancestors did repeatedly, and those who performed this kind of duty, to the great advantage of the commonwealth, earned for themselves great glory and gratitude.

[Cicero ends Book II with a couple of miscellaneous rules of expediency, regarding care of one's health and one's estate, and with a calculus of expediencies, in which health and reputation are put before riches.

Book III deals with the apparent conflict between duty and expediency, and emphasizes that to do what is morally right is the chief good, a fact which, Cicero says, escapes the notice of popular leaders like Marius and Julius Caesar. The chief example of a Roman who put duty before life itself is Regulus (see Harvey, and Horace, *Odes*, III, 5). Finally, with a last fling at the Epicureans, Cicero argues that to take pleasure as one's highest good makes doing one's duty impossible. Remembering at the end that he is supposed to be writing a letter, he tells his son that he hopes to see him in Athens, if his duty to his country permits. His duty did not permit; he at once began the series of fourteen invectives against Julius Caesar's successor Mark Antony, which resulted a little more than a year later in his death (Dec. 7, 43 B.C.) at the hands of Antony's agents.]

## NOTES TO SELECTIONS FROM CICERO'S PHILOSOPHICAL WORKS

1. W. S. Ferguson, *Hellenistic Athens* (London, 1911), pp. 24 f.

2. Aquinas' definition of Natural Law. See Introduction, above, p. 147.

3. This is the *comitia centuriata* which (see Harvey) "was organized so as to give the preponderance of power to the wealthy classes."

4. Flaminius, as tribune of the people (232 B.C.) sponsored a bill to distribute to the people certain public lands which the noblemen of the senatorial class wanted for themselves. His name was ever afterward anathema to the *optimates*, who regarded him as the leader who had first shown the people their power and "begun the dangerous policy of allowing the unstable populace to control

the government."—J. H. Breasted, *Ancient Times* (Boston, 1944), p. 650.

5. But it had, in 151 B.C., and attempts and threats of this nature were frequent. See Livy, *Epitome* XLVIII; II, 56, 13; IV, 26, 9.

6. Clodius, who as tribune in 58 B.C. brought about Cicero's exile.

7. Popilius Laenas, consul 132 B.C., was forced into exile in 124 B.C. by the tribune Gaius Gracchus in revenge for having been involved in the murder of Gaius' brother Tiberius. Ironically, one of the descendents of Popilius was the assassin of Cicero himself in 43 B.C. The tribune L. Appuleius Saturninus (see Harvey) forced into exile Q. Caecilius Metellus Numidicus (the predecessor of Marius in the Jugurthine War; cf. selections from Sallust) in a controversy over the legality of yet another law for the distribution of public lands (100 B.C.).

8. The reference is to the ostracism or exile of men like Aristides, Themistocles, or Cimon; perhaps Cicero also had in mind the fate of the Thirty Tyrants after the restoration of the democracy in 403 B.C.

9. Chrysippus of Soli (*ca.* 280–206 B.C.), the third great leader of the Athenian Stoics after Zeno and Cleanthes. He was called "the pillar of the Porch." Seven hundred and fifty works are ascribed to him, of which only fragments survive.

10. M. Pupius Piso Calpurnianus (consul 61 B.C.), orator, wit, soldier, friend of Pompey, teacher of Cicero in the art of rhetoric, and follower of the Peripatetic or Aristotelian school in philosophy.

11. Piso refers here to the art of "topical mnemonics," an aid to memory by the association of ideas, based on an imaginary town with "a certain number of districts each with ten houses, each house with ten rooms, and each room with a hundred quadrates or memory-places, partly on the floor, partly on the four walls, partly on the roof." See *Encycl. Brit.* (eleventh ed.), *s.v.* "Mnemonics."

12. Piso's memory is confused. Oedipus does ask the question (*Oedipus at Colonus*, 52). But the "tenderest of odes" is by the Chorus, much later in the play (lines 668–7 9). See the *Oxford Book of Greek Verse in Translation*, No. 331, a version by Walter Headlam. The best American translation is by Robert Fitzgerald (New York: Harcourt, Brace, 1941).

13. Phaedrus of Athens (*ca.* 138–70 B.C.), Epicurean philosopher, friend, teacher, and house guest of Cicero. Atticus dedicated a statue of him on the Acropolis at Athens.—*Hesperia* XVIII (1949), 99.

14. Terence, *Eunuch*, 59–63; the warning of the slave Parmeno to his lovesick master Phaedria.

15. Archelaus of Miletus, fifth-century Greek philosopher, one of the first to stress the moral and aesthetic superiority of men over animals. None of his works survives.

16. This may be stupid to Cicero, but to Aristotle (*Politics*, 1281b1) it made excellent sense. It is of course the principle upon which democracy is based.

17. Reading <*esse in*> *scientiam* with Klotz and Rackham.

18. Diagoras of Melos, nicknamed "the Atheist," flourished in the second half of the fifth century B.C. at Athens, whence he fled after the Athenians condemned him to death for impiety and set a price upon his head. Theodorus, who flourished about 300 B.C. was also called "the Atheist," and also banished from Athens. He took refuge in Alexandria, where he embarked on a diplomatic career under Ptolemy I (323–285 B.C.), the founder of the great Alexandrian Library.

19. Diodotus, the blind Stoic philosopher, lived in Cicero's house in Rome and instructed him in dialectic; at his death (59 B.C.) he left Cicero heir to a considerable property. Philo of Larissa (first half of the first century B.C.) was head of the New Academy until he left Athens for Rome during the Mithridatic Wars. On the others see Harvey.

20. Or "to men of our persuasion." The Latin *nostris hominibus* is ambiguous: it may mean either "my fellow-countrymen" or "my fellow-*optimates*."

21. A Stoic, a pupil of Chrysippus, *ca.* 240–152 B.C.: and later head of the school at Athens; he gave an explanation, based on physiology instead of myth, of the birth of Athena from the forehead of Zeus.

22. Cf. Lucretius, *On the Nature of Things*, V, 857–59, where the theory of the survival of the fittest is used to prove quite the opposite conclusion; viz., that animate objects get on quite well without divine interference.

23. This work, omitted from this anthology for lack of space, contains a classic statement (I, 158–59) on the importance of "liberal" education, i.e., reading in poetry, history, philosophy, and political science. This is the cornerstone of Cicero's case for the "Humanities," but it should be noted that he advocates them for an intensely practical reason: the training of the aristocratic orator to take his place in the ruling class of the Roman state. See the translator's article in the *Classical Journal*, XLIII (1948), 339–47, and compare the selections from Quintilian, below.

24. I.e., political action. See below, sec. 7, *ad fin.*

25. Literally, "in my books I have made my motions, delivered my political speeches."

26. Uncle of Jason, killed by Medea, who persuaded him to submit to being boiled to restore his youth. See Harvey, *s.v.* "Argonauts."

27. Coruncanius, consul 280 B.C., expert in the law, and the first plebeian *pontifex maximus*, was, like the others mentioned (on whom see Harvey), considered the type of old Roman virtue and frugality.

28. The references here are all to the troubles of the *optimates* rising out of concessions to the people made or proposed by the Gracchi and their friends, who, for

example, were accused of murdering Scipio Aemilianus (see *Scipio's Dream*, sec. 12), whose wife was Tiberius' sister. The "recent punishment" of Tiberius is his murder, engineered probably by another Scipio. C. Papirius Carbo (tribune of the people 131 B.C.) was an eloquent speaker in the popular cause and a close friend of C. Gracchus. The Gabinian Law (139 B.C.) required a written ballot in the election of magistrates (cf. *On the Laws*, III, 34–39); the Cassian required the same of jurymen; both were considered anti-aristocratic.

29. The term *improbi* is often used by Cicero to refer to the "popular" party as opposed to his party, the *boni*, or "decent citizens," as the Old Oligarch would call them. Cf. *For Sestius*, sec. 97.

30. Cratippus of Mitylene, appointed head of the Peripatetic School in Athens in 44 B.C., was a friend of Pompey and teacher of Brutus. He was an expert on divination. Julius Caesar, at Cicero's request, conferred upon him the freedom of the city of Rome.

31. Cf. *On the Nature of the Gods*, II, 121 ff.

32. Cf. *On the Chief End of Man*, III, 64–67.

33. Defined by Aristotle, *Ethics*, 1122A23 as "a fitting expenditure involving largeness of scale."

34. Cicero has in mind candidacy for public office, with the electioneering described at length in his brother Quintus' pamphlet of 64 B.C. on "How to Stand for the Consulship."

35. Q. Caecilius Metellus Macedonicus (consul 143 B.C.) leader of the moderate faction against Scipio in the Senate.

36. I.e., *Poetics* or *Rhetoric*.

37. Terence, *Eunuch*, 257, where the parasite explains that he has all these tradesmen at his beck and call because he has learned the art of flattery.

# SELECTIONS FROM THE POEMS OF CATULLUS

*Translated by Eric A. Havelock*

## INTRODUCTION

GAIUS VALERIUS CATULLUS (*ca.* 84–*ca.* 54 B.C.), a young gentleman of Verona, and a young man in love, is the most personal poet of antiquity; he put the whole strength of a passionate and emotional Italian nature into his many friendships, his one love, and his few poems—few, but roses, as men said of Sappho, and roses with their thorns.

His family was noble, his education impeccable, his friends the most distinguished aristocrats in Rome. He wrote lampoons, most of them obscene, against Caesar, knew Cicero, went East (a fruitless journey to forget his love) on the staff of Memmius, the man to whom Lucretius dedicated his poem. He was an intimate part of the gay, amoral, sophisticated life of the Roman ruling class in the years when the republic was falling to pieces. He died at thirty, burnt out.

A woman was responsible. Catullus called her Lesbia; her name was probably Clodia, the sister of the Clodius who had himself made a plebeian in order to engineer Cicero's exile. Lovely, passionate, nymphomaniac, she was attracted to men younger than herself—Catullus was ten years younger—and never for long. When she tired of Catullus, after four intense years, she became the mistress of a young friend of Cicero's called Caelius,* also ten years younger than she, and twenty years less experienced. He had, she said, tried to poison her, and, what was worse, he called her the lady whose price was a penny. Cicero is at his best in defending his client: "Clodia . . . a woman known not only by her noble birth but by the crowd's complete familiarity with her. . . . Is Clodius her husband or her brother? I am always getting that point confused. . . . She, a descendant of consuls, throws her house open to every Tom, Dick, and Harry, without disguise leads a courtesan's life, acts in town, in the country, at the beach, so that what she is is clear from her dress, her walk, her burning eyes, her freedom of speech,

---

* See the selections from Cicero's speech on his behalf, translated above.

her parties. . . . Her husband was poisoned: I saw him struggling to speak, his voice choked with agony, striking the wall in his paroxysms. . . ." This was the woman with whom young Catullus fell in love, and whom he immortalized.

Catullus does not take kindly to embalming in a schoolbook; his lyrical enthusiasm is alien to the educational pretense that in the classroom the heart does not exist. But though he is emotional and spontaneous, his spontaneity is highly sophisticated; his emotion is colored by a romantic feeling for gods dethroned and empires of the past. He is not two poets, the one naive and sentimental, the other learned and "Alexandrian": he is scholar, wit, and sophisticate from first to last.

As a lyric poet, he was not regarded as important by the mandarins of Latin literature. Indeed, Latin has no word for "lyric." Men like Cicero could not take Catullus seriously, because his poetry is more or less improvised; because its occasional, temporary, personal quality was considered beneath Roman dignity; and because in his love poetry Catullus is completely tender and completely serious. Yet he remains Latin literature's only authentic lyrist; the inhibitions which prevented Romans from appreciating him finally destroyed Latin literature. The Greeks in their lyric had contrived to wed strong emotion to strict form; the Romans let form master emotion almost completely, so that when a Roman took up writing he took up an attitude as well. But Catullus proves that otherwise we should find difficult to believe: that Latin is a language in which men can laugh and make love; he gives the lie to allegations that it is hard to imagine Romans dicing, dancing, or in bed. His poetry is a half-conscious protest that the lyric is worth a dozen histories or epics; frivolous, fluctuating, extravagant, emotional though he is, he is the founder in Latin literature of a new genre.

Catullus is a completely sophisticated, urbane poet, and his sophistication is sincere because his emotions were sophisticated. He expresses the spirit and essence of what we call "society"; he is at home in a milieu made up of learning and love, snobbery and sympathy, literature and politics, and founded precariously upon the labor of countless peasants. In his sophistication, his extravagance, his devastating power to turn a neat epigram, in his emotional sincerity sometimes degenerating into moral licence, he is a forerunner of the brilliant spoiled children of the Mauve Decade whose exemplar is Oscar Wilde.

The qualities most conspicuous in his poetry are elegance, gusto, irony, and affection—affection for man, for woman, and for poetry, so that for him literature is a personal relationship, and he can make of love and friendship a matter of loyalty, sincerity, and complete surrender. The Roman concept of *pietas*—loyalty to family, state, and gods—is for others a loyalty to institutions; Catullus makes of it a loyalty to individuals, like Shakespeare's in his *Sonnets*.

Ancient critics apply to Catullus the epithet "doctus," learned. But his is not learning for its own sake; rather it is for the sake of the association of ideas, making romantic use of foreign associations, using history, legend, and place-names to dignify some purely personal emotion. To call him "doctus" implies also that he was a master of form. The effect of artlessness is arrived at by the art that conceals art; as the poet of a literary revolution, Catullus appreciates the need of an exact form to express strong feeling.

Catullus' emotional power, exact form, and allusive style are characteristic of the poetic revolution of which he was a part. His successors in the Augustan age kept the last two without the first, and hence killed Latin poetry by making it a cultured classical exercise. Latin had once had a vigorous native lyric, but it had been abandoned by the phil-Hellenes of Plautus' age. Catullus and his friends, having no native source to turn to, made use of one foreign but contemporary: the poetry of Alexandria. It may have been artificial, but it was not artificial to imitate it, any more than it was for the Elizabethans to imitate Renaissance Latin. Alexandrianism released Catullus' lyrics from the clumsy ugliness of the Latin tradition. But the Augustans did not follow the lead of Catullus' better instinct, and hence they led poetry up a blind alley, though in justice to Vergil and Horace it must be said that the real failure lay in the original neglect of the native meters. It is possible to argue that, by comparison with Catullus, Horace's odes are *tours de force*, historical studies in classical form, phrase-making, sententious wisdom. Horace lasts; he composed from the brain only, Catullus from the heart; and heartbeats, however impassioned, do not last forever. Horace has the timeless appeal of mathematics; he proves that flawless poetic masonry has survival value. But Catullus' ephemeral emotions, spent so extravagantly upon dear, dead women, and dead men, make us aware at least of a heat that while it burned was very hot, and, feeling it, we are perhaps grateful if for a moment it warms us.

THE VERSIONS that follow are "imitations," not translations; that is, they try to express in contemporary equivalent the images, the social mores, the inflections, the compressed feeling of Catullus' time and Catullus' verse. Precisely because they do not pretend to be line-for-line equivalents, they may appeal more directly to this generation. They were originally published in 1939, under the title *The Lyric Genius of Catullus*, by Basil Blackwell, Oxford, to whom deep thanks are due for permission to reprint. The introduction is a summary by the present editor of the main points of Mr. Havelock's commentary. The traditional manuscript numbers of the poems appear in square brackets at the head of each selection.

—P. L. M.

---

## THE LANGUAGE OF LYRIC

### DEDICATION TO CORNELIUS NEPOS, HISTORIAN OF CISALPINE GAUL

[1]

Now has the printing-press
　Crowned my ambition
By issuing this first
　Dainty edition!
Take it, Cornelius,
　Who liked them so—

My bits of verse—and that
　Was long ago,
When you had just begun
　What was to be
Your master work, the first
　World-history.
And wasn't it profound,
　Learned, and such!
Well, here's this book. I know
　It isn't much—
A bit of a thing. And yet
　O may it stay,
My lady Muse, awhile,
　Though men decay?

### DRINKING SONG

### [27]

Boy with the brimming beaker,
　The banquet rules declare
The wine shall not grow weaker
　(A lady's in the chair).

List while her sovereign pleasure
　Decrees we drink it neat;
Then pour, O pour, a measure
　With alcohol replete.

Hence, hence, corroding water:
　Teetotallers console.
Bacchus you often slaughter,
　But here he's rescued whole!

### SALUTE TO SIRMIO

### [31]

Child of the woods and waters,
How secretly you smile,
All ocean's isles excelling—
Yourself not quite an isle!
The Neptune brothers never
Could duplicate the charm
That greets my eye returning,
And makes my heart grow warm.

And have I really left them—
Far hill and dusty plain?
And do I now before you
Stand safe and sound again?
To reach home travel-weary
Our own fireside to greet,
And slacken off the burden—
Is anything so sweet?

To sink upon the pillow
We loved in distant dreams
Is the one compensation
For toil that heavy seems.
Hail, Sirmio the lovely,
Garda, rejoice! I've come.
Laugh, rocks and waves, laugh loudly:
The master is come home.

## THE LANGUAGE OF LOVE

### BID ME TO LIVE

### [51]

To sit where I can see your face
And hear your laughter come and go
Is greater bliss than all the gods
　Can ever know.

The bright dream carries me away:
Watching your lips, your hair, your cheek,
I have so many things to say,
　Yet cannot speak.

I look, I listen, and my soul
Flames with a fire unfelt before
Till sense swims, and I feel and see
　And hear no more . . .

How rank this ease of lotus land:
I feel death in its dreamy spell.
The dreaming towers of Babylon—
　How soon they fell.

### LESBIA'S KISSES

### [5]

My darling, let us live
　And love for ever.
They with no love to give,
　Who feel no fever,
Who have no tale to tell
　But one of warning—
The pack of them might sell
　For half a farthing.

The sunset's dying ray
　Has its returning,
But fires of our brief day
　Shall end their burning
In night where joy and pain
　Are past recalling—
So kiss me, kiss again—
　The night is falling.

Kiss me and kiss again,
　Nor spare thy kisses.

Let thousand kisses rain
  A thousand blisses.
Then, when ten thousand more
  Their strength have wasted,
Let's wipe out all the score
  Of what we've tasted:
Lest we should count our bliss
  To our undoing,
Or others grudge the kiss
  On kiss accruing.

## LESBIA'S QUESTION

### [7]

And do you ask me this—
  What is the ration
Of kisses you must kiss
  To quench my passion?
Africa's desert land
  Is wide, they say:
Think of the desert sand
  Of Africa.

On shrines of Egypt beat
  Suns without pity.
White is Cyrene's street,
  That storied city.
Between, the sands roll on;
  Their count is missing:
So bid the count begone
  When you are kissing.

The stars that make the sky
  Their nightly dwelling,
Twinkling while lovers sigh,
  But never telling:
Count these if you would find
  How often given
Your kiss could cure a mind
  By hunger riven.

Then could no malice tell
  What was the measure,
Nor tongue cast dreary spell
  Over our treasure.

## WHEN LESBIA PLAYS

### [2]

On you, her singing bird,
  Her kisses fall,
Held ever at her breast,
  Loved more than all.
Her hand hovers all day
  To catch and miss
And catch again a quick
  Canary's kiss.

What thing is merrier,
  What sight is softer,
Than that bright head adored
  Bending in laughter?
So can keen merriment
  Stifle the sigh
That love puts in her heart—
  Ah, would that I
Could rest my aching love
  As she can do,
Sharing, canary bird,
  The ache with you.

## LESBIA'S TEARS

### [3]

Graces and Cupid choirs,
  Bow every head.
True lovers tune your lyres:
  Dirge for the dead.
My lady's little bird—
  Her darling one
More than her eyes preferred—
  Is dead and gone.

The tiny thing beguiled
  Her heart all day,
Charming her as a child
  Its mother may,
Hopping from room to room,
  Piping its song.
Now—what a road of gloom
  It hops along!

Must prettiness still feel
  Death's fatal sting?

Then cursed be death, to steal
  Her pretty thing.
To see her eyes all blurred
  And hear her cry
How can I bear? O bird
  Why did you die?

### LESBIA'S RIVALS (I)

#### [43]

O Lips and Nose and Hands and Feet,
Not very small or very neat:
O Eyes all languishing, that seen
More close, grow evidently green:
O Mouth extended far and wide,
Home of the Tongue that wags inside—
To charm continue, if you can,
That bankrupt bum you call a man.
Out in the provinces, I hear,
They match you with my own fair dear.
Match you! Good Lord! Are men all mad
To show taste so completely bad?

### LESBIA'S RIVALS (II)

#### [86]

They tell me Quintia's a beauty.
It's true she's fair and straight and tall.
Such qualities, considered singly,
Will help her case. She needs them all.
But how can beauty be allowed her?
O breast and thigh and arm so round,
O lump magnificent, what flavor
Of fascination have you found?

To Lesbia turn for beauty's pattern.
There every part is fair and glad.
What's more, she's stolen all the graces
That all her rivals might have had.

### MY TRUE LOVE HATH MY HEART

#### [87]

There never was a woman who could say,
  And say it true,
That she was loved of any, O my love,
  As I love you.

There never was a loyal promise given
  Faithful and free,
As loyalty to you, because I love you,
  Is given from me.

### AMANTIUM IRAE

#### [92]

Ah, my love, her lips how pretty!
  And how cruel!
Angry with me, to her anger
  Adding fuel.
Yet she loves me, and I know it:
  Here's the sign:
My tongue's as sharp, yet no heart loves her
  More than mine!

### REUNION

#### [107]

To dream of something dear, in hopeless yearning,
  And find the dream come true, is joy complete.
Dear love, I dreamt of you and your returning,
  Dreams sad and sweet.

To-day you have come back, and sorrow's over.
  I never thought, seeing you go away,
Joy could so fill the heart of any lover
  As mine this day.

## LOVE AND DEATH

### WORLD WITHOUT END

#### [101]

O'er many a sea, through many a tribe and nation,
  Brother, I come
To honor thee with mournful salutation
  Paid at thy tomb.
Only this final tribute may I tender
  In grief unheard;
Only address the dust that cannot render
  One answering word.

O thou by fate cut down, dear ghost departed
  In thy first spring,

This age-old office of the broken-hearted
    Behold I bring:
A brother's tearful offerings to cover
    Thy narrow cell,
And his slow-spoken word: Farewell for ever,
    Farewell, farewell.

## FOR QUINTILIA DEAD

### [96]

If aught of our poor grief has a returning
    To light the dead,
When our old loves come back to us in yearning
    For those long fled,
Then can Quintilia redeem great sorrow
    Of early grave,
Able a greater happiness to borrow
    From your strong love.

## THE FLOWER CUT DOWN

### IN MEMORIAM. AN EPISTLE TO ALLIUS IN RECORD OF FRIENDSHIP

### [68b]

#### I

No more refrain, O muse: declare the story
Of what I owe to Allius my friend.
Immortal may his honour stand defying
The centuries' interminable trend.

Make of my voice a message heard of millions.
Wrinkled let this poor paper still proclaim
The unforgotten service that he rendered.
Let not time's dusty webs surround his name.

#### II

Thou knowest well how on my heavy spirit
Was laid a double anguish of desire,
How tasting sweets of love I tasted sorrow,
And mingled salt tears with volcanic fire.

Then it was he who ready came to save me,
Like a calm wind to bark by tempest blown.
He lent his house and home for assignation.
So were the barriers to love torn down.

#### III

At fall of eve my love came to the threshold.
She moved on whispering feet, a goddess fair.
Poised on the trodden stone she stayed her footfall,
    Watching me there.

Her shoe creaked—that was all—and I remembered
Laodamia to her love and lord
Arriving home and waiting in the doorway
    For his first word.

One hour of fellowship they had together,
Ere Trojan service summoned him from home.
So went the gallant flower of Grecian manhood,
Sailing to Troy and their untimely tomb.

#### IV

Still in that plain are bitter ashes buried.
Alas for Troy! My brother's grave is there.
O brother, how uncomforted your passing:
How dark and comfortless my own despair!

You went, and all the fortunes of our household
Went with you and were buried with your clay,
And my own bliss, that lived by your affection,
    Died in a day.

And now far off in graveyard unfamiliar
Your lonely dust lies in an alien land.
The fateful soil of Troy holds you in keeping,
Laid by the margin of a foreign strand.

#### V

O dreamer Paris, lying with thy Helen
In stolen bowers of ease, dream thou no more.
The chivalry of Greece, for vengeance hasting,
With arms comes knocking at thy chamber door.

Laodamia, thou must leave thy lover.
Though thy life go with him, he must depart.
How fathomless the springs of thy affection!
How deep the tides that sweeping fill thy heart!

To bear the yoke of passionate submission
The heart of peerless woman still can learn.
Thy smouldering fires burn on, waiting to kindle
In that brief blissful hour of his return.

## VI

Thine image lives again, as now before me
Here in this room another woman stands
Peerless and passionate and proud, yet yielding
  Into my hands.

Light of my life, see where the little Cupid
Clad in his yellow suit, with bow and dart,
Plays hide and seek about us as I clasp you
  Close to my heart.

## VII

What though my love alone cannot content her?
She is discreet; her sins none other sees.
Why play the jealous fool? The queen of heaven
Herself must bear Jove's infidelities.

No flare of torches brought her to my dwelling;
No marriage-escort might her journey mark.
Stolen from husband's bed were her caresses,
The secrets murmured in the magic dark.

Of all her golden days can she remember
Some with a special quality of bliss?
Let her keep these for me. My short petition
  Asks only this.

## VIII

Allius, sterling friend, my verse is ended
Which celebrates your service and your praise.
May fleet tomorrow's day and then tomorrow
Never your monument with rust erase.

The gods are just, and ever have rewarded
Men of true heart and faithful to their oath.
May you and she you love enjoy their blessing:
  Peace to you both.

Peace to that house of memories immortal
In spring time of our love that saw us meet,
Peace above all to that dear life that renders
  My own life sweet.

### ONE WORD PROFANED

### [109]

And would you give a love that shall be dear
And never die—

Our love? Ah, God, give her a heart sincere
  That cannot lie,
And lips whose promises are something worth
  Nor lightly told,
That love and happiness be ours on earth
  To have and hold.

### WOMAN'S FAITH

### [70]

My lady says, None other would she marry
  But only me;
Not Jove himself, a suitor though he tarry,
  Yea, even He.
She says—but what a lady to her lover
  Softly may say—
Write it upon the wind or in the river
  That pass for aye.

### MISER CATULLE

### [8]

Poor poet, let your folly sleep:
The past is dead: bury it deep.
Time was your love 'neath sunny sky
Beckoned to you as she went by,
And your fond merriment could stir
An equal happiness in her.
The passion that you lent her then
Mocked the mere loves of common men.
Sunny the skies, and every day
Was summer—till she turned away.

Turn from her then yourself, nor strive
In futile misery to live.
Pursue no more the hope that flies:
No more remember love that dies.
Be resolute: make your heart hard—
Goodbye, my dear: I've said the word.
My heart is steeled, my love shall sleep,
Nor seek the kiss you'd rather keep.
But you when heart and hand forsake—
Yours is the hard heart that will break.
Who will make love when I am gone?
Call you his dear, his fair, his own?
Where's the heart now your heart adores?
Whose lips shall print themselves on yours
And leave their mark on them?—But stay!
Turn from her, poet, turn away.

## THE OFFICE OF MY HEART

### [75]

The office of my heart is still to love
  When I would hate.
Time and again your faithlessness I prove
  Proven too late.
Your ways might mend, yet my contempt could
    never
  Be now undone.
Yet crimes repeated cannot stop this fever
  From burning on.

## THE UNDYING FIRE

### [72]

Once you would say to me: "Your heart has found
    me
  And yours alone.
I would not have the arms of Jove around me
  More than your own."
Saying it, you became no more the fashion
  Of cheap desire,
But wife and child and home, loved with the
    passion
  Of life-long fire.

I know you now. Yet my soul goes on burning,
  As burn it must,
When you and all I gave to you are turning
  To death and dust.
Strange, do you say? How strange that love should
    cherish
  Light that is gone!
That every kindly thought of you should perish,
  Yet love last on.

## BONDAGE

### [85]

I loathe her, and I love her. "Can I show
  How both should be?"
I loathe and love, and nothing else I know
  But agony.

## JOURNEY'S END

### [76]

They say that benefits to others rendered
  Win in our memories their late reward.
They say that love, once it is loyally tendered,
  Stays sweet and keeps the lover's heart un-
    scarred.

If it is true that faith promised and given
  Is profit, and a guileless heart is gain,
How surely shall I prosper, who have striven
  So long with pain.

The gentle word, the generous intent,
  The decent things that men can do or say,
All these to gladden her I freely spent,
  But could not touch her when she turned away.

Why then, you fool, cherish your long affliction?
  Why fight against the thing that must prevail?
Put her away from you. Need resolution
  For ever fail?

'It is impossible to lay aside for ever
  In one brief point of time the love of years.'
Then do th' impossible. Steel yourself. Sever
  This knot, and wring relief from bitter tears.

O gods, if yours be pity, yours compassion
  Given to failing men even on the road
Leading to death, dispel this black obsession,
  Rescue my soul from hell. Support its load—

How like a stupor every sense pervading
  My sorrow steals! How faint I grow with grief!
How swift the sunlight of my life is fading,
  My bliss how brief!

I look no more for her to be my lover
  As I love her. That thing could never be.
Nor pray I for her purity—that's over.
  Only this much I pray, that I be free,

Free from insane desire myself, and guarded
  In peace at last. O heaven, grant that yet
The faith by which I've lived may be rewarded.
  Let me forget.

## She that I Loved

### [58]

She that I loved, that face,
   Those hands, that hair,
Dearer than all my race,
   As dear as fair—
See her where throngs parade
   Th'imperial route,
Plying her skill unpaid—
   Rome's prostitute.

## The Last Word

### [11]

Friends, who profess your ardour to explore
The ends of earth with me, on India's shore
The long wave breaking calls for evermore
   Clamorously:

Wide are the steppes and wild the Russian land:
His plains the Parthian ranges bow in hand:
Dark flows the Nile, dyeing the sea and sand
   Eternally:

Steep rise the Alpine roads that Caesar's host
Climbed to accomplish his imperial boast—
Gaul and the Rhineland and wild Britain's coast
   Afar removed:

You are prepared, you say, for each reverse
Of fate. But can you welcome something worse?

Dare you convey a last compendious curse
   To her I loved?

Tell her: God speed you, lady, to your bed,
Where thousand lovers lie, there lay your head,
Promising love to them give lust instead,
   False to the core:

Tell her how love, that in my heart one day
Blossomed unbidden as a wildflower may,
The scythe has caught, and she can throw away
   What blooms no more.

## Swan Song

### [38]

This ailing friend of yours
   Is sadly scarred.
The day is dark, and oh
   The way grows hard,
And harder every hour
   Of every day.
And you—had you one word
   Of cheer to say?
A light and little thing
   It were to spare:
You make me wild! Is this
   All that you care?
Just one small word to soothe
   My lonely fears,
Sad as Simonides'
   Melodious tears.

# SELECTIONS FROM THE *Georgics* OF VERGIL

## *Translated by Robert Fitzgerald and Smith Palmer Bovie*

## INTRODUCTION

VERGIL, THE most widely read of all Latin poets, was born in the little town of Andes, near Mantua, in 70 B.C., the son of a small farmer. His father saw to it that the boy had a good education, in several towns of northern Italy and in Rome, and probably also at the Epicurean school near Naples. In 42 B.C., while Vergil was working on the *Eclogues* (pastoral poems similar to those of Theocritus), his farm was confiscated for distribution to the disbanded soldiers of Antony and Octavian (Augustus). Vergil went to Rome to try to recover the property; aided by his friends, Pollio, Gallus, and Maecenas, he succeeded; though he presently lost it again, he received another farm in recompense. From 43 to 37 he worked on the *Eclogues*.

Probably at the suggestion of Maecenas, Vergil then undertook the four *Georgics*, with which he was busy for the next seven years. One of the ambitions of Octavian was to arouse a national feeling in Italy and an affection for her land and old ways. The *Georgics* are ostensibly a farmer's manual in verse, but they are far more important as a hymn to Italy. The first book is devoted to farming

in general and especially to climate and weather; the others are concerned with trees and vines, cattle, and bees.

When the *Georgics* were finished, Vergil, now living at Naples, embarked on his last work, the *Aeneid*. On it he spent the rest of his life, and it was not quite finished when the poet died in 19 B.C., on his way back from a trip to Greece. The story is told that he begged his literary executors to burn the poem if anything happened to him; but Augustus ordered them to publish it, with a few very minor corrections. It became popular at once, and its popularity remained; during the Middle Ages Vergil was probably regarded more highly than any other nonecclesiastical author. When Dante wrote his *Divine Comedy*, he introduced Vergil as his guide through the world below; and all the works of Vergil have been imitated many times.

*The First Georgic* is translated by Mr. Fitzgerald; *The Second* by Mr. Bovie. The Oxford Classical Text of Sir Arthur Hirtzel (1900) is the one used.

## *FROM* THE FIRST GEORGIC

### I

Until Jove let it be, no colonist
Mastered the earth; no land was marked,
None parcelled out or shared; but everyone
Looked for his living in the common wold.

And Jove gave poison to the black snakes, and
Made the wolves ravage, made the ocean roll,
Knocked honey from the leaves, took fire away—

So man might beat out various inventions
By reasoning and art.
                    First he chipped fire
Out of the veins of flint where it was hidden;
Then rivers felt his skiffs of the light alder;
Then sailors counted up the stars and named
        them;
Pleiades, Hyades, and the Pole Star;
Then were discovered ways to take wild things
In snares, or hunt them with the circling pack;

And how to whip a stream with casting nets,
Or draw the deep-sea fisherman's cordage up;
And then the use of steel and the shrieking saw;
Then various crafts. All things were overcome
By labor and by force of bitter need.

[125–146]

## II

Even when your threshing floor is leveled
By the big roller, smoothed and packed by hand
With fuller's earth, so that it will not crack,
There are still nuisances. The tiny mouse
Locates his house and granary underground,
Or the blind mole tunnels his dark chamber;
The toad, too, and the monsters of the earth,
Besides those plunderers of the grain, the weevil
And frantic ant, scared of a poor old age.

[178–186]

Let me speak then, too, of the farmer's weapons:
The heavy oaken plow and the plowshare,
The slowly rolling carts of Demeter,
The threshing machine, the sledge, the weighted
    mattock,
The withe baskets, the cheap furniture,
The harrow and the magic winnowing fan—
All that your foresight makes provision of,
If you still favor the divine countryside.

[160–168]

## III

Moreover, like men tempted by the straits
In ships borne homeward through the blowing sea,
We too must reckon on Arcturus' star,
The days of luminous Draco and the Kids.
When Libra makes the hours of sleep and day-
    light
Equal, dividing the world, half light, half dark,
Then drive the team, and sow the field with barley,
Even under intractable winter's rain . . . .
But Spring is the time to sow your beans and
    clover,
When shining Taurus opens the year with his
    golden
Horns, and the Dog's averted star declines;
For greater harvests of your wheat and spelt,
Let first the Pleiades and Hyades be hid
And Ariadne's diadem go down.

[204–211, 215–224]

The golden sun rules the great firmament
Through the twelve constellations, and the world
Is measured out in certain parts, and heaven
By five great zones is taken up entire:
One glowing with sundazzle and fierce heat;
And far away on either side the arctics,
Frozen with ice and rain, cerulean;
And, in between, two zones for sick mankind:
Through each of these a slanting path is cut
Where pass in line the zodiacal stars.
Northward the steep world rises to Scythia
And south of Libya descends, where black
Styx and the lowest of the dead look on.
In the north sky the Snake glides like a river
Winding about the Great and the Little Bear—
Those stars that fear forever the touch of ocean;
Southward they say profound Night, mother of
    Furies,
Sits tight-lipped among the crowding shades,
Or thence Aurora draws the daylight back;
And where the East exhales the yellow morning,
Reddening evening lights her final stars.

[231–251]

## IV

As for the winter, when the freezing rains
Confine the farmer, he may employ himself
In preparations for serener seasons.
The plowman beats the plowshare on the forge,
Or makes his vats of tree-trunks hollowed out,
Brands his cattle, numbers his piles of grain,
Sharpens fence posts or pitchforks, prepares
Umbrian trellises for the slow vine.
Then you may weave the baskets of bramble
    twigs . . . .
Or dip your bleating flock in the clean stream.
Often the farmer loads his little mule
With olive oil or apples, and brings home
A grindstone or a block of pitch from market.

[259–266, 272–275]

And some will stay up late beside the fire
On winter nights, whittling torches, while
The housewife runs the shuttle through the loom
And comforts the long labor with her singing;
Or at the stove she simmers the new wine,
Skimming the froth with leaves. Oh idle time!
In that hale season, all their worries past,
Farmers arrange convivialities—
As after laden ships have reached home port,

The happy sailors load the prow with garlands.
Then is the time to gather acorns and
Laurel berries and the bloodred myrtle,
To lay your traps for cranes and snares for deer,
To track the leveret, drop the running doe:
When snow is deep, and ice is on the rivers.

[291–310]

## V

What of the humors and the ways of autumn? . . . .

Just when the farmer wished to reap his yellow
Fields, and thresh his grain,
I have often seen all the winds make war,
Flattening the stout crops from the very roots;
And in the black whirlwind
Carrying off the ears and the light straw.
And often mighty phalanxes of rain
Marched out of heaven, as the clouds
Rolled up from the sea the detestable tempest;
Then the steep aether thundered, and the deluge
Soaked the crops, filled ditches, made the rivers
Rise and roar and seethe in their spuming beds.

The Father himself in the mid stormy night
Lets the lightning go, at whose downstroke
Enormous earth quivers, wild things flee,
And fear abases the prone hearts of men—
As Jove splits Athos with his firebolt
Or Rhodope or the Ceraunian ridge.
The southwind wails in sheets of rain,
And under that great wind the groves
Lament, and the long breast of the shore is
shaken.

If you dislike to be so caught, mark well
The moon's phases and the weather signs;
Notice where Saturn's frigid star retires,
Mercury's wanderings over heaven; and revere
Especially the gods. Offer to Ceres;
And let no man lay scythe against his grain
Unless he first bind oakleaves on his head
And make his little dance, and sing to her.

[311, 316–350]

## VI

When shall we herd the cattle to the stables?

The wind, say, rises without intermission;
The sea gets choppy and the swell increases;

The dry crash of boughs is heard on hills;
The long sound of the surf becomes a tumult;
The gusts become more frequent in the grove;
The waves begin to fight against the keels;
From far at sea the gulls fly shoreward crying;
The heron leaves his favorite marsh and soars
Over the high cloud. Then you will see
Beyond thin skimrack, shooting stars
Falling, the long pale tracks behind them
Whitening through the darkness of the night;
And you'll see straw and fallen leaves blowing.
But when it thunders in rough Boreas' quarter,
When east and west it thunders—every sailor
Furls his dripping sail.

A storm should never catch you unprepared.
Aerial cranes take flight before its rising,
The restless heifer with dilated nostrils
Sniffs the air; the squeaking hirondelle
Flits round and round the lake, and frogs,
Inveterate in their mud, croak a chorale.
And too the ant, more frantic in his gallery,
Trundles his eggs out from their hiding place;
The rainbow, cloud imbiber, may be seen;
And crows go cawing from the pasture
In a harsh throng of crepitating wings;
The jeering jay gives out his yell for rain
And takes a walk by himself on the dry sand.
Stormwise, the various sea-fowl, and such birds
As grub the sweet Swan River in Asia,
May be observed dousing themselves and diving
Or riding on the water, as if they wished—
What odd exhilaration!—to bathe themselves.

[355–387]

## VII

After a storm, clear weather and continuing
Sunny days may likewise be foretold:
By the sharp twinkle of the stars, the moon
Rising to face her brother's rays by day;
No tenuous fleeces blowing in the sky,
No halcyons, sea favorites, on the shore
Stretching out their wings in tepid sunlight; . . . .
But mists go lower and lie on the fields,
The owl, observing sundown from his perch,
Modulates his meaningless melancholy.
Aloft in crystal air the sparrow hawk
Chases his prey; and as she flits aside

The fierce hawk follows screaming on the wind,
And as he swoops, she flits aside again.
With funereal contractions of the windpipe
The crows produce their caws, three at a time,
And in their high nests, pleased at I know not
    what,
Noise it among themselves: no doubt rejoicing
To see their little brood after the storm,
But not, I think, by reason of divine
Insight or superior grasp of things.
[393–399, 401–416]

## VIII

But if you carefully watch the rapid sun
And the moon following, a fair night's snare
Never deceives you as to next day's weather.
When the new moon collects a rim of light,
If that bow be obscured with a dark vapor,
Then a great tempest is in preparation;
If it be blushing like a virgin's cheek,
There will be wind; wind makes Diana blush;
If on the fourth night (most significant)
She goes pure and unclouded through the sky,
All that day and the following days will be,
For one full month, exempt from rain and
    wind. . . .
The sun, too, rising and setting in the waves,
Will give you weather signs, trustworthy ones
Whether at morning or when stars come out.
A mackerel sky over the east at sunrise
Means look out for squalls, a gale is coming,
Unfavorable to trees and plants and flocks.
Or when through denser strata the sun's rays
Break out dimly, or Aurora rises
Pale from Tithonus' crocus-colored chamber,
Alas, the vine-leaf will not shield the cluster
In the hubbub of roof-pattering bitter hail.

It will be well to notice sunset, too,
For the sun's visage then has various colors;
Bluish and dark means rain; if it be fiery
That means an East wind; if it be dappled
And mixed with red-gold light, then you will see
Wind and rain in commotion everywhere.
Nobody can advise me, on that night,
To cast off hawsers and put out to sea.
But if the next day passes and the sunset
Then be clear, you need not fear the weather:
A bright Norther will sway the forest trees.
[424–435, 438–460]

## IX

Last, what the late dusk brings, and whence the
    fair
Clouds are blown, and secrets of the Southwind
You may learn from the sun, whose prophecies
No man denies, seeing black insurrections,
Treacheries, and wars are told by him.

When Caesar died, the great sun pitied Rome,
So veiling his bright head, the godless time
Trembled in fear of everlasting night;
And then were portents given of earth and ocean,
Vile dogs upon the roads, and hideous
Strange birds, and Aetna quaking, and her fires
Bursting to overflow the Cyclops' fields
With flames whirled in the air and melted stones.
Thunder of war was heard in Germany
From south to north, shaking the granite Alps;
And a voice also through the silent groves
Piercing; and apparitions wondrous pale
Were seen in dead of night. Then cattle spoke
(O horror!), streams stood still, the earth cracked
    open
And tears sprang even from the temple bronze.
The Po, monarch of rivers, on his back
Spuming whole forests, raced through the low-
    land plains
And bore off pens and herds; and then con-
    tinually
The viscera of beasts were thick with evil,
Blood trickled from the springs; tall towns at
    night
Reechoed to the wolf-pack's shivering howl;
And never from pure heaven have there fallen
So many fires, more baleful comets burned.
It seemed that once again the Roman lines,
Alike in arms, would fight at Philippi;
And heaven permitted those Thessalian fields
To be enriched again with blood of ours.
Some future day, perhaps, in that country,
A farmer with his plow will turn the ground,
And find the javelins eaten thin with rust,
Or knock the empty helmets with his mattock
And wonder, digging up those ancient bones.

Paternal gods! Ancestors! Mother Vesta!
You that guard Tiber and the Palatine!
Now that that century is overthrown,
Let not this young man fail to give us peace!
Long enough beneath your rule, O Caesar,

Heaven has hated us and all those triumphs
Where justice was thrown down—so many wars,
So many kinds of wickedness! No honor
Rendered the plow, but the fields gone to ruin,
The country-folk made homeless, and their
    scythes
Beaten to straight swords on the blowing forge!

War from the Euphrates to Germany;
Ruptured engagements, violence of nations,
And impious Mars raging the whole world over—
As when a four-horsed chariot rears away
Plunging from the barrier, and runs wild,
Heedless of the reins of the charioteer.

[461–514]

## *FROM* THE SECOND GEORGIC

### THE FRUITS OF COUNTRY LIFE

The farmer who appreciates his blessings
Knows boundless joy. A land remote from war
Pours forth her fruit abundantly for him.
Although no stately home with handsome portals
Disgorges on its steps a wave of callers
Who every morning marvel at his doors
Inlaid with tortoise shell, astonished by
His gold-trimmed clothes and his Corinthian
    bronzes;
Although his white wool is not stained with dye,
His oil not spoiled with perfumes from the East,
His rest is sound, his life beyond reproach.
His riches vary, his estates are broad—
Caves and living lakes, refreshing vales,
The cattle lowing, slumber in the shade.
Familiar with the haunts of animals,
The farmer lives in peace, his children all
Learn how to work, to honor simple fare,
To venerate their fathers and the gods:
The trace of Justice longest here remained
The last time that her footsteps graced the earth.

And as for me, may first of all the Muses,
Whose symbols I revere, inspired by love,
Receive my prayer and spread before my eyes
The planets and the stars, the sun's eclipses,
The moon's laborious turns, the earthquake's
    source;
Reveal the hidden motions of the sea,
That force the waters up and sink them down.
Show why the winter suns race toward the Ocean,
What regulates the long-delaying nights.
But if I fail to master nature's lore
Before the blood flows cold around my heart,
Let me enjoy the country, running brooks,
The woods and streams, oblivious to fame.
Oh, happy plains of Thessaly and Sparta,
Oh, joy of rest beside the hills of Thrace!

Blessed is he who knows the cause of things,
Subdues all fear and overpowering fate,
The greedy claims of roaring Acheron.
But he is happy too who knows the gods
Of country folk, Pan, Silvan, and the Nymphs.
He scorns the shouting "mandate of the people";
His not the robe of kings, not dissonance
Creating civil wars, the swift onslaught
From Balkan coalitions; not for him
The Roman State, or Empires doomed to die.
He pines not for the poor, nor hates the rich.
The boughs by their own virtue bear him fruit,
He gathers what the willing fields supply;
Has never seen the laws, engraved in bronze,
The maddening Forum, and the Record Office.
Others torment the dark sea with their oars,
Meet suicide, pay court in royal halls.
One man destroys a city and its homes
To drink from jewelled cup and sleep on scarlet;
Another hoards his wealth and broods on gold.
One gapes dumbfounded at the speaker's stand;
Applause corrupts another as it rolls
From Senators and people in the hall.
Brothers pour out their brothers' blood with joy,
And exiles make their homes in alien lands.

The farmer drives his curved plough through
    the earth:
The work sustains his home, his children's future,
His livestock and his much-deserving herds.
Without repose, the overflowing seasons
Bring in their apples, and increase the flock,
Corn sheaves load the furrows, burst the barns,
Then winter comes, the mills are grinding olives,
The pigs come home contented, stuffed with
    acorns,
Strawberries crop out in the forest groves.
Autumn brings its varied offerings:
High up, the vineyard basks in mellow heat.
The farmer's children smother him with kisses,

His home breathes purity beyond compare.
The cows give down their heavy bags of milk,
And fat kids lock horns, tussling on the grass.
The master takes a holiday at ease
Among his friends outdoors around a fire:
They twine their garlands round the drinking
 bowls,
While he makes offering to the god of wine,
Or pins a target on the elm tree's bark
For shooting, or directs the wrestling bouts.
Thus lived the Sabines, Romulus and Remus,
And thus was fashioned brave Etruria;
Thus Rome was formed, far lovelier than all,
When one wall closed in all her seven hills.
Before Jove ruled, before men slew the ox,
When golden Saturn visited the earth;
When men had never heard the bugles blow
Nor sword blades clang on stubborn anvil-irons.

[458–540]

# SELECTIONS FROM THE *Aeneid* OF VERGIL

*Translated by Rolfe Humphries*

## INTRODUCTION

EVERYBODY HAS had the experience of going to hear a distinguished speaker, who is introduced by a local chairman. The local chairman goes on and on, with jokes, anecdotes, eulogy, bibliography (after a quick glance at his sheaf of notes), biography, autobiography, and what not, until the audience begins to wonder not only when, but even whether, it is going to hear the distinguished speaker. Meanwhile that unhappy wretch, contorting his features into a grimace that he hopes will pass for a modest and affable expression, is hastily reworking his lecture, making cuts right and left, and trying to reorganize for forty minutes what he had carefully planned to take fifty-five. I take a dim view of introductions.

Moreover, what can be said, in an introduction to the *Aeneid* of Vergil, that has not been said a thousand times before? The only excuse for this one is that you, who read it, (if you do) have not read the others. Within such compass as a decent brevity permits, three or four things might be said.

First of all, the *Aeneid* is a major poem. A great poem, and, in the opinion of its author, an unfinished one. Being a great poem, its scope permits, it more than permits, it requires, a certain unevenness in the writing. To use a metaphor from geography, there must be valleys as well as peaks, dry ravines as well as upland meadows; you must expect pedestrian stretches if you are going to climb mountains. Otherwise, no matter how high above sea level you were, you would find yourself on a plateau, than which nothing is less scenically entertaining. It is evidence of design, not of carelessness, that in a work of this scope, the writing varies.

Vergil, we have been told, wanted to burn the *Aeneid*; he was not satisfied with it. This attitude, it seems to me, reflects a fatigue and exhaustion of spirit rather than a considered literary judgment. The last revisions are always the most enervating, and Vergil, one can well believe, had reached the point where he felt he would rather do anything on earth, including die, than go over the poem one more time. If we had never heard the poem was believed incomplete, we would, I think, have a difficult time in deciding which were the unsatisfactory portions. Some cutting, I suppose, could have taken place in the last six books; some of the catalogue-duels cut down, or omitted. It looks like a blunder to have Camilla's exit line read exactly the same as Turnus'. The hero might have been given a little more part in the action of Books II and III, though this might have imposed difficult problems, since the hero is himself telling the narrative. Something might have been done to brighten up Books III and VIII. Then there are the half lines—these, at least the scholars would want to see rounded off. Personally, I am just as well satisfied that they were left as is; there is a peculiar effectiveness about them, however incorrect they may be technically. The ear is a very good judge in such matters. For the reader who wants the detailed judgment of a discerning and thoughtful Latinist, the Mackail edition affords instances. With all of Professor Mackail's judgments I do not entirely agree, but they are worth your respectful attention.

The *Aeneid* labors under the charge of being propaganda. I do not know when this criticism first came to be brought; I suspect it is only our own time, with its persistent devotion to all the aspects of advertising and sloganeering, that feels sufficiently guilty about these activities to project the charge across twenty centuries. Vergil with whatever cheeriness his nature was capable of would readily have agreed that the poem was propaganda; but then he did not know the invidious pejorative semantic connotations of the word; he would have thought it meant only "things that ought to be propagated." An institute of propaganda analysis would, I think, be completely baffled by the *Aeneid*; the conclusion might be that the poem was either the best or the worst propaganda that had ever been written. What kind of propaganda is it, to begin a nationalist epic with the sorrowful sigh: "It was such a great burden—a millstone round the neck—to found the Roman race"? What kind of propaganda is it to make the enemies, by and large, more interesting and colorful and sympathetic fellows than our own side? Lausus and Mezentius, for example, are a far more engaging father and son combination than Aeneas-Anchises, Aeneas-Ascanius, or Evander-Pallas. Dido and Camilla command our admiration much more than the blushing Lavinia or the fading Creusa. We respond to Turnus, and are at best coldly respectful to Aeneas. What goes on here, anyway? Shouldn't some patriotic organization call for an investigation of this subversive writer, secretly in the pay of a foreign power? On the other hand, it is just possible that this is the very best form which national propaganda can take, the implicit and pervasive doctrine that great and good as our enemies may be, we can admire them, surpass them, be just to them, and not afraid of them, either. A good Roman, Vergil is a better human.

A word or two about the character of Aeneas. It may be that the trouble with him is really the trouble with us. We are not mature enough to accept, as epic hero, a man who is imaginative, sensitive, compassionate (everywhere except in Books IV and X), and, in short, civilized. There seems to be almost no aggression in the character of Aeneas; even in his dreams he wants to get out of trouble and avoid fighting. We don't like this; we find most satisfactory those moments when he is telling Dido off, or making bitter sarcastic speeches at Lucagus and Liger. We object, further, that when he does fight, he knows very well that he is protected by the gods and by magic armor. (We do not mind the latter in the case of, for instance, Superman; and would we rather have him sponsored by devils than by gods?) In the matter of invulnerability, we are, I think, a little unjust; Vergil takes some pains to show that Aeneas can be hurt: he rushes in, unarmed, to preserve the terms of the truce; he is grievously wounded by the death of Pallas. The surest way, I suppose, to make you dislike him even more is to argue on his behalf too strongly; let it go, and we need not feel too guilty if we are not crazy about him; there is little in the record to show that the Romans liked enthusiastic encomia, either.

It is a peculiar, paradoxical, kind of great poem, this *Aeneid*. For us, I think, the greatness can not be found in what appealed most to the Romans; it may be that, with time, we are better equipped than they may have been, to appreciate its greatness in one aspect—I mean its music. Not only the music of the lines, but the music of the whole: the pleasure comes in listening to it as you would a great symphony (and not too much attention, please, to the program notes). Remember, this is a *composition*, this *Aeneid*, carefully wrought, beautifully balanced. Professor Conway's study refers to the *architecture* of the epic; the analysis is excellent, the central metaphor

a little unhappy if it leads you to envisage the *Aeneid* as an impressive pile, frozen and static. The poem moves, in more senses than one: the thing to do is feel it, and listen to it. Hear how the themes vary, and recur; how the tone lightens and darkens, the volume swells or dies, the tempo rushes or lingers. Take in the poem with the mind, to be sure; take it in with the eye as well; but above all hearken to it with the ear.

A few words about this translation. A quick and unscrupulous job. I am not being modest; a modest man would never have started, and a scrupulous one never finished. I have, nevertheless, been not entirely without principles. For one thing, I have tried to compensate for that grievous error of American education which places major emphasis on the first six books, while admitting, in the most off-hand way possible, that there also were some others. Lately it has reached the point in secondary schools that the student reads only Books I, II, IV, and VI. This seems to me like looking at the right eye, left ear, left shoulder, and right knee of the Venus of Milo. I do not see how any intelligent American schoolboy or girl can possibly go this slowly, unless he stops to scan every line, note every example of synecdoche or synizesis, and parse all the grammatical constructions, with special attention to the poetical dative of agent, the Greek middle voice and the accusative of respect. What kind of way is this to deal with a work of art? Where the impression grew that the last six books are inferior in interest to the first I do not understand; it seems to me an unconsidered judgment. Anyway, decide for yourself; only please do not think you know much about the *Aeneid* if you know nothing about Books VII–XII inclusive.

A loose iambic pentameter has seemed to me the most convenient medium. I have tried to see to it that there should be some continuity, not merely in the run of the narrative, but also in the play of the theme; sometimes I have had no principle except that I liked the passage very much myself; more than once I have had to leave out passages that I liked, for no reason except that I could not translate them even passably. I have transposed lines, cut proper names and allusions where I thought they would slow down the reader's interest, substituted the general for the specific or the specific for the general, and in short taken all kinds of liberties, such as no pure scholar could possibly approve. But I doubt there is any such thing as a pure scholar, anyhow. I have preferred solecisms to archaisms; thus I have never used the second person singular pronoun: I have probably committed anachronisms, but, then, I think Vergil did, too. What I have tried to be faithful to is the meaning of the poem as I understand it, to make it sound to you, wherever I can, the way it feels to me. Working over it, I have been impressed, more than ever, by its richness and variety: to mention only one point, the famous Vergilian melancholy, the tone of *sunt lacrimae rerum*, is, I begin to notice, a recurring, not a sustained, theme. There is much more rugged and rough, harsh and bitter, music in Vergil than you might suspect if you have only read *about* him. You find that Hemingway is not the only hard-boiled realist in scenes of battle.

In conclusion (as even the local chairman manages to say eventually): if the translation here leads any one to conclude that the *Aeneid* must have been a pretty good poem, *in the original* (reader's italics), I shall not feel insulted. If any one, because of the strength or weakness of this translation, decides he had better read the entire poem in Latin, I shall be justified.

THE TEXT used is basically that of J. W. Mackail (Oxford, 1930), but the translation was made at different times in different places, with whatever text came to hand: school editions, the Loeb (by H. R. Fairclough), and others.

---

## Book I

### THE STORM. DIDO

Arms and the man I sing, the first who came,
Compelled by fate, an exile out of Troy,
To Italy and the Lavinian coast,
Much buffeted on land and on the deep
By violence of the gods, through that long rage,
That savage hate, of Juno's. And he suffered
Much, also, in war, till he should build his town
And bring his gods to Latium, whence, in time,
The Latin race, the Alban fathers, rose
And the great walls of everlasting Rome.

Help me, O Muse, recall the reasons: why,
Why, did the queen of heaven drive a man
So known for goodness, for devotion, through
So many toils and perils? was there slight,
Affront, or outrage? Is vindictiveness
An attribute of the celestial mind?          [1–11]

[Vergil answers his own question in the affirmative by reciting a list of Juno's grievances, going as far back into the past as the judgment of Paris, and projecting into the future with her apprehension over the Roman destruction of her favored Tyrian-descended Carthaginians. In the present situation, the Trojan voyagers, with most of their wanderings and long-suffering completed, as they think, are leaving Sicily, after Anchises' death, on the last lap of their run to the west of Italy. But Juno goes to Aeolus, god of the winds, persuading him to turn all the winds loose at once, and harry them further with a storm. He promptly obeys.]

The spear-butt struck the hollow mountain-side;
The winds, wherever they could, come sweeping
          forth,
Whirl over the world, and swoop upon the sea.

East, South, Southwest, they heave the ocean,
          howl,
Storm, roll the giant combers toward the shore.
Men cry, the rigging creaks and strains; the
          clouds
Darken the sky, and men see nothing. Dark
Broods over the deep; the heavy thunder rumbles
From pole to pole; the lightning rips and blinds;
There is no way out but death.          [81–91]

[At this point Vergil first introduces the hero of the epic. Aeneas, terribly frightened, holds up his hands in prayer and lament, speaking in envy of the men who died in the fighting at Troy, wishing he might have been among them, slain by Diomedes or Achilles. There is an echo of the storm-music in the last line of his speech, and Vergil, going on with the description of the storm, later picks up not only the cadence, but some of the same vocabulary.

If this introduction of Aeneas seems to present the hero in rather unheroic guise, the thing to remember, I think, is that Vergil is taking us here into Aeneas' own deepest feeling: his mood is expressed in soliloquy, he is not being abject in front of his men. Later, when he addresses them for the first time—but we had better leave that till we get to it. Meantime, the storm is still raging.]

A howling gust from the north strikes the sail,
          head on;
The waves are lifted to the stars; the oars
Are broken, and the prow slews round; the ship
Lies broadside on; a mountainous wall of water
Looms up, pours down: some ride the crest of the
          wave,
Some, in the trough, can see the boiling sand.
The South wind hurls three ships on the hidden
          rocks,

That sea-reef which Italians call The Altars;
The East takes three, sweeping them from the deep
On shoal and quicksand; over the stern of one
Before Aeneas' eyes, a great sea falls,
Washing the helmsman overboard; the ship
Whirls thrice in the same water, and goes down
In a devouring whirlpool; here and there
A few survivors swim, the Lycian men
Whose captain was Orontes: now their arms,
Their Trojan treasures, float with the broken
    timbers
Tossed on the waves. The storm, victorious,
Takes over other ships; Achates yields,
Abas, Aletes, Ilioneus,
Receive the hostile water; the walls are broken,
The enemy pours in.                [102–123]

[Orontes' ship is the only one actually lost; the others, making bad weather of it, and becoming separated, nevertheless manage to pull through. At this point Neptune, aware of the turmoil, and resentful of Aeolus' presumption in his domain, summons the winds to him, denounces them, and calms the storm for smooth sailing, but the fleet is too battered to try to run on to Italy. They turn south to the Libyan coast, and Vergil makes the most of the description of the harbor, by way of contrast with the storm. Both passages should be read aloud in the Latin, to note the differences in the cadence, the vowel music, the rage, on the one hand, of the line's break and roar and dart, and, on the other, the peace, the murmur, the barely perceptible rise and fall. The English can barely hint what the Latin brings out.]

There's a place, in a bay's deep curve, where the
    water lies
Unrippled even. A little island keeps
The sea-swell off, and the waves break on its sides,
And slide back harmless. The great cliffs come
    down
Steep to deep water, and the background shim-
    mers,
Darkens, and shines, the tremulous aspen moving
And the dark fir pointing still. And there is a
    cave
Under the overhanging rocks, alive
With water running fresh, a home of the Nymphs,
With benches for them, out of the living stone.
No anchor is needed here for the weary ships,
No mooring-cable. Aeneas brings them in,

Seven weary vessels, and the men are glad
To be ashore again, to feel dry sand
Under the salt-stained limbs. Achates strikes
The spark from the flint, catches the fire on the
    leaves,
Adds chips and kindling, blows and fans the
    flame,
And they bring out the soaked and salty corn,
The hand-mills, stone and mortar, and make
    ready
To crush and grind and heat the salvaged bread.
                                   [159–179]

[Meanwhile Aeneas climbs a peak to see if he can catch sight of any of the other thirteen ships; he sees none, but he and Achates do sight a herd of deer, and manage to slay seven, one for each of the surviving vessels. Some wine has also been salvaged, and after rationing out the venison and wine, Aeneas, for the second time in the narrative, opens his lips to speak.]

"O comrades, we have been through evil things
Together before this; you have been through
    worse,
Scylla, Charybdis, and the Cyclops' dwelling,
The sounding rocks; this, too, the god will end.
Recall the nerve; dismiss the fear, the gloom.
Someday, perhaps, even remembering this
Will be a pleasure. We are going on,
Through whatsoever chance and change, until
We come to Latium, where the fates point out
A quiet dwelling-place, and Troy restored.
Endure, and keep yourself for better times."
Speaking, he kept his sorrow in his heart,
Wearing, for them, a mask of hopefulness,
And they were ready for feasting. Part lay bare
The flesh from the torn hides, part cut the meat
Impaling it, still quivering, on spits,
Setting the kettles, keep the water boiling,
And strong with food again, sprawling stretched
    out
On comfortable grass, they take their fill
Of bread and meat and wine, until their hunger
Is gone, and the board cleared. And then they
    talk
For a long time, of where their comrades are,
Are, or may be, hopeful, and doubtful, both.
Can they believe them living, or would a cry
Fall on deaf ears forever! All those captains,
Brave Gyas, brave Cloanthus, Amycus,

Lycus, Orontes—in his secret heart
Aeneas mourns them.                    [198–222]

[The scene abruptly changes from the earthiness of this little cove to the spaciousness of the sky. Venus, anxious for her favored Trojans, pleads with Jupiter for reassurance as to their destiny and that of her son. The reassurance is given; Jupiter, in detailed prophecy foretells not only the immediate success in Italy of Aeneas and his heirs, but the eternal greatness of the Rome to be. He orders Mercury to earth to instruct Dido, queen of Carthage, to give the Trojans a favorable welcome, and the next day when Achates and Aeneas are reconnoitering, Venus, disguised as a native huntress, adds further information as to Dido's early history, and urges them to go on to her court, prophesying further that they will be reunited with their missing companions. So encouraged, they go on, presently come upon the wonderful activity of the construction of Carthage, and are particularly heartened by finding on the temple walls reproductions of scenes of the fighting around Troy. Venus has cast around them a protective cloud, so that they cannot be seen, but they see Dido directing the work, and then, to their great happiness, they see their own companions, with Ilioneus as spokesman, make their appeal to the queen for permission to repair the fleet until they can find Aeneas, or go on without him. The queen receives them with more than hospitality; the cloud around Aeneas and Achates dissolves, so that Aeneas' appearance is a highly dramatic one; he addresses Dido with warm gratitude, and, in view of events to come, not without unconscious irony.]

"You seek me; here I am,
Trojan Aeneas, saved from the Libyan waves.
Worn out by all the perils of land and sea,
In need of everything, blown over the great world,
A remnant left by the Greeks, Dido, we lack
The means to thank our only pitier
For offer of a city and a home.
If there is justice anywhere, if goodness
Means anything to any power, if gods
At all regard good people, may they give
The great rewards you merit. Happy the age,
Happy the parents who have brought you forth!
While rivers run to sea, while shadows move

Over the mountains, while the stars burn on,
Always, your praise, your honor, and your name,
Whatever land I go to, will endure."
                                      [595–610]

[Dido responds graciously, adding the further information that her father Belus had entertained their ancestor Teucer; she bids Aeneas enter the palace, and sends great quantities of meat to the crews at the shore. Preparations are made for a banquet in the palace; Aeneas sends Achates back to the ships to summon his son Ascanius, and orders him to bring gifts. At this point, Venus plans a new stratagem; distrusting Dido's hospitality, since she is under Juno's protection, she proposes to substitute Cupid for Ascanius, so that Dido will fall in love with Aeneas.]

Achates led the way, and Cupid came
Obedient to his mother, bringing gifts.
The queen receives them, on a golden couch
Below the royal tapestries. The spreads
Of crimson wait Aeneas and his Trojans.
Servants bring water for their hands, and bread
In baskets, and fine napkins. At the fire
Are fifty serving-maids, to set the feast,
A hundred more, girls, and a hundred boys,
To load the tables, and bring the goblets round.
And through the happy halls the Tyrians throng,
Admire the Trojan gifts, admire Iulus,
The young god with the glowing countenance,
The charming words, the robe, the saffron veil
Edged with acanthus. More than all the rest,
Disaster-bound, the unhappy queen takes fire,
And cannot have enough of looking, moved
By gifts and boy alike. She watches him
Cling to his father's neck, and come to her
For fondling, and her eyes, her heart receive him,
Alas, poor queen, not knowing what a god
Is plotting for her sorrow. He remembers
What Venus said, and she forgets a little
About Sychaeus; the heart unused to love
Stirs with a living passion.

When the first quiet settled over the tables,
And the boards were cleared, they set the great
        bowls down,
Crowning the wine with garlands. A great hum
Runs through the halls, the voices reach the rafters;
The burning lamps below the fretted gold,

The torches flaring, put the night to rout.
The queen commands the loving-cup of Belus,
Heavy with gems and gold, and fills it full,
And silence fills the hall before her prayer,
"Jupiter, giver of laws for host and guest,
Grant this to be a happy day for all,
Both Tyrians and travellers from Troy,
And something for our children to remember!
May Bacchus, giver of joy, attend, and Juno
Be kind, and all my Tyrians be friendly!"
She poured libation on the table, touched
The gold rim with her lips, passed on the bowl
To Bitias, who dived deep; and other lords
Took up the challenge. And a minstrel played
A golden lyre, Iopas, taught by Atlas.
Of the sun's labors and the wandering moon
He sang, whence came the race of beast and man,
Whence rain and fire, the stars and constella-
    tions,
Why suns in winter hasten to the sea,
Or what delay draws out the dawdling nights.
The Tyrians roar, applauding, and the Trojans
Rejoice no less, and the poor queen prolongs
The night with conversation, drinking deep
Of her long love, and asking many questions
Of Priam, Hector; of the arms of Memnon;
How big Achilles was; and Diomedes,
What were his horses like? "Tell us, my guest,"
She pleads, "from the beginning, all the tale,
The treachery of the Greeks, the wanderings,
The perils, of the seven tiresome years."
                                    [695–756]

[The contrast of the splendid luxury and richness of this scene, as compared with the simple
picnic on the landing in the peaceful cove is a
fine instance of Vergil's delight in balanced music
and imagery, as the impersonal astronomic and
philosophic song of the long-haired Iopas forms
an introduction to the story of actual human and
down-to-earth suffering in the account about to
be given by Aeneas. I am not sure whether other
people would think so, but I suspect Vergil has
intentionally had Dido make a couple of slight
*gaffes*—the summoning of Juno in the midst of
her prayer, and the use of the adjective *bona*
(kind), at which I think the Trojans must have
stirred a little uncomfortably; and the unfortunate references to Achilles and Diomedes, both of
whom had conquered Aeneas in battle. Really,

now, how big was Achilles? So that, in addition
to the obvious plot of Venus and Cupid, there is
just a trace of uneasiness in all the revelry.]

## Book II

[In the second book, Aeneas tells Dido the
story of the fall of Troy. The Greeks have
ostensibly sailed away, leaving behind them the
huge image of the wooden horse, inside which
chosen warriors have been concealed. The story
goes that it is a votive offering for their safe
return; some of the Trojans argue that it should
be immediately appropriated and lodged inside
the city; others argue for its destruction. Conspicuous among these is Laocoön, priest of Neptune—"I fear the Greeks even when they are
bringing gifts." He hurls his spear into the side
of the effigy, but the crowd pays little heed, for
at this point a Greek trickster, named Sinon, is
haled into their midst. He tells them a long story,
with calculated pauses for suspense, and subtle
appeals to their prejudices as well as their mercy,
making them think he is being persecuted by
Ulysses, and that the best thing they can do to
spite and foil the Greeks is to take in the horse.
They seem very gullible, and any skeptics among
them are dumbfounded by the destruction of
Laocoön and his two sons by twin serpents who
come in from the sea, kill the three, and glide to
safety under Minerva's shield. The horse is
brought in amid happy celebration; the Greek
fleet returns from Tenedos during the night.
Sinon lets out the warriors. Aeneas, sleeping like
the rest, is visited in a dream by the ghost of
Hector, who warns him to flee Troy, taking the
household gods and sacred objects; the city is
doomed. Waking, Aeneas pays no heed to this
warning; he climbs to the roof of his house for
a view of the city, descends to enter the fighting,
and is met by a neighbor whose alarming news
would seem to confirm the warnings of the dream.
Nevertheless Aeneas assembles a small band, determined to sell their lives dearly; they meet with
some success at first, strip their Greek victims,
and put on their armor, and their success continues until one of their number, a youth named
Coroebus, is driven desperate at the sight of
Cassandra being dragged off by the Greeks. He
rushes to her rescue, the trick is discovered, and

the Trojans are slain. A terrific fight rages at Priam's palace, to which Aeneas makes his way; a band of Trojans fight from the roof-top, where Aeneas remains during the murder of Priam by Achilles' son Pyrrhus. Aeneas finds, presently, that his comrades have gone from the roof-top (perhaps to aid Priam?), and he is thinking of making his way back to his own home to rescue his wife, son, and father, when he catches sight of Helen clinging, most ironically, to the altar of Vesta for sanctuary. Anger blazes up in him, and he is thinking of killing her, but an image of his mother Venus warns him to desist, lifts the cloud of murk that hangs low over the burning city and shows him the gods at work alongside the Greeks in the destruction of Troy. Reaching his home, Aeneas finds his father stubborn in his refusal to leave; he is too old, says Anchises, and paralyzed besides; he would rather die as Priam has. The entreaties of Ascanius, Creusa, and Aeneas are vain; but a sudden portent, thunder on the left, a comet blazing across the sky, and the appearance of a tongue of fire on the head of Iulus alter his determination. Aeneas takes Anchises on his shoulders, leading the boy; Creusa follows behind, is lost in the confusion, and in spite of Aeneas' return and desperate search, she does not reappear. A phantom of her appears to Aeneas, saying that all is well, and will be, for her; that for Aeneas a new bride waits in the western land, and he is to go on. He finds a great band of Trojans gathered at the meeting place, and with morning, makes his way with the refugees, his son, and his father, to the high mountains.

The coloring of the book is dark and somber: painting would make use of midnight blues, blacks, purples, crimsons, with occasional splashes of orange fire; music would take it slow and fortissimo, with occasional rapid staccato passages, and the brasses reaching high and shrill, possibly a melodic interlude for the wood-winds bringing the fleet back from Tenedos, *per amica silentia lunae*, a joyful chorus of the children's voices as they lead the horse into the city with rejoicing, an obligato of dissonance to accompany the lying recitative of Sinon, and some chance for the strings, and especially the cellos, to brood and cry their hearts out over the lost Creusa.]

## Book III

[Book III tells the story of the wanderings. A fleet is built at Antandros at the foot of Mount Ida, and the Trojans first sail north to Thrace. They found a city which they call Aeneadae (The *National Geographic*'s maps show a town called Enez, in the vicinity, which may preserve the original name), but they are driven out of here by an evil omen, a bleeding thicket at the grave of their kinsman Polydorus, who had been murdered there and left unburied. They turn south, stop at the holy island of Delos, and are told, oracularly, to seek their ancient mother. Anchises interprets this as meaning Crete, from where Teucer came (the oracle addressed them as *Sons of Dardanus*, which might have given them a hint, but the Trojans, at times, it seems, can be singularly obtuse.) In Crete they also attempt a settlement, but a pestilence puts an end to that. They think of returning to Delos for a new consultation with the oracle of Apollo there, but are spared the trouble when the household gods appear to Aeneas in a dream and tell him about Dardanus and the western land called Italy. Consultation with Anchises confirms Aeneas in the belief that this is sound advice to follow; they leave again, pull into islands called Strophades after a dismal experience with storm and fog, and as they are eating, are attacked by the Harpies. They fight back, and are denounced by the Harpies with the horrible threat that though they will reach Italy they will be so hungry they will have to eat their tables. They go on northward along the coast of Greece, giving Ithaca a wide berth, and presently reach the city of Buthrotum, where they find old friends, Helenus, son of Priam, now married to Andromache. The reunion is rather mournful, but there is hospitality and entertainment for the Trojans, and Helenus gives them a long prophecy of things to come: their voyage to Italy may be longer than they think, for they must steer south again, not directly across the Ionian sea, turn the peninsula, and find their landing on the western shore. They must appease Juno by every means in their power; they had better round Sicily rather than risk the straits between Scylla and Charybdis; and they must, on reaching a place called Cumae, consult there Apollo's priestess, who will unfold to them what they need know of their future in Italy. They sail on, sight Italy, land on the coast of Sicily, and there a very curious incident occurs. They are met by a ragged Greek, who flings himself at their feet, begs for mercy and death at their hands, tells them his name, Achaemenides, admits that he fought against the Trojans, and was a companion of Ulysses. He tells a horrible story of how his companions were devoured by a man-eating giant named Polyphemus, how Ulysses finally contrived an escape, and how he himself was abandoned, whether by accident or design he does not imply. The Trojans, apparently, are not at all reminded of Sinon's overtures; they pardon him immediately, and apparently take him along with them in their panic flight at the appearance of the now blind giant Polyphemus, stumbling along in that wonderful heavy onomatopoetic line, with the clump most of the way, and the trip at the end: *"Monstrum horrendum informe ingens cui lumen ademptum."* In their first rush they head back toward Scylla and Charybdis again, but get straightened out, round Sicily, eventually reaching Drepanum, where Anchises dies. They are leaving Sicily, on their way north to Italy, as they hope, when they are overtaken by the storm recounted in the first book of the epic.

Book III, by contrast with II, is staged, most of it, in daylight and the outdoors. It is a sort of timetable book, with not much more interest than a timetable has; only Book VIII, in my opinion, is anywhere near it for dullness. Perhaps it is Dido's fault; the hour was late, Aeneas reminded her, when he began the story, and perhaps he is running down. I think there must have been some yawning by the long-haired Iopas and a few others, Tyrians and Trojans alike. Aeneas takes very little part in the action; he is handed along, from one portent of Apollo to another: Anchises is more prominent than he. Artistically, it may be that this brings in the theme of Book IX, in which Aeneas does not appear at all; Iulus takes the spotlight, and Apollo also comes in as mentor.]

## Book IV

### DIDO'S PASSION AND DEATH

But the queen finds no rest. Deep in her veins
The wound is fed; she burns with hidden fire.

His manhood, and the glory of his race,
Are an obsession with her, like the sound
Of his voice, or the way he looks. By morning,
After a restless night, she seeks her sister:
"I am troubled, Anna, doubtful, terrified,
Or am I dreaming? What new guest is this
Come to our shores? how well he talks, how brave
He seems in heart and action! I suppose
It must be true; he does come from the gods.
Fear proves a bastard spirit. He has been
So buffeted by fate. What endless wars
He told of! Sister, I must tell you something:
Were not my mind made up, once and for all,
Never again to marry, having been
So lost when Sychaeus left me for the grave,
Slain by my murderous brother at the altar,
Were I not sick forever of the torch
And bridal bed, here is the only man
Who has moved my spirit, shaken my weak will.
I might have yielded to him. I recognize
The marks of an old fire. But I pray, rather,
That earth engulf me, lightning strike me down
To the pale shades and everlasting night
Before I break the laws of decency.
My love has gone with Sychaeus; let him keep it,
Keep it with him forever in the grave."
She ended with a burst of tears. "Dear sister,
Dearer than life," Anna replied, "why must you
Grieve all your youth away in loneliness,
Not know sweet children, or the joys of love?
Is that what dust demands, and buried shadows?
So be it. You have kept your resolution
From Tyre to Libya, proved it by denying
Iarbas and a thousand other suitors
From Africa's rich kingdoms. Think a little.
Whose lands are these you settle in? Getulians,
Invincible in war, the wild Numidians,
Unfriendly Syrtes, ring us round, and a desert
Barren with drought, and the Barcaean rangers.
Why should I mention Tyre, and wars arising
Out of Pygmalion's threats? And you, my sister,
Why should you fight against a pleasing passion?
I think the gods have willed it so, and Juno
Has helped to bring the Trojan ships to Carthage.
What a great city, sister, what a kingdom
This might become, rising on such a marriage!
Carthage and Troy together in arms, what glory
Shall not be ours? Only invoke the blessing
Of the great gods, make sacrifice, be lavish
In welcome, keep them here while the fierce
    winter

Rages at sea, and cloud and sky are stormy,
And ships still wrecked and broken." [1–53]

[Anna's practical way of looking at the matter encourages Dido: the sisters are careful to attend the shrines and invoke peace; Dido is scrupulous in making offerings, and seeks further reassurance by consulting the omens.]

Alas, poor blind interpreters! What woman
In love is helped by offerings, or altars?
Soft fire consumes the marrowbones, the silent
Wound grows, deep in the heart.
Unhappy Dido burns, and wanders, burning,
All up and down the city, the way a deer
With a hunter's careless arrow in her flank
Ranges the uplands, with the shaft still clinging
To the hurt side. She takes Aeneas with her
All through the town, displays the wealth of Sidon,
Buildings projected; starts to speak, and falters,
And at the end of day renews the banquet,
Is wild to hear the story, over and over,
Hangs on each word, until the late moon, sinking,
Sends them all home. The stars die out, but Dido
Lies brooding in the empty hall alone,
Abandoned on a lonely couch. She hears him,
Sees him, or sees and hears Ascanius in him,
Fondles the boy, as if that ruse might fool her,
Deceived by his resemblance to his father.
The towers no longer rise, the youth are slack
In drill for arms, the cranes and derricks rusting,
Walls halt halfway to heaven. [65–88]

[At this point Juno indignantly accosts Venus, saying, in effect, "A fine thing!" But she realizes she might as well make the best of matters, and suggests to Venus that Aeneas remain in Carthage, marry Dido, and rule jointly. This, Venus suspects, is a plot to divert the destiny of Rome, but she dissembles, intimating to Juno that it is all right with her if it is all right with the Fates, and leaving it to Juno to work out the ways and means. Juno is ready with a scheme, that on the next day's hunting party she will cause a storm, Aeneas and Dido will be driven to seek refuge in a near-by cave, and she will see to it that a marriage ceremony will hallow their union. Venus does not oppose this proposition, but she obviously has mental reservations.]

Dawn, rising, left the ocean, and the youth
Come forth from all the gates, prepared for hunting,
Nets, toils, wide spears, keen-scented coursing hounds.
She keeps the riders waiting; her own charger
Stands bright in gold and crimson; the bit foams,
The impatient head is tossed. At last she comes,
With a great train attending, gold and crimson,
Quiver of gold, and combs of gold, and mantle
Crimson with golden buckle. A Trojan escort
Attends her, with Iulus, and Aeneas
Comes to her side, more lordly than Apollo
Bright along Delos' ridges in the springtime
With laurel in his hair and golden weapons
Shining across his shoulders. Equal radiance
Is all around Aeneas, equal splendor.
They reach the mountain heights, and the hiding-places
Where no trail runs; wild goats from the rocks are started,
Run down the ridges; somewhere else, in the open,
Deer cross the dusty plain, away from the mountains.
The boy Ascanius, in the midst of the valley,
Is glad he has so good a horse, rides, dashing,
Past one group or another: deer are cowards,
And wild-goats tame; he prays for some excitement,
A tawny lion coming down the mountain,
Or a great boar with foaming mouth. . . .
                                        The heaven
Darkens, and thunder rolls, and rain and hail
Come down in torrents. The hunt is all for shelter,
Trojans and Tyrians and Ascanius dashing
Wherever they can; the streams pour down the mountains.
To the same cave go Dido and Aeneas,
Where Juno, as a bridesmaid, gives the signal,
And earth and fires of heaven alike bear witness,
And mountain-nymphs wail high their incantations,
First day of death, first cause of evil. Dido
Is unconcerned with fame, with reputation,
With how it seems to others. This is marriage
For her, not hole-and-corner guilt; she covers
Her folly with this name. [129–172]

[Whatever you think happened in the cave—and one scholar has a theory that nothing, so to speak, happens—what you might expect to happen does, namely that Rumor, personified by Vergil in an excellent description, goes flying all over the place. It is not long before she comes to Iarbas, a scorned suitor of Dido's, and you may be sure there are no understatements in her approach. He is a very rich monarch, rather ostentatious in the lavishness with which he has been a worshipper of Jupiter, and in his indignation feels that all this worship has been a great waste of time on his part, if not an actual swindle on Jupiter's. He does not ask Jupiter to do something about it, he tells him, in a wonderful burst of indignant rhetoric—*Maeonia mentum mitra crinemque madentem* is a marvelous line, not only for the scathing imagery, but in its sound of grievance, the vowel sounds of anger, the m's and n's humming, and the d's and t's spluttering with rage.

It takes him very little time to get action, for Jupiter immediately summons Mercury and tells him to go promptly to Carthage and order Aeneas to get out of there quickly and be about his business. Mercury acts with dispatch.]

Soon as the winged sandals skim the roof-tops
He sees Aeneas founding towers, building
New homes for Tyrians; and his sword is starred
With yellow jasper; he wears across his shoulders
A cloak of burning crimson, which golden threads
Run through, the royal gift of the rich queen.
Mercury wastes no time: "What are you doing,
Forgetful of your kingdom and your fortunes,
Building for Carthage? Woman-crazy fellow!
The ruler of the gods, the great compeller
Of heaven and earth, has sent me from Olympus
With no more word than this: what are you doing,
With what ambition wasting time in Libya?
If your own fame and fortune count as nothing,
Think of Ascanius at least, whose kingdom
In Italy, whose Roman land, are waiting
As promise justly due." He spoke, and vanished
Into thin air. Appalled, amazed, Aeneas
Is stricken dumb; his hair stands up in terror,
His voice sticks in his throat. He is more than
  eager
To flee that pleasant land, awed by the warning
Of the divine command. But how to do it?
How get around that passionate queen? What
  opening
Try first? His mind runs out in all directions,

Shifting and veering. Finally, he has it,
Or thinks he has: he calls his comrades to him,
The leaders, bids them quietly prepare
The fleet for voyage, meanwhile saying nothing
About the new activity; since Dido
Is unaware, has no idea that passion
As strong as theirs is on the verge of breaking,
He will see what he can do, find the right moment
To let her know, all in good time. Rejoicing,
The captains move to carry out the orders.
                                    [259-295]

[This beautifully normal masculine temporizing, however, works no more than it ever does, for Dido anticipates the project, Rumor exaggerates the news, and she tears into Aeneas bitterly: "Did you expect to sneak out of here without saying a word to me, betrayer that you are?" And from there she goes on, in anything but a regal manner, pleading with him to change his mind. Aeneas replies, with such dignity as is possible in the situation, rather austerely and coldly to begin with, telling her, among other things, that he never claimed to be married to her anyway. He quotes the orders brought him by Mercury, and ends with directly telling her off: "Cease to inflame yourself and me with your complaints; I am not going to Italy because I want to." She turns on him, then, in absolute fury, sarcastically flinging the words of Jupiter and Mercury in his face, calling down curses on his voyage, and leaves him, never to address him again in this world.

Aeneas is a little upset, but the preparations go on: Dido has evidently hoped against hope that Aeneas might change his mind, for the actual sight of the activity breaks down her resolution. She makes one more, quite abject, appeal, this time not in person, but through Anna, begging Aeneas, not to stay for good, but merely to put off his departure a little while, so that she can become more reconciled to the parting. This business of cutting the dog's tail off an inch at a time has no appeal to Aeneas; Vergil gives him credit for feeling very sorry, and all that, but just the same he is going, and immediately.]

Then Dido prays for death at last; the Fates
Are terrible, her luck is out, she is tired
Of gazing at the everlasting heaven.
The more to goad her will to die, she sees—
O horrible!—the holy water blacken,

Libations turn to blood, on ground and altar,
When she makes offerings. But she tells no one,
Not even her sister. From the marble shrine,
Memorial to her former lord, attended
Always by her with honor, fleece, and garland,
She hears his voice, his words, her husband
    calling
When darkness holds the world, and from the
    house-top
The owl sends out the long funereal wailing,
And she remembers warnings of old seers,
Fearful, foreboding. In her dreams Aeneas
Appears to hunt her down; or she is going
Alone, in a lost country, wandering,
Trying to find her Tyrians, mad as Pentheus,
Or frenzied as Orestes, when his mother
Is after him with whips of snakes and firebrands,
While the Avengers menace at the threshold.
                                    [450–473]

[With her mind made up to die, she conceals
her intent from Anna, telling her only that she
has a scheme which will either bring Aeneas
back to her, or release her from him forever.
The plan is to construct a funeral pyre in the
middle of the courtyard, to burn on it every last
relic of Aeneas, and to appeal, for the proper
charms and spells, to a Massylian priestess and
worker in magic. In thus regressing from religion to magic, Dido feels some compulsion to
offer apologies to Anna; the latter, without any
undue exercise of her imagination, complies with
the queen's wishes.]

The pyre is raised in the court; it towers high
With pine and holm-oak, it is hung with garlands
And funeral wreaths, and on the couch she places
Aeneas' sword, his garments, and his image,
Knowing the outcome. Round about are altars,
Where, with her hair let loose, the priestess calls
On thrice a hundred gods, Erebus, Chaos,
Hecate, queen of Hell, triple Diana.
Water is sprinkled, from Avernus' fountain,
Or said to be, and herbs are sought, by moon-
    light
Mown with bronze sickles, and the stem-ends
    running
With a black milk, and the caul of a colt, new-
    born.
Dido, with holy meal and holy hands,
Stands at the altar, with one sandal loosened,

And robes unfastened, calls the gods to witness,
Prays to the stars that know her doom, in-
    voking,
Beyond them, any powers, if there are any,
Who care for lovers in unequal bondage.
    Night; and tired creatures over all the world
Were seeking slumber; woods and the wild waters
Were quiet; and the silent stars were wheeling,
Their course half over; every field was still:
The beasts of the field, the brightly colored birds,
Dwellers in lake and pool, in thorn and thicket,
Slept through the tranquil night, their sorrows
    over,
Their worry soothed. But no such blessed dark-
    ness
Closes the eyes of Dido; no repose
Comes to her anxious heart. Her pangs redouble,
Her love swells up, surging, a great tide rising
Of wrath and doubt and passion. "What do I do?
What now? Go back to my Numidian suitors,
Be scorned by those I scorned? pursue the Tro-
    jans,
Obey their orders? they were grateful to me
Once, I remember. But who would let them take
    me,
Suppose they would? They hate me now; they
    were always
Deceivers; is Laomedon forgotten,
Whose blood runs through their veins? What
    then? Attend them,
Alone, be their companion, loud-mouthed sailors?
Or with my own armada follow after,
Wear out my sea-worn Tyrians once more
With vengeance and adventure? Better die.
Die, you deserve to; and the hurt with the sword.
It is your fault, Anna; you were sorry for me,
Won over by my tears; you put this load
Of evil on me. It was not permitted,
It seems, for me to live apart from wedlock,
A blameless life. An animal does better.
I vowed Sychaeus faith. I have been faithless."
So, through the night, she tossed in restless tor-
    ment.
    Meanwhile Aeneas, on the lofty stern,
All things prepared, sure of his going, slumbers
As Mercury comes down once more to warn him,
Familiar blond young god: "O son of Venus,
Is this a time for sleep? The wind blows fair,
And danger rises all around you. Dido,
Certain to die, however else uncertain,
Plots treachery, harbors evil. Seize the moment

While it can still be seized, and hurry, hurry!
The sea will swarm with ships, the fiery torches
Blaze, and the shore rankle with fire, by morn-
ing.
Shove off, be gone. A shifty, fickle object
Is woman, always." He dissolved in night.
[504–570]

[So Aeneas hurriedly wakes, gives the orders,
and the Trojans very happily and in a great rush
are on their way. The queen from her watch-
tower, as the first light whitens, sees the actual
event at last, and breaks out into her most hysterical soliloquy, wild with broken rhythms, full
of sadistic fantasies of vengeances she might
and should have taken, culminating in the famous
curse.]

"Great Sun, surveyor of all the works of earth,
Juno, to whom my sorrows are committed,
Hecate, whom the crossroads of the cities
Wail to by night, avenging Furies, hear me,
Grant me divine protection, take my prayer.
If he must come to harbor, then he must,
If Jove ordains it, however vile he is,
False, and unspeakable. If Jove ordains,
The goal is fixed. So be it. Hear my prayer.
Let him be driven by arms and war, an exile,
Let him be taken from his son Iulus,
Let him beg for aid, let him see his people dying
Unworthy deaths, let him accept surrender
On unfair terms, never enjoy the kingdom,
The hoped-for light, let him fall and die, un-
timely,
Let him lie unburied on the sand. O, hear me,
Hear the last prayer, poured out with my last
blood.
And you, O Tyrians, hate, and hate forever
The Trojan stock. Offer my dust this homage.
No love, no peace, between these nations, ever!
Rise from my bones, O great unknown avenger,
Hunt them with fire and sword, the Dardan set-
tlers,
Now, then, here, there, wherever strength is given.
Shore against shore, wave against wave, and war,
War after war, for all the generations."
[607–629]

[With this curse delivered, she calls to an attendant Barce, asking her to bring Anna so that
the proposed rites may be accomplished and witnessed; but the nurse has no sooner left on the
errand than she mounts the funeral pyre, unsheathing the sword of Aeneas. In her final words
she has come through her hysteria and frenzy
to a summing-up of great control and dignity.]

Spoils that were sweet while gods and fate per-
mitted,
Receive my spirit, set me free from sorrows.
I have lived, I have run the course that Fortune
gave me,
And now my shade, a great one, will be going
Below the earth. I have built a noble city,
I have seen my walls, I have avenged a husband,
Punished a hostile brother. I have been
Happy, I might have been too happy, only
The Trojans made their landing." She broke off,
weeping,
Face down, and rose, and cried: "So, we shall die,
Die, unavenged; but let us die. So, so,
I am glad to meet the darkness. Let his eyes
Behold this fire across the sea, an omen
Of my death going with him." [651–662]

[She stabs herself with the sword. Rumor goes
rioting through the city; Anna and the rest of the
household come running with shrieking and lamentation as Dido dies a difficult death.]

She tried to raise her heavy eyes, failed, fell,
And her wound made a gurgling hissing sound;
Three times she tried to lift herself, three times
Fell back; her rolling eyes went searching heaven,
And the light hurt when found. In pity, Juno
Sent Iris from Olympus, with compassion
For the long moaning agony, to free her
From the limbs' writhing and the struggling spirit.
She had not earned this death, she had only
sought it
Before her time, driven by sudden madness.
Therefore the Queen of Hades had not taken
The golden lock, consigning her to Orcus.
So Iris, dewy on saffron wings, descending,
Trailing a thousand colors through the brightness
Comes down the sky, poises above her, saying
"This lock I take as bidden, and from the body
Release the soul," and cuts the lock; and cold
Takes over, and the winds receive the spirit.
[688–705]

## Book V

### THE FUNERAL GAMES FOR ANCHISES

[Bound north again from Carthage, the Trojans land on the west coast of Sicily to celebrate the anniversary of Anchises' death with funeral games. The fifth is a sunshiny, outdoor book, the gayest of the entire Aeneid, and, in my opinion, the most underpraised. Contrasting with the gloomy speculations and the knowledge as to what trouble a passionate woman can stir up, the rough masculine horseplay, the rhubarbs and beefs, relieve the tension: toward the end of the book the serious theme, *Tantae molis erat Romanam condere gentem*, comes in again with the burning of the ships, and the loss of the pilot Palinurus.

The first of the games is a boat race, won by Cloanthus in the *Scylla*; Mnestheus in the *Pristis* second, Gyas in the *Chimaera* a bad third, and Sergestus in the *Centaur* dead last. The boys get a few laughs out of booing Sergestus, who has piled up on the rocks, and more out of the predicament of Gyas' pilot Menoetes, who has been heaved overboard by his captain in a fine fit of temper. The second contest is a foot race.]

The boat race over, Aeneas makes his way
To a grassy plain, with wooded hills surrounding
The racecourse in the valley. All the crowd
Come trooping after, group themselves around
The central prominence. Rewards and prizes
Draw the competitors, travellers and natives,
Trojans, Sicilians; in the foremost ranks
Are Nisus and Euryalus, the latter
Conspicuous in the flower of youth and beauty,
Whom Nisus follows with entire devotion:
Diores, of the royal house of Priam,
Was ready, Salius, an Acarnanian,
Patron, Tegean-born, and two Sicilians,
Panopes, Helymus, trained to the forests,
Companions of Acestes; and many others
Whose fame by now the darkness hides. Aeneas
Speaks to their hope: "No one goes unrewarded:
To each I give two Cretan arrows, gleaming
With polished steel, and a double-bitted axe
Embossed with silver. Everybody wins
These prizes, but the first three runners also
Shall wear the wreath of olive, and the winner

Ride home a horse equipped with splendid trappings;
For second place, an Amazonian quiver
With Thracian arrows, a broad belt of gold
With a jeweled buckle; and this Argive helmet
For the one who comes in third."
                                    They take their places,
And when the signal is given, away they go,
Like rain from storm cloud, bodies leaning forward,
Eyes on the goal. And for the lead it's Nisus,
Swifter than winds or lightning; running second,
A good way back, comes Salius, and the third one,
Third, at some distance, is Euryalus,
Helymus next; right on his heels Diores,
There's a little crowding there, the course too narrow,
Diores, full of run, is in a pocket,
He can't get through. The race is almost over,
Their breath comes hard, they are almost at the finish—
There's a pool of blood on the ground, where the slain bullocks
Fell in the sacrifice, a slippery puddle
Red on green ground, and Nisus does not see it,
Nisus, still leading, thinking himself the winner,
Is out of luck, his feet slide out from under,
He wobbles, totters, recovers himself a little,
Slips, and goes forward, in a beautiful header
Through blood and mud. But he keeps his wits about him,
Does not forget his friend Euryalus; rising,
And sort of accidentally on purpose,
Gets in the way of Salius and spills him
A cartwheel, head over heels on the flying sand.
Euryalus flashes past, an easy winner
Thanks to his friend's assistance, and they cheer him;
Helymus second; in third place, Diores.

Immediately there's a loud howl of protest,
Salius shrieking in the elders' faces
With cries of "Foul!" and "Outrage!" "I was robbed,
Give me first prize!" But all the popular favor
Sides with Euryalus, who is young, and weeping,
And better-looking, and Diores backs him,
Loudly, of course, since who would get the helmet
If Salius is first? Aeneas ends it,

"The race will stand as run; you get your prizes
As first proposed, no one will change the order;
But one thing I can do, and will do—offer
A consolation to our innocent friend."
With this, he gives a lion skin to Salius,
Heavy with shaggy hair, and the claws gilded.
Nisus is heard from: "If you're giving prizes
For falling down, what's good enough for Nisus?
I would have won it surely, only Fortune
Gave me the same bad deal she handed Salius!"
And with the words he made some kind of gesture
Showing his muddy face. Aeneas, laughing,
Ordered another prize, a shield for him,
The work of Didymaon, stolen by Greeks
From Neptune's temple sometime, but recovered.
A worthy prize for a distinguished hero.

Next is a boxing bout. "Whoever has courage
And fighting spirit in his heart, step forward,
And put the gloves on!" There are double prizes,
For the winner a bullock, decked with gold and
      ribbons,
A sword and splendid helmet for the loser.
Without delay, Dares gets up; a murmur
Runs through the crowd as this big man comes
      forward.
They know that he was Paris' sparring-partner,
And they recall his famous match with Butes
At Hector's tomb, where he knocked out that
      champion
And stretched him dying on the yellow sand.
Now Dares holds his head up for the battle,
Shakes his broad shoulders loose, warms up a
      little,
A left, a right, a left, in shadowboxing.
Who will oppose him? No one puts the gloves on,
No one, from all that throng, is in a hurry
To take on Dares. So, exultant, thinking
Himself a winner by default, he grabs
The bullock by one horn, says to Aeneas
"If no man, goddess-born, is taking chances,
How long must I keep standing here? how long
Hang around waiting? Give the order, let me
Lead home my prize!" The Trojans all applaud
      him.
But King Acestes, sprawling on the greensward
Beside Entellus, nudges him a little,
"What was the use, Entellus, of being a hero,
Or having been our bravest, under Eryx?
Where is that old Sicilian reputation,
And all those prizes hanging from the rafters?

Does Dares get away with this, no contest,
And all those prizes, and you sit here tamely?"
Entellus answers: "Oh, I still love glory
And praise; there's nothing the matter with my
      courage,
But I'm too old, the blood is slow and colder,
The strength not what it used to be. That bragger
Has one thing, youth, and how he revels in it!
If I had what he has, I'd not need prizes,
Bullocks or helmets either, to get me fighting."
From somewhere he produced the gloves of Eryx
And tossed them into the ring, all stiff and heavy,
Seven layers of hide, and insewn lead and iron.
The people stand amazed, and Dares shudders,
Wanting no part of gloves like these; Aeneas
Inspects them, turning them slowly, over and
      over,
And old Entellus adds a word of comment:
"Why, these are nothing! What if you had seen
The gloves of Hercules? He used to fight here.
These are the gloves that Eryx wore against him,
You still can see the blood and a splash of brains
That stained them long ago. I used to wear them
Myself when I was younger, and unchallenged
By time, that envious rival. But if Dares
Declines these arms, all right, make matters equal,
Don't be afraid, I waive the gloves of Eryx,
You put the Trojan gloves aside; Aeneas
Will see fair play, Acestes be my second."
He throws the double cloak from off his shoul-
      ders,
Stripped down to the great limbs, great bones,
      great muscles,
A giant in the ring. Aeneas brings them
Matched pairs of gloves.
                    They take their stand, each rising
On the balls of his feet, their arms upraised, and
      rolling
Their heads back from the punch. They spar, they
      lead,
They watch for openings. Dares, much the
      younger,
Is much the better in footwork; old Entellus
Has to rely on strength; his knees are shaky,
His wind not what it was. They throw their
      punches,
And many miss; and some, with a solid thump,
Land on the ribs or chest; temples and ears
Feel the wind of a miss, or the jaws rattle
When a punch lands. Entellus stands flat-footed,
Wasting no motion, just a slip of the body,

The watchful eyes alert. And Dares, feinting,
Like one who artfully attacks a city,
Tries this approach, then that, dancing around
    him
In varied vain attack. Entellus, rising,
Draws back his right (in fact, he telegraphs it),
And Dares, seeing it coming, slips aside.
Entellus lands on nothing but the wind
And, thrown off balance, heavily comes down
Flat on his face, as falls on Erymanthus
A thunder-smitten oak, and so on, and so on.
Roaring, the Trojans and Sicilians both
Rise to their feet; the noise goes up to heaven,
Acestes rushes in, to raise his comrade
In pity and sorrow. But that old-time fighter
Is not slowed down a bit, nor made more wary;
His rage is terrible, and his shame awakens
A consciousness of strength. He chases Dares
All over the ring, left, right, left, right, the
    punches
Rattle like hailstones on a roof; he batters Dares,
Spins him halfway around with one hand, clouts
    him
Straight with the other again. . . . At last Aeneas
Steps in and stops it, with a word of comfort
For the exhausted Dares: "Luckless fellow,
Yield to the god! What madness blinds your
    vision
To strength beyond your own?" They rescue
    Dares,
And drag him to the ships, with his knees caving,
Head rolling side to side, spitting out blood
And teeth; he hardly sees the sword and hel-
    met.
They leave the palm and bullock for Entellus,
Who, in the pride of victory, cries aloud,
"Look, goddess-born! Watch, Trojans, and dis-
    cover
Two things—how strong I was when I was
    younger,
And what a death you've kept away from Dares!"
And, with the word, he faced his prize, the bul-
    lock,
Drew back his right hand, poised it, sent it
    smashing
Between the horns, shattering the skull, and
    splashing
Brains on the bones, as the great beast comes
    down, lifeless.
"This life, a better one than Dares', Eryx,
I vow as sacrifice, and so, victorious,

Retire, and lay aside the gloves forever."
[286–484]

[The next event is an archery contest, rather
dull, because everybody is too good a shot, Hip-
pocoon hitting the mast to which the target, a
living dove, is tied, Menestheus hitting the cord,
Eurytion the flying dove; Acestes, with nothing
to shoot at, nevertheless looses his arrow, which
catches fire in the air, a prodigy sufficient to
bring him the prize without protest even from
Eurytion. Then there is an equestrian drill, led
by Ascanius, which is broken up by news of an
untoward incident: the Trojan women, who have
never been mentioned previously during the
story, have set fire to the ships, at the instigation
of Juno, who has sent down Iris disguised as an
old Trojan woman named Beroe to put them up
to this mischief. Ascanius dashes off to the rescue,
and the fire is put out, with the help of a rainfall
sent by Jupiter. Only four ships are destroyed,
but the situation is serious enough to call for a
council, at which the decision is reached to leave
the women and the weakest and weariest of the
men in Sicily, to found a town named Acesta after King Acestes. Aeneas is told by a vision of
Anchises to seek a meeting with him in the Lower
World before he attempts to found his Latian
city; Neptune gives Venus assurance that in return for one life the fleet shall reach Italy safely;
there is a nine-day period of prayer and feasting,
and finally, on a fine night with favorable breezes,
the fleet is under way.]

Fair breezes urge the fleet along the course
With Palinurus leading, and dewy night
Has reached mid-heaven, while the sailors, sleep-
    ing,
Relax on the hard benches under the oars,
All calm, all quiet. And the god of Sleep,
Parting the shadowy air, comes gently down,
Looking for Palinurus, bringing him,
A guiltless man, ill-omened dreams. He settles
On the high stern, a god disguised as man,
Speaking in Phorbas' guise, "O Palinurus,
The fleet rides smoothly in the even weather,
The hour is given for rest. Lay down the head,
Rest the tired eyes from toil. I will take over
A little while." But Palinurus, barely
Lifting his eyes, made answer: "Trust the waves,
However quiet? Trust a peaceful ocean?

Put faith in such a monster? Never! I
Have been too often fooled by the clear stars
To trust Aeneas to their faithless keeping."
And so he clung to the tiller, never loosed
His hand from the wood, his eyes from the bright
    heaven.
But lo, the god over his temples shook
A bough that dripped with dew from Lethe,
    steeped
With Stygian magic, so the swimming eyes,
Against his effort, close, blink open, close
Again, and slumber takes the drowsy limbs.
Bending above him, leaning over, the god
Shoves him, still clinging to the helm and calling
His comrades vainly, into the clear waves.
The god is gone, like a bird to the clear air,
And the fleet is going safely over its course
As Neptune promised. But the rocks were near,
The Siren-cliffs, most perilous of old,
White with the bones of many mariners,
Booming their hoarse eternal warning sound.
Aeneas starts from sleep, aware, somehow,
Of a lost pilot, and a vessel drifting,
Himself takes over guidance, with a sigh
And heartache for a friend's mishap. "Alas,
Too trustful in the calm of sea and sky,
O Palinurus, on an alien shore
You will be lying, naked."     [833–871]

### Book VI

#### THE UNDERWORLD

[Directing the fleet to Cumae, Aeneas, in compliance with earlier instructions, goes ashore,
proceeding immediately to the temple of Apollo,
over which the Sibyl, Deiphobe, presides. He
appeals to her for knowledge of the future, particularly urging that he may be allowed to enter
the lower world, through the portals of Avernus, and speak directly with Anchises. Her
prophecies about the future in Italy are por-
tentous and indicate much trouble ahead, but
there is a word of comfort in them, and she
grants that he may visit the shades.]

"Son of Anchises, from the line of gods,
By night, by day, the portals of dark Dis
Stand open; there's no trouble going down,
Down to Avernus. But to climb again,
To trace the steps back to the upper air,

There lies the task, the toil. A few, beloved
By Jupiter, descended from the gods,
A few, in whom exalting virtue burned,
Have been permitted. Around the central woods
The black Cocytus glides, a sullen stream,
But if such love is in your heart, such longing
For double crossing of the Stygian lake,
For double sight of Tartarus, if such
Mad toil attracts your eagerness, learn first
What must be done. In a dark tree there hides
A bough, all golden, leaf and pliant stem,
Sacred to Proserpine. This all the grove
Protects, and shadows cover it with darkness.
Until this bough, this bloom of light, is found
No one receives his passport to the darkness,
Whose queen requires this tribute. In succession
After the bough is plucked, another grows,
Gold-green with the same metal. Raise the eyes,
Look up, reach up the hand, and it will follow
With ease, if fate is calling; otherwise
No power, no steel, can loose it."     [125–148]

[She tells him that further rites of purification
must be performed, for one of his comrades lies
dead on the shore, and must be given proper
burial. Aeneas returns to find that the victim is
his trumpeter Misenus, who has challenged Tri-
ton in an arrogant moment and been drowned.
Aeneas takes a group to a forest, to secure wood
for the funeral pyre, hoping that his sorrow may
be alleviated by the sight of the golden bough.]

No sooner had he said so than twin doves
Came flying down before him, and alighted
On the green ground. He knew his mother's
    birds,
And made his prayer, rejoicing: "Oh, be leaders,
Wherever the way, and guide me to the grove
Where the rich bough makes rich the shaded
    ground.
Help me, O goddess-mother!" And he paused,
Watching what sign they give, what course they
    set.
The birds fly on a little, just ahead
Of the pursuing vision; when they have come
To the jaws of dank Avernus, evil-smelling,
They rise aloft, swoop down through the bright
    air,
Perch on the double tree, where the off-color
Of gold is gleaming golden through the branches,
As mistletoe, in the cold winter, blooms

With its strange foliage on an alien tree,
The yellow berry girding the smooth branches,
Such was the vision of the gold in leaf
On the dark holm-oak, so the foil was rustling,
Rattling, almost, the bract in the soft wind
Stirring like metal.                    [190–209]

[Aeneas is successful in plucking the bough,
and after the rites for Misenus have been accomplished, returns with it to Deiphobe.]

There was a cavern, yawning wide and deep,
Jagged, below the darkness of the trees,
Beside the darkness of the lake. No bird
Could fly above it safely, with the vapor
Pouring from the black gulf (the Greeks have named it
Avernus, or A-Ornos, meaning *birdless*),
And here the priestess for the slaughter sets
Four bullocks, black ones, and is pouring wine
Between the horns, and plucks the topmost bristles
For the first offering to the sacred fire,
Calling on Hecate, a power in heaven,
A power in hell. Knives to the throat are driven,
The warm blood caught in bowls. Aeneas offers
A lamb, black-fleeced, to Night and her great sister,
A sterile heifer to the queen; to Dis
An altar in the night, and on the flames
The weight of heavy bulls, the fat oil pouring
Over the burning entrails. And at dawn,
Under their feet, earth seemed to shake and rumble,
The ridges move, and bitches bay in darkness,
As the presence nears. The Sibyl cries a warning,
"Keep off, keep off, whatever is unholy,
Depart from here! Courage, Aeneas, enter
The path, unsheathe the sword. The time is ready
For the brave heart." She strode out boldly, leading
Into the open cavern, and he followed.

Vague forms in lonely darkness, they were going
Through void and shadow, through the empty realm,
Like people in a forest, when the moonlight
Shifts with a baleful light, when shadow covers
The sky, and all the colors turn to darkness.
At the first threshold, on the jaws of Orcus,
Grief and avenging Cares have set their couches,

And pale Diseases dwell, and sad Old Age,
Fear, Hunger, evil counsellor, wretched Need,
Forms terrible to see, and Death, and Toil,
And Death's own brother, Sleep, and evil Joys,
Fantasies of the mind, and deadly War,
The Furies' iron chambers, Discord, raving,
Her snaky hair entwined in bloody bands.
An elm-tree looms there, shadowy and huge,
The aged boughs outspread, beneath whose leaves,
Men say, the false dreams cling, thousands on thousands.
And there are monsters in the dooryards, Centaurs,
Scyllas, of double shape, the beast of Lerna
Hissing most horribly, Briareus,
The hundred-handed giant, a Chimaera
Whose armament is fire, Harpies, and Gorgons,
A triple-bodied giant. In sudden panic
Aeneas draws the sword, the edge held forward,
Ready to rush and flail, however vainly,
Save that his wise companion warns him, saying
They have no substance, they are only phantoms
Flitting about, illusions without body.

From here the road turns off to Acheron,
River of hell; here, thick with muddy whirling,
Cocytus boils with sand. Charon is here,
The guardian of these mingling waters, Charon,
Uncouth and filthy, on whose chin the hair
Is a tangled mat, whose eyes protrude, are burning,
Whose dirty cloak is knotted at the shoulder.
He poles a boat, tends to the sail, unaided,
Ferrying bodies in his rust-hued vessel.
Old, but a god's senility is awful
In its raw greenness. To the bank come thronging
Mothers and men, bodies of great-souled heroes,
Their lifetime over, boys, unwedded maidens,
Young men whose fathers saw their pyres burning,
Thick as the forest leaves that fall in autumn
With early frost, thick as the birds to landfall
From over the seas, when the chill of the year compels them
To sunlight. There they stand, a host, imploring
To be taken over first. Their hands, in longing,
Reach out for the farther shore. But the gloomy boatman
Makes choice among them, taking some, and keeping

Others far back from the stream's edge. Aeneas,
Wondering, asks the Sibyl "Why the crowding,
What are the spirits seeking? What distinction
Brings some across the livid stream, while others
Stay on the farther bank?" She answers, briefly:
"Son of Anchises, this is the awful river,
The Styx, by which the gods take oath; the boat-
man
Charon; those he takes with him are the buried,
Those he rejects, whose luck is out, the graveless.
It is not permitted him to take them over
The dreadful banks and hoarse-resounding
waters
Till earth is cast upon their bones. They haunt
These shores a hundred restless years of waiting
Before they end postponement of the crossing."
[237–330]

[Aeneas sees in this throng his old sea-captains,
who were drowned in the storm off Sicily, as told
in the first book of the epic, and also Palinurus,
the pilot lost just before the fleet reached Italy.
Palinurus tells his story, that he was not really
drowned, but murdered when he reached the
shore, after clinging all night to the tiller; he
begs Aeneas to take him across the river with
him. The Sibyl drives him back sternly; Aeneas
promises that when he returns to the upper world,
Palinurus shall be given due rites. Charon sculls
his boat toward them, challenging them to keep
off, warning them that he made grave mistakes
on such occasions as he ferried living beings
over. But at sight of the golden bough, he
silently accepts Aeneas, driving out a load of
spirits to make room for him, and, the craft
groaning and straining under the mortal weight,
they cross to the other shore.]

The great dog Cerberus, crouching in the cave,
Keeps the shore sounding with the dreadful bay-
ing
From his three throats; the serpents rise and
bristle
Along the triple neck. The priestess throws him
A sop with honey and drugged meal; he opens
The ravenous throat, gulps, and subsides, the den
Filled with his sprawling bulk. Aeneas crosses
And swiftly leaves the bank of the dread river
Whence none return.
　　　　　A wailing of thin voices
Comes to their ears, the souls of infants crying,

Those whom the day of darkness took from the
breast
Before their share of life. And there were many
Whom some false sentence brought to death. Here
Minos
Judges them once again; a silent jury
Reviews the evidence. And there are others,
Guilty of nothing, but who hated living,
The suicides. How gladly, now, they would suffer
Poverty, hardship, in the world of light,
But this is not permitted; they are bound
Nine times around by the black unlovely river;
Styx holds them fast.
　　　　　They come to the Fields of
　　　　　　　Mourning,
So called, where those whom cruel Love has
wasted,
Hide in secluded pathways, under myrtle,
And even in death are anxious. Procris, Phaedra,
Eriphyle, displaying wounds her son
Had given her, Caeneus, Laodamia,
Caeneus, a young man once, and now again
A young man, after having been a woman.
And here, new come from her own wound, is
Dido,
Wandering in the wood. The Trojan hero
Standing near by, sees her, or thinks he sees her,
Dim in the shadows, like the slender crescent
Of moon when cloud drifts over. Weeping, he
greets her.
"Unhappy Dido, so they told me truly
That your own hand had brought you death.
Was I—
Alas!—the cause? I swear by all the stars,
By the world above, by everything held sacred
Here under the earth, unwillingly, O queen,
I left your kingdom. But the gods' commands,
Driving me now through these forsaken places,
This utter night, compelled me on. I could not
Believe my loss would be so great a sorrow.
Linger a moment, do not leave me; whither,
Whom, do you flee? I am permitted only
This last word with you." *
　　　　　But the queen, unmoving
As flint or marble, turns away, her eyes
Fixed on the ground; the tears are vain, the words,
Meant to be soothing, foolish; she turns away,
His enemy forever, to the shadows

*The abjectly fatuous ineptness of Aeneas' speech
here does not reside entirely in the incompetence of the
translator!

Where Sychaeus, her former husband, takes her
With love for love, and sorrow for her sorrow.
                                    [417–474]

[Aeneas, Vergil says, pities her unfair lot and
weeps for her departure. He and the Sybil continue to the next area, where they meet the shades
of the famous in war. Among others they encounter Deiphobus, who tells them a long and
horrible story of mayhem and murder committed
upon him by Helen, Menelaus, and Ulysses, on
Troy's last night. Soon the pathway splits, that
on the right going on to Elysium, where they are
to find Anchises, that on the left to Tartarus,
the place of punishment.]

Wide walls beneath a cliff, a triple rampart,
A river running fire, a gate, tremendous,
Pillars of adamant, a tower of iron,
A Fury, sentinel in bloody garments,
Always on watch. Within, an endless groaning,
Blows of the lash, the clank of dragging shackles.
                                    [548–558]

[Aeneas halts, asking his guide for explanation. She tells him that she has never, with her
own eyes, seen Tartarus, but that Hecate has told
her about this place of everlasting punishment
and torture. Here, especially, the rebellious and
presumptuous suffer for their sins.]

"The giant son of Earth, huge Tityos, sprawls
Over nine acres, with a monstrous vulture
Gnawing, with crooked beak, vitals and liver
That grow as they are eaten; eternal anguish,
Eternal feast. Over another hangs
A rock, about to fall; and there are tables
Set for a banquet, gold with royal splendour,
But if a hand goes out to touch the viands,
The Fury drives it back with fire and crying.
Whoever, in his lifetime, hated his brother,
Or struck his father down; whoever cheated
A client, or was miserly—how many
Of these there seem to be!—whoever went
To treasonable war, or broke a promise
Made to his lord, whoever perished, slain
Over adultery, all these, walled in,
Wait here their punishment. Seek not to know
Too much about their doom. The stone is rolled,
The wheel keeps turning; Theseus forever

Sits in dejection; Phlegyas, accursed,
Cries through the halls forever: *"Being warned,
Learn justice; reverence the gods!"* The man
Who sold his country is here in hell; another,
Who altered laws for money; and a father
Who knew his daughter's bed. All of them dared,
And more than dared, achieved, unspeakable
Ambitions. If I had a hundred tongues,
A hundred iron throats, I could not tell
Either their crimes or punishment."     [595–627]

[They are near the entrance to Elysium, at
whose portal Aeneas affixes the golden bough,
and they enter the Groves of the Blessed.]

Here ampler air invests the fields with light,
Rose-colored, with familiar stars and sun.
Some grapple on the grassy wrestling-ground,
In exercise and sport, and some are dancing,
And others singing; in his trailing robe
Orpheus strums the lyre; the seven clear notes
Accompany the dance, the song. And heroes
Are there, great-souled, born in the happier years,
Ilus, Assaracus; the city's founder,
Prince Dardanus. Far off, Aeneas wonders,
Seeing the phantom arms, the chariots,
The spears fixed in the ground, the chargers
                                    browsing,
Unharnessed, over the plain. Whatever, living,
The men delighted in, whatever pleasure
Was theirs in horse and chariot still holds them
Here under the earth. To right and left, they
                                    banquet
In the green meadows, and a joyful chorus
Rises through groves of laurel, whence the river
Runs to the world above. The band of heroes
Is here, all those whose mortal wounds were
                                    suffered
In fighting for the fatherland; and poets,
The good, the pure, the worthy of Apollo;
Those who discovered truth, and made life nobler;
Those who served others—all with snowy fillets
Binding their temples.                  [640–665]

[Vergil's catalogue here of the saintly affords
good contrast with his earlier list of the damned:
conspicuous by their absence, it has always
seemed to me, are two groups—no business men,
no women! The poet Musaeus is found in this
company, and in reply to Deiphobe's question
directs them to Anchises. There is a moving re-

union between father and son; with Anchises at
his side, Aeneas continues to watch and marvel.]

He sees a valley, and a separate grove,
Where the woods stir and rustle, and a river,
The Lethe, gliding past the peaceful places,
And tribes of people thronging, hovering over,
Innumerable as the bees in summer
Working the bright-hued flowers, and the shining
Of the white lilies, murmuring and humming.
Aeneas, filled with wonder, asks the reason
For what he does not know. Who are the people,
In such a host, and to what river coming?
Anchises answers: "These are spirits, ready
Once more for life; they drink of Lethe's water
The soothing potion of forgetfulness.
I have longed, for long, to show them to you,
    name them,
Our children's children; Italy discovered,
So much the greater happiness, my son."
"But, O my father, is it thinkable
That souls would leave this blessedness, be willing
A second time to bear the sluggish body,
Trade Paradise for Earth? Alas, poor wretches,
Why such a mad desire for light?" Anchises.
Gives detailed answer: "First, my son, a spirit
Sustains all matter, heaven and earth and ocean,
The moon, the stars; mind quickens mass, and
    moves it.
Hence comes the race of man, of beast, of winged
Creatures of air, of the strange shapes which ocean
Bears down below his mottled marble surface.
All these are blessed with energy from heaven,
The seed of life is a spark of fire, but the body
A clod of earth, a clog, a mortal burden.
Hence humans fear, desire, grieve, and are joy-
    ful,
And even when life is over, all the evil,
Ingrained so long, the adulterated mixture,
The plagues and pestilences of the body,
Remain, persist. So there must be a cleansing,
By penalty, by punishment, by fire,
By the sweep of wind, by water's absolution,
Before the guilt is gone. Each of us suffers
His own peculiar ghost. But the day comes
When we are sent through wide Elysium,
The Blessed Fields, a few of us, to linger
Until the turn of time, the wheel of ages,
Wears off the taint, and leaves the core of spirit
Pure sense, pure flame. A thousand years pass
    over,

And the god calls the countless host to Lethe
Where memory is annulled, and souls are willing,
Once more, to enter into mortal bodies."
                                    [703–751]

[As the individual figures grow more distinct,
Anchises points out each one. The list is long, a
complete history of Rome, through its men, from
the days of the legendary kings to Vergil's own
contemporaries: Julius Caesar, Pompey, Augustus. It is of interest to note how Vergil averts
monotony by breaking from strict chronological
order, and characteristic of his sense of the tears
of things that the crowning figure is one distinguished for promise only. Toward the end
Aeneas beholds a youthful figure, of luminous
radiance, but with an aura of sadness about him,
and a dark cloud over his head. He interrupts
Anchises to ask his compelling question, and is
given the answer.]

"Great sorrow for our people! Oh my son,
Ask not to know it. This one Fate will only
Show to the world; he will not be permitted
Any long sojourn. Rome would be too mighty,
Too great in the gods' sight, were this gift hers.
What lamentation will the field of Mars
Raise to the city! Tiber, gliding by
The new-built tomb, the funeral state, bear wit-
    ness!
No youth from Trojan stock will ever raise
His ancestors so high in hope, no Roman
Be such a cause for pride. Alas for goodness,
Alas for old-time honor, and the arm
Invincible in war! Against him none,
Whether on foot or foaming horse, would come
In battle and depart unscathed. Poor boy,
If you should break the cruel fates; if only—
You will be Marcellus. Let me strew the lilies,
The dark-red flowers, honoring the shade
Of my descendant; let these gifts, this honor,
At least be paid, however vain the service."

So through the whole wide realm they walk to-
    gether,
Anchises and his son; from fields of air
Learning and teaching of the fame and glory,
The wars to come, the toils to face, or flee from,
Latinus' city and the Latin peoples,
The love of what must be.
                        There are two portals,

Twin gates of Sleep, one made of horn, where
    easy
Release is given true shades, the other gleaming
White ivory, whereby the false dreams issue
To the upper air. Aeneas and the Sibyl
Part from Anchises at the second portal.
He goes to the ships again, rejoins his comrades,
Sails to Caieta's harbor, and the vessels
Rest on their mooring lines.     [868–901]

## Book VII

### AENEAS IN ITALY

If the first six books of the *Aeneid* are to be considered
as an abbreviated *Odyssey*, then the last six are entitled
to be studied as a similar version of the *Iliad*; and if one
absolutely had to choose between *Iliad* and *Odyssey*,
which would he select? It seems to me that the last six
books of Vergil's *Aeneid* have been grossly slighted, not
only in the theorizing of scholars but in the practice of
students: I know of one quite respectable American critic
who talks about Vergil and admits, in the same breath,
that he has never read Books VII–XII inclusive. All this
in the face of Vergil's own statement: *Maior rerum mihi
nascitur ordo,/ maius opus moveo.* I have, accordingly,
given a good deal more space to selections from these
books than from the more familiar passages of I, II, IV,
and VI.

One thing to remember, reading these books, is the way
in which, book for book, they reintroduce themes from
the first half of the epic. Professor Conway's study of the
architecture of the *Aeneid* is a great help here. In Book
VII, for example, there is a great deal suggestive of Book
I: the landing on a peaceful shore, the simple picnic, the
appearance of Ilioneus as spokesman at King Latinus'
court, the original hospitable reception warped by Juno's
interference into hostility, mischief wrought by Ascanius,
and so on.

[As Book VII opens, it is apparent that at least
one of the women has not been left behind in
Sicily, for Caieta, the old nurse of Aeneas, dies
and is buried in Italy at a place which still keeps
her name. With her rites duly performed, the
Trojans are once more on their northward
course.]

The wind holds fair to the night, and the white
    moon
Reveals the way over the tremulous water.
They skirt the shores of Circe's island, where
The sun's rich daughter makes the secret groves

Ring with continual singing, where the halls
Keep light with cedar burning through the night,
And the strident shuttle running through the
    weaving.
Off shore, they hear the angry growl of lions
Trying to shake their shackles off, and roaring
In the late darkness, bristling boars, and bears
Coughing in cages, and the great wolves howl-
    ing.
All these were men, whom cruel Circe's magic
Changed into animals. But Neptune keeps
The Trojans safely seaward, fills the sails,
Carries them safely past these anxious harbors.

And now the sea is crimson under the dawn,
Aurora glowing in her ruddy car,
And the winds subside, and the air is very still,
The slow oars struggle in the marble sea,
As from the ship Aeneas sees a grove
And through its midst a pleasant river running,
The Tiber, yellow sand, and whirling eddy,
Down to the sea. Around, above and over,
Fly the bright-colored birds, the water-haunters,
Charming the air with song. The order given,
The Trojans turn their course to land; they enter
The channel and the shade.     [8–36]

[Here Vergil breaks off to invoke the muse
Erato to prompt his memory of the history of
ancient Latium: he relates that the reigning king
is old Latinus, descended, through Faunus and
Picus, from Saturn. The king's only heir is a
daughter, Lavinia, unmarried, but with many
suitors, among whom Turnus, prince of the
Rutulians, is favored by Queen Amata. But the
oracles and portents are dubious, and Latinus is
warned specifically by Faunus that Lavinia must
marry a foreign leader, and that great fame will
attend the children of their union. This news
Latinus keeps to himself, but Rumor has spread
the word around even before the Trojans have
moored their ships to the river bank.]

Aeneas and the captains and Iulus
Rest in the shade; a feast is spread; they place
The wheels of hardtack on the ground, and on
    them
Morsels of food, and sliced or quartered apples,
And after these are eaten, hunger drives them
To break the disks beneath with teeth and fingers.
"Ho!" says Iulus, "we are eating our tables!"

A boy's joke, nothing more. But the spoken word
Meant something more, and deeper, to Aeneas,
An end of hardship. He caught up the saying,
Felt the god's presence. "Hail!" he cried, re-
membering,
"Hail, O my destined land! All hail, ye faithful
Gods of our homeland! Here our country lies.
Now I remember what Anchises told me:
*My son, when hunger overtakes you, driven*
*To unknown shores, and the food seems so little*
*You find it best to gnaw the tables also,*
*There hope for home, there build, however*
*weary,*
*The city walls, the ditch, the moat, the rampart.*
This must have been that hunger, and the ending
Of our misfortunes. Come then, let us gladly
Explore what lands these are, what people hold
them,
Now pour your cups to Jove, in the light of morn-
ing,
Pray to Anchises, let the wine again
Go round in happiness."                    [107–134]

[Either Vergil, or Aeneas, here, has forgotten
the story of the third book, for the only previous
mention of the table-eating business was the
prophecy of the vindictive harpy Celaeno, and a
word of reassurance from Helenus not to worry
about it, and that Apollo would find a solution.
There had been no hint that the place where the
table-eating occurred was to be the site of the
city, nor had Anchises made any mention of such
an event. The obvious explanation is that Vergil
has made a slip; a possible one would be that
somewhere, off the record, Anchises has given
Aeneas this private comfort; or we can take it,
and this seems not too far-fetched, that Aeneas,
with his mind full of Anchises' guidance, especially on the anniversary of his death, has become, naturally, a little confused about his
father's prophecy.

To get the picture, you have to know what
the "tables" looked like, not pieces of bread, in
our sense, nor cookies or crackers. *Pillonca* is
the word for it in Italian; in the back files of the
*National Geographic Magazine,* you will find a
picture of Sardinian children, grinning and holding these up—they look like matzoth, or round
soda-crackers, or hardtack, only much bigger
than the old army ration of 1917, disks about a
foot in diameter, and maybe a half inch thick.

Next day the Trojans explore the land, and a
delegation of a hundred men, led by Ilioneus, appears in Latinus' capital, with gifts and a request
for permission to settle in the land and build their
own town. Remembering the oracle of Faunus,
Latinus welcomes them hospitably, grants their
request, and goes farther than that, in suggesting
that his daughter Lavinia might marry Aeneas.
The delegation returns to Aeneas with gifts and
this good news; meanwhile Juno, more furious
than ever, seeks out one of the Furies, Allecto,
urging her to go to Latium and stir up all possible trouble. The Fury obeys.]

Allecto, steeped in Gorgon poison, travels
To Latium and the palace, where the queen
Amata broods, anxiety and anger
Burning within her heart, for Turnus' marriage
And, fuel on fire, the coming of the Trojans.
From her own dark hair, Allecto plucks one
serpent
Meant for the queen, the intimate heart, the
bosom,
Corruption, evil, frenzy, for the household.
Between the robe and the smooth breasts the
serpent
Glides in, glides deep, unseen, unfelt; the woman,
Receives the viperous breath. The snake grows
larger,
Becomes a collar of gold, becomes the ribbon
Wound through the hair, entwining, sliding
smoothly
Over the limbs, a fluid poison, working
With slow infection, no great blaze of passion,
So that the queen, at first, speaks low and softly,
As mothers do, protesting to Latinus
Over her daughter's marriage to the Trojan.
                                              [341–358]

[She speaks mildly enough, pointing out to
Latinus that the Trojans' reputation for honor is
none too great, citing the case of Paris as an
example; and makes the added point that Turnus,
if Latinus is going to insist on the letter of the
oracle, is also eligible, since he can trace his
ancestry back to a foreign origin, through Acrisius, from Mycenae.]

Her words are vain: Latinus has decided,
She sees she can not move him. And the poison
By now has taken hold, a wild excitement

Coursing the veins; her bones are turned to
    water,
Poor queen, there is no limit to her raging,
Streeling, one end of the city to the other.
You know how schoolboys, when a top is spin-
    ning,
Snap at it with a whiplash, in a circle
Around the empty court, and keep it going,
Wondering at the way it keeps on whirling,
Driven by blows in this or that direction,
So, through the midst of cities and proud peoples,
Amata drives, is driven. Madness and guilt upon
    her,
She flies to the mountains, tries to hide her daugh-
    ter,
Deep in the woods, acts like a drunken woman,
Cries, over and over, "This girl is meant for
    Bacchus,
And not for any Trojans, only Bacchus
Is worthy of her; she honors him in dancing,
Carries his wand, and keeps for him the sacred
Hair of her head!" And Rumor, flying over,
Excites the other wives to leave their houses;
They come with maddened hearts, with their hair
    flying,
Their necks bare to the winds; they shriek to the
    skies,
Brandish the vine-bound spears, are dressed as
    tigers,
Circle and wheel around their queen, whose
    frenzy
Tosses the burning pine-brand high in gesture
To suit the marriage-hymn; "O Latin mothers,
Listen, wherever you are: if any care
For poor Amata moves you, or any sense
Of any mother's rights, come join the revels,
Loosen the hair, exult!" Allecto drives her
To the dens of the beasts; her eyes are stained and
    bloodshot,
Rolled inward to the white.    [373–405]

[Allecto, satisfied that this is enough where
Amata is concerned, takes herself next to Ardea,
capital of Turnus, the Rutulian prince. Laying
aside her natural frightening aspect, she presents herself to him, as he sleeps, in the guise of
Calybe, an old priestess of Juno's temple, pointing out to him that he is being defrauded of his
rights by the Trojan newcomers, and urging him
to go to war forthwith. Turnus takes this very
calmly.]

The young prince, smiling at her, answered:
    "Mother,
You tell me nothing new; I know a fleet
Has come to Tiber's waters; do not scare me
With fears imagined; Juno, I am certain,
Has not forgotten me. Your age, old woman,
Worn down, truth-weary, harries you with wor-
    ries,
Makes you ridiculous, a busybody,
Nervous for nothing in the wars of kings.
Back to the temple, mind your proper business,
Leave war and peace where they belong, with
    warriors."
Allecto blazed with anger; Turnus, speaking,
Was suddenly afraid, so wild her features,
So fierce her flaming eyes, the snakes of the Fury
Hissing disaster. She shoves him back; he falters,
Tries to say more; she plies her whip, she doubles
The rising serpents, and her wild mouth cries
"See me for what I am, worn down, truth-weary,
Nervous for nothing in the wars of kings!
See what I am, see where I come from, bringing
War, war and death, from the Grim Sisters'
    home."
She flung the firebrand at him, torch and terror
Smoking with lurid light. The body, sweating,
Is torn ·from sleep, he cries for arms, he seeks
Arms by his bedside, through the hallways, lust-
    ing
For sword and steel, war's wicked frenzy mount-
    ing,
And rampant anger. So a cauldron bubbles
When fire burns hot beneath, and water seethes,
Stirs, shifts, breaks out in boiling, and the cloud
Of steam goes toward the sky. The peace is
    broken.
The call to arms is given; let the captains
March on Latinus, drive the foe from Latium,
Protect the fatherland. Turnus is coming;
No matter who they are, Trojans or Latins,
Turnus will take them on.    [435–470]

Were the *Aeneid* a modern novel, it would no doubt
contain, in the front matter, a statement to the effect that
all the characters were the product of the imagination,
and any resemblance to any living person purely coincidental. I do not think this would discourage the Roman
reader from finding, in the character of Turnus, more
than a hint of Mark Antony. *Violent* is the key adjective
which Vergil uses to type him, but he is a subtler character than the single epithet makes out. As can be seen
from this first appearance, he has some tendency to a

level-headed, easy-going common sense; impulsive as he is, he is more than just a big dumb football-playing type, has some sensitivity and imagination, as will appear later, and can, when necessary, make a very good speech if sufficiently provoked.

[Allecto's next act of mischief takes place among the Trojans: Ascanius is off hunting, and the Fury puts the hounds on the scent of a stag.]

A handsome animal, with mighty antlers,
Belonging, now, to Tyrrhus and his children,
Who had raised him from a fawn. Tyrrhus, the father,
Was keeper of the royal herds, and Silvia,
The daughter, used to comb the beast, and wash him,
Twine garlands in his horns, and pet and love him,
And he, grown used to her, would wander freely
Over the woods and meadows and come home
At nightfall to the friendly door and stable.
This was the stag Iulus' hounds had started,
Floating downstream, reclining by the river
For coolness' sake, where young Ascanius, burning
For a huntsman's praise, saw him, and loosed the arrow
That pierced the belly and side, and the poor creature
Came wounded to the house he knew, and moaning
Crept into his stall, bleeding, and like a person
Asking for help, filled all the house with sorrow.
First Silvia came, beating her arms, and others,
Summoned for help, equipped themselves for vengeance,
Allecto being near them in the forest,
However silent. A club, a stake, a firebrand,
Whatever comes to hand will serve, when anger
Hurries the need for arms. Tyrrhus abandons
The oak, and the four wedges; he brings the axe,
He is out of breath with anger.        [483–510]

[Soon Allecto has the whole countryside fighting, clubs and stakes, sword and steel: Almo, Tyrrhus' oldest son, is slain, and so is a peace-loving old husbandman named Galaesus, who tries to end the strife. Allecto reports to Juno, who finds all well done, and adds a finishing touch or two, herself opening the gates of war, a

formality which Latinus, in spite of the screaming of the Latin mothers and the rage of Turnus, has resolutely declined to perform, and make the war official. The book ends with a catalogue of the Latin leaders who come to join Turnus in alliance against Aeneas. Those mentioned are:

1. Mezentius, an exiled king from Etruria. Vergil calls him *contemptor divum*. Don't think of him as an atheist; he believes in the gods, all right, but he despises them.
2. Lausus, his son, a fine handsome young man, deserving of a better father.
3 and 4. Catillus and Coras, Argive youths from Tibur.
5. Caeculus, from Praeneste, believed to be a son of Vulcan.
6. Messapus, characterized as a tamer of horsemen, said to be invulnerable, and a son of Neptune.
7. Clausus, a Sabine.
8. Halaesus, a son of Agamemnon.
9. Oebalus, from Capri, son of Telon and Sebethis.
10. Ufens, from Nersae.
11. Umbro, a priest-king, a Marsian, skilled in magic and snake-charming.
12. Virbius, sent by his mother Aricia from the groves of Egeria. He is said to be son of Hippolytus, about whose death and reincarnation a rather confusing legend is told.
13. Turnus.
14. Camilla, the Volscian soldieress.

Some of these appear, in important roles, in the later part of the story; others are never, or barely, mentioned again. The catalogue dwells a great deal on the Italian geography; the artistic effect made by Vergil lies in the contrast between the lovely pastoral landscape and the wildness and barbarity of the rush to war, this effect being heightened by Vergil's references to the outlandish armament of some of the clans, and the use of archaic terms in naming some of the weapons.]

## Book VIII

### THE SHIELD OF AENEAS

[As Turnus raises the flag of war, other allies, Messapus, Ufens, Mezentius, rally to the cause one leader, Venulus, is sent hurriedly southward to bring aid from Diomedes, who is now settled at Arpi, in Apulia. All Latium is making ready against the invader.]

Seeing it all, Aeneas tosses on
A mighty sea of trouble. The swift mind
Searches and probes, veering with every shift,
As when in a bronze bowl the light of water,
Reflected by the sun or moonlight, wavers,
Dances and flits about, from room to ceiling.
Night: over all the world the weary creatures,
The beasts and birds, were deep in sleep; Aeneas,
With warfare in his heart, stretched out for rest
Where the cold sky was awning over the river,
And sleep came late. Before him rose an image,
An aged head amid the poplar leaves,
A mantle of gray, and shady reeds around him,
Tiber, the river-god, in consolation
And comfort speaking.                    [18–35]

[The vision of Tiber tells Aeneas to be reassured: here is their home, as the sight of a white sow lying under the oaks with thirty young at her udders will confirm in the morning. Moreover, allies are at hand, the Arcadians, under King Evander, who live on the future site of Rome. Tiber promises to guide them to the place with morning, making his current mild and easy. Aeneas wakes, offers grateful prayer, chooses two galleys for the journey up river, and is heartened by the sight of the sow with the milk-white brood.]

All that long night, the Tiber calmed the flood,
The silent wave, retreating, flowed as still
As pool or mere or watery plain; the oars
Dipped without strain; the voyage went with laughter
And cheerful shouting; over the waters rode
The oily keels; and waves and woods in wonder
Beheld the shields of men, the colored vessels,
Divide the flood. Day turns to night. They traverse
The winding bends, with green shade arching over,
Parting the green woods in the quiet water,
Till it is noon, and they see walls and houses,
Evander's town, which Roman power later
Made equal to the sky, a mighty empire,
But it was little then.            [86–100]

[As they run the ships ashore, they find King Evander and his son Pallas performing annual rites in honor of Hercules. Introductions are performed; the Trojans receive a delighted welcome, they discover relationships, there is a feast, and Evander, in a somewhat long-winded narrative, explains that the feast to Hercules has been ordained in honor of his victory over a cattle-robbing giant and monster named Cacus. Thereafter he takes Aeneas on a guided tour of the future site of Rome, remarking on various points of interest, and as the day is done, asks Aeneas to be bold enough to accept simplicity, and puts him up for the night on a couch of leaves with a bear-skin covering.

Meanwhile, Venus, still anxious for her son, appeals to her husband, Vulcan, to make for him arms that will render him invulnerable. Cuckold though he is, and the son a mortal's, Vulcan responds to this invitation with amazing alacrity. The next scene is in Vulcan's workshop.]

Near the Sicanian coast and Lipare
An island rises, high with smoking rocks,
Beneath which roars a cavern, hollow vaults
Scooped out for forges, where the Cyclops pound
On the resounding anvils; lumps of steel
Hiss in the water, and the blast of fire
Pants in the furnaces; here Vulcan dwells,
The place is called Vulcania; and here
The lord of fire comes down. In the great cave
The Cyclop smiths worked iron; a thunderbolt
Such as Jove hurls from heaven, was almost finished,
Shaped by the hands of Brontes, Steropes,
And naked-limbed Pyracmon. They had added
Three rods of twisted rain, and three of cloud
And three of orange fire and winged wind,
And now they were working in the flash, the sound,
The fear, the anger, with pursuing flame.
Elsewhere a chariot for Mars was building
To harry men and cities; and for Pallas
An awful shield, with serpent scales of gold,
Snakes interwoven, and the Gorgon's head,
Awaited polish. The neck was severed, the eyes
Already seemed to roll, when Vulcan came
Crying, "Away with this! Another task
Demands your toil, your thought. Arms for a warrior!
Summon your strength, O artisans of Aetna,

Your flying hands, and all your master skill;
Break off delay!" And all, obedient, bent
To the great task; the bronze, the golden ore
Run down like rivers, and the wounding steel
Melts in the furnace, as they shape the shield,
Welding it, orb on orb, a sevenfold circle
Made one, for all the weapons of the Latins.
Some keep the bellows panting, others dip
The hissing bronze in water, and the anvil
Groans under the hammer stroke. In turn they raise
Their arms in measured cadence, and the tongs
Twist the hot metal. [416–453]

[With the next morning, Aeneas and Evander are about early, and soon discussing the practical details of their alliance. Evander has little, himself, to offer, but says that a near-by king, Tarchon, who has succeeded to the throne of the exiled Mezentius, will be glad to assist him; the only thing which has prevented the dispatch of a punitive expedition against Mezentius is an oracle saying that the avengers must have a foreign leader. Evander, to be sure, is foreign, but feels that his age is a disqualification; and his son, Pallas, is born of a native mother, hence not eligible. But Pallas, at least, will be sent, with a small force of horsemen, to help Aeneas; and the next step is to find Tarchon and arrange the alliance further. There is a pathetic parting between the old king and his son; the ships are sent back down river to bring encouraging news to the Trojans there; and Aeneas and Pallas, with attendants, ride overland to find Tarchon. The camp of Tarchon is in sight, but before Aeneas reaches it, Venus descends from the sky with her gift of armor.]

The shining goddess through the clouds of heaven
Comes bringing gifts, seeing her son alone
By the cold river in the quiet valley,
She speaks to him: "Lo, here the gifts made ready
By Vulcan's promised skill. Fear not, my son,
To dare the wars with Turnus and the Latins!"
After the word, the embrace. She placed the armor
All shining in his sight, against an oak tree;
Rejoicing in the gift, the honor, he turns
His eyes to these, over and over again,
Cannot be satisfied; takes in his hands
The helmet with the terrible plumes and flame,
The fatal sword, the breastplate, made of bronze,

Fire-colored, huge, shining the way a cloud,
Dark blue, turns crimson under the slanting sun,
The greaves of gold refined and smooth electrum,
The spear, the final masterpiece, the shield.

Hereon the great prophetic Lord of Fire
Had carved the story out, the stock to come,
The wars, each one in order, all the tale
Of Italy and Roman triumph. Here
In Mars' green cave the she-wolf gave her udders
To the twin boys; she turned half round to lick them
Each in his turn, neither afraid, but playing.
Another scene presents the Circus games,
When Romans took their Sabine brides, and war
Broke out between old Tatius and the sons
Of Romulus, and these kings together pledging
Peace at the altars over sacrifice.
Mettus, the false, by the wild horses drawn
And quartered, sheds his lifeblood over the brambles;
Porsena, the besieger, rings the city
For Tarquin's sake, exile and tyrant; Romans
Rush on the steel for freedom; Clelia breaks
Her bonds to swim the river; and the bridge
Is broken by Horatius. Manlius
Holds the high capitol, and that crude palace
Fresh with the straw of Romulus; the goose
Flutters in silver through the colonnades
Shrieking alarm; the Gauls are near in darkness,
Golden their hair, their clothing, and their necks
Gleam white in golden collars; each one carries
Two Alpine javelins; they have long shields.
Near them, the fire-god sets the priests with caps
Of wool, the miracle of shields from heaven,
The Salii dancing, the Luperci naked,
And the chaste matrons riding through the city
In cushioned cars. Far off from these he adds
The seats of Hell, the lofty gates of Pluto,
Penance for sin; Catiline, with the Furies
Making him cower; farther off, the good,
With Cato giving laws. And all this scene
Bound with the likeness of the swelling ocean,
Blue water and whitecap, where the dolphins playing
Leap with a curve of silver. In the center
Actium, the ships of bronze, Leucate burning
With the hot glow of war, and waves on fire
With molten gold. Augustus Caesar stands
High on the lofty stern; his temples flame
With double fire, and over his head there dawns

His father's star. Agrippa leads a column
With favoring wind and god, the naval crown
Wreathing his temples. Antony assembles
Egypt and all the East, Antony, victor
Over the lands of dawn and the red ocean,
Marshals the foes of Rome, himself a Roman,
With—horror!—an Egyptian wife. The sea
Boils under keel, the oar-blades churn the waters,
The triple-pointed beaks drive through the billows,
You would think that mountains swam and bat-
    tled mountains,
That islands were uprooted in their anger.
Fireballs and shafts of steel are slanting showers,
The fields of Neptune redden with the slaughter.
The queen drives on her warriors, unseeing
The double snakes of death; rattle and cymbals
Compete with bugle and trumpet. Monstrous gods,
Of every form and fashion, one, Anubis,
Shaped like a dog, wield their outrageous weapons
In wrath at Venus, Neptune, and Minerva.
Mars, all in steel, storms through the fray; the
    Furies
Swoop from the sky; Discord exults, Bellona,
With bloody scourge, comes lashing, and Apollo
From Actium bends his bow; Egypt and India,
Sabaeans and Arabians, flee in terror.
And the contagion takes the queen, who loosens
The sheets to slackness, woos the wind, in terror,
Pale at the menace of death. And the Nile comes
To meet her, a protecting god, his mantle
Spread wide, to take a beaten woman home.
And Caesar enters Rome triumphant, bringing
Immortal offerings, three times a hundred
New altars through the city. Streets resound
With gladness, games, rejoicing; all the temples
Are filled with matrons praying at the altars,
Are heaped with solemn sacrifice. And Caesar,
Seated before Apollo's shining threshhold,
Reviews the gifts, and hangs them on the portals.
In long array the conquered file, their garments,
Their speech, as various as their arms, the No-
    mads,
The naked Africans, Leleges, Carians,
Gelonians with quivers, the Morini,
Of mortals most remote, Euphrates moving
With humbler waves, the two-mouthed Rhine,
    Araxes
Chafing beneath his bridge . . . .
                    All this Aeneas
Sees on his mother's gift, the shield of Vulcan,
And, without understanding, still rejoices,

As he lifts to his shoulder all that fortune,
The fame and glory of his children's children.
                                    [608–731]

## Book IX

### NISUS AND EURYALUS. TURNUS IN BATTLE

[In the incidents of this book Aeneas takes no
part; he is absent on his mission to Tarchon. Taking advantage of his absence, Juno sends Iris to
urge Turnus to attack the camp; Aeneas had
warned the leaders in charge while he was away
not to risk open battle, but remain on the defensive.
Turnus makes the attack, finds the camp valorously
defended, and directs his wrath against the fleet,
setting fire to the ships which lie at the water's
edge. But an old promise, made by Jupiter to
Cybele, guaranteeing immunity to the ships when
the voyage has been completed, saves them from
Turnus' brands; they are turned into sea-nymphs
and glide away into the water. This does not
discourage Turnus; on the contrary. He feels that
now all possible escape is cut off from the invaders; plans a final attack in the morning; and
sets a guard which is possibly a little too confident
—there seems to be a good deal, even for soldiers,
of drinking and gambling. But the defenders take
their responsibility very seriously.

In the incident which follows, the story of
Nisus' and Euryalus' mission to seek Aeneas, some
editors have seemed to feel that Vergil has slipped
in introducing them here as if they had never appeared before, though they were conspicuous
contenders in the racing in Book V. I do not feel
that this is correct; their appearance in the games
was surely a preparation for this story: their
mutual devotion indicated, and the comic slip of
Nisus turned into victory for Euryalus, and all
coming out well, for both, in the end, surely form
a tragic contrast with Euryalus' error here, Nisus'
foolish attempts to save him, and, finally, death
for the pair. Any student of minor problems of
military tactics could point out half a dozen errors
they make in the carrying out of their mission;
this, it seems to me, Vergil must have known and
intended, and the whole sequence pathetic and
beautiful because of the young men's foolishness.]

Nisus, quick-handed with the javelin
And the light arrows, very keen in arms,

Stood guard beside the gate; Nisus, a son
Of Hyrtacus, sent by the huntress Ida
To join Aeneas; and near by his friend
Euryalus; no Trojan was more handsome
Than he was, that first bloom of youth. They
    shared
Assignments, always, side by side in the charge,
And side by side defenders. Here they were
Together, on sentry duty at the gate.
Nisus burst out: "Euryalus, what is it?
Do the gods put this ardor in our hearts,
Or does each man's desire become his god?
I want much more than this, I am not contented
With peace and calm like this; my mind keeps
    calling
To battle, or something big. Look! The Rutulians
Are far too confident; their lights are scattered,
They lie asleep, or drunk; and all is silent.
Listen! I have a plan. People and fathers
Demand Aeneas, ask that men be sent him
With information. If I can make them promise
To let you go (the glory of the action
Is all I want myself), I think that I
Can find the way around that hill, can manage
To reach the walls, the fort, of Pallanteum."
                                    [176–196]

[Nisus' proposition seems to be a little obscure:
the nearest I can make out is that he is going to
get official permission for Euryalus to perform this
errand, then actually carry it out himself, hoping
to come back undiscovered, and let Euryalus have
all the glory. At least the answer of Euryalus
to Nisus would indicate that is his understanding
of it.]

"What, Nisus? Are you planning to leave me out
Of this high enterprise, and going alone
Into such dangers? No; no, no. I am
Opheltes' son, a warrior trained among
Greek terror and Trojan suffering; and I follow
With you, great-souled Aeneas and his fortunes.
I have a spirit, not too fond of living,
Not too dissatisfied to buy with death
The honor that you strive for." Nisus answered,
"I had no fear on your account, be certain;
That would be shameless of me: so may Jove,
Or any god that looks on this with favor,
Bring me back home triumphant. But disaster,
As well you know, or god, or chance, might take
    me:
If so, your youth being worthier, I'd have you

Be my survivor, give to earth my body
Rescued or ransomed, or pay the final honor
To, it might be, an empty tomb. I would not
Cause sorrow to the only mother of many
Who scorned Acestes' city, and came on
With you, her only son." But then the other
Replied, "There is no use in all this talking,
My mind is fixed. And we had better hurry."
                                    [199–221]

[They rouse other guards to take their places,
and go to the older councillors with their proposal.
Aletes is deeply moved, at a loss for suitable rewards; Ascanius makes his presence known with
promises that are very generous, and perhaps
a little assuming. Euryalus asks one favor, that
his mission be kept a secret from his mother, and
the young men are ready to set off on their
task.]

They cross the trench, and through the shadow of
    night
Invade the hostile camp; they are bound to be
The doom of many. They see the bodies sprawling
In drunken sleep, the chariots half turned over,
Men lying under the wheels, and among the reins,
And Nisus speaks: "Euryalus, we must
Be bold; the chance is given; here lies our way.
Watch and keep back, lest some one steal upon us
Behind our track. I lead, and you will follow
Where I have cut the way; it will be a broad one."
His voice was silent; and he drew the sword
At Rhamnes, cushioned on high covers, lying
In a deep slumber, breathing deep, a king,
And Turnus' favorite augur; but his doom
No augury prevented. Nisus struck
Three servants next, and Remus' armor-bearer,
And Remus' charioteer—their necks are severed
With steel, and their lord Remus is beheaded.
The trunk spurts blood, the earth and couch are
    darkened
With blood, black flowing. Lamyrus and Lamus
Are slain, and young Serranus, handsome gam-
    bler
Who had won high stakes that night, and slept
    contented
Smiling at the god's favor, luckier surely
If he had played all night. A starving lion
Loose in a sheepfold with the crazy hunger
Urging him on, gnashing and dragging, raging
With bloody mouth against the fearful feeble,
So Nisus slaughters. And his raging comrade

Keeps pace with him: Fadus is slain, Herbesus,
Rhoetus, Abaris, all of them unconscious,
Murdered in sleep. And one, named Rhoetus,
  wakened,
And saw it all, and tried to hide, and crouching
Behind a wine bowl, took the sword, and rising,
Stumbled and sprawled and belched, the red life
  spurting
Out of the mouth, red wine, red blood. All hotly
Euryalus goes on. Messapus' quarters
Are next in line; the fires burn low, the horses
Tether-contented, graze. Then, briefly, Nisus
Sensing his comrade's recklessness in slaughter,*
Calls: "Light is near, our enemy; give over,
We have killed enough, we have cut the path we
  needed.
No more of this!" They leave behind them armor
Of solid silver, bowls, rich-woven carpets,
But must take something; Rhamnes' golden sword-
  belt
Euryalus takes up, and all that armor
That went with long tradition, from father to son,
From son to enemy, once more a trophy
For young Euryalus. He dons the armor,
Picks up, puts on, besides, a shapely helmet,
The spoil of Messapus, the long plume flowing.,
They leave the camp, are on their way to safety.

Meanwhile, sent forward from the Latin city,
Horsemen were coming, while the legion rested
Behind them on the plain, horsemen, three hun-
  dred,
With word for Turnus,, under their captain Vol-
  cens,
All armed with shields, and riding at the ready.
They are near the camp, the wall, and in the dis-
  tance
See two men turning left along a pathway,
And a helmet glimmering among the shadows,
Euryalus' prize and foolishness. They notice
At once, of course, and challenge. From the
  column
Volcens cries out: "Halt! Who goes there? Who
  are you?
What are you doing in arms? Upon what mis-
  sion?"
No answer: flight to wood and trust in darkness.

The horsemen, fanning out, block every crossroad,
Circle and screen each outlet. Wide with brambles
And dark with holm-oak spreads the wood; the
  briars
Fill it on every side, but the path glimmers
In the rare interval between the shadows.*
Euryalus is hindered by the branches,
The darkness, and the spoil he carries; terror
Makes him mistake the path. Nisus is clear,
Reaching the place that later men called Alba;
He halts, looks back to find his friend; in vain.
"Euryalus, Euryalus, where are you?
Where have I left you? What direction follow
Back through the tangled wood, the treacherous
  thickets?
Euryalus, Euryalus!" He turns,
Tries to retrace his step, is lost in the woods,
And hears the horses, hears the shouts and signals
As the pursuit comes closer, and he hears
A cry, and sees Euryalus, dragged along
Out of the treason of the night and darkness
Bewildered by the uproar, fighting vainly,
In the hands of Volcens' squadron. There is noth-
  ing
That he can do. Or is there? With what arms,
What force, redeem his friend? Or is it better
To hurl himself to death, dash in, regardless,
To glorious wounds? The spear is poised, the arm
Drawn back; he looks to the moon on high, and
  prays:
"Dear goddess, daughter of Latona, aid me,
Pride of the stars and glory of the groves,
If ever my father Hyrtacus brought honors
In my name to the altar, if ever I
Have brought gifts home from my own hunting,
  hung them
By dome or rooftop, O dear goddess, aid me!
Confound that horrible troop, direct my weapon."
The straining body flung the spear; it whistled
Across the shadows of night; and Sulmo took it
In his turned back; the point snaps off and lodges
With part of the splintered wood deep in the lungs.
Sulmo goes down, his mouth spurts blood, his
  body
Sobs, straining, in the gasp and chill and shudder
Of a cold death. They look in all directions,
See nothing. And another spear is flying,
Fiercer this time. This pierces Tagus' temples,

---

* And about time, too: this killing was a great tactical
mistake to begin with, their mission obviously requiring
them to get Aeneas with all possible dispatch and as un-
obtrusively as possible.

---

* The immediate professional competence of Volcens'
troop affords further contrast with the amateurish recklessness of the two young men.

Clings, warm in the split brain. And Volcens
rages,
And cannot find the spearman, and his anger
Has no sure place to go, but for his vengeance
Turns on Euryalus, sword drawn, and rushing
Cries, "You will pay for both of them, your blood
Be the atonement." Nisus from the darkness
Cries out in terror: "Here I am, I did it,
The guilt is mine, let him alone, come get me,
Rutulians! How could he have dared, or done it?
God knows, the only thing he did was love
A luckless friend too well." But the sword is
driven
Deep in the breast; Euryalus rolls over,
Blood veins the handsome limbs, and on the
shoulder
The neck droops over, as a bright-colored flower
Droops when the ploughshare bends it, or as pop-
pies
Bend under the weight of the heavy summer
shower.
And Nisus rushes them; he is after Volcens,
Volcens alone. They mass around him, cluster,
Buffet him back, but on and on he charges,
Whirling the blade like fire, until he drives it
Full in the face while the Rutulian shrieks, and
dying
Sees the foe die, and pierced with wounds, and
falling,
Falls over his lifeless friend, and there is quiet
In the peace of death.                    [314–445]

[By morning, the fight around the camp is on
in earnest: the Latins have made the discovery of
the carnage wrought by Nisus and Euryalus, and
as token of satisfied vengeance bring the heads
of the young men on pikes as a grim display to
the besieged camp. There is a hysterical scene in
which Euryalus' mother learns of her son's death;
Turnus comes in to attack, and the Trojans fight
fiercely in resistance: Turnus scores some spec-
tacular victories, and Ascanius kills his first man.]

There was a young man, Remulus by name,
Or, it might be, Numanus, lately married
To Turnus' younger sister, very proud
And pleased with his new royalty. He strode
Along the foremost battle-line, and taunted,
Shouting indecencies, a swollen youngster:
"What, once again, O Phrygians twice besieged,
And no shame in you, to hide behind the ramparts

A second time, a second time with walls
To ward off death? Look at the silly heroes
Who claim our brides with steel! What god, what
madness
Brought you to Italy? No sons of Atreus
Are here, no lying glib Ulysses. We
Are a tough race, we bring our new-born sons
To the cold river, dip them in for toughness,
We set them hunting till they tire the forests,
They ride, they shoot, they tame the earth, they
battle
Till cities fall; and all our life is iron,
The spear, reversed, prods on the ox; old age
Pulls on the helmet over the whitest hair;
We live on what we plunder, we revel in booty,
But you—O wonderful in purple and saffron,
Love indolence, and you delight in dancing,
And oh those fancy clothes, sleeves on the tunics,
And ribbons in the bonnets! Phrygian women,
By God, not Phrygian men! Be gone forever
Over the heights of Dindymus; pipe and timbrel
Call to the female rites; leave arms to men,
The sword to warriors!"
                              But Ascanius loosened
An arrow from the quiver, held the shaft
Nocked to the bow-string, and with arms out
spread
For shot, made prayer: "Almighty Jupiter,
Favor my bold beginning. I shall offer
The temple every year a snow-white bullock
With gilded horns, a young one, but already
Tall as his dam, butting with horn, and pawing
The sand with restless hoof." The father heard
him,
There was thunder on the left, and in that instant
The fatal bow-string twanged. The shaft came
flying
Through air, and split with steel the hollow
temples
Of that young bragger Remulus. "Go on,
Mock valor with arrogant words! This answer
The Phrygians twice besieged, the Phrygian
women,
Send back to Remulus!" The Trojans cheer him,
With joyful shouts and spirit raised to heaven.
                                        [592–637]

[Apollo adds a word of blessing and approval
from the sky, but also suggests that that will be
quite enough out of Ascanius for the moment,
and bids him desist from further battle. The fight

thickens: two big Trojans, Bitias and Pandarus,
on guard at the gate, are foolish enough to open
the door and let Turnus in, and he is foolish
enough to come in single-handed, without any
supporting heroes. He has a wonderful time for
a while, dealing out slaughter right and left, but
finally Mnestheus and Serestus rally their comrades against him, and Jupiter admonishes Juno to
send Iris to tell him he had better get out while
the getting is still good.]

The shield and sword-arm falter; darts like hail
Rain down from everywhere. The helmet rings
Around his temples, and the brass cracks open
Under the storm of stones; the horsehair crest
Is torn away; the boss of the shield is dented;
Mnestheus, with lightning force, and other Tro-
    jans
Multiply spears. The sweat over all his body
Runs in a tarry stream; he cannot breathe.
At last, with one great leap, in all his armor,
He plunges into the stream, and Tiber takes him
On the yellow flood, held up by the buoyant water,
Washing away the stains of war, a hero,
Returning, happily, to his warrior-comrades.
                    [806–818]

## Book X

### DUELS: PALLAS, LAUSUS, MEZENTIUS

[The tenth book is one of the great books of the
*Aeneid*, worthy, in my opinion, to stand with II,
IV, and VI. As in Book IV, which it balances, the
issue hangs in doubt; as in that book Aeneas shows
that when he has to he can be implacable; and as
in that book, the climax is reached in scenes of
great pity for the death of the enemy.

The opening scene is Olympus, where a brawl
is raging: Venus plaintive, Juno sarcastic, Jupiter
neutral and determined to leave the decision to
the Fates. At the scene of the Trojan camp there
is fierce fighting; down the coast the allied fleet
is coming to the rescue. A long catalogue of the
captains is given; on its course the new fleet is met
by the old, the sea-nymphs created from the ships
that Turnus had threatened. As the fleet comes in
for the landing, Turnus leads the assault; the
beachhead is established with fierce fighting—
winds warring in heaven yield to each other as
little.]

Elsewhere in the field, where a torrent had torn the
    stones
And bushes from the banks, the Arcadians fled,
Infantrymen, for once, for the rough ground
Forbade the use of chariots, and their nerve
Was at low ebb. But Pallas saw them yield,
And, being their one hope, with scorn and prayer
Rallied their courage: "Whither fleeing, friends?
By your brave deeds I beg you, by your king,
By the old wars won in Evander's name,
By my own hopes to match my father's praise,
Trust not to flight! The sword must cut the way,
And where that mass is thickest, there we go,
There Pallas leads. No gods pursue us; men,
We are being chased by men, with no more hands,
And no more lives than we have. Ocean blocks us
    off
With his great dam; earth offers us no flight;
Are we bound for Troy or the sea?"    [362–378]

[Pallas' speech, with his own example, rallies
the Arcadians, and the young warrior works havoc
in the Italian ranks. On the other side, his peer in
youth and courage, Lausus, the son of Mezentius,
does equal damage; the two strive to reach each
other.]

Two nearly matched in years, alike in worth,
Courage, and handsome manhood; two denied
Return to fatherland; and neither given
To face the other; soon each one shall find
His fate, each one confront his greater foe.

Juturna, Turnus' sister, brings him warning, *Go
To Lausus' aid;* with his swift car he drives
Between the ranks; "Break off, give way!" he
    cries,
"Room for my fighting! I alone am bound
To battle Pallas; Pallas is my prize,
My prize alone. And how I wish his father
Were here to see!" Obedient, his comrades
Give place, and as they leave, young Pallas stands
Astonished at this arrogance, this giant,
Taking the whole scene in, undaunted, proud
And fierce and high in spirit, answering
Turnus with this: "Either I win my praise
For kingly spoils or glorious death, and soon:
My father can face either: stop the threats!"
Pallas moves forward, and the blood runs chill
In all Arcadian hearts. Down from his car
Jumps Turnus; he comes nearer, like a lion

Who sees far-off a bull, intent on battle,
And stalks, and rushes; even so came Turnus.
Came within spear-cast; Pallas, watching knew it,
Took a step forward, and, that chance might favor
However uneven his strength, prayed to the heavens:
"If ever my father entertained a stranger
Who proved a god, with welcome food and greeting,
Aid me, O Hercules! Let Turnus watch me
Taking the bloody armor from his body,
His dying eyes endure me, Pallas, victor!"
The young prayer touched the god; his grief was stifled
Deep in his heart, and his tears were vain; his father
Spoke to him kindly: "Every man, my son,
Has his appointed time; life's day is short
For all men; they can never win it back,
But to extend it further, by noble deeds,
Is the task set for valor. Even my own,
My own, and other gods' brave sons have fallen
Under Troy's lofty walls. Sarpedon, Turnus,
Fate calls alike; the years for each are measured,
The goal in sight." Jupiter, having spoken,
Let his eyes turn from the Rutulian landscape.

And Pallas flung the spear, full force, and drew
The flashing blade; the shaft sped on, it struck
Where mail and shoulder meet; it pierced the shield,
It grazed the side of Turnus. And he poised
The long oak shaft with the sharp iron, hurled it,
Taunting and throwing: "See which pierces deeper,
Your shaft or mine!" Through the plates of iron,
The plates of bronze, the overlapping leather,
Through the shield's center drives the quivering point,
Through stubborn mail, through the great breast. In vain
Pallas pulls out the warm dart from the wound,
The blood, the life, come with it. Pallas falls
Doubled upon his wound; the armor rings
Over his body; he strikes the hostile earth,
Dying, with bloody mouth. Above him, Turnus,
Rejoicing, cries, "Arcadians, give heed!
And let Evander know, I am sending back
Pallas, as he deserved. Whatever honor
A tomb affords, whatever comfort lies
In burial, that much I grant, and freely:

A costly welcome, that he gave Aeneas!"
His left foot on the body, he ripped loose
The belt's great weight, with the story of a murder
Carved in its metal, the young men foully slain
On the bridal night, the chamber drenched in blood,
As Clonus, son of Eurytus, engraved it.
And Turnus glories in the spoil, exulting—
O ignorant mortal mind, which never knows
Of fate or doom ahead, or how, in fortune,
To keep in proper bounds! A time is coming
When Turnus will pay dearly, could he purchase
Pallas unharmed again, and view with loathing
Those spoils, that day. But now, with tears and weeping,
His friends lift Pallas on the shield and take him,
Great sorrow and great glory, to his father.
One day of war, one day of death, but victims
Also, for the Rutulians to remember.

No rumor, but a runner from the battle,
Comes to Aeneas, of his men endangered,
At the edge of death; they are giving way, the Trojans,
There is not much time. The sword is drawn, a harvest
Reaped through the lines; Aeneas, blazing, drives
His pathway through; it is Turnus he is seeking,
Turnus the arrogant, slaughter fresh upon him.
Aeneas, all imagination, sees
Pallas, Evander, and the friendly tables
Whereto he came, a stranger, and the pledge
Given and taken. For another pledge
He seizes four young men, the sons of Sulmo,
And four whom Ufens sired; he takes them, living,
For later sacrifice, to dye with blood
The funeral pyre of Pallas. From afar
He aimed his spear at Magus, but the latter
Ducked under it cleverly, and the shaft went over,
And Magus was a suppliant at his knees:
"I beg you, by the shades of great Anchises,
By all the hope you have of young Iulus,
Spare me, a father and a son, for son
And father. I have property and treasure,
A lofty house, talents of gold and silver,
Buried in safety, crude and minted metal.
One life like mine is nothing to the Trojans;
What difference will it make?" "Save for your sons,"
Aeneas answered, "all that gold and silver.
Turnus broke off all bargain talk, the killer,

When Pallas fell. The shades of great Anchises
Know this; my growing son, Iulus, knows it."
The left hand grasped the helmet; Magus felt
The head drawn back, mouth open in his pleading,
And the sword driven to the very hilt. [433–536]

[This is the first of three instances when Aeneas,
in his terrible rage over the death of Pallas, lets
his sense of devotion, *pietas*, become very bitter
indeed. Ordinarily an appeal made to him in the
name of the relation between father and son would
move him deeply; here, sticking to the letter of the
text of piety, he turns the appeal against the
pleader: if you want to be so devoted to your
father and sons, the way to do it is let them have
the money you are trying to bribe me with; die,
and the sooner, the better for them. He kills a
priest of Apollo, strikes off Anxur's left arm, then
intercepts Tarquitus, son of Faunus and Dryope.]

Aeneas' spear drives through the shield's huge
    weight,
Nailing it to the breast-plate; all in vain
Tarquitus struggled, pleading, wanting utterance.
Aeneas gave his head a shove; still warm, the body
Turned halfway over under his foot, and answer
Spoke from a vengeful heart: "Lie there, and
    scare me!
No mother, now, to bury the bones, no father
To build the tomb above them. Let birds of prey
Take over, or the water of the flood,
And fish, unfed, nibble and lick the wounds!"
                                    [552–560]

[This amounts to really sacrilegious vindictiveness: how could Aeneas refuse anyone the rites of
burial, and go on to gloat over his action? Even
Turnus was scrupulous in promising to return the
body of Pallas to Evander for whatever consolation there might be in funeral rites. After this,
he kills Antaeus, Lucas, Numa, Camers, and
frightens the horses of Niphaeus so badly that
they overturn the chariot and dash the driver to
the ground.]

Into the ranks ride two, Lucagus, Liger,
Brothers, in a white chariot; Lucagus
Wielding the sword, and Liger at the reins.
They burn with fury; Aeneas cannot bear
Their onslaught, rushes in against them, looming
A giant with a spear. And Liger taunts him,

"Whoa! This is not Achilles' car, these fields
Not Troy's, these horses Diomedes',
This is the end, of war and life together,
Here on this ground." Poor crazy-talking Liger!
Aeneas wastes no words; the lance comes flying,
And while Lucagus, leaning over the chariot,
Makes of his sword a whip, with left foot forward
Setting himself for action, the point comes through
The low rim of the shield, drives on, and pierces
The groin on the left side. Lucagus topples,
Writhes on the ground, and dies; and then Aeneas
Has words for him, and bitter ones: "Lucagus,
Your horses have not run away, they are brave,
They are no traitors, shying at a shadow,
You are the one, it seems, the cheap deserter,
Who jump the wheels, leave the poor beasts for-
    saken."
He pulls the horses up; and down comes Liger,
His luck all gone, his hands outstretched for pity,
"O Trojan hero, son of mighty parents,
For their remembrance, spare my life: O hear
    me—"
And there was more he would have said. Aeneas
Broke in: "That's not the way that you were
    talking
A little while ago. Should brother leave
A brother in the battle? Never. Die!"
And the sword went its deadly way, exposing
The spirit's hiding-place.              [575–601]

[With this third instance of the pious Aeneas
committing an outrage on piety, the Trojans are
sufficiently heartened to break out of their besieged camp. The scene shifts to a colloquy between Jupiter and Juno, the former pointing out,
with very little warrant, that it is Venus' power
which is keeping the Trojans going; Juno answers, very meekly for her, in a tone of resignation to the death of Turnus. Jupiter, in an indulgent mood, says that his death may be postponed
for a while at least, strictly on the understanding
that the eventual victory is to be the Trojans' and
that Turnus can not, in the end, avoid his fate.
Juno seems to hope that even in this he may yield
more than he concedes at present; at any rate, she
leaves the heavens and comes to the battlefield.]

Out of a hollow cloud she makes a figure,
Thin, weak, and curious to see, a phantom,
A false Aeneas, dressed in Dardan arms,
The shield and crest like his, and words unreal,

Voice without purpose, the image of a stride,
Like the vain forms that flit when death is over,
Like dreams that mock the drugged and drowsy
    senses.
With arrogant joy this phantom stalks before
The warriors' ranks, brandishing weapons, taunt-
    ing,
Crying a dare to Turnus. He comes on,
Hurls from afar the whirring spear; the ghost
Turns and makes off. And Turnus, swollen, feeds
An empty hope; his foolishness believes
Aeneas fleeing, gone. "What now, Aeneas,
Where do you flee? Do not desert the bride,
The marriage chamber!" And he draws the sword,
Which flashes with his challenge; he does not see
The wind sweep off his triumph.
Moored to a shelf of rock, a ship was standing,
Ladders let down, and gangplank set; a king
Had sailed therein from Clusium. The ghost,
The false Aeneas, hurrying, found shelter
Deep in the hold, and Turnus followed after,
Hotfoot through all delays, leaps onto the deck,
And has no sooner reached the bow than Juno
Breaks off the mooring-lines, and the ship goes
    scudding
Over the yielding sea. The real Aeneas
Calls Turnus to the fight, strikes down in battle
Any that cross his path. But the frail image
No longer seeks a hiding place, but sweeps
High to the darker clouds, with Turnus riding
The gale far out to seaward. Ignorant still,
Ungrateful for reprieve, he looks to shore,
Raises his hands to heaven, praying: "Father,
What have I done, to be so tricked, so sullied?
What am I being punished for? Where am I,
Who am I, for that matter? Fugitive
And coward, will I ever see again
The camp, the walls? And all that band of heroes
Who followed me and trusted me, I leave them
In death unspeakable, I see them wheeling,
I hear their dying groans. What am I doing?
What gulf, what chasm, deep enough to hide me?
Pity me, winds; dash this accursed vessel
On rocks, on reefs, on any savage quicksands,
I, Turnus, plead, with all my heart, Oh, strand me
Beyond all reach, where rumor or Rutulian
May, neither one, pursue me." The doubting spirit,
Mad with so much disgrace, is undecided
Whether to let the sword drive through the body,
Or dive and swim for it, toward camp and Tro-
    jans.

Three times he tried each way, three times the
    hand
And will were stayed by Juno, in her mercy,
And the tall ship, on wind and tide, was carried
On to Ardea, Daunus' lofty city.        [636–688]

[Back at the scene of the fighting, Mezentius,
the Etrurian king who despises the gods, enters
the fighting and at this point makes his presence
felt, slaughtering victims too numerous to mention. The Trojans gang up on him, but he is like
a wild boar whom the hunters have surrounded
and at the same time have a healthy respect for,
and keep their distance, no one having a mind to
charge him with drawn steel. Hemmed in though
he is, he attempts a successful foray every now
and then.]

There was a youth named Acron, who had come
From a Greek town, leaving his bride a virgin
At home in Corythus. Mezentius saw him
Bright in the ranks, flashing, maroon and crim-
    son,
The colors of his bride. Mezentius saw him
The way a hungry lion sees a deer,
And the jaws open, and the mane is lifted,
And after one great leap the claws are fastened
Deep in the flanks, and the mouth is red with
    slaughter.
So charged Mezentius into the midst, and Acron
Goes down, the heels drum on the ground, the
    blood
Pours over the broken spear. Orodes fled,
Or tried to, but no spear for him; Mezentius
Closed in, and struck with the sword, leaned on
    the spear
With one foot on the body, and cried aloud,
"Here lies Orodes, men, a mighty captain,
No little bit of the war!" His comrades join him
Shouting applause; with the last breath Orodes
Manages answer: "Not for long, O foeman,
Shall I be unavenged; exult a little,
Your doom keeps watch, you will hold these fields,
    as I do,
Before too long." Mezentius, smiling at him,
"Die now," he said, "and let the sire of gods,
The king of men, look after me." The weapon
Drawn from the body, iron sleep and heavy
Repose weighed down his eyes; they close for-
    ever
In night's eternal dark.        [719–746]

[There are other duels, rapidly told by Vergil, and presently Aeneas catches sight of Mezentius.]

Aeneas moves to meet him, and he stands
Unfrightened, heavy-set, waiting the foe.
He eyes the distance that the spear may need,
"Let my right hand, my god, and the dart I balance
Favor me now! And as a trophy, Lausus,
I vow the spoil stripped from this dying robber,
For you to carry, living." The spear flew on,
Glanced from the shield, wounded the knight Antores,
Between the side and thigh; Hercules' comrade,
An ally of Evander, come from Argos,
Falls by a wound meant for another; dying,
He thinks of his dear Argos. And Aeneas
Lets drive his spear; it penetrates the shield,
The triple bronze, the layers of leather, biting
Deep in the groin, not going through. And happy
At sight of Tuscan blood, Aeneas draws
Sword from his side, comes hotly on; Mezentius
Staggers, and Lausus grieves; he loves his father,
The tears stream down his face.
Mezentius, dragging back, useless, disabled,
Slowly gives ground; the hostile spear still trailing
Still fastened to the shield. Lausus runs forward,
Lifts his right arm and strikes; Aeneas parries,
Lausus is halted. But his comrades follow;
The father, under the son's protecting shield,
Has, still, a chance of safety. Missiles shower
From all sides at Aeneas; though he rages
He huddles under shelter, like a farmer
When hailstones rattle down, or any traveller
Seeking what he can find, a river bank,
An overhanging rock, or any shelter
Until the downpour stops, and the sun returns
Men to their daily tasks; even so Aeneas,
With javelins thickening, all ways, against him,
Endures the storm of war, and threatens Lausus:
"What rush is this to death? what silly daring
Beyond the limit of strength? O foolish youngster,
You love your father, but you fool yourself
With too much loving." Lausus, in his madness,
Has never a thought of stopping, and Aeneas
Feels anger rise against him; and the Fates
Tie off the ends of Lausus' thread; Aeneas
Drives with the sword; it is buried in the body,
Deep to the hilt. The little shield, frail armor,
Against so great a menace, could not hold it,

The pliant tunic, woven by his mother,
With golden thread, is no more help; the blood
Stains it another color, and through air
The life went sorrowing to the shades. And now
Aeneas changes; looking on that face
So pale in death, he groans in pity; he reaches
As if to touch him with his hand, in comfort,
Knowing, himself, how one can love a father.
"Poor boy, what proof of glory can I offer,
What recompense for glory? Keep the armor
You loved so much; if there is any comfort
In burial at home, know I release you
To your ancestral shades and ashes. Further,
If it is any comfort, you have fallen
By great Aeneas' hand." He lifts up Lausus
From the ground he stained with blood, rebukes his comrades
Over their hesitation.                [769–831]

[Aeneas is himself again, compassionate and decent. The taunts which he later lashes at Mezentius are mere conventions, compared with his scathing bitterness against Magus and Tarquitus, Lucagus and Liger. If you think that it is shockingly conceited of him to offer as comfort to the dead Lausus that it took an Aeneas to kill him, wait a minute. What should he have said? "I was lucky," or "I'm really not a very good fighter, myself"—wouldn't that have been more of an insult? Somewhere or other, in an article on British sportsmanship, I recall reading that the courteous thing to say to a beaten opponent is, "You played very badly." The same principle.]

Meanwhile, Mezentius, by the wave of the river,
Propped his slumped frame against a tree trunk, staunching
The wound with water. The bronze helmet hung,
Inverted, from the bough; the heavy arms
Lay quiet on the meadow. Chosen men
Were standing by. Sick, and with labored breath,
He let his chin fall forward, rubbed his neck,
While over his chest the flowing beard was streaming.
Over and over again, he asks, and sends,
For Lausus: *bring him back*, he tells the men,
Those are the orders from his unhappy father.
But they were bringing him back, a big man, slain
By a big wound. Mezentius knew the sound
Of sorrow from afar, before he heard it,
Fouled his grey hair with dust, flung up his arms,

Clung to the body. "O my son, my son,
Was I so fond of living that I sent
You to the sword for me, saved by your wounds,
Alive when you are dead? The wound indeed
Is driven deep, the bitterness of death
Comes home. I was the one, my son, my son,
Who stained your name with crime, with hatred, driven
From throne and scepter. I have owed too long
The debt of punishment, and here I am,
Living and never leaving men, and light.
But I shall leave." He heaved his sickened weight,
Pulling himself together, groin and all,
Slowly. The wound was deep, but he could stand.
He ordered them to bring his horse, that solace,
That pride of his, on which he used to ride
Victorious out of all the wars. He spoke,
And the beast sorrowed with the master's sorrow:
"Rhoebus, if anything is ever long
For mortal beings, you and I have lived
For a long time. Today you carry back
Those bloody spoils, Aeneas' head, avenging
The pangs of Lausus with me, or we both,
If no force clears the way, go down together,
O bravest heart, too noble to endure
The stranger's order and the Trojan rider."
He swung astride, shifted his weight a little,
The way he always did, held in both hands
A load of darts. The helmet glittered bronze,
The horse-hair plume was bristling as he rode,
Madness and grief and shame all urging on
The one heart toward the many.
"Aeneas!" and "Aeneas!" thrice he called
In a loud voice. Yes, and Aeneas heard,
Rejoiced, and recognized, and made his prayer:
"Let this be true, O father of the gods,
And high Apollo!" then, to his foe, "Come on!"
And moved to meet him with the deadly spear.
Mezentius answered: "Do you frighten me,
Think you, with all that fierceness, having taken
My son away? That was the only way
You could destroy me. Now I fear no death,
I spare no god. Be quiet; for I come
To die, but first of all I bring you this,
A present from me," and he flung the spear,
And flung another, and another, wheeling
In a great arc. The boss of gold held strong.
Three times in circles to the left he rode
Around the steady Trojan, thrice the hand
Let fly the dart, and thrice the shield of bronze
Was a great forest with its load of spears.

All this was wearisome—too many darts,
Too much defensiveness. Aeneas broke
Out of the patient watchfulness, and flung
The spear between the charger's hollow temples.
The great beast rears, with fore-hooves flailing air,
Throwing the rider, then the horse comes down,
Head foremost on him, shoulder out of joint.
Trojan and Latin noise sets heaven afire.
Aeneas, sword-blade ready, rushes in.
"Where is the fierce Mezentius now, and where
All that wild rage of spirit?" But the king,
Raising his eyes, drank in the sky a little,
Knew a brief moment of recovery,
Enough to say, "O bitter enemy,
Why all the tauntings and the threats of death?
There is no wrong in slaughter; neither I
Nor Lausus ever made such battle pledges.
One thing I ask, if beaten enemies
Have any claim on mercy. Let my body
Be granted burial. I know the hate
Of my own people rages round me. Keep
Their fury from me. Let me share the grave
Of my dear son." He said no more, but welcomed,
Fully aware, the sword-thrust in the throat,
And poured his life in crimson over the armor.
[833–908]

## Book XI

### DRANCES AND TURNUS—CAMILLA

Book XI balances Book V. There, if you remember,
the Trojans were having games in honor of Anchises,
and very happy over their deliverance from Carthage.
Here it is the despair of the Latins; the loss of Mezentius
and Lausus was a heavy blow, and the news that Diomedes
in Arpi will not come to their aid is depressing. You will
find, as you read on, other discouraging incidents in swift
succession.

I have said that if the *Aeneid* were a modern novel, it
would no doubt be prefaced with a statement by the author that all the characters were purely imaginary, and
any reference to living persons purely coincidental. But
the Roman reader, just the same, may have suspected that
Vergil might have had Cicero in mind when he drew
the character of Drances; possibly Turnus is a little like
Antony, and to some Romans Dido resembled Cleopatra.

[The book begins with Aeneas erecting a
trophy in token of his victory over Mezentius;
he proposes to strike while the iron is hot, and

attack Latinus' capital. The body of Pallas is sent home to Evander with all due honor; meanwhile envoys come from Latinus asking a twelve-day truce for the burial of the dead. This Aeneas grants. There is a pathetic scene in Evander's court while Pallas is brought home, and during the truce Venulus returns to Latinus with news of his unsuccessful mission to Diomedes. The latter has told the envoys that his luck has been all bad since the time he wounded Venus when she was rescuing Aeneas from him, and that he wants no part of any further battles with Aeneas. His advice to the Latins is to make peace. Latinus calls a council, ready to put this advice into practice: he offers either to let them share his city with them, or, if they prefer to go elsewhere, to put all possible resources at their disposal.]

Then Drances, hostile still, whom Turnus' glory
Goaded with envy's bitter sting, arose,
A man of wealth, better than good with his tongue,
And a cold hand in war, no fool in council,
A trouble-maker, though; his mother was noble,
His father no one much. His words were angry:
"Good king, you ask our guidance in a matter
Obscure to none, needing no word of ours.
All know, admit they know, what fortune orders,
They mutter, rather than speak. Let him abate
That bluster of his, through whose disastrous
      ways
Evil has come upon us, and bad omens—
I will speak out, however much he threaten—
Let us have freedom to speak frankly. Mourning
Has settled on the town, the light of the leaders
Gone down in darkness, while that confident war-
      rior,
Confident, but in flight, attacks the Trojans
And frightens heaven with arms. To all those
      gifts
Promised and sent the Trojans, add, O king,
One more; let no one's violence dissuade you
From giving your daughter in a worthy marriage,
An everlasting pledge and bond between us.
But if such terror holds our hearts, why, let us
Beseech this prince, sue for his royal favor,
To abdicate his claim, for king and country.

Why, fountainhead of all our Latin troubles,*
Consign us, wretches that we are, to danger,
Open and often? In war there is no safety;

* Drances, here, is turning to address Turnus.

Turnus, we ask for peace, and to confirm it
The only pledge that will. Even I, the first one,
The one who hates you (I'd not undeceive you),
Come to you, suppliant. Pity on your people!
Put off that pride; give in, give up, and leave us!
We have seen enough of death and desolation.
If glory moves you, you with the heart of oak,
Or if the royal dowry is your passion,
Be bold, have confidence—and face the foeman!
Let Turnus have his royal bride! No matter
If we, cheap souls, a herd, unwept, unburied,
Lie strewn across the field? O son of Mars,
If son you really are, the challenger is calling:
Dare you look him in the face?"
And Turnus' violence blazed out in fury,
A groan, or a growl, and the words pouring forth:
"A flow of words is what you have, O Drances,
Always, when wars need men; and you come
      running
Whenever the senate meets, the first one there!
But this is not the time for words, that fly
From your big mouth in safety, in a meeting,
While the wall keeps off the foe, and the dry
      trenches
Have not yet swum in blood. As usual,
Thunder on, orator! Convict me, Drances,
Of cowardice, you having slain so many
Great heaped-up piles of Trojans, all the fields
Stacked with your trophies! A trial is permitted,
The enemy are not far to seek, the walls'
Are circled with them. Coming? Why the coy-
      ness?
Will your idea of Mars be found forever
In windy tongue and flying feet? I, beaten?
Who says so? What foul liar calls me beaten,
Who has seen the Tiber red with blood, Evander
Laid low, and all his house, and the Arcadians
Stripped of their arms? Ask Pandarus and
      Bitias,
The thousands I have sent to Hell, though I was
      cut off
Inside their walls, hedged by a ring of foemen.
*In war there is no safety*. Sing that song,
Madman, to your own cause, and prince Aeneas!
Keep on, don't stop, confound confusion further
With panic fear, and praise those noble heroes
Of that twice-beaten race, despise the arms
Of King Latinus. Now the Myrmidons,
Or so we hear, are trembling, and their river
Runs backward out of fright, and Diomedes,
Is frightened—I suppose Achilles also!

Now he pretends my threats, my anger, scare
    him—
A nice artistic piece of work—he sharpens
Slander with apprehension. Listen to him!
Listen to me, I tell you, you will never
Lose such a life as yours by this right hand,
Quit worrying, keep that great and fighting
    spirit
Forever in that breast! And now, my father,
I turn to you, and more important counsels.*

If you have hope no longer in our arms,
If we are so forsaken, if we are lost
Utterly, over one repulse, if Fortune
Cannot retrace her steps, let us pray for peace,
Let us hold out helpless hands in supplication.
But, still, if only some of our valor, something—
Happy the men who died before they saw it.
But if we still have any power, young warriors
    standing
Unhurt, any Italian city, any nation,
To fight with us, if any Trojans ever
Have met with death (their glory has been costly,
As well as ours, and the storm has no more spared
    them),
Why do we fail, like cowards, on the edge
Of victory? Why do we shudder and tremble
Before the trumpet sounds? Many an evil
Has turned to good in time; and many a mortal
Fate has despised and raised. Diomedes, Arpi,
Refuse us help; so be it. There are others,
There is Messapus for one, Tolumnius
Whose luck is good, and all those other leaders
Sent by so many nations; and great glory
Will follow Latium's pride. We have Camilla
Of Volscian stock, leading her troop of horse-
    men,
Her warriors bright in bronze. If I am summoned,
Alone, to meet the Trojan, if I alone
Am obstinate about the common welfare,
If such is your decision, my hands have never
Found victory so shrinking or elusive
That I should fear the risk. Bring on your Tro-
    jan,
Let him surpass Achilles, and wear armor
Made by the hands of Vulcan! Second to no one
Of all my ancestors in pride and courage,

---

* Turnus' tone is much more temperate and controlled,
though his emotion no less felt, as he addresses the king.
But isn't that a wonderful blast he puts on Drances?
Drances may be the better orator, but Turnus certainly
has made the better speech.

---

I, Turnus, vow this life to you, Latinus,
My king and father. *The challenger is calling*—
Well, let him call. I hope he does. No Drances,
If heaven's wrath is here, will ever appease it,
Nor, out of valor and glory, be uplifted."
                                        [336–444]

[While this argument rages, Aeneas comes
nearer. Turnus breaks up the meeting, before
the king has come to any decision, by issuing
orders for the defense. He enters the battle himself and as he does so Camilla comes riding to
him, with a proposal to meet with her cavalry
Aeneas' advance guard. Turnus proposes, instead,
that she set an ambush, with Messapus beside
her, as Aeneas comes over the ridge; and he
moves in with his forces to take up the frontal
attack.

The story cuts to Olympus, where Diana tells
Opis, one of her attendant nymphs, of the early
history of Camilla: how her father, escaping from
his enemies, had to cross a flooded stream, bound
his baby daughter to a spear and flung her across
the torrent, thereafter vowing her to the worship
of Diana, by whose aid the feat had been accomplished. Now that Camilla's life is endangered in
the battle, Diana tells Opis to exact vengeance
on any warrior who harms her. We get a close-up
of Camilla fighting.]

In the thick of the fight Camilla rages, bearing
The quiver, like an Amazon, one breast
Exposed; she showers javelins, she plies
The battle-axe; she never tires; her shoulder
Clangs with the golden bow, Diana's weapon.
If ever, turning back, she yields, the arrows
Are loosed from over her shoulder; even in flight
She makes attack. Around her, chosen comrades,
Larina, Tulla, and Tarpeia, brandish
Axes of bronze. She chose them as her hand-
    maids,
Good both in peace and war, Italian daughters,
Italy's pride . . . .                  [648–658]

[She strikes down many victims: Euneus, Liris,
Pagasus, Amastrus, Tereus, Harpalycus, Demo-
phoon, Chromis; and then she sees a hunter
named Ornytus.]

Riding a native pony, in strange armor,
He wore a steer's hide over his wide shoulders,

A wolf's head for a helmet, with the jaws,
Wide open, grinning above his head; he carried
A rustic kind of pike, and he was taller,
By a full head, than all the others, easy
Target for any dart. She cries above him:
"What did you think, O Tuscan? You were chasing
Beasts in the woods? The day has come when
    boasting
Like yours is answered by a woman's weapons,
But after all, your father's shades are hearing
No little cause for pride—Camilla killed you!"
                                [677–689]

[She adds two more victims to her score:
Butes she gets with a spear blow in the back,
Orsilochus she catches up with and brains with
her axe.]

Next in her way, and stunned by terror, halted,
Was one of Aunus' sons, expert at lying,
Like all Ligurians. He could not escape her,
And knew he could not, but he could outwit her,
Or so he thought. "What's so courageous, woman,
Always on horseback? Lose the hope of fleeing,
Dismount; meet me on equal terms; try fighting
On foot for once. You will learn, I tell you,
    something,
The disillusion of that windy glory."
She took the challenge, burned with angry fury,
Turned her horse over to another, savage
In equal arms, confronting him, untroubled,
With naked sword. He leaps into the saddle,
Pleased with his own sly craft, and drives the
    rowels
Deep in the flanks, takes off. "O vain Ligurian,
Swollen with pride of heart, the slippery cunning
Will never get you home to father Aunus!"
She cries; like fire on deadly wing, she crosses
The horse's path, grabs at the bridle, hauls him
To earth, and lets his blood. A hawk in heaven
Is not more quick to seize a dove, when, driving
From the dark rock toward lofty cloud, he fastens
The talons deep, and tears, and the feathers flutter,
All blood-stained, down the sky.        [699–724]

[The camera cuts away from Camilla for a moment, to a vivid scene in which Tarchon grabs up Venulus, and rides out of sight with Venulus on the saddle before him, Tarchon riding without reins, one arm around Venulus, the other hand trying to stab a broken dart through his throat, Venulus struggling, trying to hold him off. They vanish; back to Camilla again.]

Chloreus, Cybele's priest sometime, was shining
Far off in Phrygian armor, spurring a horse
Covered with leather, scales of brass and gold,
And the rider was a fire of foreign color,
Launching his Cretan darts; the bow was golden,
The helmet golden, and the cloak of saffron
So stiff it had a metal sound, and fastened
With knots of yellow gold; some foreign needle
Had worked embroidery into hose and tunic.
Camilla picked him out from all the battle,
Either to take that spoil home to the temple,
Or flaunt the gold herself, became a huntress
In blind pursuit, dazzled by spoil, a woman
Reckless for finery. In hiding, Arruns
Caught up his spear and prayed: "Most high
    Apollo,
Soracte's warden, whose adorers feed
The pine-wood fire, and, trustful, tread the embers,
Let me wipe out this shame. I seek no plunder,
No spoil, no trophy, of Camilla beaten;
I may, perhaps, find other ways to glory,
All I ask here is that this scourge may vanish
Under a wound I give; for this I am willing
To make return, however inglorious, home."
Half of his prayer was heard; Apollo granted
The downfall of Camilla; the returning
Safe home was not to be; the south winds carried
That much to empty air. So the spear, whirring,
Spun from his hand; the sound turned all the
    Volscians
With anxious eyes and minds to watch their
    queen.
She heard no stir in the air, no sound, no weapon
Out of the sky, till the spear went to its lodging
In the bare breast, and drank the maiden blood.
Her frightened comrades hurry, they catch her
    falling,
And Arruns, frightened more than any other,
Half joy, half fear, makes off; no further daring
Is his, to trust the lance, or face encounter.
As a wolf that kills a bullock, or a shepherd,
Before the darts can reach him, down the mountains
Goes plunging through the brush, the sign of guilt
The tail clapped under the belly; bent on flight,

So Arruns sneaks to cover through the armies
Dying, she pulls at the dart, but the point is fast,
Deep in the wound, between the ribs; her eyes
Roll, cold in death; her color pales, her breath
Comes hard; she calls to Acca, her companion,
Most loved, most loyal: "I have managed, Acca,
This far; but now the bitter wound—I am done
     for,
There are shadows all around. Hurry to Turnus,
Take him this last direction, to relieve me
Here in the fight, keep off the Trojans—
Farewell." The reins went slack, the earth re-
     ceived her,
She left the body to its cold, resigning
The slumping neck, the head, to death; let fall,
For the last time, her weapons, and the spirit
Went with a moan indignant to the shadows.
                                        [768–831]

[At this Opis, whom Diana had assigned to the
task of vengeance, detects Arruns and kills him
with an arrow. But there is panic in the Rutulian
ranks over the loss of Camilla; the Trojans are
at the very walls; even the women are joining
the ranks in the desperate fighting. The news
finally reaches Turnus; reluctantly, but of necessity, he abandons the ambush he has set for
Aeneas, and comes down to rally the hardpressed defense.]

And scarcely has he done so, when Aeneas
Enters the pass in safety, crosses the mountain,
Comes out of the dark woods. And both are striv-
     ing
To reach the city, swiftly, in full column,
And close together; in a single moment
Aeneas sees the plain and the dust rising
And Turnus sees Aeneas, fierce in battle,
And hears the stamp and snorting of the horses.
There was almost time for battle, but the Sun God
Colored in crimson, brought his weary horses
To bathe in the western ocean; day was over,
Night coming on. They camp before the city.
                                        [903–915]

## Book XII

### AENEAS KILLS TURNUS IN SINGLE COMBAT.

[This book tells of the final conflict, but Vergil
is too much the artist to plunge right into it im-

mediately. The story must build, with all possible
devices of heightening the suspense. Turnus, as
he sees the Latins yielding, and the time come
when his pledge to fight Aeneas in single combat
must be redeemed, rages like a lion which begins
to fight only when he is wounded.]

He speaks to the king, as violence swells in him
To angry words: "Turnus won't keep them wait-
     ing;
No reason for these cowards to renounce
Their bargain. Start the holy ritual, father,
Arrange the terms. I go to meet the Trojan,
Let the Latins sit and watch it, if they want to,
And this right arm will send him down to Hell,
The renegade from Asia. I alone
Answer the argument that calls us cowards,
I, with one single sword. Or we are beaten,
And he takes Lavinia home."        [10–17]

[Latinus tries to dissuade him, pointing out
that he is heir of Daunus' lands, and that there
are other girls beside Lavinia. The oracles forbid the match; he has been weak in giving way
to Queen Amata's insistence. What good will it
do, to make peace with Aeneas and become an
ally of the Trojans after Turnus' death? He might
as well do so beforehand, and spare the life of
that warrior. This reasonable appeal has no effect
on Turnus, either.]

"Most kindly father, the care you have for me,
Lay down, for my sake; let me have permission
To trade death for renown. I too, dear father,
Toss no mean dart, swing no mean sword, and
     blood
Follows the wounds I give. His goddess-mother
Will not be here, this time, to hide him, running
To the folds of her gown, the cloud, the empty
     shadows."        [48–53]

[Amata also begs him not to fight, and hints
that his death also means her own; she can not
bear the thought of Aeneas as her son-in-law.
Lavinia is present, and blushes; but what she
thinks nobody knows: she is certainly dealt
with very lightly in the matter of characterization. Turnus looks at Lavinia but speaks to
Amata; he is not to be dissuaded. He sends a
message to Aeneas that he will be ready for the
duel on the next morning.]

In his own quarters, he demands his horses,
Those shining steeds Orithyia gave Pilumnus,
Whiter than snow, swifter than wind. And he is
    happy,
Looking at them, all spirit, as they nicker
Seeing their master. The drivers stand about
    them,
Grooming the manes, patting the chests with the
    hollows
Of sweating hands. And Turnus to his shoulders
Fits the stiff coat of mail, the gold, the bronze,
And he makes ready the sword, the shield, the
    double
Plumes of the reddish crest; the sword was made
By Vulcan for King Daunus; it had been glow-
    ing,
White-hot, when plunged in Stygian water for
    him.
And Turnus takes the spear, which leans on a
    pillar
In the great hall, a trophy taken from Actor,
Poises it, makes it quiver, and cries aloud:
"Be with me now, good spear that never failed
    me!
The time has come. Let me lay low that body,
With these tough hands tear off his mail, that
    eunuch's,
With crimped and perfumed hair, let me shove his
    face
Deep in the bloody dust." *

[With morning, all preparations have been
made, and both sides come trooping forth to
watch the duel. Juno cannot bear it; she summons Turnus' sister, Juturna (who has been one
of Jupiter's girls), and tells her there is nothing
more she can do, but if Juturna sees any way
of interfering, to go to it. The preliminary cere-
monial continues; solemn rites, long prayers, a
delay that must have seemed unbearable to Turnus. Our first glimpse of him, that morning,
shows him in a new and strange guise.]

Rutulian hearts were wavering; the fight
Began to seem unequal; more and more

They stir and shift and doubt. And Turnus moves
    them,
Coming with quiet footstep to the altar,
Looking down humbly, with a meek devotion,
Cheeks drawn, and pale. Juturna heard the whis-
    pers,
The muttered talk, and sensed the stir in the
    crowd,
And suddenly plunged into their midst, disguised
As Camers, noble in birth, and brave in arms,
    and son
Of a brave father. She knew what she was doing,
Putting the fuel of rumor on the fire,
And crying: "Are you not ashamed, Rutulians,
That one should be exposed for all this host?
In numbers and in strength, are we not equal?
Here they all are, the Trojans, the Arcadians,
The Etruscans, all the lot of them: and we
Are almost twice as many; man to man,
Two against one! But no, we let him
Rise to the skies on deathless praise; the gods
Receive him, by his own decision bound,
An offering at their altars, and we sit here
Sluggish as stone on ground, our country lost,
Ready to bow to any arrogant master."
They are moved; at least the young are, and a
    murmur
Runs through the ranks: the Latins and Lauren-
    tians
Are ripe for change; rest from the war, and
    safety,
Count less than arms; they want the treaty
    broken,
They pity Turnus. It's not fair, this bargain.
                                    [216–243]

[At this point Juturna seizes on an opportunity
and cries to them once more, pointing out a sight
in the skies—an eagle pursuing a troop of swans,
snatching one up, only to be driven off and compelled to let go his prey when all the other swans
rally and chase the predator to cover. The augur
Tolumnius acknowledges the omen as sent from
heaven, cries out for battle, and with the cry
lets drive his spear at the Trojan ranks. Everybody seizes up arms: Messapus rides down Aules-
tes, forcing him backward over the toppled and
desecrated altars; Corynaeus grabs burning
brands from the same altar, and sets the beard of
Ebysus on fire. One instance of sacrilege after

---

* If I translated *semiviri Phrygis . . . crinis vibratos
calido ferro* as "that pansy with the permanent," it would,
I'm afraid, be too much of an anachronism. But it's just
about what Turnus means. His conduct here has always
seemed to me very strange; why is he getting the horses
harnessed, and putting on his armor, when the fight isn't
set till the next morning? Vergil's oversight, or a master
stroke to indicate his extremely violent character?

another: Aeneas rushes in and tries to put a stop
to it.]

Head bare, and hands unarmed, Aeneas gestures,
Calls loudly to his men: "Control your anger!
Where do you rush? What sudden madness rises?
The treaty is made, and all the terms agreed on,
The fight my right alone. Let me take over,
Lay down your fear; this hand will prove the
    treaty
And make it sure; these rites make Turnus mine."
And even as he cried, an arrow flew
Winging against him; no one knew the hand
That turned it loose with whirlwind force, whether
    man,
Or god, nobody knew, and no one boasted
Of having been the one to wound Aeneas.
                                    [311–323]

[As Aeneas withdraws from the fight, Turnus,
on fire with sudden hope, dashes into the struggle.
He kills many: Sthenelus, Thamyrus, Pholus,
Glaucus, Lades; Eumedes, Asbytes, Chloreus,
Sybaris, Dares, (would this be the boxer in Book
V?), Thersilochus, Thymoetes. The battle becomes general: Aeneas, wounded, rages in anger,
trying to pull the arrowhead from the wound. A
physician named Iapyx tries to help him, but
in vain, until Venus supplies a healing herb, and
Aeneas is ready for battle again. After a quick
farewell to Ascanius, he enters the battle, looking
for Turnus alone, heedless of the duels that rage
on all sides of him.]

Juturna, frightened, overthrows Metiscus
From Turnus' chariot, far from the reins ·and
    axle.
She takes his place, plying the supple reins,
Calls with Metiscus' voice, assumes his armor.
As a dark swallow through a rich man's mansion
Flies winging through great halls, hunting for
    crumbs
For the young birds at home, and now chirps
    under
The empty courts, now over the quiet pool,
Even so Juturna, by the horses carried,
Darts here and there, quarters the field, and
    proudly
Makes a great show of Turnus, the proud war-
    rior,
Yet never lets him close in fight or grapple,

Forever wheeling and turning. But Aeneas
Is dogged in pursuit and loud in challenge.
Whenever he sees that car, and runs to meet it,
Juturna shifts the course. What can he do?
Nothing but seethe; one care against another
Makes conflict in his heart.          [468–487]

[His perplexity is resolved by the action of
Messapus who lets drive at him with a spear.
It misses, but knocks off the plume of his helmet,
and at that point Aeneas gives up his ethical quest
for Turnus; if they want to play dirty, so will
he. He kills Sucro; Turnus kills Amycus and
Diores. (Diores, you remember, came third in the
footrace.) Aeneas kills Talos, Tanais, Cethegus,
Onites—it gets to be too much of a catalogue,
on both sides. Finally Aeneas has a better idea, or
Venus has it for him—to lay direct siege to the
town. He orders his men to the assault.]

They form a wedge; a great mass moves to the
    wall,
Ladders appear from nowhere, and sudden fire;
The guards at the gates are butchered; steel is
    flying,
The sky is dark with arrows. Toward the wall
Aeneas lifts his hand, rebukes Latinus,
And calls the gods to witness that his will
Was not for battle, it was forced upon him
By the Italians, double treaty-breakers,
His foes for now the second time. The townsmen
Quarrel among themselves, "Open the town!"
Cry some, "Admit the Trojans!" and would drag
The king himself to the ramparts. Others hurry
With arms, man the defenses. When a shepherd
Trails bees to their hive in the cleft of a rock, and
    fills it
With smarting smoke, there is fright and noise
    and fury
Within the waxen camp, and anger sharpened
With buzzing noises, and a black smell rises
With a blind noise, inside the rock, and rolling
Smoke lifts to empty air.
                        And another sorrow
Came to the weary Latins, shook the city
To its foundations, utterly. The queen
Had seen the Trojans coming, and the walls
Under attack, and fire along the gables,
And no Rutulian column, nowhere Turnus
Coming to help. He had been killed, her hero,
She knew at last. Her mind was gone; she cried

Over and over, "I am the guilty one,
I am the cause, the source of all these evils!"
And other wilder words. And then she tore
Her crimson robes, and slung a noose and
fastened
The knot of an ugly death to the high rafter.
The women learned it first, and then Lavinia,
The wide hall rings with grief and lamentation,
Nails scratch at lovely faces, beautiful hair
Is torn from the head. And Rumor spreads the
story
All up and down the town, and poor Latinus,
Rending his garments, comes and stares—wife
gone,
And city falling—an old man's hair
Greyer with dirty dust.
             And meanwhile Turnus
Out on the plain pursues the stragglers, slower
And slower now, and less and less exultant
In his triumphant car. From the city comes
A wind that bears a cry confused with terror,
Half heard, but known, confusion, darkness, sor-
row,
Disturbance in the town. He checks the horses,
Pauses, and listens. And his sister prompts him,
"This way, this way! the Trojans run, we follow
Where victory shows the way. Let others guard
The houses with their valor. The Italians
Fall in the fight before Aeneas. Let us
Send death to the Trojans, in our turn. You will
not
Come off the worse, in numbers or in honor."
Turnus replies: "O sister, I have known,
A long time since, that you were no Metiscus,
When first you broke the treaty and joined this
battle.
No use pretending you are not a goddess,
But who, from high Olympus, sent you down
To bear such labors? Or was it to see your brother
Go down in cruel death? What am I doing,
What chance will fortune grant me? I have seen
A man I loved more than the rest, Murranus,
A big man, slain by a big wound, go down.
Ufens is fallen, lucky, or unlucky,
In that he never saw our shame; the Trojans
Have won his body and arms. Our homes are
burning,
The one thing lacking up to now. Do I
Endure this, not refute the words of Drances
With this right hand? Shall the land see Turnus
running?

Is it so grim to die? Be kind, O shadows,
Since the high gods have turned their favor from
me.
A decent spirit, undisgraced, no coward
I shall descend to you, never unworthy
Of all my ancient line."         [575–649]

[At this point a warrior named Saces, his face
wounded by an arrow, comes dashing up to Turnus to implore his return to the defense of the
city; he reports the suicide of Amata, says that
only Messapus and Atinas are left to hold the
lines.]

Bewildered by the shifting image of disaster,
Turnus is silent, staring; shame and madness
In that great heart boil up, and grief, and love
Driven by fury. He shakes off the shadows,
The light comes back to his mind. His eyes turn,
blazing,
To the walls of the town, from the wheels to
that great city,
Where the flame billows upward, the roaring
blast
Catching a tower, one he himself had fashioned
With jointed beams, and rollers, and the gang-
ways.
"Fate is the winner now; keep out of my way,
My sister; where the god and fortune call, I
follow.
I am ready for Aeneas, ready to bear
Whatever is bitter in death. No longer, sister,
Shall I be shamed, with you to watch me. Let me,
Before the final madness, be as mad
As ever I can."         [665–680]

[He makes his way desperately toward Aeneas,
calling, as he charges, to the Rutulians and Trojans to give up further fighting; they make way
for him. Sensing the change in the situation,
Aeneas also heads for Turnus. The spears are
thrown from too great a distance to be effective;
the first clash of the sword-play is even. Jupiter
is weighing the fates of the two men in the
balance.]

Confident, Turnus, rising to the sword
Full height, is a flash of light; he strikes: the
Trojans,
The Latins, cry aloud; they come up standing.
But the sword is treacherous; it is broken off,

With the blow half spent; the fire of Turnus finds
No help except in flight. Swift as the wind
He flies, and stares at a broken blade, a hand
Unarmed. The story is that in that hurry,
That rush of his, to arms, when the steeds were
    harnessed,
He took Metiscus' sword, not the one Daunus
Had left him, and, for a while, it served its pur-
    pose,
While the Trojans ran away. But when it met
The armor Vulcan forged, the mortal blade
Split off, like brittle ice, and the fragments glit-
    ter
Like ice on the yellow sand. So Turnus flies
For his life across the plain in devious circles;
The Trojans ring him round; a swamp on one
    side,
High walls on the other.
               Aeneas, in pursuit,
Is none too swift; the arrow has left him hurt,
His knees give way, but he keeps on, keeps com-
    ing
After the panting enemy, as a hound
Running a stag to bay, at the edge of water,
Or hedged by crimson plumes, darts in, and barks,
And snaps his jaws, closes and grips, is shaken
Off from the flanks again, and once more closes.
And a great noise goes up to the sky; the waters
Resound, and the whole sky thunders with the
    clamor.
Turnus has time, even in flight, for calling
Rutulian men, each one by name, demanding,
In rage, the sword, the sword, the good one,
The one he knows. Let anybody bring it,
Aeneas threatens, and death and doom await him,
And the town is put to ruin. Wounded, still
He presses on. They go in five great circles,
Around and back; no game, with silly prizes,
Are they playing now: the life and blood of Tur-
    nus
Go to the winner.
          A wild olive tree
Stood here, with bitter leaves, sacred to Faunus,
Revered by rescued sailors, who would give
Ex-votos to the native gods, and clothing
In sign of gratitude. For this the Trojans
Cared nothing, lopped the branches off, to clear
The run of the field. Aeneas' spear was fastened
Deep in the trunk, where the force of the cast
    had brought it,
Stuck in the grip of the root. Aeneas, stooping,

Yanks at the shaft; he cannot overtake him
By speed of foot, but the javelin is winged.
And Turnus, in a terrible moment of panic,
Cries: "Faunus, pity me, and Earth, most kindly,
If ever I was reverent, as Aeneas
And those he leads have not been, hold the steel,
Do not let go!" He prayed, and he was answered.
Aeneas tugged and wrestled, pulled and hauled,
But the wood held on. And while he strains,
    Juturna,
Once more Metiscus' double, rushes forward
With the real sword for her brother. Venus, angry
Over this wanton interference, enters,
And the root yields. The warriors, towering high,
Each one renewed in spirit, one with sword,
One with the spear, both breathing hard, are
    ready
For what Mars has to send.     [728–790]

[And at this dramatic point, Vergil shifts the
scene to Olympus, where Jupiter, with a final
display of long-suffering patience, asks Juno how
much longer she thinks she can keep this up. She
changes to an attitude of meek submissiveness,
not without a bit of the old flattering charm, asking one thing only, that the name of Troy be
forgotten, that the allied people keep the language
and name: let the new words Roman, Italian,
Latin, Alban, be the words men remember. Jupiter grants the plea, and to add force to it, sends
one of the Furies, in the form of an owl, to
frighten Juturna out of the combat and leave Turnus abandoned to his doom.]

Aeneas presses on; the flashing spear,
Brandished, is big as a tree; his anger cries
"Why the delay, why do you draw back, Turnus?
We must fight with arms, not legs! Whatever
    shape
You take, gather your strength or craft; fly up
To the high stars, or bury yourself in earth."
And Turnus shook his head and answered, "Jove,
Being my enemy, scares me, and the gods,
Not your hot words, my fierce opponent!" He
    sees
A mighty stone, which marked a boundary
In days of old, so big a stone a dozen
Men now in our degenerate time could hardly
Lift it from earth; but Turnus lifts and heaves it
At full height, with full speed. And even so
Seems not to recognize himself, in running,

Or moving, or lifting his hands, or letting the
    stone
Fly into space; he shakes at the knees, his blood
Runs chill in the veins. And the stone through
    wide air going
Fell short, fell spent. As in our dreams at night-
    time,
When sleep weighs down our eyes, we seem to be
    running,
Or trying to run, and cannot; and we falter,
Sick in our failure, and the tongue is thick,
And the words we try to utter come to nothing,
No voice, no speech. So Turnus found the way
Baffled, wherever he turned, however bravely.
All sorts of things go through his mind; he stares
At the Rutulians and the town; he trembles,
Quails at the threat of the lance; he cannot see
Any way out, any way forward. Nothing.
The chariot is gone, and the charioteer,
Juturna, or Metiscus, nowhere near him.
And the spear flung by Aeneas comes with a whir
Louder than stone from any engine, louder
Than thunderbolt; like a black wind it flies,
Bringing destruction with it, through the mail,
The sevenfold shield-rim; through the thigh it
    goes.
Turnus is down, on hands and knees, huge Tur-
    nus
Struck to the earth. Groaning, the stunned Ru-
    tulians
Rise to their feet, and the whole hill resounds,

And the wooded heights give echo. A suppliant,
    beaten,
Humbled at last, his hands reach out, he speaks
In a low voice: "I have deserved it, surely,
And I do not beg off. Make use of your luck.
But if a parent's grief has any power
To touch the spirit, I pray you, pity Daunus,
(I would Anchises), send him back my body.
You have won; I am beaten, and these hands go
    out
In supplication: everyone has seen it.
No more. I have lost Lavinia. Let hatred
Proceed no further."
Fierce in his arms, with darting glance, Aeneas
Paused for a moment; and he might have weak-
    ened,
For the words had moved him, when, high on the
    shoulder,
He saw the belt of Pallas, slain by Turnus,
Stretched dying on the ground. And Turnus wears
    it,
That belt, with the bright studs, of evil omen,
Not only to Pallas now, a sad reminder,
And a grim provocation. Terrible
In wrath, Aeneas cries: "Clad in this prize,
Shall you be taken from me? Pallas, Pallas
Inflicts this wound, exacts this vengeance. Here
Is Pallas' sacrifice." The blade went deep,
And Turnus' limbs were cold in death; the spirit
Went with a moan indignant to the shadows.
                    [887–952]

# SELECTIONS FROM THE *Odes* OF HORACE

## Translated by the Sargent Prize Translators, Paul Shorey, and Goldwin Smith

### INTRODUCTION

WITH SOME exceptions, the poems of Horace printed below are translations done by students at Harvard during the past twenty-five years. The selection, then, is of those poems most interesting to students, and the style of translation follows the traditional English verse forms of the nineteenth century—of Tennyson and Swinburne —that we accept as a pleasant standard. The poetry that Horace wrote, however, was of another kind.

> Ah child, no Persian-perfect art!
> Crowns composite and braided bast
> They tease me. Never know the part
> Where roses linger last.
>
> Bring natural myrtle, and have done:
> Myrtle will suit your place and mine:
> And set the glasses from the sun
> Beneath the tackled vine.

Perhaps this attempt by Gerard Manley Hopkins, a most untraditional nineteenth-century English poet, re-creates more nearly the fine, close-textured, seemingly illogical nature of the originals. The subject of this Ode (I, 38) is that of all Horace's poems: the preservation of one's integrity and decency in a chaotic society. The statement that the poet wants no oriental luxury but only a wreath of native myrtle and a glass of domestic wine is made in the form of intricate, perfect verse, whose language is so far from that of everyday speech that it must be studied to be understood logically. As poetry it is immediately understandable and not to be surpassed, but as a rational statement, not.

The six "Roman Odes" (III, 1-6), which are the center of Horace's poetry, present most clearly the constant theme of all that he wrote. The cycle begins: "I hate and avoid the unwashed mob. Keep pious silence, for I, the priest of the Muses, sing for the edification of the youth songs never before heard." Here is the same formula that is used by a priest before a sacrifice; the poet, in Horace's view, is a priest of the Muses who has a religious duty to improve the character of the youths for whom his poetry is written. This duty is not to be fulfilled by direct preaching; rather, the perfect, ordered beauty of poetry is to instill in the reader a sense of personal order and decency. The theme of the individual who is self-sufficient amidst disorder around him is varied as is the musical theme of a symphony: kings rule their peoples, Jupiter rules kings; indifferently, Necessity assigns high and low degree; black Care sits behind the horseman; a disciplined youth will find it sweet and fitting to die for his fatherland. The great "Roman Odes" close with the same despair that appears in some of Horace's most youthful poetry: "We must pay for our fathers' sins; our women have become impure, our men weak; our wicked generation will breed children even worse." This is no praise of the great rule of Augustus—here, Horace sees disorder and ruin without: it is only within oneself and in art that order and reason may be had.

Horace had been brought up by a father who was a freed slave. In the *Satires* that he wrote while young and in the *Epistles* of his last years, he describes how his father had devoted himself to Horace's education: at first at home in Venusia, then at the fashionable school of Orbilius in Rome; and finally how he sent him to study philosophy in Athens. In 44 B.C. when Brutus, the assassin of Caesar, came to Athens, Horace joined his forces and was made a military tribune. After Brutus' defeat, Horace, bankrupt, his father dead, returned to Rome to work for a living. His first poems, the *Epodes*, that he wrote while he was an underpaid clerk in the treasury department, reflect with frightful reality the chaotic last stage of the "Roman Revolution" into which Horace—after his comfortable and protected youth—was suddenly plunged. One (usually left out of school texts) describes a panting, stinking nymphomaniac; another, a vulgar, dishonest, newly-rich man; a third urges friends to drink and ignore the descending storm. However, beneath the bitter cynicism of these early poems, there is evident what one critic has called a certain, "sense of public decency" that attracted Maecenas, the minister of Augustus, and the patron of so many artists of the time. As the result of an interview secured by Virgil, Maecenas eventually decided to support Horace, to whom he gave a small country villa, so he might spend all the time he needed writing poetry.

The three books of Odes that were then written and that constitute the bulk of Horace's poetic creation make only a slight volume. The verses have been concentrated and polished until they are perfect: in the Epistle on the *Art of Poetry*, Horace advises that a poet should spend nine years on a poem before publishing it. Whatever subject the *Odes* present—friendship, love, fatherland, the gods, drinking songs—they are variations on the same essential theme of order within one's own life and of personal decency. The last Ode of the third book says he has made in his poetry a monument more lasting than bronze. At Augustus' insistence, he wrote a fourth book of Odes although his creative energies were already almost spent. The serious poems of the fourth book show a great weariness, and there are many loose-textured ones to fill in. Then follow some moral and literary Epistles of great wisdom but lacking the concentration and fineness of the *Odes*. Horace died at the age of fifty-seven, two months after the death of his patron, Maecenas.

—CHARLES PINCKNEY

## To Pyrrha

### *Goldwin Smith*

What slender youth, with perfumed locks,
In some sweet nook beneath the rocks,
Pyrrha, where clustering roses grow,
Bends to thy fatal beauty now?
For whom is now that golden hair
Wreathed in a band so simply fair?
How often will he weep to find
Thy pledges frail, Love's power unkind?
And start to see the tempest sweep
With angry blast the darkening deep;
Though sunned by thy entrancing smile
He fears no change, suspects no guile.
A sailor on bright summer seas,
He wots not of the fickle breeze.
For me—yon votive tablet scan;
It tells that I, a shipwrecked man,
Hung my dank weeds in Neptune's fane
And ne'er will tempt those seas again.

[I, v]

## Ignorance of the Future is Bliss

### *Goldwin Smith*

Draw not that curtain, lady mine;
Seek no diviner's art;
To read my destiny or thine—
It is not wisdom's part.

Whether our years be many more,
Or our last winter this,
Which breaks the waves on yonder shore,—
Our ignorance is bliss.

Then fill the wine-cup when you can,
And let us banish sorrow;
Cut short thy hopes to suit thy span,
And never trust to-morrow.

[I, xi]

## The Pure in Heart

### *Marshall A. Best* *

My Fuscus, cherish honor fair and keep thee pure
in heart:
You'll always be from danger free, nor know
the guilty start
When Moorish lance or bow advance, or venom-
bearing dart
By foeman drawn from heavy-laden quiver.

Then make your way where'er you may, across
the seething sand
Of Syrtis, thus, or Caucasus, inhospitable land,
No form of fear will harm you here, or on the
foreign strand
That far Hydaspes laves, the fabled river.

* Asterisks indicate Sargent Prize translators.

And well I know that this is so. Give ear unto my
tale;
As once through shades of Sabine glades I wan-
dered, past the pale,
And sang my lays in carefree praise of Lalage—
I quail
To think!—a wolf appeared, but fled unharm-
ing.

Such beast as fled was never bred beneath the
groves of oak
Whose spreading limbs Apulia hymns to guard
her fighter-folk;
Nor on the sand of Iuba's land such monster ever
woke,
The barren nurse of lion-whelps alarming.

Then set me where the murky air no grateful
comfort yields
Of summer breeze, to nourish trees in unproduc-
tive fields,
A breadth of land where Jove's stern hand
malevolently wields
O'er marshalled crowds of stormy clouds his
sceptre.

Or pack me off to learn to scoff at hot Apollo's
van,
That rides so near it leaves earth sere, untenanted
by man—
Unnumbered woes cannot dispose my Lalage's
élan;
Her gentle laugh, her gentle chaff, determine
her my captor.

[I, xxii]

TO A COY GIRL

*Goldwin Smith*

Chloe, thou fliest me like a fawn
That on some lonely upland lawn,
Seeking its dam, in winds and trees
Imaginary dangers sees.
Does Spring's fresh breeze the foliage
shake
Or lizard rustle in the brake?
At once it quakes in heart and limb.
Yet I, sweet girl, no tiger grim,
No fierce Gætulian lion am,
Then, no more, fawn-like, seek thy dam,

But bury all thy fond alarms—
'Tis time thou should'st—in true love's
arms.

[I, xxiii]

A HYMN TO FORTUNE

*W. S. Archibald* *

Goddess and Queen of Antium, hear our prayer.
Strong to uplift us to immortal heights,
And turn our triumphs into funeral rites,
O goddess, humbly we invoke thy care.

The humble tiller of the soil, to thee
With reverent eyes uplifts his simple prayer.
And toilers on the seas beseech thy care
When with their keels they cut the Cretan sea.

Cities and tribes pay homage to thy sway.
Wolf-brood of Latium, Dacian, Scythian bands,
Mothers of kings in far-off Eastern lands,
Tyrants in purple, thy commands obey,

Lest with irreverent foot thou shalt break down
The upright column; lest the people shout
"To arms! to arms!" and tumultuous shout
In royal blood the state and empire drown.

Before thee, quick to do thy stern command
Stalks dread Necessity, bearing the nails,
The wedges, and the hook that never fails—
Immutable symbols—in her brazen hand.

Hope is thy worshipper. In robes of white,
Faith walks beside thee, whom we rarely see.
And if, thy garments changed, in hate thou flee
From mighty houses, she attends thy flight.

Faith follows thee, the fickle crowd fall back,
False friends and harlots leave us when the casks
No longer feed them, nor the fragrant flasks.
Such friends forsake us when the weather's black.

Goddess and Queen of Antium, hear our prayer:
Guard Caesar bound for Britain's far-off lands.
On these, the youth, who in all-conquering bands
Will smite the orient, we invoke thy care.

Alas, our hands with brother's blood are red—
We bear in shame the scars of hateful crimes

O sinful age! What have these hardened times
Refused to touch? From what guilt have we fled?

Fear of the Gods checks not youth's impious
hands.
What altars spare they? Forge now our broken
swords,
On some new anvil: Strike them at the hordes
Of Massagetan and Arabian lands.

[I, xxxv]

## THE DEATH OF CLEOPATRA

### Richard J. Walsh *

Now to the dance!
Now to the wine
Beating of feet no fears confined!
Hey for the chance!
Feasting divine,
Feasts for the gods, now, comrades mine!

The Caecuban our fathers stored
  We had not dared to broach, for still
The mad queen and her lustful horde
Of sexless heroes turned toward
  Our empire and our sacred hill
To ruin them with fire and sword.
  Ah! they were wild enough to dare,
  Drunk with a fortune smiling fair!
But of her vessels one alone
  Escaped the flame; her madness shrank
And her unbalanced mind, o'erthrown
  By the Egyptian wine she drank,
Caesar inspired with certain dread
And back from Italy she fled,
While in pursuit his galleys sped,
  As hawk for tender doves, or where
On snowy white Thessalian plains
  The hunter swift pursues the hare,
He followed, eager to ensnare
This deadly monster in his chains.

Nobler the death she chose to die.
  She felt no woman's dread of steel,
  Nor sought to gain with speeding keel
The unknown shores that further lie.
She dared to turn her quiet gaze
  Undimmed, upon her fallen throne,
She dared the angry snake to raise
  And drink its blood into her own.

Ah! but she hated the vessel that bore her
  On to the triumph. She perished serene,
Boldest the moment her death was before her,
  Now but a woman, yet proud as a queen!

[I, xxxvii]

## SIMPLICITY

### Goldwin Smith

Leave costly wreaths for lordly brows:
  Of myrtle let my chaplet be;
Seek not for autumn's lingering rose;
  Twine but the myrtle, boy, for me.

Of all that blooms there's naught so fit
  For thee, my boy, that pour'st the wine;
For me, that quaff it as I sit,
  O'erarched by this embowering vine.

[I, xxxviii]

## A MIND UNMOVED

### R. E. Bates *

A mind, unmoved when troubles rise,
  Nor overjoyed at Fortune's smile,
  Keep, Dellius mine—a little while—
Remember—and my Dellius dies,

Whether he live forever sad,
  Or in some grassy nook recline,
  With mellow old Falernian wine
To make each festal season glad.

Huge pine and silvery poplar bring
  Their boughs to weave one friendly shade—
  Why, think you? Why this brook's delayed
Wild flight through banks meandering?

Have wines and perfumes hither borne,
  And sweet, brief-blowing roses, now
  While fortunes and while age allow—
Ere yet the Fates' dark thread be shorn.

Your villa—with its woodlands vast—
  Which Tiber's yellow waters lave—
  Your high-piled wealth—an heir shall have—
Yes, you must yield it all at last.

Unpitying Orcus waiteth nigh
  Alike, if Argive blood you claim,

Or pauper, of an unknown name,
You dwell beneath the open sky.

We all are gathered to one doom:
   The shaken Urn sends forth our lot
   Or soon or late—and we are caught
To Stygian exile's endless gloom.

                [II, iii]


## WELCOME HOME

### *Gerald F. Else* *

Pompey, old friend with whom I fought
In Brutus' army at grim odds,
Who's brought you back to your long-sought
Italian sky and tutelary gods?

Prince of companions, often we
Together drank away the hours
That lagged, and on my hair would be
The gleam of Syrian oil, and wreaths of flowers.

We fled from Philippi in haste
Together, but without my shield,
When courage failed us, and the taste
Of earth was in their mouths who would not yield.

But fleet-foot Hermes let me glide
Unseen, though trembling, past my foes,
While you went down the sucking tide
To that storm-sea of battle whence it rose.

Come, pay the feast you owe to Jove,
And, lying down to rest from war
Beneath my shady laurel, prove
Yourself the man these flagons waited for.

Pour into shining cups the wine
That brings oblivion; a shell
Will serve for perfumes—and who'll twine
A hasty wreath of myrtle, woven well,

Or parsley? Who by chance will be
Our drinking-arbiter? I'll foam
Like any Bacchanal: to me
'Tis sweet to revel when a friend comes home.

                [II, vii]


## THE GOLDEN MEAN

### *M. M. Smith* *

Licinius, to be safe from harm,
Press not forever seaward, nor
Too closely hug, through fear of storm,
   The treacherous shore.

Who makes the golden mean his guide
Shuns ruined hovels, desolate,
Avoids the envied rank, beside,
   Of high estate.

Most oft, when winds are raging, creaks
The loftiest pine; with deafening crash
Fall tallest towers; on mountain peaks
   The lightnings flash.

The heart prepared for weal or woe
In sadness hopes, in gladness fears.
Bleak winters which Jove sends below
   He likewise clears.

Think not one day the next portends:
At times Apollo, with his lyre,
Awakes the slumbering Muse, nor bends
   His bow in ire.

In strife, both bold and valiant show
Thyself to be; yet do not fail
To reef, when winds too prosperous blow,
   Thy swollen sail.

                [II, x]


## A NARROW ESCAPE

### *Elizabeth C. Evans* *

O tree! An evil day he planted thee,
Whoever nurtured thee with impious hand!
A menace to his heirs you grew to be,
And the reproach of all the neighboring land.

Full well might he who schemed this monstrous
   jest
Have choked to death a fond and doting sire;
Full well have slain by night his slumbering guest,
And stained with blood the shrine beside the fire.

With Colchian herbs he sought a deathly charm,
And every path of crime he chose to tread,
Who placed thee, hapless log, within my farm,
That fain would smite thy master's blameless
    head.

How little doth incautious man foresee
The myriad dangers that he must beware!
The Punic sailor may the Bosphorus flee,
Yet scorn on every side the hidden snare.

The soldier fears the fleeing Parthian's bow,
The Parthian dreads the bonds of Roman sway;
Yet ever 'tis death's unexpected blow
That bears the races of mankind away.

How close at hand, O thou ill-omened tree,
Did I Proserpina's dark realms behold;
Where Aeacus, the judge, I seemed to see;
Where chosen fields await the pious fold;

Where Sappho with Aeolian harp complains
Of native maids. Thy golden lyre of yore
Doth sound, Alcaeus, in yet fuller strains
The woes of ships, of exile, and of war.

Round both, the shadowy dead with wonder hear
The songs that sacred silence doth inspire;
Yet doth the throng imbibe with greedier ear
The tales of strife and tyrants' exile dire.

What wonder, if entranced by dulcet air,
The vicious watchdog droops his sable ear;
And serpents, writhing in the Furies' hair,
Are lulled to slumber by the strains they hear.

There, too, Prometheus and king Pelops' sire
From torments harsh sweet melodies beguile,
And music charms Orion from desire
To chase the lion and the lynx awhile.

                    [II, xiii]

## The Moving Finger Writes

### Paul Shorey

Alas! the fleeting seasons, my Postumus,
Go gliding onward, nor can thy piety
Delay the wrinkles, stay old age, nor
Keep thee from Death, the unconquered monarch.

What though each day, dear friend, thou pro-
    pitiate,
With blood of bullocks slain, and with hecatombs
The tearless god who binds the triple
Geryon fast and the monster Tityus?—

Beyond the wave that waiteth for all of us
Who draw from Earth's broad bounties a sus-
    tenance
To cross it, be we lords of lands or
Tillers who toil upon alien acres.

In vain we shun the weltering field of war,
In vain the noisy billows of Adria,
In vain the noxious breath of autumn,
Bearer of doom on the wings of south winds.

The dark Cocytus languidly wandering
We all must see, the daughters of Danäus,
Ill-famed and damned to toil unending,—
Sisyphus Aeolides among them.

Thou must abandon Earth and thy home and wife
So dear, and of the trees that thou waterest
None, save the dark-browed cypress only,
Shadows the tomb of its short-lived owner.

Thine heir shall waste, more worthy, thy Cae-
    cuban
Barred with a hundred bolts, and his pride shall
    spill
To stain thine inlaid floors a liquor
Richer than quaffed at the Pontiff's banquets.

                    [II, xiv]

## Regulus

### R. C. Minns *

Jove, crowned with thunder, rules the height;
Caesar this lower earth shall own,
The god who humbled Persia's might
And added Britain to his throne.

Shame on the troops that Crassus led,
True Marsians once, now sunk so low
—O shades of ancient Rome—they wed
Barbaric wives, and served their foe,

Soldiers and kinsmen of the Mede!
Can they forget their shields, their land,

The deathless flames the Vestals feed,
And still Rome's towers and temples stand?

This, this great Regulus foreknew,
And scorned peace by dishonor gained,
Tracing sure ruin to ensue
On future Rome, were mercy strained

To ransom captives better dead.
"Rome's standards I have seen adorn
The Punic shrines, and arms," he said,
"From unresisting soldiers torn;

"Free citizens these eyes have seen
Led bound like slaves, and every gate
Unshut, and fields with harvest green
Which once our swords laid desolate.

"Think you these ransomed renegades
Return the braver? Then you buy
Disgrace with gold. Can wool that fades
Regain its lustre steeped in dye?

"Can he that valor casts away
Be with some meaner thing consoled?
Sooner the hind will stand at bay,
Freed from the nets, than he be bold

"Who knows the faith those traitors keep,
Or he pursue with courage high
Who, passive, felt the bonds bite deep
On pinioned arms, and feared to die.

"He knows not, he, what life is worth,
But wages war by compromise.
Rise, Carthage, and possess the earth,
While Italy dishonoured lies!"

He shunned, they say, the last embrace
Of wife and children crowding round,
Rights his no longer; bowed his face
In manly sorrow to the ground;

Then calmed the wavering senate's fears
With counsel unsurpassed, and went
Surrounded by his friends in tears
Into heroic banishment.

Well knowing what the torturer's art
Made ready, with unfaltering stride

He pressed through kinsfolk loth to part
And thrust the hindering crowds aside,

As though he closed a long-drawn day,
Gave judgment on his client's suit,
And turned toward Tarentum's bay
Or orchards of Venafran fruit.

[III, v]

## WEALTH IN POVERTY

*Elizabeth C. Evans* *

Right well had prisoned Danaë been saved
   By doors of oak enclosed in brazen tower,
In vain had all her nightly lovers braved
   The gloomy watchdogs prowling near her
     bower,

Had Jove and Venus not Acrisius mocked,
   Pale guardian of that hidden maid of old;
For knew they not the way would be unlocked
   And opened to a god disguised in gold?

For gold, more potent than the lightning's spear,
   Stalks through the guards and shatters rocks in
     twain;
Thus fell the household of the Argive seer,
   Its glory undermined by lust for gain.

By bribery great Philip opened wide
   Strong city gates and rival kings controlled;
By bribery stern captains of the tide
   Became ensnared through greedy love of gold.

Hard on the heels of gain doth worry tread,
   Increasing wealth for wealth still greater cries.
And so, Maecenas, glorious knight, I dread
   To raise my head, the cynosure of eyes.

The more each mortal to himself denies,
   The greater riches from the gods he bears,
So, poor, I join with those who wealth despise,
   And gladly flee the camps of millionaires.

Yet richer I with my despised estate,
   Than were I said in granaries to hide
What fair Apulia's swains might cultivate,
   And yet 'mid wealth in poverty abide.

The crystal stream, the scanty wood, mine own,
   And safe assurance of the fruits of toil

My lot far happier make, by him unknown
Who boasts the sway of Afric's fertile soil.

Calabrian bees no honey bring to me,
  Nor any Laestrygonian wine I keep
In Formian jars that it may mellow be;
  For me no fleece grows rich on Gallic sheep.

Dire poverty ne'er haunts my small domain,
  Wished I for more, you would deny it not.
And if my vain desires I but restrain
  Far more will I enhance my humble lot,

Than if the Phrygian throne, the Lydian sway
  Together were mine own. Who much demand
Much also lack. Blessed by the gods are they
  Who have enough, bestowed by frugal hand.

[III, xvi]

## To a Cask of Wine Made in the Year in which Horace Was Born

### Goldwin Smith

My good contemporary cask, whatever thou dost
    keep
Stored up in thee—smiles, tears, wild loves, mad
    brawls or easy sleep—
Whate'er thy grape was charged withal, thy hour
    is come; descend;
Corvinus bids; my mellowest wine must greet my
    dearest friend.
Sage and Socratic though he be, the juice he will
    not spurn,
That many a time made glow, they say, old Cato's
    virtue stern.
There's not a heart so hard but thou beneath its
    guard canst steal,
There's not a soul so close but thou its secret canst
    reveal.
There's no despair but thou canst cheer, no
    wretch's lot so low
But thou canst raise, and bid him brave the
    tyrant and the foe.
Please Bacchus and the Queen of Love, and the
    linked Graces three,
Till lamps shall fail and stars grow pale, we'll
    make a night with thee.

[III, xxi]

## To Augustus

### C. J. Chamberlain *

Best guardian of the Roman race, and seed
  Of kindly gods, thou art too long from home;
Thy promise to the holy fathers heed,
    Hark to our prayer, and come.

O gracious prince, restore thy country's light;
  For when thy countenance, like balmy spring,
Illumines ours, the sun sheds rays more bright,
    Days flit on sweeter wing.

When southern winds o'er the Carpathian deep,
  Howling the long year through with adverse
    gales,
From his dear home the tender stripling keep,
    Lonely his mother wails.

As she with vow and prayer and omen cries,
  Nor turns her face from the bare, curving shore,
So thy land seeks for thee with yearning eyes,
    Loyal forever more.

Now safe the cattle range the quiet mead,
  The farms Ceres and rich abundance bless,
O'er peaceful waves the skimming sailors speed,
    Faith fears unfaithfulness.

By unchaste lust no homes are now defiled;
  Morals and law have conquered that foul stain;
Proud mothers trace the father in the child,
    Swift after wrong comes pain.

Who by the Mede or Scythian is alarmed,
  Or by the rough brood which the forest bears
In German gloom? While Caesar is unharmed,
    Who for the Spanish cares?

Each spends his days amid his native hills,
  Wedding the widowed elm-trees and the vine;
At evening feast to thee as god he fills
    The cup with joyous wine.

With deep libation and with prayers thy fame
  He worships, and as Greek mixed honor sends
To Castor and Alcides, so thy name
    With household gods he blends.

"Kind lord, bestow on us long holiday."
    This with dry lips at sunrise is our plea,
And this in merry evening, when his ray
        Has sunk beneath the sea.
                                            [IV, v]


NATURE AND MAN

*R. G. West* *

The snows have fled; and leaves and grasses now
    Return to trees
And meadows; earth is changing for the plough,
    And streams decrease
And flow beneath their banks; and nightly where
    None look askance,
With naked Nymphs the sister Graces dare
    Lead forth their choral dance.

But reckon not on immortality,—
    So warns the year,
And this brief hour which snatches greedily
    The day so dear:
The frosts are now dispersed by zephyrs,—aye,
    But summer fain
Would trample spring, and autumn soon is nigh
    To pour the grain

And fruitage from her horn, and by and by
    Dull winter comes again.

And though the rapid moons shall ever mend
    With heavenly fire,
Their high vicissitudes, when we descend
    Where linger sire
Aeneas, Tullus, Ancus,—we shall be
    But shades and dust! . . .
Who knows if the high gods will add a free
    Tomorrow to our trust?

So gratify yourself; life soon will pass,
    And what you spend
Will foil an heir's hot clutches. But, alas!
    When you descend,
And Minos makes his proud arbitrament
    On each offense,
Then, dear Torquatus, neither high descent,
    Nor eloquence,
Nor all your piety and good intent
    Will serve to bring you thence!
Nay, for not even Dian's self could free
    Hippolytus
From Hell; nor Theseus wrench death's slavery
    From dear Pirithoüs.
                                            [IV, vii]

# SELECTIONS FROM OVID

## *Translated by Dorrance S. White*

## INTRODUCTION

PUBLIUS OVIDIUS NASO, as he was known to his fellow Romans, perhaps the most versatile of Roman poets, was born in the year in which Cicero was murdered, 43 B.C., at Sulmo, about ninety miles east of Rome. He died in exile at Tomi on the Black Sea, A.D. 17, three years after the death of Emperor Augustus, who had sent him away forever from the gay life of Rome. It is said that he was a conspicuous figure in the social life of the capital, contrasting sharply with his contemporary, Vergil, who was twenty-seven years his senior. Just why the emperor banished this social light has never been known; Augustus never revealed his reason. But it was suspected that his earlier works, the *Amores* and the *Ars Amatoria*, which were rather frank treatises on the art of making love, or perhaps some knowledge that he possessed of corruption in the imperial court, or possibly defiance of the emperor's fiat on indecency may have angered Augustus.

Ovid's father had ambitions for his son to become versed in public and forensic life, but Ovid constantly rebelled against such a career. It is even reported that whenever he attempted to plead a case in court, his language assumed the form of verse, to the great amusement of his audiences. So, after some altercation with his father on the matter, he abandoned political life and gave himself up entirely to the writing of poetry.

Ovid's works comprise the *Amores*, or love poems in elegiac meter; *Heroides*, letters from fifteen famous women of antiquity, in the same meter; the *Art of Love*, poems on the art of winning the love of a mistress, purely sensual passion in clever verse; the *Cure of Love*, less interesting than its predecessor, but exceeding in its masterly technique, wit, and humor; the *Fasti*, a half-finished calendar of Roman festivals, vivaciously told

and containing beautiful pictures of Roman life; the *Tristia*, a "huge scroll of lament and entreaty" written, with the *Ex Ponto*, as letters to his friends from his place in exile; finally, his greatest work, the *Metamorphoses*, fifteen long books in hexameter verse, a collection of stories which Ovid gathered from Greek works on mythology no longer extant. This work is of special importance since it has been the inspiration of artists throughout the history of European art. The collection of stories concerns the transformation of human beings into stones, trees, plants, beasts, birds, and other creatures and things, cast into a continuous narrative. They well bear witness to Ovid's unusual gift of narrative and inventive ingenuity. The *Metamorphoses*, centuries after Ovid's day, became the great textbook of classical mythology.

Ovid's versatility appeared in a tragedy, now lost, the *Medea*, which Quintilian nearly 100 years later called the greatest tragedy ever written by Roman or Greek.

Ovid was one of Milton's favorite authors and many passages in the *Paradise Lost* show his influence. Chaucer and Boccaccio, Tasso and Shakespeare, all draw from Ovid's treasure store of stories. Hildebert of Tours, Abelard, John of Garland, Petrarch, Erasmus, even Martin Luther, found places for Ovid's ethical utterances and showed great familiarity with his works. Dante included Ovid among the noted Greeks and Romans whom he pictured in a pleasant greensward in the Limbo of Hell.

Ovid may not rank on a par with Vergil and Horace and Catullus, but few Roman poets created more widespread ripples in the literary pool.

THE TEXT is that of the second edition of Merkel-Ehwald in the Teubner series (Leipzig, 1931).

## *FROM THE* METAMORPHOSES

### APOLLO AND DAPHNE

The first love of Apollo was Daphne, daughter of Peneus,[1] a love that no blind chance occa-

sioned, but rather the resentful wrath of Cupid. The Delian god, vaunting himself over the serpent[2] that he had just slain, had recently spied him bending the tips of his bow with tightly-drawn string and had asked: "Ho, my pretty lad, what are you up to with that dangerous weapon? A weapon like that better becomes my manly shoulders, the shoulders of me who am able to inflict deadly wounds upon wild beast or enemy, and who have just now laid low the Python, all swollen with my innumerable arrows as he pressed down so many acres of land with his plague-bearing belly. Do you be content to stir up with your torch any fires of love that you please, but don't appropriate to yourself my own honors."

To him the son of Venus replied: "Granted, O Phoebus, that your bow can transfix all things, yet *my* bow can transfix you; and as far as all animals are inferior to a god is your glory inferior to mine." As he said that, he soared through the air with fluttering wings and quickly took his stand upon the shady pinnacle of Parnassus. From his arrow-bearing quiver he drew two darts of opposite effect: one causes love, the other puts it to flight. That which causes love is covered with gold and gleams bright with its pointed tip; that which banishes love is blunt and has a ball of lead at the end of the shaft. This dart the god fixed in the heart of the nymph, the daughter of Peneus, but with the other he wounded Apollo himself, piercing him through the very marrow of his being.

Straightway Apollo loves Daphne, but she flees from the very name of lover, rejoicing in the hidden pathways of the forests and in the spoils of the beasts that she had slain, and is a rival of the unmarried Diana. A fillet restrained her hair, caught up without care. Many young men sought her hand, but she turned away from those that sought her; impatient with men, she had nothing to do with them. She wandered through the trackless woods, unconcerned as to the meaning of Hymen or Love or marriage.

Often her father had said, "Daughter, you owe me a son-in-law"; often he reminded her, "Daughter, you owe me grandchildren." But the girl, hating the wedding torch as if it were a thing of guilt, and with her beautiful face suffused with modest blushes, clung about the neck of her father with coaxing arms and said, "Grant me, dearest father, to enjoy perpetual maidenhood. Diana's father granted her this before my day." Then her father, indeed, gave in. But that beauty of yours forbade you to be what you wish, and your charming shape, Daphne, was in conflict with your prayer.

Now Phoebus loves Daphne and, once having seen her, desires marriage and hopes to get what he desires; but, alas, his very gifts of prophecy deceive him! As the light stubble burns when the grain has been harvested, or as hedges catch fire and burn because of the firebrands that the wayfarer happens to have moved too close, or has left aflame at the break of day, so Apollo is aflame in all his breast, and feeds a fruitless love with hope.

He looks at her hair hanging about her neck uncombed and says to himself, "What if it were combed!" He sees those eyes of hers sparkling with fire like unto the stars; he sees those lips, which merely to have seen is not enough. He praises her fingers, her hands, her arms, and her upper arms bare for more than half way; [3] in fact, whatever lies hidden he esteems of greater beauty.

Now Daphne flees swifter than the light breeze, and does not stop in answer to these words, as he calls after her, "O nymph, daughter of Peneus, stay, I pray! I am not following you as an enemy; stay, O nymph! It is like this that the lamb flees the wolf, the fawn the lion, doves with frightened wings the eagle—each creature from her own enemy; Love is the cause of my pursuit. Ah, wretched me! Take care lest you fall headlong or the brambles scratch your undeserving legs, and I be the cause of your grief. Rough are the regions through which you hasten. Run more cautiously, I beg, and check a little your flight; I then shall follow with less speed. And ask who it is to whom you are so pleasing. I am no mountain-dweller, I am no shepherd, I am no shaggy-haired one who guards the flocks and herds. You don't know, rash girl, from whom you flee, and for that reason you flee. The Delphian land is mine, and Claros and Tenedos and the Patarean realm are subservient to me. Jupiter is my father. Through me is revealed what is, what has been, and what is yet to be. Through me songs sound harmonious on the lyre. My arrow indeed is sure of its mark, yet one arrow is more sure of its aim than mine, and has made a wound in my empty heart. Medicine is my discovery; I am called throughout the world the Aid-bringer, and the power of herbs is under my domination. Ah me, that love is curable by no herbs, and that the arts that are of avail to all others are of no avail to their master!"

As Apollo was about to say more, the daughter of Peneus sped on her way with frightened footsteps and left him with his words unfinished, and even then she seemed to him passing fair. The winds laid bare her body and the breezes blowing against her made her garments flutter, and the light air backward made her fair locks stream. Her beauty was increased by flight.

But now the youthful god could no longer endure to waste his caressing words, and as love spurred him on he followed her steps with unbridled speed. Even as the Gallic hound pursues his prey, when he spies the hare in an open field—one seeks his booty and the other his safety with swift feet; one, as though about to seize his prey, hopes ever and anon to hold it fast, and just grazes its heels with outstretched muzzle, while the other, for a moment in doubt whether he has already been seized or not, barely rescues himself from the bite and leaves behind the muzzle that just grazes him—so the god and the maiden raced on, the one swift because of hope, the other swift because of fear.

But the pursuing god, aided by wings of love, is the swifter and denies Daphne rest, and hangs over the very shoulder of the fleeing girl, blowing with his panting breath upon the hair that is scattered about her neck. She grew pale; with strength now gone, and overcome by the toil of her swift flight, she looks at the waters of the Peneus river and cries out, "O father, help! O mother earth, yawn open, or by changing it destroy this beauty of mine that causes me to be violated!"

Scarcely had she ended her prayer when a deep numbness seized her limbs. Her soft vitals are encircled with a thin bark, her hair is changed into foliage, her arms into branches. That foot, just now so swift, sticks fast in the ground with sluggish roots, her face and head turn into the top of a tree. Her gleaming beauty alone remains within her. This Phoebus loves too, and placing his right hand on the tree trunk, he feels the heart still beat beneath the newly formed bark, and embracing the branches as though they were Daphne's body, he imprints kisses upon the wood; yet the wood shrinks back from the kisses. At this the god spoke, "Since, indeed, you cannot be my wife, you shall certainly be my tree; al-

ways shall my hair, my lyre, and my quiver possess you, laurel tree. You shall crown the heads of the Roman leaders, when the glad trumpet shall sound forth the triumphal cry and the Capitoline height shall view the long procession. You shall have your place as the most trustworthy guardian before the entrance way on the pillars of Augustus' temple, and guard the civic crown of oak that hangs between. And even as my head is kept young with locks unshorn, so do you bear forever and ever the decoration of your beauteous leaves."

Apollo's paean came to an end, and the laurel tree nodded assent with the newly formed branches, and seemed to shake its treetop like a head.                                [I, 452–567]

## PHILEMON AND BAUCIS

On a hill in Phrygia there stands an oak tree and close by it a linden, surrounded by a low wall; I myself have seen the spot. Not far from the oak is a shallow pool of water, once a habitable bit of land, but now water thronged with diving-birds and coots. To this place came Jupiter in the guise of a mortal, and with his sire came the grandson of Atlas,[4] bearer of the caduceus, with his wings laid aside. To a thousand homes they came, seeking a place of rest. A thousand bars shut the homes against them. Yet one home did receive them, small, indeed, with a roof of straw and marsh reeds.

Now a pious old woman named Baucis and her husband, Philemon, of equal age, lived in that cottage. They had been married in early youth and had grown old there together. By admitting their poverty and by bearing it with contented minds they had made it light. It is of little use to inquire for the masters or the slaves in that cottage; the whole household consisted of two persons, and the same gave orders and the same obeyed them.

And so when the deities had reached the little home, with bowed heads they entered the humble dwelling. The old man, drawing up a bench, bade the gods rest their limbs. Over this bench the busy Baucis had spread a coarse cover. After this she pushed aside the warm ashes on the hearth, stirred up the fires of yesterday, fed them with dry leaves and bark, blew them into flame with all the breath an old woman can command, brought down cleft firebrands and dry branches from the garret,[5] split them up fine, and set over them a small brazen kettle. Then she took a vegetable which her husband had gathered from his well-watered garden and stripped it of its leaves. Philemon lifted off with a two-tined fork a dirty slab of bacon that hung from the blackened rafter,[6] cut a small portion from a choice part of the back that had been saved for a long time, and softened up the tough piece in boiling water.

In the meantime the hosts while away the intervening hours with conversation, and shake up their mattress filled with soft sedge-grass gathered from the river, and place it back on the couch, the frame of which and feet were made of willow. This they cover with a robe which they were accustomed to spread only on festive occasions— even so this was a cheap old cover, not at all unsuited to be spread upon a willow couch.

The gods reclined on the couch for their meal. The old woman, with skirts tucked up and with trembling hands, pushed up the table. But its third leg was too short, so she made it of equal length with a piece of tile. After she had put this under it and thus levelled up the sloping surface, she swept off the top with a bunch of green mint leaves. Now was set on a dish of ripe and unripe olives, autumn cornel-cherries pickled in the watery dregs of wine, endives and radishes, curdled milk, eggs lightly done in ashes not too hot, all served in earthen dishes. Beside these dishes, an embossed mixing bowl of the same kind of silver[7] is set on, and goblets made of beech-wood, whose hollowed interiors had been rubbed with yellow wax.[8]

There was but a slight delay and then the hot food was set on and wine of no great vintage was brought out; and when this had been pushed back a little, space was made for the second course. Here nuts and figs were intermingled with wrinkled dates and plums, and fragrant apples in broad baskets and purple grapes gathered from the vines, and right in the middle of it was a comb of clear white honey. In addition to all this, there were pleasant countenances and a lively and bounteous good will.

In the meantime they noticed that the winebowl, when drained, was replenished of its own accord, and the wine welled up in the bowl of itself. Astonished by the strangeness of the sight,

they were filled with fear, and with hands outstretched Baucis and the fearful Philemon began to pray, and begged to be pardoned for their scanty feast and want of preparation.

They had but one goose, the guardian of their little farmhouse, which the hosts were preparing to kill for their divine guests. But the goose was swift of wing and wore them out, since they were slowed by age; and for a long time he escaped their grasp and at last seemed to flee for help to the gods themselves. The gods forbade the couple to kill the goose. "We are gods," they said, "and these wicked neighbors of yours will be deservedly punished; but to you will be given immunity from this disaster. Do you now leave your home and come with us, and climb at once the steep slope of yonder mountain." Both obey, and aided by their staves they struggled to proceed up the long slope. When they were as far from the summit as an arrow can be shot, they looked back and saw that all things had disappeared beneath the waters of the swamp, and that only their own home remained. While they were marvelling at this and were bewailing the fate of their countrymen, that old cottage of theirs, small even for the two occupants, was changed into a temple; pillars rose up in place of the crotched poles; the straw grew yellow and seemed a golden roof; the doors were richly carved, and the ground round about became a marble pavement.

Then thus the Saturnian king[9] calmly spoke: "O honorable old man and thou, wife, worthy of so honorable a husband, tell us what you would like." After Philemon had conversed briefly with Baucis, he disclosed to the gods their joint decision. "We ask that we may be your priests and guard your shrine. And, since we have spent our years together in peace, let the same hour bear us two away together; let me never see the funeral pyre of my wife, and may I never have to be placed away in the tomb by her."

Fulfillment followed their prayer; they became guardians of the temple as long as they had life. At long last, spent with extreme old age, when they happened to be standing before the sacred steps of the temple and were reflecting upon what had happened there, Baucis saw Philemon putting forth leaves, and aged Philemon saw Baucis do the same. Now while a treetop was growing up over their two countenances, they spoke to each other the same words, while still they could, and together said, "Farewell, dear wife, dear husband," and at once the growth of foliage hid their faces from view. Even to this day the Bithynian countryman points out there the tree trunks that grew from the two bodies.

Now no frivolous old men told me this story;

there was no reason why they should want to deceive me. In fact, I myself have seen garlands hanging from the branches. And placing fresh wreaths there myself, I spoke these words: "Upright men are the concern of the gods, and those who have cherished the gods are in turn cherished."                                    [VIII, 620–724]

## *FROM THE* FASTI

### GAMES IN HONOR OF CYBELE, MOTHER OF THE GODS (APRIL 4)

Let the sky revolve three times upon its ever-turning pole; let the Sun three times yoke and three times unyoke his steeds; straightway the Berecyntian flute will blow forth a note on its curved horn, and the festive games of the Idaean Mother will be at hand. Eunuchs will march along and beat their hollow drums, and brazen cymbals clashing upon brass will give forth their jangling notes. The goddess seated on the hairless necks of her attendants, greeted with howls of ecstasy, will be borne along the streets in the midst of the city. The stage resounds, the call for the games rends the air. Look to your seats, fellow-citizens! Let the litigious forums cease their war of words.

I should like to ask many questions, but the sound of the shrill cymbal and the hooked flute of lotus-wood with its terrifying blare frighten me. Tell me, goddess, whom to consult. Then the Cybelean goddess spied her learned grand-daughters [1] and bade them aid me in my anxiety. "Mindful of her charge, ye pupils of Helicon, [2] reveal to me the reason why the Great Goddess rejoices in perpetual din." Thus did I ask; and thus did Erato reply (for to her fell the lot of Venus' month, since she had her name from tender Love [3]):

"This oracle was uttered to Saturn: 'Most gracious of kings, you shall be deprived of your sceptre by your son.' Saturn, in fear of this prediction, devoured his children, each one as it was born, and kept them confined within his vitals. Often did Rhea complain that, though so many times pregnant, she never became a mother, and she grieved because of her fertility.

"And now Jupiter was born. (Faith in so great a witness is based on antiquity; refrain from disturbing an accepted belief.) A stone wrapped in a garment stuck fast in the throat of the god. Thus the Fates would have the father deceived. Now steep Ida rang long and loud with noise as the boy squalled safely with babblings from his baby mouth. Some worshipers beat shields, some beat empty helmets with stakes. This task the Curetes assumed; this task the Corybantes, too, took on. The matter was kept hidden from the father; and even now attendants of the goddess shake the brazen cymbals and thump the raucous leathern drums in imitation of that early ritual. They beat upon cymbals instead of helmets and drums instead of shields; the flute, as before, sounds forth the Phrygian notes."

When the Muse had ceased her tale, I thus began: "Why, for her sake, should the fierce race of lions present their maned necks to the curved yoke, unaccustomed to such a task?" And when I had ceased to ask, the Muse thus began: "The fierceness of those creatures is believed to have been tamed by her; she has borne witness of that by her own car." "But why is her head adorned with a turreted crown? Did she first apply turrets to early cities?" The Muse nodded assent. "But whence came the urge," I asked, "to mutilate the private members?" When I had ceased my words, the Pierian goddess began to speak: "A handsome Phrygian boy named Attis won over the tower-bearing goddess in the woods with a chaste affection. She wanted to keep the boy to herself, to have him guard her temple, and she said, 'Make yourself always want to remain a boy.' He gave compliance to her bidding and said, 'If I lie, may that love by which I deceive you be the last love for me.' But he did break faith, and in the companionship of the nymph Sagaritis,[4] he ceased to be what he had been before.

"For that the angry goddess wreaked vengeance. By wounds inflicted upon the tree she destroyed the Naiad,[5] who thus perished, for the fate of the Naiad was the fate of the tree. Attis madly raved, and imagining that the roof of his bed chamber was falling in, he ran off and sought out the summit of Mt. Dindymus in his flight. Now he cried out, 'Away with your torches!' and now, 'Take away your whips!' Often he swore that the three goddesses[6] were present. He mangled, too, his body with a sharp stone, and he let his long hair be dragged in the filthy dust, and his cry was, 'I have deserved it! I am paying a deserved penalty with my blood! Ah, me! let my members perish which have brought harm to me! Ah, let them perish!' he kept saying, and he cut away the burden of his groin, and suddenly there was no sign left at all of his manhood. His madness set an example, and today his effeminate attendants cut their privates and toss their long hair." With these eloquent words did the Aonian Muse make answer to my question about the cause of the madness of Cybele's worshipers.

"Advise me, too, I pray, O guide in my task, whence was she brought, from what place did she come? Or was she always in our city?" "The Mother of the Gods ever loved Dindymus and Cybele[7] and Mt. Ida with its pleasant fountains, and the kingdom of Troy. When Aeneas was bringing Troy to the Italian fields, the goddess almost followed his ships that were bearing the sacred images, but she realized that her divine aid was not yet demanded by the Fates for Latium, and so she remained behind in her accustomed place. Later, when Rome, powerful in her resources, had already seen five centuries and had lifted up her head over a world subdued, the priest examined the fateful words of the Euboean oracle.[8] They report that this is what he found: 'The Mother is absent; I bid thee, Roman, to seek the Mother. When she shall come she must be received by one with pure hands.' The senators were left in doubt by the ambiguity of the hidden oracle as to who the absent parent was and in what place she was to be sought. Paean[9] was consulted, who said, 'Summon the Mother of the Gods; she is to be found on the Idaean Mountain.' Nobles were sent to Attalus,

who at that time held the royal power. He refused[10] aid to the Ausonian nobles; but then, wonderful to relate, the earth trembled with a prolonged rumble and the goddess thus spake from the depths of her shrine: 'I myself willed that I be sought. Let there be no delay; send me, since I wish it. Rome is a place worthy for every god to visit.'

"Although stricken with fear at the sound, Attalus said, 'Go forth; you still are ours; Rome returns to its Phrygian ancestors.' Straightway countless axes cut down those pine trees which the dutiful Phrygian[11] had used in his flight; a thousand hands gather them together, and a ship, adorned with colors burned into the wood, holds the Mother of the Gods within its hollow shell. . . ."

[Ovid then describes the voyage to Rome.]

She had touched the shore of Ostia, where the Tiber divides in its course to the sea and flows with a broader sweep of water. All the knights and solemn senate, intermingled with the commoners, came to meet her at the mouth of the Tuscan stream. Side by side walked mothers and daughters and daughters-in-law and those who, in unmarried state, tended the sacred hearths.[12] The men wearied their eager arms with straining at the rope; even so the foreign ship with difficulty breasted the opposing waters. For a long time had the land been dry; drought had burned the grass; the loaded ship settled down in the muddy shoals; every man who assisted in the task labored beyond his fair share, and with ringing voice aided the diligent workers. But the ship settled down like an immovable island in the middle of the sea. Astonished at the omen, the sailors stood there and quaked with fear.

Claudia Quinta claimed descent from ancient Clausus[13] and her beauty was no less than her nobility. She was really chaste, although not generally believed to be so. Unfair rumor had wronged her, and a baseless charge had been made against her; her manner of dress and her hairdos of varied decoration told against her and her tongue was quick in retort to censorious old men. Since her mind was conscious of rectitude, she laughed off the lies that went the rounds; but we, the mass of men, are inclined to believe the charge of vice. At all events, when she had stepped forth from the line of chaste women and had caught up the pure water of the river in her hands, three times she sprinkled it upon her head and three times raised her upturned hands toward the sky (all who saw her thought she was bereft of reason), and sinking to her knees, she fixed her gaze upon the image of the goddess, and with hair in disarray about her shoulders, she uttered this prayer: 'O fruitful Mother of the Gods, hear this prayer of thy suppliant, who makes this one request. I am said to be unchaste. If thou dost condemn me, I shall confess that I have deserved the charge; convicted by the verdict of a goddess, I shall wash away my guilt with death. But if I am innocent of sin, thou wilt give a pledge of the purity of my life and, as thou art chaste, so yield to my chaste hands.'

So she spoke and pulled upon the rope with slight effort (strange is my tale, but what I shall relate is attested by the stage [14]). The goddess was moved and followed her leader, and by following signified her approval. And as witness of their joy, the shout of the multitude was borne aloft to the stars.

They came to a bend in the river (men of old called it Father Tiber's Hall), where the stream turns away to the left. Night had come on. They tied the cable to an oaken stump, and refreshing their bodies with food, they gave themselves up to light sleep. When dawn had come, they loosed the rope from the oaken stump, yet not before they had set up an altar and had placed incense upon it, and had crowned the stern and had sacrificed an unblemished heifer, unused to mating and to toil.

There is a place where the smoothly-gliding Almo flows into the Tiber and the smaller river loses its name in the larger stream. There a hoary-headed priest clad in a purple robe washed the goddess and the sacred utensils with the waters of the Almo. The attendants howled aloud, the flute was blown with furious blast, and the hands of eunuchs beat the bull's-hide drums. Claudia walked on ahead with joyful countenance, attended by a very great crowd, her chastity vindicated at last by the testimony of the goddess. The goddess herself, seated in a wagon, was borne through the Porta Capena,[15] while her yoked heifers were showered with fresh flowers.

[IV, 179–276, 291–346]

# NOTES TO SELECTIONS FROM OVID

## *The* Metamorphoses

1. A river god.
2. The Python, a monster which had devastated the country around Delphi.
3. Roman women of good character were careful not to expose much of the arm.
4. Mercury, son of Maia, daughter of Atlas.
5. The driest part of a Roman house, where a poor family would keep the firewood.
6. Smoke from the fire would blacken the roof, but would preserve meat.
7. Ovidian humor for a wooden dish.
8. To keep the liquid from soaking into the wood.
9. Jupiter, son of Saturn.

## *The* Fasti

1. The Muses, whose father, Jupiter, was son of Cybele.

2. Mt. Helicon in Boeotia, favorite haunt of the muses.
3. Eros, love. April was the month of Venus.
4. Evidently a tree-nymph, as seen later.
5. Incorrectly called; for Naiads, according to Pausanias (VIII, 4, 2) were nymphs of the water.
6. The Furies.
7. A mountain, not the goddess.
8. In 204 B.C. the Sibyline Books were consulted for help against Hannibal. The Sibyl lived at Cumae, a colony of Euboea.
9. Delphic Apollo.
10. Not so, according to Livy.
11. Aeneas.
12. The Vestal Virgins.
13. Sabine founder of the gens Claudia.
14. Claudia's exploit was probably represented in some well-known drama.
15. A city gate at the southeast side of Rome.

# SELECTIONS FROM LIVY'S *History of Rome*

## *Translated by Inez Scott Ryberg*

### INTRODUCTION

THE HISTORIAN Titus Livius was born in Padua, the Roman Patavium, a town known among the Romans for its old-fashioned strictness of morals. To the ears of his literary associates in the capital, Livy's speech always betrayed a certain "Patavinity," [1] and a similar Patavinity in outlook may be detected in his condemnation of the moral standards of his own age. Born in 59 B.C., eleven years younger than Vergil, Livy was a child of only ten years when Caesar's crossing of the Rubicon plunged the state into civil war. His young manhood was spent under the shadow of the approaching conflict between Antony and Octavian, but he escaped in part the war weariness which made his older contemporaries look upon Augustus more as "Prince of Peace" than as the founder of a monarchy.

Livy's life was that of a scholar and writer. His history of "Rome from the Founding of the City" was begun in 27 B.C., the very year of Augustus' founding of the principate. The task of completing it occupied him almost to the time of his death in A.D. 17. The first book with its partly legendary account of the early kings was being written at the same time as Vergil's *Aeneid*, and it can hardly be accidental that the two together remain as the great literary monument to the glory of early Rome.

Livy was not an intimate member of the illustrious literary circle which gathered about Maecenas. He enjoyed the friendship of Augustus, however, and the emperor must have been interested in the progress of his *History* no less than in the *Aeneid* or Horace's patriotic *Odes*. Seen from the perspective of later ages, Livy numbers the third in the triad of great writers whose interpretation of Rome to the Romans made the reign of Augustus the Golden Age of a new national literature. Of the three it was Vergil who sounded the Messianic note of the new age, looking with all-but-unshaken confidence to Augustus as the hope of the future. Horace, after a struggle against disillusion and doubt, was converted to the Augustan regime as Rome's last best hope; but he was never freed from foreboding lest his own war-guilty generation might fail to realize that hope. Livy even more than Horace found Rome's best days in the time of the older republic, when the authority rested in the will of the "Fathers" supported by the citizen assemblies, and when the *gravitas* of the Senate made that body seem to a foreign ambassador an "assembly of kings." To Pompey, the champion of the senatorial government in the struggle with Caesar, he is said to have accorded such high praise that Augustus styled him a Pompeian. The same respect for republican forms of government is reflected in his query as to whether the birth of Julius Caesar had brought to the world more of good or ill. His brilliant recounting of Brutus' expulsion of Tarquin the Tyrant, with its emphasis on Roman hatred of the name of king, is a thinly veiled glorification of the contemporary Brutus' part in the assassination of the tyrant Caesar.

After Caesar's attempt to establish a divine monarchy, Augustus' restoration of the Senate and his attempt to give it a responsible part in the administration of the state must have seemed to Livy a move in the direction of good government. Other Augustan departures from Caesar's policies similarly accorded with Livy's own views: the emphasis on Italy and the West as the center and source of government; the restraint of extravagant honors and attempts to deify the emperor during his lifetime; most of all, the efforts to restore the institutions, morals, and religion of old Rome. Livy's partiality for old Roman ways made his history, in turn, serve as a bulwark to the emperor's program of revival and reform. His vivid delineation of early religious rites was contemporary with, or actually preceded, the official revival of many of these same rites. The speech which he puts into the mouth of Cato the Elder on feminine extravagance and the prevailing laxity of morals was applicable to, and without doubt aimed at, the situation of his own day. The famous speech of Camillus in praise of Rome,[2] attributing the nation's greatness and prosperity to the "peace of the Gods," embodied a message to Augustan Rome which might have been spoken by the emperor himself.

There is no reason to believe, however, that Livy entertained the same high hopes of success for the new regime as we find in Vergil or, with qualifications, in Horace. Chance has preserved for us only a fraction of the *History*—less than a third of the whole work—and that fraction exclusively from the account of those earlier times which, by his own confession in the Preface, most enthralled the narrator. We can therefore only infer what would have been his manner of recounting the decline of constitutional government in the last century of the Republic, the rise of the dictatorship, and the events leading to the establishment of the principate. His attitude toward his own times, however, is made clear not only by the sweeping condemnation stated in the *Preface* but by many other passages in which he contrasts earlier days with contemporary Rome. In describing an incident which occurred in 460 B.C. in the struggle between patricians and plebs he remarks: "Not yet did men disregard the Gods as in our generation, nor did they in those days interpret oaths and laws to suit their own purposes, but rather suited their own actions to the laws." [3] Of a mutiny in the army at Capua in 342 B.C. he comments that the army could not muster the audacity to march on Rome, "for men had not then grown so bold in shedding the blood of their fellow-citizens, and in those days knew not how to wage war except against a foreign foe." [4] After a description of the early rite of *devotio* by which in 340 B.C. Publius Decius Mus dedicated his own life to destruction in order to secure victory for the Roman army, Livy adds the remark: "These details I have thought it worth while to record in the very words in which the rite was performed, even though all memory of proper ceremony in divine and human affairs has been wiped out by our modern preference for new and foreign customs in place of the old ways of our fathers." [5]

Hopes for the future are much more tentative in tone. In a comparison between Roman military prowess and that of the Macedonians under Alexander, he concludes: "The Roman people have defeated a thousand battle lines more formidable than they, and will do so in the future, provided we preserve permanently the love of peace and the harmony within the state which we now enjoy." [6]

Livy's view of the function of history [7] encouraged him in his partiality to the earlier days of the Republic. For it is in early Rome that he finds the best of the *bona exempla*, those lessons of history by which his readers may profit. This theory of the ethical purpose of history, generally accepted among Greek and Roman writers, exerted its influence also upon his style and method. Livy regarded history as an art rather than a science. He was accordingly little concerned with historical method in

the sense of the word familiar to the twentieth century, and the criticisms often leveled at his failure to consult official documents and other primary sources are irrelevant to his aim. Livy's narrative of events is based frankly on earlier accounts. He felt no compulsion to check geographical details or to consult archives and inscriptions. On the period of the Punic and eastern wars he had available for his use a contemporary account by the most scientific of ancient historians, the Greek Polybius. This he followed with full recognition of its superiority to his other sources on the period,[8] but he made no effort to emulate Polybius' method. For Livy conceived his task as something else. His purpose was to make the events and heroes of Roman history come alive for his readers, and in this his success is unquestionably beyond cavil.

At the same time, it must be set down to Livy's credit as a historian in the modern sense of the word that he presents a reasonable and balanced version of the history of Rome, selecting his materials with judgment and good sense from earlier accounts of widely varying reliability. He is aware of prejudice in his sources even when the bias coincides with his own. For example, his partiality to the senatorial order did not blind him to the coloring of the historical tradition by private records of the senatorial families. "It is not easy to choose," he writes, "among different versions and different authorities. For I believe that the tradition has been corrupted by funeral eulogies and honorary inscriptions on portraits, as individual families with little regard for the truth seek a reputation for distinction and the credit for public achievements. From this source arises confusion in our record both of the deeds of individuals and of historical events. Nor is there any contemporary writer of those times on whom we may rely with confidence." [9]

Livy's method of presentation likewise was affected by the historiographic tradition of his age. Histories of the Roman republic were customarily written as "annals." The period of the early kings with its large ingredient of legend could be treated in comprehensive narrative, but from the founding of the Republic in 509 B.C. the historian was expected to recount the events of each year under the names of the annual magistrates preserved in the consular lists. To embark upon a year-by-year record of the events of almost five centuries challenged all the resources of the narrator. If the account was to be more than a bare report of events and official acts it must be enlivened with details of narrative, speeches, characterization, and interpretation. And herein lies the brilliance of Livy's achievement. Pursuing a middle course between the dry factual reports of the earlier annalists [10] and the fanciful exaggerations of Valerius of Antium, the Roman "father of lies" who had written a voluminous history of Rome a generation earlier, he represents the best of the ancient "historical tradition" in the best sense of the word.

Livy's smooth-flowing Latin was admirably adapted to the long continuous narrative demanded by his undertaking. The famous "milky flow" [11] of his style was as nicely suited to the annals of the five hundred years of the republic as the well-known *brevitas* of Sallust was suited to that writer's brief accounts of the war with Jugurtha and the conspiracy of Catiline. Sallust's short balanced clauses and striking antitheses were brilliantly effective in a monograph recounting a single historical event, but his terseness would have seemed choppy and monotonous in a work of great magnitude. The flowing narrative which forms the basic texture of Livy's style is constantly varied by imaginative reconstruction of the feelings, reflections, and intentions of the characters. It is varied most frequently of all by speeches, sometimes reported in detail, sometimes thrown into direct quotation. Ancient historiographic tradition permitted, and indeed expected, the historian to compose the speeches made on the occasions he recounts, and this convention offered the writer his richest resources for imparting vividness to his narrative. The historical personages in Livy's pages seem alive and real to the reader chiefly because he has imagined, in their own words, their motives and hopes and fears. The endless struggles between the patricians and the plebeians which gave birth to the Roman constitution—and, by remote ancestry, to our own democratic institutions—are carried forward in large part by the speeches for and against each hard-won liberty.[12] The speeches, of which there are some four hundred in the extant thirty-five books, served not merely to enliven the narrative. They gave the historian an opportunity to convey, most naturally and with least parade, his own interpretation of events, his understanding of their causes and their significance, his estimate of the characters portrayed. The Roman critic Quintilian [13] ranked Livy with the Greek historian Herodotus, regarding both as unsurpassed in narrative power, in fairness of judgment and, above all, in the eloquence of their speeches and their skill in adapting them not only to the circumstances but to the person by whom they are spoken. Any selection of translation from Livy, if it is to convey the quality and the flavor of the history, must not only illustrate his superb gift of storytelling but must include a sampling of the best of his speeches.

THE TEXT is that of Weissenborn and Mueller (Leipzig, 1894–1924).

---

### The preface to the History

What success may attend my effort to record the history of the Roman people from the founding of the city, I do not know, and even if I knew I should hardly presume to say. For it is a subject not only old but familiar to everyone. Time and again new writers undertake the task with the hope that they can come closer to the truth in their record of events or can surpass their predecessors in their style of writing.

Whatever my success it will be a satisfaction to have contributed, in what measure I can, to the making of a lasting record of the achievements of the greatest nation on earth. If in so vast a company of writers I fail to win conspicuous fame, I shall be consoled by the brilliance of the names which outshine my own. It is in truth a tremendous undertaking to recount the history of a state that has been in existence for more than seven hundred years, which has expanded from small beginnings to the point where now it staggers under its own weight.

Most of my readers, no doubt, will take little pleasure in the tales of the founding of the city and the earlier years of its history. They will hasten on to the events of recent years, when the energies of the nation, now long-established as supreme in the world, have been turned upon its own destruction. To me on the contrary it is one of the rewards of my labors to turn away for a little while from the multitude of evils which our own age has witnessed, and to give my whole mind to those earlier times, released from every care or consideration by which the historian's mind might be troubled and distracted, if not deflected from the pursuit of truth.[14]

The legends which cluster about the founding of the city are of the stuff of poetry rather than sober history. They shall be neither vouched for nor discredited in these pages. For it is a privilege granted to antiquity to add lustre to humble origins by mingling tales of divine miracles with the record of the deeds of men. To the Romans, if to any people, must be accorded the right to hallow the memory of their earliest years by attributing their origin to the Gods. Their glory in war surely justifies the claim that Mars was their father and founder, and the nations of the earth should allow that claim no less willingly than they have accepted Roman dominion.

Such questions as these, whatever judgment may be made of them, I hold to be of no great moment. But to this let the reader give his mind. Let him learn what way of life, what forms of government, what manner of men, what arts of statecraft and warfare have brought this empire into being and caused it to increase. Then let him note how, as discipline has been relaxed little by little, morals have conformed to lowered standards. Let him observe how succeeding generations have declined more and more until we have plunged downward headlong into the dilemma of our own times, where we can endure neither our ills nor the remedy for them.

This I hold to be the chief value and reward of history, to have examples of all kinds set forth in an illustrious record, from which you may choose what is worthy of imitation in public and private life, and what is to be shunned as wrong in inception and ruinous in outcome.

Finally, if the love of the task I have undertaken does not blind me, there has never been a nation that is greater and more worthy of veneration, or richer in examples worth imitating. There has never been a state in which the inroads of greed and extravagance have been so long resisted, or in which poverty and frugality have been held in such high regard. While our possessions were limited, our desires were moderate. But in recent years vast wealth has created greed for material things, and an overflowing abundance of pleasures has given rise to an evil will to destroy and to court destruction. But such laments, unwelcome even when they are unavoidable, should be banished at least from the beginning of such a mighty tale. I should prefer to set out under happy auspices and, if historians were accustomed to follow the tradition of the poets, to offer a prayer to the Gods and Goddesses to grant prosperous issue to the work which is now at its beginning.

### *From* Book I

[According to Roman tradition the Latin town of Alba Longa was founded by Aeneas' son Ascanius, and was ruled by his descendants for some three hundred years before the founding of Rome in 753 B.C. Ascanius, who was also called Iulus, was claimed by the Roman family of the Iulii as the ancestor of their clan.]

### *The birth of Romulus and Remus at Alba Longa*

3 . . . The ancestral kingdom of the Silvian dynasty at Alba Longa was handed down by Proca to his elder son Numitor. But neither the right of inheritance nor a father's wishes could prevail against force, and the throne was usurped by the younger brother Amulius. The usurper heaped crime upon crime. Having murdered all the male offspring of his brother's house, he enrolled Numitor's daughter Rhea Silvia among the Vestal Virgins and thus, under the guise of doing her honor, robbed her of the hope of bearing children.

4 But the Fates had decreed the foundation of the mighty city which is second in power only to the Gods. The chastity of the Vestal was violated and she gave birth to twin boys. She claimed—whether she was herself deceived, or merely anxious to find a respectable excuse for her lapse—that Mars was the father of her illegitimate family. In any case neither God nor man could protect her or her sons from the cruelty of the king. The priestess was taken into custody and the king commanded that the babies be thrown into the river.

Providentially the Tiber had overflowed its banks and the stagnant flood waters prevented any approach to the river basin itself. The henchmen who came to carry out the king's orders, thinking that they could dispose of the children anywhere in the flooded area, left them afloat in the nearest pool. This was at the very spot where now stands the Ficus Ruminalis, originally named the Ficus Romularis in memory of the event, and here, as the waters receded, the tub in which the babies had been cast adrift was stranded on dry ground.

In those days the place was a vast wilderness, and a mother-wolf coming down from the neighboring hills to drink was drawn by the sound of their wailing. She nestled down gently to shelter and give suck to the infants, and when the keeper of the royal flocks came to the place, he found her licking them with her tongue. The keeper, to whom tradition gives the name Faustulus, took the twins back with him to the sheepfold and gave them to his wife Larentia to take care of. There is another version of the story which tells that Larentia was a prostitute commonly known among the shepherds as a "she-wolf," [15] and that this was the foundation of the miraculous tale of their being nursed by a wolf.

[Brought up by Faustulus and Larentia among the shepherds of the neighborhood, Romulus and Remus eventually discovered their identity and assisted their grandfather Numitor to regain the throne.

> Now slain is King Amulius,
> Of the great Sylvian line,
> Who reigned in Alba Longa,
> On the throne of Aventine. . . .[16]]

### The founding of a new city by Romulus and Remus

6 When Numitor had been restored to the Alban throne, Romulus and Remus were seized with the ambition of founding a city in the place where they had been abandoned and had grown up. Alba Longa was now overpopulated, and they could also call on the support of numerous shepherds around the countryside. With these as a beginning they were inspired with the hope that both Alba and Lavinium would one day be insignificant in comparison with the new city which they intended to build. Then into the midst of these plans stalked their ancestral curse, the greed for power. What began as a minor disagreement turned into a fatal struggle. Since they were twins and neither had the prerogative of age, they agreed to let the Gods who watched over the place decide whose name should be given to the new city and who was to be its ruler. In accordance with the agreement, Romulus took his station on the Palatine and Remus on the Aventine Hill, to watch for a sign from heaven.

7 The story goes that Remus saw the first sign, a flight of six vultures. But this omen was immediately followed by the flight of twelve vultures within Romulus' field of observation, whereupon each brother was hailed as king by his own company of followers. One side claimed the sovereignty by priority in time, the other by the number of the birds. In the ensuing argument tempers flared to a point where the contest turned to a pitched battle, and Remus was slain in the melée.

Another version of the story, even more widely known, tells that Remus mockingly leaped over the wall which his brother was just starting to build, and that Romulus struck him down in wrath, with the words: "So dies anyone who scales my walls!" Romulus thus became the sole ruler, and the new city was called by the name of its founder.

### The establishment of a place of refuge

8 Meanwhile the city was growing in extent. One district after another was included within its circuit, more in the hope of future needs, it is true, than to accommodate its present inhabitants. To make this broad expanse something more than an empty show, Romulus, like many another city founder of early days, resorted to a stratagem. (For doubtless some stratagem of increasing the population of a new city by gathering in a multitude of poor and lowly folk lies concealed beneath the familiar tales of men miraculously sprung from the earth.) [17] In the valley between the two groves, where you see the enclosure as you go down from the Capitol to the Forum, Romulus opened a place of refuge which he called the Asylum. Thither fled all the rabble and the offscourings from the neighboring cities and from everywhere in the countryside. All who were eager for a new start in life were welcome, with no questions asked as to whether they were slaves or free. The multitudes who came to take refuge in the Asylum increased the population of the city for the first time to a number which corresponded to its ambitious size.

### The establishment of the Roman Senate

Now that there was no reason to be concerned about the city's strength in numbers, Romulus proceeded to the task of its organization. He chose a hundred men as senators, selecting this number either because it was sufficient at that time,[18] or because there were no more than a hundred eligible as "Fathers." "Fathers" was at any rate the official title of the senators, and their children were designated as "patricians." [19]

### The rape of the Sabine women

9 The Roman state was by this time strong enough to hold its own against the military force of any of its neighbors, but yet its strength seemed likely to endure no longer than one generation. Because of the great scarcity of women in the newly founded city the Romans had no hope of

children at home, nor did they as yet possess the right of marriage with women in the neighboring towns. On the advice of the senate, therefore, Romulus sent ambassadors around to the different peoples nearest at hand to make a plea for social alliance and rights of intermarriage for the new state. "Cities, like all other things," they said, "arise from lowly beginnings, and those which are aided by the Gods and by their own abilities in time attain great wealth and fame." They had sure evidence, they claimed, that the Gods had presided over the founding of Rome, and their neighbors could be equally confident that the Romans would not be found wanting in ability. Let them, therefore, recognize their common humanity by consenting to form ties of friendship and kinship with their fellow human beings. Nowhere was this embassy heard with favor. Not only did their neighbors look down upon the Romans; they also feared this new state growing so rapidly in the vicinity, lest it might prove a threat to themselves and their descendants. Often they turned the ambassadors away with the question whether they were opening an Asylum also for women. "That," they sneered, "would at least assure equality of status."

The Roman youth could not brook taunts like these, and it began to look as if the crisis must be resolved by force. To provide an occasion for such an attempt, Romulus concealed his chagrin and prepared for the celebration of the Consualia,[20] a festival of games in honor of Equestrian Neptune. He had news of the event heralded in the towns near by, and the Romans prepared for the festival with as much display as they could command, in order to make it an occasion which would draw crowds of visitors. Many people came, attracted partly by a desire to see the new city. People came from the nearest towns, Caenina, Crustumerium, and Antemnae, and also a great many Sabines with their wives and children. Hospitably received and entertained by the Romans, they admired the town, its fortifications, and its numerous buildings, and they marvelled that Rome had grown so rapidly.

The hour finally came for the races, and when the eyes and thoughts of everyone were intent upon the spectacle, the young men, leaping up at a prearranged signal, dashed here and there to seize the girls. In most cases a girl was carried off by the first man into whose hands she happened to fall. A few of exceptional beauty, however, were picked for the chiefs of the state and carried home for them by henchmen especially assigned to the task. The story goes that one in particular, who surpassed all the others in loveliness, was seized by the band of henchmen of a certain Talassius, and as people asked for whom she was intended they kept shouting "For Talassius," lest anyone might try to snatch her away. This incident, they say, was the origin of our traditional wedding cry "Talassio." [21]

As the gathering broke up in panic, the parents of the girls fled, cursing this violation of the laws of hospitality and calling down the wrath of the God at whose festival they had been so wickedly wronged. The kidnapped girls themselves were no more hopeful and no less indignant. But Romulus himself went about among them, pointing out that the fault lay in the arrogance of their parents, who had refused the right of marriage to their neighbors. He assured them that they nevertheless would be accorded the position of wives rather than captives, with full share in all the rights of citizenship and—what is most precious of all—full share in the possession of their children. Only let them mollify their wrath, he admonished, and give their hearts to the husbands to whom chance had given their bodies. Often an initial wrong might lead to greater good will, he assured them, prophesying that they would find their husbands the kinder because each would try his utmost not only to fulfill his role as husband but to assuage the longing for home and country. No less effective was the wooing of the young men, who defended their violent deed by the excuse of irresistible attraction and desire—excuses most likely to find favor in women's hearts. . . .

*In the war ensuing, the women put an end to the fighting.*

13 Then the Sabine women, on whose account the war was being waged, overcame their womanly fear under the threat of disaster. With hair flowing and garments rent in the fashion of mourning, they mustered courage to rush in between the opposing battle lines among the flying weapons, and to separate the battling armies. They calmed the wrath of the fighting men, their husbands in one array, their fathers in the other, imploring them not to stain their honor with the

slaughter of father-in-law and son-in-law, not to taint the birth of their children and grandchildren by shedding kinsmen's blood. "If the kinship between you displeases you, turn your wrath upon us! We are the cause of the war, we are responsible for these wounds, and for the slaughter of our husbands and parents. Better for us to perish than to live widowed without one or orphaned without the other!"

The deed moved both the men and their commanders. A sudden silence fell, and then the leaders came forward to conclude a truce. They not only made a treaty of peace but united the two peoples into one state, located at Rome but with the sovereignty shared between them.

[The tradition that the population of early Rome was Sabine as well as Latin is supported by archaeological and linguistic evidence. Even more certain is the evidence that in the 6th century B.C. Roman culture was strongly influenced by the Etruscans, a powerful and highly civilized people from the eastern Mediterranean, who settled in Italy and for a time held sway over a large part of the peninsula. Roman tradition preserved the names of four kings of Latin or Sabine stock: Romulus, who shared his sovereignty with the Sabine Titus Tatius, Numa Pompilius, Tullus Hostilius and Ancus Martius; the last three of the seven kings, Tarquinius Priscus, Servius Tullius and Tarquinius Superbus, belong to the period of Etruscan domination.]

*An Etruscan becomes king in Rome.*

**34** During the reign of Ancus Martius an Etruscan named Lucumo migrated to Rome, a man of ability and wealth. The chief reason for his coming was ambition and the hope of winning honors, which he had no opportunity of achieving at Tarquinii because of his foreign birth. He was the son of Demaratus of Corinth, who had been exiled from his native city by a revolution and had happened to settle in Tarquinii. Having married an Etruscan wife, Demaratus had two sons, Lucumo and Arruns. He was survived by Lucumo, who fell heir to all his wealth, while Arruns died before his father, leaving a son still unborn. The father lived only a short time after Arruns' death and, not knowing that a child was to be born to his daughter-in-law, made no provision for it in his will. Thus the

child was born to no share in the patrimony and was given the name Egerius, the needy one.

Lucumo on the contrary was fired to ambition not only by his inherited wealth but also by his marriage with Tanaquil, herself a woman of high station and not satisfied to marry beneath it. She could not endure the humiliation of the Etruscans' scorn for Lucumo, the son of an exile. Forgetting her natural attachment to her country in her determination to see honor accorded to her husband, she conceived the idea of moving away from Tarquinii. Rome seemed the most promising as a new home. In a new state where all distinctions were of recent origin and attainable by merit, there was likely to be a place for a strong and energetic man. At Rome Tatius the Sabine had been king, Numa had been called in from Cures to occupy the throne, and Ancus himself was half Sabine and had only one noble ancestor to display in his portrait gallery.[22]

Accordingly they packed up their possessions and moved to Rome. They had travelled in their covered wagon as far as the Janiculum Hill at the edge of the city, when an eagle darted down and carried off Lucumo's cap, soared above the cart with great commotion and again, as if sent on this particular mission, replaced the cap on his head and flew away. The story is that Tanaquil, who like most Etruscans was skilled in reading signs from the heavens, interpreted this as a favorable omen. She bade her husband hope for great things. For an eagle appearing from that quarter of the sky was a messenger of Jove and had given a sign which concerned the highest point of a man's life. It had removed the adornment of his head only to replace it upon him as a crown. Bringing with them such dreams and hopes they entered the city, where they bought a house and established residence, Lucumo calling himself Lucius Tarquinius Priscus.

Tarquinius was at once conspicuous among the Romans because of the novelty of a new arrival in town and because of his wealth. This prominence he himself furthered by his graciousness of address, by his hospitality of entertaining in his home, and by doing kindnesses whenever opportunity offered, until his reputation became known even to the king. Before long that first favorable introduction to the king was transformed into close friendship by the generosity and capability of his services to the state. He became an active participant in public affairs and a trusted counsellor on all questions in peace and in war. At length, thoroughly tried and tested, he was designated in the king's will as guardian of the young princes.

35 Ancus reigned twenty-four years, unsurpassed by any of his predecessors in glory and in the arts of peace and war. At his death his sons were not far from the age of manhood. Tarquinius was therefore the more insistent that the election of the new king [23] be held at the earliest possible moment, and as the time for the election drew near he sent the boys off on a hunting trip. He was the first man in our history to canvass for election to office or to make a campaign speech designed to win the votes of the populace. If he were the first foreigner to aspire to the sovereignty in Rome, he argued, men might justifiably look with surprise or disfavor upon his candidacy. But he was in no way departing from precedent. This would be the third time that the Roman throne had been occupied by a foreigner. Tatius had been made king, though he was not only a foreigner but an enemy. Numa, who was a stranger to the city, had been called in to accept the crown. He himself had lived in Rome from the time when he had come to manhood, and had made his home there with his wife and all his possessions. The years of his manhood—that part of life in which men contribute to the welfare of the state—had been spent more in Rome than in his native country. In military and civil life he had become conversant with Roman laws and institutions under tutelage at which no one could cavil, that of King Ancus himself. In loyalty and service to the king he could challenge anyone in the city. In service to the people of Rome he could match even the king.

Reminded of these many merits and recognizing the justice of his claims, the Roman people elected him by a huge majority.

[After a reign of 38 years Tarquinius Priscus was assassinated by the sons of Ancus Martius, who had always regarded him as a usurper of their claims. Tarquin's wife Tanaquil, however, managed to secure the throne for their son-in-law Servius Tullius, a man reputedly of humble origin who had been adopted by the king and brought up in the palace.

King Servius Tullius was known in Roman tradition as the great lawgiver. The principal

achievements ascribed to him were the fortification of the city by the "Servian Wall," and the establishment of the census and the centuriate assembly. The latter was an organization of the citizen body by "centuries," or companies of one hundred men, ranked in five classes according to wealth. The organization was primarily military, but the classes and centuries served also as voting units and in the course of time the assembly acquired a purely political character. (Cf. Cicero, *De Legibus* III, 44.)

In spite of Servius' efforts to avoid the enmity of Tarquinius Priscus' two sons by giving them his own daughters in marriage, he was eventually murdered by his younger daughter Tullia and her husband, who seized the throne and became famous in Roman tradition as Tarquinius Superbus. The name of Tarquinius Superbus, or Tarquin the Proud, epitomized to the Romans their hatred of monarchy, and the king is pictured as the typical "tyrant." The story of the capture of Gabii in chapter 53, for example, includes two anecdotes which are adapted from Herodotus' tales of the Persian kings. The recorded achievements of the last Tarquin bespeak the ambitious organizer and builder, under whose rule Rome attained greater stature as a city and a position of leadership in Latium. The expulsion of the kings, traditionally recorded in the story of Tarquin the Proud, represents the revolt of the Italic element in Rome against the domination of Etruscan overlords. Archaeological evidence indicates that about the end of the sixth century B.C. the Etruscans were forced to withdraw from their outposts in Latium and were pushed back within the boundaries of their original holdings in Etruria (Tuscany) north of the Tiber.]

### The reign of Tarquinius Superbus

49 Then began the reign of Lucius Tarquinius, surnamed the Proud. He forbade the payment of funeral honors to his father-in-law Servius Tullius on the pretext that Romulus himself had been accorded no funeral rites,[24] and he slew the most prominent of the senators, whom he believed to have been supporters of Servius. Fully aware that his own example of attaining the sovereignty by crime might be used against himself, he protected his life by the constant attendance of a body guard. Since he had come into possession of the kingdom without either the authority of

the Senate or the vote of the people, he could place no reliance on the loyalty of the citizens and was obliged to maintain his power through fear. To inspire terror in his subjects he made himself the sole judge in trying capital cases, and was thus able to put to death, to drive into exile, or deprive of their property any whom he suspected or hated, or whose possessions he coveted. Although the number of the senators was reduced by these practices he decided to enroll no new names, in the hope that the Senate, diminished in numbers and in influence, might be less outraged at his neglect of its counsel. For he was the first to break with the tradition, handed down from earlier kings, of consulting the Senate on all matters of public moment. He ruled the state for his own private ends, declaring war and concluding peace treaties, or forming alliances whenever and with whomsoever he wished, regardless of the will of the people or the fathers. . . .

### The capture of Gabii by treachery

*53* While the king was an unjust ruler in time of peace, he was a leader of no mean ability in war. In that field, indeed, he might have won a reputation to surpass his predecessors, had not his wickedness in other respects obscured his glory in this. He was the first of the kings to attack the Volscians, and thus to begin a conflict which continued for two hundred years beyond his own time. Having taken four hundred silver talents [about $400,000] worth of booty in the storming of the Volscian town Pometia, he conceived the idea of using it to build a temple to Jupiter—a temple which should be worthy of the King of Gods and men, worthy of the majesty of Rome, and worthy of the glory of its builder.

Next he embarked on a war with the neighboring town of Gabii, which proved to be less quickly concluded than he had hoped. After an unsuccessful attempt to take the town by storm he made preparations for a siege. But when even the besieging forces were routed he finally resorted to deceit and treachery, a means totally foreign to the Roman tradition and character. Pretending to have abandoned his plans for war, he gave his whole attention to the laying of the foundations for the temple and to other projects for the improvement of the city.

Meantime, as part of the stratagem, his youngest son Sextus fled to Gabii, bemoaning his father's intolerable cruelty to him. The tyrant, he complained, had now turned upon his own children and, irked by their presence, was bent upon creating the same desolation in his own household as he had already made of the Senate house, determined to leave alive no heir to the throne. Sextus alleged that he himself had managed to escape his father's armed guard and had come to seek refuge in Gabii, believing that he would be safe nowhere but among the enemies of Tarquin. Let them make no mistake, he warned, the war which the king had pretended to abandon was still being waged, and an attack would be made at the first opportunity. If they offered no shelter to a suppliant he would traverse all of Latium seeking shelter, he would go to the Volscians, to the Aequians and Hernicans, until he found folk willing to rescue children from the wickedness and cruelty of impious parents. Perhaps, he hazarded, he might somewhere find people ready to make war upon that worst of tyrants and his ferocious people.

As he seemed then and there on the point of going away indignant if they did not detain him, the Gabines made him welcome among them. They assured him that it was not to be wondered at that the king who had tyrannized over his own citizens and his allies should finally play the despot with his own children. He would doubtless turn his savagery ultimately upon himself if no other victims were left to destroy. They were pleased, they assured him, that he had come to them, and they hoped that with his aid it might soon be possible to carry the war from Gabine territory to the very walls of Rome.

*54* Thus received by the Gabines, Sextus was made a participant in the counsels of state. On most matters he deferred to the judgment of the Gabines, to whom the local situation was more familiar, but in military affairs he assumed a position of special competence and authority on the grounds that he knew the resources of both sides. He argued that such a king, whom his own children could not endure, was beyond a doubt hated by his subjects. Thus with steady persistence he kept inciting the leading citizens of Gabii to open hostilities with Rome, while from time to time he led the more audacious of the young men on forays and raids. Calculating every word and every act to serve his strategy, he won the confidence of the Gabines so completely that at last he was chosen commander of the military forces. A number of minor encounters with the Roman troops were managed, without arousing the Gabines' suspicion, in such a way that the Gabines came off victorious, until at length the Gabines from highest to lowest believed in Sextus Tarquinius as a leader providentially sent to their aid. The soldiers, moreover, were captivated by his sharing all their dangers and hardships, and by his generous division of booty. In short, Tarquinius was not more honored at Rome than was his son at Gabii.

When he was sure that he had support sufficient for any contingency, Sextus sent one of his henchmen to his father in Rome to inquire what he next commanded him to do, since now by the grace of the Gods his power at Gabii was unlimited. This messenger received no verbal reply, doubtless because he was not completely trusted. Instead of replying the king went into the garden, with his son's messenger at his heels, and walked about as if absorbed in thought. As he strolled in silence he struck off with his cane the protruding heads of the tallest poppies.

Finally tired of asking his question and receiving no answer, the messenger gave up and went back to Gabii, where he reported to Sextus all that had occurred. He told him how the king, either in anger or hostility, or purely because of his natural arrogance, had deigned not a single word in reply. Sextus, however, reading the riddle of his father's instructions, proceeded to bring about the destruction of the pre-eminent leaders among the citizens of Gabii. Against some he found a pretext for bringing criminal charges; in other instances he took advantage of and fostered the jealousy their high position had aroused among their fellow citizens. Some were publicly executed; others, against whom legal action would be less plausible, were secretly murdered. Some were driven into exile; others were offered the opportunity of departure from the country. The property of all his victims, killed or exiled, was confiscated and the spoils divided among the people. Thus enjoyment of private gain dulled the sense of public injustice, until finally, robbed of its defenses and leadership, Gabii fell without a struggle into the hands of the Roman king. . . .

*The rape of Lucretia* [25] *and the overthrow of the monarchy, 509* B.C.

57 The town of Ardea was inhabited by the Rutulians, a people of wealth and power by the standards of those times and that region. Ardea's wealth was, in fact, the cause of war with Rome, for the Roman king hoped to replenish the treasury which he had exhausted by the extravagance of his public buildings.[26] He needed booty also to distribute among the citizens as a means of currying their favor. For they were disgruntled and hostile because, in addition to all his arrogant and tyrannical acts, he had forced them into service in the construction of his public works.

Ardea was laid under siege, after an unsuccessful attempt to take the city by storm. In the quarters of the besieging army, as usual in a war that is long drawn out rather than vigorously waged, there was some freedom in granting leave from camp, more, naturally, for the officers than for the soldiers. The young princes of the royal house had also a good deal of time to spend on dinners and drinking parties. At one dinner party in Sextus Tarquinius' quarters Collatinus,[27] Egerius' son, happened to be present, when the conversation turned to a discussion of their wives. Each one praised his own wife to the skies. As the argument grew heated Collatinus exclaimed that there was no need of words when in a few hours they could see for themselves how far his Lucretia surpassed all the others. "Come," said he, "if we are the men we boast, why not mount our horses and in person prove the comparison? Let us agree that the character of each of our wives shall be judged by whatever greets the unexpected arrival of her husband." They were all heated with wine and with a quick reply, "Come, let us be on our way!" they started up from the table and, swiftly mounting their horses, sped towards Rome.

After a brief stop they rode on to Collatia, where they found Lucretia, not like the princesses of the royal family passing the time in luxurious parties with other young folk of the city, but seated in the great hall surrounded by her maidservants, spinning by lamplight. The prize in the contest of womanly excellence went to Lucretia.

She welcomed Collatinus and the young Tarquinii, and the triumphant husband entertained the princes with gracious hospitality, until toward morning the young men returned to camp after their night's adventure. While they were in Collatinus' home Sextus was seized with desire for Lucretia, attracted not only by her beauty but by her proved fidelity, and he conceived a dastardly plot to violate her chastity.

58 A few days later he returned to Collatia accompanied by a single attendant, without the knowledge of Collatinus. There he was received cordially by Lucretia, who had no hint of the evil intent of his visit. When they had dined and the household had retired for the night, Sextus, consumed with passion, making sure that all was safe and everyone asleep, stole with drawn sword into the bedchamber of the sleeping Lucretia. With his left hand upon her bosom holding her fast he said, "Silence, Lucretia; it is I, Sextus Tarquinius. I have a sword in my hand. If you make a sound, you shall die." When the woman, startled from sleep, saw that there was no help, no defense against imminent death, then Tarquin began to confess his love, to persuade, threaten and implore, leaving untried no plea which might win a woman's heart. But when he realized that she was immovable, and unshaken even by the fear of death, he added to that the fear of dishonor. He swore that he would kill a slave and place him naked beside her dead body, so that she would be found as if slain in adultery with a servant. With that terror his lust finally overcame her unassailable chastity, and Tarquinius departed in shameful triumph, a victor who had conquered a woman's honor.

Lucretia, crushed by this disaster, sent a servant with a message to her father in Rome and her husband at Ardea, saying that they must come at once, each with a trusted friend, for a terrible thing had befallen her. Her father Spurius Lucretius came with Publius Valerius, while Collatinus brought with him Lucius Junius Brutus, whom he happened to meet on his way back to Rome after receiving the message.

They found Lucretia, filled with sadness, sitting in her chamber. At the appearance of her husband the tears welled up, and as he asked her, "Is all well with you?" she replied, "Far from it! For how can all be well for a woman who has lost her chastity? The print of another's man's head is on your pillow, Collatinus. But I swear to you that my body alone is violated—my mind is unstained. My death shall bear witness to that. But give me your right hand as a pledge that the adulterer shall not go unpunished. It was Sextus Tarquinius who came last night, an enemy posing as a guest, and with armed violence took hence his wicked pleasure, which brought ruin upon me and, if you are men, will bring ruin upon himself as well."

They gave their pledge each in turn, and tried to soothe her grief by turning the blame from the victim to the author of the crime. "The mind alone can sin," they urged, "and where intent is absent no guilt exists." "Yours it is," she said, "to judge what is owing to him. As for me, though I absolve myself from guilt, I do not release myself from penalty. Nor shall any woman in after time find in Lucretia's name a pretext for shameful life." Drawing forth a knife which she had concealed in her bosom she plunged it into her heart, and fell dying upon the thrust.

59 Brutus, while they were all absorbed in their grief, took the knife dripping with blood from Lucretia's breast and, holding it before him, said "By this blood, unstained but for a prince's crime, I swear and call upon you, O Gods, as witnesses, that I will drive out Lucius Tarquinius Superbus with his wicked wife and all his children, by sword, by fire, by whatever force I can command, and I will suffer neither him nor any other to reign as king of Rome." He handed the knife first to Collatinus and then to Lucretius and Valerius, while they wondered whence had come this new power in the character of Brutus the dullard.[28] They took the oath at his behest and then, turning from grief to furious indignation, they followed the leadership of Brutus as he urged them to the overthrow of the monarchy. They carried the body of Lucretia from her house down into the Forum, where a crowd soon gathered, first in wonder at the strangeness of the sight and then in indignation at the crime. Each had other grievances against the wickedness and cruelty of the king, but now they were moved by the grief of the father and by the exhortation of Brutus. He scorned idle tears and passive complaints, and urged them to rise in arms, as befitted men and Romans, against those who had shown themselves enemies of the state. The boldest of the young men rushed forward as volunteers, and the rest followed their lead.

Leaving part of their number in Collatia as guards upon the gates, lest news of their uprising reach the king, they set out for Rome with Brutus in command.

Upon their appearance in the city the sight of an armed band at first created terror and tumult along its path. But when people saw that the leading citizens were at its head they realized that this was not any idle mob. The story of the horrible deed created no less indignation here than at Collatia, and men from all parts of the city gathered in the Forum. There a herald announced a call to assembly by the Tribune of the Cavalry—which was Brutus' title of office at the time—and Brutus addressed the crowd in a manner utterly foreign to the character which had heretofore masked his true nature.

He told the story of the lust and violence of Sextus Tarquinius, the rape of Lucretia and her tragic death, the grief of Lucretius Tricipitinus, who mourned for the loss of his daughter and even more for the cause of her death. He went on to speak of the tyranny of the king himself, and the toils and miseries of the common people forced into digging sewers and laying stone for public buildings. Roman citizens, he reminded them, who were victorious in war over all the peoples of the region, were now reduced to serving as stone-masons and ditch-diggers instead of warriors. He recalled Tarquin's slaughter of Servius Tullius, the callous cruelty of his wife Tullia, who had driven her carriage over the dead body of her father; and he called down upon them the wrath of the gods who punish the murder of a parent.

With such words, and others which are inspired by the excitement of the moment but not easy to recall later for the written record, he aroused the citizens to such a pitch of indignation that they abrogated the power of the king and declared him an exile along with his wife and children. Brutus himself with a band of younger volunteers set out for the camp at Ardea, to instigate the army to an uprising against the king. Lucretius was left in charge at Rome in the capacity of Prefect of the City, an office previously instituted under the kings. In the midst of the tumult Tullia fled from the palace, followed by curses and imprecations wherever she went, as people called down upon her the vengeance of the gods for the murder of her father.

*From* Book II

[The first years after the overthrow of the monarchy and the founding of the republic were filled with class struggles between the patricians and the plebeians. Not until 367 B.C. did the plebeians finally win the right to hold the chief magistracy of the state, the consulship.]

*The struggle between the patricians and plebeians,* 495 B.C.

23 War with the Volscians [29] was threatening, but at that very moment the smouldering discord within the state burst out into open strife between patricians and plebeians. The particular focus of conflict was the question of imprisonment for debt. It angered the plebeians that in spite of their having fought many a time for the liberty and protection of their country against external foes, at home they themselves were held in a state of subjection and all but slavery. The liberty of the plebeians, so it seemed, was more secure in war than in peace, and better established among the enemies of Rome than among her own citizens.

Their wrath, ready to catch fire of its own accord, was fanned into flame by the tragic plight of one old man, who escaped from prison and burst into the Forum bearing upon him the marks of the ills which afflicted them all. His clothing was ragged and soiled, his body was unkempt and wasted with starvation, his long hair and beard imparted a wild look to his pale face. In spite of his pitiable condition, he was recognized as a fellow-soldier by many of the citizens, who recalled with indignation that he had led their ranks in the army and had won the distinctions of a soldier. He himself showed them scars on his breast which testified to the battles in which he had fought. As a crowd gathered about him asking how he came to be so miserably clad and emaciated, the old man told them his story.

While he was away from home serving as a soldier in the Sabine War his fields had been untilled and devastated, his house had been burned and his property plundered, his cattle driven off by robbers. Finally he had gone into debt to meet the tax assessment which he was unable to pay at the time when it came due. The debt, as it accumulated with the accrual of the interest, had first stripped him of his inherited lands, then of everything he possessed, until finally like a disease it had attacked his body itself. He had been dragged off by his creditors not merely into slavery but to the torture chamber and slaughter house. To confirm his story he showed his back marked with fresh welts from the lash.

At this tale and the visible evidence of its truth a great tumult arose, and soon the rioting had spread from the Forum to every quarter of the city. Debtors burst into the streets, many of them in chains, and implored aid from the citizens. Volunteers from everywhere gathered to swell the crowds, and when various bands from different parts of the city had joined forces they all together made a tumultuous march on the Forum. Any patricians who happened to be there encountered them at great peril. Nor would the mob have abstained from violence if the consuls Publius Servilius and Appius Claudius had not interfered to quell the riot. To them the multitude of debtors turned, showing them their chains and other signs of their sufferings. These, they said, were their rewards for military service, and they named over the recent campaigns in which they had fought. With threats rather than prayers they demanded that the consuls assemble the Senate, and they surrounded the Senate house, determined to be themselves the arbiters of the public deliberations. . . .

24 In the midst of all this turmoil arose another and greater danger. Latin cavalrymen rode up with a hasty message that the Volscians were advancing with a large army for an assault on the city. This news was heard with far different feelings by the plebeians and by the patricians— to such a point had discord divided the state. The plebeians exulted with joy, saying that the Gods were now punishing the arrogance of the patricians. They urged that no plebeian enlist for military service. Better to perish with all of Rome than to die on the battlefield! Let the patrician fathers take up arms and serve as soldiers, so that the perils of war might be endured by those who reaped the rewards!

The Senate, alarmed and dismayed by this double threat of danger from without and from within, begged Servilius, the consul who was the less unpopular with the plebeians, to rescue the state from imminent disaster. The consul accordingly adjourned the Senate and immediately summoned the citizens to an assembly. He assured them that the Senate was deeply concerned for the welfare of the people. But their problem, though unquestionably of the greatest moment, was now overshadowed by a danger which threatened the state as a whole. With an army almost at the gates, nothing must stand in the way of mobilization for war. Indeed, even if the situation were not so desperate, it ill beseemed the citizens to demand a price in advance for defending their country, nor was it fitting that the senators should take measures for the relief of the people under constraint of force rather than of their own free will.

He pledged them his good faith and, to relieve their immediate distress, issued an edict that no one should hold a Roman citizen in chains without giving him an opportunity to appeal to the consuls; and that no one should seize or sell the property of a soldier absent in military service, or lay hands on his children or grandchildren. On the promulgation of this edict, those who had been enslaved for debt at once enlisted. From all parts of the city debtors broke away from their creditors, who now no longer had any right to detain them, and rushed to the Forum to take the oath for military service. The levy of troops was enormous, and no army during all of the Volscian war won greater distinction for bravery and zeal. . . .

*Establishment of the office of Tribune of the Plebs, 494 B.C.*

32 The senators feared that if the army were demobilized there would be a recurrence of the secret meetings and the sedition. The levy of troops had been conducted by a dictator, but they believed that the soldiers were still bound by the military oath which the consuls had administered. Accordingly the Senate decreed that the legions should be led out on a campaign against the Aequi. At this the plebs rose up in revolt. The first proposal among the mutineers was to murder the consuls, in order to be released from their oath of military obedience. But one of their number, Sicinius by name, reminded them that an oath could not be dissolved by a crime and on his suggestion, without orders from the consul, they seceded to the Sacred Mount, three miles from the city and across the Anio River.

This version of the story is more widely accepted than that of Piso, who states that the seceding plebeians withdrew to the Aventine Hill.[30] On the Sacred Mount they established a camp fortified with a palisade and moat and, with no leader in command, equipped only with what they needed to eat, they remained for some days without either making an attack or being attacked.

Panic gripped the city, and all activity was suspended in mutual fear. The plebeians who were left behind feared violence at the hands of the patricians. The patricians were afraid of those plebeians who still remained in the city, at a loss whether to hope that they would stay or depart. They wondered how long the citizens who had seceded would continue to keep the peace, and what would happen if war with a foreign foe should break out in the meantime. They saw that there was no hope except in concord within the state, and that this must be restored by any means available. They decided to send as an ambassador Menenius Agrippa, an eloquent speaker and beloved by the plebs because he was himself of plebeian origin. On being admitted to the camp, Agrippa, in the crude and uncouth manner of those early days, told them a story:

"In olden times, when the parts of the human body were not yet perfectly harmonized among themselves, each of the members had a will of its own and its own voice. It came about that the other members felt aggrieved because all their services and all the fruits of their labor were received by the belly, while the belly itself, at ease in the midst of the body, did nothing but enjoy the good things with which they provided it. The members therefore decided upon secession, agreeing that the hands would carry no food to the mouth, that the mouth would accept nothing, that the teeth would refuse to chew. While they were determined, in their wrath, to subdue the belly by hunger, the whole body and even the members themselves wasted away with starvation and weakness. Thus it became evident that the belly too had been performing a service, and that it was providing food as well as being fed, distributing impartially to the blood and all the parts of the body the nourishment which enabled them to live and grow strong." By showing them how this strife between the members and the belly was similar to the conflict between the plebs

and the senators, Menenius won over the dissenters and effected a reconciliation.

*33* As a concession to the demands of the plebeians it was agreed that there should be two magistrates of the people who, themselves sacrosanct and thus immune from interference by process of law, should have the right to intercede with the consuls in defense of the plebeians. The provision was that no patrician should be eligible for this magistracy. And thus were chosen the first tribunes of the plebs,[31] Gaius Licinius and Lucius Albinus.

### From Book IV

*Intermarriage between patricians and plebeians legalized, 445 B.C.*

*1* It was a year filled with strife at home and abroad. At the very beginning of the year the tribune Gaius Canuleius proposed a law sanctioning intermarriage between patricians and plebeians, a measure which, in the opinion of the fathers,[32] would contaminate their stock and confound the traditional rites of the *gentes*.[33] A further suggestion that plebeians might be eligible for one of the two consulships, put forward at first tentatively, finally took the form of a bill backed by nine of the ten tribunes. The bill provided that the people should have the power to elect consuls without distinction as to whether they were patrician or plebeian. To the patricians it seemed that this measure was designed, not to equalize the right of holding public office, but in effect to wrest it from the leading men of the state and confer it upon the plebs. . . .

*3* While these questions were being debated in the Senate, Canuleius spoke to the people in support of his proposal: "Many times before this have the patricians let it be known that they despise you, people of Rome, and that they think you unfit to dwell in the same state with them. But today their contempt is even more clearly evident in their savage attack upon this proposed law. For what is the intent of this new law but to remind the patricians that we are their fellow-citizens, that even if we do not possess the same wealth we still belong to the same fatherland? In one provision we propose to legalize intermarriage. This is one of the rights extended by universal custom to neighbors and to citizens of other states. But the Romans are known for exceeding universal custom in liberality. They have granted even to conquered foes the boon of citizenship, a far greater thing than the right of intermarriage.

"In the second provision we propose nothing new, but only reclaim and re-establish what has always been the people's right, to elect to office anyone it chooses. What cause have they to stir up heaven and earth? What reason had they to all but assault me as I entered the Senate house? Why did they threaten to lay violent hands on the sacrosanct person of the tribune of the plebs? If the Roman people exercise with free suffrage the right to confer the consulship on whatever candidate they choose, and if a plebeian who is worthy of the highest honor be allowed the hope of attaining it, will our state no longer survive? Will the power of Rome be at an end? If we propose that a plebeian be eligible to the consulship, is that the same as to propose that a slave or a freedman be made consul? Do you now, fellow-plebeians, begin to realize with what scorn you are regarded? If they were able they would deprive you of a share in the light of the sun! They are indignant that you breathe the air, that you speak with human voice, that you are endowed with the form of man! [34]

"We have been told that it would be a sacrilege for a plebeian to be consul. Tell me, then, even though we are not permitted to consult the religious calendars and the priestly books, are we not aware of what even foreigners know, that the consuls succeeded to the position of the kings and have no powers or privileges but those which the kings formerly held? Have they never heard the story of how Numa Pompilius, who was not a patrician—indeed, not even a Roman citizen—was called from the Sabine country and by the authority of the fathers and the vote of the people was made king of the Romans? Have they never heard that Lucius Tarquinius, who was not of Roman birth, not even of Italic stock but the son of Demaratus of Corinth and an immigrant from Tarquinii, was chosen king in place of Ancus Martius' sons? After him Servius Tullius, son of a captive woman of Corniculum, his father unknown and his mother a slave, attained to sovereignty in Rome by his own native ability and worth. Why need we mention Titus Tatius the

Sabine, whom our founder, Romulus himself, admitted to an equal share in the royal power? Those earlier days, when no man who excelled in ability was despised because of his origin—those were the days when our dominion increased! . . .

4 " 'But since the expulsion of the kings,' you say, 'no plebeian has been consul.' And I ask, What of the future? Is nothing new ever to be instituted? Because something has never been done—and in a new state there are many things which have not yet been established—is it to be rejected even if beneficial? In the time of Romulus there were no pontifices and no augurs.[35] These priesthoods were founded by Numa Pompilius. Under Numa Pompilius there was no census and no centuriate assembly. These were established by Servius Tullius. There was a time when there were no consuls. Yet after the kings were expelled consuls were elected to administer the government. At one time dictators were unknown; yet when need arose the name and the office came into existence.[36] There were once no tribunes of the plebs, no aediles, no quaestors.[37] These magistracies too were instituted without earlier precedent. The last ten years have witnessed the institution—and the abolition—of the office of "decemvir for the codification of the laws." [38] Who can doubt that, in a city established for all time and increasing as it has to unimagined dominion, new magistracies, new priesthoods, new laws of men and nations must in the course of time be introduced?

"Indeed, the very ban upon marriage between patricians and plebeians—was not this regulation passed only recently by the decemvirs, to the discredit of the Roman people, as a crowning insult to the plebeians? Could there be any greater or more conspicuous arrogance than to regard a part of the citizens as unfit to marry, just as if they were contaminated with some infection? What else is this than banishment and exile within our very walls? . . .

"Why do you not pass a law prohibiting intermarriage between the rich and the poor? A woman's right to marry, if she chooses, any man who seeks her in marriage, is properly a matter of private concern. This you would regulate by an unjust law which does away with the common rights within the state and creates two states instead of one.[39] Why is there no law that plebeians and patricians may not be neighbors, may not walk in the same street, may not attend the same social gathering, or stand beside one another in the Forum? For how do such rights differ from the right of intermarriage? What established institutions, moreover, would be altered by our proposal, inasmuch as children in any case take the status of the father? We are asking nothing but to be counted as men and as citizens. Nor is there anything in our law for you patricians to object to, unless it is your aim merely to insult and humiliate us.

5 "Finally, I ask the consuls, does the power of legislation belong to you alone or to the Roman people as a body? Did the abolition of the monarchy win dominion for you or equal liberties for all? It is right that the Roman people be free to make whatever laws they see fit. Or do you propose, whenever a new law is to be voted upon, to declare a muster of troops as a threat and a reprisal? Whenever I as tribune call the people into assembly to vote, do you intend as consul to call them to the colors and march them out to camp? As if you had not twice before discovered by experience how little weight such threats carry against the unanimous will of the plebs! [40] On those other occasions, doubtless, it was out of consideration for us that the contest stopped short of armed conflict! Or was war avoided because the more determined party was also the more reasonable? Indeed, fellow-citizens, there will be no armed conflict now. The patricians will try to intimidate you, but they will not put your strength to the test.

"Whether this levy of troops is made in good faith, or is merely an excuse to block passage of the bill, I do not know. But I assure you, consuls, the plebs are ready for your call to the colors—provided you give them a share in the state by equalizing the rights of marriage, provided they may unite with you in kinship and family ties as well as in the defense of the state, provided all citizens who are capable and courageous may have the hope of winning honor, provided all citizens with full equality may exercise as well as obey magisterial authority. If these human rights are refused to the plebeians, then prate all you please of wars to be fought, no one of us will register for the levy, no one will

take up arms, no one will march into battle at the command of haughty masters, with whom we are not permitted to share either in public office or in the rights of marriage."

[The century between the passage of the Canuleian law and the introduction of the drama, 445–364 B.C. was occupied with wars against the Volscians to the south and against the Etruscan town of Veii to the north. The destruction of Veii in 396 B.C. was followed in 390 B.C. by the sack of Rome itself at the hands of Gallic invaders. The Romans managed, however, to hold the citadel on the Capitoline Hill, and after the withdrawal of the barbarian hordes rebuilt the city and a new city wall, of which some parts may still be seen.]

*From* Book VII

*The first dramatic performances in Rome, 364 B.C.*

2 In this and the following year, when Gaius Sulpicius Peticus and Gaius Licinius Stolo were consuls, there was an outbreak of pestilence. For this reason there were no events worth recording except that a *lectisternium*[41] was performed, for the third time since the founding of the city, to placate the anger of the Gods. But the epidemic could be checked neither by human efforts nor by divine aid, and the people's minds were at length so overpowered by superstition that they sought new and unprecedented means of assuaging heaven's wrath.

Among other things they instituted theatrical performances, a new thing for a warlike nation which heretofore had had no public entertainments except the races in the Circus. This new form of entertainment was of foreign origin and, as was natural in the beginning, was established at first on a modest scale. Without any singing or mimic gestures, performers brought from Etruria danced in the Tuscan manner to the music of the flute. Shortly thereafter young Romans began to perform in the same style, exchanging gibes in crude verse form and adapting their motions to suit the dialogue. This gradually became an accepted custom, and with frequent performances its popularity grew. From the Etruscan word for "actor," the name "histriones" was given also to the native Roman players, who now no longer carried on merely a crude and impromptu dialogue like the Fescennine verses, but performed satires in verse with appropriate pantomime and flute accompaniment.

It was some time later than this that Livius Andronicus introduced regular comedies with a plot. He acted in his own plays, as was customary, and the story is told that he was so constantly in demand for performances that his voice grew hoarse, until finally with many apologies he brought in a slave to sing the parts which were set to music. He himself, being thus freed from the effort of using his voice, acted the *cantica* [42] with more elaborate pantomime. In the course of time it became customary to have special singers to accompany the actors' mimic performance of the *cantica*, while the actors themselves spoke only in the dialogue parts.

As soon as real comedies were introduced, the older jesting dialogue without plot went out of fashion. But as drama was now gradually becoming an art, the young Romans resigned the performance of regular plays to professional actors, while they themselves revived the old fashion by putting on vaudeville skits in verse form. These eventually developed into the *exodia* which are often combined with the Atellan farces. That type of entertainment, which originated among the Oscans, [43] the Roman youth kept in their own hands and refused to allow it to be taken over by professional actors. Hence it is that actors of Atellan farces do not lose their franchise and are eligible for army service just as if they had no connection with the theater. [44]

I have thought it worth while to review the modest beginnings of theatrical entertainment in Rome, to show how this institution has grown from a comparatively simple and harmless origin to the present insane craze which the wealth of kings could hardly support.

[Books VIII to X record the expansion of Roman territory in Italy, the conquest of Etruria, the colonization in Campania, and the wars with the Samnites. The lost books XI to XX described the establishment of Roman power in Magna Graecia (the Greek settlements of the southern coastal area), and the earlier part of Rome's struggle with Carthage for mastery of the western Mediterranean. Book XXI resumes

the narrative with the second Punic War, often called the War with Hannibal, 218–202 B.C. Cf. Harvey, *s.v.* Punic Wars.]

## *From* Book XXI

### *The character of Hannibal* [45]

4  Hannibal was dispatched to Spain and on his first appearance attracted the interest of the army. The old soldiers thought that a younger Hamilcar [46] had come back to them. They saw in him the same features, the same liveliness of expression, the same fire in the eyes. But shortly his resemblance to his father was only the least among their reasons for devotion to him. Never was an individual more perfectly suited both to obedience and to command. It would be hard to say whether the commander or the army loved him more. There was no one whom Hasdrubal preferred to put in charge of any assignment which demanded bravery and vigor; nor was there any leader under whom the army fought with greater confidence and daring. When danger was to be faced it was Hannibal whose spirit was the boldest, and in a crisis his strategy was the shrewdest. Under no hardship did his energy wane or his spirits flag. He could face heat or cold with equal endurance. His appetite for food and drink were controlled by hunger and not by pleasure. His waking and sleeping were not fixed by day and night. What time remained after the task in hand was done he gave to sleep, and this without any need of soft bed or quiet. Many a time he could be seen lying on the ground among the sentries and pickets off duty, covered only with a soldier's cloak. His dress was no different from that of his fellow-soldiers, but his weapons and his horses were of the finest. He was the best among cavalry and infantry alike, always the first to go into battle and the last to leave any clash of arms.

These qualities were matched by equally great flaws of character: inhuman cruelty and a worse than Punic treachery which had no regard for the truth, held nothing sacred, was stopped by no fear of the Gods or scruple at breach of faith. With such an endowment of faults and virtues he served for three years in Spain under the command of Hasdrubal, omitting no experience or training suitable for a man destined to become a great military leader.

*Hannibal addresses his army before crossing the Alps, 218 B.C.*

29 With the memory of the other war still fresh in their minds the soldiers feared the enemy, but even more they dreaded the untried journey over the Alps—a terrifying prospect to men who knew it only from hearsay. Hannibal, therefore, when he had decided to go forward into Italy, summoned his men to assembly and spoke to them, upbraiding their fears and firing their courage.

He was astonished, he said, at the sudden terror that had gripped their hearts, usually so dauntless. For years they had fought hard battles, and always with victory. On this occasion, furthermore, they had set out from Spain only after all the peoples and lands bordering on two different seas [47] had come into the possession of the Carthaginians. Then with conquered lands behind them, indignant at the demand of the Romans that the besiegers of Saguntum [48] be surrendered as if guilty of crime, they had crossed the Ebro River to wipe out the name of Rome and free the world from oppression. No one then thought the march too long, though the road stretched from the setting to the rising of the sun. Now, with almost the whole of the journey behind them, when they had traversed the heights of the Pyrenees in the midst of savage peoples, when they had crossed the Rhone, overcoming both the swiftness of the river and the resistance of so many thousands of Gauls—now, when they were actually in sight of the Alps themselves, with Italy just across the mountains, were they now going to halt exhausted at the very gates of the enemy's country?

"What do you imagine the Alps to be but high mountains?" he asked. "Granted that they are higher than the Pyrenees, no mountains touch the sky, and there are none which cannot be scaled by human beings. Indeed, the Alps are inhabited, they support living creatures, and their passes can be crossed by armies. These messengers from northern Italy whom you see before you have not flown across the Alps on wings. Their ancestors, furthermore, were not natives, but as strangers and immigrants from Gaul they crossed into Italy over these very Alps, bringing their wives and children with them. Will the same

terrain be impassable to an army carrying only equipment and implements of war?

"To capture Saguntum you endured eight long months of toil and danger. Now, when you are marching on Rome, the capital of the world, can any difficulty be so insurmountable as to delay your purpose? Are Carthaginians to despair of attacking a city which the Gauls once captured? [49] Either confess yourselves inferior in spirit and courage to a race whom you have just defeated time after time, or fix your goal in the Campus Martius between the Tiber River and the ramparts of the City of Rome."

[At the close of the second Punic War in 202 B.C. Rome found herself almost immediately involved in war with Philip V of Macedon, who had been pursuing an aggressive policy in Greece and had allied himself with Hannibal in the hope of gaining a foothold for expansion into Italy.]

*From* Book XXXIII

*The proclamation of the freedom of Greece, 196 B.C.*

32 The time had come for the Isthmian Games, a popular event even under ordinary circumstances, because the world is always eager for a spectacle with contests of skill and strength and swiftness. Moreover, because of the convenient location, [50] where wares imported over two seas were available to supply all the needs of men, the market served as a meeting ground between Greece and Asia. But on this occasion an extraordinary crowd congregated from everywhere, drawn not only by all the usual attractions but by their eagerness to know what was to be the future status and fortune of Greece. People were openly speculating as to what the Romans would do, and each individual held a different opinion. That they would withdraw from Greece no one dreamed.

When the crowd was seated ready for the spectacle a herald came forward with a trumpeter, as was customary at the solemn opening of the festival, and when silence had fallen at a blast of the trumpet, he read the following proclamation:

"The Roman Senate and the commanding general Titus Quinctius Flamininus, having conquered the armies of King Philip and the Macedonians, decree that the following peoples shall be free and independent and shall live according to their own laws," and he named all the peoples which had been subject to Philip's rule, the Corinthians, the Phocians, the Locrians, the Euboeans, the Magnesians, the Thessalians, the Perrhaebians and the Phthiotic Achaeans.

The good news was too overwhelming to be comprehended all at once. People could not believe that they had heard correctly, and looked at one another in amazement as if they thought they were seeing visions. When their own country was named they did not trust the evidence of their ears, and kept asking their neighbors to confirm what they had heard. The herald was called back to read the proclamation a second time, so eager were they not only to hear but to see the messenger who brought the announcement of their freedom. When the news was at last believed, the clamor of applause re-echoing again and again bore witness to the universal belief that of all blessings none is so precious to men as liberty.

The races and other contests were held in a perfunctory fashion, as people had no eyes for the performances, absorbed as they were with their one great joy to the exclusion of all other claims on their attention. 33 As soon as the games were ended everyone rushed up to the Roman general to offer thanks, until he was al' bu. crushed by the multitude of folk throwing garlands of flowers or crowding around him to grasp his hand. But he was a vigorous man of thirty-three years, and he was borne up by his buoyant strength as well as by the excitement of the glorious occasion.

The rejoicing which had burst forth at the moment of the proclamation lasted for days afterward in men's thoughts and conversation and in varied expressions of thanksgiving. Men marvelled that there was on earth a people who at their own cost and their own toil and risk would go to war to win liberty for others—a people who would not merely bring aid to friends or allies or neighboring nations but would actually cross seas to wage war in order that there might nowhere in the world be injustice and tyranny, but everywhere righteousness and law and liberty. For by this proclamation all the cities of Greece and Asia had been granted freedom, a boon

which it required a bold imagination to hope for and a mighty power and great good luck to achieve.[51]

### *From* Book XXXIV

*Cato's speech against repealing the Oppian Law,*[52] *195* B.C.

1 . . . The Capitol was crowded with men supporting and opposing the repeal. Even the women on this occasion forgot the modesty that ordinarily kept them in their homes, and they could be restrained by no public authority, nor even by the command of their husbands. They besieged all the streets of the city and the entrances of the Forum. As men came down to the Forum the women begged them, now that prosperity had returned and incomes were steadily increasing, to restore women's right to personal adornment. Day by day the crowds of women increased, as they congregated from outlying districts and villages, and they dared even to accost and solicit the consuls, praetors, and other magistrates. Whatever their success with the rest, one of the consuls proved to be inexorable. This was Marcus Porcius Cato, who made a speech in defense of the existing law.

2 "If each one of us," he declared, "exercised a husband's authority and jurisdiction over his own wife, we should have less trouble with the whole lot of them. As it is now our power of action, curtailed at home by our wives' insistence on having their way, is encroached upon and suppressed even here in the Forum. Because we do not control them singly, we find them formidable collectively. . . . This feminine uproar—spontaneous or instigated by you, Marcus Fundanius and Lucius Valerius—is in any case a reproach upon the magistrates. Whether it is more disgraceful to you tribunes or to us, the consuls, I hardly know: to you, if you have now resorted to stirring up women as well as men to take part in your seditious troublemaking; to us, if we are forced to pass laws by a secession of women, as we were once forced by a secession of the plebs. . . .

"Our forefathers, deeming it unwise that women should conduct even private business without the authority of a guardian, placed them under the jurisdiction of father, brothers, or husband. We now permit them—Heaven forgive us!—to take part in affairs of state, to intrude their presence even in the Forum, in public meetings and legislative assemblies! For what are they doing now in the streets and at the cross-roads but urging the passage of the tribunes' bill—indeed "casting their vote" for the repeal? Give rein to these headstrong tempers, these undisciplined creatures, and do you then expect them of their own accord to set a limit to their presumptions? Unless a limit is fixed by you, you will find that this is the least of the indulgences that women of baser nature allow themselves, laws and social usage notwithstanding. What they want is complete liberty—or, rather, complete licence, if we are to call it by its right name.

"If they succeed in this, what will they not attempt? Think of all the restrictions by which your forefathers subjected them to the control of their husbands. Even with the aid of all these you are hardly able to keep them in order! If you allow them to wheedle and extort from you a little more and a little more, and finally to be on an equal footing with men, do you think you will be able to endure them? Once they begin to be your equals, they will be your superiors! . . .

*4* "You have often heard me complain of the extravagance of women, and of the extravagance of men too, not only of private citizens but even of public magistrates. You have heard me say that our country is being corrupted by two vices, greed and luxury, the very sources of evil which have proved the destruction of all great empires. These I fear more and more, as the fortune of the state grows even more prosperous and the extent of our domain ever increases. We now cross over into Greece and Asia, lands filled with enticements to wickedness, and lay hands upon the treasures of kings. And I shudder lest those things may possess us rather than we them. To our harm, believe me, were the marble statues from Syracuse brought to the city. Too often do I now hear men praising and marvelling at the art treasures of Corinth or Athens, and deriding the earthenware adornments of the temples of our Roman Gods. But these are the gods whose blessing I prefer to enjoy—whose blessing indeed we may continue to enjoy, provided we permit them to remain in their rightful place.

"Within the memory of our fathers King Pyrrhus tried to bribe not only men but women too by offering them gifts through his agent Cineas.

Though there was then no Oppian Law to restrain feminine extravagance, not a woman accepted the bribe. And why was that, do you ask? For the very same reason that at that time no law had been passed. There was no extravagance to restrain. As a disease must precede the remedy for it, so luxury must exist before the enacting of sumptuary laws. What occasioned the passing of the Licinian Law to limit the size of farms but the growing greed for larger and larger estates? What was the reason for enacting the Cincian Law to control wages and "gifts" but the fact that the plebs were being employed as laborers by the nobles? Small wonder, then, that no Oppian Law nor any other regulation was needed to restrict the women, but that of their own accord they declined to accept the proffered gold and fine purple. If Cineas came to the city now with his gifts, he would find women standing in the streets ready to receive them!

". . . Do not fancy, fellow citizens, that things will return to the same status as before the law was passed. As it is safer for a guilty man never to be accused than to be acquitted in a trial, so extravagance never curbed would be more tolerable than it will be now, like a wild beast infuriated by chains and then released. I cast my vote against the repeal of the Oppian Law. Whatever the decision, may all the Gods bless and prosper it."

## *From* Book XXXIX

### *The character of Marcus Porcius Cato*

*40* . . . Among all the men of noble families; patrician or plebeian, the most distinguished candidate for the office of censor was the plebeian Marcus Porcius Cato.[53] In this man there was such vigor of mind and force of character that, whatever his status at birth, he would have won fame by his own efforts. There was no art, in either personal or civic affairs, of which he was not a master. He handled with equal skill the business of the city and of the country. Some men have been advanced to high position by knowledge of the law, others by the power of eloquence, others by military genius. But his ability was so perfectly adapted to all kinds of achievement that whatever he put his hand to seemed to be his special gift. In war he was a mighty soldier, distinguished in many battles; but when advanced to a position of command he was unmatched as a general. In peace he was a most learned interpreter of the law, if there was need for legal advice, or if a case was to be defended, a most eloquent advocate. Not only did he win fame as an orator during his lifetime, but his eloquence still lives among us and exerts its power, enshrined in his many writings.[54] He wrote many speeches in defense of others and of himself, many speeches of prosecution. For he was a formidable assailant, not only in bringing his opponents to trial but in arguing the case against them. He was the object of many attacks, and he himself was equally outspoken in attacking others; indeed it would be hard to say whether the nobles oppressed him or he harassed them the more. Undeniably he was a man of harsh temper and of sharp tongue too freely employed, yet at the same time unswervingly upright, incorruptible by greed, contemptuous of riches or favor. Ironclad in frugality, enduring of toil both in mind and in body, he was invincible even by death which overcomes all things. In his eighty-sixth year, still active as an advocate, he wrote and delivered a speech in his own defense; at ninety he brought Servius Galba to trial before the Assembly.

## NOTES TO LIVY'S *HISTORY OF ROME*

1. Quintilian, *Inst. Orat.* VIII, 1, 3; Harvey, *s.v.* Livy.
2. V, 51–54.
3. III, 20.
4. VII, 40.
5. VIII, 11.
6. IX, 19.
7. See the Preface, below.
8. XXXIII, 10.
9. VIII, 40.
10. Harvey, *s.v.* Fabius Pictor and Cato the Censor. Cf. Cicero, *De Oratore*, II, 52–53.
11. The phrase, "lactea ubertas," was used to describe Livy's style by Quintilian, *Inst. Orat.* X, 1, 32.
12. See IV, 3–5, below.
13. *Inst. Orat.* X, 1, 101.
14. Horace, *Odes* II, 1, describes the writing of the history of recent events, which still arouse bitter animosities, as walking on the thin crust of a crater.
15. *Lupa*, she wolf, is etymologically related to *lupanar* (den of she wolves), the common term for a brothel.
16. Macaulay's *Lays of Ancient Rome*, "The Prophecy of Capys." The legends of Romulus and Remus and other stories in Livy's early books furnished the material for the *Lays*.
17. Harvey, *s.v.* Cadmus. Cadmus, the founder of Thebes, sowed the teeth of the dragon he had slain, and from them sprang warriors. Cf. the myth of Jason, Harvey, *s.v.* Argonauts.
18. The Senate had 300 members in the time of the Republic. It was increased to 600 by Sulla, and to 900 by Julius Caesar.
19. The word "patrician" is derived from *pater* (father).
20. An early Italic harvest festival, associated by Livy with the games of the Circus because it took place in the vicinity of the Circus Maximus and because it included horse races.
21. This is an example of an etymological myth, a story invented to account for the origin of a word of which the original meaning has been lost. Harvey's explanation that Talassio was probably the name of a god of marriage (*s.v.* Talassio) is as unfounded as Livy's.
22. According to Roman custom "nobility" was attained by holding public office and carried with it the right to be represented in a portrait bust.
23. The principle of hereditary succession was never fully established in the early Roman kingdom. The earlier kings had not been succeeded by their sons, and the present episode implies a priority of claim on the part of Ancus' sons but not an undisputed right to the succession.
24. Romulus had been deified and accordingly the funeral rites performed for ordinary men were inappropriate.
25. Livy's story of the rape of Lucretia, together with Ovid's version of the tale, furnished the theme and many of the details for Shakespeare's poem, "The Rape of Lucrece."
26. To Tarquinius Superbus were ascribed the building of the great temple to Jupiter on the Capitoline Hill and the construction of the sewer (Cloaca Maxima) which drained the Forum.
27. Collatinus was the second cousin of Sextus Tarquinius, since his father Egerius was Lucumo's nephew; see above, chapter 34. His surname Collatinus was derived from his home town Collatia, a Latin city not far from Rome.
28. Brutus, meaning "dullard," was a cognomen given to Brutus because he had cloaked his abilities under a mask of stupidity, biding his time for an opportunity to overthrow the tyrant.

29. A neighboring people to the south of Latium.

30. The Aventine Hill was outside the *pomerium*, the religious boundary of the city, and a secession to the Aventine is recorded on a later occasion.

31. The tribunes, originally two in number but later increased to ten, at first possessed only the *veto*, the power to forbid any action of a magistrate directed against a plebeian. In the course of time they acquired other powers, e.g., to convene the Senate or the assembly, and to initiate legislation. See Cicero, *De Legibus*, III, 19–25, for comments on this office.

32. Livy here uses the word fathers, *patres*, as the equivalent of "senators" and also of "patricians."

33. The *gentes* were clans, or groups united by kinship; these groups were regarded as units for certain purposes in the state, e.g., eligibility for certain priesthoods.

34. Cf. Sallust, *War with Jugurtha* 85, Marius' criticism of the nobility and their contempt for men of lower birth.

35. Tradition ascribed to the second king, Numa Pompilius, the founding of the religious institutions, including most of the priesthoods. The augurs had charge over observation and interpretation of omens. The pontifices had general charge over religious rites. Cf. Cicero, *De Legibus*, II, 8 and 50 ff.

36. The date of the introduction of the dictatorship is unknown, but Livy mentions the office for the first time in II, 21, under the year 495 B.C.

37. Harvey, *s.v.* aediles, quaestors; cf. Cicero, *De Legibus*, III, 6–11.

38. In 451 B.C., for the special purpose of formulating a code of laws, ten magistrates (decemviri) were elected in place of the annual consuls, Livy, Book III, 32–33.

39. Cf. Aristotle, *Politics*, V, 12. Aristotle criticizes Plato's view (*Republic*, VIII, 551D) that in an oligarchy there are two states, one of the rich and the other of the poor.

40. The reference is to the secession of the plebs to the Sacred Mount in 495 B.C.; see II, 32.

41. An offering of a "banquet" to the gods, in which images of the gods were placed on dining couches in front of the temples. This was a Greek custom celebrated in Rome only by specific command of the Sibylline Books. Livy records the first introduction of the rite in 399 B.C. (V, 13).

42. *Cantica* are the lyric passages of a Roman comedy, written in more elaborate verse forms than the dialogue and intended to be sung. Plautus' liberal use of *cantica* makes his plays somewhat akin to musical comedies. See Plautus, *The Haunted House,* and Harvey, *s.v.* Comedy.

43. Inhabitants of southern Italy, who spoke a dialect related to Latin. The farces of Atella, one of the chief Oscan towns, were probably written in this dialect. Harvey, *s.v.* Oscans and Atellan farces.

44. Actors in the theater were of low social status, ordinarily slaves or freedmen. Eligibility for army service was a privilege of Roman citizenship and in the period of the republic required also the ownership of some property; cf. Livy I, 43.

45. Cf. Sallust's characterization of Sulla and Marius in *The War with Jugurtha,* chapters 95–96, 98, 100.

46. Hannibal's father, one of the Carthaginian leaders in the first Punic War. Hasdrubal was his brother and his successor to command in Spain.

47. Lands on the northern and southern shores of the Mediterranean.

48. Saguntum was a Roman outpost in Spain. Its capture by the Carthaginians was the occasion of the second Punic War; cf. Livy XXI, 6–16.

49. See introduction to VII, 2.

50. The games were held at Corinth, located on an isthmus which commanded access to the Aegean and the Adriatic Seas.

51. The "liberation" of the Greek cities by the Roman general Flamininus was in part prompted by his admiration for Greek arts and letters, an attitude which was much in vogue among the Romans at the time. It was also in accord with the consistent Roman policy of establishing friendly free states as "buffers" to secure her own territory from border invasion.

52. The Oppian Law, which forbade the use of gold and costly purple-dyed materials for feminine adornment, had been passed as a wartime emergency measure. After the close of the Macedonian War it was no longer necessary for reasons of economy.

53. Cf. the characterization of Hannibal in XXI, 4, (p. 276, above).

54. In addition to his speeches, Cato wrote a history of Rome, *Origines,* and a work on agriculture, *De Re Rustica.*

# The Deeds of the Deified Augustus

## Translated by Charles F. Edson, and Carl Schuler

### INTRODUCTION

THE YEAR before he died (A.D. 14) Augustus had composed or revised, sealed, and deposited for safekeeping four documents, which were opened and read before the Senate immediately after his death. The first of these documents was his will, the second made provisions for funeral arrangements, the third summarized his achievements, and the fourth was an appraisal of the military and financial resources of the state. It is the summary of his achievements, the *Res Gestae* (Deeds) with which we are here concerned. The original has disappeared—although Suetonius (A.D. 70–160) appears to have had access to it—and so has the primary copy of it, the Monumentum Romanum, which Augustus had ordered inscribed on bronze pillars next to his tomb. Fortunately, copies of the *Res Gestae* have been found elsewhere, for they seem to have been set up in every province. Most notable of these copies and the most complete is that still in its original site at Ankara (ancient Ancyra, now the capital of Turkey). Its existence has been known to the modern world since 1555 and it has been published many times. It is inscribed in both Latin and Greek; the Latin seems to be a direct copy of the Monumentum Romanum, while the Greek is a translation of the Latin, intended especially for the inhabitants of a province to whom Greek was the mother tongue. The Greek version is invaluable in that it fills in occasional gaps in the Latin. Fragments of a second copy, less well known, have been found at Apollonia in Pisidia, and when pieced together —much of the job of piecing has taken place since 1930— help fill in the gaps in the Greek version of the Monumentum Ancyranum. A third copy, in Latin only, fragments of which were first found in 1914 in Antioch, supplements our knowledge of the Latin text of the Monumentum Ancyranum. Both the Monumentum Ancyranum and the Monumentum Antiochenum clearly stem from a common source, the original manuscript of Augustus or the Monumentum Romanum.

Augustus (63 B.C.–A.D. 14) was not the first Roman general to leave a memoir of his achievements, but none of his predecessors in that genre had felt the need for such hypocrisy as he showed, nor had they had the skill for it; none "fabricated history with such calm audacity." * The style of the document is deceptively plain —Augustus' admiration of the Ciceronian style was not so great that he sought to imitate it; the *Res Gestae* is far more important for its omissions than for what it says, and the reader must never forget that Augustus was writing self-justification, not history.

THE TEXT used is that of J. Gagé (Paris, 1935).

A COPY SUBJOINED OF THE EXPLOITS OF THE DEIFIED AUGUSTUS BY WHICH HE SUBJECTED THE INHABITED WORLD TO THE IMPERIUM OF THE ROMAN PEOPLE, AND OF THE MONIES WHICH HE EXPENDED FOR THE REPUBLIC AND THE ROMAN PEOPLE. THE ORIGINAL IS INSCRIBED ON TWO BRONZE PILLARS WHICH ARE PLACED AT ROME.

*1* At the age of nineteen years on my own responsibility and at my own expense I raised an army with which I liberated the Republic from domination by a faction. In acknowledgment of this the Senate, in the consulship of Gaius Pansa and Aulus Hirtius [43 B.C.], elected me into its order by honorific decree with the right to vote as one of consular rank, and granted me the imperium. Together with the consuls I was ordered as propraetor to see to it that the Republic suffered no harm. Moreover, in the same year, when both consuls had fallen in war, the people made me consul and triumvir for the ordering of the Republic.

*2* In the legally constituted courts I took vengeance upon the murderers of my father [1] by driving them into exile, and afterwards, when

---

* R. Syme *The Roman Revolution*, p. 522.

they waged war upon the Republic, I twice defeated them in battle.[2]

3 Many times I waged wars, both civil and foreign, throughout the inhabited world, and as victor I spared all citizens who sought mercy. I preferred to preserve rather than to destroy those foreign nations which could safely be treated with clemency. About five hundred thousand Roman citizens were bound to me by the military oath. When their service had expired, I settled in colonies or sent back to their municipalities somewhat more than three hundred thousand of these, to all of whom I either assigned land or gave money as a reward for their military service. I captured six hundred warships, in addition to those which were smaller in size than triremes.

4 I twice held triumphal ovations and three times curule triumphs. I was hailed as imperator twenty-one times, but when the Senate would have decreed more triumphs to me, I refused them all. I dedicated the laurel from my fasces in the Capitol after the fulfillment of those vows which I had publicly pronounced in each war. Fifty-five times the Senate decreed thanks to the immortal gods for the successes achieved by me or by my lieutenants under my auspices. Moreover, there were 890 days on which thanks were given in accordance with a decree of the Senate. Nine kings or children of kings were led before my chariot in my triumphs. I had been consul thirteen times and was in the thirty-seventh year of my tribunician power [A.D. 14] as I wrote this.

5 I did not accept the position of dictator, offered to me by the Senate and the People during the consulship of Marcus Marcellus and Lucius Arruntius [22 B.C.], either when I was absent or when I was present in Rome. When there was a very severe shortage of grain I did not refuse the management of its supply, and I so administered it that within a few days by my efficiency and at my expense I freed the entire state from fear and danger. I did not accept the annual and perpetual consulship which was also then offered me.

6 In the consulship of Marcus Vinicius and Quintus Lucretius [19 B.C.], again in that of Publius Lentulus and Gnaeus Lentulus [18 B.C.], and a third time in that of Paullus Fabius Maximus and Quintus Tubero [11 B.C.], although the Senate and the Roman People were in agreement that I should be created sole curator with final authority over the laws and public morals, I did not accept any magistracy proffered contrary to the custom of our ancestors. It was through my tribunician power that I completed those tasks which the Senate then wished to be performed, and five times I asked for and received from the Senate a colleague in that power.

7 For ten consecutive years [43–33 B.C.] I was a triumvir for the ordering of the Republic. I was princeps of the Senate for forty years up to that day when I wrote this. I was Pontifex Maximus, an Augur, one of the College of Fifteen for making sacrifices, one of the College of Seven for religious feasts, an Arval Brother, a Titian fellow and a Fetial.

8 In my fifth consulship [29 B.C.] at the command of the People and the Senate. I increased the number of patricians. Three times I reviewed the membership of the Senate. In my sixth consulship [28 B.C.] with Marcus Agrippa as colleague, I held a census of the people. I held the lustrum after a lapse of forty-one years. Four million sixty-three thousand Roman citizens were counted in this lustrum. And again, with the consular imperium, I held a lustrum, this time alone, in the consulship of Gaius Censorinus and Gaius Asinius [8 B.C.]. Four million two hundred and thirty-three thousand Roman citizens were counted in this lustrum. I held a third lustrum, with my son Tiberius as colleague in the consular imperium. This was in the consulship of Sextus Pompeius and Sextus Appuleius [A.D. 14]. In this lustrum four million nine hundred and thirty-seven thousand Roman citizens were counted. By new laws which I introduced I restored many ancestral traditions which were already falling into decay in our time, and I myself have handed on to posterity many examples worthy of imitation.

9 The Senate decreed that the consuls and priests should offer up prayers on behalf of my health every fifth year. In accordance with these prayers, games were often held during my lifetime, sometimes by the four most distinguished priestly colleges, sometimes by the consuls. Moreover, all the citizens, both as private individuals and as

members of the municipalities, sacrificed continually with one accord upon all the altars on behalf of my health.[3]

*10* By a decree of the Senate my name was included in the Saliar Hymn, and it was enacted in law [23 B.C.] that I be permanently sacrosanct and possess the tribunician power as long as I lived. I refused to be made Pontifex Maximus in the place of my colleague while he was yet alive, although the People offered me that priesthood, once held by my father. Some years later, after this man [4] who had taken advantage of civil disturbance to seize that priesthood was dead, I accepted it. This was in the consulship of Publius Sulpicius and Gaius Valgius [12 B.C.]. From all over Italy a multitude flocked to Rome for my election, such as had never been reported before this time.

*11* In celebration of my return the Senate dedicated a shrine to Fortune the Homebringer [5] near the Capene Gate in front of the Temple of Honor and Virtue, and ordered the Pontiffs and Vestal Virgins to perform an annual sacrifice there on that day on which, in the consulship of Quintus Lucretius and Marcus Vinicius [19 B.C.], I returned to the City from Syria, and the Senate named that day the Augustalia from my cognomen.

*12* At the same time, by a decree of the Senate, a part of the praetors and the tribunes of the plebs, together with the consul Quintus Lucretius and the foremost men of the state, were sent to meet me in Campania. This was an honor which had up to that time been decreed for no one else. In the consulship of Tiberius Nero and Publius Quintilius [13 B.C.], when I had returned to Rome from Spain and Gaul, where affairs had been successfully settled in commemoration of my return, the Senate decreed that an altar of the Augustan Peace be dedicated on the Field of Mars. The Senate ordered the magistrates, the priests, and the Vestal Virgins to make annual sacrifices upon this altar.

*13* Though the portal of Janus Quirinus, which our ancestors ordered to be closed whenever peace had been secured with victory both on land and sea throughout the entire realm of the Roman

People, is recorded to have been closed but twice in all since the founding of the city and before my birth, the Senate on three occasions when I was *princeps* voted that it should be closed.

*14* As an honor to me the Senate and the Roman People designated my sons Gaius and Lucius Caesar, whom fortune was to snatch from me while they were still young men, as consuls-to-be in their fifteenth year, so that they might enter upon that magistracy five years later. The Senate also decreed that they be present at the deliberations of state beginning with the day on which they were conducted into the Forum. Moreover, the entire order of Roman equestrians hailed both as *principes* of the young men and presented them with silver shields and spears.

*15* To each member of the Roman Plebs, I distributed [44 B.C.] in accordance with my father's will, three hundred sesterces, and in my own name at the time of my fifth consulship [29 B.C.] I distributed four hundred sesterces from the spoils of war. Again in my tenth consulship [24 B.C.] I paid out to each individual as a gift from my own patrimony four hundred sesterces. In my eleventh consulship [23 B.C.] also I made twelve distributions of grain, after having purchased it at my own expense, and in the twelfth year of my tribunician power [12 B.C.] I gave four hundred sesterces to each person for the third time. My gifts never reached less than two hundred and fifty thousand individuals. In the eighteenth year of my tribunician power, when I was consul for the twelfth time [5 B.C.], I gave sixty denarii to each of three hundred and twenty thousand of the urban plebs. And in my fifth consulship I gave to each person settled in the colonies of my soldiers one hundred sesterces from the spoils of war. About one hundred and twenty thousand men in the colonies received this grant, which was in celebration of my triumph. In my thirteenth consulship [A.D. 2], I gave sixty denarii to each of the plebs who was then receiving grain at public expense; they numbered somewhat more than two hundred thousand persons.

*16* In my fourth consulship [30 B.C.] and afterwards in that of Marcus Crassus and Gnaeus Lentulus the Augur [14 B.C.] I allotted to the municipalities monies in payment for those lands of theirs I had given to the soldiers. The total sum for lands in Italy was about six hundred million sesterces, for lands in the provinces about two hundred and sixty million sesterces. Of all those who established colonies of soldiers in Italy or the provinces I was the first and the only one in the memory of my own time to make such recompense. Afterwards in the consulships of Tiberius Nero and Gnaeus Piso [7 B.C.], Gaius Antistius and Decimus Laelius [6 B.C.], Gaius Calvisius and Lucius Pasienus [4 B.C.], Lucius Lentulus and Marcus Messalla [3 B.C.], and Lucius Caninius and Quintus Fabricius [2 B.C.], I granted rewards in cash to the soldiers whom I brought back to their own municipalities after their discharge. For this purpose I expended about four hundred million sesterces.

17 Four times I came to the assistance of the public treasury with my own funds, to the extent of handing over one hundred and fifty million sesterces to those in charge of it. And in the consulship of Marcus Lepidus and Lucius Arruntius [A.D. 6] I transferred one hundred and seventy million sesterces from my own patrimony to the Military Treasury, which had been founded upon my advice in order that bonuses might be given to discharged soldiers who had served twenty years or more.

18 Beginning with the year in which Gnaeus and Publius Lentulus [18 B.C.] were consuls, whenever the provincial taxes were insufficient, I contributed grain or money, sometimes to one hundred thousand men, sometimes to more, from my own grain stores and my own patrimony.

19 I constructed the Senate house, the Chalcidium adjoining it, the temple of Apollo on the Palatine Hill along with its porticoes, the temple of the Deified Julius, the Lupercal, the portico at the Circus Flaminius which I permitted to be called the "Octavian" after the name of him who had built the former portico on the same site, a shrine at the Circus Maximus, the temples of Jupiter Feretrius and Jupiter the Thunderer on the Capitoline Hill, the temple of Quirinus, the temples of Minerva, of Juno the Queen and of Jupiter Liberty on the Aventine Hill, the temple of the Lares at the end of the Sacred Way, the temple of the Penates in the Velian district,

the temple of Youth, and the temple of the Great Mother on the Palatine Hill.

20 I repaired both the Capitoline Temple and the Theater of Pompey at enormous expense and without inscribing my name. I repaired the conduits of aqueducts which in many places were collapsing from age, and I doubled the flow of the aqueduct known as the "Marcian" by bringing a new source of water into its conduit. I completed the Julian Forum and the basilica which was between the Temple of Castor and the Temple of Saturn, works begun and nearly finished by my father, and when that same basilica was destroyed by fire I began its reconstruction in the name of my sons on an enlarged site. I have ordered that it be completed by my heirs, if it is not so done in my lifetime. In my sixth consulship [28 B.C.] in accordance with the authority of the Senate I rebuilt eighty-two temples in the City, omitting none which needed to be rebuilt at that time. In my seventh consulship [27 B.C.] I repaired the Flaminian Way from the City up to Ariminum [Rimini] and all the bridges save the Mulvian and Minucian.

21 On privately owned land I constructed from the spoils of war the temple of Mars the Avenger and the Forum of Augustus. Next to the temple of Apollo on land largely purchased from private individuals I built a theatre in the name of my son-in-law Marcellus. Gifts from the spoils of war to the value of about one hundred million sesterces I consecrated in the Capitoline Temple, in the temples of the Deified Julius, of Apollo, of Vesta, and of Mars the Avenger. To the municipalities and colonies of Italy I remitted, during my fifth consulship [29 B.C.], thirty-five thousand pounds of "crown gold" which they had contributed to my triumphs, and afterward, whenever I was hailed as Imperator I would not accept "crown gold," which the municipalities decreed as willingly and as liberally as before.[6]

22 Three times I gave gladiatorial shows in my own name and five times in the name of my sons or grandsons. About ten thousand men fought in these shows. Twice in my own name and a third time in the name of my grandson I offered to the People an exhibition of athletes who had been assembled from every region.

Four times I held games in my own name and twenty-three times I did so in the place of other magistrates. In the consulship of Gaius Furnius and Gaius Silanus [17 B.C.], with Marcus Agrippa as my colleague, I held the Centennial Games on behalf of and as master of the College of Fifteen. In my thirteenth consulship [2 B.C.], I inaugurated the Games of Mars, which thereafter in subsequent years, by a decree of the Senate, were held by the consuls. Twenty-six times I gave for the People, in my own name or in that of my sons and grandsons, fights of African beasts in the Circus, in the Forum or in the amphitheater. In these fights about 3500 animals were expended.

23 I provided for the People the spectacle of a naval battle in that place across the Tiber where the Grove of the Caesars is now. The earth there was excavated to a length of eighteen hundred and a width of twelve hundred feet. In this space thirty beaked ships, triremes or biremes, and many smaller vessels waged battle. In addition to the rowers about three thousand men fought in these fleets.

24 As victor I restored to the temples of all the cities of the province of Asia the ornaments which he [7] with whom I waged war had taken and possessed as his own. There were about eighty silver statues of me in the city, standing, on horseback, or in a chariot; these I removed, and from the monies so obtained I placed golden dedications in the temple of Apollo in my name and in the names of those who had honored me with the statues.

25 I swept the sea free of pirates. In that war [8] I handed over to their masters for punishment nearly thirty thousand slaves who had run away and were captured. All Italy voluntarily swore an oath in my name and begged me to be its commander in that war in which I won the final victory at Actium. The Gallic and Spanish provinces and Sicily and Sardinia also took the oath in my name. More than seven hundred senators fought at that time under my standard. Among them were eighty-three men who either had been consuls or were to hold that office before the day on which this was written, and about one hundred and seventy priests.

26 I extended the frontiers of all those provinces of the Roman People which bordered nations not obedient to our command. From the ocean and Gades [Cadiz] to the Elbe River I pacified the Gallic and Spanish provinces and Germany. I pacified the Alps from the region nearest the Adriatic to the Tuscan Sea, in the process waging war unjustly on no tribe. My fleet sailed upon the Ocean from the mouth of the Rhine eastward as far as the frontiers of the Cimbri, whither no Roman had hitherto gone either by land or sea. And the Cimbri, the Charydes, the Semnones, and other German peoples of the same region sought my friendship and that of the Roman People through their legates. At my bidding and under my auspices two armies were conducted almost simultaneously into Ethiopia and that part of Arabia which is called the Blessed. Large numbers of the enemy of both countries were slain and very many towns were captured. In Ethiopia the town of Nabata was reached, next to Meröe; in Arabia the army proceeded to the frontiers of the Sabaei to the town of Mariba.

27 I added Egypt [9] to the empire of the Roman People. Though I could have made Greater Armenia a province upon the murder of the king, Artaxes, I preferred to follow the example of our ancestors and turn its rule over to Tigranes, son of King Artavasdes and grandson of king Tigranes. This was done through the agency of Tiberius Nero, at that time my stepson. And later, after that nation had revolted and had been subdued by my son Gaius, I entrusted its rule to king Ariobarzanes, son of Artabazus, king of the Medes, and after his death to his son, Artavasdes. After he had been murdered, I sent to that kingdom Tigranes, a member of the Armenian royal family. I recovered all the provinces across the Adriatic Sea in the East, and also Cyrene, from the kings who had usurped the greater part of them; this after I had recovered Sicily and Sardinia, which had been seized during the servile war.

28 I founded colonies of soldiers in Africa, Sicily, Macedonia, the two Spains, Achaea, Asia, Syria, Narbonese Gaul, and Pisidia. Moreover, Italy has twenty-eight colonies, founded by my

authority, which, in my own lifetime, are flourishing and populous.

29 From Spain, Gaul, and the Dalmatian regions I have recovered from defeated enemies many military standards which were lost by other commanders. I forced the Parthians to return to me the spoils and standards they had taken from three Roman armies [10] and humbly to seek my friendship. I deposited the standards in the temple of Mars the Avenger.

30 After their defeat at the hands of Tiberius Nero, then my stepson and legate, I subjected the Pannonian tribes, which no Roman army had ever attacked before I was princeps, to the imperium of the Roman People, and I extended the frontiers of Illyricum to the banks of the Danube. An army of the Dacians which had crossed the Danube was defeated and almost destroyed under my auspices, and afterwards my army was conducted across the Danube, and it forced the tribes of the Dacians to submit to the commands of the Roman People.

31 Embassies from kings of India were often sent to me, such as had never been seen before by any other Roman commander. Through their legates the Bastarnae, the Scythians, the kings of the Sarmatians who lived on both sides of the Don River, and the kings of the Albani and the Iberi and of the Medes sought our friendship.

32 These fled to me as suppliants: Tiridates and then Phraates son of King Phraates, kings of the Parthians; Artavasdes, king of the Medes; Artaxares, king of the Adiabeni; Dumnobellaunus and Tincommius, kings of the Britons; King Maelo of the Sugambri; and [. . . . .]rus, king of the Suebian Marcomanni. Phraates, king of the Parthians, son of Orodes, sent all his sons and grandsons to Italy, not because he was defeated in war, but because he was seeking our

friendship by pledging his own children. During my principate many other nations have proved by experience the good faith of the Roman People, nations that had never previously had any exchange of embassies or friendship with the Roman People.

33 The nations of the Parthians and of the Medes asked me for kings through their legates, who were the leading men of these nations, and received them at my hands. The Parthians accepted Vonones, son of king Phraates and grandson of king Orodes; the Medes, Ariobarzanes, son of king Artavasdes and grandson of king Ariobarzanes.

34 In my sixth and seventh consulships [28 and 27 B.C.] after I had put an end to the civil wars and had acquired, by unanimous vote, supreme control, I transferred the Republic from my power over to the authority of the Senate and the Roman People. In return for this service of mine, I acquired the title of Augustus in accordance with a decree of the Senate, and the doorposts of my house were publicly wreathed with laurel and a civic crown was fastened above the entrance. A golden shield was placed in the Julian Senate house which, as the inscription upon it bears witness, the Senate and the Roman People gave to me because of my virtue, clemency, justice, and piety. After this time I exceeded all in prestige, but I had no more power than those who were my colleagues in each magistracy.

35 While I was holding my thirteenth consulship [2 B.C.], the Senate, the equestrian order and the whole Roman People gave me the title "Father of my country" and decreed that this be inscribed in the entrance way of my house, in the Julian Senate house and in the Augustan forum beneath the chariot which was set up for me in accordance with a decree of the Senate. I was in my seventy-sixth year when I wrote this.

## NOTES TO *THE DEEDS OF THE DEIFIED AUGUSTUS*

1. In his will, opened and read after his death [44 B.C.], Julius Caesar had made the future Augustus, born Gaius Octavius, heir to his name and fortune. By blood he was a grandnephew of Julius Caesar (see table on p. 370).

Upon his adoption into the Julian house he acquired the legal designation of Gaius Julius Caesar Octavianus. He never referred to himself as Octavianus, however; he had been born into a family, which, though respectable and wealthy, lacked nobility, and he preferred not to be reminded of his origin. In 27 B.C. he assumed the name of Augustus. When Augustus refers to "sons," he means his grandsons (by blood), Gaius, Lucius and Agrippa II, and his stepson Tiberius, all of whom he adopted. The "grandsons" are Germanicus (adopted by Tiberius) and Drusus II.

2. At Philippi in Macedonia, October and November, 42 B.C. His enemies accused the future Augustus of having run away in the first battle.

3. Until 24 B.C., when Augustus was dangerously ill, his health had always been precarious. Cold baths, prescribed by his physician Antonius Musa, pulled him out of this illness, and henceforth he was to enjoy a miraculous good health.

4. This was Aemilius Lepidus, a member, along with Antony and Octavian, of the Triumvirate of 43 B.C. He made a singularly ill-timed bid for power in 37 B.C. (see note 6), but the will to fight of his troops was successfully undermined by Octavian, and he had to beg publicly for mercy. He was stripped of his triumviral power and was banished, but Octavian allowed him to retain the title of Pontifex Maximus.

5. See Harvey, article *Ara Pacis*. Considerable fragments of the altar have been found, and it has been re-erected as far as possible, near its original site in Rome.

6. "Crown gold" was a contribution in gold demanded from his province by a victorious general, to pay the expenses of his triumph.

7. This was, of course, Antony; this is the only reference to him in the *Res Gestae*. For some time before the battle of Actium the propaganda machine of Augustus had labored to picture the civil war between Octavian and Antony as a war between Rome and the East, the latter personified by Cleopatra. For diverging views on Cleopatra see R. Syme, *The Roman Revolution*, and W. W. Tarn's chapters in *Cambridge Ancient History*, Vol. X.

8. The war with Sextus Pompey, son of Pompey the Great. Octavian pictures him as a mere pirate-adventurer. The war [38–37 B.C.] was no mere skirmish. At one point Octavian barely escaped with his life, and it was primarily due to the lack of ability of his opponent to rally around him the dissident elements that Octavian finally came out ahead. It was after the defeat of Sextus Pompey that Lepidus made his bid for power.

9. Egypt had a special status. It was governed by a Prefect of equestrian rank who was directly responsible to Augustus. Senators and persons of senatorial rank were forbidden to set foot in Egypt. The province was one of the principal sources of Augustus' wealth; it was actually administered as his private property.

10. That of Crassus in 54 B.C. It appears also that Antony incurred two defeats in his Parthian wars.

# SENECA'S *Medea*

## *Translated by Elizabeth C. Evans*

## INTRODUCTION

THE THEME of the quest of the Golden Fleece and the Argonautic expedition is popular in both Greek and Latin literature. Pindar's use of it in Greek lyric poetry, that of Apollonius Rhodius in late Greek epic, and of Valerius Flaccus in Roman epic of the first century of our era, are familiar examples in the more majestic forms. In ancient drama it is the Medea story that attracted the interest of Euripides, and of Ennius and Ovid as well as of Seneca. The brilliant success of Robinson Jeffers' version on Broadway, adapted from Euripides' play, with Judith Anderson playing the title role, bespeaks an intense modern interest in the portrayal of the desertion and suffering of the Colchian woman.

If the quest of the fleece is a recurrent theme in ancient literature, the story of the Argonautic expedition in search of it is likewise one of the oldest in Greek legend.[1] It was probably based on some real adventure that may have had its origin in or around Miletus in Asia Minor, which engaged in the Black Sea trade as far east as Colchis. The heroic leader of the expedition was Jason, son of Aeson, who sought to regain from his stepuncle, Pelias, the throne rightfully belonging to Aeson. To achieve this end he is sent by Pelias on the almost impossible task of finding the fleece. In the voyage he is accompanied by a band of glorious heroes like himself, fifty all told, who pass through a series of breathless adventures in unknown lands until they reach their goal in Colchis. There Jason is in turn confronted by the demand of the king Aeetes that he perform certain terrible feats before he is permitted to receive the fleece. Medea, daughter of the king, captivated by the marvelous appearance of the leader of the Argonauts, secretly aids him by her power of magic in carrying out the command of the king. Her name, "the scheming one," indicates her true nature, and her capacity for wizardry makes her a dread figure in Greek mythology. She is, furthermore, the granddaughter of Helios (the Sun), and the niece of the enchantress Circe, and thus belongs to a family given to the practice of strange magic. Her overwhelming love for Jason compels her to abandon her home and family and to flee with the Argonaut. The return to Iolcus in Thessaly is filled with horror, for Medea, determined to divert the Colchians from pursuit, kills her brother, whom she has taken with her as a hostage, and scatters his dismembered body on the sea. At Iolcus she continues to exercise her magic powers: she persuades the daughters of Pelias to boil their father in a vat which Medea pretends contains a drug to restore his youth, so that she and Jason are forced to flee to Corinth, where they live in happiness for some years, and where their two sons are born. Jason, however, in looking for the betterment of his own position, deserts Medea in favor of an advantageous marriage with the daughter of Creon, king of Corinth. It is at this point that Seneca's play, *Medea*, opens.

"Our Seneca"—Lucius Annaeus Seneca (4 B.C.–A.D. 65)—belongs to that group of Roman literary figures born in Spain. His father was a wealthy merchant at Corduba and a writer himself of considerable importance in the field of rhetoric. He was, furthermore, the father of Gallio, provincial governor of Achaea, whose connections with St. Paul we know from the Book of Acts, and of Mela, whose son in turn was the epic poet Lucan, author of the *Pharsalia* and staunch defender of republican ideals in Roman government. In this distinguished family, the Seneca who composed the *Medea* pursued the usual Roman course of education and was soon launched on a successful career of Roman public service as well as of writing. His early essays gave promise of the growth intellectually and spiritually of a great adherent of the Stoic view of life.[2] During the reign of Claudius he suffered, through complicity in intrigue at court, a period of exile on the island of Corsica that lasted some eight years. It is possible that during this time of banishment he wrote the tragedies which have formed such vital connecting material betwen the work of the Greek tragedians and that of the Elizabethan theater. After he was recalled to Rome in A.D. 49 to serve as tutor to the young Nero, the interests of that prince gradually turned to the theater, and Tacitus describes for us Nero's passion for acting. It has usually been thought that the nine tragedies of Seneca were composed directly as chamber drama for the delight of Nero's court. Whether or not they were actually produced in Seneca's lifetime (though we do know they were presented in the Renaissance in England) there is no evidence. They seem far more likely to have served as excellent reading pieces for a dilettante, cosmopolitan Roman court audience, and to have provided that instantaneous pleasure in rhetorical brilliance that characterizes their literary distinction and bespeaks the interest of the audience to which Seneca's tragedies appealed.

The ten tragedies that have come down to us in Seneca's name are rightly his save for the *Octavia*, a Roman historical play which may be the work of a later hand. They are derived and adapted from the originals of all three great Greek tragedians, but the most important source is Euripides, from whom Seneca drew material for five of his plays. All suffer badly by comparison with the originals. His *Medea*, in contrast to that of Euripides, concentrates markedly on the sorceries of Medea, and on her fury at the desertion of Jason. The preoccupation with magic and spells is the result of a deep interest on the part of Seneca in lore of this type and the introduction of it with the fullest rhetorical effect. It is important to compare the incantation scene in Seneca's play with the witches' scene in Shakespeare's *Macbeth*. In contrast to the 'throes of despair in the *Medea* of Euripides, the manifest anger constantly present in the person of Seneca's heroine expresses the maenad-like character of Medea perhaps derived from Ovid's concept of Medea in his lost play. The Roman play, which dramatically has a certain power, loses when compared with the Greek original in the skillful psychological analysis of a woman scorned. For Seneca paints a more sympathetic picture of Jason than of Medea, and the chorus of Corinthians is allied with Jason. It gains in horror, however, at the direct murder of the second son by Medea, in the very presence of Jason, whose cry of torture at the end of the play sums up the cruelty of the tragedy:

"Go through the lofty spaces of the aether, and wherever you are borne, bear witness that there are no gods."

If we compare the two plays we find the plots essentially the same. The roles of Aegeus and the Paedagogus, however, have been omitted in Seneca. In the treatment of the two main figures, the Roman playwright has emphasized the inhuman nature of the barbarian sorceress, Medea, against the insignificant and weaker character of Jason, who has been forced by circumstances into the marriage with Creusa. Jason has chosen this course of action in fear that resistance to the brutal Creon may bring death to his two sons, for whom he holds a very genuine and deep-seated affection. Throughout the Roman play the concern is less for dramatic action than for setting a tone of dread and terror. The lyrics of Seneca's *Medea* include a wedding song of joy (not in Euripides' play) at the marriage of Jason and the Corinthian

princess. Two other lyrics deal with the glorious achievements of the Argonauts and their leader, but are foreboding for the future. Another lyric, briefly descriptive of Medea's fury, dwells on the ominous and fiendish magic used in the Colchian's revenge on Jason, and points to the horrible finale of the spectacle.

An important contribution of Seneca to the history of drama is his crystallization not only of themes of Greek drama, but also of dramatic devices into a fixed form, which are inherited and imitated in a later period. The prologue, stemming primarily from Euripides, and often separated from the rest of the play, sets the tone for the play, be it of revenge, fury, or sheer horror. The play is written in verse, iambic trimeter, and is divided into three episodes, plus prologue and exode or its equivalent, separated by choral odes in lyric meters. Many of these odes contain current philosophical ideas, especially Stoic beliefs, such as the vagaries of fortune, the need of moderation in life. There is a definite limitation on the number of characters speaking at any one time. The stock characters—the ghost, the messenger, the villain or tyrant, the confidante or nurse—all appear. The long speech, either that of the messenger or the soliloquy, and the short, rapid dialogue of one-line exchange, often epigrammatic in type, are an important part of Seneca's art.

The *Medea* was first translated into English in 1566 by John Studley. A collection of individual translations of Seneca's tragedies called "Seneca: His Tenne Tragedies," edited by Thomas Newton in 1581, was reproduced in the Tudor translations in 1927, with an introduction by T. S. Eliot. Eliot begins with this statement: "No author exercised a wider or deeper influence on the Elizabethan mind or upon the Elizabethan form of tragedy than did Seneca." The example that may be cited as the most popular play written under Senecan influence is Kyd's *Spanish Tragedy* (ca. 1586). Of later adaptations of the *Medea* the most important are the *Médée* of Corneille (1634), the *Medea* of Glover (1763) and the *Medea* of Grillparzer (1822), the final play of his trilogy, *Das Goldene Vliess*.

For a striking use of one chorus of the *Medea* we may turn to the field of history. In Samuel Eliot Morison's *Admiral of the Ocean Sea*, a life of Christopher Columbus, we find at the head of the chapter on "The Enterprise of the Indies"[3] a quotation from the famous lines of Seneca's play: "An age will come after many years when the Ocean will loose the chains of things, and a huge land lie revealed; when Tiphys[4] will disclose new worlds and Thule no more be the ultimate." In the copy of these tragedies owned by Ferdinand Columbus was the note written in Latin on the margin beside these lines: "This prophecy was fulfilled by my father, the Admiral Christopher Columbus, in the year 1492."

GRATEFUL acknowledgment is made to Miss Winifred Smith, Professor Emeritus of Drama, Vassar College, for a careful reading of the translation in manuscript. The text translated is that of R. Peiper-G. Richter (Leipzig: Teubner, 1921), except for lines 98–99, 1012–1013, where the text of F. Leo (Berlin, 1878–79) is preferred, though the translator has rejected his bracketing of the latter pair of lines.

---

### CHARACTERS

MEDEA, Princess of Colchis, wife of JASON
NURSE
CREON, King of Corinth
JASON
TWO CHILDREN
MESSENGER
CHORUS OF CORINTHIANS

*The scene is the home of* JASON *in Corinth.*

MEDEA *enters.*

MEDEA. O gods of marriage and the wedding couch; O Lucina, and Pallas, who once taught skilled Tiphys how to guide his new built ship upon an unknown sea; and you, cruel master of the depths, and Titan, that divides the brightness of the day from dark—on you I call; on you, O awful three-faced goddess, Hecate, who gives a helping light to silent rites. And you upon whose strength it is Medea's right to call—chaos of eternal night, kingdoms scorned by gods of the upper world, hated spirits of the dead; you, lord of a dreary realm, and you, O queen of that darkness, who were brought from the world in better faith than that Medea found—to you I turn with my ill-omened prayer.

Be close at hand, I beg you, avenging hags of crime, with hair all foul with filthy crawling snakes, clutching the hellish torch in your bloody fists; be close, as once you appeared in a savage mood beside my wedding couch. Bring death to the new bride, death to the king, death to Creon's royal line! But to my Jason—for this shall be my curse on him—grant a yet more fearful woe: let him live on! But let him roam through distant towns, needy, beggared, and fearful, a homeless exile, begrudged an unknown hearth. Let him be driven to find a stranger's door, he who is now an honored guest. And, what is worse, let him still yearn for me, his wife, and—a far more evil prayer—let him long for his children, like himself indeed, but always like their mother too. Enough! Revenge in full is won, for I have borne these children. Why do I utter these useless complaints? Why do I not rush against my foes, to shake the wedding torches from their hands, and snatch the light from heaven?

Does not the sun, the very founder of my line, behold this wrong? Is he not still seen, seated in his lofty car, as he glides through spaces of the shining firmament? Will he not soon return upon his eastern path, and measure once again the day? Let me be carried high through the winds in my father's chariot; resign to me, O Sun, your reins, and let me drive the fiery yoked team with its blazing bridle. Then Corinth, whose twofold shore brings delays to ships,[1] may burn with flames, and join its double seas.

Yet this one task remains for me—to bear the bridal torch to the wedding chamber and slay the victims with proper sacrificial prayers at holy altars. But through this very sacrifice now, my soul, find a way for vengeance, if any life rest in you, if your earlier strength abides within your breast. Drive out all foolish fear and set the cold of Caucasus within your heart. Whatever crime Pontus or Phasis has ever seen, the Isthmus shall now behold. My mind contrives wild, unknown, evil; fiendish deeds, hated in heaven and hell. Wounds, slaughters, death creeping from limb to limb—I dwell too much upon such trivial acts. These I accomplished in my girlish years. Let sharper grief stir deadlier ills; greater crimes befit me, now that I have borne the pangs of childbirth. Prepare yourself with hate, and stir your fury to bring complete destruction. Let the tale of your divorcement match the horror of your wedding. How will you leave your husband? As you have followed him. Break off now; end your slow delays. A home that has been got by guilt, by guilt must be resigned.

*The* CHORUS OF CORINTHIANS *enters, singing the wedding hymn for* JASON *and* CREUSA.

To the home of kings, to the royal wedding, let the gods draw near who rule the sky and sea with gracious will, and let our people duly give their assent. First to the scepter-bearing Thunderer on high the mighty bull, all sleek, shall bear his proud and lofty neck. Our gift to you, Lucina, is a heifer, white as snow, untouched by the yoke. And that kindly goddess,[2] who restrains the bloody hands of fiendish Mars, who bestows upon the warring nations peace and calm, who holds within her rich horn a bounteous plenty, shall now receive a tender offering. And you [3] who will attend the lawful torches of the wedding rites, dispelling the darkness of the night with favoring signs, draw near with reeling drunken steps, with a rosy garland on your head. You, too, O star that goes before the twilight hour, too late you return to eager lovers. For you the mothers long, from you brides await the spreading of your bright beams.

Our maiden's grace far surpasses the beauty of Athenian brides or that of Spartan girls, who freely, like their brothers, roam the ridges of Taÿgetus from Lacedaemon's unwalled town, or any whom Theban springs may bathe, or sacred Alpheus' waters.

To Aeson's son that youth must yield in beauty, who is the child of the resistless thunderbolt, who yokes the savage tigers [4]; and he who makes the tripods tremble,[5] brother of a cruel goddess; and those bright twins, Castor and his brother Pollux, who rejoices in his skill of fist. And so, O heaven dwellers, I make my prayer. May thus our bride outshine all other wives, our groom excel by far all other men.

When she finds her place among her train, her fair face shines far brighter than the beauty of the rest, as when the starry light declines with coming of the sun, and the clustered Pleiades lie dim, when moon with her encircling horns binds full her disk with borrowed light. While the youthful groom gazes on such a face, a rosy flush steals up the new bride's cheek. So snowy color grows red when dipped in purple dye; so a shepherd waits the shining light, all dewy with fresh dawn.

And now, O Jason, rescued from the halls of savage Phasis, where with reluctant hand you once caressed the breast of a barbarian wife, now take your sweet Aeolian bride, and receive your girl with her parents' glad consent.

Sport, boys, in ribaldry and bantering song in turn; rare is the freedom given you against your masters. Fair free-born son of thyrsus-bearing Bacchus, now is the time to kindle the cleft stick of pine; hurl high the sacred fire with shaking fingers! Let boisterous verses shout their witty jests, and let the crowd bawl out its unruly taunts. But if any exiled woman weds a foreign man, let her slink off in silent darkness.

*The* NURSE *enters.*

MEDEA. We are undone! The wedding hymn has reached my ears. I did not think till now that treachery so base existed. Could Jason be so cruel, could he do this—deprive me of my father, of my land, and of my royal honor, and then forsake me thus on a foreign shore? Has his stony heart so scorned my help to him, after he has seen the fiery breath of bulls and the swelling surge of the sea subdued by my enchantments and my crimes? Does he conceive that all my powers of wickedness are spent? Bereft of wit, distraught with wavering mind, perplexed on every side I turn in turmoil. Where to find vengeance for this wrong? Would that the man had a brother! Yet he has a wife; let my sword be driven deep into her! Is this a vengeance great enough for all the pain I have endured? No, Medea; if there is any vast, notorious crime which lands of Greece have known, or any monstrous deed barbarian towns have seen, which your own hands have left untouched, now let it be devised. Let your past guilt bid you take hope and all your former feats return to your mind.

The glory of my land [6] was spirited away, and the little brother [7] of a hated girl, companion of my flight, was cut to pieces by the sword and strewn dismembered on the sea within his father's sight. The body of a doddering Pelias was boiled inside a brazen vat. How often have I spilled such lifeblood shamelessly! And yet there is no crime that I have tried in wrath; misguided love always persuaded me.

How else could Jason have behaved, forced by another's will and power? Rather than yield he should have bared his breast to Creon's sword. Oh, speak not so, my maddened grief! If it can be, may Jason live as mine, as once he was. If not, may he yet live, and, still remembering me, keep safe my gift of life. The fault is wholly Creon's, who by his proud scepter dissolved our marriage ties. He takes a mother from her sons and breaks a pledge of love held by the strictest bond. Let him be sought for vengeance; let him alone receive his just deserts. His palace I shall heap with ashes, and Malea, that causes delays for lingering ships, shall see his blackened roofs pierced deep with all-devouring flames.

NURSE. Peace, I beg you. Vent your secret griefs in hidden plaints. Whoever has endured a heavy wound with patience and serenity may yet repay it. Anger hid deep harms most the foe; confessed hates destroy the chance for hurt.

MEDEA. Light is the grief that can take thought and mask itself. Great wrongs do not lie hid; to fight against them is a bitter joy.

NURSE. Calm this fierce anger, child. For even silence barely saves you now.

MEDEA. The grave is feared by fortune, but the coward is outdone.

NURSE. If courage has a place, then it must be esteemed.

MEDEA. There cannot lack a place for courage.

NURSE. No hope points out a way in your cruel adversity.

MEDEA. He who cannot hope, cannot despair.

NURSE. The Colchians have cast you off; as for your husband, Jason, put no trust in him; and nothing is left for you from your vast wealth.

MEDEA. Medea remains—in me you see water and earth and sword and fire and gods and deadly thunderbolts.

NURSE. The king is always to be feared.

MEDEA. My father was a king.

NURSE. Have you no dread of arms?

MEDEA. No, though they spring from earth.

NURSE. You will die.

MEDEA. Would God I might.

NURSE. Escape!

MEDEA. I was ashamed of flight.

NURSE. Medea——

MEDEA. Medea shall become Medea indeed.

NURSE. You are a mother.

MEDEA. You see for whom I am a mother!

NURSE. Do you still hesitate to flee?

MEDEA. I must go, but first I'll take my vengeance.

NURSE. Avengers will follow.

MEDEA. Perhaps I shall devise delays.

NURSE. Be still, refrain from desperate threats, you senseless girl, and curb your pride. Adapt yourself to time's demands.

MEDEA. Fortune may carry off my wealth but not my spirit. Now do the hinges of the royal door creak sharply? Oh, it is that cursed Creon, puffed up with Grecian power.

*The* NURSE *departs.* CREON *enters.*

CREON. Has not Medea, the wicked daughter of Colchian Aeetes, yet departed from my realms? She goes about some mischief. We know too well her trickery of old, and her cunning hand. Whom will she spare, whom will she leave secure from harm? It was my purpose to destroy this evil plague by the sword, but Jason turned me from my good intent; my son-in-law pleaded with constant prayers to let her live. Her life is given her; but let her go, let her leave the country without fear and go in safety from our land. See, here she comes toward me with lowering look. Keep off, my men; she must not touch you; bid her be silent, and let her learn to yield her haughty self to royal power. Be off in hasty flight! Out of my sight, you hated, fiendish, monstrous being!

MEDEA. What crime of mine, my lord, what fault is punished thus by exile?

CREON. The guileless woman asks what cause compels this edict.

MEDEA. If you be judge, then hear; if you be king, command.

CREON. The power of a king you must obey, whether just or unjust.

MEDEA. Unjust power in a king cannot endure.

CREON. Go. Complain to the Colchians.

MEDEA. I shall go. Yet let me take him who brought me here to my home.

CREON. Your prayer has come too late; when the decree is fixed entreating words cannot avail.

MEDEA. The man who has pronounced a fixed decree and has heard one side only, though he may judge the case most fairly, has not been fair at all.

CREON. Was Pelias heard by you before the doom of death was sealed? But speak, we'll give you place for all your glorious plea.

MEDEA. My royal rank at home has taught me well to understand how hard a task it is to soothe the angry heart, once stirred to rage. He who has grasped the scepter with haughty hands conceives it his duty to display his greater might and to pursue the course he has begun. Though in sad, piteous plight I am now crushed, banished, a suppliant, hunted from place to place, deserted on every hand, yet once I shone as a princess in my home, descended from a high and noble line, through my father and through Phoebus, my own grandfather, the sun. Whatever Phasis floods with its slow stream, whatever coast the roaming Scythian waters leave behind, where seas grow sweet from marshy fen, all this my father rules with royal sway. The lands included by the banks of Thermodon are his, where fearful troops of warrior maids [8] with curved crescent shields hold all the earth in fear. Once happy there I shone, endowed with royal birth. Then suitors sought my hand and bed, the suitors whom I now must seek. Rash, fickle, wavering fortune cast me forth from my royal pomp to feel the crushing weight of exile. Put trust in scepters, when some chance may toss your mighty wealth to the winds? No, this is the gift of kings, a great and glorious boon, which time can never bear away: to succor those in misery, to shield a suppliant at a welcoming hearth.

This is the only gift I brought from out the Colchian realm: in safety I restored the very hope of Greece; I saved the flower of chivalry, the bulwark of the Achaean race, the offspring of the gods. My gift is Orpheus, who soothes the rocks with song, and draws the listening forests with his spell. The heavenly twins are given back to Greece, and Boreas' sons, and Lynceus, who, with sharper sight can behold the land on distant banks, and all the Minyae that sought the fleece. I shall not mention the leader of the host. For him no debt is owed me; I ask no recompense for him. The rest I brought for you, him only for myself.

Come, heap abuse upon me, I admit my guilt; but one charge alone can stand: the Argo has returned. Yet if it had pleased my sense of right (*she sees the scene before her*), and if my father's good had been foremost in my mind, the whole Pelasgian land would be undone, and all its leaders fallen! and your new son, my Jason, blasted by the fiery breath of bulls! But whatever fortune may crush my cause, I never shall repent of saving such a host of kings. Whatever guerdon or reward for crime like this I've earned, lies in your hands, O Creon. Condemn me as guilty, if you will, but give me back the man who was the cause of the crime. That I am guilty, Creon, I confess. You knew what I was, when first I clasped your knees and asked the help of your protecting hand. I beg within this land some quiet place, some poor retreat, for all my woe. If you must drive me from this place, a wanderer in exile, let some far corner in your realm be mine.

CREON. My choice of son-in-law would seem to prove that I am not a tyrant prone to bear the scepter in proud haughtiness or tread with vaunting foot upon the down-trodden. For he, a wanderer, in exile, too, in dread affliction and in fear of death, found refuge here, a man whom King Acastus, when he had gained Thessalia's crown, pursued for vengeance. And rightly so, for he laments that aged Pelias, trembling with weak old age and burdened down with years, was foully slain and his body cruelly cut to bits, when his devoted sisters, beguiled by treachery, ventured in piety an impious deed of crime. If you give up your claim, Jason can purge himself of wrong. No blood, no sword has touched his guiltless hands. He has stood aloof and free from your conspiracies. But you, contriver of vile crime, to you belongs a woman's shameless brain and a man's stout strength; in you there is no wish for good or a happy name. Leave now, and free this land from crime. Take forth your deadly herbs and rid this people of its fear. Away, into another tract of earth, to settle there and to provoke the gods!

MEDEA. You force me to go? At least restore to me my ship or else the partner of my voyage. Why do you bid me go alone? I came not so. If you have fear of wars, drive out the two of us. Why part a pair of guilty culprits? For Jason's sake, not mine, does Pelias lie dead. Add to this our treacherous flight and plunder, my father forsaken, and my brother's mangled body, and all the crimes the husband teaches his new wives—those ugly deeds are surely none of mine. So many times have I been guilty in my acts, but never for myself.

CREON. Your time to leave is gone. Why do you make delays?

MEDEA. One boon I ask before I leave. Let not a mother's guilt harass her guiltless sons.

CREON. Go. With a loving parent's arms I shall receive your boys within my home.

MEDEA. By this good-omened marriage, by the bright hopes and future of your crown, which Fortune, ever changing in her fickle state, torments, grant a brief delay to exile, and let me give a mother's kiss to my sons' lips, and say my last farewell.

CREON. You ask this time for treachery.

MEDEA. What fraud can be feared in such a space of time?

CREON. No jot of time is overshort for those intent on harm.

MEDEA. Cannot a jot of time be lent a mother's tears?

CREON. My deep-set fear rebels against your plea. Still, one day I shall give you to prepare.

MEDEA. That is too much. Lop off a part, for haste is what I plan.

CREON. Your life is forfeit if, before bright Phoebus scatters far his dawning beams, you do not take leave of this land forever. The holy rites of marriage and prayers to Hymen call me now.

CREON *and* MEDEA *leave.*

CHORUS. Too bold was he who first in fragile bark ploughed through the treacherous seas and, gazing back to view the land left far behind, dared trust his life to the winds' inconstant course. The slender vessel cleft the waves asunder upon an unknown way, too finely drawn, between hope of life and dread of death.

Our fathers saw the golden age, set far apart from fraud. All sought to till the land, each one content, grown old upon his father's soil; each one rich, though with but little, save what his native earth brought forth. Not yet had any man the need of planets, nor used the stars which paint the firmament; not yet did ships avoid the rainy Hyades, or the She-Goat's glimmering light. The sailor did not fear the Attic Wain which slow Boötes wheels about, nor yet was Boreas or Zephyr known by name. Tiphys [9] first dared to spread his sails upon the deep, and to decree new laws for the winds; now to stretch the hoisted sail full to the breeze, to hold the slanting south-wind with the close-hauled sheet, to set the yards midway upon the mast and now to bind them at the top, while eager sailors long for every puff of breeze, and trembling ruddy topsails flutter on the mast. Thessalian pine has brought together worlds lying distant; seas endure the oars' unwonted beat, and waters set apart become our dread. That impious ship has paid a grievous price, tossed through the deep, where clashing rocks, the barriers of the sea, gave forth a thundering roar, and soaring spray, caught by the force of wind, dashed every height and struck the clouds themselves. Dismayed at this, Tiphys with trembling hand loosed his grip upon the helm, Orpheus grew still with muted lyre, and Argo lost her voice.[10] When on Pelorus' shores the mongrel dogs of Scylla yelped from her monstrous paunch, what terror did that barking not convey? Or when the loathsome Sirens with a dulcet air soothed the sailors of the Ausonian sea, Orpheus upon his soft Pierian lyre beguiled the mermaid to follow him, she who had stayed the ships upon those waves. What was the prize of this vast voyage? A golden fleece, and an evil greater than the storms of sea, accurst Medea— these were the wages of that venture in the deep.

Now the sea has yielded, and endures all laws. No longer is a proud Argo sought, built by Pallas' hands, and bearing oars of kings. Each little boat scuds freely on the deep. All limits of the world are gone, and cities raise their walls in newly-opened lands. The circuit of the earth may now be passed, and nothing has been left as once it was. The Indian drinks the deep Araxes' icy stream, the Persian quaffs the Elbe and Rhine. But in later years an age shall come when the ocean will relax her bonds and a vast extent of earth will be revealed, when Tethys [11] will disclose some new-found world, and Thule will no longer mark the limit of the lands.

*The* NURSE *returns.*

NURSE (*To* MEDEA, *appearing from the house*). My child, where do you go so quickly outside the palace? Stand still, suppress your hate, and check your frenzied rage. (*To herself*) As some wild Maenad follower of Bacchus, who has felt the god, runs in frantic madness up and down the heights of snowy Pindus or the lofty ridges of Nysa, so does my lady rush with frenzied step distracted fury in her face, which manifests the bitter pangs of sorrow, her cheeks flush red; she summons from the depths her sobs of pain and floods her eyes with overflowing tears. In turn she blithely smiles, and then assumes a look of tortured rage. Where does the weight of such a pondering brain incline? Where does she aim her threats? I cannot tell. She fumes with burning wrath; then in turn she weeps. Where will this wave of woe spend its full fury? A surge of madness overwhelms her mind. She must intend no simple crime, no modest mischief; she will surpass herself in wickedness. Too well I know the familiar signs of her fiendish anger. She is possessed of some wild, monstrous, impious plan. I see her face of fury; may the gods disprove my fear!

MEDEA (*To herself*). If now you wish a limit to your hate, study the depth of your love, and hate as deeply. Shall I endure without revenge these royal wedding torches? Shall this day pass me by in slowly moving hours, so humbly asked for, so barely granted at my prayer? While earth shall hold the heavens in balance, while the shining world shall roll its endless round of seasons, while sands cannot be numbered, and the day shall follow on the sun, and night on the stars, while the pole shall turn the never-setting Bears, and rivers flow into the sea, my wrath shall never cease from vengeance, but increase. What brutish beasts, what Scylla or what wild Charybdis, sucking deep the neighboring seas, what Aetna crushing hard the gasping Titan,[12] shall spew forth flames and vapors with such smoldering threats as I? No whirling river, no raging stormy sea, no Pontus, tossed by northwest blasts, nor flash of fire, fanned by the boisterous wind, can check my violence and my rage. My anger shall destroy, shall sweep to ruin all before it. Has Jason feared cruel Creon and the wars of the Thessalian king? True love can never yield to fear. But be it that, forced hard, he has succumbed to Creon's might, and given way, he might have come to me, his wife, to make his last goodbye. This also he has feared to do, the bold in heart! Surely to Creon's son the chance was given to stay the length of heartless banishment. One day I have to take leave of my sons. Yet I do not complain that the time is short. Much shall be gained. This day shall see a deed so wrought that length of time shall never wipe away its memory. I will assail the gods and shake the very universe.

NURSE. Set your vexed heart at rest, my lady; compose your troubled spirits.

MEDEA. That only is peace—to watch all hurled in headlong ruin; with me let all things perish. It is a sweet delight to drag down others with me.

NURSE. If you persist in this folly beware what must be feared. For none may dare contrive against a king.

JASON *enters.*

JASON. Oh, luckless fates, unkind and bitter fortune, cruel when she smites or when she hopes to spare! How many times the cure that God has given us is harsher than the dangers we have faced! If I wish to make amends to my Medea for all I have received from her, I must face death, but if I will not die, then I must live in misery for want of loyalty. It is not fear that overcame my faithfulness to her, but anxious piety. And why? Lest my sons should share their father's death. Holy Justice, if you abide in heaven above, I call you to witness my deed. I take my children's part. Medea herself, though fierce of heart, and not inclined to bear restraint, would rank her sons above her marriage bed. It was my purpose and intent to reach her angry heart with pleading. But at the sight of me (MEDEA *approaches*) she now starts back, flies into rage, and bears her deadly hate upon her face. All her grief is in her eye.

MEDEA. I leave you now, my Jason, I go. To change my home is nothing new—the cause of banishment alone is new—for I used to wander far on your behalf. I shall depart, whom you force to leave your hearth. Where will you have me go? Shall I return to Phasis, and the Colchian lands, my father's kingdom, and the fields my brother's blood has stained? What lands do you appoint? What seas can you ordain for me to pass? The jaws of Pontus through which I brought a valiant band of kings, through the roaring rocks of the Symplegades, where I followed you, the wanton hero of the voyage? Is it little Iolcus, the home of Pelias, that I must visit, or Thessalian Tempe? Whatever passage I have gained for you is closed for me forever. Where would you send me? You order exile to an exile but assign me no dwelling place. Now let me go. The royal son-in-law has ordered this. I can refuse nothing. Heap up cruel punishments; I have earned them. Let royal anger torment your mistress with cruel penalties. Let Creon load her hands with chains, and shut her fast in some fearful hole in bleak, eternal night.

Yet I shall suffer less than I deserve. Consider, thankless man, the fiery breath of the Colchian bulls, amid the mighty terrors of an unconquered folk, the flaming herd Aeetes raised in weapon-bearing fields, the hateful spears of sudden-rising foe, when, by my wish, an earth-born army fell in mortal fight. Add, too, the long-sought spoils of Phrixus' ram; the sleepless dragon, made to close his watching eyes in unfamiliar sleep; my brother yielded up to death, a crime not finished in a single act of guilt; add, too, the daughters, lured by trickery to carve to bits the body of an aged man who shall not live again. By your hope for your children and a happy hearth, by monsters overcome, by hands which for your sake I did not spare, by dread of the dangers we have shared, by sky and waves that witness marriage ties, have mercy, in your happiness, on a suppliant. I went into another's realm, and so forsook my own. With all that wealth, which the Scythians have carried off from the distant sunburnt Indians, we Colchians deck our groves with gold, for the palace could not hold the treasure piled so high. Yet I carried with me none of this. An exile from my land, I bore my brother's body. This, I expended for your sake. My country I gave up for you; for you my father and my brother yielded place, for you my honor and my name. With such a dowry as this I wedded you. Restore her goods again to one whom you would send away.

JASON. When Creon in malicious mood wished you slain, he granted exile, persuaded by my tears.

MEDEA. I thought it then a punishment. But banishment now seems to me a gift.

JASON. Leave now while you have time. Away! Hard is a king's displeasure.

MEDEA. You urge this course on me? No, Creusa is the one for whose sake you ask! You would remove a hated wanton.

JASON. Medea upbraids me with a breach of love?

MEDEA. With murder, too, and treachery.

JASON. What charge of guilt can you impute to me?

MEDEA. Whatever I have done.

JASON. Then this one thing is left for me, that all your guilt should be mine.

MEDEA. My crimes are yours; who profits by a crime commits it. All blame your shameless wife; do you alone protect her, call her innocent, and let the woman be guiltless who was guilty for your sake.

JASON. That life is thankless which is kept with shame.

MEDEA. A life that brings one shame must not be kept.

JASON. Calm now your angry heart; for your dear children's sake, allay your hate.

MEDEA. I give them up, renounce, deny them. Will now Creusa's sons be brothers to mine?

JASON. A queen's sons shall be kin to an exile's children, a monarch's sons to offspring sore afflicted.

MEDEA. May such a cursed day never shine on my poor sons, which mixes baseborn boys of Sisyphus with Phoebus' line.

JASON. Why, wretched woman, would you drag yourself and me to woe? Away!

MEDEA. King Creon heard my plea.

JASON. What would you then require of Jason?

MEDEA. On my behalf? An ugly crime.

JASON. Two kings have set stark terror in my path.

MEDEA. There is a greater fear before you— Medea. Let us contend, the kings and I, and let Jason be the prize.

JASON. I must yield to cruel necessity. But recall that fate, too often tried, may still prove fatal to your cause.

MEDEA. All the vagaries of Fortune lie forever crushed beneath my feet.

JASON. Acastus is at hand.

MEDEA. Our nearer foe is Creon; but you can escape them both. Medea does not bid you arm yourself against your father, or stain with a kinsman's blood your unstained hands. Leave this land a guiltless man.

JASON. Who can resist them both if a double war breaks out? If Creon and Acastus enter battle with their armies joined?

MEDEA. To these add the Colchians and Aeëtes; join Scythians to Greeks. I shall destroy them all.

JASON. I dread the scepter's power.

MEDEA. Be sure that you do not long for it.

JASON. Have done with this long harangue. We stir suspicion.

MEDEA. O Jove on high, let thunder roar, stretch forth a threatening arm, and order avenging flames of lightning's fire to shake all the world from rifted clouds above. Now hurl your bolts with careless hand on him or me. Whichever of us two shall fall by your right hand shall perish guiltily, for never can your lightning err in aim.

JASON. I beg you now, come back to reason, and speak with calm. If you wish any gift from Creon's home to ease your banishment, bid me but get it.

MEDEA. My mind can scorn the wealth of kings, and often has. This gift alone I ask: let me have my sons as partners of my flight, and let me shed my streaming tears with them. New sons await you here.

JASON. My wish is to consent to your request, but love for my dear sons forbids. Not even Creon could force me with harsh torments to such pain. These children are the very strength of life, the comfort of my tortured heart, worn out with care. Far sooner would I endure the want of breath, or use of hands and feet, or light of day.

MEDEA (*To herself*). So, he loves his sons? That's good! I have him now. The place for hurt lies ·open. (*To Jason*) Ah, grant me this, since I must leave, to say a last goodbye, to take a last embrace of my sweet boys. This will be comfort to my woe, and I ask no more. If, in my tortured grief, I have said unkind words, let them not linger in your mind. Let memory of my milder self stay with you, and thoughts of wrath be blotted out.

JASON. I have forgotten all. I beg you, check your qualms of mind, and stay your hate. For quietness brings ease to troubled souls.    (*Exit.*)

MEDEA. He's gone. Shall it be thus? Do you sneak away, and slyly forget what I have done for you? Do you no longer bear us in your mind? It shall never be. (*To herself*) Enough, come, fetch your wits again and gather all your strength and arts. The fruit of sin is to count no mischief as a sin. There is no chance for fraud; we are distrusted. Attack where none can dream of danger. Now courage! To your task, and try what lies within Medea's power, and what does not. (*To the* NURSE) My faithful nurse, companion of my woe and changing fate, come, aid my unhappy plans. I have a robe, a gift from Heaven, the glory of our palace and the realm, a present from my grandfather, the Sun, a pledge to King Aeëtes of his birth; and a necklace, too, that shines with golden threads, and a golden snood as well, adorned with sparkling gems, with which I bound my hair. Let my children bear these treasures to the bride, but let me smear them first with deadly magic poison. Now, Hecate, I call on you. Prepare the fearful sacrifice; let the altars be set in place, while crackling fire resounds within the halls with awesome sound.

CHORUS. No force of flame or boisterous wind or a whirling spear can drive such terror to the heart as when a wife, deprived of her marriage rights, must seek revenge with all-consuming hate. Not when the cloudy southwind sends the gushing winter rains and the raging Danube rushes with its flood to sweep away the bridges in its path, and wanders wildly, far afield; not when the Rhone drives headlong to the sea, nor when in streams of melting snow and under rays of hotly-burning sun Haemus' summit slowly wastes away. Blind is the power of love, spurred on by wrath that does not care for guides and brooks no curbs, dreads not even death, and is prepared to meet the sword's sharp blade. Show mercy, gods; we beg your grace that he who has tamed the sea may live in safety. But Neptune, master of the deep, still seethes with anger that this second realm lies now within men's power. The boy [13] who dared to drive the everlasting chariot of the sun, forgetful of his father's course, himself was burned by fires he madly sought to spread throughout the sky. The beaten path has cost mankind no peril. Pass where it has been safe for earlier folk to tread, and never, impetuous man, break the bonds of heaven's inviolable laws. Whoever put hands on Argo's valiant oars and laid bare the thick, dark shade of Pelion's sacred grove, whoever entered first the Wandering Rocks and measured out so many toils, whoever set his anchor cable on barbarian soil in the hope of a quick return with the loot of foreign gold—he has paid forfeit by a dreadful end for this emprise, because he transgressed the laws the gods have made for men. The sea, provoked, demands cruel payment for such crime.

[Seneca then recalls in great detail the fate of many of the Argo's crew, since they dared to share that impious venture in the quest of the golden fleece; Tiphys, Orpheus, the sons of Boreas, Periclymenus, Ancaeus, Meleager, Hylas, Idmon, Mopsus, Peleus, Nauplius, Palamedes, Ajax, and in addition Pelias himself and Alcestis.]

O gods, the sea is now revenged enough; spare Jason, who was ordered to the task.

NURSE (*To herself*). My mind is terrified, aghast! Such vengeance is at hand, such vast disaster! Grief rises full again and finds its earlier power. I've seen her rage in frantic fits, attack the gods, and drag down heaven itself to suit her magic charms. But greater mischief is at hand, for which Medea now turns her hate. For as she made her way with quickened steps, and came into the inner shrine, she summoned forth her dreadful knowledge, and brought to light all she loathed before, and set in front a whole disordered mass of evils, her hidden rites, kept close, unseen. She touches the sacred altar now with her left hand, she calls upon all pestilential plagues, whatever Libya's burning sands now breed, or Taurus' height, stiff with the Arctic snow—on every fiendish monstrous thing. Lured by such magic spells the scaly tribes of vipers leave their desert cells, and crawl to her. Here the cruel serpent twists its cumbrous length along, darting its tri-forked tongue; now it espies with piercing gaze its victim. But hearing once her soft alluring song it sinks beguiled, and winds its swollen body into twining knots and links them into coils.

"Too small," says she, "the plagues, too slight the weapons which the depths of earth bring forth. From heaven itself I shall call down my poisons. Now is the time for me to try such spells as never common witch may use. Crawl down, grim dragon, like a river with rushing stream, between the great and little Bears, by which both Greek and Sidonian sailors guide their passage on the deep. Let now the Serpent-holder loosen his twofold grip, and lend his venom to my plan. O slimy Python, that has dared attack the heavenly twins, come now in answer to my chants. Let Hydra now return to life, whose awful heads the mighty Hercules cut cruelly with his sword, come, bring me aid. Help, too, O wakeful dragon, once lulled to slumber by my song; leave Colchian lands, and aid my magic here." When she has thus called forth a filthy rout of snakes, then does she pick each kind of poisonous herb, and heaps them closely piled. Whatever pathless Eryx yields on its jagged slopes, whatever plants the heights of Caucasus may grow in hoary frost, where now Prometheus' bloody gore spurts on the ground; whatever venoms rich Arabians use to smear their arrows, or fearless Mede or swiftly-moving Parthian, or those vile juices that the noble Suebian women, beneath their icy pole in dark Hyrcanian groves, wring from the poisonous roots; or what the smiling earth creates in the nest-building spring, or when the churlish winter freezes hard the beauty of the woods with ice-congealing cold, all pestilential flowers that grow or deadly sap that lurks in twisted roots be-

neath the earth for breeding bane—all these she gathers for her use. Haemonian Athos brought these herbs to her, and Pindus; these shoots were fetched from high Pangaeus, when bloody sickle lopped them to the ground. The Tigris nourished these beside its whirling flood, the Danube those; these the rich Hydaspes grew, gem-bearing river, which flows with lukewarm stream in torrid tracts, and those the river Baetis gave to the land of Spain, beating its way against the western sea with languid course. These herbs were cut by sword at dawn, while Phoebus brings the day, and those in depths of silent night were snapped, and others still were pinched from off their stems by fingernail to a chant of charmed words.

She culls these deadly herbs, and squeezes serpents' clotted blood, she mixes in the brew more filthy birds, the heart of moping owl, the dirty guts of raucous screeching owl, cut out alive. All these the framer of such arts now sets in vast array. In some the greedy force of fire is found, in some the icy cold of sluggish frost. She mutters to these poisons magic words, as fearful as the vile concoctions. But look, how she appears with maddened dance and sound, and chants her incantation. Nature trembles at her frantic shrieks.

MEDEA (*Chanting*). I now entreat the silent throng, gods of the lower world, and gloomy chaos, and the shadowy home of dismal Dis, and wretched tortured souls, bound to the wailing shores of Hell by the abyss of Death—let loose your woes and hurry on with quickened pace to the new wedding couch. Let the whirling, twisting wheel now pause, and let the racked Ixion touch the ground; let Tantalus safely gulp the waters of Pirene's spring, and you Danaids, whom fruitless labor mocks with sievelike urns—come, aid me now; this day has need of you. Now let the brutal Creon bear the weight of heavier pain, and may the sliding stone roll Sisyphus again upon the rocks. And so, my lady, torch of the night, all garbed in murky guise, come in your threefold shape, bring terror to this house.

In the usage of my country I have unbound my hair, and with naked foot have walked the sacred groves, and called from out the dry, unwatered clouds the showers of hard rain. Through me the seas are driven back to their lowest depths, and ocean's swell drives mighty waves to shore, its tides outdone. The laws of heaven are now reversed; and sun and glimmering stars at once together show their beams, while in the sea the never-setting Bears have dipped their light. I have changed the seasons by my charms: the summer blossoms like the spring, and Ceres sees the grain grow ripe in winter's cold. Phasis returns its raging stream to its source, while Danube's channel, cleft in many mouths, has checked its rushing course, and slowly flows within its banks. The waves have thundered, the tameless sea swells up, though the winds are silent. The hearts of aged groves, at my command, will spread no shade when day returns. Phoebus has stood still at noon, and at my charms the watery Hyades glide down on their way. O moon, the hour is come to honor you with sacred rites!

These garlands were twined with bloody hands for you, with a serpent's coil, bound tightly round with nine enfolding circles; for you the serpent flesh of cruel Typhoeus, who shook the home of Jove. Here is the poisoned blood which dying Nessus, faithless bearer, gave. The pyre of Oeta has bestowed these ashes, dyed with the poisoned blood of Hercules. The fatal brand lies here, the gift of Althaea, a pious sister but an impious mother. The Harpy left these feathers far behind in trackless hollows in flight from Zetes' hot pursuit. And here the plumes of that Stymphalian bird, galled by the shaft of Lerna's dart.[14] But now, as in the past, my altars echo with strange sounds, and tripods shake at the favouring presence of the goddess I entreat.

I see the swift and gliding car of Trivia,[15] not that wherein she rides in darkened sky with shining face, but that in which she drives when with sad and lurid light she skirts the heavens with close-drawn rein beneath the spell of wild Thessalian charms. Thus pour your cloudy, pallid light amid the darkening sky, and smite the heart of people with new fear. Let the brazen pans[16] of Corinth ring to aid you, goddess, with such magic spells as draw you down from heaven to earth. To you, in solemn worship, we begin these rites on bloody turf; for you a kindled torch, sought from the funeral pyre, has raised the fires of night; for you, with neck bent down and tossing head, I offer muttered, magic words; for you a band around my head holds fast my unkempt hair; and this somber branch from the Stygian waves is offered you, while, like a Maenad with my naked breast, I strike my arms with sacred knife to call forth the bubbling blood. (*She cuts her arm to let the blood flow.*) Now let it stream upon the altar; now learn to draw the sword, and to brook, with hardened heart, the sight of precious lifeblood. (*She lets the blood flow on the altar.*) Self-struck I make this sacrifice.

But if you wearily lament that too often you hear my sad complaints, I ask your pardon, Perses' child; the only cause of all my prayers and of my begging for your help is Jason.

Now tinge Creusa's robes with magic drugs (*she pours poison on the robe*) to work her woe when she shall wear the gift, and let the fire of poison deep consume the marrow of her bones. A secret fire, closed fast in yellow gold, lies hid. (*She takes a box.*) Prometheus gave me this, and taught me well to store its strength. He now has paid the price of his daring theft of fire upon the crags of Caucasus, where vultures feast unendingly upon his maw. For my sake, too, has Vulcan showed his fires in sulphur fumes; this flash of living fire my cousin Phaethon gave to me. I have received the gift of flame from the Chimaera's goat; I have the scorching fumes from Colchis' bull, mixed with the fell Medusa's bitter gall; and I have bidden them keep their potent lurking evil. Breathe on these poisons, Hecate, and in return for all these gifts preserve the hidden seeds of flame. Let them deceive her sight and bear her touch. Let burning fire probe deep her heart and veins, infuse her arms, and darken her bones with smoke. Let the bride's blazing hair outshine the brightness of her wedding torches!

My prayers are heard. Three times the fearful Hecate has barked, and has displayed her sacred flash of fire with its hideous glare.

The force of my magic spells is now complete. (*To the* NURSE) Call here my sons, let them bear these precious gifts to the new bride.

*The* CHILDREN *enter.*

Go now, my boys, from your unhappy parent, and with an earnest plea win grace from your new queen and mother by these gifts. Go, and come swiftly home again, for I must take a last embrace.

*The* CHILDREN *leave.*

CHORUS. Where does this bloodstained Maenad rush in maddened love? What crime does her unbridled rage conceive? Her wrath-frozen face is stiff and set. She stalks with haughty tossing head, and threatens Creon. Who would think her a banished exile? Her cheeks flush red, then the cold of death puts the color of her face to flight. Her changing looks can hold no pallor long. She turns her step this way and that, like a tigress tearing through the jungles of the Ganges, looking for the tracks of her helpless cub. Medea knows not how to stay her wrath. If love and passion join their strength, what will the outcome be? When will this barbarous Colchian woman take her way out of Pelasgian fields and ease this land and its kings of terror and of fright? Let Phoebus drive his chariot without delaying rein, and let fair night conceal the day, and Hesperus, harbinger of eventide, drench deep the dreaded light.

*A* Messenger *enters.*

Messenger. All things have perished utterly, our kingdom is brought to nothing. Father and daughter lie dead, with ashes blended.

Chorus. By what snare are they dead?

Messenger. By treacherous gifts which often prove a snare to kings.

Chorus. In gifts like those what guile can be?

Messenger. I marvel at this hideous thing, and cannot yet divine how such woe came to pass, now that it is here. What limit can there be to murder? Wildly through every corner of the royal house the flames have raged like fire required to sweep all in its path. The palace has fallen in ruin to the ground, and we fear the city may be doomed.

Chorus. Let water quench the greedy flames.

Messenger. No, in this peril something strange occurs. The water feeds the fire; the more we try to put it out, the more it blazes forth. It glories in the very things we get for our defense.

Medea *enters.*

Nurse. Medea, in haste depart from Pelops' house. Away to any land you may desire.

Medea. Shall I depart? No, even had I already fled, for this I should return. (*To herself*) I see strange weddings here. Why hesitate, my soul? Pursue the way of death, for good success may come. How small is the revenge in which

you now rejoice! You still must love this man within your maddened heart, if you are satisfied with Jason's loss of a newly wedded wife. Does this suffice for grief? Look not for common vengeance, but devise unpractised art. Have no respect for justice; let all sense of honor go. Light is the rod of vengeance which pure hands bear. Yield now to anger, and find your faltering self again. Fetch up your former strength laid deep within. Let what you have done till now be called your duty. Do this, and let them know how trivial were the feats I have achieved before; my grief was only practice through such acts. What crimes could my unpractised hands essay? What, this madness of a girl? Now I am become Medea. Through evil deeds my skill has grown. Joy, it is a joy, to have slashed my brother's head and torn to bits his body; to have robbed my father of his sacred fleece; to have brought old Pelias to his death, and lured his pious daughters to that killing. O grief, devise a way! To every crime you bring a skillful hand.

Where, anger, do you bear your power, and with what weapons will you strike the treacherous foe? I little know what my own fiendish mind has now contrived and dares not confess to itself. In my rash and foolish haste I speed too much. Oh, that my enemy had children by his wanton wife! All the sons you have by him, Medea, consider Creusa's boys. This kind of vengeance pleases me, and rightly so. My final deed of crime can now be planned; I know it well. Ah, children, once my own, now bear your father's crime.

My heart shudders at the deed; my body stiffens numb with cold, my breast quakes with ghastly fear. Now wrath is banished from the wife, and mother's mercy takes the place of rage and malice toward my Jason. Oh, shall I shed my children's guiltless blood? Oh, madness, think again! Let not this heinous, wicked deed be done! For what appalling crime will these unhappy children pay? Their father, Jason, is their sin; their greater sin is Medea, their mother.

No, let them perish, they are not mine! Let them die? They are my own; they are without blame or fault. Alas, they are mere innocents—but such my brother was. Why do you falter so, my soul? Why do these tears course down my face? Why, wrath and love, with wavering thoughts drive me thus to and fro? A double tide of feeling bears me on. As when the boisterous winds raise maddened war, and on all sides discordant waves drive on the seas, and swelling floods of water wrangle fiercely—so is my heart within. Wrath chases out devotion, and my love displaces hate. Ah, yield to love, my aching heart!

Come here, dear children, here, the only comfort of this home, and put your close-embracing arms about me. May your father keep you safe from harm, so your own mother may enjoy you, too. Exile and flight come close upon me now, and they by force shall be pulled from my arms, in tears and sobbing at my kisses.

No; let them die before their father's eye, since they are lost to me. Once more consuming grief begins to rise, and deadly hate possesses me. The fury of revenge, as in the past, starts up again, claims my unwilling hand. O wrath, where you may lead, I must follow there. Oh, that the brood of Niobe had issued from my womb and I had been the mother of twice seven sons! My barren womb has yielded little for revenge, but for a father's and a brother's shades enough—two sons. (*She sees a vision of the Furies, and her brother's ghost.*) Where does that horde of fiends rush now? Whom do they hunt, for whom prepare their brandished whips of fire? For whom does that cruel Stygian host of hell intend their bloody, blazing torches? Whom will you crush, Megaera, with your stake? Whose is the shade that rushes up from Dis, with scattered limbs? My murdered brother's ghost, who wants revenge; due vengeance I shall give, and it shall be complete. Dig, rend, and squeeze the eyes from out my head. My breast lies open to the Furies' strokes. O brother, bid these hags of hell depart from me, and go their way down to the silent ghosts below. Let me be left here by myself, alone, to use my hand, my brother (*she slays one son*), to make this sacrifice upon the altar to your shade. What means this sudden sound that strikes my ear? A band of armed men prepare my death and my destruction. Up to the palace roof I go, to end the slaughter that I have begun. (*To the other son*) Come with me, child. (*To the dead child*) Your body I shall bear up with me. Come now, do this, my soul! No secret murder earns renown; proclaim in people's eyes your cruel and bloody skill.

JASON *enters, accompanied by Corinthian citizens.*

JASON. If any faithful man grieves loyally for Creon's daughter, come to this spot to take the wretched perpetrator of this ghastly deed. Here, here raise arms against this fiend, and burn the palace to the ground.

MEDEA (*On the house top*). I have regained my scepter's power, my father, and my slain brother. The golden fleece returns to Colchian hands. My kingdom is restored to me, and my virginity. O gods, kindly and favoring at last, O joyous wedding day, the deed is done! Yet my vengeance is not finished. Go on, while your hand can do the task. My soul, why do you delay? You have the power. Yet now my anger cools. The pain of sorrow pricks my heart and shames me for my act. What have I done? I do repent, but though I am ashamed, yet I have done it. A wild delight possesses me and drives me on. (*She sees* JASON *below.*) Ah, this is what I lacked, a witness to my crime. For nothing he has not beheld is done.

JASON (*Seeing her*). Look, there she is, above us; she leans upon the very edge of the steep palace roof; fling here a torch to make her fall to death, enkindled by her own flames!

MEDEA. Go, Jason, go; prepare the funeral pyre for your sons, and build them a tomb. Your bride and Creon are now entombed by me; their rites are finished. One child has met his doom, and soon the other boy shall lose his life, within your sight.

JASON. By all the sacred powers of heaven, by the exile we have shared, by the marriage bed that never was betrayed by me, now spare my helpless son, and yours! If there is any crime, lay it to me. Make me the sacrifice of death, and strike this guilty head.

MEDEA. Here, where you will not have it so, you must endure the pain. Here will I drive the sword. Go then, proud man, and find a young girl's bed! Cast off the unwanted mother of your sons!

JASON. One can suffice for vengeance.

MEDEA. If a hand of mine could find sure vengeance with the blood of one, I would have sought no death. If I slay only two the number is too small, for all my pain. If any pledge of love for you lies in me still, I shall search out my womb with the sword, and draw it forth.

JASON. Now finish off your ghastly deed, I pray for nothing. But grant at least, I beg, no cruel delay to my full punishment.

MEDEA. No; linger, anguish! hurry not, slow death. The day is mine. We use the time given by Creon.

JASON. O, hateful fiend, destroy me too.

MEDEA. You ask for pity. (*She slays the second son.*) Oh, it is well! All now is done! This is the only sacrifice that I can offer you, my grief. Unthankful Jason, raise your swollen eyes to me. Do you behold your wife? This is my way to exile. The path to heaven lies open now to me. Two flying dragons bend their scaly necks to bear the yoke. Receive your sons, my Jason. (*She hurls the bodies to the ground.*) I shall be carried high through upper air in my swift winged car (*she is borne away*).

JASON. Go through the lofty spaces of the aether, and wherever you are borne, bear witness that there are no gods.

## NOTES TO SENECA'S *MEDEA*

### Introduction

1. A striking modern treatment of this theme is to be found in Robert Graves' novel, *Hercules, My Shipmate* (New York, 1945).

2. But for a recent analysis of Seneca's neurotic cast of mind observable in his literary work, cf. E. P. Barker, *s.v.* "Seneca" in *The Oxford Classical Dictionary* (Oxford, 1949).

3. S. E. Morison, *Admiral of the Ocean Sea* (Boston, 1946). Chap. VI.

4. More correctly Tethys.

### Medea

1. The Isthmus of Corinth forced ships to sail around the Peloponnesus. In the Roman Empire a notable attempt was made by Nero to cut a canal across the Isthmus, but that project was not successfully carried out until modern times.

2. Venus. Compare the beginning of Book I of Lucretius, above, p. 63.

3. Hymen, god of marriage.

4. Dionysus.

5. Apollo.

6. The golden fleece.

7. Absyrtus, Medea's brother.

8. The Amazons.

9. Pilot of the Argo.

10. The figurehead of the Argo, made of wood from Dodona, had the power of speech.

11. Goddess of the sea; name used for the sea itself.

12. Typhoeus, who was buried beneath Aetna because of his defiance of Jove.

13. Phaethon.

14. The Stymphalian bird was shot by an arrow dipped in the poisoned blood of the Lernaean hydra by Hercules.

15. Diana of the Crossways. She is worshipped in three aspects, on earth as Diana, in heaven as the moon, and in the lower world as Hecate.

16. The beating on bronze to produce a loud noise was thought to remove the spell of magic from the moon in eclipse.

# SELECTIONS FROM THE *Satyricon* OF PETRONIUS

*Translated by Alston H. Chase*

## INTRODUCTION

THERE IS now fairly general agreement that the author of the picaresque novel called the *Satyricon* was the same Petronius whom Tacitus so vividly describes (*Annals*, XVI, 18–19; cf. Professor Leon's translation, below) as Nero's *elegantiae arbiter* or final authority on matters of taste, a man of polished luxury, indolent in his ordinary life, but capable of energy in public affairs, who made of his enforced suicide a matter of jest and mockery of the Emperor.

The novel written by this extraordinary man is unfortunately extant only in very limited fragments of its once vast bulk. It is the first picaresque novel and retails the escapades of three quite unsavory characters among the cities and towns of southern Italy at the time of Nero. The trio consists of Encolpius, the narrator, his friend Ascyltus, a young freedman, and a handsome serving lad, Giton, for whose favors they are rivals. Our fragments are so broken that it is hard to see the main thread of the plot, which was probably not a very weighty one in any case. The longest extant episode is the account of a banquet given by a rich parvenu, Trimalchio, in which the author satirizes the tasteless display of wealth which is characteristic of that class in all ages. From this scene several excerpts will be found in the following selections. The story of the werewolf is related by one of the guests at the banquet. Similarly, the tale of the widow of Ephesus, recently treated in amusing

verse by Christopher Fry in *A Phoenix Too Frequent*, is inserted in a later episode of adventures on board a ship. The story of the legacy hunters of Croton comes from the last extant portion of the book, in which the adventurers go to seek their fortune at that city.

The form of the book is that of the Menippean satire of Varro—largely prose with verses interpolated now and then. Despite its frequent coarseness, the book has an engaging liveliness and naturalness, quite refreshingly in contrast with the self-conscious dignity of most classical Latin. It is an invaluable picture of the manner of life and the manner of speech of the lower classes of imperial Italy. Its language has been a happy hunting ground for philologians in search of the words from which many words in the Romance languages descend.

Some think they see a strain of social criticism in the novel, an underlining of the truism that great wealth does not bring happiness. The American novelist F. Scott Fitzgerald evidently had this interpretation in mind when he considered naming "The Great Gatsby" after Trimalchio. But it is probably idle to look for any very serious purpose in the author. He wished to amuse by a clever and realistic satire upon the foibles of low life—always a favorite study with a corrupt aristocracy.

THE TEXT translated is that of M. Heseltine in the Loeb Classical Library (London, 1913).

---

## THE WEREWOLF

*61* "While I was still a slave, we lived in a narrow street—the house is now Gavilla's. There, as luck would have it, I fell in love with the wife of Terentius the innkeeper—you know Melissa of Tarentum, a pretty little number. But hell, it wasn't for her body or her bedroom manners that I cared for her, but rather because she had a beautiful nature. Whatever I asked her, she never refused me. If she made two bucks, I got one. Whatever I got I tossed in her lap, and I was never cheated.

"Her husband died on the estate. So I racked my brain how to get to her. You know, a friend in need is a friend indeed. *62* The master happened to have gone to Capua to take care of some trifle or other. I seized the opportunity and persuaded a guest of ours to come with me as far as the fifth milestone. He was a soldier, as brave as hell. We started off about cockcrow; the moon was shining as bright as noon. We reached the place where the way ran through some tombs. My man began to look around among the epitaphs and I sat down all set for a song and began to count the inscriptions. Then, when I glanced at my companion, he stripped and put all his clothes beside the road. My heart was in my mouth and I stood like a dead man. Then he pissed around his clothes and suddenly turned into a wolf.

"Don't think I'm joking; I wouldn't lie for any man's fortune. But, as I started to say, when he had turned into a wolf, he began to howl and ran off into the woods. At first I didn't know where I was at; then I went to pick up his clothes, but they had turned to stone. No one could be nearer dead from fright than I was. However, I drew my sword and kept killing shadows all the way until I got to my girlfriend's place. I was like a corpse when I went in and just about passed out, the sweat running down my crotch, my eyes glazed. I could hardly be brought round.

"My Melissa started wondering that I was out so late. 'If,' she said, 'you had come sooner, you could at least have helped us, for a wolf came on the place and attacked all our flocks and bled them like a butcher. But he didn't have the laugh on us even if he got away, for our slave stuck a spear through his neck.'

"When I heard this, I couldn't keep my eyes shut any longer, but as soon as it was light I ran home to our Gaius' place like a cheated tavern-keeper, and when I got to the place where his clothes had turned to stone I could find nothing but blood. And it's a fact that when I got home my soldier was lying in bed like an ox and the doctor was dressing his neck. I realized that he was a werewolf and I couldn't eat a crumb with him afterwards, not if you killed me."

## THE WIDOW OF EPHESUS

*111* There was a matron of Ephesus so famous for her virtue that she drew women even from neighboring countries to look at her. When she buried her husband, she was not content, after the usual way at funerals, to follow his bier with dishevelled hair or to beat her naked breast in the sight of the crowd; she followed the dead even into the tomb, and when the body, in accordance with Greek custom, was placed in an underground vault, she began to guard it and to weep over it night and day. Neither her parents nor her relatives could dissuade her from thus tormenting herself and from courting death by starvation. Finally, the very magistrates were forced to go away rebuffed. Lamented by all, this extraordinary woman was already on her fifth day without food. A faithful maid sat at the bereaved woman's side, shed tears of sympathy for her mourning, and refilled the lamp set in the tomb as often as it failed. The city talked of nothing but the fact, admitted by people of every class, that this was the one true and shining example of chastity and love.

At that same time, the ruler of the province ordered the crucifixion of two bandits close by the small structure in which the matron was mourning the newly dead. On the next night, therefore, when the soldier who was watching the crosses lest anyone remove a body for burial noticed a light shining quite plainly among the tombs and heard the groans of the mourner, out of natural human weakness he desired to know who it was and what he was doing. Accordingly, he went down into the vault and, upon seeing a very beautiful woman, stopped at first as if frightened by some horror or some hellish ghosts. Then, as he caught sight of the body of the dead man and noticed the woman's tears and her nail-scarred face, taking it for what it was, that the woman could not bear her longing for her dead, he brought his little supper into the tomb and began to urge the weeping woman not to persist in her unavailing sorrow or break her heart with profitless lamenting. All, he said, come to the same end and go to the same home. And he added the other commonplaces by which wounded hearts are healed. But she ignored his condolences and beat and tore her breast more violently than ever and snatched out her hair and laid it upon the body of the dead. The soldier, however, did not withdraw, but with more of the same sort of encouragements tried to give the little woman food, until the maid, weakened, no doubt, by the smell of the wine, first herself gave in and reached out her hand to accept his kindly offer, and then, refreshed by food and drink, began to break down her mistress's obstinacy and said, 'What good will it do you if you faint from hunger? If you bury yourself alive? If you give up your life before it is doomed or the Fates demand it?

" 'Do you think ashes or the buried dead can sense this?' [1]

"Do you want to come to life again? Do you want to shake off this womanish weakness and enjoy the good things of life as long as you may? The very body of the dead ought to warn you to stay alive."

No one turns a deaf ear when he is urged to take a meal or to live. And so the woman, dry after a fast of several days, allowed her resolution to be overcome and filled herself with food no less greedily than had her maid, who had been the first to give in.

*112* Now you know what temptation usually assails people who have filled their bellies. The same soft arguments by which the soldier had won her to live served him in an assault upon her virtue. The young fellow seemed to the chaste lady to fall short neither in looks nor in eloquence, and the maid urged her to favor him and added,

" 'Will you fight love, even one that pleases?
  Or do you not remember in whose lands you
      are?" [2]

Why labor the point? The woman did not refuse even this part of her body and the victorious soldier won both arguments. They lay together not only that night, which was their wedding night, but the next day too, and the third, with the doors of the tomb closed, of course, so that whatever acquaintance or stranger came to the tomb should think that this supremely loyal wife had breathed her last above her husband's body.

Now the soldier, delighted with the woman's beauty and the secret affair, would buy every good thing he could afford and bring it to the tomb at nightfall. So the parents of one of the crucified bandits, when they saw the guard relaxed, carried off his hanging body by night and gave it proper burial. The soldier, outmaneuvered while derelict in duty, upon seeing the next morning one cross without its corpse,

feared punishment and told the woman what had happened. He would not, he said, await the court-martial's sentence but would punish his neglect with his own sword. Let her, therefore, make a place for one about to die and make the same vault fatal to her husband and her lover. But she, no less tender-hearted than chaste, said, "God forbid that I should at the same time look on the two corpses of the two men dearest to me. I had rather make some use of the dead than kill the living."

After this speech, she ordered her husband's body taken out of the coffin and nailed upon the empty cross. The soldier profited by the shrewdness of this most far-seeing woman and the next day people wondered how the dead man had gotten on the cross.

## THE LEGACY-HUNTERS OF CROTON

*116* We set out on our appointed journey and in a short time, not without sweat, climbed a mountain from which we saw, at no great distance, a town set on a lofty hill. Having lost our way, we did not know what town it was until we learned from some farm manager that it was Croton, a very ancient city, once the first of Italy. When we went on to ask, with greater interest, what sort of men dwelt on so famed a soil and what sort of business they particularly liked, since their wealth had been wasted by incessant war, the manager replied, "My friends, if you are business men, change your plans and look for some other way of making a living. But if you are men of a smoother brand and can stand it to be always lying, you are on the highway to wealth. For in this city there is no interest in learning, no place for eloquence; frugality and decency bear no fruit or honor. All the people you see in this city you may be sure are divided into two groups, for they are either the objects of legacy-hunters or legacy-hunters themselves. In this city no one brings up children because anyone who has heirs of his own blood gets no invitations to dinner or the theater but is deprived of all advantages and lives an obscure and despised existence. But those who have never married and have no near relatives attain the highest distinctions; I mean, are alone considered soldierly, excellently brave, and even virtuous. You are entering a town," he said, "that is like a field of pestilence on which there lie nothing but bodies that are being torn and crows that are doing the tearing." ³ . . .

*117* "Well then," said Eumolpus, "why should we hesitate to put on an act? So make me your master, if you like the business."

No one dared find fault with a trick which could do no harm. So, in order that we might all keep to the same story, we swore to obey Eumolpus, to be burned, bound, beaten, butchered, or anything else at Eumolpus' orders. Just like regular gladiators, we solemnly bound ourselves body and soul to our master. After taking the oath, we bowed to our master in slavish fashion and all learned that Eumolpus had lost a son, a young man of vast eloquence and promise, and that Eumolpus had on that account left his own city a pitiful old man, so that he might not every day be brought to tears by the sight of the friends and followers and tombstone of his son.

This sorrow had been increased by a recent shipwreck, in which he had lost over two million sesterces. It was not the loss that troubled him, but the fact that, deprived of servants, he had lost the sense of his own importance. Furthermore, he had thirty million sesterces invested in estates and bonds in Africa. He had so large a corps of slaves scattered over the fields of Numidia that he could have taken even Carthage by storm.

According to this plan, we told Eumolpus to cough a good deal, to be troubled with indigestion now and then, and to find fault openly with all his food; to talk about his gold and silver and his disappointing farms and forever barren soil; to sit daily over his accounts and to revise the pages of his will every month. And that nothing might be lacking from the act, as often as he tried to call any one of us, he should call one by another's name, so that it might easily be plain that the master had in mind even those slaves who were not present.

Having made these preparations, we prayed the gods for good luck and set out. But Giton could not stand up under his unaccustomed load and Corax, our hired man, a shirker, kept setting down his bundle, cursing us for hurrying, and saying that he was either going to throw away his bundles or run away with his load. "What do you think I am," he said, "a pack horse or a stone barge? I hired out as a man, not a

nag. I'm just as much a free man as you are, even if my father did leave me poor." Not content with curses, he kept lifting his leg and filling the road with nasty sounds and smells. Giton laughed at his impudence and matched his break for break. . . .

*124* At last we reached Croton. The next day, when we had refreshed ourselves at a little inn, we went looking for a more elegant house and fell in with a crowd of legacy-hunters who asked what sort of men we were and where we came from. According to the prearranged plan of our common council, we told them with an eager flow of words who and whence we were, and they readily believed us. They immediately fell into a fierce rivalry to heap their wealth upon Eumolpus.

[Encolpius is the hero of an intrigue with a passionate and beautiful woman named Circe, but is at length dismissed as tried and found unsatisfying. He is unfortunate enough to slay a sacred goose. Our fragments end with an account of his provision in his will that the beneficiaries shall eat him after his death.]

## TRIMALCHIO'S BANQUET

*26* The third day had now come, and with it hope of a free meal, but we were so battered and bruised that we were more inclined to run away than rest. So, as we were sadly considering how we should escape the present storm, one of Agamemnon's ⁴ slaves broke in upon our dithering and said, "Don't you know who's giving it today? Trimalchio, a very smooth chap; he has a clock and a liveried bugler in his dining room to keep him constantly informed how much of his life he has lost beyond recall."

So we forgot all our troubles and got dressed and ordered Giton, who had so far been very willing to play servant to us, to follow us to the baths. *27* Meanwhile, we began to stroll about in our dinner clothes, or rather to pass jokes and mix with the groups of players, when suddenly we saw a bald-headed old man, clad in a reddish shirt, playing ball with some long-haired boys. It wasn't so much the boys that had caught our eye, though they were worth watching, as daddy himself, who, in his slippers, was busy with a green ball. He never picked up any that touched the ground; a slave stood by with a bag full of them and passed them out to the players. We also saw an innovation in the game, for two eunuchs stood at different points of the field, one holding a silver chamber pot, while the other counted the balls, not those which flashed from hand to hand in the speed of the game but those which fell to the ground. While we were marvelling at these elegancies, Menelaus ran up and said, "That is the man at whose house you are bending the elbow; indeed, you are witnessing the overture to the dinner."

Menelaus had just finished when Trimalchio snapped his fingers. At this signal, one eunuch held the pot for him as he went on playing. When he had emptied his bladder, he called for water to wash his hands, and after dipping his fingers in it a little wiped them on a boy's head. . . .

28 We came to the door with Agamemnon. On the doorpost was nailed a notice with these words: "Any slave leaving the house without the master's orders shall get a hundred lashes." Just at the entrance stood a porter in green uniform with a cerise belt, shelling peas into a silver dish. Over the door hung a gold cage with a spotted magpie in it which greeted those going in. 29 While I was gaping at all this I almost fell backwards and broke my leg. On our left as we entered, not far from the porter's lodge, a great dog was painted on the wall and over him was written in black letters, "Beware of the dog." My friends laughed at me, and I plucked up my courage and went on to examine the whole wall. There was a picture of a slave market with names to identify the figures. In it, Trimalchio, with long hair and carrying a caduceus, was entering Rome under Minerva's guidance. Then the painstaking artist had faithfully pictured his whole career, with explanatory notes—how he had learned to keep accounts and how he at last had been made a household manager. Just where the portico ended, Mercury was taking him by the chin and quickly lifting him up to his high seat of office. Fortune was there with an overflowing horn of plenty, and the three Fates spinning threads of gold. I also noticed in the portico a group of runners training under a coach. Furthermore, I saw in a corner a large cupboard with a small shrine, in which stood household gods of silver, a marble statue of Venus, and a gold box of no small size, in which they said Trimalchio's first beard was kept. . . .

I started to ask the porter what pictures they had inside. "The *Iliad* and the *Odyssey*," he said, "and the gladiatorial show Laenas put on." There was no time to take it all in. . . .

31 So at length we took our places and boys from Alexandria poured snow-cooled water on our hands. Others followed and fell at our feet and with great skill pared away our hangnails. Not even during this most unpleasant task were they silent, but sang as they worked. I wanted to find out whether the whole staff could sing, and so asked for a drink. At once a boy took my order and repeated it in a chant just as shrill. . . .

Elegant hors d'oeuvres were served, for now all but Trimalchio himself had taken their places. For him, according to the latest fashion, the head of the table was reserved. On a tray was a little donkey in Corinthian bronze, carrying two panniers of olives, white on one side, black on the other. The donkey was flanked by two dishes with Trimalchio's name and their weight in silver engraved on the rim. Soldered to them were little bridges bearing dormice rolled in honey and poppy seeds. There were hot sausages lying on a silver grill, and under the grill Syrian plums with pomegranate seeds.

32 We were busy with these delicacies when Trimalchio was brought in to the music of an orchestra. The sight of him lying upon the tiniest pillows drew a laugh from the unprepared. His shaven head emerged from the folds of a scarlet cloak, and over his neck, burdened with its wrappings, he had placed a broad-striped napkin with fringes hanging down on all sides. On the little finger of his left hand he had a large gilt ring, on the first joint of the next finger a smaller one, of pure gold, so far as I could see, but absolutely starred, so to speak, with small particles of iron. Lest he display only this wealth, his right arm was uncovered and was adorned with a gold bracelet and an ivory circlet clasped with a bright metal plate.

33 As soon as he was brought in, picking his teeth with a silver quill, he said: "My friends, it was not convenient for me to come down so soon to dinner, but I gave up all my own pleasure in order not to delay you any longer by my long absence. You will, however, permit me to finish my game."

A slave followed him with a board of terebinth wood and crystal pieces, and I witnessed the height of refinement, for in place of black and white counters he had gold and silver coins.

Meanwhile, as he kept passing all kinds of remarks throughout the game, while we were still eating hors d'oeuvres, a tray was brought in with a basket in which was a wooden hen with wings extended as though she were setting. At once two slaves came up and, with the orchestra playing *fortissimo*, began to search the straw. From it they drew peahens' eggs and handed them to the guests.

Trimalchio turned his face toward this scene and said: "My friends, I ordered peahens' eggs put under a common hen and, by Hercules, I'm afraid the chicks are already formed. Let's see, however, whether the eggs are still good enough to suck."

We were given spoons weighing not less than half a pound and tapped the eggs, which were covered with rich meal. As a matter of fact, I almost threw away my share, for it seemed to me already to have formed a peachick. Then, as I heard an old hand at these dinners say, "There ought to be something good here," I poked a finger through the shell and found a very fat beccafico wrapped in peppered egg-yolk.

*34* Trimalchio had now stopped his game and asked for all the same dishes and had, in a loud voice, invited anyone of us who wished to have another glass of mead. Suddenly the orchestra struck a note and the hors d'oeuvres were spirited away by a group of singing waiters. In the confusion, a dish fell and a boy picked it up from the floor. Trimalchio noticed it and ordered the boy given a box on the ear and the dish thrown down again. A litter-bearer came up and began to sweep out the silver with a broom, along with the other rubbish. Then two long-haired Ethiopians came in with little wine-skins, like the men who sprinkle the sand in the amphitheatre, and gave us wine to wash our hands in, for no one offered any water.

When the master was praised for these refinements, he said, "Mars loves a fair field. So I gave orders that each should be given his own table. In that way these filthy slaves won't make us so hot by crowding about us."

At once, glass jars carefully sealed with gypsum were brought in. On their necks were tied labels bearing this legend: "Hundred-year-old Falernian of Opimius' vintage." While we were reading the labels, Trimalchio clapped his hands and said: "Dear, dear, wine lives longer than mere man. So let's get pickled. Wine is life. I'm serving genuine Opimian. Yesterday I didn't put on such good stuff, and the guests were of a much higher class."

As we were drinking and curiously observing the luxuries, a slave brought in a silver skeleton, so joined together that its limbs and vertebrae could be bent and twisted in every direction. When he had thrown it down on the table once or twice and the supple joints had fallen into several positions, Trimalchio added:

Unhappy we, man's nothing but a breath.
So shall we all be when we're snatched by Death.
So let us live, while happy we may be.

*35* The applause was followed by a dish of unexpectedly small size but of a novelty which caught the eyes of all. A round platter had the twelve signs of the zodiac in order around the edge, and on each the artist had placed food fit and proper to the sign: on the Ram, ram's-head peas; on the Bull, a piece of beef; on the Twins, testicles and kidneys; on the Crab, a crown; on the Lion, an African fig; on Virgo, a sterile sow's womb; on Libra, a pair of scales with a muffin in one pan and a cake in the other; on Scorpio, a small sea fish; on Sagittarius, a bull's eye; on Capricorn, a lobster; on Aquarius, a goose; on Pisces, two mullets. In the center, a bit of turf cut out with the grass still on it held a honeycomb. An Egyptian boy carried bread around in a silver baking dish. . . . And he himself in a terrible voice murdered the hit from *Halitosis*. We turned with understandably low spirits to food so cheap.

*36* "Let's eat," said Trimalchio. "There is sauce for the dinner." As he said this, four dancers ran up in time with the orchestra and took off the cover of the dish. When this was done, we saw in the lower part fat fowls and sows' bellies and in the center a hare decked out with wings to look like Pegasus. We also noted in the corners of the dish four Marsyases from whose wineskins a sauce spiced with pepper poured out over fish, which swam in a sort of tide rip. The slaves started an applause which we all took up, after which we laughingly attacked these delicacies. Trimalchio was no less delighted at a gag of this sort and called out,

"Carver!" At once a serving-man came forward and, with gestures timed with the orchestra, so tore apart the dish that you would think a chariot-fighter was battling to the music of a water organ. Nonetheless, Trimalchio kept repeating in a very soft voice, "Carver! Carver!" I suspected that the word repeated so often had something to do with a joke and I was not ashamed to ask the man next to me this very question. He, who had a more frequent acquaintance with shows of this sort, said: "You see the one who is carving the dish? He is called Carver. So whenever Trimalchio says, "Carve 'er!" he calls him by name and gives him his orders at the same time."

37 I couldn't eat anything more, but turned to this man to pick up as much information as I could. I began to try to drag tall stories from him and to ask who the woman was that kept running hither and yon. "Trimalchio's wife," he said. "She's called Fortunata and counts her coin by bushel baskets. And just a little while ago, what was she? You must forgive me if I say you wouldn't have wanted to take a bit of bread from her hand. Now, without rhyme or reason, she's risen to the skies and is Trimalchio's nonpareil. In a word, if she says it's night at high noon, he'll believe it. He himself doesn't know what he has, he is so filthy rich, but this vixen looks out for everything, even when you wouldn't think it. She is sober, temperate, prudent—you see their wealth—but she has a mean tongue and henpecks him. She likes whom she likes, dislikes whom she dislikes. Trimalchio has estates that reach as far as a kite can fly; he has millions upon millions. There's more plate lying in his porter's room than ordinary people have in their whole house. As for his slaves—oh boy! By Hercules, I don't think one out of ten knows his master by sight. 38 Nor must you suppose that he buys anything. Everything is home-grown—wool, citrons, pepper; you'll get cock's milk if you ask for it. For instance, his wool wasn't turning out well: he bought rams from Tarentum and mated them with his flock. To have Attic honey made at home, he had bees brought from Athens; and, incidentally, the native bees will be improved by the Greek. Just within the past few days he wrote to have mushroom spawn sent him from India. Why, he hasn't a single mule not gotten by a wild ass. You see all the pillows—every one has either purple or scarlet stuffing. That's the extent of his blessings."

.    .    .    .    .    .    .

40 The servants came and spread on the couches coverlets painted with hunting nets and men lying in wait with hunting spears and all the equipment for the hunt. We didn't yet know what to make of this, when a great shout arose outside the dining room and Spartan hounds dashed in and began to run around the table. After them a tray was brought in with the largest size of wild boar upon it, decked with a cap of freedom and with two little baskets woven of palm twigs hanging from its tusks, one full of dried dates, the other of fresh. Smaller piglets, made of cakes of some pounded material, were grouped around the wild boar, seemingly hanging to the teats, and thus showing that a sow was being served. These were for the guests to take home. The Carver who had dismembered the fowls did not step up to tear apart the boar; instead, a huge, bearded fellow, with his legs wound with bands and sporting a light damask hunting jacket, drew a hunting knife and plunged it smartly into the side of the boar, whereupon thrushes flew out of the wound. Fowlers, ready with limed rods, caught them in a moment as they flew around the dining room. Then, when Trimalchio had told each guest to take his portion, he added, "Now you see what elegant acorns that woodland boar has eaten." At once, boys stepped up to take the baskets which hung from the tusks and properly distributed fresh and dried dates to the guests. 41 Meanwhile, I, having gotten myself a private corner, was turning over many possible explanations as to why the boar had come in wearing a cap of freedom. So, after I had canvassed all the possible reasons, I decided to ask that old informant of mine the question that was troubling me. He replied: "Certainly; your humble servant can explain this too. There's no riddle; the thing's quite clear. This boar, after it had been the main course at yesterday's dinner, was sent back untouched by the guests. So he returns to the banquet today as a freedman." I cursed my own stupidity and asked no more questions, lest I seem never to have dined in decent society.

After this course, Trimalchio got up and went to the bathroom.

[During Trimalchio's absence there is much discursive conversation among the guests. One, a ragman, invites Agamemnon to visit him at his country place.]

46 "Could I persuade you to come down to my country property some day and see our little place? We'll find something to eat—a chicken, some eggs. It'll be fun, even if the weather this year has brought everything along at the wrong time; we'll find something to stuff ourselves with. My small boy is already growing into a follower of yours. He can do short division now. If he lives, you'll have a little servant at your side. What spare time he has, he never lifts his head from his writing pad. He is clever and has good stuff in him, even if he is crazy about birds. I just lately killed three of his goldfinches and said a weasel had eaten them. But he's found another hobby and loves to paint. He's about finished his Greek and has begun rather to enjoy his Latin, even though his teacher is conceited and never spends long on any one thing. The boy comes asking me to give him something to write, though he does not like to work. The other boy is no student but has a natural curiosity and can teach more than he knows. He usually comes home on holidays and is happy with whatever you give him. So I have now bought the boy some books with red letter headings because I want him to have a taste of law, with an eye to managing the property. There's bread and butter in the law. He has absorbed enough literature. But if he turns restless, I've decided to teach him a trade, either that of barber or auctioneer or at least a lawyer's, something nothing but Death can do him out of. So I shout to him every day, 'Believe me, Primigenius, whatever you learn you're learning for your own good. Look at Phileros the lawyer; if he had not studied, he wouldn't be able to keep the wolf from the door today. Not so long ago he used to carry a pack of things for sale around on his back; now he struts his stuff even against Norbanus. A liberal education is a treasure and a trade never dies.'"

47 Conversations of this sort were going on when Trimalchio came in, mopping his brow, and washed his hands in perfume. After a very brief pause, he said: "You must excuse me, my friends. My bowels haven't been in order for several days and the doctors are at a loss. Pomegranate rind has helped me some, however, and pitch-pine in

vinegar. I hope, though, that my belly will now resume its former good manners, for all that it rumbles like a bull. So if any one of you wishes to retire, he doesn't need to be shy. None of us is born without an inside. I think there's no worse torture than holding oneself in. That's one thing Jupiter himself cannot forbid.

"Why do you laugh, Fortunata, when you are the one that keeps me awake all night? I don't even forbid anyone's relieving himself in the dining room; the doctors tell us not to hold in. Or, if its something more serious, there's everything ready outside—water, towels, and all the other little things. Believe me, the vapors mount to the brain and cause a disturbance throughout the body. I know of many who have died that way, because they wouldn't admit the truth to themselves."

We thanked him for his generous kindness and then drowned our laughter with frequent drinks. Nor did we yet realize that we were only halfway through the delicacies and had an uphill task before us, as they say. For when, to the music of the orchestra, the tables had been cleared, three white pigs, decked out with muzzles and bells, were led into the dining room. The master of ceremonies said one was two, one was three, and one was all of six years old. I thought some rope-dancers had come in and that the pigs would do some wonderful tricks, such as they do for street gatherings. But Trimalchio ended our suspense by saying, "Which of these do you want to have turned into dinner at once? Mere country people can cook a fowl, a mixed grill *à la* Pentheus, or such trifles; my cooks are accustomed to cooking whole calves in a cauldron." And he had the cook called at once, and, without waiting for us to choose, ordered the oldest pig killed. "What division of the property do you come from?" he shouted to the cook, and, when the man answered that he came from the fortieth, Trimalchio asked, "Were you bought or born on the place?" "Neither," said the cook, "I was left to you in Pansa's will." "See to it then that you serve this carefully; otherwise I'll have you thrown into the messengers' division."

48 The cook, having been duly reminded of his master's power, rode off to the kitchen on the course that was to be. Trimalchio turned a mild face upon us and said, "If you don't like the wine, I'll change it. You'll have to admit it's good.

God be thanked, I don't have to buy it. Anything here that makes your mouths water comes from a country place of mine I've not yet seen. It's said to be near Terracina and Tarentum. I want to make an unbroken line of properties in Sicily and then when I want to go to Africa I can go all the way on my own property.

"But tell me, Agamemnon, what lecture did you give today? Even though I'm no court lawyer, I learned literature for use at home. Just so you won't think I look down on learning, I have three [*sic*] libraries, one Greek and one Latin. Give me then, please, an outline of your lecture."

When Agamemnon said, "A poor man and a rich man were enemies—" Trimalchio broke in, "What is a poor man?"

"Very clever," said Agamemnon, and proceeded to summarize some set speech or other. At once Trimalchio said, "If this happened, it's not a problem; if it didn't happen, it's nonsense."

As we were heaping this and other bright remarks with the most effusive praise, Trimalchio said: "I wonder, my dearest Agamemnon, whether you have ready the twelve labors of Hercules or that tale of Ulysses and how the Cyclops twisted his thumb with the tongs. I used to read these things in Homer, when I was a boy. As a matter of fact, I saw the Sibyl with my own eyes at Cumae, hanging in a cage, and when boys would say to her, "Que veux-tu, Sibylle?" she used to answer, "Je veux mourir." [5]

49 He still had not finished sounding off when a dish holding the huge pig filled the table. We began to express our surprise at the speed and to swear that not even a fowl could have been cooked so quickly, especially as the pig seemed to us much larger than the boar had a little while ago. Trimalchio kept looking at it more and more intently and then cried, "What's this? What's this? This pig hasn't been gutted! By Hercules, it hasn't. Call in the cook! Call in the cook!" When the cook had taken his stand before the table with a gloomy air and said that he had forgotten to gut it, Trimalchio shouted, "What? Forgot? You'd think he had failed to put on pepper and cummin. Strip him!"

Without a moment's delay, the cook was stripped and stood dejectedly between two executioners. Everyone began to plead for him and say, "These things will happen. Please let him off. If

he does it again, none of us will say a word for him."

I, being extremely severe by nature, could not restrain myself and leaned over and said in Agamemnon's ear. "This slave really must be the world's worst. Can you imagine anyone forgetting to gut a pig? By Hercules, I wouldn't let him off if he had missed gutting a fish."

But not Trimalchio. His face broke into a smile. "Well then," he said, "since you've so bad a memory, gut it in front of us." The cook was given back his shirt, picked up a knife, and made timid stabs at the pig's belly on either side. Immediately the slits were widened by the weight within, and sausages and black puddings poured out.

. . . . . .

52 The more Trimalchio was praised, the happier he was in his cups, and now, very nearly tipsy, he said: "None of you asks my Fortunata to dance. Believe me, no one does a better cancan."

Thereupon he raised his hands over his head and did a take-off of the actor Syrus, while the whole household sang in unison:

Madeia!
Perimadeia!

He would have come out into the middle of the room if Fortunata had not whispered in his ear. I suppose she said that such low humor was beneath his dignity. He was the most inconsistent thing in the world—one minute he was afraid of Fortunata, the next he would revert to type.

53 His passion for dancing was brusquely interrupted by a clerk, who read, as if from a government bulletin: "July 26. Born on Trimalchio's place at Cumae: 30 male slaves, 40 female; 500,000 pecks of wheat taken from threshing-floor to granary; 500 oxen broken in. On the same day, 10,000,000 sesterces were put in the safe for want of proper opportunity for investment. On the same day there was a fire in the gardens at Pompeii, originating in the house of Nasta the manager."

"What's that?" said Trimalchio. "When did I buy any gardens at Pompeii?"

"Last year," said the clerk. "That's why they haven't appeared on the books yet."

Trimalchio grew white with rage and said: "If any estates are bought for me and I don't know of it within six months, I forbid it to be entered on my books."

Next came a reading of police reports and the wills of some overseers in which Trimalchio was cut off in one clause. Then came names of managers and that of a freedwoman who had been divorced by her husband, a watchman, for having been caught with a bathman; and then that of a porter who had been banished to Baiae. There was also the name of a steward who was accused of something or other, and a judgment rendered in a dispute between some valets.

At last the acrobats came in. A stupid ass stood there with a ladder and made a boy dance to various tunes on the rungs and at the top, then jump through burning hoops and hold a wine jar in his teeth. Trimalchio was the only one to care for this, and he kept saying that it was a thankless profession. But, he said, there were two things in the world he most liked to watch— acrobats and trumpeters. All other shows were nothing but nonsense. "Why," he said, "I once bought a company of comic actors. But I preferred to have them act an Atellan farce and I told my flutist to play Latin airs."

*54* At this point in Trimalchio's speech the boy slipped and fell on top of him. There was an uproar from the household and from the guests as well, not because of that wretched fellow, whose neck all would have gladly seen broken, but because of the bad end it would have made to the dinner. People didn't want to have to weep over the death of a perfect stranger. Trimalchio himself gave a deep groan and bent over his arm as if it were hurt; doctors rushed up to him, and right in the lead was Fortunata, carrying a cup, her hair down her back. She cried that she was wretched and luckless. As for the boy who had fallen, he had for some time been crawling about at our feet and begging for pardon. I was very much afraid that the outcome of these petitions would be some comic surprise. I still hadn't forgotten the cook who had forgotten to gut the pig. So I began to glance all around the dining room to see if some machinery wouldn't pop out of the wall, particularly after they began to beat a slave who had bandaged his master's bruised arm in white wool instead

of purple. My suspicions weren't far wrong, for instead of any punishment for the boy came Trimalchio's decree that the boy should be made a free man, so that no one might be able to say that so great a man had been wounded by a slave.

*59* A troupe which gave readings from Homer came in and at once began to beat their spears and shields together. Trimalchio himself sat on his cushion, and when the actors talked together in Greek in their rude way, he read in a loud voice from a book in Latin. When silence had been restored, he said, "Do you know the episode they're putting on? Diomede and Ganymede were twin brothers and Helen was their sister. Agamemnon abducted her and put off Diana by sacrificing a deer in Helen's place. So Homer is now telling how the Trojans and Parentines went to war. Of course Agamemnon won and married his daughter Iphigenia to Achilles. That's why Ajax went crazy. He will act you the whole story in a minute." As Trimalchio said this, the actors raised a shout and the slaves scattered to let a boiled calf be brought in on a hundred-pound platter. The calf had a helmet on. Ajax went after it with drawn sword and fell upon it like a madman. He made passes with the edge and the flat of the sword and then picked up slices and divided the calf among the astonished guests.

*70* Now Fortunata had begun to want to dance and Scintilla was clapping her hands more often than she spoke, when Trimalchio said: "Philargyrus, and you too, Cario, even though you are a notorious Green, you may sit down; and tell Menophila your mate that she may too." I needn't say that we were thrown off our couches by the way the slaves took over the whole dining room. Anyhow, I noticed the cook seated just above me—the one who had made a goose out of a pig and smelled to high heaven of pickle and sauces. He was not content just to sit down, but began at once to do an imitation of Ephesus the tragic actor and then to challenge his master to make a bet on the Green taking first place at the next races.

*71* At this dispute, Trimalchio cheered up and

said: "My friends, slaves are human beings too and drank the same milk as we did, even if an unkind fate has overtaken them. Yet if I live, they shall soon taste the water of freedom. In a word, I'm freeing all of them in my will. I'm even leaving Philargyrus a farm and his mate, and to Cario too an apartment house and his manumission tax and a bed with its bedding. For I'm making Fortunata my heir and commending her to all my friends. I'm disclosing all this so that my household may love me now as much as they will when I am dead."

As they all began to express their thanks for their master's kindness, he forgot his fun and ordered a copy of his will brought in and read the whole thing aloud from beginning to end, to the moans of the household.

Then he looked at Habinnas and said: "What say, my dear friend; are you building my monument as I ordered you? I insist that you put at the foot of my statute my little bitch puppy and wreaths and perfume bottles and all Petraites' [a famous gladiator] fights, so that, by your kindness, I may live after death. The monument is to have a frontage of one hundred feet and be two hundred feet in depth. I want all sorts of fruit to grow around my ashes, and quantities of vines. It's quite wrong for a man's house to be carefully tended while he's alive but for that to be neglected where we must make a longer stay. Therefore, above all, I want added to the inscription: 'This monument does not descend to the heir.' But I'll see to it that I take measures in my will to protect myself from injury when I am dead. I'll appoint one of my freedmen to take care of my tomb, so people won't run and use my monument as a privy. You are to carve ships under full sail on my monument, and a statue of me sitting in my chair of office, wearing five gold rings and doling money out to the people from a bag. You know I gave a free dinner worth two denarii a plate. I'd like a dining room represented too, if you don't mind. And you're to show the whole populace having a good time. On my right you're to set a statue of my Fortunata holding a dove and leading a little dog with a sweater on. And my little boy, and big jars sealed with gypsum so the wine can't run out. And you may carve a broken urn and a boy weeping over it. And a sundial in the center, so that anyone who looks at the time shall read my name willy-nilly. Now think carefully whether this inscription seems quite appropriate to you: 'Here lies C. Pompeius Trimalchio Maecenatianus. He was appointed Priest of Augustus *in absentia*. Though he could have been an attendant upon any magistrate in Rome, he refused the honor. Pious, strong, faithful, he rose from humble beginnings to leave thirty millions, and never went to college. Farewell, Trimalchio, and thou who readest this.' "

## NOTES TO THE *SATYRICON* OF PETRONIUS

1. This quotation, from Vergil, *Aeneid*, IV, 34, made by a servant, may be used as evidence both of the wide use of the epic as a schoolbook and of the wide extent of education in the first century A.D. But the ridiculous inappositeness of the situation and the quotation would not have escaped Petronius.

2. Vergil, *Aeneid*, IV, 38–39.

3. There is a gap in the manuscript, and a part of a chapter has been omitted.

4. A professor of rhetoric.

5. In the original the Sibyl's words are Greek. This sentence has been used by T. S. Eliot as the epigraph to "The Waste Land," to epitomize the pessimism of an age of anxiety.

# SELECTIONS FROM QUINTILIAN'S
## The Training of the Orator

### Translated by Paul MacKendrick

## INTRODUCTION

MARCUS FABIUS QUINTILIANUS, professor of rhetoric, was born in northern Spain about A.D. 35 and died in Rome about A.D. 95. Like his fellow Spaniard, elder contemporary, and rival, Seneca, he was educated in Rome, returning afterward for a short time to Spain, whence he came back to the capital with the future emperor Galba in A.D. 68. The emperor Vespasian appointed him to an endowed chair of rhetoric, which he occupied for twenty years, numbering among his pupils many of the distinguished names of literature and the Roman bar. The emperor Domitian recalled him from retirement to become tutor to his two grandnephews. Quintilian married, apparently late in life, a young wife (she died at nineteen), who bore him two sons, both of whom died in early childhood. His one surviving work, *The Training of the Orator* (*Institutio Oratoria*) was intended as a textbook for his own children, whose death he mourns with real pathos in the preface to Book VI, translated below.

Quintilian's textbook is the heir of a long tradition, reaching back at least to the "Sophists" of fifth-century Athens, and including such names as Isocrates, Aristotle, and Cicero. His subject, rhetoric or the art of persuasion, was of central importance to literature, law, and politics from the time of Homer to far beyond the end of the classical age, and indeed classical literature cannot be understood without it. From the Embassy to Achilles in *Iliad* IX to Juvenal's diatribe upon women, its resources were consciously used by the authors of every age and of both languages; it was used in the courtroom by the Attic orators and by Cicero, and it made them invincible in a good cause and not easily bested in a bad one; in politics, it was equally necessary to the tyrant who wished to justify his position and to the democrat who sought to attack it.

Though the orators of Quintilian's age no longer enjoyed the freedom of speech which had given point to the periods of Demosthenes and Cicero, law courts were still in session, and Quintilian aims to train the practising trial lawyer. It is one of the ironies of our time that in an age when rhetoric is perhaps more important than ever before—we call it "propaganda"—most educated people lack a knowledge of its principles; equally ironic is the fact that university professors are often somewhat scornful of their colleagues in departments of speech, whose subject is actually one of the most time-honored in the curriculum.

The present selections are intended to portray Quintilian under his least technical aspect. Noteworthy throughout is his characteristically professorial insistence upon the importance of his own subject, especially as compared with philosophy. The quarrel between philosophy and rhetoric is at least as old as Plato and Isocrates (Isocrates attracted the more distinguished pupils); Quintilian would heal the breach, but it is not exactly clear how, since he makes no concessions to the philosophers. His tone is that of a modern business-man reproaching a professor for living in impractical and sheltered retirement; he himself stresses practicality and common sense throughout his book.

This note is at once obvious in Book I, on elementary education. Quintilian obviously knows, understands, and loves talented children, and his ideas will seem surprisingly "modern" to those who have not discovered that it is not the classics that are new, but the problems that are old. Among his "new" ideas are making education into play for very young children, allowing for individual difference, abolishing corporal punishment, requiring a high standard for the elementary teacher, recognizing that if the child does not love learning it is not entirely his fault, and stressing the influence of the home environment upon the student. What is most old-fashioned about him is his insistence upon hard work and discipline, especially memory work. Old-fashioned, too, is his satisfaction with large lecture classes and his doubts about the efficacy of private tutoring. To Quintilian, Mark Hopkins would be better off on the rostrum than on the end of his log.

In the teacher, Quintilian insists upon strict morality, dignity without stand-offishness, clarity, patience, perseverance without too much pressure, and the golden mean in giving and withholding praise. Modern students are always interested in testing their own teachers by this standard.

The selection from the prologue to Book VI will remind the student that professors are also human beings, capable of human affection and of grief at the death of those they love, at the snuffing out of promise in the young. If Quintilian appears to make his children almost superhuman paragons, let the reader remember first that parents are seldom the harshest judges of their children, and that the rhetorical style of the early Empire was not noted for its restraint. The picture of the old man grieving for a child wife as for a daughter, and continuing for the edification of other men's children the labor of love he had begun for his own, is one of the most intimate and personal glimpses of heartbreak that we have from classical antiquity.

The sad circumstances under which they were written make the merits of Books X and XII all the more remarkable. The survey of Greek and Roman literature is remarkable for its brevity, practicality, and common sense. There is no question of art for art's sake; literature is to be used as a quarry or gold mine for the orator; Homer is great because he could write speeches; Cicero gets most space because he is Rome's greatest orator and Quintilian's ideal; the assessment of Seneca, whose style and turn of mind were anathema to Quintilian, is a model for critics who would learn the delicate art of praising with faint damns. The survey, like Hamlet, is full of quotations— Livy's "creamy richness," Sallust's "immortal brevity," Horace's "curious felicity"; unfortunately it is also admirably devised to pass from the professor's notes to the student's notebook without passing through the minds of either. The omissions, too, are characteristic, especially Sappho and the Lesbia poems of Catullus, which were, of course, not in keeping with the moral standards of a "good man skilled in speaking."

For if the touchstone of a classic is that it should inculcate a moral lesson, then Quintilian passes the test, for his whole work insists strongly—perhaps too strongly for modern taste—upon morality, in parents, nurses, teachers, pupils, and especially in the finished product, the ideal orator himself. Perhaps he even protests too much, and we are justified in inferring from his insistence that the ethical standards of the Roman bar were none too high.

At any rate, the capstone of the work, Book XII, sets a standard borrowed from the golden age of republican Rome for an era when men strove to stand well with truth and yet not ill with tyrants. The negative cast of Quintilian's mind comes out even more strongly here than elsewhere; it is the dangers of the evil orator, and not the services of the good one, that he stresses; the tone is milder than that of Tacitus and Juvenal, but the defeatism is there, and it darkly presages the decline and fall.

One's estimate of Quintilian will depend upon the importance one attaches to maintaining the *status quo*. For Quintilian is a mandarin, and mandarins have many virtues not always appreciated by our impatient age. In education, he sees with keen penetration the importance of sound method; he has a rare respect for childhood; he sees education as understanding, and teaching as a stimulus to self-development, not the mere imposition of tasks, the Penelopean practice of undoing each morning what has been done the night before. He is the founder of the science of comparative literature, and his critical judgments are illuminated by wide reading and sound common sense. In an age where nothing succeeded like rhetorical excess, he preferred that Ciceronianism which has ever since been the touchstone of good Latin. But a language which canonizes its past has no future; the Pope who would not read the Vulgate for fear it would spoil his Latin prose style would have Quintilian's blessing, but he, like Quintilian himself, contributed to making Latin a dead language. The rhetoric that once, on the lips of Demosthenes, had galvanized Athenian democracy to a brave last stand against oppression and tyranny now looked upon the greatest works of Greek and Roman genius as a sort of Bartlett's *Familiar Quotations* from which to draw suitable commonplaces in the defense of a Roman accused of throwing his wife out of a window. One overharsh critic has described Quintilian's book as "a treatise upon Lying as a Fine Art for those fully conscious of their own rectitude." Form had become more important than content; in the words of Professor Robert Ulich, "the art of expression was set above the deeper experiences from which we draw our convictions," and when that happens to a culture, we call it decadence.

THE TEXT translated is that of E. Bonnell (Leipzig: Teubner, 1869–72, 2 vols.). The commentaries of F. H. Colson on Book I (Cambridge, 1924), and W. Peterson on Book X (Oxford, 1891) have provided a number of happy renderings.

PREFACE

*Quintilian's ideal: to educate the perfect orator, by means of the marriage of philosophy and rhetoric, in the science and art of oratory, producing "the good man skilled in speaking." But the prerequisite is talent, without which no textbook is of any use.*

*1* After the granting of my request for retirement from twenty years spent in teaching the young, several friends insisted on my putting together a work on the theory of rhetoric. Naturally I fought for a long time against the proposal, because I was well aware that the best-known authorities both in Greek and Latin had left as their legacy to men of after time many a painstaking volume on this subject. *2* Now it is difficult to choose among the diverse and often mutually contradictory opinions of earlier authors, and this was my ground for high hopes that my friends would let me off, but it only made them the more enthusiastic. The result was that I thought them not unreasonable in asking me to go to the trouble not so much of doing original research as of making critical judgments. *3* I yielded finally less out of confidence that I could supply their need than out of shame at refusing. Though as the scope of my subject widened the burden proved to be more than I had bargained for, I took it up gladly, moved by a desire both to do for my dearest friends more than they had asked, and to avoid walking in other people's footsteps, even though I had taken a well-travelled road. *4* Nearly all other writers on rhetoric have started from the premise that they were giving the finishing touches of eloquence to students who had already mastered all the rest of their education. This they did either out of contempt for "trifling" primary studies, or because they thought, given the prevailing division of labor among teachers, that primary work was not in their department; or, most likely, because they expected to get no credit for brilliance out of treating a subject which, however vital, gives no opportunity for show. Towering structures are admired; their foundations lie hidden. *5* Now in my view everything is related to rhetoric, which is admittedly indispensable to the orator's education, and you never get to the advanced part of a subject until you have gone through the fundamentals; therefore I shall not refuse to descend to those lower levels which, if neglected, cut off access to the higher ones; in fact, if an orator should be assigned to me to educate, I should begin his training in his infancy. *6* This work I dedicate to you, Marcellus Victorius. You are my dearest friend, and you love literature dearly, but these, important as they are, are not the reasons why I judged you most worthy of this token of our mutual affection; rather it is because these volumes may be of some little use in the education of your son Geta, who, young as he is, shows clear promise of talent. My book starts from the very elements of education, and proceeds through all the subjects having anything to contribute to the future orator, until finally it aims to bring him to the peak of his art. *7* I am the more eager to publish because there are already two books on the art of rhetoric circulating under my name which I neither edited nor composed for publication. One is the notes of a two-day session, taken down by professional stenographers, the other contains as much of a several days' lecture series as my students could take down in shorthand—good lads, but too fond of me; they were rash enough to honor the notes by publication. *8* This edition will contain some of the same matter, but the changes are many, the additions innumerable, and the whole is, to the best of my ability, better planned and executed.

*9* The orator whom we aim to educate is the "perfect" one, who cannot be so unless he is a good man, and therefore we demand of him not merely extraordinary skill in speaking, but every intellectual virtue as well. *10* I am by no means so ready as some to concede the point that the regulation of an upright and honorable life is a job for the philosophers: it is the orator and not the philosopher who is the true citizen, fitted to administer public and private business; it is the orator whose advice rules cities, his constitutions are their cornerstone, his judicial decisions provide their moral standard. *11* So, while I admit that I intend to use philosophical sources, yet I should argue—with right and truth on my side—that they are relevant to my work and that they belong properly to the field of rhetoric. *12* Speakers often have to deal with topics like justice, courage, and temperance; indeed research would uncover scarcely a single brief in which one or another of them was not discussed, and the utmost eloquence and ingenuity are required to expound them. But is there any doubt that, wherever talent and facility are required, it is the orator and not the philosopher who plays the leading role? *13* There was a time, as Cicero very soundly concludes, when the two fields were so closely united in theory and in practice that the same men were held to be both philosophers and orators. But later on the two subjects were divorced, and neglect of science led to the multiplication of sciences. For as soon as there began to be money in oratory, and rhetoric began to be abused, men with reputation for eloquence abandoned ethical conduct. *14* Rhetoric, thus deserted, became as it were the prey of lesser men. The result was that some, scorning the difficult profession of rhetoric, turned to intellectual discipline and the laying down of laws for the guidance of life, thus reserving for themselves the more important role, if indeed it is possible to make a distinction. But they had the effrontery to appropriate for their sole use the names "philosopher" and "scholar," an effrontery unmatched by great generals or by the best-known experts in councils of state or public administration, who have preferred noble deeds to noble pretensions. *15* That many ancient philosophers taught and lived by high ethical standards I would willingly admit; but in our time the name "philosopher" covers a multitude of sins. For it is their ambition to earn the title not by character and scholarship, but by a dour expression and eccentric dress, as a front for their low morals. *16* The fact is that what they claim as philosophy's private property is something we all constantly deal with. For who, unless he is an utter villain, does not discuss what is just, right, and good? Who is there, even among country people, who has not some interest in science? Correct and discriminating speech ought to be the joint concern of all who care about language. *17* But the man who will know and express this best is the orator. If there had ever been a perfect one, he would not go to the philosophical schools for his moral precepts. But, as it is, we must occasionally have recourse to those authorities who have pre-empted that abandoned but superior branch of rhetoric which I have mentioned already, and ask for our own back, not to use as their discoveries but to

show up as their borrowings. *18* Let the orator then be a man worth calling a true philosopher, not only morally perfect (for, despite dissenting voices, I think morality is not enough) but perfect in scholarship and in oratorical ability as well. *19* It may be true that so far no such person has ever existed, but that does not excuse us from aiming at perfection; we should take as our example several ancient philosophers who passed on the precepts of philosophy even though they thought no true philosopher had yet been found. *20* Consummate eloquence is certainly important, and there is nothing in the nature of the human intellect which prevents its attainment. But even if we should not attain it, those whose goal is the very pinnacle will at any rate mount higher than those who stay stuck at the bottom because they have assumed before they started that they cannot get to where they want to go.

*21* Therefore I should be the more readily forgiven, if I do not omit even minor points, provided they are relevant to the plan of my work, which will be as follows, subject to my own shortcomings and limitations:

|  |  |
|---|---|
| I | Preliminaries to instruction in rhetoric |
| II | Elements of rhetoric; research into its content |
| III–VII | Gathering and arranging of materials (*22*) |
| VIII–XI | Delivery, memorizing, pronunciation |
| XII | The education of the orator: his character; his method in taking, preparing, and pleading cases, the various kinds of oratorical style; the proper age for retirement; proper studies after retirement. |

*23* In addition to all this I shall insert, as the occasion demands, remarks on teaching methods. My goal is not merely to instruct students in the technicalities to which some would restrict the science of rhetoric, nor to interpret its "laws." Rather I am to give eloquence something to feed on and to increase its strength. *24* Generally speaking, the outline manuals affect an oversubtlety which cuts into bits and pieces the noblest part of oratory; they suck out the lifeblood of talent and lay bare the bones and ligaments, which, however necessary they are, ought to be covered with flesh. *25* Therefore I shall gather together and treat briefly not a small corner of the subject, as is the usual practice, but the whole field, whatever I consider useful for training an orator. I say "briefly," because if I set down in entirety as much as can be said on each topic, I should never come to the last page. *26* One point is to be stressed at the outset, that rules and handbooks are of no avail without the help of natural ability. Therefore this book is no better suited to the untalented than a work on agriculture to unfruitful soil. *27* There are also various innate qualities: a good voice, physical stamina, good health, pertinacity, a good appearance; if the student has some share of these, they can be increased by application, but lack of them frequently cancels out the advantages of talent and hard work, while their presence in itself means nothing without an experienced teacher, constant study, and unremitting practice in writing, reading, and speaking.

## I. ELEMENTARY EDUCATION

*1* As soon, then, as his son is born, the father should be as optimistic as possible about his future, and will be careful about it from the beginning. There is no basis for the common complaint that very few men have any power of understanding, and that slowness of wit makes most of them not worth time or trouble. On the contrary, you would find that most of them are quick-witted and apt pupils. Indeed this is an innate human quality: just as birds are born to fly, horses to run, and wild beasts to growl, so our peculiar property is mental activity and reason; hence the human mind is held to be of heavenly origin. *2* Stupid and unteachable people are no more a normal product of nature than giants and freaks are, and there are remarkably few of them. As for the argument that boys shows sparks of promise in many fields, which are snuffed out as they grow older, this clearly shows a defect not in their innate ability but in their schooling. *3* I grant that there are gradations of talent, but they will produce either progress or relapse; there is no such thing as getting *nowhere* with study. The new parent who sees the truth of this should at once devote his keenest attention to the prospects of the orator-to-be. *4* First of all, the child's nurses should not make mistakes in speech. Chrysippus [1] wanted

them to be philosophers, if that were possible, or at any rate to be the best applicants available. Of course in nurses character is unquestionably the first consideration, but they should speak well, too. *5* These will be the first persons the baby will hear talking, and he will try to imitate their pronunciation. And our memories are naturally most retentive of what we learn in our earliest years, as the old odor persists in refilled bottles, and as dyed cloth cannot be washed white again. And the worse the faults are the harder they stick. For what is good easily deteriorates, but when did you ever turn bad to good? Therefore the child should not get used, even before he can talk, to any form of speech which he will have to unlearn.

*6* I should prefer the parents to have as much education as possible. And I am not referring to fathers only. For it was Cornelia, mother of the Gracchi, who according to tradition contributed much to their eloquence, and the elegance of her style is preserved to posterity in her letters; Laelia the daughter of Gaius Laelius is said to have reproduced her father's nicety of expression in her own speech, and the oration of Hortensia, Quintus Hortensius' daughter, to the triumvirs is still read, and not merely because it was spoken by a woman. *7* Parents who have not themselves had an opportunity for education should not on that account pay less attention to teaching their children; let them for this very reason work all the harder at it.

What has been said about nurses applies equally to the slave-boys among whom our future orator is brought up.

*8* This further note on the footmen: [2] they should either be well educated, which I should prefer, or they should know their limitations. Nothing is worse than those who because they have made a little progress beyond their ABC's assume a false air of knowledge. For they are indignant at giving up the office of teacher, and, with that rush of authority to the head which characterizes their class, they inculcate their own stupidity into their charges with a high and mighty air and sometimes with savage growls. *9* Their character can be as pernicious an influence as their mistakes, if it is true, as related by Diogenes of Babylon, that Leonides, the footman of Alexander the Great, taught him certain bad habits, which, as a result of that instruction when he was a boy, persisted in him when he was a grown man and a great king.

*10* If anyone thinks me too demanding, let him remember that training an orator is a hard job, even when everything necessary is at hand. Further and more serious difficulties lie ahead; there is need for constant study, the best instructors, and a great variety of subject matter. *11* Therefore we have need of the best system, and if anyone balks at it, it is the pupil and not the system that will suffer.

If the child cannot have the sort of nurses, slave-boys, and footmen I should prefer, he should have at least one constant companion with a good pronunciation, who will correct on the spot any errors of diction committed by the servants in his charge's presence, and not allow them to insinuate themselves into the child's speech, provided it be understood that the first method is the good one, while the other is a mere substitute.

*12* I prefer the boy to begin with Greek, because Latin, being in wider use, is a language he will get his fill of whether we want him to or not; besides, his first instruction will be in Greek subjects, from which our own are derived. *13* But I should not want this practice so literally followed that he should speak or study Greek too long at a time, as often happens. The result will be that he will fall into a foreign accent and idiom; when Greek inflections become ingrained through constant habit, they very stubbornly persist even when a different language is being spoken. *14* Latin ought therefore to follow not long after Greek and should soon be running parallel with it, so that, since from the beginning we are equally watchful of both languages, neither will stand in the way of the other.

*15* Some authorities think that boys should not be taught to read before they are seven, on the ground that children cannot grasp the content nor endure the discipline before that age. . . . *16* The view of men like Chrysippus, that no year of a child's life should be empty of learning, is a better one. He would entrust the child to the nurse for the first three years, but thinks that she ought to shape the baby's mind by the best possible instruction. *17* Besides, why should not the age at which character is being formed not be appropriate also for the learning of letters? I am well aware that in all the time of

which I speak scarcely as much can be done as one year can accomplish later on; but those who disagree with me in this matter appear to have more sympathy for the teacher than for the pupil. *18* What better occupation can children have than study, from the time they learn to talk? For they must occupy their time somehow. Or why should we look down our noses at the advantages involved, slight as they are, until the child is seven? For certainly however little the earlier years have contributed, the child will learn something more important in his first year of school, because he has learned the elements beforehand. *19* This advantage, carried from year to year, will add to his total profit, and whatever head start he gets in infancy will stand to his credit in his early teens. The same principle applies to later years, especially since the elements of reading depend on memory alone, which not only exists in small children, but is most retentive then. *20* I am not so poor a judge of maturity that I think one ought to stand threateningly over a tiny child and simply force work out of him. For the first thing to avoid is that he should hate the studies he cannot yet be fond of, and acquire a distaste for study which he cannot shake off in maturity. Let it be play; ask him questions, praise him, let him feel pleasure at being faithful about his lessons; from time to time when he is balky, teach someone else, to arouse his jealousy. Hold an occasional competition; let him have a frequent sense of victory, and stimulate him by prizes appropriate to his years.

*21* These are minor points of doctrine for a man who professes to be educating an orator; but studies, too, have their age of infancy. The training of future athletes begins with their mothers' milk and the cradle; in the same way the future ideal orator once upon a time uttered the birth cry, first tried to talk in a stammering voice, and got stuck on shapes of letters. The inadequacy of any form of learning does not prove that it can be dispensed with. *22* But if no one blames a father who thinks he ought not to neglect the primary education of his son, why should the man be criticized who publishes to the world the correct methods he uses in his own household? Another argument in favor of my proposal is that little children are quick to learn little things; and, just as the body cannot be trained to certain movements of the limbs unless it is taken in hand young, so the strength of the mind itself inures it to further exercise. *23* Would Philip of Macedon have wanted Aristotle, the foremost philosopher of his age, to teach his son Alexander his alphabet, or would Aristotle have taken on the job if he had not thought that elementary education was best handled by the best possible teacher, and that it contributes to the final result? *24* Suppose then that Alexander is entrusted to my care, a child placed in my lap, and worthy, as every man's child is, of my best teaching: should I be ashamed, as I taught the elements, to give some short rules about teaching?

I am not at all pleased with the standard practice of making youngsters learn the names and order of the letters before learning all their forms. *25* This interferes with their recognizing them, because their minds are not fixed upon the outlines of them immediately after they have memorized their names. This is the reason why teachers, when they see that the child has well enough fixed in mind the order in which the letters ought first to be written, then arrange them in reverse order and mix them up in various combinations, until the pupils recognize the letters by their shape and not by the order in which they appear. The best method, then, is the same as the one used in getting acquainted with a person: to learn what he looks like and what his name is at the same time. *26* But the method which is bad with individual letters will do no harm with syllables. I do not leave out of account the well known practice of humoring children's impatience with learning by giving them ivory letters to play with, or any other available toy that suits their years, which they enjoy handling, looking at, and calling by name. *27* As soon as the child can follow the outlines of the letters, it will not be a bad idea to have them carved as carefully as possible upon a board, so that his pen can be guided by them as though they were furrows. Thus he will not make mistakes, as he would on wax, (for his pen will be confined by the edges of the letters on each side and will not be able to go beyond the bounds of his model) and he will be able to work faster and oftener by following a fixed pattern, thus strengthening his fingers so that he will not need the help of the teacher's hand placed on top

of his to guide it. *28* Related to this is a good rapid handwriting, a matter usually neglected by persons of social position. For writing is paramount in education, and by it alone can true progress resting on solid foundations be assured. Slow writing delays the very flow of thought; an unformed and jumbled hand makes no sense; the result is an extra step: dictating what has to be copied. *29* Therefore always and everywhere, but especially in private correspondence and letters to friends, it will be a satisfaction not to have left even good handwriting neglected.

*30* There is no quick and easy way to master syllables; they must all be learned by heart, and one should not follow the common practice of putting off the hardest till last, which results in getting stuck in writing out the declensions of nouns. *31* And we should certainly put no rash confidence in the child's memory of syllables even when it is fresh; it will be more practical to repeat the syllables and pound them in over and over, and it is better not to rush the child into continuous prose or rapid reading, unless a passage can be found with no stumbling-blocks and a perfectly clear juxtaposition of letters, so that there is not even need to stop to think. Then the child should begin to make up words with his syllables, and to make connected sentences out of the words. *32* Unbelievable delay is caused by reading too fast. Children who undertake more than they are able fall into stammering, pauses, and repetition, and then, when they have made mistakes, they begin to lose confidence in what they already know. *33* At the beginning, then, reading must be sure, then connected, and quite slow for a long time, until speed and accuracy have been attained by practice. *34* For looking to the right (the universal method) and looking ahead are matters of practice as well as of theory; since the student has to pronounce what comes first while he is looking at what follows, and he must concentrate on two things at once, a most difficult feat, while his voice does one thing and his eyes another. When the boy begins to follow the standard practice of writing out nouns, the teacher will not be sorry to have taken pains that the pupil did not waste his time with common words chosen at random. *35* For he can readily learn by heart the interpretation of rare words, which the Greeks call *glosses*, while he is doing something else, and thus acquire, while he is learning his ABC's, knowledge which otherwise would demand a separate time later on for learning. And since we are lingering on minor matters, I hope that the lines set for writing practice may contain not pointless sentiments but moral precepts. *36* The memory of them will persist until old age, and what is impressed upon an unformed mind will have a good effect upon character. Even the sayings of famous men, and especially selections from the poets (children like to learn poetry) may be got by heart as a sort of game. For an orator has a special need for a good memory (as I shall mention when the time comes),[3] and memory develops and grows strong by practice. At the age of which we are now speaking, when children have almost no power of original thought, memory is almost the only faculty which can be enhanced by teaching. *37* It will be appropriate to demand of young children, for the sake of better pronunciation and more distinct speech, that they reel off as fast as they can a string of nouns and lines hand-picked for difficulty, made up of polysyllables that go harshly and unevenly together; these the Greeks call "tongue-twisters." It is a minor matter, but if it is neglected many an error in pronunciation, unless it is rooted out in early years, persists into after life as an incurable quirk.

## II. Is SCHOOL PREFERABLE TO PRIVATE TUTORING?

*1* But let us suppose our pupil has gradually begun to grow up, leave the apron strings, and take his schooling seriously. This then is the best place to treat the question whether it is more practical to confine the student within the walls of his own home or to send him to a large school and so-called "public" instructors. *2* I note that the most eminent authorities,[4] and those who have been responsible for the moral tone of the most famous cities,[5] have preferred the latter course. But there is no blinking the fact that a number of authorities dissent from "public" schooling for private reasons. The lines of reasoning that they follow are mainly two: (1) it is better for the pupil's morals to avoid a crowd of people at an age which is especially given to vice. I should like to deny, but cannot, the allegation that immoral acts have often resulted from these contacts. (2) Regardless of the teacher, he is

likely to be more prodigal of his time with one pupil than if he has to share it with many. *3* The first argument is a very serious one. For if it were an established fact that schools, while increasing knowledge, undermine morality, I should make the moral life a more important consideration even than speaking superlatively well. But, at any rate in my view, the two are inseparably linked. For in my judgment it is not even possible to be an orator unless you are a good man, and if it were possible I should not want it so. This point first, then.

*4* The opposition thinks that morals are corrupted in schools; this may sometimes happen, but it happens at home as well, as many examples prove, of reputations both damaged and held inviolate in both places. Whether one or the other happens depends entirely on the individual nature and training of the pupil. Given a mind easily tempted, given a careless and unobservant upbringing at the age when chastity first becomes important, then privacy will provide plenty of opportunity for wrongdoing. For the household tutor can be immoral, too, and it is just as risky to associate with bad slaves as with immoral freemen. *5* But if the pupil's character is sound, if the parents are not blind, shiftless, and lulled into a false security, then a tutor can be chosen of the most upright life (and sensible parents will be especially careful about this), discipline can be extremely strict, and besides, a serious-minded and mature friend or a faithful freedman can be assigned as bodyguard to the child, whose constant companionship may even improve the morals of those who caused the worry in the first place.

*6* This worry is easily removed. I could wish that we were not ourselves often the ruination of our children's character. Before they can talk we begin to spoil them. That flabby upbringing which we call "indulgence," weakens all the sinews of mind and body. What will be the limit of his lust when he is grown, if his very creeping is done upon purple? Though he has not yet spoken his first word, he already recognizes the cook and insists upon oysters. *7* We train their taste before we train their morals. They spend all their time in their baby-carriages; if their feet touch the ground, there is someone to hold their hand on either side. We are delighted if they say something off-color. Words that we would not take even from a favorite Alexandrian slave-boy are greeted with a laugh and a kiss.[6] No wonder: we are their teachers; it was from us they heard it. *8* They see our concubines and our catamites; every dinner party echoes with smutty songs; they have in full view scenes too shameful to mention. Thus habit is formed and becomes a part of their personality. The unfortunate children learn vice before they recognize it; wishy-washy and effete, they do not contract these diseases at school; they actually bring them there.

*9* Now for the objection that if a master has only one pupil, he will have more time for him. First of all, there is nothing to prevent our hypothetical tutor from spending time with the boy out of school hours. But even if the two methods could not be combined, I should still prefer the full daylight of a well-conducted school room to the hole-in-corner privacy of tutoring. For every first-rate instructor likes a large class and thinks he ought to have a larger lecture-room, *10* but usually poorer teachers, aware of their own limitations, do not think it beneath them to attach themselves to a single pupil and do what is essentially a footman's job. *11* But suppose a person has enough pull, income, or connections to acquire the world's best scholar as a private tutor. Is such a man likely to spend the whole day on a single pupil? Or can any student concentrate so steadily that his mind does not get tired, as his eyes do, from constant application? Especially since study requires that the student spend most of his time on his own. *12* The instructor does not look over the pupil's shoulder while he is writing, committing to memory, or thinking. When a student is concentrating, interruption by anybody, no matter who, is a nuisance. Furthermore, not every reading assignment requires someone to go over it first and interpret it. For in that case how would the student ever get all his authors read? Only a short time, then, is required to get the pupil's day's work organized. *13* Even when individual assignments have to be made, many can be dealt with in a few minutes. Many subjects are of such a nature that they can be taught to all the students at once by a single lecturer, to say nothing of outlines of themes and set speeches by professors of rhetoric, in which the class may be of any size, since each member still receives the full benefit. *14* At a banquet, the less food there is

the fewer are fed, but this does not apply to the lecturer's voice, which, like the sun, is single but pours forth light and heat for all. The same applies to secondary school teachers. Whether their subject is theory of grammar, explanation of difficulties, notes on the text, or higher criticism, no matter how many are in the class, they all will learn. *15* It may be argued that when individual mistakes are to be corrected, or an assignment read aloud, large numbers are an obstacle. They may be unwieldy (what method is universally satisfactory?) but I shall soon come to the contrast of the merits with the defects. Still I do not want the boy sent where he may be neglected. But a good instructor will not take on a larger teaching load than he can handle; and we must take great pains to make him a personal friend, to whom teaching is not a chore but a passion. *16* In that way no class will ever be overcrowded. Of course no teacher with even a smattering of culture will fail to give special attention to a pupil in whom he spots enthusiasms and talent, for such students reflect credit upon him. But even granted that large schools are to be avoided (and I do not even grant this, if the size is a reflection of good teaching), still that does not mean that schools are to be avoided altogether. Boycott is one thing, selection is another.

*17* If this is an adequate refutation, let me now set forth my own viewpoint. *18* It is of the first importance that the orator-to-be, who must pass his life surrounded by people and in the full glare of politics, should get used even from his earliest years to not being shy nor acquiring a scholar's pallor from a sheltered and solitary life. His mind needs stimulation and drawing out of itself, but in retirement it either goes soft and musty like something left in the dark, or at the other extreme grows puffed up with empty self-conceit, for the man with no standard of comparison will invariably give himself too much credit. *19* Then when the results of his study have to be given to the public, he gropes in clear light and stumbles over everything new, as is natural in one who has learned in solitude what has to be put into practice in public. *20* I say nothing of the friendships made at school, which last quite unbroken to old age and have an almost religious sanctity about them. Being initiated into the mysteries of education has about it the same spiritual quality as being initiated into the mysteries of religion. Where will the student learn sympathetic human relations when he has cut himself off from the associations natural to human beings and to dumb animals as well? *21* Besides, at home he can learn only what is taught to him; at school he can learn also what is taught to others. Every day he will hear much praise and much criticism; he will profit from hearing laziness rebuked and hard work commended. *22* Approbation will rouse his competitive instinct; he will consider it a disgrace to be beaten by a classmate, but a fine thing to beat out an upperclassman All this sharpens the mind, and, though ambition may be a vice, still it is often the stimulus to virtue. *23* I know that my own teachers' device was a practical one: when they divided the boys into classes, they made them speak in the order of their marks, so that a boy's place in the program indicated the progress he had made. *24* The order was the result of a previous trial. We competed keenly to get on this list, but to lead the class was the finest prize of all. But this post was not assigned once and for all; every month the losers had a chance to try again. Thus the winner's success did not go to his head, and the loser's disappointment was an incentive to remove the stigma. *25* I would wager that as far as I can remember this practice did more to kindle the flame of oratorical ambition than all the fight-talks by our teachers, the watchful eye of our footmen, or our parents' fond hopes. *26* But just as competition with their professors favors progress in advanced students, so for beginners, still of tender years, it is more fun to imitate their classmates than the teacher, precisely because it is easier. For elementary pupils will hardly dare to compete on the same basis with what they regard as polished eloquence; rather they will seek their own level, like a vine trained on a tree, which by first twining about the lower branches finally emerges at the top. *27* This is so true that it is the teacher's own job, at any rate if he puts practical considerations before his own ambitions, to bear in mind that he is dealing with minds not yet fully developed, and so must not overburden the immaturity of his pupils, but should dilute his mixture, as it were, and come down to the level of his audience. *28* A small-mouthed bottle will take only so much liquid poured into it at once,

but it can be filled if you pour gradually or even drop by drop: boys' mental capacity should be estimated in the same way.[7] For what is over their heads will not penetrate their minds, which are as it were not open wide enough to take it in. *29* It is a practical advantage, therefore, for a boy to have classmates, whom he will want first to imitate and then to surpass. This will gradually inculcate also the hope of higher things. To this let me add that the instructors themselves cannot work up the same keenness and enthusiasm in lecturing to individuals as they can under the well-known inspiration of a larger audience. *30* For eloquence is over 50 per cent state of mind, which must be set in motion, put the imagination to work, and adjust itself to the nature of the subject under discussion. Moreover, the nobler and more exalted it is, the greater the forces that move it; so it thrives on praise, is developed by exercise, and rejoices in glorious action. *31* Though one may not put the feeling in words, one scorns to put the oratorical ability so painstakingly acquired to the service of a single listener; one is ashamed to raise the voice above the level of ordinary conversation. Imagine a teacher assuming the manner, voice, gait, accent, gestures, and figures of speech of an orator or declaimer, to say nothing of his toil and sweat, all for the sake of a single listener! Why, he would seem little better than a madman. There would be no such thing in the world as eloquence, if we simply talked with people one at a time.

### III. BOY NATURE: SOME HINTS TO THE TEACHER

*1* When a boy is entrusted to his care, an experienced teacher will first of all make inquiry into his talent and his character. The best index to intelligence in small children is their memory. Its qualities are twofold: quick grasp and faithful retention. Next comes ability to imitate, also the sign of a teachable nature; but the child must imitate what he is taught, and not some idiosyncrasy of bearing or gait, or some failing that he happens to notice in someone. *2* I get no impression of promise from a child who likes to make fun of people just for laughs. For a boy of real talent will be a good boy as well; if not, I would rather have a boy slow-witted than naughty. Now a good boy is quite different from a lazy or an indolent one. *3* My hypothetical ideal student will learn easily, and will even ask questions, but he will follow his teacher, not run ahead of him. It is no accident that the precocious type never is really productive. *4* Precocious children do small things easily, grow bold at their progress, and are quick to show off their petty talents, which are extremely superficial; they can recite a string of words without the slightest stage fright or any modest restraint. They have not much to offer, but they are quick. *5* There is no real basis of strength, and what they have is not deep-rooted; they are like seed scattered on the surface of the ground, which grows too fast; the little shoots look like the full ear of grain, but the kernels are empty, and turn yellow before the harvest. One's satisfaction with them proceeds from considering how young they are, but then their progress stops, and admiration wanes.

*6* When he has assessed his pupil's character, the teacher should next consider how to handle his mind. Some students are slack unless you keep after them, others do not take kindly to discipline; intimidation keeps some in line, while it makes others nervous; steady application hammers some into shape, a quick attack on a problem does more for others. *7* Give me the boy who is spurred on by praise, benefited by success, and moved to tears by failure. He will feed on his own ambition, be cut to the quick by criticism, be stimulated by honors, and in him I will never worry about laziness.

*8* Every student ought to have some relaxation. In the first place, there is no such thing in nature as a perpetual-motion machine, and even tools, unintelligent and inanimate as they are, if they are to preserve their properties, need to relax their tension with intervals of rest; but, more important, study is a matter of will power, and that cannot be forced. *9* And so students who are fresh and rested will tackle their work with more energy, but against compulsion the mind is likely to rebel. *10* I like to see boys play; it is a sign of mental alertness; and I would never expect a boy who is always gloomy and depressed to prick up his ears with eagerness for study, if he lacks the drive which is natural to boys of his age. *11* But there must be a limit to relaxation for fear that a holiday refused will breed hatred of studies, or too long a vacation make idleness a habit. There are even a number of games which are handy for sharpening boys' wits, as for instance when they fire childish questions at one another and compete in answering. Character, too, reveals itself more openly in play. *12* But the teacher must realize that no child is so immature that he cannot readily [even in play] learn the difference between right and wrong; character is best formed while the child is still innocent of guile and still malleable in the hands of his teachers. A character of hardened depravity will break before it will submit to correction. *13* A boy ought early to be cautioned to unselfishness, honesty, and self-control; Vergil's line [*Georgics*, II, 272] must constantly be borne in mind: "Great is the force of habit in the young."

I am definitely opposed to corporal punishment, though it is the general practice and Chrysippus does not condemn it. In the first place, it is an ugly practice, fit only for slaves. *14* It is certainly insulting, which is an appropriate argument if you apply it to a later age. Secondly, if a boy's mind is so boorish that scolding does not set it right, it will simply grow hardened to the blows, like an incorrigible slave; finally, there will be no need for this form of punishment, if an unflagging taskmaster stands always at the boy's side. *15* As it is, we seem to make up for the footmen's neglect, not by forcing the boy to do what is right, but by punishing him when he has done wrong. Finally, when you have whipped your pupil as a youngster, what are you going to do with him when he is no longer subject to this discipline and yet has harder tasks to do? *16* Besides, when a boy is whipped, pain and fear cause accidents which are unpleasant to mention, and a source of shame in later life. This shame breaks and depresses the spirit, and makes the boy thoroughly antisocial. *17* And if too little trouble has been taken in choosing footmen and tutors of good character, I am ashamed to say how indecently perverts may take advantage of their licence to administer corporal punishment, or how often the poor schoolboy's terror may give opportunity to others. I will not labor this point; I have done more than enough if I have made myself understood. So let me say this and have done; children cannot defend themselves and are easily imposed on, and so no one should have unbridled power over them. *18* I will now begin to speak of the necessary courses of instruction for a boy who is to become an orator, and the age at which each subject should be taken up.

## IV. LITERATURE

*1* As soon as the pupil has learned to read and write, it is time for the secondary school teacher. What I have to say applies equally to Greek and Latin, though I prefer that the student start with Greek. In either language the method is the same. *2* Now though this profession may be summarily divided into two parts, the science of correct speech and the expounding of the poets, it is like a property which is deeper than its frontage indicates. *3* For right method in speech is connected with right method in writing, correct reading comes before expounding of texts, and critical judgment is involved in all these procedures. Indeed professors of literature in the old days carried criticism so far that, not content with marking some lines as spurious and ejecting some books with false titles from the family of literature as though they were foundlings, they drew up canons of authors [8] from which they omitted some names altogether. *4* And it is not enough to have read the poets; one must ransack all sorts of authors, not only for content but for style, which often derives its authority from the authors who use it. Again, literature, which has to do with rhythms and meters, cannot be complete without music, and a teacher ignorant of astronomy cannot understand the poets, who (other considerations aside) so often use the rising and the setting of the constellations in establishing the time of the action; and he cannot afford to be unacquainted with philosophy, both on account of the number of passages in almost every poet which are based on an intimate and detailed knowledge of physics, and because of Empedocles in Greek, and Varro and Lucretius in Latin, who have turned philosophy into verse. *5* There is need also of no mean oratorical ability in order to speak appropriately and at length on each of the topics I have mentioned. Therefore those who carp at the study of literature as trivial and inadequate ought all the less to be tolerated, since unless literature well and truly lays the foundations of the orator-to-be, whatever is built upon it will fall to the ground; literature is indispensable to childhood, pleasant to old age; it is the sweet partner of our privacy, and is the only subject in the curriculum with more gold than glitter.

[The rest of Book I deals with details of grammatical instruction. The last chapter, translated below, discusses the question whether the student should pursue several subjects at once or take them up one at a time.]

## XII. CAN BOYS STUDY A NUMBER OF SUBJECTS AT ONCE?

*1* I am frequently asked whether, even granted all these subjects ought to be studied, they can all be taught and grasped at the same time. Some say no, on the ground that the mind is mixed up and worn out by so many courses with such different points of view, which overload the mind, the body, and the timetable, and that even though mature students can endure this, the years of childhood ought not to be overburdened. *2* But these critics are not keenly enough aware of the natural power of human intelligence, which is so quick, nimble, and perfectly adaptable, that it is impossible for it to do only one thing at a time; it expends its energy upon more than one object, not only on the same day, but even at the same instant. *3* Do not players upon stringed instruments use, at the same time, their memories and the tone and modulations of their voices, while their right hand runs over their strings, and their left plucks, stops, or mutes the strings, and not even their foot is idle, but beats time—and all simultaneously? *4* Again, when we are caught unprepared and have to plead a case on the spur of the moment, do we not say one thing while we are thinking ahead to another, while a plan of argument, choice of words, organization, gestures, diction, expression, and bodily movements are all demanded of us at once? But if, as it were, under the stress of a single effort of will, such different faculties all obey us at once, why should we not divide our time among various interests? Why, the variety itself tends to refresh and reinvigorate the mind, whereas it is considerably harder to keep continually at a single job. Hence reading gives the pen a rest, and when reading itself becomes boring, a change of subject supplies relief. *5* However many irons we have in the fire, we are still somehow refreshed by any new beginning. How can the keen edge of attention help being blunted if a student must endure a single teacher of any subject, no matter what, all day long? A change of subject will revive us like a change of diet, which by varying the menu stimulates the digestion and makes it less finicky. *6* If there is any other method of learning, let my opponents state it to me. If we first dance attendance exclusively upon the teacher of literature, and then upon geometry, we should forget in the interval what we had learned before; if we should go next to the music master, our previous studies would fall by the wayside; and, while we were studying Latin literature, we would not keep up with Greek. To make a long story short, should we work at nothing but the last subject we studied? *7* Why do we not give the same advice to farmers: not to cultivate fields and vineyards at the same time, nor olive grove and orchard; not to adjust their working days to the needs of meadow, cattle, garden, bees, and poultry? Why do we professional men divide our time every day among duties in court, the demands of our friends, our household accounts, physical exercise, and even recreation? Any one of these occupations, pursued without let-up, would tire us out. This will show how much easier it is to do many jobs than to stick to one.

*8* That our pupils might not bear up well under the weight of their studies ought to be the least of our worries. As a matter of fact, no time of life is less subject to fatigue than theirs. This may seem remarkable, but try it and see. *9* One reason for their tirelessness is that their minds are more teachable before they get set in their ways. What clinches the argument is the obvious fact that within two years of the time when a child begins to form words correctly it can, no matter how little encouragement it gets, pronounce nearly every word in the language, yet what a hard time our new slaves have with colloquial Latin! You would appreciate this if you tried to teach an adult to read: how right people are who say of a man who is good at his job, "He's been doing it since he was knee-high to a grasshopper!" *10* Children naturally take to school work better than adolescents. When children fall down, as they do so often, they are not so badly hurt, and they are not so worn out by crawling on their hands and knees, nor, a little later on, by their constant running and playing from dawn

till dark, because they are not very heavy and so are not dragged down by their own weight; in the same way their minds, I think, do not tire as easily as grown-ups', because it takes less effort to get them started, and, besides, they do not embark upon their studies on their own incentive but simply hand themselves over to the teacher to be educated. *11* Besides, another advantage of their youth is that they obey instructions more single-mindedly, and do not measure their distance from the goal. Indeed they still cannot even judge how hard an assignment is. In fact, as my own experience has repeatedly shown, being aware that exertion is needed tells on us more than the exertion itself.

*12* The time element enters in also; students will never have more of it than when they are children, because then they make most progress by listening to the teacher. When a boy graduates to writing, when he has to make something up himself and compose it, he will have neither leisure nor inclination for purely literary studies. *13* Therefore since the teacher of literature cannot and should not take up the whole day, lest boredom breed aversion to study, on what subjects shall we set our student to work, to occupy, as it were, his odds and ends of time? *14* I do not want to spread the student too thin: I would not make a composer of him, nor does he need to be able to take down a tune in musical notation; he need not explore the most specialized levels of geometry, and I do not want his diction to be like a play-actor's, nor his gestures to be like a ballet-dancer's, though even if I required all this, there would still be time. A long time is spent in school, and I am not talking about dunces. *15* Finally, why, [unless all these subjects are valuable] which I think ought to be in the curriculum of the orator-to-be, did Plato take the trouble to shine in them? Not content with the range which Athens had to offer, nor with the Pythagoreans, whom he made the object of a special trip overseas to Italy, he also visited the priests of Egypt and thoroughly learned their lore.

*16* Using the plea of difficulty as a pretext, we make it stand sponsor for our laziness. For we do not love our work, and we do not aim at eloquence for its own sake because it is honorable and the fairest of the professions. We strip for action because there is profit in it, for the sake of the sordid gain. *17* Many make an income at the bar without these talents, but if income is all that matters, the huckster is richer, and the auctioneer's voice is his fortune. And I do not even want a reader for my book, if he is going to calculate how much profit there is for him in these studies. *18* But the man who by God's good grace can imagine what true eloquence is like, the man who, to quote no mean tragic poet,[9] sets oratory before him as the queen of the arts, and seeks his reward not in the lawyer's fee but in the wisdom and activity of his own mind—a reward that never fails and does not depend upon mere chance—such a man will easily persuade himself to spend his time, not in shows or circuses or gambling or idle conversation, to say nothing of frittering away precious hours in sleep or dinner parties; rather he will devote himself to geometry and music, and will derive far more pleasure from it than from those other pastimes so unworthy of a scholar. *19* The capacity to enjoy the things of the mind is the gift of Providence to man. But it is this very enjoyment that has carried me away in too long a digression. Enough, then, on the subjects a boy should study before he begins to specialize; the next book will make a fresh start, and pass to the duties of the professor of rhetoric.

### *From* Book II

[The first chapter of Book II advocates beginning rhetoric early, and dividing the instruction in its first stages with the teacher of literature; chapter II, translated below, discusses the qualifications of the ideal teacher, and his proper relation to his pupils.]

#### II. THE IDEAL TEACHER

*1* When the boy has developed his powers of application to the point where his mind can grasp what we have called the elements of rhetoric, he should be sent to the professors of this subject. It will be of the first importance for us to look into their character. *2* I take up the treatment of this subject precisely here, not because I underestimate the importance of such investigations in the case of other teachers—as Book I has shown—but because the pupil's time of life makes it more necessary to mention it. *3* For boys are usually almost full grown when they are promoted to these instructors, and they

continue with them even after they have become young men; and therefore greater care has to be taken at this level, so that the respect which the teacher inspires may keep the younger students from harm, while his influence keeps flaming youth within bounds. *4* And it is not enough for him to set an example of complete restraint, unless by strict discipline he makes his pupils' character match his own.

First of all, then, he should assume the attitude of a father toward his pupils, and should consider that he has assumed the place of those who have entrusted their children to his care. *5* He should neither have vices of his own nor tolerate them in others. When he is on his dignity he should not be stand-offish; when he meets his pupils socially he should not be servile, so that he will not be hated for the one attitude and despised for the other. His main subject of conversation should be good and upright conduct; for the more cautionary tales he tells, the less punishing he will have to do. He should not fly off the handle; on the other hand he should not be one to mince words when there is a fault that needs correction; he should be straightforward in his teaching; capable of hard work; persevering, but not to excess. *6* When his students put questions, he should give willing answers; if no questions are put, he should ask them himself. He should neither stint his praise of student recitations nor be lavish with it; for if he stints, the students get bored; if he is lavish, overconfident. *7* When he corrects mistakes, he must not be carping, and above all not insulting; for teachers who criticize their pupils as though they hated them discourage many good intentions. *8* Besides criticizing his pupil's speeches, he should himself discourse at length every day, giving his listeners something to take away with them. For however many examples to follow the assigned reading supplies, there is more meat in the so-called *viva voce* instruction, especially if it comes from a teacher whom the pupils, provided only they have been properly brought up, both love and venerate. It is impossible to overemphasize how much readier we are to imitate a person of whom we are fond.

*9* The prevailing practice of allowing students to leap from their seats and jump up and down by way of applause is an excess which should be strictly forbidden. Even young men should applaud a speech with reserve. Then the proper result will follow, that the pupil depends upon his teacher's judgment and derives from his master's praise the conviction that he has spoken well. *10* The most vicious practice of all is what is now called "manners," which means indiscriminate praise of every speech in turn. This is in bad taste, theatrical, and out of keeping with proper school discipline, and specifically, it is the worst enemy of real scholarship. For painstaking hard work seems to be a complete waste of time if every random effusion gets its meed of praise. *11* The pupils in the audience should keep as careful an eye as the speaker on the instructor's expression; in that way they will learn to be discriminating in their approval and disapproval; for just as writing builds style, so listening fosters critical ability. *12* But as it is, the boys are poised ready for the spring; at the end of every sentence they do not merely rise to applaud; they actually run to the front of the room with loud and unseemly shouts of congratulation. They agree beforehand to do this for each other, and the fate of the speech depends on it. As a result, they grow swelled-headed and complacent without reason, to the point where, puffed up as they are by the noisy applause of their classmates, they hold it against their teacher if he praises them too little. *13* But this applies to teachers too, whose wish should be for an attentive and sober hearing; for the master should not speak to please his students, but the other way round. Actually, if possible, he should note with special attention the content and the basis of each student's approval, and his pleasure at his success should rise no more from his own sense of self-satisfaction than from seeing his pupils use sound critical judgment.

*14* I do not approve of a seating plan which mixes children with adolescents in a class. For even if the sort of man who ought to be in charge of curriculum and character can keep boys in their teens under control, the immature should still be separated from the more developed, so as to avoid not only the charge of vice, but even the suspicion of it. *15* I thought I ought to make brief mention of this, though I thought it unnecessary to lay down the law that both teacher and school should be free of the coarser vices. And if any parent overlooks obvious moral defects in choosing a teacher for his son, I warn

him that if he shirks this part of his duty, all the rest of my program to improve the youth is wasted on him.

[In chapters III to VIII, Quintilian discusses the early stages of education in rhetoric. The best teachers, he says, should be used early, and should help their students with the elementary exercises, including simple narrative, proof and refutation; praise and blame, commonplaces, and fictitious declamations, remembering always that different methods suit different pupils. In chapter IX, translated below, Quintilian enlarges on his statement in chapter II that teachers should stand to their students *in loco parentis*.]

IX. THE TEACHER AS THE PARENT OF THE MIND

*1* Much as I have said about the teacher's duty, I have for the moment only one piece of advice for students: "Love your instructors just as you love your studies, and think of them as your parents, not indeed in the physical but in the intellectual sense." *2* Such a feeling of loyalty will contribute a great deal to their studies; it means they will be willing listeners, will believe what they hear, want to be like the teacher, come to school cheerfully on time, not sulk at being corrected, beam at praise, and compete enthusiastically to be first in their master's affections. *3* The teacher's job is to teach, the student's to prove himself teachable; neither can get on without the other. Both parents contribute to the birth of a child; seed is sown in vain unless the furrow has been prepared to receive and protect it; in the same way eloquence cannot wax strong unless he who imparts it and he who receives it come together in harmony.

[The rest of Book II is devoted to rhetoric in general: its rules, its subdivisions, various definitions, its utility, its place among the virtues, the materials with which it works, which are the subject matter of what we should call a "liberal" education. This is a transition to Book X, which deals with what to read and how to write, but first Quintilian devotes seven highly technical books (III–IX) to the preparation, arrangement, and delivery of a speech. Of these the most interesting section to the general reader, and the most moving passage in the whole work, is the prologue to Book VI, translated below, in which the author mourns the death of his young wife and two boys.]

## *From* Book VI

PROLOGUE: THE LAMENT OF A HUSBAND AND
FATHER

*1* My book, Marcellus Victorius, begun at your
express wish, continued in the hope that I might
be of some practical use to young men of good
family, I have worked hard on lately as if it were
almost a requirement of my tutorship; but it was
pleasure as well as work, for I had a son who
showed promise well worth a father's earnest attention, and I had hoped to leave him this book
as the best part of his heritage, so that if, as
was right and desirable, I died before him, he
could still have the benefit of his father's teaching
through the book. *2* But as I was working away at
it day and night and hurrying for fear I would
not live to finish, fate suddenly dealt me so
crushing a blow that there is no one who has less
personal interest in the fruits of my labor than
I have myself. For the wound of bereavement has
been reopened, and I have lost the son for whom
I had made such plans, the sole prop of my old
age. *3* What shall I do now, or how can I believe
myself of any use to anyone, since the gods are
against me? For, as it happens, I had just begun
to write my previous book, *On the Causes of
Decadence in Oratory*, when I was struck down by
a blow of the same kind. Surely then it would
have been better to throw that unlucky book, and
every other product of my ill-starred pen, on the
untimely pyre to be consumed by the flames that
are to burn what I hold dearest in life, and not
to burden with any further labor an existence
accursed by the gods. *4* For what good parent
would forgive me if I am able to go on studying?
Or not despise my obstinacy if I use my voice for
anything else but to reproach the gods for leaving
me the sole survivor of my family? Let me bear
witness that no Providence looks upon this
earth, not so much because *I* have suffered, for
I have no complaint to make except that I am
alive; it is *their* sufferings I complain of, who
in their innocence were doomed to an untimely
death. The first to be taken from me was the
mother of my boys, who, though she was not yet
nineteen, died happy, though it was far too soon
for her to die, because she had brought into the
world two sons. *5* This blow alone was so crushing that no good fortune could ever again make

me happy. For she had every womanly virtue,
and her death brought her husband inconsolable
sorrow, especially because she was so young,
particularly in comparison with me, so that I
grieved for her as for a daughter. *6* Yet her children survived her, and—a rank injustice, but it
was what she wished—so did I. And she escaped the height of suffering by the shortest way.
My younger son, who was just going on six, was
the first of the two to pass away. *7* I have no
wish to parade my troubles, or to make the reasons for my mourning greater than they are; I
wish I had the means to make them less. But how
can I forget the charm that was in his face, his
pleasant voice, his little flashes of wit, the quality
of his calm and almost unbelievably lofty mind?
Even in someone else's child it would have earned
my affection. *8* It was a freak of fate, which added
to my suffering, that he used to throw his little
arms around my neck and love me better than
his nurses, his grandmother with whom he lived,
or any other persons who watch over children of
that age. And therefore I was glad to bear the
sorrow that had been mine a few months before
at the death of his mother, that best of women,
who far exceeds our praise. For I had less cause
for grief on my own account than for joy that she
was spared it. *9* All my hope and joy thereafter
was centered in my little Quintilian, and he might
well console me. For his talent was not merely
in bud, like my younger son's; he was going on
ten, and his education had already shown clear
and unmistakable signs of bearing good fruit.
*10* I take to witness my own grief, my broken
heart, the shades of my loved ones, the symbols
of my grief, that I saw in him qualities of mind
unsurpassed in all my wide experience, and not
in comprehension of his studies only, though
he never had to be made to work, as his teachers
know. He was as well the soul of honor, a dutiful
son, full of human sympathy, a perfect little
gentleman. I should have had a foreboding that
the thunderbolt would strike, for it is well known
that precocious children die young, and that there
exists a mysterious cosmic jealousy that nips such
promise in the bud, for fear, I suppose, that our
happiness should exceed the lot of man.[10] *11* Fate
had even granted him all her random gifts: a
clear and pleasant voice, sweetness of expression
both in Greek and in Latin (he spoke both
tongues like a native), and precise pronunciation

of every letter. But these were qualities still in the promising stage; he already had those more mature virtues, courage, dignity, strength of character in the face of fear and pain. How the doctors marvelled at the fortitude with which he faced eight months of illness! How he tried to comfort me in his last hours! As his life was fading, and he was already no longer mine, his delirious thoughts were all about his studies. *12* O son in whom my vain hopes were centered, did I see your eyes clouded in death, your spirit flee away? Did I embrace your cold pale body, and catch with my lips your last breath, and can I still breathe the breath of life? I deserve the cross I bear, I deserve the heartache. *13* Your recent adoption by a man of consular rank had given you every right to be preferred to high office; a marriage had been arranged for you with your cousin, a praetor's daughter; everyone had the highest hopes for you; as a candidate, you would have shown the keenest oratorical sense. And now your father, the sole survivor, has nothing but pain to bear. May my fortitude, if not my lust for life, make me worthy of you all the rest of my days. For it is no use blaming fate for all our sorrows. No man's long mourning is of any but his own making. *14* But I live on, and I must find some excuse for living; I must believe the wise, who find literature the one ever-present help in time of trouble. If I ever recover from the present shock, so that any thought but of my troubles can enter my head, I shall have a right to be forgiven for my delay [in publishing this book]. For who should be surprised that my studies are postponed when the wonder ought to be that they are not broken off forever? *15* If in any way my work is less effective than what I began when my sorrow was still endurable, lay it to the charge of imperious fortune, which has weakened if not destroyed whatever modest talents I may once have possessed. But I have one more reason to square my shoulders doggedly in the face of trouble: it is hard to bear, but scorning it comes easy. It can do me no further harm, and after these afflictions it has brought me a peace of mind which is a sorry thing, to be sure, but I can count on it. *16* If my critics are kindly, they will look on my work in this light. I continue it with no selfish motive. I take all my trouble with a view to profiting others, if indeed there is any

profit in anything I write. I must unfortunately bequeath to others the heritage I intended for my sons. So let it be with my book.

[In spite of Quintilian's pessimism, some of his best work is still to come, especially in Books X and XII. In Book X, chapter I, he draws up a sort of list of the "hundred best books" in Greek and Latin, to be read for the strictly practical purpose of improving the orator's vocabulary and stock of commonplaces. The list includes many of the authors translated in this anthology and contains many shrewd critical judgments in capsule form. A selection follows.]

*From* Book X

I. WHAT TO READ

*20* For a long time we must read only the best authors, the ones least likely to let us down. We must read carefully, taking almost as much pains as if we were copying it down; and it is not of parts of the work only that we must do our close reading; the book must be read all the way through, and then taken up again from the beginning, especially speeches, whose virtues are often deliberately concealed. . . . *24* The reader ought not to be too ready to believe that everything the best authors have said is in every way perfect. They slip sometimes, and stagger beneath their burden; they indulge their fancy; they sometimes relax and grow weary. Cicero thought that Demosthenes sometimes nodded; Horace thought the same of Homer himself. *25* For though they are the best, they are still men, and those who elevate whatever they find in them into a law of language may imitate the inferior parts (which is quite easy) and congratulate themselves that they are fair copies, if they succeed in imitating the shortcomings of the great. *26* Still, critical judgments about men as important as these should be made with balance and breadth of view; otherwise we may fall into the common error of condemning what we do not understand. But if the reader must miss the mean one way or the other, I should rather have him indiscriminate in his likes than in his dislikes.

*Poetry in general*

*27* Theophrastus says that reading the poets contributes a great deal to the orator, and many agree with him, not without reason. For the poets have what the orator wants: sublimity of content, loftiness of style, power to play on our heartstrings, propriety in character-drawing, and—a matter of prime importance—minds jaded by daily pleading in the courts derive their ideal refreshment from the honeyed words of poetry. This is why Cicero thinks that this sort of reading should provide recreation. *28* We should bear in mind, however, that the orator should not go the whole way with the poet. Poetic licence, either in vocabulary or in figures of speech, is not for him; it is a type of literature invented for show, and it aims, besides, at entertainment only, seeking its ends by fictions not merely untrue to life but even in some cases quite beyond belief. Poetry depends also on another device [which is not for the orator]. *29* Bound by the fixed requirements of his metre, the poet cannot always use the appropriate turn of phrase; instead he is driven off the highroad and must take refuge in the byways of the language, being forced not only to change one word for another, but to lengthen them, shorten them, reverse them, or split them in two. But the orator must stand armed to the teeth in the front line, struggle for the highest stakes, and strive for victory. *30* Therefore I would not have him in rusty or mildewed armor; it should have a natural and fearsome sheen, like steel, to dazzle both mind and eye, not like gold and silver which are non-combatant dress and oftener than not dangerous to the wearer.

### History

*31* History also can nourish the orator with its rich and pleasant infusion, but we must read it, too, with the full realization that many of its virtues must be avoided by the orator. History is closely related to poetry and is a sort of prose poem; it is written to tell a story, not to prove a point; the whole work is composed not for a current case or a modern lawsuit but for posterity to remember, and to enhance the author's reputation; and therefore it avoids monotony in its story by the use of highly archaic and figurative language. *32* And so, as I have said, we who must deal with absent-minded and often uneducated jurors ought not for instance to adopt the famous terseness of Sallust, which is ideal for undivided attention of a cultured listener; again

the creamy richness of Livy is not sufficiently informative for the man who is looking not for charm but for credibility in the exposition.

[But history supplies the orator with material useful for digressions.] . . . *34* And it has another value, a very important one, though irrelevant to our present purpose: it gives a knowledge of the past and a stock of precedents which the orator cannot afford to be without, since otherwise he must depend for the proof of all his points on his client's depositions. He should derive most of his arguments-from-analogy out of a carefully acquired knowledge of the past; such arguments are the more effective for being peculiarly free from the bias or the odium of the case in hand.

### Philosophy

*35* Granted that the reading of the philosophers ought to be of much service to us, this is a state of affairs for which the orators themselves are responsible, for having let the philosophers take over the best part of their own field. For the bulk of their speeches, and their sharpest arguments, involve justice, honor, expediency, and their opposites, as well as matters of religion; and for arguing at the bar and cross-examination the orator-to-be can prepare himself no better than by reading the Socratics. *36* But here, too the same sort of discrimination must be used as in the other cases; otherwise we fail to recognize that even though the subject matter is the same, a lawsuit is not a philosophical dialogue, a courtroom is not a lecture hall, a moral maxim is not a matter of life and death.

*37* Most readers, I think, will insist that, in view of the practical importance I attach to reading, I append a list of authors and their chief merits. But to list them all individually would be a never-ending task. . . . *39* The safest course was that followed by Livy in his letter to his son: "First read Demosthenes and Cicero, and then, whoever most resembles Demosthenes and Cicero." *40* Still, I have no right to keep from the public a summary of my own views. In my opinion there is hardly to be found a single author who has stood the test of time, from whom a critical reader will not derive some profit. Cicero even admits that he got most help from the oldest authors of all, who were men of sense, though they lacked polish. My own opinion of modern authors is not far different. *41* For how many can be found so witless as not to have the slightest confidence that posterity will remember any part of their work? But if there are any such, the fact can be detected within the first few lines, and we can take our leave of the book before sampling it has wasted too much of our time. *42* But a book which has a bearing on one branch of knowledge or another may not be readily adaptable to use for forming style, which is our present concern.

But before I take up the authors one by one, I ought to say a word or two in general about differences of critical opinion. *43* Some think only ancient authors worth reading, maintaining that no others have any innate eloquence or manly vigor; others revel in the excesses of modern style, dedicated entirely to pampering the uncritical mob. *44* Even among those who want to follow an orthodox oratorical fashion some hold that the succinct and simple colloquial style is the only sensible and genuine "Attic" one; others vote for the more elevated, rousing and spirited style, which gives more scope to the mental powers; there is even no small number who favors the smooth and polished composite style. I shall go into more detail on the differences between them, when I discuss kinds of style.[11] Meantime I shall touch briefly on what should be read, and why, by those who want to develop their powers of speech. *45* I intend to select only a few authors, but those the most illustrious. Students can easily make their own selections of authors who most resemble these; so that no one should grumble that his special favorites happen to have been omitted. For I admit that more ought to be read than those I specifically mention.

But now I proceed to the actual types of reading which I think especially suitable for those who aim to become orators.

### Greek poetry

*46* Therefore, as Aratus[12] thinks "we ought to begin with Jupiter," so it seems fitting and proper that I should begin with Homer. For we may say of him what he has said[13] of Ocean, that every stream and spring has its source therein; for every branch of rhetoric he sets the pattern, he is the source. Surely he has not his

equal for sublimity in a major key, or simplicity in a minor one. He is at once flowery and terse, grave and gay, equally remarkable for his fullness and for his brevity; he excels as orator *and* as poet. *47* To say nothing of the examples in his work of praise, exhortation, and consolation, do not Book IX—the embassy sent to Achilles, Book I—the strife of kings, and Book II—the council of war, set forth all the rules for legal and political oratory? *48* As for the emotions, whether mild or violent, the veriest ignoramus will admit that the Master can manipulate them as he will. And further, the invocations to the *Iliad* and the *Odyssey*, in a minimum number of lines, do not merely observe the rules for introductions; they lay them down once and for all. For by his invocation of the goddesses believed to have poets in their charge, he wins over his audience; by setting forth the greatness of his theme, he fixes their attention; and by giving a quickly-grasped summary, he holds them in the palm of his hand. *49* In exposition who can be more succinct than the messenger of Patroclus' death,[14] or more graphic than he who tells of the battle between the Curetes and the Aetolians?[15] His similes, enlargements upon themes, citation of precedents, digressions, evidences of fact, and inferences, and methods of proof and refutation are so numerous that even the textbook writers, by and large, borrow from this poet their examples of these devices. *50* In peroration who will ever be able to equal the prayer of Priam to Achilles?[16] Again, in vocabulary, aphorisms, figures of speech, and arrangement of a work as a whole, does he not pass the bounds of mere mortal intelligence? It follows that it is a sign of greatness, I will not say to imitate his merits, for that is impossible, but even to come to critical conclusions about them. *51* But he has unquestionably left all his rivals in every field of rhetoric far behind, especially the epic poets, in whose case the contrast is most striking because the material is the same. . . .

*55* Theocritus is admirable in his field, but his rustic and pastoral Muse shyly avoids cities in general, to say nothing of the forum. . . .

*61* Of the nine lyric poets, Pindar is far and away the chief because of the splendor of his inspiration, his maxims, his figures of speech, his boundless store of subjects and of language: he is a veritable flood of eloquence, and for all these reasons Horace quite properly thought that no one could equal him. . . .

63 Alcaeus in some of his work deserves his prize of a golden quill,[17] when he attacks the tyrants and makes himself a guide to conduct; his rhetoric is curt, lofty, painstaking, and in many ways like an orator; but he is not serious; he descends to the level of love poetry, though he is better suited to loftier themes.[18]

64 Simonides, for all his simplicity, deserves honorable mention for his *mots justes* and his charm; he is at his best in moving our pity, and some critics place him in this respect at the head of all the poets in this field.

### Greek comedy

65 Old Comedy is almost unique in retaining the famous pure grace of Attic speech. In particular, it is most eloquent in its freedom of speech, and though its forte is the indictment of vice, it is most forceful in other respects as well. For its style is lofty, polished, and charming, and I know of no other but Homer—who like Achilles is always the exception that proves the rule—which is more like oratory or better suited to the education of orators. 66 There are several masters of Old Comedy, of whom the chief are Aristophanes, Eupolis, and Cratinus.

### Greek tragedy

Aeschylus was the first to produce tragedies; he is elevated, solemn, and florid to a fault, but often uncouth and jarring; therefore the Athenians allowed more modern poets to submit his plays for competition in revised versions, and many of them in this way won the crown.

67 But Sophocles and Euripides cast the other tragedians far in the shade; there is much argument which in his own way of speaking is the better poet, a question which I shall leave open, as irrelevant to my present theme. This at least must be universally admitted, that for those who are training themselves to be trial lawyers, Euripides is of far more practical use. 68 For his style (though criticized by those who think that Sophocles' solemnity, grand manner, and ringing tones are more elevated) is closer to rhetoric; it is packed with aphorisms, and on philosophical themes he positively rivals the philosophers, and in quick debate he brooks comparison with any of the famous trial lawyers of antiquity; in ability

to appeal to the emotions he is remarkable, both generally and particularly in evoking pity, where he stands easily first. . . .

### Greek history

73 In history there have been many famous writers, but everyone agrees that there are two to be preferred far beyond the rest, who, despite their different talents, have won almost equal critical acclaim. There is Thucydides, close-packed, terse, and always in a hurry; and Herodotus, fascinating, crystal-clear, as he saunters along; the first superior in expressing violent emotion, the second relaxed; the first superior in speeches, the second in conversations; the first in vigor, the second in charm.

### Greek oratory

76 There follows a mighty company of orators; Athens alone, for instance, produced ten in a single century. Of these Demosthenes stands head and shoulders above the rest; he virtually set the standard for oratory; his style is so forceful, so packed with meaning, so sinewy, so economical, so temperate, that you find in him neither excess nor defect. 77 Aeschines is fuller and more diffuse; in him it is easy to mistake looseness for the grand style. Hyperides is remarkable for charm and keenness, but better suited, not to say more practical, for less important cases. 78 Lysias belongs to an older generation than these; he is subtle and elegant, and, if to be instructive is an adequate function for an orator, you could ask for no one better. For there is no nonsense about him; nothing far-fetched; yet he is more like a clear spring than a mighty river. 79 Isocrates, in a different style of oratory, is polished, well groomed, and better suited to the practice ground than to the battlefield. His whole aim is rhetorical grace, and with good reason, for he had trained himself for lecturing, not court-room appearance. He is of a ready inventiveness; full of enthusiasm for what is honorable, painstaking to a fault in word order. . . .

### Greek philosophy

81 Among the philosophers whom Cicero acknowledges as the source of most of his eloquence, Plato is unquestionably the leader, whether we consider his keenness in dialectic or his god-given ease of style, in which he rivals Homer. For he

rises far above prose and what the Greeks call "pedestrian" style; I think of his inspired genius as not so much that of a mere mortal as of the Delphic oracle itself. . . . *83* As for Aristotle, I hesitate to make up my mind whether his fame rests more on his factual knowledge, the number of his works, the charm of his style, the shrewdness of his discoveries, or the variety of his subject matter. . . .

*Roman poetry*

*85* In dealing with Roman authors I shall follow the same order. Vergil in our language, like Homer in Greek, will supply our most promising introduction, for of all epic poets, Greek and Roman, he is certainly the closest to Homer. *86* I shall use the same language as I heard from Domitius Afer [19] when I was a young man; when I asked him who in his opinion came closest to Homer, he replied, "Vergil is second, but he is nearer first than third." Of course we must bow before Homer's deathless and godlike qualities, but Vergil is a more careful and painstaking workman, because he had to work harder, and perhaps Vergil's general high level of excellence compensates for Homer's superiority in the purple passages. *87* All our other poets follow a long way behind. For . . . Lucretius is certainly worth reading, but not to shape style, which is the core of eloquence; . . . he is eloquent in his field, but difficult. . . .

*96* Iambics are not much written by Romans as a separate *genre;* instead, they alternate with other meters. They are used to express bitterness by Catullus . . . and Horace in his *Epodes.* In Roman lyric Horace is almost the only one worth reading. For at times he rises above himself; he is full of jollity and grace, and in the variety of his figures and his choice of words he is both bold and happy. . . .

*Roman comedy*

*99* Latin lags behind especially in comedy, though Varro says the Muses would speak in the language of Plautus, if they wanted to talk Latin . . . and Terence's plays have been ascribed to Scipio Africanus; these last are still the most elegant of their kind and would be still more pleasing if they were confined to iambic trimeters. But Roman comedy hardly succeeds in being even the faint shadow of the Greek, so that I am forced to conclude that Latin does not seem to lend itself to that famous charm which was vouchsafed, apparently, to the Athenians alone, since not even the other Greek dialects were able to achieve it. . . .

*Roman history*

*101* In history, however, we need not, I think, yield the palm to the Greeks. I should not be afraid to match Sallust with Thucydides. And Herodotus would not resent comparison with Livy, either in the marvelous attractiveness and limpid clarity of his narrative, or in the indescribable eloquence of the speeches, where everything that is said fits both the situation and the characters; and as for emotions, especially the pleasanter ones, it is mild praise to say that no historian has portrayed them better.

*102* And so, though his talents are different, he has achieved an immortality on a par with that of Sallust's rapid brevity. . . .

*Roman oratory*

*105* It is our orators, of course, who enable us to compare Latin eloquence with Greek. I would dare to match Cicero with any one of them. I am fully aware what a controversy I will stir up, especially since it is not my intention at this time to compare him with Demosthenes. There is no point in it, since I too think Demosthenes ought above all authors to be read or rather learned by heart. *106* I think the two are for the most part alike in their excellences, which include judgment, orderly arrangement, their method of subdividing, introducing, and using logic in their speeches, and finally in the whole department of "invention." They are somewhat different in their style; Demosthenes is more compact, Cicero more diffuse; Cicero ends his sentences with looser rhythms than Demosthenes; the latter's weapon is the sharp edge of his wit; the former's, repeated blows of the bludgeon; from Demosthenes nothing can be taken away; to Cicero nothing can be added; the Athenian is more painstaking, the Roman more unstudied. *107* Certainly in wit and in pathos, which make the most powerful appeal to the emotions, we hold the field. And perhaps the custom of his city barred Demosthenes from using perorations, but the different nature of the Latin language, it may be argued, gives us, too, less opportunity to use the style the "Atticists" admire. In their letters, which exist from both authors, and in the dialogue form, which Demosthenes never attempted, Cicero wins without a struggle. *108* But Cicero must bow before Demosthenes because the Greek came first, and largely made possible Cicero's greatness. For Cicero, in my view, who devoted himself entirely to the imitation of the Greeks, has copied Demosthenes' vigor, Plato's vocabulary, and Isocrates' charm. *109* He did not merely reproduce pedantically the best features of each of these; most or rather all of his excellences were self-made, the result of the blessed richness of his immortal genius. For he does not, as Pindar says, "collect rain water, but overflows from a living fountain," since he was born with a gift of Providence, whereby eloquence might in his person make trial of all her powers. *110* For who can be a more painstaking teacher, a more powerful stirrer of the emotions? Who has ever had such charm? You would think he had obtained as a favor what actually he has wrenched from a juror by constraint, and the juror whom he has carried away with him by main force seems to go voluntarily, not under compulsion. *111* He invariably speaks with such a voice of authority that one is ashamed to disagree with him; his is not merely the enthusiasm of an advocate; he carries the conviction of a witness or a juror. And at the same time all those accomplishments, which an ordinary mortal could even with the most painstaking study acquire only with difficulty, and one by one, flow effortlessly from him; and yet his oratory, which is the most beautiful ever heard, gives every evidence of felicity and ease of expression. *112* Therefore it was not without reason that his contemporaries called him the "King of the Courts," while in the eyes of posterity he has achieved such heights that "Cicero" is considered not so much to be the name of a man as the synonym for eloquence. Let us therefore look to him, let him be the example set before us, let the recognized touchstone of progress be a genuine appreciation of Cicero. . . .

### Roman philosophy

*123* There remain the philosophers; of whom Roman literature has so far produced very few

eloquent examples. So Cicero is again our instance; he stands out as a rival of the Greeks in general, and in this field of Plato in particular. . . .

### Seneca

*125* I have purposely separated my discussion of Seneca from my treatment of the various branches of rhetoric on account of a false impression of me that has got about, to the effect that I condemn and even hate him. This happened through the efforts I made to raise the standards of oratory in general, which was corrupt and full of flaws of every description. *126* Moreover at that time Seneca's works were practically the sole reading of the younger set. My efforts were directed, not to snatching his works from their hands entirely, but to preventing his being rated higher than more important authors, men whom he had consistently inveighed against, because he knew his style was different, and had no confidence in his ability to please those who were fond of his rivals. But he had more admirers than he had imitators, and his admirers were as far inferior to him as he was to the classics. *127* For I wish the impossible had happened, and someone had shared the first prize with him or at least come in second. But they loved him for his faults alone, and each of his partisans aimed unswervingly at reproducing them, as far as he could; then when he boasted that he talked just like Seneca, it hurt Seneca's reputation. *128* There is no denying that he had many striking virtues, a quick and well-stocked mind, a capacity for hard work, a wide range of factual knowledge, though his research assistants sometimes misled him. He had an almost encyclopedic range. *129* Speeches, poems, letters, and dialogues are ascribed to him. In philosophy he was not very painstaking, yet he was noted for his indictments of vice. His works contain many famous quotations, much that is worth reading for its ethical effect; but generally speaking his style is corrupt, and most pernicious precisely because of the attractive vices with which it abounds. One finds oneself wishing that in speaking he had used his own intelligence, but someone else's critical judgment. *130* For if only he had been critical of some single item in his work, if only there was a part of it he did not dote on, if only he had not been in love with every line he wrote, if only he had not reduced his work to triviality by his excessive use of ellipsis in epigram, he would win his fame as the common choice of scholars, not as a school-boy fad. *131* But even so he ought to be read by those who are already mature and well-grounded in the discipline of a severer style, if for no other reason than that he can supply material for criticism both pro and con. For, as I have said, there is much in him to approve, much to admire, but one must select carefully, as I wish he himself had done. For his nature was worthy of better aims, since whatever ends it aimed at, it achieved.

[The rest of Book X discusses imitation, writing (manner, matter, and form) and extemporaneous speaking. The author especially emphasizes the fact that mere imitation, without talent, is not enough. Book XI deals with the fitting of the speech to the circumstances, with memory and mnemonic devices, and with delivery, gesture, and costume. The twelfth and final book concerns the culture and character of the orator. The first two chapters, selections from which are printed below, stress (I) the central theme of Quintilian's work, that the good orator must also to be a good man, and (II) the importance of the study of philosophy as a prop to character.]

*From* Book XII

I. THE GOOD ORATOR MUST ALSO BE A GOOD MAN

*1* Let my hypothetical orator, then, be the one defined by Marcus Cato, "a good man, skilled in speaking." In this definition what Cato put first, and what is in the very nature of the case more important and farther reaching, is that he must be a good man. This is important not merely because there is nothing more detrimental to public and private life than eloquence, if rhetorical power becomes the armament for evil men, and not merely because I, who have tried with might and main to make some contribution to the art of oratory, would deserve a minimum of credit from mankind, if I put these weapons into the hands of a thief instead of a soldier. *2* No, personal reasons are not enough. Mother Nature herself will have turned out to be but a stepmother in granting what appears to be her greatest gift to mankind, the gift which distinguishes us from the other animals, if she has designed the faculty of speech as a partner in crime, an adversary to innocence, an enemy of truth. For it would have been better to have been born speechless and altogether bereft of reason than to turn the gifts of Providence to mutual self-destruction. *3* My view of the matter has further implications. For I say not merely that the orator must be a good man but that he will never even be an orator unless he *is* a good man. For certainly you would not concede that a man has theoretical wisdom who, when faced with a choice between a good and an evil way, prefers always the wicked course; nor that he has practical wisdom when, by a turn of events he has not himself foreseen, he subjects himself to the gravest penalties often of the law, but always of a guilty conscience. *4* But if the time-honored philosophical and popular view is correct, that no one is wicked unless he is also ignorant, certainly an ignorant man will never become an orator. Besides, no mind which is the slave of every vice can be free to concentrate on the fairest of the professions: first, because good and evil cannot dwell together in the same breast, and the same mind can no more think the highest and the lowest thoughts at once than the same individual be simultaneously good and bad; (*5*) second, because a mind fixed upon so important a subject must be free from every other preoccupation, even from innocent ones. For only the free and single-minded man, with no distractions or ulterior motives, will focus his attention solely on what he is being trained for. *6* But if too much attention to one's estates, undue devotion to household finances, the joys of hunting, or whole days devoted to gladiatorial shows steal time from books (for whatever time other interests gain, study loses): what are we to suppose will be the effect of unbridled thoughts, greed, avarice, and envy, which trouble even sleep and dreams? *7* For there is nothing so distraught, so schizophrenic, so hacked and mangled by its various emotions as a guilty conscience. For while the plot is being laid, the conscience is torn by hope, responsibility, and overwork; and even when it has got what it sinned for, it is tortured on the rack of worry, remorse, and anticipation of every kind of punishment. What room is there in the midst of all this for literature or any of the arts and sciences? No more than there is for crops in a bramble-tangle. *8* Look at it this way: given the slim rewards of scholarship, does not a man have to live simply? What then can he get out of a life of lust and luxury? Does not desire for approval whet our appetite for the literary life? But what does approval matter to bad men? Who can fail by now to see that oratory consists in large measure of the discussion of what is just and right? But will the unjust or the wicked man speak with due consistency on these subjects? *9* Finally, suppose I yield the central point in the argument and grant the impossible, that there can be the same talent, industry, and learning in the worst of men as in the best of them: which will be called the better orator? Surely the one who is also the better man. The same person, then, can never be a wicked man and a perfect orator. *10* For nothing is perfect, if anything better than itself exists. But, to avoid the appearance of imitating the Socratics, who rig the answers to their own questions, let us suppose that there exists a person so stubbornly opposed to truth that he dares call a bad man, endowed with equivalent talent, industry, and learning, as good an orator, potentially, as a good one: let us convict this objector, too, of self-delusion. *11* For certainly no one will doubt that the aim of every speech is to convince the jury that its brief is true and honorable. Who will have an easier job of persuasion, the good man or the bad? At least the good man will more often say what is true and honorable. *12* But even if sometimes, under the stress of duty, he tries to make the worse appear the better reason (which can happen, as I shall show), he must still gain greater credence. But bad men are sometimes so careless of their reputation and so ignorant of the right that they drop all pretence, and are extravagant in their brief and shameless in their assertions. *13* Next, though they cannot get away with it, come unseemly harping on the same theme and labor in vain. For their wicked hopes are as high in their lawsuits as they are in their lives. Moreover, it often happens that such men are not believed even when they tell the truth, and if they plead a case, it is taken for a sign that it is a bad one.

[Quintilian then replies to the charge that Demosthenes and Cicero were not thoroughly good men. Next, he argues that command of speech divorced from morality is not persuasive, and therefore not true eloquence. Nevertheless the teacher of rhetoric must discuss wrong principles as well as right ones, so that the student will not be caught unprepared. And sometimes even good men find that they must argue against truth and defend an apparent wrong. Chapter II discusses the role of philosophy, in all its branches and schools, in the orator's education.]

## II. THE MORALS OF THE ORATOR

*1* Since then the orator is a good man, and this cannot be understood without virtue, virtue, though it gets some of its stimulus from nature, must still get its finishing touch from education: the most important thing for the orator to cultivate in his studies is morality; he must be thoroughly familiar with every subject having to do with honor and justice, without which no one can be either "a good man" or "skilled in speaking." *2* Unless perhaps we agree with those who hold that morality is innate and that education contributes nothing to it. According to these worthies, manual labor, even of the lowest kind, admittedly has to be taught, while virtue, the gift which brings man closest to the immortal gods, lies ready to hand without working for it, and is ours simply by right of birth. But will a man be self-controlled who does not know what self-control is? *3* Or brave who has not completely purged himself of the fear of pain, death, and superstition? Or just, who has never discussed in an intellectual conversation the nature of the just and the good, natural law—which is a universal gift to all peoples—and the law of nations, especially laid down for particular nationalities? O how little thought has been given to such matters by those who think them so easy! *4* But I pass over this point, on which I think there can not be the slightest doubt on the part of anyone who has even a bowing acquaintance with literature. I shall proceed instead to my second point, that a man will never be sufficiently skilled in speaking who has not made a deep study of physics and formed his character by study of principles and by practical application. *5* Lucius Crassus in the third book of [Cicero's] *On the Orator* quite soundly maintains that all statements on what is right, just, true, good, and their opposites are the property of the orator, and that the philosophers, when they use their powers of speaking to defend them, are using the rhetorician's weapons, not their own. But he also admits that we must go to philosophy for these virtues, apparently because she has staked out more of a claim on them. *6* This is why Cicero, in many of his books and letters, bears witness that the ability to speak well takes its rise from the inmost founts of wisdom, and that this is the reason why for a long time ethics and rhetoric were taught by the same teachers. Therefore the point of my advice is not that I want the orator to be a philosopher, since no way of life is more remote from political duties or from every function of the orator. *7* For what philosopher haunts the courts or is a familiar figure in political meetings? Which one of them is versed in public administration, though they teach it often enough? But I want my pupil to be a wise man in the Roman manner, who shows himself to be a political figure not by hole-and-corner hairsplittings but in the active give and take of practical life. *8* However, because philosophy, abandoned by those who have devoted themselves to rhetoric instead, no longer operates where it belongs, in the full light of the courtroom, but has withdrawn, first into the Athenian arcades and gymnasia, then into the Roman lecture halls, the orator's needs, unsupplied by the professors of rhetoric, must be supplied by those in whose keeping philosophy has remained; the authors who teach virtue must be painstak-

ingly read, so that the orator's life may come into contact with the knowledge of things human and divine. *9* How much more important and beautiful these subjects would seem if they were taught by those who could give them most eloquent expression! I look forward to the day when some perfect orator, such as I hope to see, may take over the field of philosophy, unpopular as it is because of its lofty pretensions and the shortcomings of some who are turning its virtues into vices, and, coming into his own again, may lead philosophy back into the fold of rhetoric. *10* It is divided, of course, into three parts, physics, ethics, and logic, no one of which is without its connection with the work of the orator.

[The rest of chapter II discusses these three divisions of philosophy, ending with advice to the orator to follow no one philosophical school, but to be an eclectic. Quintilian next stresses (like Cicero in *On the Laws*), the importance to the orator of a knowledge of civil law. Successive chapters deal with the orator's necessary stock of examples and precedents, his need to be firm and resourceful, and to cultivate his natural advantages, the proper age to begin a career, kinds of cases, fees, the need to study each case carefully, the proper aim in pleading, the styles of oratory, and how the orator may spend the years of his retirement. The author ends his long work with an encomium on the virtues of oratory, an exhortation to perseverance, and the characteristically Roman hope that his book will prove to be of some *practical* value to the student.]

## NOTES TO *THE TRAINING OF THE ORATOR*

1. See note to Cicero, *On the Chief End of Man*, I, 44, above p. 202.

2. *Paedagogus*, the slave who escorted children to and from school.

3. XI, ii; cf. the second note to Cicero, *On the Chief End of Man*, V, 2, above p. 202.

4. E.g., Plato.

5. E.g., Lycurgus of Sparta.

6. Cf. Ben Jonson, *Every Man in his Humor*, II, ii:
Ere all their teeth be born, or they can speak,
We make their palates cunning! The first words
We form their tongues with, are licentious jests!
Can it call whore, cry bastard? O, then kiss it!

A witty child! Can 't swear? The father's darling!
Give it two plums.

7. Ben Jonson, *Discoveries* (Nonesuch ed.), p. 979: "If you pour a glut of water upon a bottle, it receives little of it, but with a funnel, and by degrees, you shall fill many of them, and spill little of your own; to their capacity they will all receive and be full."

8. See the note in the introduction to selections from the Attic Orators.

9. Pacuvius, an early Roman tragedian (220–*ca.* 130 B.C.), in his *Hermione*, now lost.

10. This is the theme of the interview between Solon and Croesus in Herodotus, I.

11. XII, x, 63–70.
12. Greek astronomical poet of about 315–240 B.C.
13. *Iliad*, XXI, 196.
14. *Ibid.*, XVIII, 18.
15. *Ibid.*, IX, 529.
16. *Ibid.*, XXIV, 486.

17. A pick for plucking the lyre.
18. On this characteristic Roman attitude, cf. the *Introduction* to Catullus.
19. An orator much admired by Quintilian, though his technique was more distinguished than his character. He died A.D. 59.

# SELECTED LETTERS OF THE YOUNGER PLINY

*Translated by John Paul Heironimus*

## INTRODUCTION

AN INTERESTING and valuable writer of the early second century of the Christian era is Pliny the Younger (so called to distinguish him from his uncle, the author of a famous Natural History). He was born in A.D. 62 in the North Italian city of Comum. His father, wealthy and locally prominent, died when Pliny was but a boy, leaving him to the guardianship of Verginius Rufus, who enjoyed the rare distinction of having more than once declined the imperial purple when his troops offered to set him on the throne. Pliny's education, however, was supervised by his maternal uncle, who eventually adopted him and gave him the name by which he is commonly known. At the age of seventeen he lost his uncle also, the victim of scientific curiosity, which tempted him to investigate too closely the phenomenon of the eruption of Vesuvius in 79.

After receiving an education appropriate for his wealth and rank, Pliny embarked upon a senatorial career, taking the necessary steps of office until he reached the consulate in the year 100. A dozen years later he was called by the Emperor Trajan to assume the governorship of the troubled province of Bithynia, in which post he apparently met his death, some time before 114.

Although he wrote assiduously in many fields, even including poetry, only two of his works have survived. One is the *Panegyric*, or speech of thanks and praise, which he delivered in honor of Trajan during his consulate; it was admired by contemporaries and imitated by later ages, but seems a rather dull performance to modern readers. The other is more to our taste; it is the collection of his private letters to various correspondents, published at intervals from 97 to 107, in nine books, and a tenth book devoted to an exchange of correspondence with the Emperor Trajan. Most of these latter date from the period of Pliny's proconsulship in Bithynia. It was his custom to refer to his imperial master all difficult problems, such as how to deal with the troublesome sect of religious fanatics known as Christians.

In Pliny's letters we have a vivid picture of the daily life of the Roman upper classes. Travel, social intercourse, city and country residences, activities in the law courts and Senate, literary pursuits, and many other aspects are abundantly illustrated. One also gets a pleasant impression of the writer's personality. A generous friend, devoted public servant, benevolent philanthropist, humane master, loving husband, he has hardly any fault except perhaps too great a consciousness of his own virtues, and of posterity, for which he wrote.

---

### PLINY TO SOSIUS SENECIO

*The unpopularity of public recitations*

This year has brought a big crop of poets. In all the month of April there was hardly a day when someone did not give a public recitation. I am delighted that literature is thriving and that men of letters bring themselves forward and display their talents, though people are a bit reluctant to come and listen. Lots of men sit in the lounging-places and waste the time by gossiping with each other when they should be listening. From time to time they send to ask whether the performer has made his appearance yet and spoken his introductory remarks; whether he is most of the way through his manuscript by now. Then at last, still slowly and reluctantly, they arrive. Even so they do not wait till the end, but retire before, some of them in stealthy embarrassment, others quite nonchalantly. But, so help me, in the days of our forefathers it is recorded that the Emperor Claudius was once walking in the palace when he heard a shouting. He asked the cause and was told that the historian Nonianus was giving a recitation; so, to the complete surprise of the performer, Claudius dropped in to listen. But now the idlest citizen, invited long in advance and repeatedly reminded of the coming event, either does not come, or if he does, complains that he has wasted his time, when he has really been spending it profitably. But so much more praise and admiration are due to the authors who are not deterred from reading and writing by this attitude on the part of their hearers—I don't know whether to call it laziness or insolence. Well, *I* have hardly ever failed to come. To be sure most of the performers were my friends—almost anybody who is devoted to literature is automatically a friend of mine. For these reasons I have spent more time in the city than I had planned. I can now seek seclusion in the country to write something which I *won't* recite—for I do not want to seem to have come to those recitations just to ensure an audience for my own. Just as in everything else, any gratitude for coming to listen disappears if repayment is required.          [I, 13]

## PLINY TO AVITUS

### *A stingy host*

It would take too long to recount (nor does it particularly matter) how it happened that I, though far from an intimate friend, was the dinner guest of a fellow who seemed to himself an elegant yet a thrifty soul, but who impressed me as simultaneously extravagant and stingy. For he served excellent fare to himself and a few others, while to the rest he gave cheap scraps. He even served his wine in small bottles of three different kinds, not to give his guests a choice, but to deny them the right of refusing; one kind was for himself and us, another for his lesser friends (he has friends in degrees), the third for his own freedmen and ours. The guest next to me observed this and asked me whether I approved of it. I replied that I did not. "Well, what is your custom?" "I set the same before everybody; for I invite my guests to receive a meal, not an insult; and I treat alike in every respect those whom I have invited to the same couch and table." "Even

freedmen?" "Yes, for I regard them as guests then, not as freedmen." And he said, "Does it cost you a lot?" "Far from it." "How is that possible?" "Why, obviously, my freedmen don't drink what I do, but I what they." And really, if one restrains one's gluttony it is not difficult to share with a number what one enjoys oneself. So it is gluttony which must be restrained and humbled, if you must spare expenses; which you can deal with better by self-restraint than by insulting other people.

Why all this? To keep you, my young friend, from being taken in, in spite of your excellent disposition, by the extravagance of certain folks in their table practice, with its appearance of economy. It is my duty, feeling as I do toward you, to give you a word of warning what to avoid when something like this occurs. So remember that nothing is more to be shunned than this incongruous combination of extravagance and stinginess; qualities bad enough by themselves, but worse when combined.          [II, 6]

## PLINY TO BAEBIUS MACER

### *Pliny the Elder*

It gives me great pleasure that you read the books of my uncle so eagerly that you want to have them all and ask for a complete list. I shall act as a bibliography, and shall let you know also in what order they were written; for this information is likewise not without interest to devotees. "On Throwing the Javelin from Horseback," in one volume; he wrote this, with equal skill and hard work, when he was serving as a cavalry captain. "The Life of Pomponius Secundus," in two volumes; a great friend of his, he paid this as if it were a debt he owed to his memory. "The German Wars," in twenty volumes, in which he included all the wars we have waged with the Germans. He began it while serving in the army in Germany, being prompted by a dream. In his sleep there appeared to him the ghost of Drusus Nero,[1] who after extensive victories in Germany had died there; he commended his memory to Pliny and prayed to be rescued from the humiliation of oblivion. "The Student," in three books, but published in six volumes because of their size; in this he described the training and perfection of the orator from the cradle onward. "Questionable Language," in eight volumes; he wrote this during the last years of Nero, when slavery had made it dangerous to engage in literary activity with any pretension to a bold and liberal spirit. "Continuation of the History of Aufidius Bassus," in thirty-one volumes. "Natural History," in thirty-seven.[2] This is a work of varied content and deep learning, as many sided as Nature herself.

Do you wonder that so many volumes, and among them so many of a minute scholarship, were completed by a busy man? You will wonder the more when you learn that he pleaded cases in court for a while, died in his fifty-sixth year, and spent the interval between his retirement from the bar and his death amidst the distractions and impediments of public offices and friendship with the emperor. But his intelligence was keen, his enthusiasm beyond belief, his capacity to work late superlative. He would begin lighting a lamp before dawn at the Vulcanalia,[3] and not just for good luck, but for study, long before daylight; in the winter, an hour after midnight, or at the latest, within two hours; often it was midnight. To be sure he had the power of falling asleep at will; sleep would sometimes come upon him in the midst of his work, then leave him again. He would go before dawn to the Emperor Vespasian (who also used the hours of the night), then to the task assigned him. On his return home he would devote to his writing whatever time was left. After some food (his morning meal was easily digested and simple, in the old fashion) he would lie in the sun in the summer, if he had any time, and would listen to the reading of a book, while he took notes and copied passages. He did that with everything he read; he used to say that no book was so bad that it was not useful in some part. After his sun bath he would usually take a cold shower; then he would eat a bite for lunch and take a short nap. Then he would start working again as if it were another day, until dinner time. During dinner he would have a book read to him, and notes taken down, and at a brisk rate. I remember that once when the reader made a mistake in pronunciation, one of our friends called him back and made him say it right. "I suppose you understood him?" said my uncle. When the friend admitted he had, "Well, why did you stop him? We have lost ten

or more lines by this interruption of yours." Such was his economy of time. In summer he would get up from the dinner table while it was still light, in winter, within an hour after sunset; this as if some law compelled him. Such his practice amidst his official work and the uproar of the city. When on vacation at one of his estates, only the time of the bath was denied to his study; and when I say "bath," I mean the time of actual immersion; for while he was taking off his clothes and being dried he would listen to something or dictate. While traveling, as if released from other concerns he would concentrate on this one. At his side was a secretary with book and stenographic pad; gloves protected his hands in winter, so that not even bitter cold could rob any time from the work. For the same reason he got about Rome in a sedan chair. I recollect being scolded for walking: "You could have avoided losing those hours." He thought all time not spent on studies was lost. By such concentration he completed all those volumes, and he left to me 160 notebooks of excerpts, written on both sides in a very minute hand, by which consideration the number is really multiplied. He used to say that when he was serving as procurator [4] in Spain he could have sold these notebooks to Largius Licinus for four hundred thousand sesterces,[5] and they were somewhat fewer at that time.

When you recollect how much he read and wrote, does it not seem impossible that he was involved in any public duties or in the friendship of an emperor? On the other hand, when you hear what toil he devoted to his literary work, does it not seem that he did not write nor read enough? For what is there which such tasks could not hinder, or that such concentration could not effect? So I laugh when some people call me a diligent student—me, who if compared to him am extremely lazy. But am I the only lazy one, I, who am distracted by duties, partly public and partly private? Who of those who devote all their lives to letters would not blush at comparison to him, as if they were found to be mere sleepyheads and lazybones?

I have lengthened this letter, though I had intended to write only an answer to your question, what books he left. Yet I am sure these details will be of no less interest than the titles; for they can inspire you, with the stimulus of rivalry, not only to read his books but also to produce something similar.                    [III, 5]

PLINY TO TACITUS

*The eruption of Vesuvius* (A.D. 79)

You ask me to write an account of my uncle's death so that you may report it accurately to posterity. I thank you, for I see that immortal glory is in store for his death if it be recorded by you. Though he perished as nations and cities perish, in a disaster involving the fairest lands, in a catastrophe never to be forgotten, so that it might seem he could never be forgotten, though he was himself the author of many immortal works, yet the eternity of your writings will contribute much to the perpetuation of his memory. I regard men as happy who have been given by the gods either the power to do things worth writing about or to write things worth reading, but those are happiest who have received both gifts. My uncle will be found in this number, thanks to his own books and to yours. So I undertake the more willingly, or rather. I demand, the task you require.

He was at Misenum [6] in personal command of the fleet. On August 24, about the seventh hour, he was informed by my mother that a cloud was visible of unusual size and shape. Having had a sun bath and then a cold shower, he had taken a light luncheon and was now reclining at his studies. He called for his slippers and climbed to a height from which the strange phenomenon could best be observed. A cloud was rising— from what mountain distant observers could not tell, but it was later learned to have been Vesuvius; its likeness and shape are best compared to a pine tree. For it rose on a long trunk and then spread out in branches; I suppose it was lifted up by the fresh blast, then, when no longer supported by its failing force, or overcome by its own weight, it thinned out and spread laterally. It was white in some places, in others dark and spotted, according to whether it had picked up earth or ashes.

Being a man of learning, he thought this was something important and worthy of closer investigation. He had a Liburnian galley got ready; he gave me a chance to accompany him if I wished. I replied that I preferred to study; it happened that he had himself set me a topic to write on. He was just leaving the house when he received a message from Rectina, the wife of Tascus; she was terrified by the impending danger (for her villa lay at the foot of the mountain, nor was it possible for her to escape except by ship): she begged him to rescue her. He altered his plan and carried out in the spirit of a hero what he had begun in the spirit of a scientist. He launched quadriremes and went on board, intending to rescue not only Rectina but many others, for the charming shore was thickly populated. He hastened toward the place from which others were fleeing, and held a straight course, without any shifting of the rudder, toward the danger. He was so free from fear that he commented on and noted down all changes and phases of the awful spectacle. Ashes were now falling on the ships, hotter and denser the closer they drew; now pumice stones and other kinds, black and scorched and broken by the fire; now there was a sudden shoaling as the shore, built up by the debris of the mountain, blocked his path. He deliberated a little as to whether he should turn back, but when the helmsman advised him to do so, he replied, "Fortune aids the brave; head for Pomponianus." The latter was at Stabiae,[7] far across the bay, for the sea nestles between the gradually curving shores. There, though the danger was not yet approaching, it was clearly visible, and would be very close indeed if it should grow worse. Pomponianus had loaded his possessions on ships, intending to flee if the on shore wind should die down. This wind was most favorable for my uncle's course; he sailed in and clasped his frightened friend, offered him consolation and encouragement, and to relieve his fear by his own *sang froid*, he asked to be taken to the bath. After his ablutions he took his place at the table and dined, either in a cheerful mood or (what is equally admirable) a good imitation of it.

Meanwhile from Mount Vesuvius in numerous places widespread and towering flames were shining; their gleam and brightness were intensified by the darkness of the night. To allay his companions' fears he declared that farm dwellers had left their hearths lighted when they fled, and that now their deserted houses were burning with no one to stop them. Then he turned to rest, and slept in quite unfeigned sleep; for his breathing, always rather noisy and heavy because of his bulk, was heard by those moving about before his door. But the courtyard outside his apartment was so filled with ashes that its level was rising and there was danger that if he should stay in his chamber any longer it would be impossible to leave. On being aroused he came forth and rejoined Pomponianus and the others who had stayed awake. They took counsel together as to whether they should stay under cover of the roof or wander about in the open. For the building shook with frequent and violent tremors and as if starting from its foundations seemed to move this way and that. Beneath the open sky, on the other hand, one had to fear the fall of pumice stones, light and porous though they were. Yet this course seemed preferable from a comparison of dangers. With him, one argument outweighed another, with the others one fear overcame a second. They put pillows over their heads, and tied them on with napkins as a protection against falling objects. Now there was daylight elsewhere, but here a night blacker and denser than any other, though many torches and other lights relieved it. They decided to go to the shore and investigate from close at hand whether the sea would yet permit the launching of a boat; but it was still rough and contrary. My uncle lay down on a sail cloth which was spread out and asked for some cold water, which he drank. Then flames and a smell of sulphur that warned of coming flames startled the others into flight, and aroused him. Leaning on two slaves he rose, but immediately collapsed; as I infer, it was because his breathing was impeded by the denser atmosphere, and his throat blocked; it was naturally weak, narrow, and subject to frequent inflammation. When day was restored (the second after the last he saw) his body was found, intact, uninjured, still dressed in the clothes in which he had started out; the posture suggested sleep rather than death.

Meanwhile at Misenum my mother and I— but this does not concern history, and you asked only about his death. So I shall stop. I shall add one point, that I have related only what I myself witnessed or what I heard immediately afterward, when the truest accounts are given. You will select what material you desire to use. For it is quite a different thing to write a letter and to write a history, to write for one friend as compared with writing for the public in general. [VI, 16]

## PLINY TO TACITUS

### *The eruption of Vesuvius (continued)*

You say that the letter I wrote at your request about the death of my uncle makes you want to hear about the terrors, and dangers as well, which I endured, having been left behind at Misenum—I had started on that topic but broken off. "Though my mind shudders to remember, I shall begin." [8] After my uncle departed I spent the rest of the day on my studies; it was for that purpose I had stayed. Then I took a bath, ate dinner, and went to bed; but my sleep was restless and brief. For a number of days before this there had been a quivering of the ground, not so fearful because it was common in Campania. On that night, however, it became so violent that everything seemed not so much to move as to be overturned. My mother came rushing into my bedroom; I was just getting up, intending in my turn to arouse her if she were asleep. We sat down in the rather narrow courtyard of the house lying between the sea and the buildings. I don't know whether I should call it iron nerves or folly—I was only seventeen: I called for a book of Titus Livy and as if at ease I read it and even copied some passages, as I had been doing. Then one of my uncle's friends, who had recently come from Spain to visit him, when he saw my mother and me sitting there, and me actually reading a book, rebuked her apathy and my unconcern. But I was as intent on my book as ever.

It was now the first hour of day, but the light was still faint and doubtful. The adjacent buildings now began to collapse, and there was great, indeed inevitable, danger of being involved in the ruins; for though the place was open, it was narrow. Then at last we decided to leave the town. The dismayed crowd came after us; it preferred following some one else's decision rather than its own; in panic that is practically the same as wisdom. So as we went off we were crowded and shoved along by a huge mob of followers. When we got out beyond the buildings we halted. We saw many strange and fearful sights there. For the carriages we had ordered brought for us, though on perfectly level ground, kept rolling back and forth; even when the wheels were chocked with stones they would not stand still. Moreover the sea appeared to be sucked back and to be repelled by the vibration of the earth; the shoreline was much farther out than usual, and many specimens of marine life were caught on the dry sands. On the other side a black and frightful cloud, rent by twisting and quivering paths of fire, gaped open in huge patterns of flames; it was like sheet lightning, but far worse. Then indeed that friend from Spain whom I have mentioned spoke to us more sharply and insistently: "If your brother and uncle still lives, he wants you to be saved; if he has died, his wish was that you should survive him; so why do you delay to make your escape?" We replied that we would not allow ourselves to think of our own safety while still uncertain of his. Without waiting any longer he rushed off and left the danger behind us at top speed.

Soon thereafter the cloud I have described began to descend to the earth and to cover the sea; it had encircled Capri and hidden it from view, and had blotted out the promontory of Misenum. Then my mother began to plead, urge, and order me to make my escape as best I could, for I could, being young; she, weighed down with years and weakness, would die happy if she had not been the cause of death to me. I replied that I would not find safety except in her company; then I took her hand and made her walk faster. She obeyed with difficulty and scolded herself for slowing me. Now ashes, though thin as yet, began to fall. I looked back; a dense fog was looming up behind us; it poured over the ground like a river as it followed. "Let us turn aside," said I, "lest, if we should fall on the road, we should be trampled in the darkness by the throng of those going our way." We barely had time to consider the thought, when night was upon us, not such a night as when there is no moon or there are clouds, but such as in a closed place with the lights put out. One could hear the wailing of women, the crying of children, the shouting of men; they called each other, some their parents, others their children, still others their mates, and sought to recognize each other by their voices.

Some lamented their own fate, others the fate of their loved ones. There were even those who in fear of death prayed for death. Many raised their hands to the gods; more held that there were nowhere gods any more and that this was that eternal and final night of the universe. Nor were those lacking who exaggerated real dangers with feigned and lying terrors. Men appeared who reported that part of Misenum was buried in ruins, and part of it in flames; it was false, but found credulous listeners.

It lightened a little; this seemed to us not daylight but a sign of approaching fire. But the fire stopped some distance away; darkness came on again, again ashes, thick and heavy. We got up repeatedly to shake these off; otherwise we would have been buried and crushed by the weight. I might boast that not a groan, not a cowardly word, escaped from my lips in the midst of such dangers, were it not that I believed I was perishing along with everything else, and everything else along with me; a wretched and yet a real consolation for having to die. At last that fog dissipated into smoke or mist, and then vanished; soon there was real daylight; the sun even shone, though wanly, as when there is an eclipse. Our still trembling eyes found everything changed, buried in deep ashes as if in snow. We returned to Misenum and attended to our physical needs as best we could; then we spent a night in suspense between hope and fear. Fear was the stronger, for the trembling of the earth continued, and many, crazed by their sufferings, were mocking their own woes and others' by awful predictions. But as for us, though we had suffered dangers and anticipated others, we had not even then any thought of going away until we should have word of my uncle.

You will read this account, far from worthy of history, without any intention of incorporating it; and you must blame yourself, since you insisted on having it, if it shall seem not even worthy of a letter. [VI, 20]

## PLINY TO THE EMPEROR TRAJAN

### *The official treatment of the Christians*

It is my custom, Sire, to refer to you all matters in which I am in doubt. For who can better guide my hesitancy or instruct my ignorance? I have never been present at trials of Christians; therefore I do not know what is sought and punished, nor to what extent. I have been puzzled in no small degree as to whether there is any difference in the treatment of ages or if the young, no matter how young, are treated just like more mature defendants; whether pardon is given to those who repent or it avails not at all to have given up the aberration if one has once been a Christian; whether the name itself, if free from criminal practices, is punished or only the abominations that are associated with the name.

For the present I have followed this procedure in the case of those who were denounced to me as Christians: I asked the defendants in person whether they were Christians. If they admitted it I asked them for a second and third time, threatening punishment; if they persisted, I ordered them to be executed. For I had no doubt that whatever it was they were confessing, their persistence and unbending stubbornness deserved to be punished. There were others of similar folly whom I sent to Rome, since they were Roman citizens. Soon the accusation became common, as usual, from the very fact that cases were being tried, and several variations appeared. An anonymous information was lodged listing a number of names. If defendants who denied that they were now Christians or had been in the past would, following my example, pray to the gods and offer incense and wine to your statue, which I had had placed beside those of the gods for this purpose, and if they would curse Christ, they should, I thought, be dismissed; for it is declared that real Christians cannot be compelled to do any of these acts. Others, named by an informer, said that they were Christians but later denied it; they had indeed been, but had given up the practice, some of them several years ago, one even twenty years ago. All of these also worshipped your image and the statues of the gods, and cursed Christ. However, they asserted that their guilt or mistake had amounted to no more than this, that they had been accustomed on a set day to gather before dawn and to chant in antiphonal form a hymn to Christ as if to a god, and to bind themselves by a pledge, not for the commission of any crime, but rather that they would not commit theft nor robbery nor adultery nor break their promises, nor refuse to return on demand any treasure that had been entrusted to their care; when this ceremony had been completed, they would go away, to reassemble later for a feast, but an ordinary and innocent one. They had abandoned even this custom after my edict in which, following your instruction, I had forbidden the existence of fellowships.[9] So I thought it the more necessary to extract the truth even by torture from two maidservants who were called deaconesses. I found nothing save a vile superstition carried to an immoderate length.

So, postponing further trials, I have resorted to consulting you. For it seemed to me a subject worthy of consultation, especially because of the number of people charged. For many of every age and rank, and of both sexes, are being brought to trial, and will be. The contagion of the superstition has pervaded not only the cities but the villages and country districts as well. Yet it seems that it can be halted and cured. It is well agreed that temples almost desolate have begun to be thronged again, and stated rites that had long been abandoned are revived; and a sale is found for the fodder of sacrificial victims, though hitherto buyers were rare. So it is easy to conjecture what a great number of offenders may be reformed, if a chance to repent is given.

[X, 96]

TRAJAN TO PLINY

*The Emperor's answer about the Christians*

You have followed the proper course, my friend, in examining the cases of those who have been denounced to you as Christians. It is impossible to establish a hard and fast procedure for general use. They are not to be sought out; if they are accused, and the case is proved, they are to be punished, with the restriction, however, that if one denies that he is a Christian and makes it manifest in very deed, that is, by offering sacrifice to our gods, he shall be pardoned because of his repentance, however suspicious his past conduct was. Information lodged anonymously ought not to be regarded in dealing with any charge; it is of an abominable tendency, and not consonant with our enlightened age.

[X, 97]

# NOTES TO SELECTED LETTERS OF THE
## YOUNGER PLINY

1. Elder stepson of Augustus and heir presumptive at the time of his death in 9 B.C.

2. The only one of the works listed which has survived.

3. It was customary to celebrate the festival of the god of fire on August 23 by lighting a lamp before dawn (about 4:45 A.M.) ; a mere ceremony for most Romans, but for Pliny the time when he regularly began to study.

4. A fiscal agent of the emperor.

5. Roughly equivalent to $20,000, but with far greater purchasing power.

6. A promontory at northwest end of the Bay of Naples; one of the principal bases of the imperial fleet.

7. Misenum is roughly west of Naples; Stabiae is about 17 miles to the southeast. Rectina, who probably lived in the vicinity of Herculaneum, seems to have been forgotten at this point.

8. Vergil, *Aeneid*, II, 12.

9. The emperors tended to regard all associations of citizens or provincials with suspicion, as possible masks for seditious movements.

# SELECTIONS FROM TACITUS

*Translated by Harry J. Leon*

## INTRODUCTION

LITTLE IS known about the life of Publius Cornelius Tacitus, generally regarded as Rome's greatest historian. He was born about A.D. 55 and outlived Trajan, who died in 117, but the year of his death is quite unknown. Coming from a family of good station, he held the various offices of the *cursus honorum* and attained the consulship in 97. Later, probably about 112–113, he was proconsul (governor) of the province of Asia. He was distinguished as a lawyer and orator.

The extant works of Tacitus include the following: *Dialogue on Orators*, a discussion of the oratory of his time and the reasons for its decline from the golden era of Cicero. *Agricola*, a biography of his father-in-law, Gnaeus Julius Agricola, who conquered much of Britain under Domitian; this work is considered the finest example of Roman biographical writing. *Germania*, a valuable ethnographic study of the Germans of his day. *Histories*, a work originally dealing with the period A.D. 69–96 (the reigns of Galba through Domitian) in perhaps fourteen books, of which only the first four books and part of the fifth have survived. *Annals*, his masterpiece, a work in sixteen books, which covered the period A.D. 14–68 (the reigns of Tiberius through Nero); of this we still have most of the portions dealing with the reigns of Tiberius (Books I–VI), of Claudius (XI–XII), and of Nero (XIII–XVI).

As a historian, Tacitus made conscientious use of all the sources available to him, such as the writings of his predecessors, the senatorial archives, private memoirs, and eyewitness accounts. While possessed of strong prejudices with a marked bias toward his own aristocratic class, he presents the facts honestly, so that it is possible to reconstruct the true picture despite the rhetorical coloring which sometimes distorts it. This is particularly true of Tacitus' portrait of the Emperor Tiberius, who is represented as a grim tyrant but whom modern historians have demonstrated, largely from Tacitus' own narrative, to have been a capable, conscientious ruler.

As a prose stylist, Tacitus is ranked among Rome's greatest masters. He developed a strikingly original style far removed from that of his great predecessors, Cicero and Livy. His sentences move rapidly with an astonish-

ing variety of word and phrase, an epigrammatic incisiveness, biting satire, and vivid coloring, which defy adequate reproduction in any translation. His descriptive powers, his skill at dramatic narration, his unforgettable character sketches, his effective use of stinging innuendo, have established him as one of the great writers in world literature.

A brief comparison of Tacitus with other historians may be appropriate here. Both as a writer and as a historian Tacitus may well be regarded as of equal stature with Thucydides, the greatest historian of Greece. While lacking the austere objectivity of his Greek predecessor, he surpasses him in emotional coloring and in richness and variety of style. Though less expansive in his narratives than either Herodotus or Livy, Tacitus has the supreme art of concentrating on a few dramatic details by throwing upon them, in a Rembrandt-like manner, a vivid spot of light against a somber background. In the *Annals* one may note especially the account of the death of Britannicus (XIII, 16) and of Agrippina (XIV, 8). Tacitus resembles, and is probably influenced by, Sallust in his sententiousness and his fondness for rhetorical phrasing, but he has a far deeper insight into the causes and motives of events. As compared with Livy, Tacitus is more critical of his sources, more concerned about presenting a completely accurate account, more inclined to delve into the deeper psychological motives of his characters, more prone to philosophize over the forces which brought on the tragic events which he must relate. The pride and joy which Livy felt in the greatness and destiny of Rome have in Tacitus given way to a gloomy pessimism and the conviction that the Empire is crashing toward its doom. To compare Tacitus with historians of the modern era would be less than fair, since the scientific objectivity of a von Ranke and our newer techniques for the evaluation of sources can hardly be expected of an ancient author. But in spite of this, Tacitus must still be included among the greatest writers of history, whether ancient or modern.

The selections presented here offer substantial portions of two of Tacitus' most significant works, including a fairly complete account of Nero and his court from the

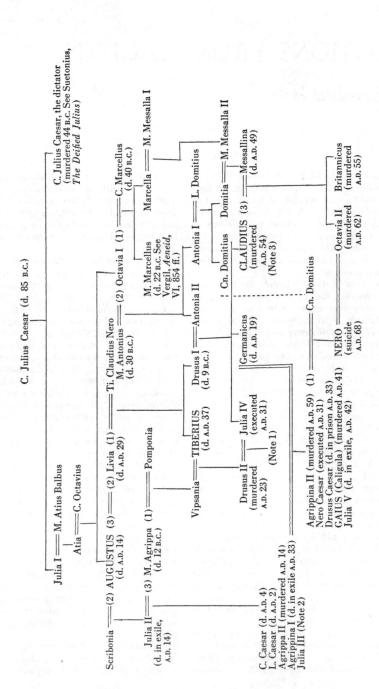

# GENEALOGICAL TABLE OF THE JULIO-CLAUDIAN CAESARS

NOTICE that Julius Caesar left no descendants, but adopted his great-nephew Augustus. Connections with Augustus were later traced by descent from his daughter Julia, his stepsons Tiberius and Drusus, or his sister Octavia. The names of emperors are in capitals. Numerals in parentheses show the order of marriages. Single lines indicate blood relationship; double lines, marriage; the dotted line, that the Cn. Domitius is the same person.

C. Julius Caesar (d. 85 B.C.)

C. Julius Caesar, the dictator (murdered 44 B.C. See Suetonius, *The Deified Julius*)

Julia I ══ M. Atius Balbus

Atia ══ C. Octavius

Scribonia ══(2) AUGUSTUS (3) ══(2) Livia (1) ══ Ti. Claudius Nero
(d. A.D. 14) (d. A.D. 29)

Julia II ══(3) M. Agrippa (1)
(d. in exile, A.D. 14) (d. 12 B.C.)

Pomponia

Octavia I (1) ══(2) M. Antonius
(d. 30 B.C.)

C. Marcellus (d. 40 B.C.)

Marcella ══ M. Messalla I

M. Marcellus (d. 22 B.C. See Vergil, *Aeneid*, VI, 854 ff.)

Antonia II ══ Drusus I (d. 9 B.C.)

Antonia I ══ L. Domitius

Domitia ══ M. Messalla II

Cn. Domitius

CLAUDIUS (murdered A.D. 54) (Note 3) ══ Messallina (d. A.D. 49)

Vipsania ══ TIBERIUS (d. A.D. 37)

Drusus II (murdered A.D. 23) ══ Julia IV (executed A.D. 31) (Note 1)

Germanicus (d. A.D. 19) ══ Agrippina II (murdered A.D. 59)

Cn. Domitius ══ (1)

NERO (suicide A.D. 68) ══ Octavia II (murdered A.D. 62)

Britannicus (murdered A.D. 55)

C. Caesar (d. A.D. 4)
L. Caesar (d. A.D. 2)
Agrippina I (murdered A.D. 14)
Agrippina II (d. in exile A.D. 33)
Julia III (Note 2)

Nero Caesar (executed A.D. 31)
Drusus Caesar (d. in prison A.D. 33)
GAIUS (Caligula) (murdered A.D. 41)
Julia V (d. in exile, A.D. 42)

NOTE 1. A daughter of Drusus II and Julia IV married Rubellius Blandus; their son, Rubellius Plautus, was executed by Nero. NOTE 2. Julia III had a daughter who married Junius Silanus; several of their descendants were executed by Nero. NOTE 3. After the death of Messallina Claudius married his niece Agrippina II; there were no children.

*Annals* (Books XIII–XVI) and the greater portion of the *Germania* (Chapters 1–27).

THE BASIC text used for the translation of the *Annals* is that of C. D. Fisher in the Oxford Classical Texts (1906).

Some readings are adopted from the excellent text of E. Koestermann in the Teubner series (1936). For the *Germania* the text of H. Furneaux, revised by J. G. C. Anderson (Oxford: Clarendon Press, 1922) has been largely followed.

# THE ANNALS

## Book XIII

### Beginning of Nero's reign (A.D. 54)

*1* The first to die under the new reign was Junius Silanus, the proconsul of Asia, whose death was arranged without Nero's knowledge through the guile of Agrippina. It was not an overviolent disposition that provoked his ruin, for he was a do-nothing and was held in such complete disdain under the previous rulers that Gaius Caesar [1] used to call him the golden sheep. Agrippina, however, who had contrived the murder of his brother, Lucius Silanus, feared he might take revenge, in view of the widespread talk among the public that instead of Nero, who was scarcely more than a boy and had attained the imperial power through an act of crime, it was better to have a man of mature years, of unblemished reputation, of noble family, and—what was an important consideration in that day—a direct descendant of the Caesars; for, as a matter of fact, Silanus also was a great-great-grandson of the Divine Augustus. This was the reason for his murder. The deed was carried out by Publius Celer, a Roman knight, and the freedman Helius, who were in charge of the emperor's private possessions in Asia. These two had the proconsul poisoned at a banquet, but too openly to escape detection. With no less haste Narcissus, the freedman of Claudius, whose clashes with Agrippina I have already reported, was driven to suicide because of the severity with which he was confined and by extreme want, though against the will of Nero, to whose still latent vices he was remarkably congenial on account of his greed and extravagance.

*2* There would have been more assassinations but for the intervention of Afranius Burrus and Annaeus Seneca.[2] These two guardians of the youthful emperor, acting in harmony—a rare phenomenon where power is shared—exercised equal influence, though by different means: Bur-

rus, through his military responsibilities and his rigorously upright character; Seneca, through his lessons in oratory and his genuine courtliness. They both worked together in order the more effectively to maintain control over the emperor's unstable youth by granting him permissible pleasures in case he should scorn the virtuous life. Their one joint struggle was against the overbearing disposition of Agrippina, who was fired with all the selfish passions of a corrupt regime and had the support of Pallas,[3] at whose instigation Claudius had brought destruction on himself by that incestuous marriage and the fatal act of adoption.[4] Nero, however, had not the disposition to be ruled by slaves, while Pallas, through his surly arrogance, had so overstepped the bounds of an ex-slave as to make himself unbearable. Nevertheless, publicly every honor was heaped on Agrippina, and when the tribune asked for the customary military password, Nero gave him "The Ideal Mother." The Senate also voted her two lictors, made her priestess of Claudius, and at the same time proclaimed a censor's funeral for Claudius, to be followed by his deification.

*3* On the day of the funeral the emperor started his eulogy. While he was reviewing the ancient history of the family and the consulships and triumphs of his ancestors, both speaker and audience were serious. His references to the deceased's cultural attainments and to the fact that during his reign the nation had suffered no disaster abroad were listened to with favor; but when he turned to Claudius' statesmanship and wisdom, no one could suppress a smile, although the speech, which had been written by Seneca, displayed considerable literary polish, for that writer had a talent well suited to the taste of his day. It was observed by the older men, who have the leisure time to compare past and present, that Nero was Rome's first ruler to need a ghost writer. Caesar the Dictator had rivaled the greatest orators; Augustus had a spontaneous, fluent speaking style, such as was becoming to an emperor; Tiberius also was expert in the art of weighing his words and, besides, was forceful in expressing his meaning, or else deliberately ambiguous; even Gaius Caesar's muddled mind did not ruin his power as a speaker; and Claudius, when delivering a prepared address, showed no want of elegance. Nero, however, had even from boyhood turned his mental energies to interests of a different sort, such as engraving, painting, music, or horsemanship, and in his occasional attempts at writing poetry he showed some degree of training in the fundamentals.

4 When the period of make-believe mourning was ended, Nero entered the Senate chamber, and after some introductory remarks on the authority of the Fathers and the cooperative spirit of the army, he pointed out that he had available to him good advisers and precedents for a notably successful rule, and that the years of his youth had not been steeped in civil wars or family discord. He was bringing with him no hatreds, no resentments, no lust for revenge. Next he outlined the policies of his future administration, taking particular care to repudiate those practices which had aroused a still rankling resentment. He asserted that he would not act as judge in all kinds of cases so as to shut up the prosecutors and defendants under one roof and allow the power of a few to go unchecked. In his house nothing would be for sale or vulnerable to secret influence. Palace and state would be kept separate. The Senate should retain its traditional functions, Italy and the public provinces should appear before the tribunals of the consuls, who in turn should grant them access to the Fathers, while he himself would be responsible for the activity of the armies entrusted to him.

5 He was sincere in what he said, and in fact many measures were adopted by senatorial decision; for instance, that no lawyer's services for pleading a case should be sold for either a fee or gifts, and that the quaestors-elect should be relieved of the obligation to produce gladiatorial shows. Despite the opposition of Agrippina, on the ground that the enactments of Claudius were being abrogated, this last measure was passed by the Fathers, who were now being convened in the palace in order to make it possible for her to station herself at a special doorway in the rear, where she could be screened by a curtain which kept her from being seen but not from hearing. Still worse, when envoys from Armenia were pleading the cause of their people before Nero, she started to ascend the dais of the emperor and would have presided with him but that while all were frozen with horror, Seneca prompted Nero to step down and meet his mother. Thus a scandal was averted by a pretense at filial courtesy.

[Chapters 6–10 give an account of Rome's war with the Parthians in Asia.]

### Breach between Nero and Agrippina

11 In the consulship of Claudius Nero and Lucius Antistius [A.D. 55] when the new officials were swearing to abide by the enactments of the emperors, Nero forbade his colleague Antistius to swear allegiance to his own enactments and thereby aroused warm applause among the Fathers in the hope that his youthful mind, encouraged by the acclaim even of lesser deeds, might go on to greater ones. He followed this up with an act of clemency toward Plautius Lateranus by restoring him to the Senate, from which order he had been removed for adultery with Messalina, and he pledged himself to a lenient policy by a series of speeches in which Seneca used the emperor as a mouthpiece to broadcast the high moral tone of his teachings, or perhaps in order to display his talents.

12 Now his mother's influence was gradually weakened as Nero lapsed into an affair with a freedwoman named Acte. His confidants in this intrigue were Marcus Otho [5] and Claudius Senecio, a pair of fashionable young men, the former of consular family, the latter the son of one of Caesar's freedmen. Without his mother's knowledge, and afterward in the face of her opposition, this woman had worked her way into his affections through her sensuous appeal and mysterious intimacies. Not even the emperor's older friends offered opposition to letting an insignificant woman gratify his passion without harming anyone, seeing that he detested his wife Octavia [6] despite her high birth and exemplary character, be it through fate or because the unlawful has a greater charm. Besides, there was the danger that he would break

into outrages upon women of rank if he were forbidden this outlet.

*13* Agrippina raged away about having a freedwoman for a rival, a servant girl for a daughter-in-law, and so on, as women do, without waiting for either repentance on her son's part or repletion. But the more offensive her scolding became, the more she inflamed him, until at last, completely under the spell of his infatuation, he cast off all obedience toward his mother and put himself under the guidance of Seneca. One of Seneca's friends, Annaeus Serenus, under the pretense of an amour with the same freedwoman, had covered up the first passionate impulses of the youth by lending his name and openly lavishing on the woman those gifts which the emperor sent her in secret. Then Agrippina reversed her tactics and began to play up to the young emperor with endearing words, offering him the privacy of her own chamber to conceal that which his time of life and supreme rank demanded. She even went so far as to confess that her harshness had been ill-timed and she laid at his disposal the full use of her own resources, which were not much inferior to those of the emperor. Extreme as she had lately been in restraining her son, so now did she humble herself without moderation. This transformation did not deceive Nero. His closest friends were alarmed and begged him to be on guard against the schemes of a woman who had always been violent and was now deceitful as well. At this time it so happened that as Nero was inspecting the robes with which the wives and mothers of the emperors had arrayed themselves in splendor, he picked out a dress and some jewelry and sent them to his mother as a gift, an act by no means ungenerous, since without being asked he presented to her some very choice things, such as other women would covet. Agrippina, however, cried out that this added nothing to her own wardrobe, but that she was being deprived of the remainder and that her son was just doling things out to her from a store which he owed entirely to her.

*14* There were plenty of persons to report an exaggerated account of her words. Infuriated with those on whom the woman's arrogance relied for support, Nero removed Pallas from the high responsibilities to which he had been appointed by Claudius to become virtually the power behind the throne. The story went around that as Pallas was coming down from the Palatine escorted by a great crowd of retainers, Nero observed rather aptly that he was on the way to take the oath of abdication. As a matter of fact, Pallas had bargained that there was to be no investigation of any of his past acts and that his official accounts should be accepted as fully balanced. Thereupon Agrippina plunged recklessly into intimidation and threats and did not even restrain herself from asserting in the emperor's hearing that Britannicus[7] was now grown up and that he was the legitimate and rightful heir to succeed to his father's power, which a pretender, an adoptee, was exercising, thanks to the sins of his mother. No, she had no objection to permitting absolutely all the evils of the ill-fated house to be exposed: her own marriage to Claudius, first of all, and how she poisoned him. The one safeguard provided by the gods and her own precautions was that her stepson was alive. With him she would go to the Camp.[8] The soldiers would hear on the one side the daughter of Germanicus, on the other the cripple Burrus and the exile Seneca, those two who, apparently, claimed the right with a maimed hand and a professorial tongue to be the rulers of the whole world. As she spoke, she flung out her arms, uttering a stream of abuses and calling upon the deified Claudius, the spirits of the dead Silani, and all her fruitless crimes.

## Death of Britannicus

*15* Nero was worried by her conduct, and as the fourteenth birthday of Britannicus was near, he began to think over now his mother's violent outbursts, now the lad's own character, as recently revealed by an incident which, though insignificant in itself, had yet gained him widespread sympathy. During the festival of Saturn,[9] when among other games the boys were selecting their "king" by lot, the choice fell on Nero. Accordingly, he ordered the others to perform a variety of tasks, such as would cause them no embarrassment; but he commanded Britannicus to rise up, step into the middle of the room, and begin to sing, hoping thereby to secure a laugh at the expense of a boy who knew nothing even of sober parties, not to mention drunken revels. Britannicus, however, quite calmly started a song, the theme of which was his expulsion from his father's place and from the supreme power. This aroused expressions of pity which were all the more outspoken because the night and merrymaking had eliminated all pretense. Sensing the feeling against himself, Nero redoubled his hatred, and pressed by Agrippina's threats but having no formal charge against his brother, he did not dare openly to order his death and so planned to proceed secretly. He ordered the preparation of a poison to be arranged by Julius Pollio, tribune of a praetorian cohort, who had in his custody the woman named Locusta, a convicted poisoner and widely celebrated for her crimes. That none of those nearest to the person of Britannicus should have any regard for right or honor had long since been arranged. He received the first dose of poison from his own tutors, but suffered only a diarrhea and passed it off because it was not strong enough or perhaps it had been diluted so that he would not be violently affected right away. Nero, impatient at the slow progress of the crime, threatened the tribune and ordered Locusta the poisoner to be punished, asserting that in their worry about gossip and their preparing of an alibi they were interfering with his safety. Thereupon they promised that the murder would be accomplished as swiftly as with the sword, and so, right next to Caesar's chamber, a venomous potion was brewed, the quick action of which was assured by a previous test of the ingredients.

16 It was an established custom for the children of the royal house to take their meals in the presence of their relatives along with the other nobles of their age, seated at a more modest table of their own. Britannicus used to eat at this table and a specially chosen attendant tasted his food and drink. In order not to omit the taster or have the crime betrayed through the death of both persons, the following scheme was devised. A drink which was still harmless, but excessively hot, was pretasted and handed to Britannicus. When he refused it because it was too hot, the poison was poured in with some cold water, and it worked through his whole body so swiftly that his speech and breathing were cut off simultaneously. Confusion arose at the table; the undiscerning fled, but those with deeper understanding remained motionless in their places with their eyes upon Nero.

He just reclined there, the picture of innocence, and remarked that this was a common thing with Britannicus because of the epileptic condition with which he had been afflicted ever since he was a baby and that he would gradually recover his sight and consciousness. Agrippina, however, betrayed such terror, such consternation, though she tried to control her features, that it was perfectly clear that she was just as innocent as Octavia, the sister of Britannicus. She realized in fact that now her last resource had been torn from her and that here was the precedent for matricide. Octavia also, despite her tender years, had already learned to conceal sorrow, affection, every emotion. So, after a brief hush, the merriment of the party was resumed.

17 That same night combined both the murder of Britannicus and his pyre, the preparations for his modest funeral having been made in advance. He was entombed in the Campus Martius during a rainstorm of such violence that the public regarded it as a forewarning of the wrath of the gods against a crime which human beings generally were inclined to forgive, as they recalled the traditional discord between brothers and the fact that royal power tolerates no partner. A number of the writers of the time report that on several occasions before the murder Nero had violated the boyish purity of Britannicus, so that we may look upon his death as not so untimely and cruel after all, although it was amid the sanctity of the table, with no time given him to embrace his sisters,[10] and before the eyes of his enemy that a hurried death was visited on that last of the blood of the Claudians, whom dishonor had defiled even before the poison. Caesar issued an edict explaining the hasty funeral as due to the traditional custom of withdrawing the prematurely dead from the public eye without waiting for eulogies or processions. He added that for his own part, having lost his brother's support, he placed all his remaining hopes in his country, so that the Fathers and the people ought to be all the more solicitous of their emperor, who was the sole survivor of a family born to the supreme power.

18 Following this he enriched his most influential friends with lavish gifts. While there was considerable criticism of men who made a point of their moral integrity for having at a

time like this divided up city houses and country estates like so much loot, others felt that pressure had been brought to bear on them by an emperor with a guilty conscience who hoped to win forgiveness by putting all the most powerful men under obligations to him with bounteous presents. But his mother's anger could be appeased by no generosity. She took Octavia to her bosom and continually held secret meetings with her friends. With more than her natural avarice she grabbed up money from every source, apparently for an emergency fund. She graciously received tribunes and centurions and accorded high honor to the names and virtues of the still-existing nobles, as though she were in search of a leader and a party. Nero, who was well aware of her activities, ordered the removal not only of the military guard, which had been assigned her as the emperor's wife and now as the emperor's mother, but also of the personal bodyguard of Germans, which had recently been given her as an additional mark of honor. To prevent her being visited by the throngs of callers at the palace, he gave her a separate house, transferring her to what had been Antonia's [11] residence, and whenever he paid her a visit there, he came surrounded by a crowd of centurions and departed after a hasty kiss.

### A plot against Agrippina

19 There is nothing in human affairs so undependable and transitory as a reputation for power if it is based on a strength other than its own. Immediately Agrippina's threshold was deserted. No one offered her comfort, no one visited her, with the exception of a few women, whether prompted by love or hate is hard to tell. One of these was Junia Silana, who had been forced by Messalina to give up her husband, Gaius Silius, as I have related above [*Ann.* XI, 12]. This woman, who was conspicuous for her high birth, beauty, and profligacy, had long been a very dear friend of Agrippina's, but afterward a secret feud had sprung up between them, because when Sextius Africanus, a young noble, was going to marry Silana, Agrippina had frightened him off by telling him that she was an immoral woman and well on in years, not that she wished to keep Africanus for herself, but in order to prevent a husband from getting control of the wealth of the childless Silana.

Seeing a good chance for revenge, Silana got two of her own clients, Iturius and Calvisius, to accuse Agrippina, not of such old, familiar charges as her mourning the death of Britannicus or broadcasting the mistreatment of Octavia, but that she had formed a conspiracy to set up a new government headed by Rubellius Plautus, who was descended on his mother's side from the Divine Augustus in the same degree as Nero, and that by marrying him and making him emperor, she planned once more to get her hands on the control of the state. Iturius and Calvisius revealed these charges to Atimetus, a freedman of Nero's aunt Domitia. Delighted at the opportunity, for there was a bitter rivalry between Agrippina and Domitia, he induced the actor Paris, who was himself a freedman of Domitia, to go speedily and present the charge as a dangerous threat.

20 The night was well on, and Nero was prolonging it over the wine, when Paris entered. Normally his appearance at that hour would stimulate the emperor's revelry, but on this occasion Paris assumed a solemn demeanor, and as he exposed the details of the plot, he got his hearer so frightened that he expressed his determination not only to put his mother and Plautus to death but also to remove Burrus as prefect on the ground that as he owed his promotion to Agrippina's support, he was now discharging his obligation to her. According to Fabius Rusticus, Nero actually wrote out a dispatch to Caecina Tuscus appointing him to the command of the praetorian cohorts, but through Seneca's influence Burrus was retained in his post. Pliny and Cluvius report that no doubt whatever was cast on the loyalty of the prefect. We must realize that Fabius shows a tendency to glorify Seneca, through whose friendship he prospered. For my part, I intend to follow the authorities where they agree, but where the reports differ, I shall cite the variations with the names of their sources.

In his alarm and his impatience to kill his mother Nero could not be put off until Burrus promised her execution if she should be proved guilty of the crime. After all, anyone, not alone one's mother, should be given an opportunity for self-defense. He pointed out further that the accusers were not present, but that all they had was the word of one man coming from the house of Agrippina's enemy. He must take into consideration the darkness, the lateness of the night spent in revelry, and the whole environment, which was conducive to reckless and uninformed judgments.

21 Thus the emperor's fears were quieted, and at daybreak a call was made on Agrippina to inform her of the charges and allow her either to refute them or pay the penalty. Burrus carried out his instructions in the presence of Seneca. There were also some freedmen who witnessed the interview. After explaining the accusations and naming their authors, Burrus assumed a threatening attitude. Agrippina, maintaining her defiant spirit, replied: "I am not surprised that Silana, who has never borne a child, knows nothing of a mother's feelings. Children cannot be changed by their parents as lightly as an immoral woman can change her lovers. If Iturius and Calvisius, after squandering all their fortunes, are paying the old lady this latest service of undertaking an accusation for her, that is no good reason why either I must incur the infamy of seeking to murder my son or Caesar must have matricide on his conscience. I should, in fact, thank Domitia for her enmity if she were contending with me in good will toward my Nero. But in reality, aided by her bedfellow Atimetus and the actor Paris, she is composing what looks like the scenario for a play. She was beautifying the fish preserves of her Baian estate during the time when my efforts were securing Nero's adoption, his proconsular powers, his appointment as consul-designate, and all the other necessary steps toward succeeding to the sovereignty. Or else let someone come forward to prove that the cohorts in the city have been tampered with, that the allegiance of the provinces has been shaken, and finally that the emperor's slaves or freedmen have been corrupted to commit a crime. Could I have remained alive with Britannicus in power? And if Plautus, or any other man, were to become master of the state and be my judge, I do not have enough accusers, I suppose, to bring up against me not merely words, indiscreet at times because of my impetuous affection, but crimes so grave that none but a son could acquit me of them." Her words moved her hearers deeply, and when they even tried to calm her indignation, she demanded an interview with her son. At this interview she uttered not a word in her defense, so as to show

no misgivings, and she refrained from seeming to reproach him by mentioning her services, but she secured vengeance on the informers and rewards for her friends.

[Chapters 22–24 relate minor events in Rome.]

*Riotous conduct of Nero*

25 In the consulship of Quintus Volusius and Publius Scipio [A.D. 56], there was peace abroad but scandalous disorder in Rome, in that Nero, disguised as a slave, prowled through the streets, dives, and taverns of the city, escorted by companions who would seize merchandise offered for sale and inflict injuries on those they encountered, while their victims were so ignorant of the identity of their assailant that even Nero himself received some blows and bore the marks on his face. Then, after it became generally known that the marauder was Caesar and the indignities committed on distinguished men and women were multiplied, for once such conduct became legitimate, other hoodlums, operating with impunity under Nero's name, carried on the same riotous practices with gangs of their own, the nights were spent as though Rome were a city captured by an enemy. One Julius Montanus, a member of the senatorial order, though he had not yet held office, chanced to collide with the emperor in the dark, but because he fought back vigorously against his attacker and then upon recognizing him begged for pardon, he was regarded as having rebuked Nero and was forced to die. This made Nero more fearful thereafter, so that he surrounded himself with soldiers and a number of gladiators under instructions to keep hands off any brawls which started mildly and on a private scale; if, however, the victims put up too good a fight, the men were to interfere with arms. In addition, Nero stirred up the disorders at the theater and incited the partisans of the actors to what were virtually pitched battles by granting them impunity and even prizes, while he himself watched them from hiding or, quite often, in plain view. Things got to the point where the populace became so riotous and the fear of a more serious disturbance was so grave that the only remedy which could be found was to expel the actors from Italy and to restore the military guard at the theater.

[Chapters 26–44 treat politics in Rome and the wars in Asia.]

## Nero and Poppaea

45 A no less conspicuous scandal in that year [A.D. 58] was the starting point for grave misfortunes to the state. There was in Rome a certain Sabina Poppaea, who, though her father was Titus Ollius, had taken the name of her maternal grandfather, Poppaeus Sabinus of illustrious memory, a consular who had won the high distinction of the triumphal insignia, whereas Ollius had been ruined through his friendship with Sejanus [12] before holding the higher offices. This woman had everything except a decent character. Her mother, the most beautiful woman of her day, had endowed her with her fame and her beauty alike. Her fortune was adequate to the distinguished position of the family. She was gracious in conversation and had a ready wit. She paraded her modesty and yet indulged in dissipation. She appeared in public but rarely, and when she did, she kept her face half veiled so as not to satisfy men's gazes, or because this style was becoming to her. Never was she scrupulous about her good name, making no distinction between a husband and a lover. Untouched by any sentiment involving either herself or another person, wherever material advantage was indicated, there she transferred her lust. While she was still living as the wife of Rufrius Crispinus, a Roman knight by whom she had a son, she was attracted to Otho because of his youth, his lavish mode of life, and his reputation as one of Nero's warmest friends. With no loss of time adultery was followed by marriage.

46 It may be that the indiscretion of love caused Otho to praise the beauty and charm of his wife in the presence of the emperor, or he may have intended deliberately to inflame him, with the idea that if both possessed the same woman, this might be an additional bond to strengthen his influence. Many a time, as he rose from Caesar's table, he was heard to remark that he was going to his wife, that in her he possessed high birth, beauty, that which all men crave and the fortunate enjoy. Through the use of such stimuli as these there was no long delay before Poppaea got access to the emperor. First she gained a hold over him by her flatteries and wiles, pretending to be overpowered by her passion and captivated by Nero's personal charm; later, when the emperor's love was already ardent, she changed over to a haughty attitude, reminding him, in case he detained her for more than a single night or two, that she was a married woman and couldn't allow herself to lose her husband, for she was attached to Otho because he really knew how to live in a way no one else could equal; Otho was truly royal both in mind and in style; with him she had before her eyes only that which was worthy of the highest rank, whereas Nero, tied down as he was to a slave mistress through his connection with Acte, had gained not a thing from his cohabitation with a slave but what was low and degrading. Otho was first dropped from his position of intimacy with Nero, then from attending his functions and escorting him, and finally, in order to eliminate him as a rival in Rome, he was appointed governor of the province of Lusitania.[13] In that position he remained until the civil war,[14] and in contrast with his disgraceful reputation in the past, he conducted himself uprightly and honorably, intemperate in his private life, but fairly restrained in his exercise of power.

## Banishment of Sulla

47 Up to this time Nero had sought to veil his outrages and crimes. He was particularly suspicious of Cornelius Sulla, whose apathetic disposition he interpreted as being exactly the opposite, so that he regarded him a sly hypocrite. Graptus, one of Caesar's freedmen, who through a long life of experience was thoroughly familiar with the ways of the imperial household ever since Tiberius, increased Nero's fears by the following deceit. In those days the Mulvian Bridge [15] was popular for its nocturnal attractions. Nero would often go out there so that he could carry on his revels with greater freedom outside the city limits. Graptus made up the yarn that as Nero was returning by the Flaminian Way, an ambush was laid for him, which he escaped providentially by turning off on a different road to the Gardens of Sallust, and that the author of this plot was Sulla. This lie was inspired by the fact that as the emperor's servants were returning to Rome, it so chanced that they were given a needless scare by some young roisterers such as were carrying on everywhere at the time. As a matter of fact, not one of Sulla's slaves or clients was recognized

among them, and the man's character, which was held in low regard and was quite incapable of any act of daring, made such a charge absurd. Yet, as though actually proved guilty, he was ordered to leave the country and confine himself within the walls of Massilia.[16]

[Chapters 48–58 recount miscellaneous affairs in Rome and Germany.]

## Book XIV

### *Murder of Agrippina*

*1* In the consulship of Gaius Vipstanus and Gaius Fonteius [A.D. 59] Nero postponed no further his long-planned crime, now that several years of rule had strengthened his audacity, while his love for Poppaea was growing more intense each day. Since the woman had given up hope of having him marry her and divorce Octavia as long as Agrippina was alive, she nagged at him continually and often sneered at him, calling him a ward who had to take orders from others and who, far from being an emperor, did not even possess his personal liberty. She would ask why he was putting off his marriage with her. Presumably he did not approve of her looks and the military triumphs of her grandparents; or perhaps it was her childbearing ability and her sincere devotion that he found fault with. It was feared, she charged, that once she became his wife, she would expose the indignities inflicted on the Fathers and the popular resentment against the arrogance and greed of his mother. If Agrippina would tolerate no daughter-in-law except one that was her son's enemy, she for her part wanted to be restored to her marriage with Otho. She was prepared to go to any place on earth where she might rather hear of the emperor's humiliation than witness it while being personally entangled in his dangers. Such reproaches, uttered with all the tears and guile of a wanton woman, made a deep impression, and there was no attempt to stop her, since all were eager to have the mother's influence broken and no one believed that the son's hate would go to the extreme of murder.

*2* Cluvius reports that Agrippina went to such lengths in her eagerness to hold her influence that on several occasions, when Nero was getting heated with wine and feasting at midday, she offered herself to him in his drunken state attractively dressed and ready for incest. When those near by began to notice the lustful kisses and caresses preparatory to an act of shame, Seneca tried to counteract these feminine allurements through another woman by bringing in the freedwoman Acte, who, concerned as she was for both her own peril and Nero's disgrace, was to inform him that his incestuous conduct was widely known, since his mother bragged about it, and that the troops would never tolerate the rule of a sinful emperor. According to Fabius Rusticus, this immoral relationship was desired not by Agrippina but by Nero himself and was foiled by the cleverness of this same freedwoman. The other authorities, however, as well as popular report, agree with Cluvius' version, whether because Agrippina actually did conceive a sin of such enormity or because it seemed easier to believe this woman capable of contriving a novel form of vice, seeing that as a mere girl she had committed adultery with Lepidus in the hope of winning power and had with the same motive stooped to improper relations with Pallas and then had prepared herself for any degree of sin by marrying her own uncle.

*3* Consequently Nero avoided meeting her in private, and when she withdrew to her gardens or her country estates at Tusculum or Antium,[17] he praised her for taking a vacation. Finally, convinced that she was just too dangerous no matter where she kept herself, he decided to kill her, deliberating only as to the method, that is, whether by poison, steel, or some other form of violence. At first he favored poison, but if it were administered at the emperor's dinner table, what happened could not be explained as accidental after the way Britannicus had died; also it seemed impracticable to tamper with the servants of a woman who through her own experience with crime was on the alert against treachery. Besides, she had fortified her system by dosing herself with antidotes in advance. As for murder with steel, no one could figure out a way to keep it hidden, and there was the danger that whoever was chosen for so dreadful a crime might disobey orders. In this emergency the freedman Anicetus offered his talents. He was prefect of the fleet at Misenum and had been a tutor of Nero's boyhood, and he hated Agrippina as heartily as she hated him. He demonstrated that a ship could be built a portion of which should through some device come loose right on the sea and plunge the unsuspecting woman into the water. Nothing, as he pointed out, was so rich in possibilities of accident as the sea, and if she should be taken by shipwreck, who would be so unreasonable as to attribute to human crime what was the fault of the wind and the waves? The emperor would build a temple and altars to the dead woman and do whatever else was needed to display his devotion as a son.

4 This scheme was approved and it was aided also by the occasion, for Nero was celebrating the Quinquatrus festival at Baiae.[18] He lured his mother there by repeatedly asserting that one really ought to put up with angry outbursts on the part of one's parents and it was one's duty to appease their feelings. In this way he hoped to spread a rumor that he was reconciled and to get Agrippina to accept it, since women readily believe what they enjoy believing. When she arrived, he went out onto the beach to meet her (she was coming from Antium), lent her his hand, embraced her, and escorted her to Bauli. This is the name of a villa at the edge of the winding shore between the Cape of Misenum and the Lake of Baiae. Among the ships stationed here there was one more elegantly adorned than the rest, apparently as an additional mark of honor to his mother, who was regularly accustomed to sail in a trireme manned by members of the fleet. Besides, she was invited to dinner on this occasion so that night should aid in concealing the crime. It is well established that someone betrayed the plot and that Agrippina, on hearing of this, was uncertain whether to believe it, but traveled overland to Baiae in a sedan chair. There Nero's caresses banished her fears. She was graciously received and given a place above the emperor himself. Nero talked to her volubly, now with boyish intimacy and again gravely, as though sharing important confidences with her, and so the party was continued to a late hour. When she left, he escorted her, warmly kissing her eyes and clinging to her bosom, whether in order to carry hypocrisy to its limits or because his last sight of his doomed mother touched even Nero's savage breast.

5 A bright, starry night and a perfectly calm sea were provided by the gods as though for the purpose of exposing the crime. The ship had not traveled far. Agrippina was attended by two of her friends, one of whom, Crepereius Gallus, was standing nearby, not far from the pilot; the other, Acerronia, was leaning over the foot of the couch where Agrippina lay and happily discussing the son's change of heart and the mother's restoration to favor, when suddenly at a signal the heavy, leaded ceiling of the cabin collapsed and Crepereius was crushed and instantly killed. Agrippina and Acerronia were saved by the projecting framework of the couch, which proved strong enough to hold up under the weight. The ship did not immediately break apart because of the general confusion, as those not in the plot interfered with those who were. Thereupon the crew decided to throw all their weight on one side and so capsize the boat, but they failed to work together promptly in the emergency, while others, pressing down on the opposite side, made it possible for the passengers to slide more gently into the sea. While Acerronia, unaware of the plot, was screaming that she was Agrippina and calling for help to the emperor's mother, she was killed with poles and oars and whatever other naval implements came to hand. Agrippina herself, keeping silent and thus remaining unrecognized (she did, however, receive one wound on the shoulder), swam off, and then on meeting with some fishing boats, she was taken to the Lucrine Lake and conveyed to her villa.

6 There she reflected that this explained why she had been invited through a treacherous letter and shown such distinguished honor and why a ship, close to shore, driven by no winds, colliding with no rocks, had collapsed in its upper portion like any land mechanism. Also, as she thought over how Acerronia had been killed and she herself had been wounded, she realized that her only protection against the plot was to ignore it. So she sent her freedman Agerinus to report to her son that thanks to the favor of the gods and Nero's own good luck she had escaped a terrible accident. She begged him that despite his alarm about his mother's danger he should postpone his concern to visit her, since what she needed for the time being was quiet. In the meantime, pretending to be unworried, she had her wound dressed and got warm applications for her body. She gave orders that Acerronia's will be found and her property sealed, her one act in which she showed no pretense.

*7* Meanwhile, as Nero was waiting for the report that the deed had been accomplished, he received the news that she had escaped with a slight wound only, after having been endangered just enough so as to leave no doubt as to who was responsible. Frightened to death, he avowed that she would show up at any moment bent on revenge, and if she were to arm slaves or inflame the troops or go before the Senate and the people denouncing him for the shipwreck and her wound and the murder of her friends, what protection did he have against her? Unless possibly Burrus and Seneca could suggest something. He had them waked up and summoned immediately, though it is uncertain whether they were previously informed of the plot. They were both silent for a long while, either because they felt it would be useless to dissuade him or they thought the situation had so far deteriorated that Agrippina had to be stopped in order to save Nero from destruction. Seneca first broke the silence by merely turning to Burrus and asking whether the troops should be ordered to carry out the execution. Burrus replied that the praetorians were loyal to all the house of the Caesars and that with the memory of Germanicus [19] still alive they would commit no outrage against his daughter. Let Anicetus finish what he had promised. The latter showed no hesitation in demanding the entire management of the crime. Upon hearing this, Nero exclaimed that his reign started with this day and that the author of this great boon was a freedman. Let him go speedily and take along men who would most readily carry out his orders. Nero himself, on hearing of the arrival of Agerinus as Agrippina's messenger, arranged the setting for an accusation on his own part by throwing a sword between the man's feet while he was delivering his message and then ordering him cast into chains as though caught in the act, thus making it possible to pretend that his mother had plotted to assassinate the emperor and that through shame at the discovery of the crime she had taken her own life.

*8* In the meantime, with the spreading of the news of Agrippina's harrowing experience, which was thought an accident, everyone on hearing of it came running down to the shore. They climbed up on the breakwater, they mounted the nearest boats, others waded into the sea as deep as they could, some stretched forth their arms, the whole beach was confused with lamentations, prayers, and shouts, amid a jumble of questions and unintelligible answers. A huge crowd came pouring in with lights, and at the news that Agrippina was safe, they were pressing forward to offer their congratulations, when they were scattered at the appearance of a threatening troop of armed soldiers. Anicetus threw a guard around the villa, broke down the door, seizing those slaves whom he encountered, and reached the entrance of the bedroom. Here only a few were standing by, as the rest had been frightened away by the invaders. The room was dimly lighted, and just one of the maids remained, while Agrippina's anxiety increased momentarily that there was no messenger from her son and not even Agerinus was back. If all were well, things would look different. Now she was deserted and there was a sudden uproar, all indications of extreme danger. Then as the maid started to leave, she exclaimed, "So you are leaving me, too," and turning her head she saw Anicetus, accompanied by the trierarch Herculeius and the naval centurion Obaritus. If he had come to call on her, she said, he could report that she was feeling better, but if his purpose was to commit a crime, she did not believe it of her son. He had not ordered his mother's murder. The assassins surrounded the bed, and first the trierarch brought a club down on her head. As the centurion was already drawing his sword for the deathstroke, she thrust forth her abdomen, and screaming "Strike my womb!" she was dispatched with many wounds.

*9* These facts are supported by all the authorities. That Nero actually viewed his dead mother and praised her beautiful body is asserted by some writers and denied by others. She was cremated that same night on an ordinary dinner couch and with a common funeral ceremony. As long as Nero was emperor, her grave had no mound or enclosure. Later through the efforts of her household it received a low mound near the highway to Misenum and the villa of Caesar the Dictator, which stands on a high elevation overlooking the bay. After her pyre was lighted, a freedman of hers, named Mnester, stabbed himself to death either through affection for his patroness or through fear of execution. Agrippina had believed many years before that she would have this end, but she regarded it with indifference. When she was consulting the Chaldaeans about Nero's future, the soothsayers replied that he would some day be emperor and would kill his mother, and she exclaimed, "Let him kill me, provided he is emperor!"

*10* Only after the crime was done did Caesar at last realize its enormity. He spent the rest of that night now lying silent, more often leaping up in terror, and in a helpless state of mind he awaited the daylight which he thought would bring his end. The first note of encouragement came when, at Burrus' suggestion, he received the flatteries of the centurions and tribunes, who grasped his hand and congratulated him at his having escaped the unforeseen danger and his mother's deed. Then his friends flocked to the temples, and following this example the neighboring towns of Campania gave proof of their joy by offering sacrifices and sending deputations. Nero himself, following a different type of hypocrisy, acted as though he were dejected and angered at his own survival, and he shed tears over his mother's death. Still, because natural scenery cannot be changed as easily as the human countenance and he had ever before him the grim view of that sea and shore (some, in fact, believed that a trumpet call was heard in the surrounding heights and that wails rose from the mother's grave), he withdrew to Naples and sent a dispatch to the Senate, the substance of which was that the would-be assassin, Agerinus, one of Agrippina's most trusted freedmen, was caught with a sword and that Agrippina, conscience-stricken over her attempted crime, had now made expiation.

*11* He added some charges which went back rather far: that she had aimed at joint rule with the emperor and at having the praetorian cohorts take the oath of allegiance to a woman and inflicting the same degradation on the Senate and people, and that when frustrated in this ambition, she was so incensed at the troops and the Fathers and the people that she had opposed his granting a bonus to the army and the people and had framed capital charges against prominent citizens. He called attention to his own efforts in preventing her from bursting into the Senate chamber and from giving official replies to foreign nations. With an indirect slap at the Claudian era he blamed all the outrages

of that reign upon his mother, interpreting her destruction as a national blessing. He even told of the shipwreck; after that who could be found that was stupid enough to believe that this was only an accident or that a shipwrecked woman had sent just one man with a weapon to force his way through the cohorts and fleets of the emperor? The resulting criticism was no longer aimed at Nero, whose brutality now went beyond all protest, but rather at Seneca for having written a speech which was virtually a confession.

*12* Nevertheless, with astonishing rivalry on the part of the leading men, decrees were passed proclaiming thanksgiving services at all the temples, and ordering that the Quinquatrus, the festival on which the plot was discovered, be celebrated with annual games, that a gold statue of Minerva be set up in the Senate chamber with a portrait of the emperor next to it, and that Agrippina's birthday be one of the accursed days on the calendar. Thrasea Paetus, who had been accustomed to pass over previous acts of flattery in silence or with brief assent, walked out of the Senate on this occasion, thus providing a basis for endangering himself without offering the others any leadership toward freedom. There was also a profusion of omens which proved meaningless: a woman was delivered of a snake; another was killed by lightning while lying with her husband; there was a sudden eclipse of the sun, and the fourteen districts of Rome were struck by lightning. So little were the gods concerned with these prodigies that Nero's rule and his crimes continued for a number of years thereafter. In order to aggravate the feeling against his mother and to demonstrate that with her removal his own leniency was increased, he restored to their native soil the noblewomen, Junia and Calpurnia, and the former praetors, Valerius Capito and Licinius Gabolus, all of whom had been formerly exiled by Agrippina. He even permitted the return of the ashes of Lollia Paulina and the building of her tomb. He also released from punishment Iturius and Calvisius, whom he had himself banished recently. As for Silana, she had already died after returning to Tarentum from her distant exile, when Agrippina, through whose enmity she had fallen, was already losing her influence or else had softened her attitude.

*13* Nevertheless Nero lingered in the towns

of Campania, worried as to how he should enter Rome and whether he would encounter a submissive Senate and a favorable public. To reassure him, the vilest characters, such as flourished in his court as never before, argued that the, name of Agrippina was hated and that the enthusiasm of the populace had been aroused by her death. He should go unafraid and experience in person their reverence for him. At the same time they claimed the right to go on ahead. They found everything even more favorable than they had promised: the tribes out to meet him, the Senate in holiday dress, columns of women and children arranged by age and sex, stands for spectators erected along his route, just as when triumphal processions are viewed. Thus, as an arrogant conqueror of the servile populace, he proceeded to the Capitol, offered his thanks, and then plunged recklessly into all those forms of dissipation which, though ill suppressed, had previously been held in check by some small degree of respect toward his mother.

*Artistic interests of Nero*

14 Nero had long entertained an ambition to compete in the four-horse chariot race and a no less disgusting interest in playing the lyre on the professional stage. He argued that horse racing was a royal sport, indulged in by leaders of olden times, heralded in the praise of poets, and celebrated in honor of the gods; that music was in fact sacred to Apollo and that the mighty god of prophecy stood garbed in the robes of a musician not only in the cities of Greece but also in Roman temples. When he could no longer be restrained, Seneca and Burrus thought it best to concede him the one so that he should not end by doing both. An area was enclosed in the Vatican valley, where he could drive his horses without being exposed to public view. Soon the Roman public was actually invited in, and they praised him to the skies, as the common people will do, eager as they are for amusements and gratified if their ruler has the same interests. Still, the advertising of his shame did not bring the expected satiety, but only stimulated him all the more. Thinking that the disgrace would be lessened if more persons were defiled, he brought upon the stage descendants of noble families, men made venal through poverty. Since these men have passed

away, I feel that out of respect for their ancestors I should refrain from naming them; for the disgrace must be shared by the ruler who gave them money to do wrong rather than to keep them from it. With huge gifts he also induced well-known Roman knights to offer their services in the arena, but we must realize that a reward from one who has the power to command is equivalent to compulsion.

15 Refraining as yet from disgracing himself by an appearance on the public stage, he initiated the games called Juvenalia, for which volunteers enrolled quite generally. No one was deterred by high rank, age, or the offices he had held from performing as a Greek or Latin actor even to the extreme of indecent gestures and rhythms. Even worse, noble ladies acted in shameful roles. In the park with which Augustus had surrounded the Naval Pool,[20] lounging places and taverns were built and incentives to vice were offered for sale. Tokens were distributed, which the respectable spent through necessity and the immodest as a means of display. This brought on a general increase in vice and scandal, and in fact nothing contributed more to the further corruption of our long degraded morals than that filthy crowd. It is difficult enough to uphold decency even in a respectable environment, so that it is not surprising that in an atmosphere of competition in vice there could be no place for purity or modesty or honor in any form. As a climax, Nero appeared in person on the stage, tuning his lyre with great care and playing a preliminary number with his voice teachers standing by. To escort him there was a military cohort, with centurions and tribunes, and Burrus heartsick but applauding. On this occasion Roman knights were enrolled for the first time under the title of Augustians, men conspicuous for their youth and physique and motivated either by a natural love of pleasure or by the hope of winning influence. They made day and night noisy with applause, praising the emperor's beauty and voice with such names as are used of gods. They conducted themselves as though they were gaining fame and high honor through meritorious conduct.

16 To show the world that the emperor had not the talents of an actor only, he took up also an interest in poetry and brought together a

group of men possessed of some skill in versifying but not yet well known as poets. After dinner they would sit down with him and weave together verses which were brought in or thought out on the spot, and they finished out Nero's own words which he threw out haphazardly, a method of composition indicated by the appearance of the verses themselves, which do not flow with any momentum and inspiration or uniformity of style. He devoted some time also to teachers of philosophy as an after-dinner function and in order to amuse himself with their disagreements as they argued their opposing views. There were in fact some individuals who by assuming a solemn aspect and demeanor sought to be regarded among the diversions of the court.

[Chapters 17–21 describe minor events in Rome.]

### Banishment of Plautus

22 It was at this time (A.D. 60) that a comet blazed forth. The opinion among the common people is that this phenomenon means a change of ruler. Consequently, on the supposition that Nero was already deposed, people began asking who would be his successor. All lips mentioned Rubellius Plautus, who was a noble of the Julian house on his mother's side. He lived by the teaching of his ancestors, dressing plainly and keeping his home pure and private, but the more inconspicuous he tried to be through caution, the more publicity he acquired. The rumors about him were increased through an equally senseless interpretation of a thunderbolt. As Nero was reclining for dinner in the villa called Sublaqueum at the Simbruine lakes,[21] a bolt of lightning struck the dinner table, scattering it, and because the scene of this accident was in the territory of Tibur, the native district of Plautus' family on his father's side, people thought Plautus must be the person destined to rule by divine will, and he began to be courted by many of those persons who have a selfish and generally deluded ambition to offer the first homage to new and still uncertain fortunes. Worried by this development, Nero wrote a letter to Plautus suggesting that out of regard for the peace of the city he should remove his presence from these malicious rumors, and reminding him that he had ancestral estates in Asia, where he could enjoy the prime of his life in safety and tran-

quillity. Consequently, Plautus retired there with his wife Antistia and a few intimate friends. At about the same time an intemperate impulse to self-indulgence brought Nero unfavorable publicity and personal danger when he went swimming in the spring of the Aqua Marcia, which is piped to the city. It was felt that he had polluted the sacred drinking waters and the religious sanctity of the spot by washing his body there. A severe illness which followed confirmed the displeasure of the gods.

[Chapters 23–50 describe campaigns in the East, the British revolt under Boudicca, and events in Rome.]

### Death of Burrus

51 While the evils of the state grew worse every day, the means of defense were weakened with the death of Burrus, whether from illness or poison is uncertain. A natural end was indicated by the fact that he had been suffering from a swelling in his throat which as it gradually increased blocked the windpipe and stopped his breathing. It was more widely asserted that at Nero's orders his palate was painted with a poisonous drug under pretense of a remedy and that Burrus detected the crime; when the emperor came to see him, Burrus avoided his gaze and replied to his inquiry only with these words: "*I* am all right!" He was missed greatly and for a long time by his countrymen, who remembered his fine character, and because of the innocuous inefficiency of one of his two successors and the outrageous crimes of the other. Caesar had now appointed two men to command the praetorian cohorts: Faenius Rufus, on account of his popularity after handling the distribution of grain without graft, and Sofonius Tigellinus, whose hardened shamelessness and scandalous reputation appealed to him. In fact, both men lived up to their past characters, Tigellinus having a stronger position in favor of the emperor and being made a party to his most intimate orgies, while Rufus enjoyed a high repute with the people and the soldiers, a circumstance which he discovered to be a handicap with Nero.

### Retirement of Seneca

52 The death of Burrus impaired the influence of Seneca, now that the cause of virtue was weakened through the loss of one of its

two champions and Nero was beginning to lean toward the worse elements. These began attacking Seneca with a variety of accusations, alleging that he was continuing to add to his wealth, which was already too vast for the fortune of a private citizen, that he was drawing popular support to himself, and that he was outdoing the emperor in the beauty of his gardens and the grandeur of his villas. They charged also that he was trying to monopolize fame as an orator and had become much more active in writing poetry after Nero had taken a fancy thereto. They stated that openly hostile as he was to the emperor's amusements, he belittled his skill at driving horses and ridiculed his tone-quality whenever he sang. How long was nothing to be regarded as excellent in the nation unless Seneca were deemed its originator? Nero's boyhood was surely over and he was enjoying the full prime of youth. Let him discard the schoolmaster, since he was blessed with sufficiently accomplished teachers in his own ancestors.

*53* Seneca was not unaware of these charges, for they were revealed to him by those who had some regard for honor and Caesar was increasingly avoiding his society. He asked for an interview and on receiving it, began as follows: "It is the fourteenth year now, Caesar, since I have been associated with your career, the eighth of your tenure of power. Within this period you have heaped upon me such honors and riches that all I need to complete my happiness is contentment with my good fortune. I shall cite great precedents, drawn not from my station of life but from yours. Your great-great-grandfather Augustus permitted Marcus Agrippa to withdraw to private life in Mytilene and granted Gaius Maecenas the privilege of retirement in Rome itself as though in a foreign land. The former had been his associate in war, the latter had fought through even more struggles in Rome, and both were rewarded amply, to be sure, but in payment for really great services. But what have I been able to offer in return for your generosity other than my studies, fostered as it were in scholarly seclusion and owing their distinction to my reputation for having aided your youthful training, indeed a great reward for such service? But you, on the other hand, have surrounded me with prestige so unlimited, with wealth so unnumbered, that often I reflect within myself: 'Am I, born in an equestrian and provincial station, now numbered with the leaders of our nation? Among nobles who can boast of generations of honors does my new arrival shine so conspicuously? Where is that spirit which was content with little? Has it laid out these fine gardens, does it stroll through these suburban estates, does it luxuriate in such vast stretches of land and such widespread investments?' The only excuse which comes to my mind is that I had no right to oppose your generous gifts.

*54* "But now both of us have completed the measure to the full, you as far as a prince could be generous to a friend, and I as far as a friend could receive generosity from a prince. Everything beyond this only increases prejudice. Although such prejudice, like all things mortal, lies beneath your greatness, it rests heavily upon me and I am in need of relief. Just as, if I were campaigning or on the highway, I might ask for a staff when weary, so in this journey of life, now that I am an old man, unequal even to the lightest responsibilities and unable to sustain my wealth any longer, I beg support. Issue orders for my fortune to be managed through your procurators and included among your property. I shall not be reducing myself to poverty, but by surrendering those possessions which now blind me with their glitter, I shall restore to my spirit that time which I have been devoting exclusively to the management of my gardens and villas. You are now more than strong enough by yourself after experiencing the control of the supreme power through all these years. We, your older friends, can now claim our right to relax. Your glory will also be enhanced by your having raised to the highest place men who would have been content even with a moderate station."

*55* To these words Nero replied about as follows: "That I am now able to reply spontaneously to your prepared speech I owe first of all to you, for you taught me how to express myself not only in premeditated words but also extemporaneously. My great-great-grandfather Augustus did permit Agrippa and Maecenas to retire after their labors, but he had himself reached an age the authority of which could justify his concessions, no matter how great or what their nature; but even so, he did not strip either of these men of the rewards which he had given them. They had earned them in war and in personal dangers, for it was amid these conditions that Augustus had passed his youth. I also should not have found your sword and physical prowess lacking if I were engaged in arms. But as my situation at the time demanded, you fostered first my boyhood, then my youth with your wisdom, counsels, and teachings. Your gifts to me will be with me forever, as long as my life endures; but those things which you have from me, gardens, capital, villas, are exposed to the accidents of life. Numerous though they may seem, yet a good many persons, who did not remotely equal your talents, have possessed more. I am ashamed to mention even freedmen who are conspicuously richer. As a result, I must blush that though you stand first in my affections, you have not yet surpassed all in fortune.

*56* "But you are still in the vigor of life and equal to your duties and the fruits of them, whereas I am only in the first laps of my reign; unless possibly you rate yourself below Vitellius, who was three times consul, or me below Claudius, and unless my generosity is unable to supply in your case as much wealth as a long life of thrift accumulated for Volusius.[22] Besides, if at some point the unsteady time of my youth slips off the path, why do you not recall my steps to safety and guide my strength with greater zeal, fortifying it with your support? It will not be your moderate spirit if you give back your money, not your retirement if you abandon the emperor, but my avarice and fear of my cruelty that everyone will talk about. However great the praise which your self-restraint may inspire, it would hardly be ethical for a philosopher to win glory for himself if thereby he brings dishonor on his friend." This speech was followed by an embrace and kisses, since Nero was fashioned by nature and trained by habit to veil his hatred with deceptive marks of affection. Ending the interview as every interview with a ruler must end, Seneca expressed his thanks. But he changed the routine of his former position of power, stopped the crowds of visitors, avoided escorts, and scarcely ever appeared in the city, pretending that ill health or his philosophical studies were keeping him at home.

## Murder of Sulla and Plautus

*57* With Seneca overthrown it was easy enough to undermine the position of Faenius Rufus by charging him with friendship toward Agrippina. Tigellinus grew more powerful every day, and thinking that the evil devices on which alone his strength depended would be more effective if he could bind the emperor to himself as an accomplice in crime, he began to explore his secret fears. When he learned that the two chief objects of his dread were Plautus and Sulla, and that Plautus had recently been removed to Asia and Sulla to Narbonese Gaul, he kept harping on their noble birth and the proximity of the armies of the East to the former and of the armies of Germany to the latter. He claimed that he did not, like Burrus, have a divided allegiance, but that he was concerned for the safety of Nero alone. Nero could be protected against treachery in the city well enough by immediate measures; but if there were uprisings far away, how could they be crushed? The provinces of Gaul were tense at the name of the great Dictator Sulla and the peoples of Asia were no less under the spell of the renown of Plautus' grandfather Drusus. Sulla was a poor man—a major stimulus to daring—and one who pretended indolence until he should find an opening for recklessness. Plautus, a man of wealth, did not even pretend to a love of retirement, but was parading his imitation of the old-time Romans; he had in addition adopted the arrogance of the Stoics, a sect which made its adherents restless and eager for trouble. There was no further delay. On the sixth day the assassins had reached Massilia, and before Sulla had even time to be frightened or to hear any reports, he was murdered while reclining at dinner. When his head was brought to Nero, the emperor made fun of it as ugly with its premature grey hairs.

*58* The plan for Plautus' murder was not kept a secret so successfully, because more persons were concerned for his safety, and the long distance by land and sea and the interval of time had set rumors going. A false story was widely spread that he sought out Corbulo, who was then commander of large forces and who would be particularly exposed to danger if distinguished and blameless men were going to be murdered.

It was even rumored that Asia had taken up arms out of sympathy for the young man and that the soldiers sent to murder him, because of inadequate numbers or lack of enthusiasm for their mission, had failed to carry out their orders and had joined the revolt. These empty rumors, like most gossip, were increased through the indolence of the credulous hearers. Actually, a freedman of Plautus, aided by swift winds, arrived ahead of the centurion with a message to him from his father-in-law, Lucius Antistius, advising him to avoid a cowardly death as long as there was a way out. Through the sympathy aroused by his great name he could find the support of good citizens and ally daring men to his cause. In the meantime he should reject no kind of support. If he would but repel sixty soldiers, the number of men that were coming, then while the news was traveling back to Nero, while a new force was on its way through, many things would happen which might develop even into war. At least, he would either save his life by such a course, or else suffer no worse a fate through an act of daring than through inglorious submission.

*59* These arguments did not influence Plautus, whether because he felt that an unarmed exile had no resource, or because he was weary of his precarious life, or out of love for his wife and children, to whom he felt the emperor would be more mercifully disposed if no trouble were caused him. Some authorities state that another message came to him from his father-in-law indicating that no serious danger threatened, and two teachers of philosophy, the Greek Coeranus and the Tuscan Musonius, advised firmness in awaiting death as preferable to a life of uncertainty and fear. At any rate, the soldiers came upon him at midday as he was stripped for exercise. While in that condition he was slain by the centurion in the presence of the eunuch Pelago, whom Nero had placed over the centurion and his company, like the emissary of a king over his satellites. The head of the murdered man was brought back to Nero, who upon seeing it (I quote him exactly) exclaimed: "Why, Nero, [did you fear a man with a nose like that]?" [23] Now putting aside his fears, he made arrangements to hasten his marriage with Poppaea, which had been delayed by such worries as these, and to get rid of his wife Octavia, who,

despite her discreet conduct, was dangerous on account of her father's name and the sympathy of the people for her. He sent a message to the Senate, making no confession of the slaying of Sulla and of Plautus, but asserting that both men had seditious temperaments and that he was deeply concerned for the security of the state. On this pretext the Senate decreed thanksgiving services and decreed that Sulla and Plautus should be expelled from the Senate, a farce which was even worse than the evils themselves.

### Divorce and death of Octavia

*60* Upon receiving the decree of the Fathers and seeing that all his crimes were accepted as meritorious deeds, he drove out Octavia on the charge of sterility, and then was united to Poppaea, who had long been his mistress and had controlled Nero first as a paramour, then as her husband. She now induced one of Octavia's servants to accuse her of a love-intrigue with a slave. The alleged guilty party was a native of Alexandria named Eucaerus, a professional flute player. The maidservants were examined about this charge, and while some of them were overcome by the torture into making a false confession, most of them persisted in upholding the purity of their mistress. One of the maids, when questioned insistently by Tigellinus, replied to him that Octavia's pudenda were cleaner than his mouth. Nevertheless she was at first removed under the pretense of a civil separation and received the house of Burrus and the estates of Plautus, gifts of ill omen. Afterward she was banished to Campania and placed under a military guard. As a result there were persistent and unconcealed complaints among the common people, who have less discretion and fewer dangers because of their insignificant station. A rumor arose that Nero, regretting his outrageous act, had recalled Octavia as his wife.

*61* Thereupon the people joyfully climbed the Capitol and paid homage at last to the gods. They threw down the statues of Poppaea, carried busts of Octavia on their shoulders, covered them with flowers, and set them up in the Forum and the temples. They even went to the point of praising the emperor for recalling her. They were already filling the Palatine with their shouting multitude when bands of soldiers dashed forth and dispersed the mob, driving them with whips and drawn swords. Everything that had been overturned in the rioting was put back and Poppaea's honors were restored. She herself, always savage in her hatred and now infuriated also by the fear that the mood of the populace would increase in violence or that Nero's attitude would be affected by the sympathies of the mob, threw herself at his knees, crying that her own fortunes had not merely reached a pass where she had to fight for her marriage, though this meant more to her than life, but her life itself was brought into grave danger by the clients and slaves of Octavia, who claimed for themselves the name of the people, daring in time of peace what would hardly happen even in war. Those arms were raised against the emperor. All that was lacking was a leader, who would be found readily enough once a revolt was started, let but Octavia leave Campania and come to Rome in person, when at her mere nod, without her presence, such riots could be stirred up. Besides, what crime had she committed? Whom had she ever offended? Was all this because she was going to present a legitimate heir to the household gods of the Caesars? Would the people of Rome rather have the brat of an Egyptian flute player [Eucaerus] raised to the imperial heights? Finally, if this were to his best advantage, let him voluntarily, rather than under compulsion, summon back a woman to rule over him, or else let him take measures for his own safety. It had required only legitimate punishment and mild remedies to quell the first uprising, but if the mob were to lose hope that Octavia would be Nero's wife, they would give her a husband.

*62* This appeal, cleverly adapted to arouse both fear and anger, at once terrified Nero and enraged him as he listened to her. But the suspicion involving the slave failed to work out and it was thwarted at the examination of the maids. Accordingly it was decided to secure a confession from some individual on whom the charge of a plot to overthrow the government could be attached as well. The appropriate man appeared to be Anicetus, the murderer of Nero's mother, commander of the fleet at Misenum, as I stated above. After perpetrating this crime he had enjoyed some slight favor, which was followed by all the deeper hatred, since the agents of one's evil deeds are looked upon as an ever-

present reproach. Summoning him, Caesar reminded him of his former service, when he alone had come to the rescue of the emperor's life against the treacherous plots of his mother. Now the opportunity was present for no less great a service if only he would repel the hostility of his wife. Here no violence or weapon was required; he need only confess to adultery with Octavia. The rewards which he promised him, though concealed for the time being, would be considerable and would include his retirement to a delightful place; the alternative, if he refused, was death. With his natural tendency to mad recklessness, aided by his experience gained from crimes in the past, he invented even more than he was asked and made a confession in the presence of the friends whom the emperor had called in as a sort of advisory council. Then Anicetus was banished to Sardinia where he endured a comfortable exile and ended his days naturally.

*63* Nero announced in an edict that Octavia had corrupted the prefect in the hope of gaining the support of the navy. Forgetting his recent charge of sterility, he accused her of having committed abortion when conscience-stricken over her unchastity, and he affirmed that he was reliably informed on all this. Then he confined Octavia on the island of Pandateria.[24] No other exile aroused greater compassion in the eyes of all beholders. Some people still recalled Agrippina,[25] banished by Tiberius, and there was the still fresher memory of Julia, banished by Claudius. But those women were fully mature; they had seen some happiness and could relieve the cruel suffering of the present with recalling their better fortune of the past. But as for this girl, first of all her wedding day was like a funeral, when she was brought into a home where she found nothing but sorrow, with her father taken from her by poison and then her brother[26] immediately afterward; then to have a servant girl ranked above her mistress, and Poppaea, whose marriage meant only ruin to Nero's wife, and last of all, this charge more bitter than any death.

*64* Now this girl, in her twentieth year, surrounded by centurions and common soldiers, already taken from life by the presentiment of doom, was not yet granted even the peacefulness of death. With the passing of a few days she was ordered to die, though she cried that she was no longer his wife, but was only his sister, and called on their common kinsmen, the Germanici,[27] and lastly on the name of Agrippina, during whose lifetime her marriage had, to be sure, been an unhappy one, but without destruction to herself. She was bound tightly with cords and the blood vessels were cut open in each of her limbs. As the blood, congealed by her fright, flowed but slowly, she was suffocated in the heat of a steaming bath. Another even more horrible atrocity was added in that her head was cut off and brought to Rome, where Poppaea viewed it. What use is there for me to record that offerings were decreed to the temples because of this act? Whoever learns of the events of those times either through my account or that of other historians may take it for granted that on every occasion when the emperor ordered an exile or an execution, services of thanksgiving were offered to the gods, so that a function which in former times betokened happy occasions had now become a mark of national calamity. Even so, I shall not keep silent about any decree of the Senate which reached new heights of flattery or depths of servility.

65 In the same year Nero was believed to have poisoned two of the most powerful of his freedmen, Doryphorus for opposing his marriage with Poppaea, and Pallas for tying up his enormous wealth by a prolonged old age. Romanus had brought a secret accusation against Seneca as an associate of Gaius Piso, but it recoiled on him when Seneca retaliated more vigorously with the same charge. As a result, Piso was alarmed, and thus was born a conspiracy against Nero, a movement formidable and unsuccessful.

## Book XV

[Chapters 1–22 are concerned with war in the East and minor events in Rome.]

### Birth and death of Nero's daughter

23 In the consulship of Memmius Regulus and Verginius Rufus [A.D. 63], Poppaea bore Nero a daughter, which he welcomed with more than human joy, naming the child Augusta and giving Poppaea the same title. The place of the child's birth was the colony of Antium, which was Nero's own birthplace. Earlier the Senate

had commended Poppaea's womb to the gods and had assumed vows in the name of the state; these vows were now multiplied and paid. Thanksgiving services were held in addition, and a temple to Fecundity was decreed along with athletic contests modeled after the Actian ceremony. Gold images of the two goddesses of Fortune were to be set up on the throne of Capitoline Jupiter and circus races were to be held at Antium in honor of the Claudian and Domitian houses, similar to those at Bovillae in honor of the Julian house. All this proved ephemeral, since the infant died before it was four months old. Again there was a flood of fulsome decrees proposing the honor of deification for the infant and the couch of a goddess with a temple and priestess. Extravagant as had been Nero's joy before, so now was his grief. It was noticed that when the entire Senate flocked to Antium right after the child was born, Thrasea was forbidden to attend and that he received this indignity, which was a forewarning of his impending doom, entirely unmoved. There is a report that Nero afterward made some statement in which he boasted before Seneca that he had been reconciled with Thrasea and that Seneca had offered Caesar his congratulations. The consequence of this incident was that the glory of these two distinguished men was increased, but so also were their dangers.

[Chapters 24–32 are concerned with affairs in the East.]

### Nero on the public stage; other excesses

33 In the consulship of Gaius Laecanius and Marcus Licinius [A.D. 64], Nero was driven on by a desire which grew keener daily to appear on the public stage. Hitherto he had sung at his palace or gardens in the Juvenalian games, which he now scorned as too private and too cramped for his great voice. Not daring, however, to make his debut in Rome, he selected Naples as being a Greek city. After starting there he would cross over to Greece and by winning the celebrated, time-honored wreaths, he would with his greater fame bring out the enthusiasm of his fellow Romans. At the performance a crowd of townspeople gathered in addition to those persons whom the report of this event attracted from the neighboring colonies and municipalities and those who habitually accom-

pany Caesar to show him honor or to render various services. With these and with the maniples of soldiers the theater of Naples was filled.

*34* Here an incident took place which most people regarded as an evil omen but which Nero preferred to interpret as providential and a sign of divine favor. After the crowd had left and the theater was empty, it collapsed without anyone being hurt. Thereupon Nero composed an elaborate song of thanksgiving to the gods, heralding the recent accident as a miracle. Then on his way to the passage of the Adriatic he stopped over at Beneventum,[28] where a gladiatorial show was being given by Vatinius before large crowds. Vatinius was one of the most hideous freaks of Nero's court. A graduate of the shoemaker's shop, misshapen in body and scurrilous of wit, he was first taken in as a buffoon, but afterward, by slandering all the finest men, he attained to such importance that through his influence, wealth, and power of doing harm he became pre-eminent even among scoundrels.

*35* While Nero was attending this function, he did not permit even his pleasures to interrupt his crimes. It was during those days that Torquatus Silanus was forced to die because in addition to the glory of belonging to the Junian house he was a great-great-grandson of Divine Augustus. The accusers were instructed to charge that he had been so extravagant with his gifts that his only hope was in an overthrow of the government; that he even had freedmen whom he styled Secretaries of Correspondence, of Petitions, and of Finance, titles associated with the supreme position and the steps preliminary thereto. All his most confidential freedmen were arrested and carried away. When his condemnation was inevitable, Torquatus severed the blood vessels of his arms. Nero followed with his usual speech asserting that although the accused was guilty and had with reason despaired of defending himself, he would have lived if he had only awaited the clemency of his judge.

*36* Not much later Nero, who had given up his Greek trip temporarily for some unknown reason, returned to Rome, harboring secret fancies about a trip to the eastern provinces, particularly Egypt. Then he issued an edict proclaiming that he would not be absent for long

and that all the affairs of state would be as undisturbed and prosperous as before. With reference to this trip he paid a visit to the Capitol, where he worshiped the gods, but when he entered the Temple of Vesta also, he suddenly began to tremble in all his limbs, either because the goddess inspired him with terror or because the recollection of his crimes never left him entirely devoid of fear. So he abandoned his plan, asserting that love for his country outweighed all his private interests; he had beheld the sorrowful faces of his countrymen; he heard their secret complaints that he was going on so long a journey when they could hardly endure even his brief departures from Rome, accustomed as they were to comforting themselves against the accidents of fortune with the sight of their ruler. Consequently, even as in one's private relationships those nearest and dearest come first, so the Roman people meant most to him and he felt obligated to yield to their desire to keep him. All this was agreeable to the common people, eager as they were for amusements and disturbed more than anything else with the fear of a grain shortage if Nero were absent. The Senate and the leading men were not quite sure whether to regard him as more to be dreaded abroad or at home. Afterwards, as is usual in times of great terror, they believed that what actually happened was the worse alternative.

*37* In order to make people believe that nowhere else was he so happy as in Rome, he held his banquets in public places and used the whole city as though it were his house. The most conspicuous of his parties in lavishness and notoriety was one arranged by Tigellinus, which I shall describe as an example in order not to have to repeat similar instances of extravagance. In the pool of Agrippa [29] he constructed a float on which a banquet was set, to be kept in motion by other vessels towing the float. These vessels were resplendent with gold and ivory and the oarsmen were sex perverts arranged according to their age and accomplishments in vice. He had secured birds and wild beasts from distant lands and sea creatures all the way from the Atlantic Ocean. On the banks of the pool stood brothels well filled with women of high rank, while opposite them one could view stark-naked prostitutes. Obscene gestures and motions were under way, and as darkness came on, all of the adjacent grove and surrounding buildings rang with music and blazed with lights. Nero himself, defiled by natural and unnatural pleasures alike, had omitted no vile practice which could add to his depravity, except that he capped all a few days later by actually becoming the bride of one member of that degenerate crew, an individual named Pythagoras, and marrying him in a formal religious ceremony. The bridal veil was placed over the emperor's head; the regular witnesses were used; the dowry, marriage bed, and nuptial torches were there; in short, they displayed in full view everything which the night conceals even when the bride is a woman.

## The great fire

38 There followed a catastrophe, whether through accident or the design of the emperor is not sure, as there are authorities for both views, but it was the most disastrous and appalling of all the calamities brought on this city through the violence of fire. It had its beginning in the part of the Circus [30] next to the Palatine and Caelian hills among the shops where inflammable merchandise is sold. Here the fire broke out and, immediately gaining strength, was fanned by the wind and swept through the length of the Circus. No houses surrounded by enclosures or temples girded by walls or any other obstruction served as a check. First the blaze, as it rushed ahead, overran the level stretches, then rose to higher ground and again descended to devastate the low-lying areas, moving so swiftly in its destructive path as to outstrip all efforts to fight it, and aided by the fact that the city was vulnerable to fire because of the narrow streets winding in every direction and the irregular blocks of houses, such as old Rome had. To aggravate the situation there were the terrified outcries of the women, of the old and feeble, and of the helpless young children, and there were the people who were trying to save either themselves or others, carrying the infirm or waiting for them to come up, some tarrying, some hurrying, all getting in the way of everything. Often while they looked behind them, they were cut off at the sides or in front, or if they escaped to some near-by refuge and this too was seized by the flames, they would discover that even places which they thought

beyond range of the blaze were also on fire. Finally, bewildered as to what to shun and what to seek, they crowded the roads and spread out over the fields. Some, who had lost all they possessed, even their means of livelihood, and others, despondent at the loss of their loved ones whom they had been unable to save, allowed themselves to perish though they could have escaped. And yet no one dared to fight the fire, since they were prevented by men who repeatedly threatened those that sought to extinguish the flames while others openly threw firebrands, shouting that they did it on authority, either in order to carry on their looting with greater freedom or because they really were so ordered.

39 During this time Nero was at Antium and did not come back to Rome until the fire approached his palace, with which he had joined the Palatine to the gardens of Maecenas.[31] Even so the fire could not be stopped until the Palatine and the palace and everything in the area were devastated. To relieve the homeless refugees he opened up the Campus Martius and the public buildings of Agrippa and even his own gardens, and he built temporary structures to shelter the helpless multitude. Supplies were brought up from Ostia and the neighboring towns and the price of wheat was reduced to three sesterces.[32] These measures, though in the public interest, were wasted, because a rumor had spread abroad that at the very time when the city was burning, Nero had mounted on his private stage and sung of the destruction of Troy, comparing the present disaster with that ancient catastrophe.

40 It was not until the sixth day that the fire was stopped at the foot of the Esquiline by demolishing buildings over a vast area so as to oppose an open space and, as it were, a clear sky to the uninterrupted fury of the flames. But fear was not yet dismissed nor did hope return to the people, for once again the fire began raging in the less crowded sections of the city, so that while the loss of life was smaller, there was a more extensive destruction of shrines of the gods and the colonnades which beautified the city. This phase of the fire aroused more adverse criticism because it broke out in the Aemilian estate of Tigellinus, and it looked as though Nero was after the glory of building a

new city and naming it for himself. Rome, of course, is divided into fourteen districts: four of these remained untouched, three were razed to the ground, and the other seven had only a few mutilated and scorched remains of buildings left in them.

*41* To attempt an enumeration of the private mansions, tenement blocks, and temples which were lost would hardly be practical. Among others the most ancient and venerable temple built by Servius Tullius to Luna and the great altar and shrine which Evander the Arcadian had dedicated to Hercules in his presence, the Temple of Jupiter Stator [33] vowed by Romulus, the royal residence of Numa and the sanctuary of Vesta, together with the Penates of the Roman people, all were destroyed. Then there were the treasures acquired through so many victories and the masterpieces of Greek art, and in addition the uncorrupted records of the genius of the ancients, so that, despite the great beauty of the rebuilt city, the older men remembered many an object which could not be replaced. There were some who noted that the nineteenth of July, on which the fire began, was also the date on which the Senones [34] had captured and burned Rome. Others went so far in their calculations that they counted up an equal number of years, months, and days between the two conflagrations.[35]

*42* Nero took advantage of the destruction of his city by building a palace in which it was not so much the precious stones and gold that were remarkable, since luxury had made these familiar and common enough, as the fields and lakes and, reminiscent of uninhabited places, forests on one side and open stretches with long vistas on the other. The planners and architects were Severus and Celer, who had a daring genius for attempting by artificial means even that which nature denied and for playing with the resources of an emperor. They had actually promised to dig a ship channel from Lake Avernus [36] all the way to the mouths of the Tiber along the barren shore or right through the mountains, despite the fact that the only source of water along the route is the Pomptine Marshes, while all the rest consists of steep cliffs or sandy stretches, so that even if they could break their way through, the amount of labor would be prohibitive and without justification. Nero, how-

ever, eager as always to achieve the impossible, did make an effort at digging through the hills nearest to Avernus. There still remain some traces of this fruitless undertaking.

*43* Those parts of the city which were left unoccupied by the palace were not, as after the Gallic fire, built up without a plan or promiscuously, but the streets were laid out in a measured pattern and with broad avenues; the height of buildings was limited and open spaces were to be left between them, while porticoes were to be built as a protection for the fronts of the tenement blocks. These porticoes Nero promised to build at his own cost and to clear the areas and turn them back to their owners. He added rewards proportioned to the rank and financial resources of each individual, with a time limit set for completing the private houses or tenements in order to receive the reward. He made arrangements for the debris to be dumped into the marshes of Ostia and for the boats which brought wheat up the Tiber to return with a load of debris. The buildings themselves were to be constructed up to a certain height without any timbers, but of solid blocks of Gabine or Alban stone, which is fireproof. In order to insure that there would be a stronger water pressure available at more places for public use, he set up guards at the aqueducts, which had been illegally tapped by private individuals. It was required that everyone have fireextinguishing apparatus in an accessible place and that houses have no party walls, but must in every case be surrounded by their own walls. These measures, adopted for practical purposes, contributed also to the beauty of the new city. There were, however, some who felt that the old arrangement was more healthful, since the narrow streets and tall buildings could not so easily be penetrated by the hot sun, whereas now the wide open spaces with no protecting shade were exposed to a more oppressive heat.

*44* All these precautions involved human counsels, but afterward means of expiating the gods were sought and the Sibylline Books were consulted, according to which prayers were addressed to Vulcan and Ceres and Proserpina, and Juno was propitiated by the matrons, first on the Capitol, then at the nearest point of the sea, from which water was drawn and used to sprinkle the temple and statue of the goddess. Sacred banquets and all-night vigils were observed by women with living husbands. But no amount of human effort, no acts of generosity on the part of the emperor or appeasement of the gods could save Nero's reputation from the general belief that the fire had been set at his command.

In order to put an end to these rumors Nero provided scapegoats and visited most fearful punishments on those popularly called Christians, a group hated because of their outrageous practices. The founder of this sect, Christus, was executed in the reign of Tiberius by the procurator Pontius Pilatus. Thus the pernicious superstition was suppressed for the while, but it broke out again not only in Judaea, where this evil had its origin, but even in Rome, to which all obnoxious and disgraceful elements flow from everywhere in the world and receive a large following. The first ones to be seized were those who confessed; then on their information a vast multitude was convicted, not so much on the charge of incendiarism as because of their hatred of humanity. Their executions were made into a sport in that they were covered with skins of wild beasts and torn to pieces by dogs, or they were fastened to crosses or wrapped with inflammable materials, so that when the daylight waned, they could be burned to serve as torches in the night. Nero, who had offered his own gardens [37] for this spectacle, gave a chariot-racing exhibition in which he mingled with the crowd dressed as a charioteer or drove a chariot. The result was that despite the fact that these people were criminals worthy of the worst kind of punishment, a feeling of sympathy arose for them, since they were being destroyed not for the public good but to satisfy the cruelty of one man.

*45* In the meantime, in order to raise the necessary funds, Italy was plundered and the provinces were ransacked, as well as the allied nations and so-called free states. Even the gods made their contribution to the loot, as the temples in the city were despoiled and robbed of the gold which every generation of the Roman people had dedicated in triumphs and in payment of vows, in times of prosperity or fear. Throughout Asia and Greece not only the offerings to the gods but their very images were carried off under the direction of Acratus and Secundus Carrinas, who were special envoys to these provinces. The former was a freedman available for every kind of rascality, the latter was a man versed in Greek

learning, as far as lip service went, but he had not clothed his heart in good practices. It was said that Seneca, in order to avert from himself the odium of sacrilege, requested permission to retire to a remote place in the country, but when this was refused, he pretended to be suffering from rheumatism and did not leave his room. Some historians report that a poison was prepared for him by his own freedman, named Cleonicus, acting on Nero's orders, but that Seneca escaped when the freedman betrayed the plot, or perhaps through his own caution, for he supported life with a very simple diet of fruits of the fields and running water to quench his thirst.

[Chapters 46–47 are concerned with minor events.]

### Conspiracy of Piso

*48* When Silius Nerva and Atticus Vestinus entered their consulship [A.D. 65], a conspiracy had started and immediately grown, since it was eagerly joined by senators, equestrians, soldiers, and even women, prompted both by their hate of Nero and their liking for Gaius Piso. A member of the Calpurnian house, he united on his father's side many distinguished noble families and had a splendid reputation with the public on account of his high character, or an outward appearance of high character. He employed his talent as a speaker in defense of his countrymen; he was lavish with gifts to his friends; he was also affable with strangers in his conversation and contacts. Besides, he had the incidental advantages of being tall and good-looking. But far removed from him were solidity of character or restraint in gratifying his pleasures. He indulged in frivolity and ostentation and at times in dissipation, a trait which was approved by a good many who, because of the powerful fascination of vice, prefer that the supreme ruler should not be too narrow or puritanical.

*49* The conspiracy did not arise from Piso's own ambition. Still, I cannot readily report who the originator was, who inspired and set in motion a cause in which so many participated. Among the most aggressive members were Subrius Flavus, tribune of a praetorian cohort, and Sulpicius Asper, a centurion, as was proved by the courage with which they met their deaths. There were also Annaeus Lucan [38] and Plautius Lateranus, who contributed violent hatred. Lucan was inflamed by private motives because Nero was trying to suppress his fame as a poet and, out of a vain spirit of rivalry, had forbidden him to display his talents. Lateranus, the consul-elect, was brought into the conspiracy by no personal sense of injury but through patriotic motives. Flavius Scaevinus and Afranius Quintianus, both members of the senatorial order, took the lead in this great enterprise quite contrary to their earlier reputation, for Scaevinus' character had so degenerated through dissipation that his life was spent in drowsiness, while Quintianus, who was notorious as a moral pervert, had been vilified by Nero in a scurrilous poem and now sought to avenge the insult.

50 While discussing among themselves or with their friends the crimes of Nero and the imminent destruction of the Empire and the urgent need of selecting someone to rescue the prostrate nation, they added to their numbers Claudius Senecio, Cervarius Proculus, Vulcacius Araricus, Julius Augurinus, Munatius Gratus, Antonius Natalis, and Marcius Festus, all Roman knights. Out of this group, Senecio, who had been one of Nero's most intimate friends, still retained the outward appearance of friendship and was exposed to all the more dangers for that reason; Natalis shared Piso's every secret; the rest hoped for personal advantage in a change of ruler. Besides Subrius and Sulpicius, to whom I have already referred, other military men were added in the persons of Gavius Silvanus and Statius Proxumus, tribunes of the praetorian cohorts, and the centurions Maximus Scaurus and Venetus Paulus. But their chief strength was thought to be in the prefect Faenius Rufus. Though this man was highly praised for his character and reputation, Tigellinus surpassed him in the favor of the emperor because of his cruelty and shamelessness, and he persecuted him with accusations, often arousing Nero's fears by charging that he had been a lover of Agrippina and that through his grief for her he was bent on revenge. When the conspirators were assured by repeated statements from his own lips that the praetorian prefect had joined their cause, they began more aggressively to plan the time and place for the assassination. Subrius Flavus was reported to have conceived the impulse of attacking Nero while he was singing on the stage or when his palace was burning and he was rushing hither and yon unguarded in the night. In the latter case, there was the opportunity of his being alone; in the former, Subrius was thrilled by the thought that a huge crowd would be the fairest witness of his glorious deed. But he was held back by the desire to escape punishment, ever an obstacle to great endeavors.

51 In the meantime, while they were hesitating and putting off their hopes and fears, a certain woman named Epicharis (it is not known how she learned of the movement, for she had never before shown the slightest interest in anything honorable) began to stir up and to criticize the conspirators, and finally out of disgust with their slowness, while staying in Campania, she tried to break down the loyalty of the officers of the fleet at Misenum and to involve them in the conspiracy by the following means. There was in the fleet a captain, Volusius Proculus, who had been one of the agents in the murder of Nero's mother but had not, in his opinion, been advanced as far as the importance of the crime merited. He was known to the woman from before, or perhaps their friendship was of recent origin, and while he was telling her of his services toward Nero and how they had been in vain, and was expressing his dissatisfaction and his determination to get even should the opportunity arise, she began to entertain the hope that he could be induced to join the conspiracy and bring in many more. The fleet would afford no slight assistance and frequent opportunities, since Nero often enjoyed the sea at Puteoli and Misenum. So Epicharis argued with him at length, beginning with all the emperor's crimes and his leaving no powers to the Senate. But plans, she said, had been made to punish him for ruining the state; let Proculus but prepare himself vigorously to do his part and bring the most aggressive of his men into the cause and he could expect worthy rewards. Nevertheless, she kept secret the names of the conspirators, so that the evidence of Proculus proved of no value, although he reported to Nero all that he had heard. Epicharis was summoned and when confronted with the informer, easily refuted him, as he had no witnesses to support him. But the woman was retained under custody, since Nero suspected that the story was not false even

though its truth had not been well established.

*52* The conspirators, however, stimulated by fear of betrayal, decided to hasten the assassination at Baiae in Piso's villa, the beauty of which attracted Caesar to visit there frequently and to take his baths and dinners without bodyguards and the usual trappings of his rank. But Piso turned the plan down on the ground of the odium it would cause if the sanctity of the table and the gods of hospitality were stained with the blood of an emperor, however bad. Better let them accomplish it at Rome in that hateful palace built by despoiling the citizens, or let them carry out in some public place a deed which they had undertaken in the public interest. This is what he said before the others, but actually he harbored a secret fear that Lucius Silanus, a distinguished noble, trained by Gaius Cassius, at whose home he was reared so that he was qualified to attain the highest station, would seize the imperial power, and that this would be readily offered to him by those who had no part in the conspiracy and would feel sympathy for Nero as the victim of murder. Many have believed that Piso shunned also the aggressive spirit of the consul Vestinus, for fear that he would rise to the cause of freedom or, by choosing a different emperor, would make control of the government a matter of his own gift. In any case, Vestinus had no share in the conspiracy, although it was on this charge that Nero satisfied his long-standing hatred against an innocent man.

*53* They decided at last to carry out their plans on the day of the circus races in honor of Ceres,[30] because Caesar, who rarely went out and kept himself secluded in his palace or his gardens, would always attend the shows of the circus, and thus it would be easier to approach him during his enjoyment of the spectacle. The planned sequence for the plot was that Lateranus should plead with Nero as though asking support for his private fortunes and falling at the emperor's knees, should throw him off balance unexpectedly and pin him down, since he was a man of resolute spirit and physically huge. Then, as Nero lay there unable to move, the tribunes and centurions and all the rest, according as their courage prompted, were to rush up and kill him. Scaevinus claimed the privilege of dealing the first blow with a dagger which he had taken from the Temple of Safety or, according to other authorities, from that of Fortune in the town of Ferentinum, and which he wore as though consecrated to some great deed. In the meantime, Piso was to be waiting at the Temple of Ceres, where the prefect Faenius and the others were to fetch him and escort him to the Camp, accompanied by Antonia, the daughter of Claudius Caesar, in order to win the favor of the multitude, as Gaius Pliny relates. I have preferred not to conceal this detail, whatever the account is worth, although it seems absurd to me that Antonia should have lent her name and endangered her personal safety for an empty hope or that Piso, whose love for his wife was well known, should have obligated himself to marry someone else, unless it be that the lust for power burns more intensely than all other emotions.

*54* It is astonishing how in a group involving such different classes, ranks, ages, sexes, both rich and poor, all was kept absolutely secret until the betrayal, which started in the household of Scaevinus. On the day before the planned attack he had had a long talk with Antonius Natalis, then had gone home and sealed his will. Unsheathing the dagger which I have mentioned above, he complained that it was dulled with age and ordered it sharpened on a stone and polished to a keen point, assigning the task to his freedman Milichus. At the same time he took dinner more lavishly than usual and rewarded his favorite slaves with freedom and others with money. He himself was gloomy and obviously wrapped in deep thought, though he pretended to cheerfulness with disjointed conversation. Finally he admonished the same Milichus to prepare bandages and materials for checking the flow of blood, whether this man was aware of the conspiracy and had been loyal up to then, or he was uninformed and his suspicions were first aroused at that time, as most authorities assert on the basis of what followed. When his slavish mind thought over the rewards for treachery and visions of vast wealth and power began to pass before him, all moral scruples and the safety of his patron and the memory of the freedom he had received gave way. Besides, he followed his wife's advice, which coming from a woman was for the worse. She went so far as to work on his fears, reminding him that many freedmen and slaves had been present to see what he had seen. The silence of one man would be of no use, while the rewards would go to the one person who came first with the information.

55 At daybreak Milichus hastened to the Servilian gardens and when stopped at the gate, cried that he had serious and dreadful news, whereupon he was escorted by the gate-keepers to Nero's freedman Epaphroditus, who in turn took him before Nero. Telling the emperor of the pressing danger, the formidable conspirators, and everything else that he had heard or sur-mised, he even showed him the weapon intended for his assassination and urged that the man he accused should be summoned. When dragged in by the soldiers, Scaevinus began his defense by saying that the dagger of which he was accused had long been a sacred object in his family and had been kept in his room, from which it had been stolen through the treachery of the freed-man. As for the tablets of his will, he sealed these quite often with no special attention to the date. He had awarded money and freedom to his slaves on previous occasions as well, but he had done it more liberally this time because his private fortune was so reduced and his creditors so insistent that he had no confidence in his will. Furthermore, he had always dined on a generous scale, enjoying a life of luxury hardly approved by stern critics. He had ordered no first-aid remedies for wounds, but because all the man's other charges were manifestly absurd, he was merely adding an accusation in which he could make himself both informer and witness. These words were spoken with complete self-assurance. He even denounced the freedman as an un-principled scoundrel, controlling his voice and features so perfectly that the information would have broken down had not Milichus been re-minded by his wife that Antonius Natalis had had a long secret conference with Scaevinus and that both were intimate friends of Gaius Piso.

56 Accordingly, Natalis was summoned and they were questioned separately as to their conference and what it was about. At that point suspicion was aroused, because their replies did not agree, and they were thrown into chains. They broke down before the sight and threat of torture. The first to give way was Natalis, who was better informed on the entire conspiracy and was also more experienced as an accuser. He confessed first about Piso, then brought in Annaeus Seneca, either because he had been the intermediary between Seneca and Piso or with a view to gaining the favor of Nero, who in his hatred of Seneca sought every means to ruin him. Upon hearing that Natalis had confessed, Scaevinus showed equal cowardice, or perhaps believing that all was revealed, he saw no gain in silence, and he betrayed the others. Lucan, Quintianus, and Senecio persisted long in their denials, but afterward they were corrupted by the promise of impunity, and in order to justify their slowness in confessing, Lucan named his own mother Acilia, while Quintianus named Glitius Gallus and Senecio named Annius Pol-lio, the closest of their friends.

57 In the meantime Nero remembered that Epicharis was being held in custody on the information of Volusius Proculus, and thinking that a woman's body would be unequal to pain, he ordered her to be racked with tortures. But neither the scourging nor the flames nor the wrath of the torturers, who worked all the more fiercely so as not to be scorned by a woman, succeeded in breaking down her denial of the charges. Thus she defied the first day of the inquisition. On the following day, while she was being carried in a sedan chair to a re-sumption of the tortures, for her legs had been so dislocated that she was unable to stand, she removed the breastband from her bosom and fastening it in the shape of a noose to the arched top of the chair, she thrust her neck into it and pressed down with the full weight of her body, until she forced out the feeble breath that still remained in her. Thus a mere freedwoman under such extreme agony displayed so glorious an example in protecting strangers whom she hardly knew, while men, freeborn, Roman knights and senators, untouched by any tortures, betrayed the very dearest of their relatives and friends. For even Lucan and Senecio and Quin-tianus did not cease to reveal their accomplices right and left, while Nero grew more and more terrified, although he had surrounded himself with greatly increased bodyguards.

58 He went so far as to virtually place the city under military guard by having companies of troops occupy the walls and placing garrisons at the sea and the river. Through the fora,

through private houses and even the farm districts and the neighboring towns dashed infantrymen and cavalrymen, with a sprinkling of Germans, whom the emperor trusted because they were foreigners. Men in chains were dragged in unending lines through the streets and lay beside the gates of the emperor's gardens. When they entered to plead their defense, a mere smile at any of the conspirators or a casual conversation or a chance meeting or having attended a dinner party or a show together with one of them was regarded as incriminating; and in addition to the furious questioning of Nero and Tigellinus, Faenius Rufus also assailed them fiercely, for he had not yet been named by the informers and sought to give assurance of his own innocence by being violent against his accomplices. When Subrius Flavus, who stood near him, asked with a sign if he should draw his sword and carry out the murder then and there at the investigation, Rufus shook his head, thus checking the man's impulse as he was in the act of placing his hand upon the hilt of his sword.

59 After the betrayal of the conspiracy, while Milichus was being heard and Scaevinus was wavering, there were some who urged Piso to proceed to the Camp or to mount the Rostra and attempt to win the support of the soldiers and the people. If his accomplices were to join him in this effort, those outside the plot would follow, and a revolt once started would arouse widespread report, a very valuable aid in a rebellion. Nero, they argued, had taken no steps against such an attempt. Even brave men were frightened by sudden emergencies, so one could hardly expect that stage player, accompanied of course by Tigellinus with his concubines, to work up any armed opposition. They said that by taking a chance, many things were accomplished which would seem impossible to the cowardly. It was no use hoping for silence and good faith where the minds and bodies of so many accomplices were involved; tortures or bribes could break through anything. Men would be coming soon who would arrest him also and finally inflict on him an ignominious death. How much more gloriously could he die embracing the cause of the state and rallying aid to liberty! Let the soldiers rather fail and let the people desert him, provided he himself, if his life must

be cut off, met a death acceptable in the sight of his ancestors and his descendants. Unmoved by these pleas, Piso appeared in public for a little while, then he secluded himself in his house and was strengthening his spirit for the end until a band of soldiers arrived, consisting of raw recruits or men recently in the service, all selected by Nero, for he was suspicious of the veterans as affected by partiality. Piso died by cutting the blood vessels of his arms. His will with its disgusting flattery of Nero was a concession to his love for his wife, a low-born woman with only her beauty to recommend her, whom he had taken away from her marriage with a friend of his. The woman's name was Satria Galla, that of her former husband Domitius Silus. He by his submissiveness and she by her unchastity added to Piso's dishonor.

60 Next to be killed by Nero was Plautius Lateranus, the consul-elect, and in such haste that he was not permitted to embrace his children or to take the brief time of choosing how to die. Hurried off to a place set aside for the execution of slaves, he was slain by the hand of the tribune Statius, meeting death with unshaken silence and without accusing the tribune of complicity in the same plot.

Following this came the murder of Annaeus Seneca, most gratifying to the emperor, not because he had positive information that he was guilty of conspiracy, but because he now sought to dispatch him with the sword after poison had failed. No one but Natalis had mentioned him, and he only to the extent of saying that he was sent to visit Seneca in his illness and to complain over his keeping Piso from coming to him; it would be better if they would keep up their friendship by intimate contact. Seneca had replied that exchanges of conversation and frequent interviews would be useful to neither one, but that his welfare rested on the safety of Piso. Gavius Silvanus, tribune of a praetorian cohort, was ordered to report this testimony to Seneca and to question him as to whether he acknowledged the words of Natalis and his own reply. Seneca had, either by chance or purposely, returned from Campania on precisely that day and had stopped over in his suburban estate at the fourth milestone from Rome. To that place the tribune came towards evening and surrounded the villa with bands of troops. Then he delivered the emperor's instructions to Seneca, who was at dinner with his wife, Pompeia Paulina, and two friends.

*61* Seneca replied that Natalis had indeed been sent to him and had complained in Piso's name that he was being kept from seeing him and that he had offered as his excuse the state of his health and his love of quiet. As to why he should place the welfare of a private individual above his own safety, he could give no reason; his was not a nature prone to flattery, and no one knew this better than Nero, who had more frequently experienced Seneca's outspokenness than his servility. When the tribune reported this answer to Nero in the presence of Poppaea and Tigellinus, who formed the most intimate of the savage emperor's advisory councils, Nero asked whether Seneca was preparing for a voluntary death. The tribune asserted that he had detected no signs of fear, no sadness in his words or his face. Thereupon he was ordered to go back and announce his death sentence. Fabius Rusticus reports that he did not go back by the road he had come, but turned aside to the prefect Faenius, whom he informed of Nero's orders and asked whether he should obey, and that Faenius advised him to carry out his orders, such being the fatal cowardice shown by all of them. For Silvanus also was one of the conspirators, and he was now adding to those crimes to avenge which he had joined the conspiracy. Still he spared his own voice and eyes by sending in one of the centurions to Seneca to inform him of his doom.

*62* Unafraid, Seneca asked for the tablets of his will. When the centurion refused, he turned to his friends and declared that since he was prevented from showing them his gratitude for their services, he was leaving them the one and yet finest legacy within his power, the image of his life, and if they kept this before their minds, their loyal friendship would be rewarded with a name for virtuous deeds. At the same time he tried to recall them from tears to composure, now with conversation, now in the sterner tone of rebuke, asking where were those precepts of philosophy, where was that rational attitude which they had cultivated through so many years as a protection against whatever happened. Who of them had not known Nero's cruelty? The only thing left for him after the killing of his mother

and brother was to add the murder of his guardian and teacher.

*63* When he had made such remarks as these more or less publicly, he embraced his wife, and for the moment softening his manner in contrast to the firmness he had been showing, he asked and implored her to restrain her grief and not keep it up forever, but rather through contemplation of a life virtuously spent to endure the loss of her husband with noble consolations. She, on the contrary, insisted that she was determined to die with him and she called for the hand of the executioner. Seneca, not averse to her winning glory and, out of his affection for her, not wishing to leave his dearly beloved exposed to mistreatment, said, "I showed you how to find comfort in life; you, however, prefer the glory of death. I shall not begrudge you the example. May firmness in meeting death bravely be shared alike by both of us, but greater be the glory of your end!" Then with one stroke of the knife they slashed their arms. As his aged body, weakened by a spare diet, allowed his blood to escape but slowly, he severed also the blood vessels of his lower legs and thighs. Exhausted by the excruciating pain and fearing that his suffering would break down his wife's courage and the sight of her agony might weaken his own endurance, he persuaded her to go into another room. As his eloquence did not desert him even in his very last moments, he called in scribes and dictated at length, but since these utterances have been published in his own words, I dispense with giving a version here.[40]

*64* Since Nero did not feel any personal hatred against Paulina and was concerned that her act might increase his reputation for cruelty, he ordered that her suicide be prevented. Prompted by the soldiers, her slaves and freedmen bandaged up her arms and checked the flow of blood, but whether without her knowledge is uncertain. Prone as people are to accept the less creditable version, there were some who believed that as long as she feared that Nero would be implacable, she sought the glory of sharing her husband's death, but afterwards when a more kindly prospect was presented, she was overcome by the attractions of life. She lived on for a few more years, showing a praiseworthy devotion to her husband's memory, while her face and body displayed such a pallor that it was obvious that much of her vital spirit had been drained out. Seneca meanwhile, as death came on slowly and with prolonged agony, begged Statius Annaeus, in whom he had great confidence as a loyal friend and skilled physician, to bring him a poison which he had previously prepared, the kind used to execute those condemned by the people's court of Athens. When it was brought to him he drank it down, but in vain, since his limbs were already cold, so that his system was immune to the power of the poison. Finally he stepped into a pool of hot water, and sprinkling the slaves who were near him, he added that he was offering this liquid as a libation to Jupiter the Liberator. Then he was carried into a bath, and after being suffocated by its heat, he was cremated without any funeral ceremony, as he had prescribed in his will at a time when, though still at the height of wealth and power, he was yet concerned about his end.

65 There was a rumor that Subrius Flavus had plotted with the centurions secretly, but not without Seneca's knowledge, that once Nero was murdered with Piso's assistance, Piso should also be killed and the imperial power be handed to Seneca under the pretense that those innocent of the conspiracy chose him for the sovereign power because of his distinguished reputation for high character. In fact, Flavus was widely quoted as having remarked that as far as the disgrace was concerned, it didn't matter if a lyre player were removed and a tragic actor put in his place; for as Nero sang to the lyre, so did Piso in the costume of a tragedian.

66 The military phase of the conspiracy remained concealed no longer, as the informers were enraged to the point of unmasking Faenius Rufus, whom they could not tolerate as both fellow-plotter and inquisitor. Accordingly, as Faenius persisted and threatened, Scaevinus remarked to him with a smile that no one knew more about it than did Faenius himself, and he urged that he should of his own free will show his gratitude to so excellent an emperor. No reply came from Faenius, nor yet silence, but stumbling over his words, he betrayed his terror, and when the rest, particularly the Roman knight Cervarius Proculus, combined to denounce him, he was seized at the emperor's order and bound by

Cassius, a soldier who was standing by on account of his unusual physical strength.

67 Next the testimony of the same individuals ruined the tribune Subrius Flavus, who at first based his defense on the contrast between his character and theirs, asserting that he, a man of arms, would not have associated himself in so formidable an enterprise with such unwarlike, effeminate creatures. Then, finding himself hardpressed, he embraced the glory of a confession. When asked by Nero what motives had brought him so far as to forget his oath of allegiance. he exclaimed, "I hated you. No other of your soldiers was more loyal to you as long as you deserved to be loved. I started to hate you when you became the murderer of your mother and your wife, a chariot driver and an actor and an incendiary." I have quoted his exact words because they have not, like Seneca's, been published, and it seemed no less appropriate that the unpolished, forceful expressions of a military man should be known. It is certain that nothing in the entire conspiracy fell more unpleasantly on Nero's ears, for though ready enough to commit crimes, he was not used to being reminded of what he did. The execution of Flavus was assigned to the tribune Veianius Niger. He had a grave dug in a field near by, but Flavus criticized it as shallow and narrow, saying to the soldiers who stood around, "This isn't by military standards either." When urged to extend his neck bravely, he said, "I only hope you will strike as bravely!" The executioner, his hands trembling, scarcely severed the head with two blows, then boasted of his cruelty before Nero, stating that he had killed him with a stroke and a half.

68 The next display of fortitude came from the centurion Sulpicius Asper. When Nero inquired of him why he had conspired to kill him, he replied briefly that it was the only possible remedy for Nero's many crimes. Then he submitted to the required punishment. The other centurions also showed no cowardice in suffering their punishments. Faenius Rufus, however, did not show similar courage, but carried his lamentations even into the text of his will. Nero was waiting for the consul Vestinus also to be incriminated, as he regarded him a violent and dangerous character; but none of the conspirators had taken Vestinus into their confi-

dence, since some had long-standing disagreements with him, more felt that he was an impulsive man, incapable of cooperation. Nero's hatred of Vestinus had sprung from their intimate association, in that Vestinus despised the emperor's degenerate character, with which he was thoroughly familiar, while Nero feared his friend's independent spirit after being frequently ridiculed with sharp jests which, when largely based on the truth, leave behind a bitter memory. There was a more immediate cause in the fact that Vestinus had married Statilia Messalina, though fully aware that Nero also was numbered among her lovers.[41]

69 So, because he was unable in the absence of a charge or an accuser to assume the appearance of a judge, he resorted to the violence of a despot and sent the tribune Gerellanus with a cohort of troops under instructions to forestall the consul's attempts, to seize what he called his fortress and overwhelm his picked band of youths, because Vestinus owned a house overlooking the Forum and had handsome slaves matched in age. Vestinus had performed all his consular duties for that day and was having a dinner party, either disturbed by no fears or in order to conceal his fears, when the soldiers entered and told him that he was wanted by the tribune. He arose immediately and the entire procedure was rushed through all at once: he was shut up in a room, a doctor was on hand, his blood vessels were cut open, while still strong he was taken to the bath and immersed in hot water, during all which time he uttered not a single word of self-pity. In the meantime, his dinner guests were surrounded by guards and not released until late at night, after Nero had gleefully visualized their terror as they awaited destruction following their dinner and remarked that they had paid dearly enough for their consular banquet.

70 Next he ordered the execution of Annaeus Lucan. As Lucan's blood was gushing forth and he felt his feet and hands getting cold and the vitality gradually ebbing from his extremities, while his breast was still warm and he was fully conscious, he recalled some verses of his own [42] in which he had described a wounded soldier as dying in a manner of death like his, and so he recited these very lines as his last words. After him Senecio and Quintianus and

Scaevinus died in a manner that contrasted with the earlier degeneracy of their lives; then the rest of the conspirators perished with no act or utterance worth recording.

71 The city meanwhile was filled with funerals, the Capitol with sacrificial victims. Because of the execution of a son in one case, of a brother in another, or a kinsman or friend, men gave thanks to the gods, decorated their houses with laurel, groveled at the emperor's feet and plied his right hand with kisses. Taking all this for joy, Nero paid Antonius Natalis and Cervarius Proculus with impunity because of their prompt information. Milichus, enriched with rewards, assumed as a surname the Greek equivalent of the word savior. Of the tribunes, Gavius Silvanus, though acquitted, took his own life; Statius Proxumus spoiled the pardon he received from the emperor by the folly of his death.

[Chapters 72–74 relate various minor consequences of the conspiracy.]

## Book XVI

### A treasure hunt

1 Now fortune made a fool of Nero, thanks to his own stupidity and the promises of Caesellius Bassus. The latter, a Carthaginian by birth, was a man with a disordered mind, who interpreted a dream of the night as promising certain fulfillment. So he traveled to Rome, and buying his way to the emperor's presence, revealed that he had discovered on his land a cavern of immense depth containing a great quantity of gold, not in minted coins but in unworked, ancient masses. Ponderous bars were lying all around and in another part there were whole stacks of gold. The treasure had remained concealed for such an age in order to enhance the blessings of the present era. As he explained it, Phoenician Dido, when a refugee from Tyre, had, on founding Carthage, hidden away these treasures for fear that her new nation might be demoralized with excessive wealth or that the Kings of Numidia, who were hostile enough as it was, would be stirred to war through greed for this gold.

2 Accordingly, without carefully checking the trustworthiness either of the man or his story

or sending anyone to investigate whether there was any basis of truth, Nero magnified the rumor on his own account and sent an expedition to bring back the booty as though it were all ready to be taken. Triremes were assigned with picked crews to speed the journey. During those days nothing else was talked about by the people in their credulity, though the more intelligent discussed it in quite a different vein. It so happened that the quinquennial games were then being celebrated on the occasion of the second lustrum,[43] and so the orators made this treasure the chief theme in their eulogies of the emperor: not alone ordinary crops or gold blended with baser metals came forth, but the earth was blossoming with a new fertility and the gods were presenting Nero with riches right to hand; and such other servile flatteries as they invented with great eloquence and no less sycophancy, taking their confidence from Nero's ready credulity.

3 His extravagance meanwhile was increased on the strength of these empty hopes, and long-accumulated reserves were used up with the idea that there was a new supply for him to squander over a period of many years. He was actually drawing on the expected treasure for generous gifts, and in fact the anticipation of riches was one of the causes for the impoverishment of the state. After Bassus had dug up his own land and the neighboring fields over a wide area, always asserting that now this place, now that, was the site of the promised cave, and he was followed around not only by soldiers but by a crowd of farm laborers hired to do the work, he finally put aside his delusion, and expressing astonishment that his dreams had never been false before and this was absolutely the first time he was ever deceived, he escaped his shame and fear by a voluntary death. Some historians report that he was imprisoned and then released after his property was confiscated in order to make up for the royal treasure.

### Nero's artistic exhibitions

4 In the meantime, as the quinquennial contest was already approaching, the Senate, in the hope of averting the disgrace, offered the emperor the championship in music and added the wreath for eloquence so as to cover over the humiliation of the stage. Nero, however, asserted that he did not need any personal influence or the prestige of the Senate, and that he would compete on equal terms with his rivals and depend on the impartial decision of the judges in winning whatever glory he merited. He first declaimed a poem on the stage; then, in response to the clamors of the mob that he should display all his talents (those were their very words) he made his appearance in the theater, observing all the rules of the lyre, such as not sitting down when tired, not wiping off the sweat except with the garment he was wearing, not allowing any saliva or nasal mucus to be seen. When he finished, he bent his knee, paid homage to that rabble with a gesture of the hand, and awaited the decision of the judges with pretended nervousness. The common people of Rome, accustomed as they were to encourage the gestures even of the regular actors, cheered with organized rhythms and a regulated type of applause. You would have supposed they were happy about it, and perhaps they were, in their indifference toward the national disgrace.

5 There were some spectators present from distant communities and that section of Italy which was still strict in its morals and retained something of the old-time standards, as well as some from faraway provinces, who were inexperienced in wanton practices. Having come as special envoys or for personal reasons, they could neither endure such a spectacle nor keep up with the degrading effort as their unpractised hands grew weary, and so they confused the skilled applauders and were often beaten by the soldiers who were stationed in the various sections to make sure that not a moment passed with unrhythmic applause or passive silence. It is a fact that a number of knights were crushed to death while struggling through the narrow entrances and the pressing crowd and that others were seized with fatal illnesses by remaining constantly in their seats day and night. It was actually a graver danger to leave a performance, as there were many spies openly and more of them secretly making note of the names and faces of the audience and their enthusiasm or distress. As a result, those of lesser station were at once visited with punishment, but Nero's resentment toward prominent persons, though concealed for the present, was satisfied at a later time. There was a story that Vespasian was re-

buked by the freedman Phoebus for having dozed off and that he was saved with difficulty through the appeals of men of higher rank, and later escaped the threatening danger because of his higher destiny.[44]

### Death of Poppaea

6 After the festival was over, Poppaea met her death as the result of a sudden fit of rage on the part of her husband, who gave her a violent kick while she was pregnant. I am unable to believe that poison was involved, although this is reported by some writers through hate rather than conviction; for Nero was certainly desirous of children and he was affectionately devoted to his wife. Her body was not consumed by fire, as is the Roman custom, but was embalmed with aromatic substances after the fashion of foreign rulers and placed in the tomb of the Julii. Still, a public funeral was held and Nero himself delivered the eulogy from the Rostra, praising her beauty and the fact that she had been mother of a deified child and the other advantages of fortune as if they were virtues.

[Chapters 7–17 describe the prosecution and death of various persons and recount minor events at Rome and abroad.]

### Death of Petronius

18 There is a little more to be told about Gaius Petronius.[45] He was a man who spent his days in sleep, his nights in the functions and pleasures of society. While others are raised to fame through their industry, he became famous through idleness; yet he was not regarded as just a libertine and spendthrift, as are most of those who waste their property, but as a refined voluptuary. The more unconventional were his words and acts and the more they showed a certain disdain of consequences to himself, with all the greater favor were they received as evidence of his frank nature. Nevertheless, as proconsul of Bithynia and later as consul, he proved himself an efficient administrator and equal to his responsibilities. After that, reverting to his life of vice, or only pretending to do so, he was taken in as one of Nero's few intimate friends, serving as the dictator of etiquette, in that Nero deemed nothing really aesthetic and gratifyingly luxurious without the approval of Petronius. Consequently, the jealousy of Tigel-

linus was aroused against an apparent rival who was his superior as an expert in the art of dissipation. He therefore appealed to the emperor's cruelty, which was stronger than all his other emotions, and accused Petronius of friendship with Scaevinus, after bribing a slave of his to give evidence and depriving him of any opportunity for defense and arresting the greater part of his household.

19 As it happened, Caesar had just at that time made a trip to Campania, and Petronius, on reaching Cumae, was detained in that city. Deciding to put off no longer his fears or hopes, he did not, however, hurry to expel life, but after cutting into his blood vessels he bandaged them up whenever he felt like it, then opened them again and chatted with his friends, but not on serious topics such as might win him the glory of fortitude. He listened to no discussions on the immortality of the soul or the teachings of philosophers, but rather to light songs and racy verses. Some of his slaves he rewarded with lavish gifts, others with whippings. He joined in a banquet, then took a nap, so that his death, though under compulsion, might resemble a natural one. Even in his will he did not, like most of those who died, flatter Nero or Tigellinus or any other of those in power, but he listed the shameful acts of the emperor, itemized under the names of the sex degenerates and the women involved, and recorded the novel aspects of his debauchery in each case, then sealed the document and sent it to Nero. He broke his seal ring so that it might not be used afterward to endanger anyone.

[Chapter 20 describes how Petronius' fall proved disastrous to other persons.]

### Deaths of Thrasea and Soranus

21 After murdering so many illustrious men, Nero finally set his heart on wiping out virtue itself by killing Thrasea Paetus and Barea Soranus. While he had for a long time hated both these men, he had additional reasons for resentment against Thrasea because he had walked out of the Senate when the motion concerning Agrippina was put, as I have related above, and because his services at the Juvenalian games had been hardly noteworthy. The latter offense rankled the more deeply because in his native city of Patavium [46] this same Thrasea had ap-

peared as a singer, dressed in a tragedian's robes, at the games founded by Trojan Antenor. Furthermore, on the day when the death penalty was being voted against the praetor Antistius for composing insulting verses about Nero, Thrasea moved and carried a milder sentence; and when divine honors were being voted for Poppaea, he was deliberately absent from the Senate and did not appear at her funeral. It was Capito Cossutianus who did not permit these acts to be forgotten, for in addition to a character prone to wickedness he bore a grudge against Thrasea because he had been ruined through the prestige of Thrasea's support of the Cilician envoys when they prosecuted Capito for extortion.

22 He brought against him the following charges in addition: that on the first of each year Thrasea avoided the formal oath of allegiance; that he did not appear for the offering of prayers for the safety of the state, though he was a member of the Quindecimviral priesthood; [47] that he had never offered a sacrifice for the emperor's health or his heavenly voice; that though he had formerly been conscientious and indefatigable in supporting or opposing even routine resolutions of the Fathers, he had for three years not entered the Senate chamber; that quite recently, when all the senators vied with one another in their rush to suppress Silanus and Vetus, he preferred to occupy himself with the private affairs of his clients. This attitude amounted to secession and the forming of a faction, and if many should dare to do the same thing, it would come to war. "Just as in olden times," he cried, "men talked of Gaius Caesar and Marcus Cato,[48] in the same way do the people now, in their eagerness for discord, talk of you, Nero, and of Thrasea. And he has his followers, or rather satellites, who while they do not yet imitate the insolent spirit of his record in the Senate are copying his dress and looks, showing themselves stiff and austere, in order to reproach you with looseness of character. He is the only man to whom your safety is of no concern, your talents without honor. He despises the emperor's successes: is he not even satisfied with his afflictions and sorrows? It belongs to the same disposition not to believe in the divinity of Poppaea as not to swear loyalty to the enactments of the Divine Augustus and the Divine Julius. He scorns our religious in-

stitutions, he annuls our laws. People throughout the provinces and the armies read the daily journal of Rome all the more eagerly in order to see what it is that Thrasea has not done. Let us either go over to his system of government, if that is so superior, or else let us deprive the subversive elements of their leader and agitator. It was this philosophy which produced the Tuberones and the Favonii,[49] names odious even to the old republic. In order to overthrow the government they cry freedom; once they overthrow it, they will attack freedom itself. It was useless for you to get rid of Cassius,[50] if you are going to allow the imitators of the Bruti to increase and flourish. Finally, you need not personally send any message about Thrasea; just let the Senate be our judge." Nero himself stimulated Cossutianus' spirit, furious enough as it was, and he gave him the cooperation of Marcellus Eprius, a speaker of fiery eloquence.

23 The prosecution of Barea Soranus had already been claimed for his own by Ostorius Sabinus, a Roman knight, in connection with Barea's proconsulship of Asia, during which he increased the emperor's resentment by his uprightness and efficiency and through having given his energies to opening up the harbor of Ephesus and having failed to punish the people of Pergamum for their violence in preventing Acratus, Caesar's freedman, from carrying away their statues and paintings. The specific charges against him were friendship with Plautus and a plan to win over the province to the side of rebellion. His conviction was deliberately timed for the arrival of Tiridates to receive the crown of Armenia, in order that the crime at home might be obscured by diverting the talk of the public to foreign affairs, or perhaps in order to give Nero an opportunity to display the emperor's greatness by executing distinguished men as though this were a royal prerogative.

24 Accordingly, when the entire population of Rome poured out to welcome the emperor and to see the King, Thrasea was forbidden to appear; but not becoming discouraged, he composed a note to Nero asking for the charges against him and asserting that he would clear himself if only he had some knowledge of the accusations and the opportunity to refute them. Nero received this note eagerly in the hope that Thrasea had been frightened into writing something that

might redound to the glory of the emperor and degrade his own reputation. Since this did not happen and Nero was afraid to come face to face with the bold and independent spirit of this innocent man, he issued a call for a meeting of the Senate.

25 Now Thrasea consulted with his closest friends whether to attempt a defense or disregard it. Contradictory advice was offered. Those who were in favor of his appearing before the Senate argued that they were completely confident that he would be resolute and would say nothing except what would enhance his glory. Only the submissive and the cowardly veiled their last moments in secrecy. Let the public behold a man face to face with death; let the Senate hear his words as though they were more than human, emanating from some divine being; possibly the very miracle of it would stir even Nero. But if he persisted in his cruelty, posterity at least would make a distinction between the record of a noble end and the cowardice of those who died in silence.

26 Those on the other hand who advised him to await the outcome at home expressed the same opinion about Thrasea personally but thought that there was danger of ridicule and insults. They advised him to withdraw his ears from vituperation and abuse. Cossutianus and Eprius were not the only ones ready to do evil; there were many others who might perhaps go so far in their brutality as to lay hands upon him and even strike him; then good men also would follow through fear. Let him rather spare the Senate, on which he had brought great honor in the past, the disgrace of such an outrage and let it remain uncertain what the Fathers would have decreed had they actually seen Thrasea on trial. Any hope that Nero would be seized by shame for his crimes was utterly futile; it was much more to be feared that he would turn his rage on Thrasea's wife and daughter and his other dear ones. Accordingly, unviolated, undefiled, following the glorious example of those whose footsteps and teachings had guided him in his way of life, let him seek his end. Present at this conference was Rusticus Arulenus, an impetuous young man, who in his eagerness for glory offered to interpose his veto to the decree of the Senate, for he was then tribune of the people. Thrasea checked his impulsiveness for

fear that he might start some foolish action which would be of no help to the accused and be fatal to the vetoer. He argued that his own life was done and he must not abandon the principles which he had maintained unbroken through so many years; but Rusticus was holding only his first office and his career still lay intact before him. Let him weigh carefully what course of public life he would follow in these times. Whether it would be appropriate for himself to come before the Senate he left to his own further consideration.

27 Early the following morning two armed praetorian cohorts occupied the Temple of Venus Genetrix.[51] A band of men wearing togas stood guard at the entrance to the Senate with their swords unconcealed, and bodies of troops were distributed through the fora and basilicas. In this threatening atmosphere the senators entered the chamber, where the emperor's speech was read by one of his quaestors. Without mentioning anyone by name he rebuked the Fathers for neglecting their public functions and by their example causing the Roman knights to assume an indifferent attitude. In fact, what wonder was it that men didn't bother to come from distant provinces, when many who had attained the consulship and priesthoods preferred to devote themselves to beautifying their gardens? This speech was seized upon by the accusers as a weapon.

28 After Cossutianus started things off, Marcellus shouted with greater violence that the welfare of the nation was at stake; through the insolence of his subjects the ruler's kindheartedness was being handicapped. The Fathers had been too lenient up to that day in that the rebellious Thrasea and his son-in-law, Helvidius Priscus, who showed the same madness, and at the same time Paconius Agrippinus, who had inherited his father's hatred toward emperors, and Curtius Montanus, the composer of repulsive poems, were permitted to mock them with impunity. He failed to see a certain ex-consul in the Senate, a priest at the offering of the vows, a citizen at the taking of the oath of allegiance, unless Thrasea in defiance of the institutions and ceremonials of their ancestors had openly assumed the role of a traitor and a public enemy. Let him at least, accustomed as he had been in the past to play the part of a senator and to

shield those who disparaged the emperor, come in and express his opinion as to what he wanted corrected and changed. They could more easily tolerate his criticisms of specific things than put up with his present attitude of silently condemning everything. Was it the world-wide peace that he didn't like or the victories without losses to the armies? If the man was unhappy over the prosperity of the nation, if he regarded the fora, theaters, and temples as so many desolate places, if he held out his own exile as a threat, let them not permit him to gratify his perverse ambition. In his eyes, these were no senatorial decrees, no magistrates, no city of Rome. Let him now cut off his life from that country toward which he had long since abandoned all affection and even the sight of which he had now cast off.

**29** As Marcellus in his usual ferocious and threatening manner uttered these and similar words with fire in his voice, face, and eyes, it was not the usual melancholy, such as had already become normal through the frequency of their dangers, that now came over the Senate, but there was a new and deeper terror as they beheld the soldiers with weapons in their hands. At the same time there passed before their minds the revered aspect of Thrasea. There were some who felt sorry also for Helvidius, who was to pay the penalty for his innocent relationship. What charge was there against Agrippinus other than the tragic fate of his father, who had with equal innocence fallen victim to the cruelty of Tiberius? Furthermore, Montanus, an honorable young man, no writer of libelous verse, was being banished only because he had displayed his poetic talent.

**30** In the meantime Ostorius Sabinus, the prosecutor of Soranus, entered and began his attack with the charge that Soranus had been a friend of Rubellius Plautus and that Soranus had administered his proconsulship in Asia so as to further his own distinction instead of the common welfare by fostering rebellion in the various states. These were old charges. Then came a new charge, by which he involved Soranus' daughter in her father's danger, to the effect that she had lavished money on astrologers. This had actually happened through Servilia's devotion (that was the girl's name), for out of love for her father and the indiscretion of youth she had consulted fortune-tellers, but only

concerning the safety of her family and whether Nero would relent and whether the trial before the Senate offered no serious danger. Accordingly, she was summoned before the Senate, and so the two stood facing each other in front of the tribunal of the consuls, on one side the elderly father, opposite him the daughter, a girl in her twentieth year, who had recently been left bereaved and desolate when her husband, Annius Pollio, was driven into exile, now not even looking her father in the face, for she felt that she had increased the burden of his dangers.

**31** Then while the prosecutor questioned her as to whether she had sold her trousseau and a necklace taken from her neck in order to raise money for conducting magic rites, she first threw herself to the ground and wept long and silently, then embracing the shrine and the altar she cried, "I invoked no evil spirits, resorted to no imprecations, and in my ill-advised prayers I asked for nothing else than that you, Caesar, you, Fathers, should keep unharmed this best of men, my father. I gave my jewels and my clothes and the ornaments of my rank, just as I would have given my blood and my life if they had demanded them. It is for those fortune-tellers, whom I had never known before, to see to it what name applies to them, what arts they practise. I never even mentioned the emperor except among the gods. In any case, my unhappy father knows nothing of it, and if it is a crime, I alone am guilty."

**32** Before she finished speaking, Soranus interrupted to cry that she had not gone to the province with him, that she was too young to have been known to Plautus, that she was not involved in the charges against her husband. Let them separate the case of a girl guilty only of excessive devotion, while he himself would undergo any fate whatsoever. At the same time he rushed to embrace his daughter, who ran to meet him, but the lictors stepped between them and kept them apart. Next the witnesses were called upon, and great as had been the sympathy which the savagery of the prosecutor had excited, no less was the indignation aroused by the testimony of Publius Egnatius. This man, a client of Soranus, had on this occasion been bought so as to ruin his friend. Parading the dignity of the Stoic sect, he had trained himself to present in his demeanor and speech the appearance of high character, but at heart he was treacherous, crafty, harboring greed and lust. When money brought these vices to light, he gave the world a lesson to guard not only against those who are wrapped in deceit or stained with crime, but also those who under the pretense of honorable conduct are really hypocrites and betrayers of friendship.

*33* The same day, however, presented also the noble example of Cassius Asclepiodotus. A leading citizen of Bithynia on account of his great wealth, he had been a devoted friend of Soranus in prosperity and now with the same devotion refused to desert him in his fall. He was stripped of his entire fortune and driven into exile, as the gods showed themselves indifferent toward good and evil conduct alike. Thrasea, Soranus, and Servilia were allowed to choose their manner of death: Helvidius and Paconius were banished from Italy; Montanus was pardoned out of regard for his father, but with the proviso that he stay out of political life. The prosecutors, Eprius and Cossutianus, were each awarded five million sesterces, while Ostorius received twelve hundred thousand sesterces [52] and the insignia of a quaestor.

*34* Thrasea was in his gardens when the consul's quaestor was sent to him as evening was already approaching. He had assembled a considerable group of distinguished men and women, but was giving his closest attention to Demetrius, a teacher of the Cynic philosophy, with whom, as one could gather from the intent expression of his face and the occasional louder remarks that were overheard, he was discussing the nature of the soul and the separation of spirit and body, when Domitius Caecilianus, one of his closest friends, arrived and advised him of the verdict of the Senate. As all those present wept and uttered their complaints, Thrasea urged them to depart immediately and not endanger themselves by being involved in the doom of a condemned man. Arria tried to share her husband's death and follow the example of Arria her mother,[53] but he advised her to keep on living and not deprive their daughter of her only mainstay.

*35* Then he walked to the portico, where the quaestor found him in a happier mood, for he had learned that his son-in-law, Helvidius, was only barred from Italy. Then, on receiving the Senate's decree, he led Helvidius and Demetrius into the room with him. Offering both his arms for the blood vessels to be cut, he let the blood flow out and sprinkled it on the ground. Then he called the quaestor to come near and said to him, "I am pouring a libation to Jupiter the Liberator. Look, young man, and may the gods avert the omen, but you have been born into times when it is useful to strengthen one's heart with examples of fortitude." Then, as the slowness of his end brought grievous tortures, he turned to Demetrius. . . .

[Here the text of the *Annals* breaks off and the rest of the work, which originally extended probably to eighteen books, is lost.]

# GERMANIA

Tacitus published the *Germania* in A.D. 98, soon after the *Agricola*. While Herodotus and other predecessors of Tacitus in historical and geographical writing had introduced ethnographical material into their larger works, the *Germania* of Tacitus is the only example from antiquity of a monograph devoted exclusively to the study of a people, although there are indications that there were other works of this character.

The *Germania* is the most important of the sources for our knowledge of the ancient Germans. It would be a mistake to regard it, as some scholars have done, as primarily a political pamphlet or a satire on the decadence of morals at Rome in Tacitus' own time. Undoubtedly, Tacitus chose this subject because he was interested in the Germans and thought that his countrymen would be interested in a treatise concerning them. It was inevitable that the satirist in Tacitus should emerge whenever an opportunity was offered for some pungent comparison between the relatively unspoiled Germans and the too sophisticated Romans.

## Geography and early history

*1* Germany, taken inclusively, is separated from Gaul, Rhaetia, and Pannonia by the rivers Rhine and Danube, from Sarmatia and Dacia [1] by mutual fear or by mountains; the rest is bounded by the ocean, which embraces broad peninsulas and islands of vast size. Some of the tribes and kings here have only recently become known, as war has revealed them. The Rhine, which has its source in a steep, inaccessible summit of the Rhaetian Alps, turns with a slight bend to the west for some distance and then flows into the northern ocean. The Danube, starting its flow in low, gently-sloping Mount Abnoba, passes through a number of nations, finally discharging into the Pontic Sea [2] through six mouths, the seventh being lost in the marshes.

2 As for the Germans themselves, I am inclined to believe them indigenous with hardly any mixture occasioned by immigrations or friendly intercourse with other tribes, because in former times those who sought to migrate came not by land but by sea, and the ocean, extending as a boundless and, I might say, hostile barrier, is but rarely ventured on by ships from our part of the world. Besides, apart from the dangers of the rough, unknown sea, who would ever leave Asia or Africa or Italy to seek Germany, a land so hideous in its scenery, so harsh in its climate, so cheerless to live in or to behold, unless it were his native land? In their ancient lays, the only type of tradition and historical record among them, the Germans celebrate the earth-born god Tuisto and his son Mannus as the original ancestors and founders of their people. To Mannus they attribute three sons, after whose names those nearest the ocean are called Ingaevones, those in the middle Herminones, the rest Istaevones. Some, in view of the liberties taken with antiquity, assert that the god produced more sons and so more tribal names, the Marsi, Gambrivii, Suebi, Vandilii, and that these are genuine ancient names. The name Germany, however, they claim is a modern one, which has only recently been applied to the country, since the first people who crossed the Rhine and drove out the Gauls and are now the Tungri were then called Germans. Thus what was the name not of a nation but only of a tribe, gradually became so formidable that at first the whole people was called Germans by the conquering tribe in order to inspire fear; subsequently, once the name was invented for them, they adopted it themselves.

3 They recall Hercules also as having been among them, and before going into battle they sing of him as foremost of all heroes. They have also those songs by the rendering of which (called

*barditus*) they work up their spirits and they foretell their fortunes in the coming engagement by the way they sing; for they create terror or become terrified, according to the sound produced by their battle line, so that this seems a harmony not so much of voices as of valor. They try especially to produce a hoarse kind of effect and a spasmodic roar, placing their shields against their mouths so that the reverberation will cause a fuller and deeper noise to swell forth. Some believe that Ulysses also in the course of his long, fabled wanderings came to this part of the ocean and visited the lands of Germany and that Asciburgium,[3] a city on the Rhine, which is inhabited to this day, was founded and named by him. They even say that an altar dedicated to Ulysses, with the addition of the name of his father Laertes, was long ago found on this same spot and that certain monuments and mound tombs inscribed with Greek characters still exist at the border of Germany and Rhaetia. It is not my intention to offer proof either for or against these statements. Each reader may follow his own inclination in disbelieving or believing.

*Physical characteristics of the people and the country*

4 I for my part favor the views of those who think that the peoples of Germany are not mixed by intermarriage with any other nations and so form a distinct, pure, and entirely unique race. This accounts for the uniformity of their physical characteristics despite their large population. They all have fierce blue eyes, red hair, large frames, powerful only for a sudden onset. This strength is not matched by any power to endure hardship or work, and they are not used at all to standing thirst or heat, though their climate and soil have accustomed them to cold and hunger.

5 Although the landscape shows some differences in aspect, on the whole the country is covered with either wild forests or foul swamps, and it is wetter on the side toward Gaul, windier on the side toward Noricum and Pannonia. While productive of grain crops, it does not grow fruit-bearing trees, but is rich in livestock, which is for the most part undersized. Even the cattle lack their natural attractiveness or frontal adornment. It is numbers that appeal to them and these are their only and their most prized form of wealth. Silver and gold the gods have denied them,

whether out of goodness or anger I cannot say. I shall not, however, go so far as to affirm that there is no vein bearing silver or gold in Germany, for who has ever looked for any? They are ʌot particularly affected by the possession and use of these metals. One may see among them silver vessels, presented as gifts to their envoys and chiefs, regarded as cheaply as earthenware. Those, however, who are nearest to us value gold and silver for their use in trade, and they recognize certain types of our coins and choose these. Those in the interior use the older and more primitive system of barter. They favor our old coins which have been known to them for a long time, those with saw-toothed edges and two-horsed chariots. Likewise, they accept silver in preference to gold, not through any special partiality but because a supply of silver pieces is more convenient for the cheap, common articles in which they trade.

*Military customs*

6 They do not even have an abundance of iron, as one can tell from the character of their weapons. They rarely employ swords or long lances. They carry spears, called *frameae* in their language, the metal part of which is narrow and short, but so sharp and so manageable that they use the same weapon, as occasion demands, for fighting at either short or long range. Their cavalry are content with shield and *framea,* their infantry fling showers of darts also, each throwing a considerable number, and they can hurl them a great distance, since the men are naked or lightly covered with a cloak. There is no display of ornament. They adorn only their shields with carefully chosen colors. A few have chest protectors; hardly one or two have a helmet of metal or leather. Their horses are conspicuous for neither beauty nor speed. They are not even taught to perform a variety of evolutions, like ours, but they guide them straight ahead or carry out just the one maneuver of wheeling to the right in such a way that the arc is kept together with no one falling behind the line. Judged as a whole, their chief strength is in their infantry. Therefore they fight with infantry and cavalry intermingled, adapting the speed of the footsoldiers so as to keep up with the cavalry battle, these footsoldiers being men selected from the entire body of young men and placed in the front

part of the line. The number of these also is fixed; there are one hundred from each district and their name is derived from the number. What was at first only a number has now become a title and an honor. Their battle formation is by wedge-shaped divisions. To yield ground, provided you advance again, is regarded as a strategic maneuver rather than cowardice. They carry away the bodies of their fallen even when the battle is in doubt. To abandon one's shield is the greatest of disgraces and one so dishonored is not allowed to be present at religious rites or attend the assembly. In many cases, those who survive the fighting end their ignominy with the noose.

7 They select their kings according to birth, their generals according to courage. The power of the kings is not unlimited and arbitrary, and the generals lead by example rather than authority, through admiration due to their being aggressive, conspicuous, and fighting in the forefront. The power to punish by death or to imprison or even to flog is granted to none but the priests, and that not as a penalty or at orders of the general, but as though at the behest of the god whom they believe to be their aid in war. They carry into battle certain figures and emblems taken from the sacred groves. Their greatest stimulus to courage is that the basis for the troop or division is not chance or a casual arrangement but family and kinship. Besides, their loved ones are close by, so that they can hear the shrieks of their women, the cries of their babies. These are each warrior's most sacred witnesses, these their chief applauders. To their mothers and their wives they take their wounds, nor do the women shrink from counting and even insisting on wounds, and they bring food and encouragement to the men while they fight.

*Respect for women*

8 Tradition reports that certain armies which were already giving way and cracking had their spirits restored by their women, who courageously pleaded with them, holding out their breasts and showing them that captivity was close at hand, a fate of which they have a dread all the more unendurable on account of their women, so that those states are more effectively held bound to their obligations which are required to include maidens of noble birth among the hos-

tages. They actually believe that women possess some holy and prophetic power, and so they neither scorn to ask their advice nor neglect their replies. In the reign of the Divine Vespasian we saw Veleda, who was long looked on as a divinity among many Germans; and in earlier times they worshiped Aurinia and a number of other women, but not, however, out of servility, and without making goddesses of them.[4]

*Religion*

9 Mercury is the god they most worship, considering it proper on certain days to sacrifice even human victims to him. Hercules and Mars [5] are appeased with legitimate animals. Some of the Suebi sacrifice to Isis also. The cause and origin of this foreign rite I have been unable to determine, except only that the emblem itself, which is shaped like a Liburnian boat, indicates that the cult came from abroad. They think, however, that it is not in keeping with the grandeur of the heavenly beings to confine gods within walls or represent them in any semblance of the human countenance. They consecrate groves and woods to them and they apply the names of gods to that mysterious element which they behold with reverence alone.

10 In observing auspices and lots they are surpassed by no other people. They follow only one method of drawing lots. They cut a twig off a fruit-bearing tree and split it into strips, which they label with certain marks and then scatter them quite indiscriminately and at random over a white cloth. Then, if it is a public consultation, the priest of the community, if private, the father of the household, prays to the gods, and, raising his eyes to the sky, takes up three strips, one at a time, then interprets these according to the marks previously scratched on them. If the signs are negative, there is no further consultation on the same matter during the same day; [6] but if they are favorable, confirmation by auspices is required in addition. Here also they are familiar with the method of consulting the cries and flight of birds. What is unique with this people is their use of horses also for prophecy and warnings. These are maintained by the community in the above-mentioned forests and groves, and they use only white horses that have never been tainted by mortal labor. These are yoked to a sacred chariot and accompanied by the priest and the king or chief of the state, who observe their whinnies and snorts. No other form of augury is more trusted not only by the common folk but by the nobles and the priests, who look upon themselves as servants of the gods but upon the horses as acquainted with the divine will. They have still another method of observing omens, that by which they test the issue of serious wars. Capturing by some means a warrior of the tribe against which they are fighting, they match him in combat with a picked man of their own people, each armed with his native weapons. The victory of the one or the other is taken as a prediction of the outcome.

*Communal organization*

11 On minor matters the chiefs deliberate, on major ones the entire assembly, with the provision, however, that even such business as the people must decide is previously discussed by the chiefs. The assemblies are regularly held, except for unforeseen emergencies, on fixed days, when the moon is either new or approaching the full, since they regard these times as most auspicious for starting any business. They figure time not by the number of days, as we do, but by the number of nights. On this principle they make their appointments and their agreements. The night is regarded as preceding the day. One defect resulting from their independent spirit is that they do not assemble at the same time or when ordered, but two or three days are wasted by the slowness of the arrivals. When the crowd sees fit, they sit down fully armed. Silence is ordered by the priests, who then have the right also of enforcing order. The king or chief, according to each one's age or birth or glory in war, is heard through power of persuasion rather than right to command. If the speech displeases them, they reject it with a roar; if they approve, they clash their spears. The most complimentary form of approval is applause with weapons.

12 Before this assembly they are permitted to bring accusations and capital charges. The punishment is made to fit the crime. Traitors and deserters they hang from trees; the timid and cowardly and sex perverts they submerge in the mud of a swamp, placing a net of osiers over them to hold them down. The different methods of execution are based on the principle that crimes should be exposed while being punished.

but disgrace should be concealed. The less serious crimes also are punished appropriately. Those convicted are fined so many horses or livestock. Half of the fine is paid to the king or the state, half to the injured party or his kin.

In these councils they also choose the chiefs who dispense justice in the districts and villages. Each of these has one hundred associates from the common people to form a group of advisers and sponsors.

13 They transact no business, either public or private, without wearing arms. It is their custom, however, not to permit anyone to carry arms until the community has passed favorably on his ability. Then at the council meeting one of the chiefs or the candidate's father or a kinsman invests the youth with shield and spear. With them this is the equivalent of the toga, this the first honor of youth. Before the ceremony he is regarded as a member of the household, after this of the state. Outstanding nobility of birth or great services on the part of their fathers confer the rank of chief even upon very young men. These attach themselves to the others who are more robust and have long since passed the test, and they do not blush to be seen among the retainers. Even the retinue itself has its gradations of rank, according to the judgment of the man they follow. There is a considerable rivalry not only among the retainers for the first place with their chief, but also among the chiefs to see which will have the largest number of retainers and the most energetic ones. This is their prestige, this their strength; always to be surrounded by a large band of picked young men is their glory in peace, their bulwark in war. Not only in their own tribe but also with neighboring states they win distinction and glory if their retinue is conspicuous in numbers and valor. Such chiefs are courted by embassies, honored with gifts, and frequently decide a war by the sheer prestige of their name.

14 When they come into battle, it is degrading for the chief to be surpassed in valor, degrading for the retinue not to match the valor of the chief. It brings one infamy and reproach for life to leave the battlefield surviving one's chief. To defend him, to watch out for him, to assign one's own deeds of valor to his glory, is the most important feature of their oath of allegiance. The chiefs fight for victory, the retainers for the chief. If their native state has grown sluggish through prolonged peace and inaction, a good many of the young nobles voluntarily seek out those tribes which are at that time waging some war, because this race hates inactivity and can more easily win fame amid doubtful fortunes; besides, one cannot keep up a large retinue except through violence and war, for the retainers insistently claim of the chief's liberality the war horse and the bloody, victorious spear. Feasts and table fare, which though unelaborate is on a plentiful scale, are their only pay. The means for this generosity are secured through war and plunder. It is less easy to prevail on them to plough the land or await the year's crop than to challenge the foe and earn wounds. They actually regard it as lazy and tame to gain with sweat what you can win with blood.

15 When they are not entering on a war, they spend some little time in hunting, but still more in idleness, occupying themselves with sleeping and eating, since the bravest and most warlike do nothing at all, but assign care of house and home and fields to the women and the old men and all the weakest members of the family. They themselves lounge around slothfully, with an astonishing inconsistency of character, in that the same men are so fond of idleness and yet hate tranquillity. It is customary for the states to contribute a portion of their cattle and crops to the chiefs, who accept this as a sign of honor but also as a means of supplying their needs. They are especially pleased with gifts from neighboring tribes, sent not only by individuals but also by communities, such gifts as choice horses, heavy weapons, medallions, and neck chains. In modern times we have taught them to accept money also.

*Houses and dress*

16 It is a well-known fact that the peoples of Germany live in no cities and do not even tolerate houses closely joined. They live well scattered and in different types of places, choosing a spring, a meadow, or a grove, as they prefer. In arranging their settlements they do not, as we, place their buildings in groups and joined to each other, but each has a clear space around his house either as a protection against fire or because of lack of skill in building. They make no use of masonry or tiles. For all purposes they employ rough timbers with no concern for ornament or attractiveness. They smear over some parts more carefully with

a refined and glossy earth, so that it resembles painting or colored designs. They are accustomed also to excavate dugouts, heaping piles of manure on top, so that these serve as a shelter in winter and as storage places for the crops, for by such an arrangement they mitigate the severity of the frost, and if an enemy comes, he plunders the open country, but those places which are concealed underground either remain unknown or are not discovered because they would have to be looked for.

17 They all wear the same kind of garment, a cloak fastened with a safety pin or, lacking this, a thorn. Naked in other respects, they pass their entire days beside the hearth fire. The wealthiest are distinguished by a garment, not of the loosely flowing type, such as the Sarmatians and Parthians wear, but a tight-fitting one, so as to bring out the separate limbs. They wear also the skins of wild animals, those near the river bank wearing them in a careless fashion, those in the interior with more discrimination, since they receive no fine clothes through trade. They select certain animals and removing the hides they vary them with patches from the skins of beasts produced in the outer ocean and unknown part of the sea. The women dress like the men, except that in addition they frequently put on a linen scarf, which they adorn with red, not extending the upper portion of the garment so as to form sleeves, and thus leaving arms and shoulders bare and even the nearest part of the bosom exposed. Nevertheless, matrimonial standards among them are strict, and there is no phase of their morals deserving higher praise. They are almost the only barbarians content with one wife, the only exceptions being those few who are approached with many offers of marriage not for lustful reasons but because of their high rank.

### Women and children ⸗

18 The dowry is brought not by the wife to the husband but by the husband to the wife. The parents and relatives are present and approve the gifts, gifts not adapted to feminine vanity or for the adornment of the bride, but oxen and a horse with bridle and a shield with spear and sword. In consideration of these gifts the bride is received, while she herself in turn brings some weapons to her husband. This they look on as their chief bond, these their mystic rites, these

their gods of wedlock. That the woman may not regard herself as exempt from thoughts of valor, exempt from the fortunes of war, she is reminded by the ceremonies marking the very beginning of her marriage that she comes as a partner of his toils and dangers, to suffer and to dare alike with him in peace and in battle. That is what the yoked oxen, the bridled horse, the gift of arms signify. So she must live and so die, receiving what she must hand down inviolate and honorable to her children, that which her daughters-in-law will receive and which will in turn be passed on to the grandchildren.

19 Consequently, their chastity is well protected and there are no allurements of shows, no attractions of parties to corrupt them. Secret love notes are unknown to men and women alike. In so populous a nation there are very few cases of adultery and for these the punishment is immediate and left to the husbands. The adulteress' husband cuts off her hair, strips her naked, and in the presence of the kinsmen expels her from his house and drives her with a whip through the entire village. If a woman surrenders her chastity, she can receive no pardon. Not beauty nor youth nor wealth will find her a husband. Vice is no laughing matter there and seducing or being seduced is not called the modern fashion. Even higher is the moral standard of those states where only virgins get married and so the wife's hopes and expectations are settled once for all. Thus they receive just one husband, as they receive one body and one life, so that they may have no thought beyond, no further desire, and love their husband not so much as an individual but as representing the state of marriage. To practice birth control or destroy any of the later-born offspring [7] is regarded as criminal, and good morals are more effective there than good laws elsewhere.

20 In every house the children, naked and dirty as they are, grow up with those limbs, those bodies that we marvel at. Each child is suckled at its own mother's breasts and they are not turned over to maidservants and nurses. You can distinguish master and slave by no refinements of rearing. They are brought up among the same livestock, on the same dirt floor, until time separates the freeborn and valor acknowledges them. Sex indulgence comes late for the young men and therefore their

young manhood is unexhausted. Neither are the girls hurried into marriage.[8] They have the same youthfulness, the same tall bodies. They are united as equals in age and in vigor, and their children reproduce the strength of the parents. The sons of one's sisters are as highly esteemed by their uncle as by their father. Some think that this is an even holier and closer blood tie and so insist by preference on nephews when taking hostages, in the idea that these have a stronger hold on the affections and a wider influence on the family. Each one's heirs and successors are his own children and they make no will. If there are no children, the nearest degrees for purposes of inheritance are brothers, paternal uncles, maternal uncles. The more blood kinsmen and marriage relations a man has, the more favored is his old age. There are no rewards for childlessness.[9]

*Social life*

21 It is obligatory to take over the feuds of one's father or kinsman as well as their friendships. But these feuds do not endure irreconcilably. Even homicide is expiated by paying a fixed number of cattle and sheep, and the whole family thus receives satisfaction, a useful arrangement for the community, since feuds are more dangerous when combined with freedom. No other people indulges more lavishly in feasting and the entertainment of strangers. To bar any human being whatsoever from one's house is regarded as sinful. Everyone receives strangers with feasts proportioned to his means. When these give out, the man who has been serving as host designates another host and accompanies the stranger to him. Without any invitation they go to the next house, and it makes no difference: they are received with the same courtesy. No one discriminates between acquaintance and stranger as regards the right of hospitality. On the guest's departure it is customary to give him anything he asks for, and there is the same readiness about asking something in return. They enjoy gifts, but claim no return for what they give and feel no obligation for what they receive.
22 Immediately on waking from sleep, which they commonly prolong well into the day, they wash, generally with warm water, for winter takes up most of the year in their country. After washing they take food, sitting on separate seats, each at his own table. Then they proceed to their business, or no less frequently to feasts, wearing their arms. It is no disgrace for anyone to spend the entire day and night drinking. The frequent brawls, such as are natural among heavy drinkers, rarely end with mere verbal abuse, but more often with murder and wounds. Yet such matters as the mutual reconciliation of enemies, joining marriage alliances, and selecting chiefs, or even deciding peace and war, are generally discussed at feasts, with the idea that there is no other time when the mind is either more open to sincere thoughts or warmed up to great ones. Since this people is not very keen or shrewd, they open the secrets of their hearts still further amid the relaxation of merriment; accordingly, the minds of all are stripped and laid bare. On the following day the matter is reconsidered, and so, full consideration is paid to both occasions: they deliberate when they are incapable of pretending, they decide when they cannot err.
23 Their beverage is a liquor made of barley or wheat, fermented to something that resembles wine. Those near the river bank also buy wine. Their food is simple: wild fruits, fresh-killed game, or coagulated milk. Without elaboration, without condiments they banish hunger. Toward thirst, however, they do not show the same temperance. If you indulge their drunkenness by supplying them with all the drink they want, they will be conquered by their vices quite as easily as by arms.
24 They have only one type of spectacle and this is used at every gathering. Naked youths, who are trained to play this game, leap among swords and exposed spears. Practice has given them skill, skill gracefulness, but not for gain or fee. However reckless the sport, the only reward is the enjoyment of the spectators. Astonishingly, they gamble with dice even when sober, as a serious activity and with such recklessness in winning or losing that after they have lost everything, they stake on the very last and final throw their freedom and their bodies. The loser goes into voluntary slavery; though younger, though stronger, he allows himself to be bound and offered for sale. Such is their stubbornness in a perverse cause: they themselves call it honor. The slaves acquired by these conditions they pass on through trade, in order to

deliver themselves also from the shame of such a victory.

25 They employ their other slaves without having their duties severally assigned within the household, as is our custom. Each slave controls his own home, his own household gods. The master requires of him a definite amount of wheat or livestock or clothing, as of a tenant farmer, and the slave is in subjection to this extent only. The other functions of the household are performed by one's wife and children. The flogging of a slave or punishing him with imprisonment and hard labor is rare. They are in the habit of killing slaves, not out of discipline or severity, but by impulse in a fit of rage, as one would kill an enemy, except that the killing of a slave goes unpunished. Freedmen rank not much above slaves, rarely exerting any influence in the household, never in the state, except only in those tribes which have kings. In these they rise above even the freeborn and the nobles. Among the others the inferiority of the freedmen is an indication of freedom.

26 The business of lending money and making capital bear interest is unknown. Therefore usury is better guarded against than if it were expressly forbidden. The fields are occupied by entire communities according to the number of settlers and then they parcel these out on the basis of rank. Ease of distribution is assured by the large amount of available territory. They change their cultivated fields each year and still there is land left over; for they do not put forth any effort to get the utmost out of the fertility and extent of the soil by planting orchards, marking off meadows, and irrigating gardens. Only a grain crop is required of the land. Consequently, they do not even divide the year into as many aspects as we do. Winter, spring, and summer have a meaning to them and receive names; but as for autumn, both its name and its gifts are unknown.

27 In their funerals there is no ostentation. The only exception is that they burn the bodies of illustrious men with special kinds of wood. They do not heap up the pyre with garments or spices. Each warrior's own weapons and, in some instances, his horse also, are thrown on the fire. A mound of turf is raised over the grave. They scorn the heavy, elaborate honor of monuments as only a weight upon the dead. Their wailing and weeping they put aside soon, their grief and sadness late. It is honorable for women to lament but for men to remember.

## NOTES TO SELECTIONS FROM TACITUS

### *The* Annals

1. Better known as the Emperor Caligula.

2. Burrus held the powerful position of prefect of the praetorian guards. Seneca was the famous philosopher and tragic poet. (See his *Medea.*)

3. Pallas was one of the most important freedmen during the reign of Claudius.

4. Claudius' marriage to Agrippina, his brother's daughter, was incestuous according to the law forbidding marriage between uncle and niece. His adoption of his stepson Nero was regarded as a fatal step bringing on his poisoning by Agrippina so as to place her son upon the throne.

5. The future emperor, who reigned for a few months in A.D. 69.

6. Nero's wife Octavia was the daughter of the Emperor Claudius. A play about her is extant under the name but not by the pen of Seneca, as already noted.

7. Britannicus was the son of Claudius and regarded by many as the rightful heir to the throne. The French playwright Racine produced a tragedy about him (1669).

8. The Camp, which is frequently referred to, was the Praetorian Camp of the praetorian guards. It lay in the extreme northeastern part of Rome.

9. The Saturnalia, celebrated December 17–19 with exchange of gifts, general merriment, and something of the atmosphere of an old-fashioned Christmas.

10. Besides Octavia, Britannicus had a half-sister, Antonia.

11. This Antonia was the mother of Claudius and grandmother of Agrippina.

12. The fall of Sejanus, the trusted but treacherous minister of Tiberius, dragged down many of his friends and supporters in A.D. 31. Tacitus' account of this dramatic episode is unfortunately lost with nearly the whole of the fifth book of the *Annals*. Ben Jonson's drama, *Sejanus His Fall*, is a noteworthy literary treatment of an event which made a profound impression on later times and was to be paralleled in England by the fate of Cardinal Wolsey.

13. The province of Lusitania occupied the southwest-

ern part of the Spanish peninsula and included most of what is now Portugal.

14. This was the revolt against Nero in 68. Otho became emperor the following year.

15. Two miles north of the city, where the Via Flaminia crossed the Tiber.

16. An important city (founded by Greeks about 600 B.C.) in southern Gaul, now Marseille. It was a favorite place of exile. Cf. Cicero's speeches above, p. 126.

17. Tusculum was a popular villa site in the Alban Hills, fifteen miles to the southeast of Rome, near what is now Frascati, the scene of Cicero's *Tusculan Disputations*. Antium, now Anzio, was on the coast, thirty-three miles south of Rome.

18. The Quinquatrus was a festival of Minerva, celebrated March 19–23. Baiae was a celebrated resort on the Gulf of Naples, to which Petronius' Trimalchio banished a slave.

19. Germanicus, father of Agrippina, had been the idol of the soldiers as well as of the populace. His premature death in A.D. 19 had caused unprecedented grief throughout the Empire.

20. This pool, used for mock naval combats, lay across the Tiber from the Campus Martius.

21. Nero's villa was in the Sabine Mountains about fifty miles east of Rome. The modern town of Subiaco takes its name from Sublaqueum.

22. L. Volusius Saturninus had died immensely wealthy a few years before this (in A.D. 56) at the age of 93.

23. There is a gap in the manuscript here, a few words being lost. The words in brackets are supplied from the account of a later historian, Cassius Dio, LXII, 14.

24. Pandateria, now Ventotene, is a small island in the Tyrrhenian Sea, some forty miles west of Naples.

25. This was the elder Agrippina, mother of Nero's mother. The Julia mentioned here was her youngest daughter, banished on the charge of adultery with Seneca.

26. It was generally believed that her father, the Emperor Claudius, was poisoned by his wife Agrippina, Nero's mother, so that her son might become emperor. For the death of Octavia's brother, Britannicus, see above, XIII, 15–17. The "servant girl" is Acte, the freedwoman who was Nero's mistress for a while; see XIII, 12.

27. The first to be called Germanicus was Drusus, the younger brother of Tiberius, grandfather of Octavia and great-grandfather of Nero. His son, who also bore the name, was Octavia's uncle and Nero's grandfather.

28. Beneventum, now Benevento, was an important city on the Via Appia, about thirty-five miles northeast of Naples.

29. This was a large artificial pool in the Campus Martius near the Pantheon.

30. The vast Circus Maximus filled the valley between the Palatine, Aventine, and Caelian Hills.

31. These were on the Esquiline at a considerable distance from the Palatine.

32. This would be approximately thirty cents a peck. The regular price seems to have been substantially higher.

33. For the temple of Jupiter Stator, see Livy, I, 12. Jupiter was so named ("the Stayer") because at this spot he "stayed" the retreat of the Romans in their battle with the Sabines.

34. The Senones were a tribe of Gauls who in 390 B.C. routed the Romans at the stream of the Allia and then sacked and burned the city.

35. Precisely how this was calculated is uncertain. It has been conjectured that the interval of 453 (or 454) years may be expressed as approximately 418 years plus 418 months plus 418 days.

36. A canal from Lake Avernus, west of Naples, to the mouths of the Tiber would have been more than 150 miles long.

37. These gardens were on the Vatican Hill about where St. Peter's now stands.

38. Lucan, Seneca's nephew, and the most celebrated poet of the Neronian period, wrote the epic poem *Pharsalia*, which still survives.

39. The Cerealia were celebrated from April 12 to 19. The circus races were on the last day.

40. These last words of Seneca have not come down to us.

41. Nero married this Statilia Messalina after the death of Poppaea.

42. The verses here referred to may be the weird passages in the *Pharsalia* (III, 635–646) where the poet describes the death of a warrior whose body was severed at the middle, the upper part falling in the water, while his comrades hung on to his nether part by his legs, and the blood gushed forth all at once in a great stream. While the lower half of the body speedily lost its vital powers, life lingered for a while in the upper half with its palpitating lung and warm entrails, but after a struggle yielded here also.

43. The lustrum was properly a purification ceremony held every five years; then the word came to be used to denote a five-year period.

44. Vespasian was to be emperor of Rome (A.D. 69–79).

45. This Petronius has been plausibly identified with the author of the brilliant satiric novel, called the *Satyricon*, which contains the famous episode of Trimalchio's Dinner, included in this book.

46. Patavium, now Padua, was the birthplace of Livy. It was at that time the most important city of northern Italy.

47. The Quindecimvirs were the college of fifteen priests who had charge of the Sibylline Books and may have had supervision over foreign cults. Tacitus was himself a member of this priestly college.

48. Cato, a champion of the old Republic, was an uncompromising opponent of Julius Caesar, as Sallust records in a selection above. After his suicide in 46 B.C. he was regarded as a martyr to the cause of freedom.

49. Aelius Tubero and Marcus Favonius were Stoics who opposed the Gracchi and Julius Caesar, respectively.

50. Gaius Cassius was an eminent jurist, banished after the Pisonian conspiracy.

51. This temple was just behind the Senate house (Curia Julia) in the Forum of Julius Caesar.

52. These are enormous sums. On 1952 standards they would come to at least $500,000 and $120,000, respectively.

53. The elder Arria had stabbed herself as an example for her husband, Caecina Paetus, who was condemned to death for conspiring against the Emperor Claudius. She handed the bloody dagger to him with the words, "Paetus, it doesn't hurt."

## Germania

1. Gaul bounded Germany on the west, Rhaetia and Pannonia on the south, Sarmatia and Dacia on the east.

2. Mount Abnoba is now the Black Forest. The Pontic Sea is the Black Sea.

3. The name survives in that of the modern village of Asberg, north of Cologne.

4. Tacitus is alluding to the Roman practice of deifying female members of the royal house. Examples are Nero's wife, Poppaea, and his infant daughter.

5. Mercury corresponds to Wodan, Hercules to Thor, Mars to Tiu. The Romans made a practice of identifying the gods of foreign peoples with those familiar to themselves.

6. The Romans, on the other hand, kept on consulting the omens until they got favorable ones.

7. These are the children born after their heirs have been decided. Among the Romans it seems to have been legitimate to do away with such children if the father saw fit.

8. In contrast with Roman girls, who might marry at as early an age as twelve.

9. A satiric reference to the activities of Roman legacy hunters, who courted the rich and childless. Cf. the Croton section of Petronius' *Satyricon*.

# SELECTIONS FROM The Sixth Satire OF JUVENAL

## Translated by John Paul Heironimus

### INTRODUCTION

DECIMUS JUNIUS JUVENALIS, the last of the great Roman satirists, was the son or foster son of a wealthy freedman, according to a biography which appears in widely varying forms in several manuscripts. Born at Aquinum about A.D. 55, he spent most of his life at Rome, where he frequented the schools of rhetoric, more for amusement than for profit, and did not turn to writing until he was middle-aged. Some lines deriding the political influence of an actor who was a favorite of an emperor led to an exile, which took the bizarre form of appointment to a military post in distant Egypt. One suspects that a period of military service in earlier life has been confused with the exile. There is no agreement about which emperor inflicted the exile, nor whether the poet survived it. He seems to have lived to A.D. 130 or even later.

As Roman literary critics proudly pointed out, satire was one literary form developed independently by Roman talent. Lucilius, a contemporary of the younger Africanus, was regarded as its founder. His works survive only in fragments, but we have in complete form the satires of Horace and Persius, writing under Augustus and Nero respectively. Many would give the palm to Juvenal, who

closes the series of Roman satirists. Lacking the urbanity and subtlety of Horace and the moral earnestness of Persius, he yet attains to first rank in his chosen field because of his unflagging energy, grim humor, and brilliant rhetoric. His sixteen satires are devoted to various aspects of Roman vice and folly. The sixth, which is translated almost entire, catalogues the shortcomings of Roman women, ranging from harmless peccadilloes such as too much fondness for books or athletics to the grossest immorality and crime. The nominal occasion was the proposed marriage of Ursidius Postumus, who as a reformed rake should know too well the frailties of the opposite sex. It exhibits some of the defects as well as the merits of the author: on the credit side, a real detestation for the morally base, and a graphic power in delineating it; on the other hand, the lack of a sense of proportion which blinds him to the difference between trifling eccentricities and serious transgressions, and a bigoted form of patriotism which makes him sneer at everything foreign.

THE TEXT translated here is that of S. G. Owen (Oxford 1902).

---

### The antiquity of adultery

I believe that Chastity lingered on earth in the good old days of Saturn, and that she was long seen while a chilly cavern furnished a tiny home and hearth and household altar, and sheltered both flock and family in a common shade; while a hill-billy wife made up a sylvan bed of leaves and hay and the hides of beasts that were their neighbors; a wife very different from you, Cynthia,[1] or you whose bright eyes were dimmed by the death of the sparrow.[2] With

her breasts bulging with milk for her brawny brats to drink, she was often a grimmer spectacle than her husband, belching over his meal of acorns. Yes, men lived far otherwise than we when earth was new and the heavens freshly created;[3] men who had to burst their way forth from oak trees to be born, or were moulded from clay, for they had no parents. Many traces, perhaps, or at least some, remained of Chastity even in Jove's reign—but before Jove grew a beard, before the Greeks were ready to take an oath on somebody else's life; when no one feared a thief would steal his cabbages and apples, and everybody lived with garden unfenced. Gradually then Justice retired to the heavens with Chastity as her companion, and the two sisters fled hand in hand. It is an old and hackneyed business, O Postumus, to meddle with somebody else's bed and to flout the deity that watches over the holy couch of matrimony. It was the Iron Age which later gave rise to all other crimes; the Age of Silver saw the first adulterers.

### Suicide preferable to matrimony

Yet, in our time, you are preparing a marriage pact and covenant and a betrothal; already you are groomed by the master barber; perhaps you have placed a ring on her finger! Surely, you used to be of sound mind. What, getting married, Postumus? Tell me what snaky-haired Tisiphone is hounding you. Can you endure a female boss, when there are so many ropes available, so many windows of dizzy height, when the Aemilian bridge is right at hand? Or if you don't care for any of these numerous forms of suicide, don't you think it better to have a lad sleep with you? A lad who won't scold you at night, nor demand any gifts as he lies there, nor complain that you are sparing your forces and not laboring as ordered.

### Rarity of decent wives

But Ursidius wants to comply with the Julian law; [4] he's planning to get a dear little heir, though he will have to give up the fine pigeons and bearded mullets and everything else that the legacy hunters buy for him in the provision market. What can you consider impossible if Ursidius takes a wife, if the most notorious of adulterers foolishly puts his neck in the matrimonial halter, after hiding so often in a chest like Latinus [5] to save his life? Yes, and he's looking for a wife with old-fashioned morals! Ye doctors, tap his vein, his pressure is too high! The presumption of the fellow! Fall down on your face and adore the Tarpeian [6] threshold, sacrifice a heifer with gilded horns to Juno, if you can find a matron of chaste repute. Few indeed are worthy to wear the ribbons as a priestess of Ceres, few whose kisses a father need not fear. Well, go on and tie a wreath to

your door and hang ivy clusters over your lintel: [7] is one man going to satisfy Hiberina? [8] You'll find it easier to compel her to be satisfied with one eye. Yet high is the repute of a certain lass who lives on her father's farm. Let her continue to live at Gabii or Fidenae [9] as she lived on the farm, and I'll accept the tale of her good behavior under papa's care. Yet who can affirm that nothing happened to her in the mountains or in the caverns? Have Jove and Mars grown so old?

### Craze for actors, musicians, gladiators

Is any woman such as you pray for to be found in the public colonnades? Do the shows have anywhere in all their benches a woman you can safely love and take from there? When Bathyllus, that sissy, dances the role of Leda, with lots of arm-flapping, Tuccia cannot control herself, your Apulian wench suddenly gives a long sad moan as if she were in his arms; Thymele [10] gives heed; she can learn from them, poor naive Thymele! But when the awnings are taken down and the theater is closed and empty, and only the law-courts ring with voices, and it's a long, long time from the Plebeian festival to the Megalesian, other ladies sadly clasp as souvenirs the mask and wand and tights of Accius. Urbicus in the concluding Atellan farce gets a laugh with his gestures as Autonoë; Aelia, poor wretch, falls in love with him. For others a comedian unbends—at quite a price. Some keep Chrysogonus too busy to sing. Hispulla rejoices in a tragic actor. Do you expect her to fall in love with Professor Quintilian? [11] You take a wife in order that the crooner Echion may become a father, or Glaphyrus, or Ambrosius the flautist. Let us crowd the streets with long scaffolds, let your portals and door be adorned with huge laurel branches, that your noble son in his richly inlaid cradle, O Lentulus, may smile beneath the mosquito net with the features of Euryalus or some gladiator.

### Notorious case of Eppia

Eppia, the wife of a senator, ran off with a troupe of gladiators to Pharos and the Nile and the notorious walls of Lagus, while even Canopus was revolted at the monstrous morals of Rome.[12] She forgot her household and husband and sister; had no thought of her native Rome, nor of her weeping sons, the hard-hearted hussy; still more surprising, she gave up the Roman theater and the actor Paris. Though from girlhood she had slept in the lap of luxury, on downy beds in her father's house, and in a richly inlaid cradle, she thought nothing of the sea voyage. Long ago had she scorned her fair repute—that's the lightest thing to be given up amidst the chaises longues of these easy ladies. So she braved the Tuscan waves and the far-roaring Ionian deep with intrepid breast, though she must pass from sea to sea. If there is a good and honorable reason for the hazard, a gentlewoman is afraid; her frightened bosom grows cold at the thought; she cannot stand on her trembling feet. But they show a valiant heart when their daring is in a base cause. If her husband should bid her, she swears it is an awful thing to have to board ship; the smell of the bilge is nauseating, the sky reels before her dizzy eyes. But a woman who goes off with her lover has a strong stomach. The other vomits all over her husband; but our heroine joins the sailors at mess, and strolls about the deck, and rejoices to haul on the hard ropes. Yet what beauty was it that set Eppia on fire, what youthful charm that captivated her? What did she see that made her willing to be called a gladiator's wench? Why, her little Sergius had long since been scraping his chin; he hoped they would let him retire with his wounded arm; there were plenty of scars on his face; there was a huge wart on the middle of his nose where the helmet rubbed it; his sweet little eyes ran continually with a chronic inflammation. But he was a gladiator! That makes a man as handsome as Hyacinth; that was what she preferred to her children and home-town, to her husband and sister. If this same Sergius had been put on the retired list, he would have begun to seem as unattractive as old Veiento. . . .[13]

[1–113]

### Love potions

Shall I speak of love potions and charms, of poison concocted and served to a stepson? They do worse things when compelled by the tyranny of their feminine nature; their lust is the least of their sins.

### Some husbands are silent for money,

"Yet why is Censennia an excellent woman, by the testimony of her husband?" She brought him a dowry of a million sesterces; that's his price for calling her virtuous! It is not Venus quiver that makes him lean, nor her torch that burns him; it's from her cash that the torch gleams for him, it's from her dowry that the arrows shoot. She has bought her freedom: before his very eyes she may wink at a lover or write a billet doux; a wealthy woman who has married a covetous man is as free as a widow.

### Others are temporarily blinded by beauty.

"Why does Sertorius blaze with desire for Bibula?" If you will shake the truth from him, it is a face, not a wife, that *he's* in love with. Let three wrinkles develop and her skin grow dry and loose; let her teeth lose their gleam and her eyes their lustrous size: his agent will tell her, "Pack up your bags and be on your way; we're tired of you, and you blow your nose too often; be on your way, and hurry up about it; another bride with a dry nose is coming." But for the present she is in high favor and plays the queen, demanding Canusinian flocks and shepherds, Falernian vineyards—that's a small item: she wants all his slaves, domestic and rural; and anything her house doesn't have, and a neighbor's does, he'll have to buy! Come December,[14] when the mural of merchant Jason and his armed sailors disappears behind the canvas booths, she carries off huge goblets of crystal and bigger ones of agate; then the famous diamond which gained even greater worth from the finger of Queen Berenice: [15] the barbarous Agrippa gave it in days of yore to the sister who shared his bed, in the land where kings dance on naked feet to celebrate the Sabbath, and long established clemency lets pigs die of old age.

### Intolerable pride of upper-class women

"Does none seem worthy to you out of such herds of women?" Though she be beautiful and discreet, rich and fertile, though she have a gallery full of ancestral portraits, though she be chaster than any of the Sabine women [16] who rushed in with dishevelled hair to part the battle lines—in short, a rare bird on earth, comparable to a black swan—who can stand a wife in whom all virtues meet? I'd rather have a country lass from Venusia than you, O "Cornelia, Mother of the Gracchi," [17] if along with your undoubted virtues you bring a haughty nose and count the family triumphs as part of your dowry. Pack up your Hannibal and Syphax routed in his camp, and get you gone with all Carthage! [18]

### Niobe is typical.

"O Healer God, be merciful, and thou, O goddess, lay aside thy arrows; my children are guilty of nought—shoot thou their mother!" implores Amphion. But the Healer God continues to bend his bow. So Niobe was the death of her flocks of children and of their father, for she thought herself nobler than the race of Latona and more prolific of offspring than the white sow.[19] What dignity of character or what beauty is worth so much that you would be willing to have it constantly thrown in your teeth? For there is no enjoyment in this rare and supreme "blessing" when she, corrupted by the spirit of pride, has more of the bitterness of aloe than the sweetness of honey. And what husband is so devoted that he does not secretly loathe and curse seven hours a day this rare prize he publicly extols?

### Affectation of talking Greek

There are certain practices which are indeed unimportant, yet for a husband intolerable. For what is more nauseating than the fact that no Italian woman considers herself charming until she has made herself into a Greek instead of a Tuscan, a purebred Athenian instead of a lass from Sulmo? They say everything in Greek, though it is more of a disgrace to our people not to know Latin. But in Greek they must express their fears, their wrath, their joys, their worries; in this tongue they pour out all the secrets of their hearts. Can one go further than this? They talk Greek in the transports of love! Yet one may allow this foible to the sweet young things: are *you* still to sigh in Greek, you, tottering on the verge of eighty-six? This is no seemly speech for an old lady! How often comes that lustful "Zoê kai psychê!" [20] You take words

from under the bed-clothes and use them in public. What man's desire is immune to a sweet, naughty voice? It stirs him like a nudge! Yet though you utter these phrases more wantonly than Haemus or Carpophorus,[21] your face tells the tale of your years, so that all his ardor subsides.

### Kindly and devoted spouses are victimized.

If you, sir, aren't going to love the wife so lawfully betrothed and wedded, there does not seem to be any reason to marry her. Why should you waste your money on a wedding feast, and cakes to give the obsequious guests as they depart well stuffed? Or the bride-gift for the first night's bliss—the effigy of our Dacic and Germanic prince, gleaming on his lettered gold coins, presented to her on a costly platter? But if you are a uxorious simpleton, with a soul devoted to but one, you may bow your head with neck ready to receive the yoke; you'll find no woman will spare her devoted slave! Though she too feel the flame, she delights to torment and rob her lover. So a wife is a worse disaster for any good and desirable husband. You will never make any present without her approval; you won't sell anything if she opposes; you won't buy anything if she says no. She will dictate your feelings for you: let that friend be turned away, whose downy beard your door saw long ago. Though the right of making their own wills is allowed to panders and prize-fight trainers, and gladiators have the same privilege, *you* will have to inscribe as your heirs your rivals for her love—and several of them. "To the cross with this slave!" "By what crime did the fellow earn that fate? Who bears witness against him? Who told on him? Hear what he has to say; it's never too long to deliberate when a man's life is at stake." "You fool, so a slave is a man? Suppose he did not do anything: I wish it, I order it, let my wish stand for a reason."

So she lords it over her husband; but soon she abandons her kingdom and seeks another house, and wears out her wedding veil; then she flies away from there and retraces her steps to the couch she scorned. She's off from the door so lately adorned, the awnings hanging on the house front, the branches still green over the lintel. So she runs up her total; thus she gets eight husbands in five years—a record well worth inscribing on her tombstone!

*Sinister influence of mothers-in-law*

You may give up any hope for harmony as long as your mother-in-law is alive. She teaches her daughter what fun it is to rob her husband of his very shirt; she coaches her, when a letter arrives from a seducer, to write a smart and sophisticated reply. She fools the guards or bribes them. She calls in a doctor when the girl is perfectly well, and heaps the blankets on her. Meanwhile the lurking lover silently waits in the offing, chafing at the delay. Well, do you expect the mother to impart honorable ways, different from her own? Besides, it's useful to the old hag to have a daughter as bad as herself.

*Fondness for litigation*

There is hardly a lawsuit that some woman did not start. Manilia sues somebody else if she is not the defendant. They draw up and arrange the indictments themselves—they could dictate an exordium or topics for Professor Celsus [22] himself.

*Female athletes*

Who does not know about the purple sweat-shirts and the feminine wrestling oil? or has not seen them whack at the fencing post? She pounds away with sword and shield, and goes through the whole drill; a matron who well deserves to blow a trumpet at the Floralia [23]—unless she is planning something still worse in that bosom, and is getting ready to fight in the real arena. What virtue can you expect in a woman with a helmet, one who casts off her sex and is mad about strength? Yet even she would not be willing to turn man; for how slight is our pleasure in comparison to theirs! What a fine thing for you if your wife's property were put up for sale—her belt and gauntlets and crests and greaves for the left leg. Or if she turns to some other kind of fighting, what a lucky fellow you will be when your little woman sells her shin guards! Are these the ladies who find a gauzy tunic too heavy, whose delicate skin is hurt by a scrap of silk? Listen to her grunt as she deals home the prescribed strokes! How heavy the helmet that bows down her head!

See how big and thick the roll of bandages of bark about her legs! And laugh when she lays aside her arms and retires to the ladies' room. Tell me, ye daughters of Lepidus or of Metellus the blind or of Fabius Gurges: [24] what carnival wench ever put on such garb? When did the wife of Asylus pant at the fencing-post?

*Impossible to best a woman in argument*

Any bed that contains a wife is always the scene of wrangles and mutual recrimination; there's not much sleep in it! Though she is always a nuisance to her husband, she is worse than a tigress robbed of her cubs when she really has her own hidden peccadilloes on her conscience but pretends to groan over *his* misdeeds; she hates his boy-loves, or weeps about the imaginary mistress he keeps—weeps with an ever plentiful stock of tears, always at their post, waiting like soldiers for their orders to flow forth. You think it is love; you smirk with self-satisfaction, you poor worm, and kiss away the teardrops. What letters would you find to read, what compromising billets-doux, if you should open up the desk of this jealous wife of yours? But suppose you actually find her in the arms, be it of a groom or of a knight. Suggest some line of defense for her, Professor Quintilian. "I'm really puzzled." Well, let *her* try. "We made a bargain long ago," says she, "that you should do what you liked, and that I might indulge my fancy. Though you bellow and make the welkin ring, I'm a human being." There's nothing like their audacity when you catch them in the act; their guilt just makes them angry and bold.

*Only in the frugal past was Rome virtuous.*

Do you ask whence come these enormities, what can be their source? It was poverty that kept the Latin women chaste in days of old; no vice could enter their humble doors when all was work and hours of sleep were brief, their hands were hard and calloused from spinning Tuscan wool, Hannibal was at the gates, and their husbands were on guard at the Colline tower. Now we suffer the woes of long peace. More dire than war, luxury has descended upon us, and avenges the conquered universe. [25] No disgrace or abomination is missing since Roman poverty has ended. Thus upon these hills has poured old Sybaris, thus Rhodes and Miletus and Tarentum, wanton and drunken beneath her garlands. It was filthy money that first brought in foreign ways, it was dissolute wealth that has enervated the age with shameful luxury. . . .

[133–300]

### The scandal of Clodius and Pompeia

I wish the ancient rites and public ceremonies at least were kept free from these abominations. But everybody knows, even the Moors and Hindus, what "singing girl" [26] brought an organ bigger than Caesar's two books *Against Cato* [27] to a place whence even a mouse would flee, conscious of his masculinity—a place where they even have to hang a veil over any picture that represents the opposite sex. What mortal in the good old days despised the gods? Who dared laugh at the cup and black dishes of Numa, and the fragile saucers of Vatican clay? But now what altar lacks its Clodius?

### Extravagance in their whims

I hear what you keep telling me, old friends: "Put her under lock and key, keep 'em off!" But who will guard the guards? Your wife is clever enough to begin with them! They all have the same lust, high and low alike; no difference between the common woman who must pound the black pavement on foot, and the lady who rides in a sedan chair on the necks of tall Syrians. To go to the games, Ogulnia rents a dress, hires some attendants, a sedan chair, a pillow, and some lady friends and a nurse-chaperone, and a blonde servant girl to take her messages; yet she gives away to smooth athletes whatever is left of the ancestral silver service, yes, the very last plates. Lots of them are hard up, but none show the self-restraint of poverty, or measure themselves by poverty's standards. Yet men eventually realize what expediency demands; some learn from the example of the ant to anticipate cold and hunger. But the extravagant woman does not realize that the family fortune is going. Just as if money grew again in the bottom of the empty money chest, and was drawn from a pile that ever keeps renewing itself, she never gives a thought to how much her pleasures cost. . . .[28]

[335–365]

### Fanatical enthusiasm for musicians

If her taste is for singing, no public performer can keep himself safe. Her favorite's harp is always in her hands, while her rings glitter here and there all over the sounding board, and the nimble quill darts up and down the row of strings. She clasps the instrument on which Hedymeles (oh so ravishing!) once performed; this is her consolation; she lavishes her kisses on the quill that gave such delight. One lady of the line of the Lamiae and the Appian gens consulted Janus and Vesta with sacrifice of flour and wine whether Pollio should hope for the crown of oak leaves at the Capitoline games and should enter the fiddlers' contest. What more could she do if it were a question of her husband's recovery from illness, or if the doctors looked grave over the prospects of her little son? She stood before the altar and thought it no disgrace to veil her head in behalf of a harpist, and she uttered the prescribed formulae as custom demands, and when the lamb was cut up for examination she lost all color. Now tell me, most ancient of gods, Father Janus: do you give answer to such as these? Heaven must be a terribly lazy place; you gods apparently have an idle time of it. Another woman consults you about comic actors, another will want to commend a tragedian to your favor; the soothsayer will have to stand at his task until his legs are swollen.

### Love of gossip

But let her sing rather than gad all about the city, a bold hussy who can appear in gatherings of men and in the presence of her husband can with unembarrassed look and unfeminine breasts talk to uniformed generals. This creature knows what's going on all over the world, what the Chinese and Thracians are up to, the secret doings of a stepmother and her stepson, who is in love, what lady-killer is scrambled for by all the girls. She'll tell you who got the widow with child and in what month, what patter, what technique each belle employs in her love scenes. She's the first to see the comet [29] that threatens woe to the king of Armenia and Parthia, she catches all rumors and canards fresh at the city gates; some she starts herself: that the Niphates river has overflowed the country and all the fields there are under water; cities are tottering, the ground is sinking—she tells it at any cross-roads to anybody she meets.

*Brutality toward neighbors and discourtesy to guests*

Yet this failing is not any worse than hers who is accustomed to have her humble neighbors seized and flogged with thongs—providing she is in a mild mood. For if her sweet sleep is disturbed by some dog's yapping, "Get the cudgels in a hurry," she says, and bids that first the owner be pounded, then the cur. A formidable creature to encounter, with grim countenance, she enters the bath by night, orders her oil flasks and whole retinue to set out by night; she likes to get up a sweat with a rousing workout, when her arms fall wearied by the heavy dumbbells, and the shrewd masseur explores her frame with his fingers, and loudly slaps milady's hams. Meanwhile her unhappy dinner guests get sleepy and hungry. At last she comes, all flushed of face, thirsty enough to drink a whole jug of wine, which is set before her feet, holding full three gallons. She quaffs a second pint before she starts to eat; it's just to whet her appetite, for up it comes again and hits the floor after bathing her stomach. Rivers of it run over the marble pavement, or a golden basin catches the fragrant Falernian; for as if a long snake had fallen into the tall jug, she drinks and then vomits. So her husband turns queasy and covers his eyes while he retches.

*The lady critic of literature*

Yet *she* is still worse who when she takes her place at table, praises Vergil, finds an excuse for poor Dido, doomed to the grave, pits the bards against each other and compares them, sets Vergil on one side of the scales and Homer on the other. Teachers of literature yield the floor, professors of rhetoric retire in defeat, the whole crowd falls silent; neither a lawyer nor a town crier will say a word—not even another woman! Such a flood of words rolls out, you'd think somebody was pounding tin pans or bells. Let no one bother to blow a trumpet or clash the cymbals; all by herself she can save the failing moon.[30] A wise man sets a limit even to virtues; a woman who wants to appear too clever and eloquent might as well wear a tunic to the middle

of her leg like a man, sacrifice a pig to the man's god Silvanus, and pay the men's fee at the baths. Let the matron who shares your table have no oratorical style, nor wield the rounded syllogism in hurtling phrases. Let her not know all history; let there be some things in books that she *doesn't* know. I loathe a woman who consults and thumbs the grammar of Palaemon, who always observes the rules and laws of good diction, and in her antiquarian erudition quotes verses I never heard before; one who corrects the mistakes of a less gifted friend—mistakes no man would bother about. A husband ought to have the right to use careless grammar!

*Disgusting use of cosmetics*

There is nothing that a woman does not allow herself, nothing at which she blushes, when she can afford to adorn her neck with a string of emeralds, or stretch her lobes with pearl earrings; there is nothing more intolerable than a wealthy woman. For the time being, her ugly and ridiculous face is plastered with a bread poultice, or smells of greasy Poppaean ointment—what a sticky mess for her poor husband to kiss! But they wash their skins clean when they go to meet their lovers. When does she bother to appear beautiful at home? It's for her lovers that she buys the perfume of nard and whatever else the slender Hindus export to us. Finally she reveals her face and takes off the innermost layer of enamel; she begins to be recognizable, and applies a soothing lotion of asses' milk—for its sake she takes the she-asses with her wherever she goes, though she should be sent to exile beneath the bleak sky of the arctic. Yet such a face, when it is coated and bathed with so many changing cosmetics and plastered with bits of damp breadcrust—is it a face or shall it be called a running sore?

*A typical day shows their cruelty to slaves.*

It is worth while to learn in detail how they employ themselves throughout the day. If her husband turned his back on her last night, it's too bad for the overseer of the spinning women, her hairdressers take off their clothes to receive their whippings, the Liburnian coachman is accused of coming tardily, and pays the penalty for somebody else's slumbers; he has the rod broken over his back, another is whipped with thongs till his back runs red, still another gets the cat-o'-nine-tails. Some women hire the torturer by the year! Wham! goes the whip, while she coolly applies her cold cream, chats with her lady visitors, or admires the wide gold border of her pretty dress; wham! and she reads the newspaper to the last line; wham! until finally the torturers are exhausted, and she growls, "That's all," the "examination" having been completed. Her rule over her household is no milder than a Sicilian tyrant's court. For if she has made a date with a lover and wants to look prettier than usual, and is in a hurry, for she's already overdue at the park, or perhaps rather at the temple of the obliging Isis, the wretched Psecas dresses milady's hair while her own hair has been tugged and her tunic torn off her shoulder and breast. "Why is this curl too high!" and instantly the lash of bull's hide punishes the outrageous crime of misplacing that lock. What has Psecas done? How is the girl at fault if you aren't pleased with your nose? Another maid works at the left side and combs the locks and sets her wave. An aged crone, the slave once of milady's mother, now the overseer of the spinning women, for she is discharged from the curling-iron post, sits as assessor; hers will be the first vote; after her, those inferior in age and skill will voice their views, as if their lady's honor were at stake, or life itself. Such is her concern to be beautiful; with so many layers she loads her head, one after another with so many tiers she builds it up. You'll find her as majestic as Andromache, viewed from in front; but she is shorter from the rear view; you'll think her somebody else! But what can a woman do, if nature has allotted to her a short waist, so that without high heels she seems shorter than a Pygmy girl, in fact she has to jump up on tiptoe for a kiss?

*Extravagant devotion to outlandish cults*

Meanwhile, no thought of her husband—no allusion to the frightful expenses she causes him. She lives as if she were just a neighbor, closer only in that she makes a point to hate his friends and servants and to wreck his budget. Look, a chorus of frenzied Bellona and of the Mother of the Gods comes dashing in, at their head a huge eunuch, an awful personage to the lesser obscenities. Long ago he seized a pots-herd and sacrificed his tender virility; the howling mob and the kettledrums of the common herd make way for him as he enters, with the Phrygian headdress draping his cheek. He booms a warning that she must dread the advent of September and the southwest wind unless she shall buy immunity with a hundred eggs and bestow on himself her wine-colored gowns—they're getting rather old, anyhow—so that any sudden danger that threatens may be diverted to the tunics, and she shall be free for a whole year at one stroke. In winter she will break the ice and jump into the river; thrice at dawn will she plunge into the Tiber and bathe her cowering head in its eddies; then, naked and trembling, she will crawl on bleeding knees the whole length of the haughty king's field.[31] If white Io shall bid, she will go to the limits of Egypt and get water from torrid Meroë to bring to Rome to sprinkle in the temple of Isis, rising beside the ancient sheepfold.[32] For she thinks it is the voice of the Lady herself that utters the warning—what a mind and heart for the gods to commune with at night! So the highest honors go to the charlatan who, amidst a train of priests, linen-clad and shaven of pate, parades in the role of Anubis, sneering all the while at the wailing mob. He intercedes whenever a wife has failed to keep ritual chastity on the solemn days of sacrifice and some heavy atonement is due for the couch profaned; and the silver serpent is seen to nod its head in acceptance; obviously, his studied tears and muttered prayers prevail on Osiris not to deny indulgence for the sin. A fat goose and a thin pancake—that's all it takes to bribe a god.

When he makes way, a palsied old Jewess who has left her basket and straw [33] whines a secret plea into milady's ear—an authority, she, on the laws of Jerusalem, a powerful open-air revivalist, a reliable medium of communication for heaven's will. She too gets a handout, but a smaller one; the Jews sell their nonsense, whatever one wants to hear, for small change.

*Credulous victims of fortune-tellers*

A fortune-teller from Armenia or Commagene, after pawing the lungs of a freshly slaughtered dove, assures her that she will have a smooth lover or a fat legacy from some childless old man. He'll scrutinize the bosom of chickens, the entrails of a dog, or even of a child, sometimes; he will commit the crime so that he can threaten to turn informer against his patroness. But the Chaldaeans have even greater sway over her credulity. Whatever an astrologer tells her she will regard as straight from the fount of Hammon—since oracles are no more spoken at Delphi, and the human race is condemned to darkness as to the future. Yet the mightiest of these is one who often suffered exile, a man by whose friendship and mercenary horoscope died the great citizen whom Otho feared.[34] These charlatans are trusted only if they have worn iron chains on their wrists and have long languished in a military prison. No astrologer will be credited with talent if he has never been sentenced in court; only he who barely escaped the death penalty and was lucky to get off with banishment to the Cyclades, and who finally was released from tiny Seriphus. Your Tanaquil[35] will consult him as to why her jaundiced mother is so slow to die (but first she'll ask about *you*): when she may expect to bury her sister and her uncles; and whether her lover will survive her— for what greater favor can heaven vouchsafe?

*Some profess the art of divination themselves.*

Yet such as these do not themselves profess to discern the menace of the gloomy star of Saturn, or in what conjunction the rise of Venus is lucky, what month is doomed to disaster, what season is granted for gain. Avoid even meeting a woman in whose hands you see a well-thumbed almanac, carried around like a sticky ball of amber.[36] *She* seeks no professional assistance— by this time people consult *her*. When her husband must go to a foreign post or must return home, she will refuse to accompany him if the calculations of Thrasyllus forbid; if it is only a question of a drive to the first milestone, a suitable hour must be determined by the book. If the corner of her eyelid itches when she rubs it, she will consult her horoscope before she puts salve on it. Though she lie ill, the only right hour for taking nourishment is drawn from the book of Petosiris.

*Rich and poor alike consult soothsayers*

If she be in humble circumstances, she will stroll around the goal posts in the Circus and will draw lots, and offer hand and brow to some fortune-teller, who urges her to smack her lips repeatedly.[37] To the wealthy, a Phrygian seer or Indian wise woman will interpret the future, or some sage observer of the stars and sky, for a fee; or an elder priest who expiates lightning strokes for the state; but the destinies of the humble are determined in the Circus or on the causeway.[38] A woman who wears all her scanty wealth in a gold necklace about her naked neck consults the Towers [39] and the Dolphins' Columns as to whether she should desert her tavern keeper and marry the old-clothes peddler.

*Rich women won't bear children;*

Yet these poor wenches undergo the risk of bearing children and all the annoyances of nursing them, as their condition compels; but rarely indeed are children born in golden beds. So effective are the techniques and the drugs of this witch who gives release from pregnancy and contracts to kill human beings in the womb. Rejoice, you poor husband; with your own hand administer the potion, whatever it is. For if she should consent to burden her womb with a lusty infant, you might find yourself the reputed father of an Ethiope, and your will must name as heir a mulatto, an unlucky sight, never to be witnessed by you in daylight hours.

*They pass off foundlings as their own children.*

I won't mention spurious children—a father's joys and prayers cheated at the foul reservoirs, and pontiffs and Salii who come from there to bear the noble name of Scaurus in their masquerade.[40] Mischievous Fortune stands there by night, smiling at the naked babies; she clasps them to her bosom with fondest affection, then hands them over to lofty houses, and makes a secret comedy for herself; these she loves, these she showers with gifts, and ever promotes them as her own darlings.

*They drive their husbands crazy with love potions.*

Here is a vendor of magic charms, here one offers Thessalian potions for sale—potions that enable a wife to overturn her husband's reason, so that she can turn him over her knee and spank him with her slipper. That's the cause of your wandering wits, your mental fog, and your utter forgetfulness of things you did     minute ago. Yet you may consider yourself lucky if you don't go raving mad as well, like Nero's well-known uncle,[41] for whom Caesonia mixed the entire forehead of a shivering colt. What woman will not follow the example of the emperor's wife? All the world was bursting into flame and falling into ruin, its framework shattered, as if Juno had driven *her* husband to insanity. Less guilty was the mushroom that Agrippina served Claudius; it only stopped the heart of one old dotard, and bade his palsied pate descend to heaven,[42] and his lips that drooled with saliva. But this potion of Caesonia calls for fire and sword, for tortures and slaughter of senators, mingling their blood with that of knights. Such was the cost of the mare's offspring, and of one witch's mischief!

*They kill their stepsons—or even their own children.*

They loathe their husbands' sons by their predecessors; let no one oppose or forbid that! In fact, it is now perfectly proper to kill a stepson. But I warn you, fatherless children, if you have any property worth mentioning: guard your lives and distrust every dish! Pastry that your mother has poisoned leads to pallor and fever. Let someone taste in advance anything that she has offered you, yes, though she be your own mother; let a quaking old slave sample your cups first!

*Real life equals the most extravagant stories of mythology.*

I am making this up, I suppose you think, and Satire is putting on the high buskins of Tragedy;

I have wandered far from the literary limits and rules decreed by my predecessors and am indulging in fabulous rant like the tragedies of Sophocles. Would that mine were an idle tale! But Pontia proclaims, "I did the deed, I admit, and brewed the aconite for my children; the facts were detected and are public knowledge; but with my own hands I perpetrated the crime!" What, you abominable snake, you killed your two children at one meal? Two of them? "I would have killed seven, had there been seven!" Let us believe the tragic poets in their tales of the cruel Colchian[43] and Procne; I make no demur; they too dared awful crimes for those days, but not for money. We need feel less surprise at atrocious crimes when it is anger that drives this sex to guilt; when rage fires their spleen they are swept on as impetuously as rocks from a cliff when the whole mountain side gives way beneath. But I can't stand a woman who calculates and commits a terrible deed in cold blood. They go to the play and see Alcestis[44] dying for her husband; if a similar choice arose for them, they would want to sacrifice a husband's life to save a lapdog! Any day you will meet plenty of women like the daughters[45] of Danaus or like Eriphyle; in every street there will be a Clytemnestra. The only difference is that the famous daughter of Tyndareus held a rude and uncouth axe in both hands; but now the business is performed with subtle extract of toad's lungs. But they too will resort to the steel if their Agamemnon, like the thrice-conquered king of Pontus,[46] has been cautious enough to fortify himself in advance with antidotes.
[379–661]

## NOTES TO *THE SIXTH SATIRE* OF JUVENAL

1. Beloved of the Augustan poet Propertius; actual name Hostia.

2. Lesbia (Clodia), beloved of Catullus.

3. Cf. Lucretius, V, 925 ff.

4. A law of Augustus, enacted in 18 B.C., to encourage matrimony and the rearing of children.

5. An actor in the period of Domitian. He played the part of an adulterer in a farce, and hid in a chest to escape detection.

6. Refers to the Capitoline temple of Jupiter, who with Juno had particular charge of marriage.

7. In celebration of the approaching ceremony.

8. Presumably the bride-elect of Postumus.

9. These were sleepy country towns; but even there an energetic matron could find an adulterer.

10. A notorious actress.

11. Eminent author and teacher of rhetoric, A.D. 35–95.

12. Pharos, the lighthouse of Alexandria; Lagus, founder of the Ptolemaic dynasty which ruled there; Canopus, a suburb of the city.

13. Possibly the husband whom Eppia deserted. Notorious as an informer under Domitian, and evidently repulsively ugly.

14. The Saturnalia, December 17–23, was the occasion

of exchange of gifts, and of much extravagant purchasing. Stalls for the exhibition of merchandise were erected in or near the Saepta in the Campus Martius, and their canvas would conceal the frescoes of the portico of Agrippa, depicting Jason and the Argonauts.

15. Sister of Agrippa II, King of Judaea (A.D. 50–100). The emperor Titus loved her but was forced to part with her because of her odium in the eyes of the Roman populace. Juvenal as a confirmed xenophobe is of course strongly anti-Semitic.

16. See Livy I, 9.

17. A traditional phrase, inscribed on the statue of the mother of the martyred leaders of the Roman plebeians, Tiberius and Gaius Gracchus (cf. Plutarch, *Tiberius Gracchus*, 1).

18. Cornelius Scipio Africanus, father of Cornelia, triumphed for his victory in 203 B.C. over Syphax, the Numidian ally of the Carthaginians, and over Hannibal at Zama a year later.

19. It was foretold to Aeneas that he should build his city where he found a white sow with thirty pigs (*Aeneid*, VIII, 42–45).

20. "My life and soul."

21. More actors.

22. Probably the rhetorician Cornelius Celsus, author of an encyclopedia of which one section, dealing with medicine, survives.

23. The Floralia (April 23–May 3) were celebrated with licentious exhibitions by actresses.

24. Typical Roman aristocrats; Asylus was evidently a gladiator.

25. Sallust gives a similar account of the growth of vice at Rome; cf. *Catiline*, 6–12 or *Jugurthine War*, 41.

26. Clodius, the bête noire of Cicero, disguised himself as a female musician to visit the rites of Bona Dea in 62 B.C. at the house of Caesar's wife Pompeia, with whom Clodius was carrying on an intrigue.

27. Cicero's laudation of Cato of Utica in 46 B.C. elicited a counterblast in two volumes from Caesar.

28. At this point one Oxford manuscript adds thirty-four lines (not included here) on loathsome satellites introduced into the household by matrons. Discovered in 1899, they have been the subject of considerable controversy among scholars, and their authenticity is still open to question.

29. This comet appeared in November, A.D. 115. The Armenian campaign of Trajan ended in 114, the Parthian campaign in 116.

30. In eclipses of the moon the superstitious, believing that witches were making away with the luminary, raised a din to drown out their incantations.

31. The Campus Martius, originally the property of King Tarquin the Proud.

32. The building more commonly called the Saepta, in the Campus Martius.

33. Used to keep food warm over the Sabbath, when Jewish law forbade the use of fire. The Jews seem to have used a public park in Rome for their conventicles; hence the sneer about "open-air revivalist."

34. The emperor Galba (A.D. 68–69), murdered by his successor Otho. The name of the astrologer who encouraged the hopes of Otho is variously given as Ptolemaeus or Seleucus.

35. Wife of Tarquin the First, given here as the type of woman skilled in divination.

36. Roman ladies liked to fondle amber balls for their agreeable fragrance when warmed.

37. Part of the ceremony from which the charlatan predicted his client's fortune.

38. An earthwork of the regal period on the east side of Rome, used by later ages as a promenade.

39. Temporarily erected for sham fights in the Circus; the seven Dolphins' Columns were used to indicate how many laps remained in the current race.

40. A typical Roman aristocratic family. High priesthoods such as the colleges of the pontiffs and Salii were the perquisites of noble birth—here usurped by these nameless foundlings, abandoned by their mothers at the water tank and adopted and reared by childless matrons of great families.

41. The emperor Caligula (A.D. 37–41), supposed to have been driven mad by a love potion given him by his wife Caesonia. A membrane growing on the forehead of a new-born colt was traditionally a favorite ingredient in such concoctions (*Aeneid*, IV, 515).

42. Intentionally paradoxical; nominally worshipped as a god in heaven, his real destination was Hades. Seneca's satire *Apocolocyntosis* describes the deceased emperor's ignominious rejection when he knocked at the door of Olympus.

43. Medea, who like Procne, wife of Tereus, killed her children to get revenge on a faithless spouse. See the plays of Euripides and Seneca.

44. Heroine of a famous play by Euripides. The wife of Admetus, she volunteered to die to save her husband from death.

45. Like Eriphyle and Clytemnestra (daughter of Tyndareus, wife of Agamemnon) murderers of their husbands.

46. Mithridates, King of Pontus (111–63 B.C.), defeated by three Roman generals, Sulla, Lucullus, and Pompey, was reputed to be the inventor of a universal antidote against poisons. According to another account he established an immunity by repeated small doses of poison. Cf. A. E. Housman, *A Shropshire Lad*, LXII. Housman was a famous editor of Juvenal.

# SELECTIONS FROM *The Deified Julius* OF SUETONIUS

## *Translated by John Paul Heironimus*

## INTRODUCTION

GAIUS SUETONIUS TRANQUILLUS, the biographer of the first twelve Roman emperors, was the son of an army officer. Born about A.D. 75, from youth he devoted himself to a life of study. Influential friends, including the younger Pliny, secured for him certain imperial favors, such as the *ius trium liberorum*, which conferred special privileges on the father of three or more children, and appointment to a military tribunate, the latter of which he declined, however, in favor of another friend. A still more powerful patron, Septicius Clarus, to whom the *Lives* was dedicated, obtained for him appointment as one of the secretaries of Hadrian (emperor, A.D. 117–138). He held this post for only a few years, since both he and his patron, who was commander of the imperial guard, were dismissed when they incurred Hadrian's displeasure by not showing sufficient respect toward the emperor's wife. We do not know how long Suetonius lived after this event, which occurred in 122, but he was a voluminous writer on a variety of subjects, so it is probable that he enjoyed a long life. Though numerous fragments of his writings are imbedded in the writings of later authors, his only work which time has spared in its entirety is the series of imperial biographies. A rather extensive portion is also preserved of another series of biographies, of Roman grammarians and rhetoricians; and several of his biographies of Roman poets have come down in connection with the manuscripts of their works. The most important are his lives of Terence and Horace.

Suetonius has considerable merit as a biographer. He is temperate in his judgments, systematic in method, and indefatigable in the investigation of disputed points. He frequently quotes original sources. He has an eye for picturesque detail. He is sometimes criticized as excessively fond of salacious gossip, but this too contributes to the effect of candor he produces. He does not have the power, nor does he attempt, to analyze such complex personalities as Julius Caesar or Augustus; in comparing his work with Plutarch's, one is struck by his relative lack of psychological insight. But in compensation he gives us an abundance of well-documented detail; that is, he gives us the material from which we can form our own estimate of his subjects.

The popularity of his work was such that for centuries thereafter Roman historical writing tended to take the biographical form. But a comparison of the feeble efforts of the authors of the *Historia Augusta* with the Suetonian model redounds to the credit of the latter. His method may seem mechanical and easy, but his imitators have not found it so.

THE TEXT translated is that of M. Ihm (Leipzig: Teubner, 1927).

---

*Early youth—persecuted by the dictator Sulla*

*1* In his sixteenth year he lost his father.[1] Under the consuls of the next year he was appointed Priest of Jupiter;[2] and divorcing Cossutia, a lady of only equestrian rank, though exceedingly wealthy, who had been betrothed to him before he came of age, he married Cornelia, the daughter of the Cinna who was four times consul. His daughter Julia was presently borne by her, nor could he be compelled in any way by the dictator Sulla to divorce her. Wherefore he was deprived of his priesthood, the dowry of his wife, and the family inheritance, and was regarded as a member of the opposing party, so that he was even forced to withdraw from public view. Though he was suffering from a quartan fever, he must seek a new hiding-place almost every night and bribe his hunters to let him go; until by the intercession of the Vestal Virgins and Mamercus Aemilius and Aurelius Cotta, who were relatives or in-laws, he obtained a pardon. It is well known that though Sulla had for some time denied this favor to his close friends, men of highest position, who were pleading for Caesar, they stubbornly insisted; and Sulla was finally overborne, exclaiming, whether by prophetic insight or some rational conjecture, that they should prevail and have their man, provided they realized that the one for whose safety they were so desirous would some day be the ruin of the conservative party, for which they had fought along with himself; for in Caesar were many Mariuses.

[His first military service in Asia was attended with some scandal but also some honors for valor. He returned to Rome on learning of the death of Sulla, but refused to join the conspiracy of Lepidus.]

*He is captured by pirates.*

4 But, when the uprising [3] had been subdued, he prosecuted Marcus Dolabella, who had held the consulate and enjoyed a triumph, on a charge of extortion. When Dolabella was acquitted, Caesar decided to withdraw to Rhodes, both to avoid the unfavorable reaction and to study at leisure under Apollonius Molo, the most famous professor of rhetoric of the time. While sailing there in the winter season, he was captured by pirates near the island of Pharmacussa, and remained in their hands for almost forty days, though in high dudgeon, his only attendants being a physician and two valets. For he had sent off his other companions and servants at the very beginning to collect the funds to ransom him. When the sum of fifty talents was paid, he was set on shore, and he did not delay an instant to collect a fleet and pursue the pirates as they went off; and when he had got them in his power, he put them to death, as he had often warned them in jest that he would do.

[He helped defend the Roman interests in Asia against Mithridates, and on returning to Rome began his career of honors with the military tribunate and quaestorship, in which latter office he

lost his wife, Cornelia. As quaestor he was stationed in Spain, and was inspired by a statue of Alexander the Great to seek advancement more vigorously. He planned to arouse the Latin colonies in Italy to revolt, but was thwarted by the consuls.]

*Engages in a plot to seize the government.*

9 In spite of this [4] he did not fail to undertake still greater projects presently in the city; a few days before he entered upon his aedileship he was suspected of having joined a conspiracy [5] with Marcus Crassus the ex-consul, likewise with Publius Sulla and Autronius, who had been elected to the consulate but set aside on grounds of bribery. Their plan was that at the beginning of the year they should attack the Senate and kill such members as it pleased them; then Crassus was to assume the dictatorship, Caesar was to be appointed his Master of Horse, and when the constitution had been revised to suit their desires, Sulla and Autronius were to be restored to the consulate. This conspiracy has been mentioned by Tanusius Geminus [6] in his History, by Marcus Bibulus in his edicts, and by Gaius Curio the elder in his orations. Cicero also seems to allude to it in a certain letter to Axius, remarking that in his consulate Caesar had established the royal power at which he had aimed in his aedileship. Tanusius adds that Crassus, whether from a change of heart or from fear, failed to appear on the day appointed for the slaughter, and for this reason Caesar did not give the signal previously agreed upon; Curio adds that the agreement was that he should drop his toga from his shoulder. Curio again and Marcus Actorius Naso as well vouch for the fact that he likewise conspired with the youthful Gnaeus Piso, who had in rather irregular fashion been appointed governor of the province of Spain because of a suspicion that he was forming a conspiracy at Rome. Their bargain was that simultaneously they should lead revolutionary uprisings, Piso abroad, Caesar at Rome, with the help of the Ambrani and the Transpadanes; but both plans were dropped when Piso died.

[As aedile he spent money lavishly to win popular favor; but his attempt to gain a special command in Egypt was blocked by the conservatives. He retaliated with various measures to humiliate and annoy his opponents, and was elected pontifex maximus over two aristocratic rivals.]

*He pleads for leniency toward the Catilinarian conspirators.*

14 As praetor-elect, when the conspiracy of Catiline had been exposed and the whole Senate was in favor of inflicting the supreme penalty on those implicated in the crime, he alone proposed that they should be distributed among the Italian towns and held in custody, after their property had been confiscated.[7] Indeed he inspired such fear in those who urged harsher measures, repeatedly showing what resentment on the part of the Roman plebs awaited them, that Decimus Silanus, consul-elect, was not loath to soften his proposal by explanation (for to change it would be humiliating), intimating that it had been interpreted more rigorously than he had intended. And Caesar would even have carried the day, for he had brought a majority to his view, including Cicero, the brother of the consul, had not an oration by Marcus Cato stiffened the wavering body. Not even then did Caesar cease to obstruct the progress of the affair, until a force of Roman knights, who stood in arms around the Senate as a guard, threatened him with death as he persisted beyond all measure. They menaced him with drawn swords so that those sitting near him retreated, and only a very few saved him by taking him in their embrace and covering him with their togas. Then indeed he was frightened and not merely yielded the point, but stayed away from the Senate house for the rest of the year. [As praetor he continued his daring opposition to the conservatives, who tried to bring him to justice as an accomplice in the late conspiracy, but failed dismally.]

*Propraetor in Spain; candidate for consulate*

18 After his praetorship the province of Spain was allotted to him. When his creditors attempted to keep him in Rome, he got rid of them by having some rich men guarantee his loans, and in defiance of custom and law he set out for his post before the funds for the provincial administrations had been voted. It is uncertain whether this was due to his fear of a prosecution, with which he was threatened as soon as he should return to private life, or to his desire to come sooner to the aid of the provincials, who

were appealing for help. After he had restored order in the province, in equal haste, without waiting for his successor, he returned, expecting to win both a triumph and the consulate. But inasmuch as the election date had already been set, and he could not be admitted as a candidate unless he entered the city as a private citizen and many opposed his negotiations to have a decree passed exempting him from the legal requirement, he was compelled to give up his triumph in order not to be kept out of the consulate. 19 Of his two rival candidates for the consulate, Lucius Lucceius and Marcus Bibulus, he took the former into partnership, with the understanding that Lucceius, being unpopular but wealthy, should promise money in the name of both of them throughout the centuries of voters. On learning of this arrangement the conservatives, seized with the fear that he would stop at nothing if he had a friendly and cooperative colleague in the highest magistracy, authorized Bibulus to promise a similar amount. Many also contributed to this fund, not even Cato denying that this bribery was in the public interest.

So he was elected, along with Bibulus. For the same reason pains were taken by the conservatives to have provinces of the least importance, mere woods and cattle paths, decreed to the future consuls. Goaded on by this slight, he courted with every attention the favor of Gnaeus Pompeius, who was already on poor terms with the senate because his arrangements after conquering King Mithridates had been grudgingly confirmed. And he effected a reconciliation between Pompeius and Marcus Crassus, an old enemy since the days of their consulate, which they had held simultaneously but most discordantly; and he formed a partnership with both, so that no public measures could be passed which displeased any one of the three.[8]

*He overbears his colleague in the consulate.*

20 When he entered upon his office, he introduced a novelty, that the daily acts of the senate, and of the people as well, should be recorded and published. He also revived the antique custom that in the months when he did not have the fasces an orderly should precede him and the lictors follow. He introduced a bill for the distribution of public lands; and when

his colleague tried to thwart his proceedings by religious technicalities he drove him from the forum by arms. On the next day Bibulus complained in the Senate, but no one could be found who dared bring up the question of such a high-handed procedure or make any motion about it, such as had often been voted in far less outrageous situations. So Caesar forced him to such despair that until his term expired he skulked at home and did nothing save issue obstructive edicts.[9]

From that time on Caesar alone managed everything in public affairs, and to suit his own pleasure, so that some of the wits, when signing something by way of a joke, dated it not in the consulate of Caesar and Bibulus but of Julius and Caesar, giving the same man twice, by name and surname. And the following verses later enjoyed a vogue: "Not under Bibulus but under Caesar did something happen lately; for I can't remember a thing that happened in the consulate of Bibulus."

[He enacted measures for the benefit of impoverished citizens and equestrian tax collectors. Individuals who tried to oppose him were cowed by threats or violence. He married Calpurnia, the daughter of the man who was to succeed him as consul, and gave his own daughter Julia in marriage to Pompey.]

*He chooses Gaul as his province.*

22 So, with the support of his father-in-law and his son-in-law, from the whole number of provinces he chose the Gauls in preference to all others, since their wealth and strategic position afforded a suitable opportunity for triumphs. And at the beginning he received Cisalpine Gaul [10] with Illyricum, by a law sponsored by Vatinius; later he received Gallia Comata as well through the Senate, whose members feared that if they refused, the people would give him that too. Transported with pleasure at this, he did not refrain from boasting a few days later in a full Senate that despite the ill will and groans of his foes he had got what he wanted; so from now on he would trample on all of their heads. When some one insultingly replied that this would not be easy for any woman, he replied as if in jest that in Syria Semiramis had ruled and the Amazons had once held a great part of Asia.

[At the end of his term of office, the conservatives showed their intention of attacking him in his absence, but he took pains to have friendly candidates elected to some of the key offices. When the triumvirate showed signs of disintegrating, he summoned his colleagues to a conference at Luca and revived their coalition. His proconsular authority was prolonged, and he began an ambitious program of conquest in Gaul.]

*Summary of his years in Gaul*

25 In the nine years in which he held the command, his accomplishments were approximately as follows: All of Gaul, which is bounded by the Pyrenees, Alps, and Cévennes ranges and by the Rhine and Rhone rivers, and which extends 3200 [Roman] miles in circumference, he reduced to the form of a province, with the exception of certain allied states which had served the Romans well; and he imposed an annual tribute of 40,000,000 sesterces. He was the first of the Romans to take the offensive against the Germans who dwell beyond the Rhine; building a bridge, he inflicted heavy losses on them. He also invaded the Britons, hitherto unknown, and subduing them levied money and hostages from them. Amidst all these victories he suffered adverse fortune on only three occasions: in Britain, when his fleet was almost destroyed by a violent storm; in Gaul, when a legion was routed before Gergovia; and in the territory of the Germans, when his generals Titurius and Aurunculeius were ambushed and killed.

*Break with Pompey looms.*

26 In the same period he lost first his mother, then his daughter, and soon his grandson.[11] In the midst of these events, the state being in a turmoil because of the murder of Publius Clodius, after the Senate had voted that a single consul should be elected, specifically Gnaeus Pompeius, he arranged with the tribunes of the people who were planning to have him chosen as Pompey's colleague that they should rather present a bill to the people to give him the right of candidacy for the consulate in his absence, when the period of his proconsular authority should begin to expire; he did not

wish to leave too soon, before the war was finished, for that purpose.

[Still absent in Gaul, he began to court popular favor at Rome by magnificent public works and entertainments. He also sought the support of important individuals by showering favors.]

28 With no less energy he courted kings and provinces all over the world, offering to some a thousand captives as a gift, to others sending troops as an aid wherever and whenever they wanted them, without the authority of the Senate and people; and adorning with splendid public works not only the chief cities of Italy and Gaul and Spain but of Asia and Greece as well; until all were amazed and began to reflect on the object of all these measures. And Marcus Claudius Marcellus, the consul, first announcing by an edict that he was going to present a matter of gravest import to the state, proposed to the Senate that a successor should take Caesar's place before the proper time, inasmuch as the war was over and peace prevailed and the victorious army ought to get its discharge. He also proposed that Caesar should not be considered as a candidate in absence at the elections, inasmuch as Pompey had not abrogated the plebiscite on that matter. It had happened that when Pompey proposed a law concerning magistracies, a law in which he had denied candidacy to absentees, he had failed by oversight to make an exception even of Caesar; afterwards, when the law had been engraved in bronze and deposited in the treasury, he had corrected the error. Not satisfied with depriving Caesar of his provinces and of his special dispensation, Marcellus also proposed that citizenship should be taken away from the colonists Caesar had established at Novum Comum according to the terms of the Vatinian law; he proposed this on the ground that it had been given to further Caesar's private interests and at variance with legal prescription.

*He tries to arrange a compromise.*

29 Aroused by this attack, and judging, as they say was often heard from his lips, that it would be harder to shove him from the first rank to the second in the state than from the second to the last, he resisted with all his power, partly by the veto of tribunes, partly through Servius Sulpicius, the other consul. Likewise

in the following year when Gaius Marcellus, the successor of his cousin Marcus in the consulate, was attempting the same measures, Caesar bought for a huge price the services of Aemilius Paulus, Marcellus' colleague, and of Gaius Curio, the most reckless of the tribunes, to defend his interests. But when he saw that all these measures were too resolutely pushed, and that even the consuls-elect were opposed to him, he pleaded with the Senate by letter not to take from him the favor conferred by the people, or else that the rest of the generals should likewise retire from their armies; trusting, as men think, that whenever he wished he could call his veterans together again more rapidly than Pompey could assemble new soldiers. He tried to bargain with his opponents that he should give up eight legions and Transalpine Gaul, but be allowed to keep two legions and the Cisalpine province, or even one legion with Illyricum, until he became consul. 30 But when the Senate refused to intervene and his adversaries declared that they would make no bargain concerning the welfare of the state, he crossed to Nearer Gaul; and after holding the assize courts he halted at Ravenna, intending to resort to arms if the Senate should take severe measures against the tribunes of the people who were intervening in his behalf.

[However, informed opinion holds that he was driven to war by his fear of prosecution, or at least of losing his position of power.]

*Outbreak of war*

31 When, therefore, he heard that the right of veto of the tribunes had been suspended and that they had withdrawn from the city, sending ahead secretly some cohorts, so as to arouse no suspicion, he both attended a public show, to disguise his intentions, and considered the plans of a gladiatorial school he was planning to build; and he was present at a large dinner party, according to his custom. Then after sunset he had some mules from a near-by bakery hitched to his carriage and started out on a most secret journey with a modest retinue. Travelling along without lights, he lost his way; after long wandering, finally toward daybreak he found a guide and reached his destination on foot by the narrowest paths. On overtaking his cohorts at the Rubicon, which was the boundary of his prov-

ince, he halted for a little; and reflecting on how great an enterprise he was essaying, he turned to those about him and said, "Even now we can return; but if we cross this little bridge, everything must be settled with arms." *32* As he hesitated, the following omen was revealed to him: a man of extraordinary size and figure suddenly appeared sitting near by, playing on a reed pipe. When not only shepherds but a number of soldiers ran from their posts to hear him, among them some trumpeters, he snatched a trumpet from one of them and sprang toward the river; and with a great blast he sounded the advance and went on across. Then Caesar said, "Let us go where the portents of the gods and the injustice of our enemies call us. The die is cast."

[Having entered Ariminum, he inflamed his troops by a violent harangue and lavish promises.]

### Résumé of civil wars

*34* This is a summary, in chronological order, of his movements thereafter. He overran Picenum, Umbria, and Etruria; he overpowered Lucius Domitius, who had been designated Caesar's successor under martial law, and who occupied Corfinium with a garrison; but Caesar let him go and went on along the Adriatic to Brundisium, where the consuls and Pompey had fled, intending to cross over at the earliest opportunity. After vain attempts to keep them from sailing away, by all hindrances he could contrive, he turned away toward Rome. Summoning the senators to discuss the state of the nation, he set out against Pompey's strongest forces, which were in Spain under three generals, Marcus Petreius and Lucius Afranius and Marcus Varro. Before leaving Caesar remarked to his intimates that he was setting out against an army without a leader, and would return to face a leader without an army. Though delayed by the siege of Marseilles, which had closed its doors to him as he marched along, and by stringent lack of supplies, he soon subdued all opposition. *35* Then he went back to the city and crossed to Macedonia. For a space of nearly four months he blockaded Pompey with great siege works; in the end, he routed him at the battle of Pharsalus and pursued him in his flight to Egypt. Learning there that Pompey

had been killed, he engaged in a very difficult war with King Ptolemy, when he saw that the king was trying to trap him also. Neither the place nor the season was convenient; it was winter, and he had to fight inside the city walls of a foe abundantly supplied and shrewdly active. After winning the struggle, he bestowed the kingdom of Egypt upon Cleopatra and her younger brother, being afraid to make a province of it, lest it should prove a good base for a revolution if it fell into the hands of an unscrupulous governor. He moved from Alexandria to Syria, and from there to Pontus, because of urgent news about Pharnaces. This was the son of Mithridates the Great; he was taking advantage of the situation to start war, and was now cocksure because of repeated successes. But within five days after he reached the land, and within four hours after he came in sight, Caesar destroyed him in a single battle. He often alluded to the good luck of Pompey, who had attained great military glory at the expense of so weak a foe. Next he conquered Scipio and Juba, who were reviving the remnants of the senatorial party in Africa, and then the sons of Pompey in Spain.

[His defeats were only temporary, and mostly suffered through his subordinate commanders rather than in person.]

### Domestic legislation

*40* Turning then to setting the state in order, he reformed the calendar, which had long since fallen into such confusion, thanks to the pontiffs who had mismanaged the intercalary [12] months, that the harvest festivals no longer came in summer nor the vintage festivals in autumn. He adapted the year to the course of the sun so that it consisted of three hundred and sixty-five days. The intercalary month was dropped, but an extra day was to be inserted every fourth year. That the new system might go into effect on the first day of January, he put two extra months between November and December; the year in which this change was adopted had fifteen months, counting in the usual intercalary month which had fallen in that year. *41* He filled up the Senate and created new patricians; he increased the number of praetors, aediles, quaestors, and minor magistrates. He restored to their rights senators who had been degraded by the censors or condemned in court for fraud in elections. He divided the elections with the people, so that with the exception of the consulate, half of the candidates chosen for each office should be those the people named, half those he nominated. . . .

[He reduced the number of people receiving free grain, and sent 80,000 to colonies abroad, but restricted opportunities for prolonged foreign travel.]

42 . . . Ranchers were required to have free men form at least a third part of their herdsmen. He gave citizenship to all physicians at Rome and to all teachers of the liberal arts, so that they might be more willing to dwell there, and that others might be attracted. As for debts, he disappointed the hope of a general cancellation, which was often proposed, but at last decreed that debtors should pay off their creditors by yielding property estimated at its prewar value,[13] deducting from the total of the debt whatever had been paid or assigned by way of interest; approximately a fourth part of the principal was wiped out by this arrangement. He disbanded all guilds except those of ancient standing.

[Penalties for crimes were increased, and laws more rigorously enforced, particularly those restricting luxury. He entertained plans for grandiose public works and for a campaign against the barbarian nations that threatened the eastern provinces.]

### Personal details

44 In the midst of such undertakings and plans death cut him off. Before I tell of it, it will not be amiss to describe briefly his appearance, garb, care of his person, and habits, and also his practices in civil and military life.

45 He is reported to have been tall, of light complexion, with well-rounded limbs, a rather full mouth, bright black eyes; his health was sound, except that toward the end he often had sudden fainting spells and nightmares. He was twice seized with epilepsy while transacting public business. He was rather fastidious in the care of his body, so that he was not only carefully shaved and trimmed but had superfluous hairs plucked out, as some have charged. He was very

sensitive about his baldness, having often found it a target for the jests of his ill-wishers. Consequently he used to comb his thinning locks down from the top of his head, and of all the honors bestowed on him by Senate and people the one he was most pleased to accept and use was the right to wear a laurel wreath perpetually.

[Plunder from his campaigns gave him the income for luxurious and sensuous living, especially with Cleopatra, queen of Egypt, by whom he had a son. He was famous both as an orator and as an author, the severe style of his *Commentaries* on his campaigns in Gaul being especially praised.]

### Physical prowess and daring

57 He was highly skilled in arms and horsemanship, and incredibly tough in enduring hardships. On the march he sometimes went ahead on horseback, but more often on foot, with bare head, in sunshine or rain. He completed the longest journey with incredible speed, travelling light, in a hired carriage, a hundred miles a day; if rivers blocked his course, he would swim across, or would float over on inflated skins, so that he often anticipated the messengers who were to announce his approach. 58 In his campaigns it is hard to say whether he was more noteworthy for caution or daring. He never led his army along a route exposed to ambush without reconnoitring the lay of the land; and he did not transport it to Britain until after he had himself investigated the harbors and problems of navigation and all approaches to the island. Yet when he heard the news that his camp was besieged in Germany he passed through the enemy lines disguised as a Gaul to join his men. He crossed in winter from Brundisium to Dyrrachium amidst a blockading enemy fleet; and when the troops he had ordered to follow close after him failed to do so, he vainly sent several messages to summon them, and finally boarded a small boat secretly by night, with veiled head, nor would he reveal his identity or allow the pilot to yield to the adverse weather until he was almost overwhelmed by the waves.

[A bold campaigner, he had many narrow escapes. His skill in handling men kept his soldiers loyal.]

## Treatment of friends and enemies

72 He always treated his friends with such consideration and kindliness that when Gaius Oppius,[14] who was his companion on a journey through a wooded area, was seized by a sudden illness, Caesar gave up to him the only lodging that was available and himself slept on the ground under the open sky. And when he was master of the state he promoted some men of very lowly origin to highest offices, declaring, when criticized for this, that if he had had the help of footpads and cutthroats in maintaining his honor, he would have shown equal gratitude even to such men.

73 On the other hand he never entered into feuds so bitter that he was not glad to end them if opportunity offered. He had replied to the biting denunciations of Gaius Memmius [15] with equal bitterness, but he later supported him in his candidacy for the consulate. When Gaius Calvus,[16] after writing notorious epigrams against Caesar, negotiated for a reconciliation through friends, Caesar took the lead of his own accord and wrote to him. When Valerius Catullus offered an apology for his lines concerning Mamurra,[17] which Caesar admitted had imprinted a lasting stigma, Caesar invited him to dinner the same day; and he continued to accept the hospitality of the poet's father, as was his wont. . . .

## His arrogance causes unfavorable reaction.

78 But he aroused especial and deadly hatred above all by this act. When the whole body of the Senate came to him to present numerous highly complimentary decrees, he received them sitting in front of the temple of Venus. Some think that he tried to rise but was restrained by Cornelius Balbus; others, that he did not try to rise at all, and even when Gaius Trebatius advised him to do so, Caesar gave him an unfriendly look. This act seemed the more unforgivable because when he was riding in triumph past the tribunes' benches and Pontius Aquila alone of the body failed to rise in his honor, Caesar was so indignant that he exclaimed, "Then try to take the government out of my hands, Aquila, you tribune!" And for several days he would not promise anything to anybody except with the proviso, "If Pontius Aquila will permit it."

[He deposed two tribunes who had restrained attempts to urge kingly honors for him. His action in refusing a crown offered him by Marcus Antonius failed to convince the populace of his democratic intentions. Rumors spread that Rome was to be abandoned in favor of some eastern capital, and that the Senate was to be urged to grant him the title of king because the Sibylline Books demanded it.]

## A great conspiracy formed against him

80 . . . So everybody merged the plots which had hitherto been formed independently, often by only two or three participants. Not even the people were happy about the existing state of affairs, but in private or in public were chafing at his tyranny and calling for defenders. When foreigners were admitted to the Senate a lampoon was posted: "In the name of the law: Let no one direct a new senator to the Senate house!" and the following ditty gained popularity: "Caesar led the Gauls in his triumph, and likewise into the Senate; the Gauls put off their trousers [18] and donned senatorial tunics." When Quintus Maximus, a suffect [19] consul for a three months' term, entered the theater and a lictor admonished the audience to receive him with the customary ceremony, the whole audience shouted that that was no consul. After Caesetius and Marullus were deposed as tribunes, a number of ballots were found at the next election naming them as consuls. Somebody wrote on the base of the statue of Brutus,[20] "Would that you were alive!" and likewise on the base of Caesar's statue, "Brutus, for casting out the kings, was made the first consul; this man, for casting out the consuls, was at last made king." The conspiracy was joined by more than sixty men, of whom Gaius Cassius and Marcus and Decimus Brutus were the leaders. They at first hesitated whether to wait until he was summoning the tribes to cast their ballots at the election in the Campus Martius, and, dividing their roles, some to pitch him from the bridge,[21] others to catch and stab him; or to attack him on the Sacred Way or at the entrance of the theater. But after a meeting of the Senate was announced for the

Ides of March in the Senate house of Pompey, they preferred the easy time and place.

### Caesar warned by portents

*81* But Caesar was forewarned of his coming murder by manifest signs. A few months before, when colonists settled at Capua by the Julian law were tearing down ancient tombs in order to build farm houses, and were doing so more eagerly because in their search they had found some vessels of ancient workmanship, there was found in the tomb in which Capys, the founder of Capua, was said to be buried, a brazen tablet in Greek and with Greek letters, to the effect that whenever the bones of Capys should be uncovered, one of his descendants would be slain by the hands of kinsmen and would presently be avenged by great disasters to Italy. That no one may think this a fabulous invention, Cornelius Balbus, a most intimate friend of Caesar, vouches for it. A few days before the event, Caesar learned that the herds of horses which he had dedicated at the crossing of the Rubicon and allowed to wander without keeper were stubbornly refusing to graze and were weeping copiously. And when he was offering sacrifice, the soothsayer Spurinna warned him to beware of a danger which would come not later than the Ides of March. Moreover, on the day before the Ides a kingbird flying with a sprig of laurel into the Senate house of Pompey was set upon by birds of various kinds from the near-by grove and torn to pieces. On that night indeed which preceded the day of his death he himself dreamed, now that he was flying above the clouds, now that he was shaking hands with Jupiter; and his wife Calpurnia dreamed that the gable of their house collapsed and that her husband was stabbed as she clasped him in her arms. And suddenly the doors of their bedroom flew open of their own accord.

### The assassination

Both for these reasons and for ill health he hesitated for some time whether he should stay in and postpone the matters he had intended to discuss with the Senate; but finally, when Decimus Brutus urged him not to disappoint the well-attended meeting which had long been waiting for him, he set out about the fifth hour of the day; and when a document giving information about the plot was handed to him by some one passing by, he put it with the other documents which he held in his left hand, as if he intended to read it presently. Then he offered sacrifice, but could obtain no favorable omens, though several victims were slain; so, scorning the religious scruple, he entered the Senate House with a gibe at Spurinna as a false prophet, since the Ides of March were at hand without harm to himself—though Spurinna replied that they had indeed come but not yet gone. *82* As he took his seat the conspirators, as if to do him honor, gathered about him, and straightway Tillius Cimber, who had undertaken the initial role, came up closer to him as if to ask some favor. Caesar shook his head and with a gesture put him off to some later time; then Cimber snatched his toga from both his shoulders. As Caesar exclaimed, "This is indeed violence!" one of the Cascas stabbed him from behind a little below the neck. Caesar seized the arm of Casca and pierced it with his writing stylus; but as he tried to spring up he was checked by another wound; and when he saw drawn daggers aimed at him on every side, he wrapped his head in his toga, and at the same time with his left hand drew its skirt down about his legs so as to fall in more seemly fashion, with the lower part of his body covered. And so he was stabbed with twenty-three blows, uttering only one groan at the first stroke, but no articulate word, though some have reported that as Marcus Brutus came at him Caesar said in Greek, "You too, child?" After all had fled, he lay lifeless for some time, until three humble slaves placed him on a litter and carried him off home, with one arm dangling. Nor in all those wounds, in the opinion of Antistius the physician, was any found to be fatal except the one he had received second in his chest. . . .

### His funeral

*84* After the time of his funeral had been announced, a pyre was built in the Campus Martius next to the tomb of his daughter Julia, and a gilded temple was set up on the Rostra, a model of the temple of Venus Genetrix. Inside it was an ivory couch, spread with gold and crimson; at its head, a trophy with the garment he had worn when slain. People bringing in offerings were bidden, since it seemed that the day would not be long enough, to give up their procession and to bring them to the Campus Martius by any route they chose through the city. In the funeral plays certain verses were recited to arouse pity and indignation at the murder from the *Judgment of Arms* of Pacuvius: [22] "That I should have saved them, so that they might destroy me!" and a passage of similar content from the *Electra* of Acilius. By way of a funeral eulogy the consul Antonius had a herald recite the decree of the Senate in which it had voted all honors, human and divine, to him; likewise the oath by which all its members had bound themselves to guard his safety. To these the consul added a very few words of his own. Magistrates and former office holders carried the couch on the Rostra into the Forum. While some intended to cremate it in the shrine of Capitoline Jupiter, others in the Senate House of Pompey, suddenly two men with swords at their waists, brandishing two javelins in their hands, set it alight with blazing torches, and immediately the crowd of bystanders heaped on dry twigs and the judges' platforms, along with the benches, and in addition whatever was at hand by way of offering. Then the musicians and actors took off and tore up the robes which they were wearing for that day, from the triumphal wardrobe, and cast them into the flames; veteran legionaries threw in the arms with which they had adorned themselves for the solemn occasion; many matrons, the ornaments they were wearing and the amulets and gowns of their children. . . .

*His willingness to die*

86 Caesar left the impression on some of his intimates that he had no desire or care for longer life, because he was suffering from poor health, and for that reason ignored the warnings of omens and the information of his friends. There are some who think he relied upon that final decree and oath of the Senate and dismissed his Spanish guards, who had attended him with drawn swords. Others, however, believe that he preferred to face once and for all the plots that threatened him from every side rather than always to be on guard, and they say that he was wont to remark that it concerned not so much himself as the state that he should be preserved; he had long since gained all the power and glory he wanted; if anything should happen to him, the state would enjoy no peace, but would undergo civil wars of a more ruthless type. 87 This is pretty well agreed by all, that such a kind of death was almost exactly what he wanted. For once when he had read in Xenophon that Cyrus in his final illness had given certain instructions for his funeral, he scorned so slow a death and wished for a sudden and swift one for himself. And the day before he was killed, in a conversation that arose at dinner in the house of Marcus Lepidus about what end of life was best, he had given the preference to a sudden and unexpected one.

88 He died in his fifty-sixth year, and was exalted to the number of the gods, not merely by the perfunctory vote of the Senate but in the conviction of the folk. For at the games which his heir Augustus gave for the first time after his deification, a comet shone for seven successive days, arising about the eleventh hour, and it was believed to be the soul of Caesar, received into the heavens; for that reason a star is added to the crown of his statue.

It was decided that the Senate house in which he was slain should be walled up, and that the Ides of March should be named the Day of Murder, and that the Senate should never meet on that day. 89 Hardly any of his assassins lived for more than three years after that, or met a natural death. All were condemned and died in various ways, part by shipwreck, part in battle, some slew themselves with the same daggers with which they had stabbed Caesar.

## NOTES TO *THE DEIFIED JULIUS*

1. The abruptness of this opening is due to the loss of several pages at the beginning of the archetype of our manuscripts.

2. A position of considerable honor, reserved for patricians.

3. An attempt in 78 B.C. to overthrow the Sullan constitution.

4. An unsuccessful attempt made by Caesar, returning from his quaestorship in Spain in 68 B.C., to lead the Latin colonies in a demonstration for full citizenship.

5. This is usually called the first conspiracy of Catiline, but Suetonius does not connect that leader with it.

6. The sources here quoted are all lost.

7. Sallust's *Catiline*, 51, 52, gives a version of Caesar's speech on this occasion, and also of Cato's reply.

8. The triumvirate was certainly formed before rather than after the election, but was not revealed until later.

9. He would announce that he was going to watch the sky for omens; this was supposed to halt all public business.

10. I.e., the part of Italy between the Alps and the river Rubicon; Gallia Comata ("Longhaired Gaul") was beyond the Alps, but at this time extended only to the Cévennes on the north.

11. The infant son of Julia, who died in 54 B.C.

12. When the calendar consisted of three hundred fifty-five days, an extra month was inserted every two or three years to correct the shortage.

13. Many properties had been thrown on the market, causing a severe deflation.

14. The author of a book of memoirs (lost) from which this and many others of these intimate accounts were no doubt derived.

15. Patron of Lucretius, who dedicated his poem to him.

16. Friend of Catullus, well known for oratory and poetry (lost).

17. Friend of Caesar, and commander of the engineering corps of Caesar's army; a rival of Catullus in certain amours.

18. To the Romans a sign not of male dignity but of barbarism.

19. One elected to fill out an unfinished term.

20. The Liberator, who had led the revolt which overthrew the Roman monarchy in 509 B.C.

21. A raised gangplank over which the voters passed in single file.

22. Nephew of Ennius; the subject of his play was the contest of the Greek leaders before Troy for the arms of the dead Achilles.

MAPS

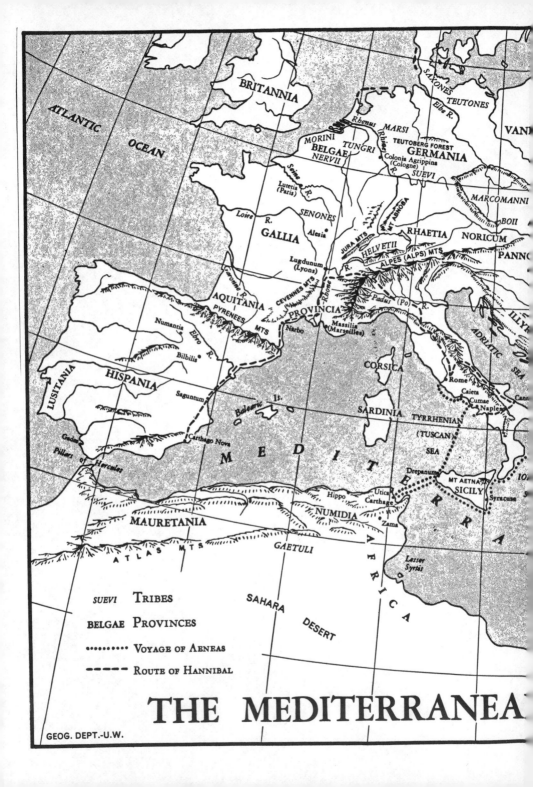

# THE MEDITERRANEA

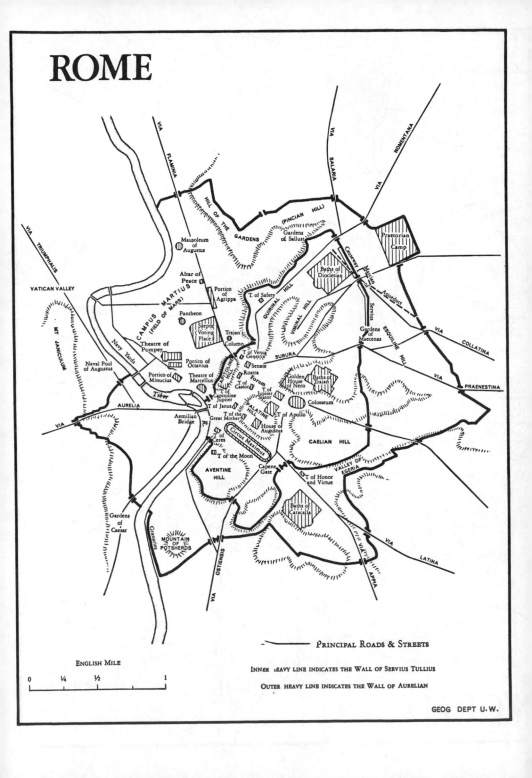

# ROME

VIA FLAMINIA

VIA SALARIA

VIA NOMENTANA

VIA TRIUMPHALIS

VATICAN VALLEY

MT JANICULUM

HILL OF THE GARDENS

(PINCIAN HILL)

Mausoleum of Augustus

Gardens of Sallust

Praetorian Camp

Baths of Diocletian

Altar of Peace

Portico of Agrippa

T. of Safety

QUIRINAL HILL

Aqueduct

Pantheon

CAMPUS MARTIUS (FIELD OF MARS)

Septa Voting Place

Trajan's Column

VIMINAL HILL

Servius

Gardens of Maecenas

ESQUILINE HILL

VIA COLLATINA

Theatre of Pompey

T. of Venus Genetrix

SUBURA

VIA PRAENESTINA

Navy Yards

Portico of Octavius

Senate

Rostra

Golden House of Nero

Baths of Trajan

Naval Pool of Augustus

Portico of Minucius

Theatre of Marcellus

Forum

T. of Castor

Tiber

ESQUILINE

T. of Jupiter Stator

Colosseum

AURELIA

Capitoline Jupiter

T. of Janus

T. of the Great Mother

PALATINE HILL

House of Augustus

T. of Apollo

Aemilian Bridge

T. of Ceres

Circus Maximus

CAELIAN HILL

T. of the Moon

AVENTINE HILL

Capene Gate

T. of Honor and Virtue

VALLEY OF EGERIA

Gardens of Caesar

MOUNTAIN OF POTSHERDS

Granaries

Baths of Caracalla

VIA OSTIENSIS

VIA APPIA

VIA LATINA

ENGLISH MILE

0    ¼    ½    1

——— PRINCIPAL ROADS & STREETS

INNER HEAVY LINE INDICATES THE WALL OF SERVIUS TULLIUS

OUTER HEAVY LINE INDICATES THE WALL OF AURELIAN

GEOG DEPT U.W.

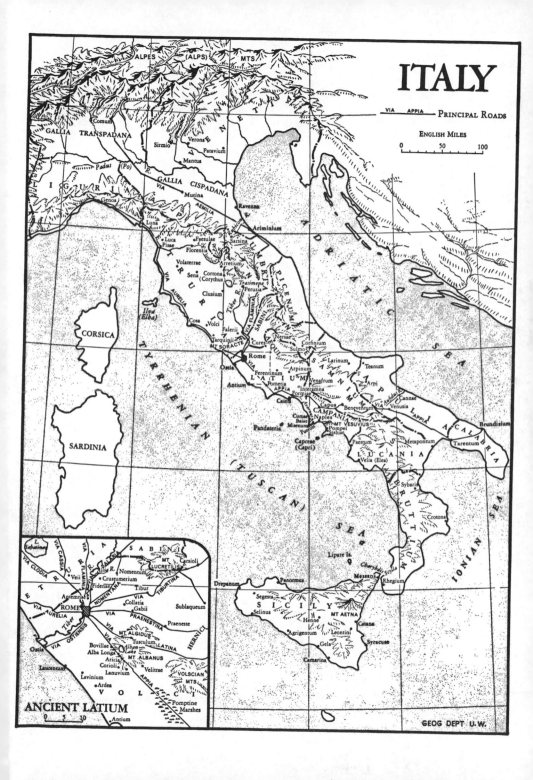

# ITALY

VIA APPIA — PRINCIPAL ROADS

ENGLISH MILES
0    50    100

ALPES    (ALPS)    MTS

GALLIA TRANSPADANA

Comum
Sirmio
Verona
Patavium
Mantua

LIGURIA

Padus (Po) R.

GALLIA CISPADANA

Genoa
Mutina
Luna
Ravenna

AEMILIA

Luca
Pisae
Faesulae    Sarsina
Florentia
Volaterrae    Arretium
Sena    Cortona (Corythus)
Clusium    Perusia
L. Trasimene

VIA AURELIA

Ilva (Elba)

CORSICA

Cosa
Volci
Falerii
Tarquinii
MT SORACTE
Rome
Ostia

ETRURIA

Tiber

UMBRIA

PICENUM

SABINI

Cures
Nersae
Corfinium
Sulmo

ADRIATIC SEA

TYRRHENIAN (TUSCAN)

SARDINIA

VIA APPIA

Antium
Ferentinum
Pomeria
Caieta
Formiae
Interamna
Arpinum
Larinum
Teanum

LATIUM

SAMNIUM

Venafrum
Capua
Beneventum
Cannae
Arpi
Venusia

APULIA

CALABRIA

Brundisium

Cumae
Baiae
Misenum
Naples
Pompei
Stabiae
MT VESUVIUS
Puteoli

CAMPANIA

Pandateria
Capreae (Capri)

Paestum
Metapontum
Tarentum

LUCANIA

Velia (Elea)

SEA

Sybaris

BRUTTIUM

Crotona

IONIAN SEA

Lipare Is.

Drepanum
Panormus

Messana
Cherybdis Scylla
Rhegium

Segesta
Selinus
Henne
Agrigentum
Leontini
Gela
Camarina

SICILY

MT AETNA
Catana
Syracuse

## ANCIENT LATIUM

0    5    10

L. Sabatinus
VIA CASSIA
VIA CLODIA
VIA FLAMINIA
Veii
Fidenae
Antemnae
ROME

ETRURIA

Allia R.
Nomentum
Crustumerium
Collatia
Gabii
Praeneste

SABINI

MT LUCRETILIS
Carsioli
Sublaqueum

VIA NOMENTANA
VIA TIBURTINA
Tibur
VIA PRAENESTINA
VIA LATINA

VIA AURELIA
Ostia
Tiber
VIA OSTIENSIS
Laurentum

Bovillae
Tusculum
Alba Longa
Aricia
Corioli
Lanuvium
Lavinium
Ardea

MT ALGIDUS
Alban Lake
MT ALBANUS
Velitrae

HERNICI

VOLSCIAN MTS

VOLSCI

VIA APPIA

Pomptine Marshes

Antium

GEOG DEPT U.W.